Reducing Emissions of Short-Lived Climate Pollutants

International Environmental Law

Series Editor

Makane Moïse Mbengue

VOLUME 20

The titles published in this series are listed at *brill.com/iel*

Reducing Emissions of Short-Lived Climate Pollutants

Perspectives on Law and Governance

Edited by

Yulia Yamineva, Kati Kulovesi, Eugenia Recio

BRILL | NIJHOFF

LEIDEN | BOSTON

Library of Congress Cataloging-in-Publication Data

Names: Yamineva, Yulia, editor. | Kulovesi, Kati, editor. | Recio, Eugenia, illustrator.
Title: Reducing emissions of short-lived climate pollutants : perspectives on law and governance / edited by Yulia Yamineva, Kati Kulovesi, Eugenia Recio.
Description: Leiden ; Boston : Brill/Nijhoff, 2024. | Series: International environmental law, 1873-6599; vol. 20 | Includes index. | Identifiers: LCCN 2023034637 (print) | LCCN 2023034638 (ebook) | ISBN 9789004684072 (hardback) | ISBN 9789004684089 (ebook)
Subjects: LCSH: Climatic changes–Law and legislation. | Greenhouse gas mitigation–Law and legislation. | Carbon dioxide mitigation–Law and legislation. | Emissions trading–Law and legislation. | Carbon offsetting–Law and legislation. | Climate change mitigation. | Pollutants–Environmental aspects.
Classification: LCC K3593 .R43 2023 (print) | LCC K3593 (ebook) | DDC 363.7–dc23/eng/20230919
LC record available at https://lccn.loc.gov/2023034637
LC ebook record available at https://lccn.loc.gov/2023034638

Typeface for the Latin, Greek, and Cyrillic scripts: "Brill". See and download: brill.com/brill-typeface.

ISSN 1873-6599
ISBN 978-90-04-68407-2 (hardback)
ISBN 978-90-04-68408-9 (e-book)
DOI 10.1163/9789004684089

This book is printed on acid-free paper and produced in a sustainable manner.

Contents

Illustrations

Tables

Figures

Graph

Acronyms

AMAP	Arctic Monitoring and Assessment Programme
APS	Announced Pledges Scenario
BC	black carbon
BCM	billion cubic meters
CAFE	Corporate Average Fuel Economy Standards
CCA	Clean Cooking Alliance
CCAC	Climate and Clean Air Coalition
CDM	Clean Development Mechanism
CFC	Chlorofluorocarbon
CLRTAP	Convention on Long-Range Transboundary Air Pollution
CMA	Conference of the Parties serving as the meeting of the Parties to the Paris Agreement
CO	Carbon monoxide
CO_2	Carbon dioxide
CO_2e	Carbon dioxide equivalent
COP	Conference of the Parties
DOC	Diesel oxidation catalyst
DPF	Diesel Particulate Filter
EB	Executive Body of the United Nations Economic Commission for Europe
EC	European Commission
ECA	Emission Control Area
EEAP	Environmental Effects Assessment Panel of the Montreal Protocol
EECCA	Eastern Europe, the Caucasus and Central Asia
EGBCM	Expert Group on Black Carbon and Methane
EMEP	European Monitoring and Evaluation Programme
EPA	United States Environmental Protection Agency
ETS	Emissions trading scheme
EU	European Union
GGFR	Global Gas Flaring Reduction Partnership
GHG	Greenhouse gas
GMI	Global Methane Initiative
GMP	Global Methane Pledge
GP	Gothenburg Protocol
Gt	Gigaton
GWP	Global warming potential
HCFCs	Hydrochlorofluorocarbons
HFCs	Hydrofluorocarbons

HFOS	Hydrofluoroolefins
I&M	Inspection and Maintenance
ICCT	International Council for Clean Transportation
IEA	International Energy Agency
IMO	International Maritime Organisation
INDOEX	Indian Ocean Experiment
INTERTANKO	International Association of Independent Tanker Owners
IPCC	Intergovernmental Panel on Climate Change
ISO	International Organisation for Standardisation
LNG	liquefied natural gas
LPG	liquefied petroleum gas
MARPOL	International Convention for the Prevention of Pollution from Ships
Med ECA	Mediterranean Emission Control Area
MEPC	Marine Environment Protection Committee
MOU	Memorandum of Understanding
MRV	Monitoring, reporting and verifying
MRV&E	Monitoring, reporting, verifying and enforcement
NAFTA	North American Free Trade Organisation
NDC	Nationally Determined Contribution to the Paris Agreement
NGO	Non-governmental organisation
NH_3	Ammonia
NOC	National Oil Corporation
NO_X	Nitrous oxides
NZE	Net-zero Emissions by 2050 Scenario
ODP	Ozone depleting potential
ODS	Ozone depleting substance
OGCI	Oil and Gas Climate Initiative
OGMP	Oil and Gas Methane Partnership
PM/PM_{10}	Particulate matter
$PM_{2.5}$	Fine particulate matter
POPS	Persistent organic pollutants
ppm	Parts per million
RDI	Research, development and innovation
RTA	Regional trade agreement
SAO	Senior Arctic Officials
SAP	Scientific Assessment Panel of the Montreal Protocol
SDGS	Sustainable Development Goals
SDS	Sustainable Development Scenario
SEE	South-Eastern Europe
SEforALL	Sustainable Energy for All

SLCF	Short-lived climate forcer
SLCP	Short-lived climate pollutant
SO_2	Sulphur dioxide
SO_x	Sulphur oxides
STC	Specific trade concern
STEPS	Stated policies scenario
TBT	Technical barriers to trade
TEAP	Technology and Economic Assessment Panel of the Montreal Protocol
TFA	Trifluoroacetic acid
UAE	United Arab Emirates
UK	United Kingdom of Great Britain and Northern Ireland
UN	United Nations
UNEA	United Nations Environment Assembly
UNECE	United Nations Economic Commission for Europe
UNEP	United Nations Environment Programme
UNFCCC	United Nations Framework Convention on Climate Change
US	United States
USD	US Dollars
UV	ultraviolet
VAT	Value-added tax
VOCS	Volatile organic compounds
WEO21	World Energy Outlook 2021
WG	Working Group
WGSR	Working Group on Strategies and Review of the United Nations Economic Commission for Europe
WHO	World Health Organisation
WLTP	Worldwide Harmonized Light Vehicles Test Procedure
WMO	World Meteorological Organisation
WP.29	World Forum for Harmonization of Vehicle Regulations
WTO	World Trade Organisation

Notes on Contributors

Editors

Yulia Yamineva
is Senior Researcher at the Center for Climate Change, Energy and Environmental Law (CCEEL) of the University of Eastern Finland Law School. She holds the title of Docent in Climate Law and Policy. Her research focuses on international climate change law, governance and negotiations, as well as law on air pollution prevention, and the science-policy interface, and has been published in leading academic journals including Nature Climate Change, Transnational Environmental Law, and others. She previously worked for the UN Climate Change Convention Secretariat and the International Institute for Sustainable Development.

Kati Kulovesi
is a Professor of International Law and Co-Director of the CCEEL at the University of Eastern Finland. She has published widely on international, EU, and national climate change law, as well as international economic law. Kulovesi has led several large multidisciplinary research projects funded by the European Research Council, the Finnish Strategic Research Council and Academy of Finland.

Eugenia Recio
is Postdoctoral Researcher at the UEF CCEEL. Her main research interests are international and national climate law and governance and international environmental negotiations, with a focus on biodiversity and forests. Eugenia has worked at the local, national and international levels, both in developing countries in Latin America and the Caribbean, and Europe.

Chapter Authors

Pami Aalto
is Jean Monnet Professor in international relations at the Politics Unit, Faculty of Management and Business, Tampere University, Finland, and Principal Investigator of the university's research platform Climate Neutral Energy Systems and Society (CNESS). He has worked on all major sources of energy

and components of the energy system and has interests in interdisciplinary studies of energy transitions and international environmental governance alongside energy geopolitics and great power relations. The bulk of the work has revolved on the European, Arctic, Eurasian and East Asian regions.

Thomas L. Brewer
is a member of the Emeritus Faculty of Georgetown University in Washington, DC. He has been Visiting Senior Research Fellow at Oxford University in the Smith School for Enterprise and the Environment, Visiting Scholar at the MIT Center for Energy and Environmental Policy Research, and Schöller Foundation Senior Research Fellow at Friedrich-Alexander University in Nuremberg, Germany. He was a Lead Author of the chapter on International Cooperation for the Fifth Assessment of the IPCC. He has made presentations at conferences of the Harvard-China bilateral cooperation project on climate change, the Centre for European Policy Studies, UNFCCC COP side events, WTO side events, and the EU's Florence School of Regulation. He has been a consultant to the World Bank, the United Nations Conference on Trade and Development, and the Organization for Economic Cooperation and Development.

Adam Byrne
has a PhD in Geography, Law and Policy which he completed at University College London (UCL) and a Master's degree in Environmental Law and Sustainable Development awarded by SOAS, University of London. At the time of writing his chapter in this book, he was a Visiting Postdoctoral Research Fellow at the Department of Geography at UCL. Adam has research interests in both climate change and air pollution law. His doctoral research explored the origins, design and implementation of the UK Climate Change Act 2008. He has researched and published on the history of transboundary air pollution law.

Anna Claydon
is a Doctoral Researcher in international relations at the Politics Unit of the Faculty of Management and Business in Tampere University, Finland. The focus of her dissertation is on the dynamics of black carbon governance and the possibilities for enhanced mitigation. She approaches these issues through the structuration of knowledge on black carbon, stakeholder interests, policy entrepreneurship, science diplomacy, and the formation of an epistemic community around black carbon.

Medy Dervovic
is a PhD Candidate at Reykjavík University, Iceland, where he focuses on the normative impact of climate change on the law of the sea in the Arctic. He holds an LL.M degree in Polar Law from the University of Akureyri, Iceland. Medy is also a visiting researcher at the Arctic Centre, University of Lapland (Rovaniemi, Finland), a researcher at the Stefansson Arctic Institute (Akureyri, Iceland), and a researcher at the Centre for Law on Climate Change and Sustainability (Reykjavík, Iceland). His fields of research include the law of the sea, Arctic law and governance, public international law, environmental law, and human rights.

Louise du Toit
is Lecturer in Law at the University of Southampton and Visiting Fellow at the College of Social Sciences, University of Lincoln (United Kingdom). Her research focuses on strengthening environmental law and governance to respond to current earth system challenges, including climate change, stratospheric ozone depletion, and plastics. Louise holds a PhD in Public Law and an LLM in Environmental Law from the University of Cape Town and is an admitted attorney of the High Court of South Africa.

Minna Hanhijärvi
is a Doctoral Researcher in international relations at the Politics Unit of the Faculty of Management and Business in Tampere University, Finland. Her doctoral study explores the nexus of truth-subversion in climate politics and inter-state trust in global climate governance in the framework of the Paris Agreement and the Russia-Ukraine conflict and war. As a case study, the focus is on the international cooperation on climate change in the Arctic and its global effects accelerated by black carbon and methane emissions linked to the flaring of the associated petroleum gas in the Russian oilfields.

Gørild Heggelund
PhD, Research Professor at the Fridtjof Nansen Institute (FNI), has carried out research on China's environmental, energy and climate change policy for three decades, including China in the Arctic. Heggelund leads a newly initiated research project on China's changing role in global environmental governance (2023–2027) working with partners in Norway and China – funded by the Norwegian Research Council. She is international advisor/expert for the China Council for International Cooperation on Environment and Development (CCICED), currently for the policy study on Carbon Dioxide Emissions Peaking and Carbon Neutrality Policy Measures and Implementation Pathways. She

also has extensive experience from evaluation projects in the energy sector in China. From 2009–2014 she was Senior Climate Change Advisor at UNDP China. Gørild has lived and worked in China for more than 16 years and is fluent in Chinese having studied at Peking University.

Matthew Hengesbaugh
is a Policy Researcher supporting Institute for Global Environmental Strategies (IGES) Integrated Sustainability Center with action research on the 2030 Development Agenda. Mr. Hengesbaugh has worked extensively in the Asia-Pacific region advocating and delivering sustainable development policy objectives since 2006, over which time he has advised and consulted with the United Nations, including the International Labor Organization and the United Nations Economic and Social Commission for Asia and the Pacific (UNESCAP) on issues including climate change and air pollution, green economy, and sustainable consumption and production.

Mikael Hildén
has a PhD in resource management from the University of Helsinki. He led the Climate Change Programme in Finnish Environment Institute SYKE in 2010–2022. He served as chair of the EGBCM 2017–2019. Currently he is vice chair of the Finnish Strategic Research Council and holds a position as Expert Councellor in the Supreme Administrative Court. He has gained expertise in combining legal, economic, social, technical, and scientific research on environmental policy.

Kateryna Holzer
is Senior Researcher with the CCEEL at the University of Eastern Finland Law School, where she leads a project on regulatory cooperation on carbon standards and teaches a course on international economic law and green transitions. Kateryna Holzer holds a PhD in Law from the University of Bern and a PhD in Economics from Ukraine. She has many years of experience in climate change and energy research, teaching and consultancy, with a focus on trade rules and measures supporting sustainable development.

Tuula Honkonen
is a Senior Lecturer of International Law at the University of Eastern Finland CCEEL. She holds an LLM (London School of Economics and Political Science) and a PhD in Environmental Law (University of Eastern Finland). She is specialized in international environmental law and policy. Tuula's research focuses largely on climate change law and policy at different levels of governance: from

global and transnational to the national level. Her recent research interests also include law on air pollution and climate resilience.

Alice Karanja
is a Post-doctoral Research Scientist at the World Agroforestry (ICRAF) in Nairobi, Kenya where she works on the interplay between agrobiodiversity, food environment and nutritional issues. She holds a PhD (Sustainability Science, University of Tokyo, 2019) in which she focused on clean cooking in rural Kenya from the perspectives of adoption dynamics, impacts, national policies, and stakeholder engagement.

Stefan Kirchner
is Research Professor of Arctic Law and head of the Arctic Governance Research Group at the Arctic Centre of the University of Lapland in Rovaniemi, Finland. Prof. Dr. Kirchner is a member of the bar in Frankfurt am Main, Germany, and is working at the intersection of human rights and the protection of the natural environment. He has taught international law at universities in Finland, Germany, Greenland, Italy, Lithuania, and Ukraine and currently (2023) serves as Chair of the Disaster Law Interest Group of the American Society of International Law and as Visiting Professor of Human Rights at Vytautas Magnus University in Kaunas, Lithuania.

Timo Koivurova
is Research Professor at the Arctic Centre, University of Lapland, Finland. He is focused on Arctic law and governance but has also conducted broader research on global law (including authoring an English-language textbook on international environmental law). Some of his research areas include: the legal status of the indigenous peoples of the Arctic (e.g. the Sámi); regulations and politics regarding climate change in general and in the Arctic; regulating mining industry practices; and the continued development of the Arctic Council as an intergovernmental forum. He has been involved as an expert in several international processes globally and in the Arctic region and has published on the above-mentioned topics extensively.

Harri Kokkola
is a research professor at Atmospheric Research Centre of Eastern Finland at the Finnish Meteorological Institute and a professor of aerosol-cloud interactions at the Department of Technical Physics at the University of Eastern Finland. His expertise is studying aerosol-cloud interactions and their effects

on the atmosphere and climate, having especially focused on the development of large-scale numerical models.

Kaarle Kupiainen
works as a Ministerial Adviser at the Finnish Ministry of the Environment where his main areas of responsibility concern international cooperation in climate and environmental policies. He represents the Finnish Government in the OECD, the UNFCCC, the IPCC, as well as the Arctic and Nordic cooperation in different duties. Prior to his public office, he worked in director and managerial duties in environmental business as well as in academia, where his work mainly focused on emissions of air pollutants and greenhouse gases.

Thomas Kühn
is Head of the Research Group 'Climate Change and the Cities of the Future' at the Finnish Meteorological Institute. He holds the title of Docent in Global Aerosol-Climate Modelling at the UEF. Kühn's expertise is in climate modelling, short-lived climate forcers, and model development. His main research interests are in aerosol-climate interactions, secondary organic aerosol, and black carbon, with a special focus on the Arctic regions.

Kari Lehtinen
is Professor of Atmospheric Physics and Chemistry as well as Dean of the Faculty of Science, Forestry and Technology at UEF. His main research interests are aerosol microphysics theory and modeling related to various applications in atmospheric science and climate change. Lehtinen has published more than 200 peer reviewed international journal articles (3 in 'Science') and supervised 25 PhD theses. Together with Kühn and Miinalainen, he has been working with the editorial team in joint interdisciplinary projects on SLCPs since 2014.

Niklas Löther
is a Project Researcher at the CCEEL, UEF Law School. He holds degrees in Politics and International Relations from the University of Aberdeen and Environmental Policy and Law from UEF. His research focuses on the intersection of environmental law and global politics, including the influence of non-state actors and the role of science.

Tuuli Miinalainen
conducted her PhD studies in the global climate modeling team, Aerosol Physics group, UEF Department of Technical Physics. Her dissertation was in global climate modeling with a focus on the impact of mitigating black carbon

emissions, particularly on the differences between different regions. Currently she is a postdoctoral researcher at the Finnish Meteorological Institute, continuing in the field of terrestrial biosphere modelling.

Tade Oyewunmi
is an Assistant Professor of Law and Director of the Energy, Environment, and Natural Resources Certificate Program, at the University of North Dakota School of Law, Grand Forks, North Dakota, US. His research and teaching areas include property, energy law and policy, and international business transactions. He obtained his Doctor of Laws (LL.D) in International Energy Law and Policy at the University of Eastern Finland School of Law, Finland; his LL.M in Oil and Gas Law at the University of Aberdeen, Scotland, UK; and Bachelor of Laws (LL.B) from the University of Ibadan, Nigeria.

Veera Pekkarinen
is a doctoral researcher in climate law at the UEF Law School. Her research focuses on global legal and regulatory framework for methane, particularly on examining opportunities to strengthen action on methane in developing countries and informal initiatives targeting methane. Her research was a part of the European Research Council funded project "ClimaSlow: Slowing Down Climate Change: Combining Climate Law and Climate Science to Identify the Best Options to Reduce Emissions of Short-lived Climate Pollutants in Developing Countries". Her other research interests include climate change loss and damage.

Malgorzata (Gosia) Smieszek
is a postdoctoral fellow at UiT The Arctic University of Norway in Tromsø, a visiting researcher at the Arctic Centre, University of Lapland in Rovaniemi, Finland, and an adjunct fellow of the East-West Center (EWC) in Honolulu, Hawaii. Her research interests include international environmental and Arctic governance, science-policy interface, science diplomacy, Arctic scientific cooperation, and gender-environment nexus. Smieszek was the Chair of International Arctic Science Committee (IASC) Action Group on Communicating Arctic Science to Policy Makers, a representative of IASC to meetings of the Arctic Council, and the Co-chair of the Arctic Observing Summit 2022. She is a co-founder of a non-profit "Women of the Arctic".

David D. Sussman
is an Associate Professor in the Department of Global Studies at Tokai University in Japan, and most recently served as a Fellow at the Institute for

Global Environmental Strategies (IGES) and a Visiting Scholar at the Global Development and Environment Institute. As a scholar-practitioner his research examines global interconnectivity and conflicts over natural resources, linking use of material resources to the environmental and social impacts in communities where they are sourced. David earned his B.A. from Dartmouth College, and M.A. and PhD degrees from the Fletcher School at Tufts University.

Charlotte Unger
is a Senior Research Associate at the Research Institute for Sustainability Helmholtz Centre Potsdam (RIFS), which she represents in national and international climate fora, such as the UNFCCC, the IPCC or the Deutsches Klima Konsortium. Her work focuses on global climate governance, climate clubs and non-traditional alliances, carbon markets; as well as climate policy in Germany, the EU, and the US. She was also involved in the Berlin Climate Citizens Assembly. Charlotte draws from fifteen years of experience in the field of environmental policy, gained in civil society, governmental and scientific institutions. She holds a PhD in political sciences from the Technical University of Munich. Her dissertation focused on the international linking of EU Emissions Trading System.

Eric Zusman
is a senior policy researcher/area leader at the Institute for Global Environmental Strategies in Hayama, Japan. Dr. Zusman holds a bachelor's degree in Mandarin Chinese from Rutgers University, a dual Masters Degree in public policy and Asian studies from the University of Texas at Austin, and a PhD in political science from the University of California, Los Angeles. For much of the past two decades he has conducted research on environmental issues in Asia. This has included working with China's Yellow River Conservancy Commission, the Chinese Research Academy on Environmental Science, Woodrow Wilson Center's China Environment Forum as well as Taiwan's Academia Sinica. He has published books and articles on water scarcity, air pollution regulation, environmental law, multilevel governance, sustainability transitions, low carbon development and the Sustainable Development Goals. He is currently serving as a lead author for the sixth assessment report of the IPCC (Chapter 17).

Introduction

Reducing Emissions of Short-Lived Climate Pollutants: Perspectives on Law and Governance

Yulia Yamineva, Kati Kulovesi and Eugenia Recio

1 Introduction

At the time of finalising this book in 2022–2023, the world seems to have entered a new stage of 'permacrisis' amid the pandemic, rising inflation, and international conflicts. Russia's invasion of Ukraine shook the very core of the international legal order and has clearly led to reshaping of geopolitical and energy relations with further manifestations of this transformation still unfolding. Impacts of the resulting economic and energy perturbations are already acutely felt in many countries and especially in the global South. Geopolitical tensions elsewhere in the world are also deepening. Many have been casting serious doubts as to the potential of multilateral approaches to address global problems.

Against these developments, the climate problem appears to be taking a second seat in public opinion and media. However, it shows no signs of diminishing: global average temperatures are expected to rise by 2.4 degrees Celsius based on the current climate mitigation commitments.[1] It is evident that further endeavors are required, and reducing emissions of short-lived climate pollutants (SLCPs) has been identified as a promising avenue to pursue in order to effectively and cost-efficiently attain climate objectives. This book provides a thorough analysis of the past decade's evolution of the legal and governance frameworks on SLCPs on a global and regional scale, and we anticipate that scholars, policymakers, and practitioners engaged in climate and environmental policy matters will discover valuable insights and learnings for the future within these pages.

1 Climate Action Tracker, 'CAT Climate Target Update Tracker' <https://climateactiontracker.org/climate-target-update-tracker-2022/> accessed 16 May 2023.

 | DOI:10.1163/9789004684089_002

2 Background, Purpose and Scope of the Book

Most global climate mitigation efforts have centred on reducing CO_2 emissions due to their dominant role in long-term global warming. Non-CO_2 greenhouse gases and aerosols also warm the climate though at a shorter timeframe. In the past decade, the potential of reducing their emissions for slowing down near-term climate change has become part of the discussion on ways to step up global climate action. This discussion has focused on the SLCPs, an umbrella label created to refer to a group of substances – methane, black carbon, hydro-fluorocarbons (HFCs), and tropospheric ozone – all of which have a relatively short lifetime in the atmosphere and a climate warming impact.

In the face of increasing climate change and due to the need of identifying quicker solutions to address it, an increasing focus on mitigating emissions of SLCPs has become a powerful argument of how countries and society in general can contribute significantly to achieving the objectives of the Paris Agreement and the Sustainable Development Goals. According to the Intergovernmental Panel on Climate Change (IPCC), limiting global warming to 1.5°C which is one of the more ambitious temperature targets set by the Paris Agreement is in fact impossible without action on SLCPs as it involves 'deep reductions of methane and black carbon emissions, 35 per cent or more of both by 2050 relative to 2010'.[2] As such, from a policy-makers' perspective, the focus on SLCPs offers an opportunity to achieve significant gains relatively quickly and help bridge the gap between current mitigation efforts and climate goals. Indeed, current national mitigation actions under the Paris Agreement are insufficient in bringing the world to lowering global temperature rise to well below 2°C and pursuing 1.5°C.[3] Finally, the focus on SLCPs is also attractive for associated co-benefits of their emissions' mitigation: methane and black carbon emissions' reductions lead to improved air quality and public health gains and hence have high institutional and socio-cultural feasibility.[4]

Against the multiple apparent advantages from reducing SLCPs' emissions, it is not surprising that the topic is becoming more and more salient

---

2 Intergovernmental Panel on Climate Change (IPCC), 'Summary for Policymakers' in V. Masson-Delmotte and others (eds.), *Global warming of 1.5°C. An IPCC Special Report on the impacts of global warming of 1.5°C above pre-industrial levels and related global greenhouse gas emission pathways, in the context of strengthening the global response to the threat of climate change, sustainable development, and efforts to eradicate poverty* (CUP 2018), 14 para. C.1.2.

3 UNEP, *Emissions Gap Report 2022: The Closing Window – Climate Crisis Calls for Rapid Transformation of Societies* (UNEP 2022).

4 IPCC (n2) 316.

in the global policy discourse around climate action. Prominent international organisations such as the UN Environment Programme (UNEP), World Meteorological Organisation, IPCC, and Arctic Monitoring and Assessment Programme have published several influential reports synthesising the science of SLCPs.[5] A global state-led partnership to tackle SLCPs – the Climate and Clean Air Coalition (CCAC) – was established under UNEP in 2011 and has since become a key actor in driving policy responses at global and national levels. Other international and regional fora have also made concrete legal and policy steps to mitigate specific SLCPs. In 2012, black carbon emissions were integrated into the targets to reduce particulate matter pollution under the Gothenburg Protocol to Abate Acidification, Eutrophication and Ground-level Ozone of the Convention on Long-Range Transboundary Air Pollution (CLRTAP). In 2015, the Arctic Council agreed on the Framework for Action on Enhanced Black Carbon and Methane Emission Reductions. In 2016, the Montreal Protocol on Substances that Deplete the Ozone Layer was complemented with the Kigali Amendment on the phase out of HFCs. Under the Paris Agreement, some countries have included SLCP mitigation targets or policies in their Nationally Determined Contributions, and various global cooperation efforts have also been launched to address methane emissions, most recently the Global Methane Pledge in 2021.

It is clear that SLCPs – in their entirety and each of them individually – have taken a firm place in the global climate policy discourse and governance. However, somewhat surprisingly, little scholarly work has been conducted to evaluate the global and regional regulatory frameworks and governance initiatives that have emerged to mitigate SLCPs' emissions. The few scientific works that have been published discuss specific institutions, sectors or geographies such as: CCAC,[6] transportation sector,[7] transnational law

---

5 AMAP, *AMAP Assessment 2021: Impacts of Short-lived Climate Forcers on Arctic Climate, Air Quality, and Human Health* (AMAP 2021); IPCC, 'Chapter 6: Short-Lived Climate Forcers' in V. Masson-Delmotte and others (eds.), *Climate Change 2021: The Physical Science Basis* (CUP 2021); UNEP and WMO, *Integrated Assessment of Black Carbon and Tropospheric Ozone: Summary for Decision Makers* (UNEP and WMO 2011); UNEP, *Near-term Climate Protection and Clean Air Benefits: Actions for Controlling Short-Lived Climate Forcers* (UNEP 2011).

6 Charlotte Unger, Kathleen A Mar and Konrad Gürtler, 'A Club's Contribution to Global Climate Governance: The Case of the Climate and Clean Air Coalition' (2020) 6 Palgrave Communications 1.

7 Thomas Brewer (ed), *Transportation Air Pollutants: Black Carbon and Other Emissions* (Springer International Publishing 2021) <https://www.springer.com/gp/book/9783030596903> accessed 11 December 2020.

characteristics,[8] Arctic perspectives,[9] and China.[10],[11] Despite the detailed case studies, we still lack a full picture and an overall stocktake and analysis of the novel policy issue. This book seeks to fill the gap.

The main purpose of this book is to provide a comprehensive and critical evaluation of global law and governance on SLCPs. In particular, the book delves into the science behind the concept of SLCPs and assesses the concept's evolution and nature as a boundary object between science and policy realms. The book further evaluates the legal and governance responses developed to mitigating SLCPs' emissions under various international and transnational arenas. These include such treaties as the UNFCCC and Paris Agreement; Gothenburg Protocol; and Montreal Protocol; as well as other international and transnational fora like CCAC and the Arctic Council.

The policy responses to mitigating SLCPs' emissions are spread across various governance and jurisdictional levels. The landscape is also characterised by the multiplicity of law-making actors and stakeholders, which owns to the variety of emissions' sources, and the global and local nature of their impacts. These characteristics warrant a multi-level pluralistic approach to considering legal and governance responses to mitigating SLCPs' emissions. While much of the volume engages with international and transnational law and governance, many chapters evaluate their interface with laws and policies at the domestic level. Importantly, the book also delves into the specifics of several case studies to illustrate the unique challenges and common features of multilevel regulatory efforts, for instance in relation to emissions from cookstoves, maritime

8 Kati Kulovesi, 'Exploring Transnational Legal Orders: Using Transnational Environmental Law to Strengthen the Global Regulation of Black Carbon for the Benefit of the Arctic Region' in Veerle Heyvaert and Leslie-Anne Duvic-Paoli (eds), *Research Handbook on Transnational Environmental Law* (Edward Elgar Publishing 2020) <https://www.elgaronline.com/display/edcoll/9781788119627/9781788119627.00010.xml> accessed 21 April 2023.

9 Sabaa Ahmad Khan and Kati Kulovesi, 'Black Carbon and the Arctic: Global Problem-Solving through the Nexus of Science, Law and Space' (2018) 27 Review of European, Comparative & International Environmental Law 5; Sabaa A Khan, 'The Global Commons through a Regional Lens: The Arctic Council on Short-Lived Climate Pollutants' (2017) 6 Transnational Environmental Law 131; Seita Romppanen, 'Arctic Climate Governance via EU Law on Black Carbon?' (2018) 27 Review of European, Comparative & International Environmental Law 45; Yulia Yamineva and Kati Kulovesi, 'Keeping the Arctic White: The Legal and Governance Landscape for Reducing Short-Lived Climate Pollutants in the Arctic Region' (2018) 7 Transnational Environmental Law 201.

10 Yulia Yamineva and Zhe Liu, 'Cleaning the Air, Protecting the Climate: Policy, Legal and Institutional Nexus to Reduce Black Carbon Emissions in China' (2019) 95 Environmental Science and Policy 1.

11 Many of these publications have been authored by the contributors to this edited volume.

and road transportation, and oil and gas operations. In discussing national cases, the authors draw on a wide selection of country examples across developed and developing countries in Europe, North and South Americas, Africa, and Asia.

The book brings together some of the most experienced legal and governance scholars, most of which have dedicated years to researching and evaluating specific aspects of the global law and governance of SLCPs. In addition, the author collective includes atmospheric physicists to provide for a science-based approach to law and policy.

The book is structured accordingly: The volume opens with a scientific overview on characteristics, sources and impacts of SLCPs' emissions. The rest of the book consists of two parts: the first part is dedicated to overarching global and regional legal and governance responses to SLCPs, while the second part of the book discusses specific sectoral case studies.

To adopt an evaluative approach to SLCPs, the book is structured around three key policy questions: What is the existing state of global law and governance concerning SLCP mitigation? What accomplishments have been made and what gaps remain? What lies ahead for the SLCP policy agenda? The concluding chapter synthesizes the responses to these inquiries.

The subsequent sections in the introduction offer a concise overview of the book's contributions.

3 What Are SLCPs?

Providing scientific context is paramount for discussing the regulation and governance of SLCPs as underlying complexity, knowledge gaps and uncertainties pose significant challenges for the development and formulation of policy responses. The opening chapter, authored by Thomas Kühn, Tuuli Miinalainen, Harri Kokkola and Kari Lehtinen, provides a comprehensive overview of the science behind SLCPs (Chapter 1). It covers emissions sources, characteristics, and impacts, emphasizing the difficulties associated with evaluating climate effects through climate models and the existing scientific uncertainties.

The authors explain that methane and HFCs are greenhouse gases where HFCs are emitted primarily from refrigeration and air conditioning, and methane emissions result from agriculture, landfills, and natural gas and petroleum systems. Black carbon is not a greenhouse gas but an aerosol and occurs as a result of burning of fossil fuel and biomass in energy production, transportation, and domestic cooking and heating, and agricultural open burning. Tropospheric ozone is not an emitted pollutant but forms as a result of chemical reactions of methane, carbon monoxide, nitrogen oxides, and volatile organics.

What unites these substances is their short lifetime in the atmosphere – from days to years – and a warming impact on the climate. SLCPs are typically co-emitted with other pollutants which may have a cooling impact on the climate. This characteristic presents a challenge for formulating appropriate policy responses, as they must account for the cumulative effects of various policy measures. In addition, most SLCPs – except HFCs – have a detrimental effect on air quality and human health as well as ecosystems and agriculture (ozone) implying that any measures to reduce their emissions bring co-benefits for other public policy goals.

What the authors of this chapter underline is that the science of SLCPs is very complex due to multiple parallel interactions among various atmospheric processes. The analysis of SLCPs' effects is conducted using complex climate models which have their own shortcomings. Furthermore, there are still unresolved scientific inquiries that lack definitive answers. One example is the uncertainties surrounding the overall climate impacts of mitigating black carbon emissions, a question directly relevant to policy-making decisions.

4 Global Perspectives on Law and Governance of SLCPs

The opening chapter of the book's first part highlights the challenge of bringing together diverse substances under the umbrella term of SLCPs. Niklas Löther's contribution, titled 'A conceptual history of SLCPs', focuses on SLCPs as a policy concept and traces its development (Chapter 2). Specifically, the chapter delves into the history of how and why different scientific aspects were amalgamated under the term of SLCPs, as well as the resulting political ramifications. This exploration leads the author to intriguing conclusions, highlighting the significant influence of the growing epistemic community and the CCAC partnership, alongside the role of the United States in shaping global priorities regarding SLCPs on the climate policy agenda.

In the following part, the book attempts to make sense of the polycentric and fragmented global legal and governance landscape on SLCP mitigation. Here, the book takes stock of the various approaches taken to regulating and governing SLCPs' emissions under international treaties and transnational initiatives and assesses their problem-solving potential, achievements, and options for further strengthening.

Individual chapters employ a variety of theoretical and analytical approaches to their subjects. Some have legal discipline as a starting point engaging in a legal doctrinal analysis of relevant international treaties; others draw upon literature from the domains of global environmental governance, international relations, and environmental policy research. Several chapters take a historiographical approach, necessitating meticulous document tracing. Many of the book's contributions delve into novel thematic areas, often lacking prior scholarly work on the subject.

Considering the climate impacts of SLCPs, the international climate change regime appears as a logical avenue for regulating SLCPs' emissions. However, Chapter 3 of the book, co-authored by Yulia Yamineva and Veera Pekkarinen, questions whether the UNFCCC regime is truly 'right home for SLCPs'. The authors explain that the regime has primarily focused on mitigating CO_2 emissions, considering them as the primary driver of long-term global warming. Consequently, they highlight the comparatively limited attention given to non-CO_2 greenhouse gas emissions such as HFCs and methane. The chapter further delves into the significance of the UNFCCC's comprehensive approach to greenhouse gases and its reporting framework for mitigating SLCPs. Additionally, it discusses the possibilities and challenges associated with addressing SLCPs through countries' Nationally Determined Contributions under the Paris Agreement. The authors conclude that the most significant potential for action lies in expanding mitigation efforts related to methane emissions, while other international avenues appear more suitable for addressing HFCs and black carbon.

Continuing the discussion, Chapter 4, authored by Louise du Toit, examines the global regulation of HFCs under the Montreal Protocol on Substances that Deplete the Ozone Layer. Initially designed to address concerns related to stratospheric ozone depletion, the Montreal Protocol is widely regarded as a successful international agreement. However, from a climate change perspective, the Protocol has been problematic due to the substitution of ozone-depleting substances with HFCs, which are potent greenhouse gases. Consequently, the Protocol has inadvertently contributed to increased HFC consumption and, in turn, climate change. In 2016, after substantial resistance and deliberation, HFCs were added to the list of substances controlled and restricted by the Montreal Protocol. In light of these developments, the chapter explores potential avenues to further strengthen the ozone regime, ensuring its ongoing success. This includes addressing gaps within the regime and effectively coordinating measures across different international legal frameworks.

The most advanced approach to regulating black carbon emissions has been developed under a regional treaty aimed at preventing air pollution in the Northern hemisphere. This treaty is known as the 1999 Gothenburg Protocol to Abate Acidification, Eutrophication, and Ground-level Ozone, which was later amended in 2012. The Gothenburg Protocol was developed under the 1979 Convention on Long-Range Transboundary Air Pollution. In Chapter 5, Adam Byrne explores the progress and challenges associated with addressing SLCPs and developing an integrated approach to air pollution and climate change under the Protocol. The chapter elucidates the reasons behind the inclusion of black carbon in the agreement, the resulting commitments for participating Parties, and the implementation of these provisions. Additionally, Byrne delves into the latest round of the periodic review of the Gothenburg Protocol (2020–22), discussing further potential for strengthening actions to mitigate SLCPs under this treaty.

While the previous three chapters have focused on traditional international legal instruments, the subsequent chapter, Chapter 6 by Charlotte Unger, delves into a less conventional yet increasingly prevalent approach to governing common environmental issues. Transnational institutions have emerged as crucial actors in global environmental and climate change governance. One such prominent transnational institution in the realm of SLCP governance is the CCAC. Established in 2012, the CCAC is a government-led voluntary network that now brings together a diverse range of over 150 countries, intergovernmental organizations, non-governmental organizations, and scientific members. Chapter 6 provides an overview of the Coalition's structure, operational approach, and activities, including fostering policy dialogue, assessing scientific knowledge, developing technical expertise and a knowledge network, and implementing on-the-ground projects. Unger also evaluates the past, present, and future role of the Coalition within the international policy landscape and global governance of SLCPs, while addressing associated challenges.

In addition to the global perspective, the regional scale holds significant importance when considering existing and potential regulatory approaches for mitigating SLCPs' emissions. An example of this is the noteworthy impact of black carbon emissions on warming and the loss of snow-ice cover in the Arctic region, attributed to the reduction in the reflectivity of snow and ice.[12] The Arctic is already experiencing a much faster rate of warming compared to the global average, and there is growing evidence suggesting that the Arctic Ocean may become ice-free during summers as early as the late 2030s.[13] These dramatic transformations not only present significant challenges for the

12 AMAP, *AMAP Assessment 2015: Black Carbon and Ozone as Arctic Climate Forcers* (AMAP 2015).

13 AMAP, *Snow, Water, Ice and Permafrost in the Arctic* (AMAP 2017); AMAP, *Arctic Climate Change Update 2019: An Update to Key Findings of Snow, Water, Ice and Permafrost in the Arctic* (AMAP 2019).

vulnerable ecosystems and nature-based livelihoods of people residing in the Arctic but also contribute to the acceleration of global and regional climate change. This is due to the Arctic's crucial role in regulating global climate and environment.

Chapters 7 and 8 focus on the Arctic governance of black carbon and methane emissions. The Arctic Council, recognized as the primary institution for governing the region, has played a pioneering role in knowledge generation and action on SLCPs, both regionally and globally. Chapter 7 is authored by a collective of writers including Timo Koivurova, Stefan Kirchner, Malgorzata Smieszek, Medy Dervovic, Mikael Hilden, and Kaarle Kupiainen, many of whom have had a first-hand experience with the Council and its workstream on SLCPs. The chapter outlines the development of the Council's workstream on SLCPs, highlighting the scientific assessments conducted and how their findings have influenced and interacted with policy decisions and processes led by the Senior Arctic Officials and Ministerial meetings. The authors emphasize that the Council's unique ability to address emerging environmental concerns stems from its strong polycentric features.

Maintaining the focus on the Arctic region, the subsequent chapter shifts from regional governance to inter-state relations, delving into the contents and impacts of bilateral science diplomacy. The authors, Pami Aalto, Gørild Heggelund, Anna Claydon, and Minna Hanhijärvi, investigate the science diplomacy efforts of Norway and Finland towards China and Russia, respectively, in order to mitigate black carbon emissions. The diplomatic endeavors of these two Nordic nations aimed to foster research, development, and innovation initiatives in the major economies of China and Russia, and involved collaboration between various governmental, public, and private sector actors. The authors examine how shared problem definitions and similar interests, or the lack thereof, have shaped the relative successes and failures of the Norwegian-Russian and Finnish-Russian cases, unraveling the dynamics at play in each context.

5 Case Studies on SLCP Mitigation

The second part of the book offers a comprehensive examination of sectoral approaches to mitigating SLCPs, along with an exploration of the potential for a co-benefits assessment in responding to these pollutant emissions. Some of chapters are based on key sectors responsible for high volumes of SLCPs' emissions or the sectors where for one or another reason regulating SLCPs' emissions has been problematic or ineffective. Other case studies present examples of innovative action to reduce emissions of SLCPs at global or local levels.

Emissions from household cookstoves used for cooking and heating are significant, especially in developing countries, and intersect with many policy agendas including public health, climate change, energy access, and development. However, regulating cookstove emissions poses a challenge due to the involvement of multiple governance levels, diverse actors, and varied policy objectives that must be effectively addressed. In Chapter 9, Tuula Honkonen and Alice Karanja examine clean cooking policies and regulations in India and Kenya, two countries heavily reliant on cookstoves. Their objective is to extract lessons that can guide the development and implementation of national regulatory frameworks. The authors emphasize the significance of the legal nature of regulations, ease of implementation, administrative coordination, and the availability of reliable information. This analysis highlights that cookstove emissions represent a multidimensional problem that requires polycentric forms of governance. However, most regulatory efforts are primarily driven by the state. In this context, the authors propose that transnational networks could play a more substantial role in the future in addressing and controlling cookstove emissions.

The subsequent chapter, authored by David Sussman, Eric Zusman, and Matthew Hengesbaugh, delves into the necessary policy and institutional reforms required to attain multiple co-benefits from reducing SLCP emissions in terms of health, climate, and food security. The authors specifically advocate for the crucial role of the science-policy-society interface, multi-sectoral and multi-level governance, as well as just transitions. These concepts are explored within the context of clean transportation, clean cookstoves, and the reduction of open burning of biomass residue in Asia. The chapter proposes specific measures to be taken, including strengthening policy coherence, enhancing interagency coordination, and promoting vertical integration. Additionally, the authors emphasize the importance of establishing deliberative decision-making platforms for stakeholders and implementing compensation programs. These recommendations aim to foster effective collaboration and facilitate the realization of desired outcomes in the pursuit of reducing SLCP emissions.

Chapter 11, authored by Thomas Brewer, addresses the complexities, multi-level nature, and polycentric governance and regulation pertaining to black carbon emissions in international maritime shipping. Brewer examines the scope and effectiveness of regulatory frameworks across four levels: the International Maritime Organization (IMO), regional Emission Control Areas, national jurisdictions, and local levels such as ports. The chapter highlights the significant advancements in technologies and policies regarding the measurement, reporting, and verification of black carbon emissions in the shipping industry. However, it also acknowledges the lack of explicit regulation of black carbon emissions in both international and national laws. Particularly at the global level, the chapter demonstrates that the IMO has yet to adopt any limits on black carbon emissions from ships, leaving a notable gap in guidance. Additionally, enforcement measures for breaching emissions limits in shipping are generally weak.

Chapter 12, authored by Kateryna Holzer, examines another significant source of black carbon emissions: road transport. The author identifies varying emissions restrictions across countries as the primary obstacle to more effective emission regulations. This issue is particularly pronounced in developing countries, which often have more lenient regulations regarding car emissions. Holzer proposes potential solutions to this problem. One approach involves promoting the global diffusion and harmonization of car emission standards. This entails leveraging market forces to incentivize automakers to adhere to stricter emission standards in order to gain access to larger and environmentally conscious export markets. Another complementary approach involves adopting international car emission standards through relevant international and regional platforms.

The concluding chapter of this part, Chapter 11, authored by Tade Oyewunmi, focuses on another significant short-lived climate-warming substance: methane. Methane emissions from oil and gas operations account for a substantial portion of global methane emissions. These emissions are addressed on a global scale through various transnational initiatives and frameworks, including international best practices. The chapter explores how industry-led groups, governmental bodies, and intergovernmental institutions have established multinational partnerships and developed best practice guidelines to tackle methane emissions in the oil and gas sector. Oyewunmi illustrates how such transnational norms, either directly or indirectly, become integrated into national regulatory frameworks to manage environmental risks and mitigate climate change in oil and gas-producing countries. However, he concludes that greater cooperation is necessary at both national and transnational levels, fostering collaboration among operators and institutions to effectively address methane emissions.

The book concludes with a final chapter in which the editors aim to synthesize the diverse research presented throughout the book and address the initial questions posed at its outset. These questions relate to the current state of global law and policy regarding SLCP mitigation, achievements and gaps in this area, and the future of the SLCP policy agenda. This section highlights the crucial role of the science-policy interface and the intricate interactions between science and policy in shaping agendas and formulating policy responses. The polycentric and fragmented nature of the global landscape of SLCP law and governance is explored, along with the growing significance of transnational law and institutions in this domain. Here, the chapter explains how the regulation and governance of SLCP emissions reflect broader trends observed in global environmental law and governance. The concluding section also delves into the future of the global SLCP policy agenda and identifies potential pathways for further science-based research on the subject.

Acknowledgements

The book has received financial support from the European Research Council through the Starting Grant awarded to Professor Kati Kulovesi for the period from 1 January 2017 to 31 July 2022 (project number 678889). The book has further benefited from the support provided through the Academy of Finland flagship project 'ACCC – Atmosphere and Climate Competence Center'.

The editors would also like to express their gratitude to research assistant Niklas Löther for his invaluable assistance in finalizing the book manuscript.

Bibliography

AMAP, *AMAP Assessment 2015: Black Carbon and Ozone as Arctic Climate Forcers* (AMAP 2015).

AMAP, *AMAP Assessment 2021: Impacts of Short-lived Climate Forcers on Arctic Climate, Air Quality, and Human Health* (AMAP 2021).

AMAP, *Arctic Climate Change Update 2019: an Update to Key Findings of Snow, Water, Ice and Permafrost in the Arctic* (AMAP 2019).

AMAP, *Snow, Water, Ice and Permafrost in the Arctic* (AMAP 2017).

Brewer T (ed), *Transportation Air Pollutants: Black Carbon and Other Emissions* (Springer International Publishing 2021) <https://www.springer.com/gp/book/9783030596903> accessed 11 December 2020.

Climate Action Tracker, 'CAT Climate Target Update Tracker' <https://climateactiontracker.org/climate-target-update-tracker-2022/> accessed 16 May 2023.

IPCC, 'Chapter 6: Short-Lived Climate Forcers' in V. Masson-Delmotte and others (eds.), *Climate Change 2021: the Physical Science Basis* (CUP 2021).

IPCC, 'Summary for Policymakers' in V. Masson-Delmotte and others (eds.), *Global warming of 1.5°C. An IPCC Special Report on the impacts of global warming of 1.5°C above pre-industrial levels and related global greenhouse gas emission pathways, in the context of strengthening the global response to the threat of climate change, sustainable development, and efforts to eradicate poverty* (CUP 2018).

Khan SA, 'The Global Commons through a Regional Lens: The Arctic Council on Short-Lived Climate Pollutants' (2017) 6 Transnational Environmental Law 131.

Khan SA and Kulovesi K, 'Black Carbon and the Arctic: Global Problem-Solving through the Nexus of Science, Law and Space' (2018) 27 Review of European, Comparative & International Environmental Law 5.

Kulovesi K, 'Exploring Transnational Legal Orders: Using Transnational Environmental Law to Strengthen the Global Regulation of Black Carbon for the Benefit of the Arctic Region' in Veerle Heyvaert and Leslie-Anne Duvic-Paoli (eds), *Research Handbook on Transnational Environmental Law* (Edward Elgar Publishing 2020) <https://www.elgaronline.com/display/edcoll/9781788119627/9781788119627.00010.xml> accessed 21 April 2023.

Romppanen S, 'Arctic Climate Governance via EU Law on Black Carbon?' (2018) 27 Review of European, Comparative & International Environmental Law 45.

UNEP, *Near-term Climate Protection and Clean Air Benefits: Actions for Controlling Short-Lived Climate Forcers* (UNEP 2011).

UNEP and WMO, *Integrated Assessment of Black Carbon and Tropospheric Ozone: Summary for Decision Makers* (UNEP and WMO 2011).

Unger C, Mar KA and Gürtler K, 'A Club's Contribution to Global Climate Governance: The Case of the Climate and Clean Air Coalition' (2020) 6 Palgrave Communications 1.

Yamineva Y and Kulovesi K, 'Keeping the Arctic White: The Legal and Governance Landscape for Reducing Short-Lived Climate Pollutants in the Arctic Region' (2018) 7 Transnational Environmental Law 201.

Yamineva Y and Zhe L, 'Cleaning the Air, Protecting the Climate: Policy, Legal and Institutional Nexus to Reduce Black Carbon Emissions in China' (2019) 95 Environmental Science and Policy 1.

CHAPTER 1

Scientific Overview on SLCPs

Characteristics, Impacts and Uncertainties

Thomas Kühn, Tuuli Miinalainen, Harri Kokkola and Kari Lehtinen

1 Introduction

Most human activities result in emissions of pollutants that not only affect our health through degrading air quality but also accelerate global warming. Such activities include for example various means of energy production, transportation, agriculture, industrial processes, waste management, cooking and residential heating and cooling. Emissions originating from human activities are called anthropogenic emissions. In contrast, natural emission sources include, for example, forest fires and volcano eruptions. The origin of the term *short-lived climate pollutants* (SLCPs) arises from the life cycle of the emitted pollutants: the removal mechanisms of those climate warming pollutants are so effective that they don't stay in the atmosphere for very long (Table 1.1). The short, or relatively short, lifetimes make emission mitigation of SLCPs attractive: if their emissions can be reduced, their amounts in the atmosphere will then also rapidly decline. This is very different compared to carbon dioxide (CO_2), the lifetime of which is tens to hundreds of years, which means that the effects of emission reductions can be seen only after a very long time in actual atmospheric amounts.

However, the same processes that emit SLCPs typically also emit other, *co-emitted pollutants*, such as sulfate aerosols, which may actually have a cooling effect on climate. If such a pollutant also has a short lifetime in the atmosphere, it is called *a short-lived climate forcer* (*SLCF*), but not an SLCP. SLCFs include all short-lived climate altering substances, both warming and cooling, and are thus a more general class of substances than SLCPs. It is important to consider both SLCFs as a whole and SLCPs in particular because they originate from the same sources, interact within the atmosphere and, therefore, affect each other's atmospheric abundances. This means that, in general, mitigating of one pollutant entails changes in other pollutants' emissions and atmospheric abundances. The term 'SLCF' is more commonly seen in the field

 | DOI:10.1163/9789004684089_003

TABLE 1.1 Main sources and lifetimes of the most important SLCPs

SLCP	Sources	Lifetime
Black carbon	Burning of fossil fuel and biomass in energy production, transportation, cooking, agricultural open burning	Days to weeks
Hydrofluorocarbons	Poor maintenance and equipment failure related to refrigeration and air conditioning, aerosolized propellants	Days to years
Methane	Agriculture, landfills, fugitive emissions from natural gas and petroleum systems	12 years
Ozone	Chemical reactions of methane, carbon monoxide, nitrogen oxides, volatile organics (so not an emitted pollutant)	Hours to weeks

SOURCE: INTERGOVERNMENTAL PANEL ON CLIMATE CHANGE (IPCC), *CLIMATE CHANGE 2021: THE PHYSICAL SCIENCE BASIS. CONTRIBUTION OF WORKING GROUP I TO THE SIXTH ASSESSMENT REPORT OF THE INTERGOVERNMENTAL PANEL ON CLIMATE CHANGE* (HEREAFTER IPCC AR6; CUP 2021).

of natural sciences. For instance, the latest IPCC Assessment Report (AR6)[1] analyses the total effect of SLCFs, not only SLCPs. In this chapter, we use both terms, because focusing only on SLCPs would omit some important co-effects that play a major role when analysing the climatic effects of, for example, black carbon.

How does the emission of a pollutant lead to a change in the Earth's climate? To answer this question, an in-depth understanding of many complex and inter-connected processes is needed. These include consideration of the emission of the pollutants, their atmospheric transport and transformation, interaction with solar radiation, and their removal mechanisms. To estimate the climate effects, complex computer programs called Earth-System Models are required to integrate knowledge from several scientific fields, including physics, meteorology, chemistry, and biology. Here, we try to give a general overview of these processes and concepts, especially targeted to readers who are not part of the natural science community.

1 Ibid.

The main removal mechanisms for SLCFs in aerosol form, such as black carbon, include wet deposition (capture by rain or snow and ending up on the ground) and gravitational settling (i.e., gravity pulling aerosols towards the ground). Both the emission and removal rates of SLCFs vary considerably by geographical location, causing the effects of black carbon to change considerably depending on location. Methane and ozone removal both include complicated atmospheric chemistry,[2] in which the amount of methane in the atmosphere plays a crucial role. For instance, reducing methane emissions can also lead to decreased surface ozone levels due to atmospheric chemical processes.

This chapter first introduces some basic concepts used in assessing climate impacts of pollutants and other changes in the Earth system (Section 2), then introduces SLCPs and their past, present, and future impacts on the global climate (Sections 3 and 5). In Section 4, we give a short overview on how the climate impacts of SLCPs are assessed using climate models, the problems which occur in these modelling exercises, and how they are solved. Finally, in Section 6, we explain the meaning and origin of scientific uncertainty about SLCPs, and how uncertainty estimates can be interpreted.

2 Radiative Forcing and Surface Air Temperature

In this chapter, we describe, how the impact of a change in the Earth system, for instance the increase of atmospheric abundance of a pollutant, leads to a change in the Earth's climate and more particularly the surface air temperature. We introduce the two central terms of radiative forcing and climate feedback, how they are assessed, and where the related and often cited uncertainties in their estimates come from.

2.1 *The Radiative Balance of the Earth System*

While much of the public discussion concerning climate change is centred around surface temperatures, the natural sciences deal first and foremost with *energy* and how it is gained, lost, and re-distributed in a system. Much of the uncertainty in the assessed surface temperature response to an atmospheric pollutant originates from climate feedbacks due to radiative forcings, two terms that will be explained below. By restricting the scientific discussion to

2 See, for example, John H. Seinfeld and Spyros N. Pandis, *Atmospheric chemistry and physics: from air pollution to climate change* (John Wiley & Sons, 2016).

energy and its gain and loss in the Earth system, we can obtain more robust comparisons between the climate impacts of different pollutants.

The Earth system constantly gains energy (is warmed) by absorbing a large portion of the incoming sunlight. At the same time, the Earth also loses energy (is cooled) as it emits thermal radiation, i.e., releases heat, back to space. Because these two processes both vary in time and occur unevenly across the Earth, the energy contained in the Earth system is constantly re-distributed. This leads to daily and seasonal variations in, e.g., temperature and precipitation, which we call weather. Even though these weather variables change constantly, we can still find repeating patterns if we look for long enough. On a global scale, such timeframe is of the order of 30 years.[3] In an unchanging climate, the Earth's energy gains and losses, averaged over such time scales, are equal. Hence, the amount of energy in the Earth system remains almost unchanged. In this case, we say that the Earth system is in *equilibrium*.[4] Keep in mind, though, that over shorter time scales, be it days, months or even several years, the Earth's energy gains and losses are not equal. Therefore, when climate scientists talk about the Earth's energy balance, it is always with respect to climate-relevant time scales.

If the radiative balance of the Earth system is disturbed (on a climate-relevant time scale), the Earth system will start to either gain or lose energy, which will ultimately lead to a warming or cooling of the planet, respectively. Such a disturbance in the radiative balance is called a *radiative forcing*: The Earth system is forced out of its equilibrium and starts to change. Over time the Earth system will adjust by emitting respectively more or less thermal radiation to space and thereby find a new equilibrium. This adjustment results in the observed and projected changes in, e.g., long-term average surface temperatures and precipitation patterns. A radiative forcing can be caused by any kind of persistent disturbance in the Earth system including changes in atmospheric composition, vegetation, snow and ice cover, solar irradiation, and cloud cover. In the following part, we will limit the discussion to the change in abundance of an atmospheric pollutant.

Defining and determining a radiative forcing is not easy, and both definitions and methods used have changed over time. It is nonetheless important to do this in a rigorous manner in order to produce comparable and repeatable results. Radiative forcing is usually determined with the help of climate

3 IPCC (n1) Annex VII: Glossary, pp. 2215–2256.

4 Note here that the term equilibrium according to its thermodynamic definition is used quite loosely. A better term would be *dynamic steady state*, but for simplicity we stick with equilibrium.

models. The AR6[5] of the IPCC defines three different categories of radiative forcing: instantaneous radiative forcing (IRF), stratospheric-temperature-adjusted radiative forcing (SARF) and effective radiative forcing (ERF). IRF only considers the change in the Earth's radiative budget due to the interaction of the additional pollutants with radiation. In addition, SARF is calculated after the stratosphere has adjusted in response to the IRF, which affects the total computed radiative budget. ERF further accounts for cloud effects and tropospheric adjustments, which happen after stratospheric adjustments and again affect the total computed radiative budget. The definitions of IRF, SARF and ERF deviate somewhat from the definitions used in earlier assessment reports but are still qualitatively comparable. The extent to which the atmosphere is allowed to adjust to a change in abundance of an atmospheric pollutant has direct implications on the estimated magnitudes of climate change as well as the involved uncertainties. Before the Fifth Assessment Report (AR5)[6] of the IPCC, most of the discussion was based on a quantity similar to SARF, but since AR5, discussion has shifted to ERF instead, which is considered a more robust measure of a pollutant's effect on the climate.

2.2 *Climate Feedbacks and Climate Response*

To estimate how much the climate changes in response to the increased amount/abundance of a pollutant, two principal components are to be considered: the radiative forcing that the pollutant induces and the *climate feedbacks* that occur after the Earth's surface starts to warm. A climate feedback is defined as a process that occurs in response to the warming of the Earth's surface. Climate feedbacks can be both negative and positive: a negative climate feedback counteracts global warming, thereby stabilising the climate, while a positive climate feedback enhances global warming. A good example of a negative climate feedback is the fact that a warmer planet emits more thermal radiation, which has a cooling effect on the climate. An example of a positive climate feedback is the Arctic sea ice melt in a warming climate, which increases the amount of sunlight absorbed by the surface, which in turn results in further warming.

In principle, the total response of the Earth system to a given radiative forcing, i.e., the combination of all climate feedbacks, can be estimated with help of a numerical value, called the net feedback parameter. However, the

5 IPCC AR6 (n1).

6 IPCC, *Climate Change 2013: The Physical Science Basis. Contribution of Working Group I to the Fifth Assessment Report of the Intergovernmental Panel on Climate Change* (hereafter IPCC AR5; CUP 2013).

magnitudes of different climate feedbacks are not known precisely. Depending on the feedback mechanism, estimates of its strength in different climate models may differ quite a lot. Also, estimates based on other methods, e.g., satellite and ground-based observations, vary. This means that, instead of obtaining one number for the net climate feedback parameter, we obtain a range of values. Based on this range of values, we can calculate a central value (the best estimate) and an uncertainty range for this best estimate: The smaller the spread of values, the smaller the uncertainty. According to the AR6, the uncertainty of the estimated net feedback parameter is of the order of 50 %, i.e., the estimated lower and upper bounds for the most likely net feedback parameter values are either 50% lower or higher than the best estimate.[7] Estimates of radiative forcing in different climate models vary as well, contributing further uncertainty to the estimated magnitude of the climate response (see more about uncertainty in Section 6).

In practice, it is more feasible to estimate climate response using Earth System Models (see Section 4) since they also model the oceans and hence make it easier to consider the warming of the ocean surface, which in turn allows to model climate feedbacks directly. However, as the use of Earth System Models is computationally very expensive (see Section 4), the scientific discussion is often constrained to the estimation of radiative forcings, thereby omitting the net feedback parameter. This can be done using different models, such as atmospheric global circulation models which, compared to Earth System Models, are computationally less demanding (i.e., fewer processors, less time, and/or data storage capacity are needed to run a global circulation model compared to an Earth System Model). This is because Earth System Models are more complex and include more physical processes to be modelled, and additionally have to model much longer time periods compared to global circulation models. The output from global circulation models provides information mostly about radiative forcings but does not provide rigorous values for surface temperature changes, which may not be as feasible for policy-making. However, by comparing the radiative forcings, the discussion about the climate response to different pollutants can still be held in a scientifically rigorous manner. Furthermore, because climate feedbacks are not (or only partly) included in global circulation model simulations, the overall uncertainty of the results is smaller. Also, physical descriptions of SLCFS in Earth System Models are usually not very detailed, because Earth System Models are already computationally demanding. The more light-weight global circulation

7 IPCC AR6 (n1).

models, on the other hand, allow for more detailed physical descriptions of the processes governing SLCFs. Some Earth System Model-derived metrics exist, which can be used to convert the radiative forcings from global circulation models into rough estimates of climate response.

Like in the real atmosphere, modelled meteorological variables, such as temperature and precipitation, vary in time. This is both a necessary and wanted feature of a climate model. Scientifically we express this variability as an uncertainty. Such uncertainty can also be estimated when computing radiative forcings. As stated in Sub-section 2.1, radiative forcing estimates as well as the associated uncertainties depend on the type of the radiative forcing. For instance, the definition of SARF allows the stratosphere to adjust to a change in pollutant abundance. This does result in some uncertainty, which is nonetheless rather small. ERF, on the other hand, additionally allows for tropospheric adjustment, including changes to atmospheric water vapour, clouds, and transport of pollutants. Especially in the case of modelling the effects of pollutants with relatively short atmospheric lifetimes, atmospheric abundances can vary significantly both in terms of geographical location and time. This can lead to large uncertainties in the resulting ERF estimates. For the same reason, the estimated values for SARF and ERF can differ quite a lot. During the past years, quantification of climate effects has moved from a quantity closely related to SARF to the nowadays standard ERF.[8] This is one of the main reasons why the estimated effects of the mitigation of some SLCPs have changed so much over the last few years.[9]

3 Short-Lived Climate Pollutants

Here we list the most common SLCPs—ozone, methane, hydrofluorocarbons, and black carbon—and how they affect the Earth's radiation budget. Although not considered as an SLCP, we also include a short discussion about carbon dioxide (CO_2) to provide comparative references.

3.1 *Carbon Dioxide*

CO_2 is the most abundant of all atmospheric greenhouse gases (GHG) which (at least partly) originate from human activities. Without anthropogenic emissions, the natural greenhouse effect (due to clouds, water vapor, CO_2 and other

8 IPCC AR5 (n7); IPCC AR6 (n1).

9 Arctic Monitoring and Assessment Programme (AMAP), *AMAP Assessment 2015: Black carbon and ozone as Arctic climate forcers* (AMAP 2015); IPCC AR6 (n1).

natural GHGs) is necessary to uphold the equilibrium energy balance of the Earth (see Section 2.1) and with it the favourable climate for life on Earth as we know it. GHGs contribute to the greenhouse effect by absorbing part of the thermal radiation emitted by the planetary surface. As this thermal radiation is re-emitted by the GHGs, part of it travels back to the surface, inducing additional warming.

Since pre-industrial times, the abundance of CO_2 in the atmosphere has increased by about 50 %. By pre-industrial times we here refer to the year 1750.[10] The golden standard of all climate response estimates is the change in average global surface temperatures due to a theoretical doubling of the pre-industrial abundance of CO_2. For this change in CO_2 abundance, the IPCC best estimate for the resulting ERF is 3.93±0.47 W/m^2, which is estimated to lead to a global warming between 1.3°C and 3.1°C after 70 years or between 1.5°C and 7.7°C once a new equilibrium in the radiative balance is reached.[11] From these values alone it becomes already apparent why discussing radiative forcings instead of temperature changes is useful: radiative forcing values contain uncertainties, but these uncertainties are small compared to the uncertainties in the climate response.

One important consideration to remember is that in these theoretical studies it is assumed that the atmospheric CO_2 abundance is doubled instantly. In reality, CO_2 abundance has grown gradually, which also means that the radiative balance of the Earth system has been disturbed gradually. Therefore, the observed past climate responses and the projected future climate responses, based on realistic scenarios, differ from the ideal values provided above. The IPCC estimate for the present-day ERF value of CO_2 is 2.156±0.259 W/m^2. Realistic values for the climate response since pre-industrial times (1750) are 0.75–1.41°C for 2019.[12]

3.2 *Ozone (O_3)*

O_3 is a short-lived gas which is not emitted by any natural or anthropogenic sources. Instead, O_3 is formed in the atmosphere through photochemical reactions with a range of chemical compounds, including nitrogen oxidants, carbon monoxide (CO) and organic compounds such as methane (CH_4). O_3 is naturally present in the atmosphere,[13] but human activity can significantly

10 Ibid.

11 Ibid.

12 IPCC AR6 (n1).

13 Stephen O. Andersen, Marcel L. Halberstadt & Nathan Borgford-Parnell, 'Stratospheric ozone, global warming, and the principle of unintended consequences—An

alter its atmospheric abundance. Most of the atmospheric ozone resides in the upper part of the atmosphere at an altitude of 10–50 km (stratosphere), and only 10 % in the lower part, between 0 and 12 km altitude.[14]

The amount of O_3 in the atmosphere depends on various mechanisms, like chemical production and losses. For instance, increased water vapor concentrations in the stratosphere can increase the amount of ice clouds which, in combination with direct sunlight, leads to depletion of ozone. Furthermore, ozone can react directly with various chemical compounds such as chlorides. In addition, there is exchange of ozone between stratosphere and troposphere, and ozone depletion due to deposition at the Earth's surface.[15] O_3 acts as a greenhouse gas by trapping some of the thermal radiation escaping to space. The net climatic effect of ozone strongly depends on both its vertical and horizontal location. There is no method to measure the radiative forcing due to ozone directly. Instead, the estimates for O_3 radiative forcing are entirely based on models. Besides direct effects on the Earth's radiative balance, ozone can add a substantial positive radiative forcing via the effects on terrestrial vegetation.[16]

Near the Earth's surface, ozone has adverse effects on human health.[17] Besides health effects, O_3 pollution has negative impacts on agriculture and natural vegetation.[18] Ozone can damage plant tissue, which can result in reduced crop yields,[19] suppressed forest growth[20] and negative impacts on terrestrial ecosystems.[21]

In the stratosphere, on the other hand, ozone has a vital role for life on the Earth: stratospheric O_3 absorbs UV-C and UV-B light, and thereby prevents some portion of the UV radiation from reaching the lower part of Earth's atmosphere. UV-B is known to have severe effects on human health, plants,

---

ongoing science and policy success story' (2013) 63 Journal of the Air & Waste Management Association 6, 607–647.

14 IPCC AR6 (n1).

15 Ibid.

16 Ibid.

17 Ibid.

18 Gina Mills and others, 'Evidence of widespread effects of ozone on crops and (semi-)natural vegetation in Europe (1990–2006) in relation to AOT40-and flux-based risk maps' (2011) 17 Global Change Biology, 592–613.

19 Ibid.

20 Maxime Cailleret and others, 'Ozone effects on European forest growth—Towards an integrative approach' (2018) 106 J Ecol. 4, 1377–1389.

21 Evgenios Agathokleous and others, 'Ozone affects plant, insect, and soil microbial communities: A threat to terrestrial ecosystems and biodiversity' 6 Science Advances 33, eabc1176.

and animals. The group of substances that are known to destroy stratospheric ozone, such as chlorofluorocarbons (CFCs) and other halogenated compounds containing chlorine and bromine, are labelled as ozone-depleting substances (see Chapter 4 for a detailed discussion of the international ozone regime).

3.3 *Methane*

Methane is the second most important anthropogenic greenhouse gas. While the abundance of methane in the atmosphere is much lower than that of CO_2, the per-molecule warming potential of methane is drastically larger than for CO_2. This makes the radiative forcings due to CO_2 and methane comparable (see Table 1.2). Because the lifetime of methane is relatively short, its mitigation is a promising option to slow global warming in the next decades. Methane originates from both natural sources, such as peatlands and thawing of permafrost, and from anthropogenic activities, such as agriculture and natural gas production and distribution. In a warming climate, the permanent thawing of permafrost regions may drastically increase natural methane emissions, which makes methane a major player in one of the climate feedback mechanisms which exacerbate global warming (see section 1.2.2).

Methane is involved in a chain of atmospheric chemical reactions which facilitate the production of tropospheric ozone. In the stratosphere methane is a major source of water vapour through oxidisation by hydroxyl (OH).

3.4 *Hydrofluorocarbons* (HFCs)

Hydrofluorocarbons (HFCs) are a group of compounds that do not have any natural sources but instead are completely synthetic. HFCs are used in both household and industrial air conditioners, refrigerators, and heat pumps. At room temperatures, most of HFCs are in a gaseous form. HFCs are used as a replacement for ozone-depleting substances as they do not directly deplete stratospheric ozone. However, there are indications that HFCs can weaken the stratospheric ozone layer indirectly, and thus, could be considered weak ozone-depleting substances.[22]

The atmospheric lifetimes of different HFC compounds vary from a year to hundreds of years. Furthermore, HFC molecules have a vast warming potential compared to CO_2 and methane. However, the total amount of HFCs in the atmosphere is still very small compared to CO_2 and methane, and that is why

22 Margaret M. Hurwitz and others, 'Ozone depletion by hydrofluorocarbons' (2015) 42 Geophys. Res. Lett. 20, 8686–8692.

the present-day warming impact of HFC is very small.[23] However, they are projected to increase significantly in the future.[24]

3.5 *Aerosols and Black Carbon*

Aerosols are either solid or liquid particles suspended in a gaseous media, e.g., in the air. There are both primary and secondary sources of atmospheric aerosols: they are either directly emitted from, e.g., industrial processes, road transport and other anthropogenic activities, or they can be formed in the atmosphere via chemical reactions or as a result of the condensation of some atmospheric trace gases. In addition, natural aerosols such as sea salt or mineral dust make up a large portion of the total aerosol burden. The atmospheric properties of aerosols depend on their size and chemical composition, as well as the prevalent atmospheric conditions. The diameter of an aerosol particle can be in the approximate range of 3 nanometres to 10 micrometres.

The lifetime of aerosols varies from days to months, and they can be transported thousands of kilometres from one region to another. During their time in the atmosphere, the composition and size of aerosol particles are subject to changes due to physical processes and chemical reactions. For instance, two small aerosols particles can form one larger particle by colliding with each other. Typically, aerosols are removed from the atmosphere either via wet removal (precipitation) or by depositing on surfaces.

As an opposite to well-mixed greenhouse gases, the climatic effects of aerosols can be more local and more dependent on the emission source horizontal and vertical location. For instance, aerosol emissions from flat terrain in the Arctic region can have very different effects than emissions that originate from elevated mountain areas near the equator. This is due to their relatively short lifetime, which causes the concentration and composition of aerosols to strongly vary with geographic location, which is in strong contrast with, for instance, the concentrations of methane and CO_2.

Black carbon is a carbonaceous aerosol compound that is typically formed in incomplete combustion processes. Typical sources of black carbon are forest fires, residential biomass burning, and transportation. In addition, one distinct source of black carbon in the Arctic region is the flaring of natural gas.

---

23 IPCC AR6 (n1).

24 Guus J.M. Velders, David W. Fahey, John S. Daniel, Stephen O. Andersen, Mack McFarland, 'Future atmospheric abundances and climate forcings from scenarios of global and regional hydrofluorocarbon (HFC) emissions' (2015) Atmospheric Environment, Volume 123, Part A, 2015, Pages 200–209, ISSN 1352–2310, https://doi.org/10.1016/j.atmosenv.2015.10.071.

A well-known characteristic of black carbon is its ability to absorb sunlight, and thereby warm the air that surrounds it. Other aerosol substances, such as sulfate or organic carbon, can scatter solar radiation, and as some portion is reflected back to the space, have a cooling effect in the atmosphere. These climatic effects are directly caused by aerosol-radiation interactions and commonly termed as *direct climate effects* of aerosols.

In addition, aerosols also have *indirect effects* on the climate, also called aerosol-cloud interactions. All cloud droplets are formed by condensation of water vapor onto atmospheric aerosol particles. An increased concentration of aerosol particles in general results in a larger amount of cloud droplets. However, because approximately the same amount of water vapour is divided among more cloud droplets, these cloud droplets are also smaller. Clouds with more but smaller droplets both reflect more sunlight back to space and have a longer lifetime than clouds containing a smaller number of larger droplets. Both of these effects have a cooling effect on the climate. Black carbon containing aerosols can also act as such cloud seed aerosols, which can increase the reflectivity of clouds and partly cool the climate. Thus, mitigating black carbon emissions can reduce this indirect cooling effect, and make a warming contribution on the climate.

The direct and indirect effects of black carbon containing aerosols thus affect the climate in opposite directions, which means that the sign of the total effect can only be determined via careful studies. Furthermore, decreasing black carbon emissions also affects the emission strength of co-emitted aerosol species such as organic carbon and sulfate, which are known to have a net cooling effect on global climate. Recent studies have corroborated this.[25] It was found that there is large uncertainty in the total climate effect of mitigating black carbon emissions because of these competing processes and especially the uncertainty due to modelling the aerosol-cloud interactions.

3.5.1 Black Carbon and Albedo Effects

The reflectivity of a surface for radiation depends strongly on surface colour: darker surfaces absorb much of the incoming sunlight (more warming) while bright surfaces reflect more sunlight back to space (more cooling). The climate warming effect of black carbon is strongly dependent on this

25 IPCC AR6 (n1); Thomas Kühn and others, 'Effects of black carbon mitigation on Arctic climate' (2020) 20 Atmos. Chem. Phys., 5527–5546; Tuuli Miinalainen, Harri Kokkola, Kari E.J. Lehtinen, and Thomas Kühn, 'Comparing the radiative forcings of the anthropogenic aerosol emissions from Chile and Mexico' (2021) 126 Journal of Geophysical Research: Atmospheres 10, e2020JD033364.

phenomenon. If dark black carbon containing aerosols are floating above or deposited on a bright surface such as snow, ice, or clouds, the warming effect of black carbon is enhanced. In the Arctic region, this mechanism is of importance as the reflectance of snow and sea ice are weakened by black carbon deposition. In contrast, if the surface itself is dark, such as ocean surfaces, the climatic warming effect of black carbon is weaker because not much additional sunlight is absorbed by the black carbon. All in all, the underlying surface can cause large differences in the black carbon effects on climate. This partly explains why the climatic impact of black carbon is highly dependent on the geographical location and altitude.

Besides the impact on surface air temperatures, aerosols can alter both large-scale and regional weather patterns and magnify or cause pollution episodes. For instance, due to various interaction mechanisms in the atmosphere, anthropogenic aerosols have generated anomalies in large-scale precipitation patterns since pre-industrial times.[26] Wei et al studied the effects of COVID-19 restrictions and how the changes in black carbon emissions affected local weather patterns in Northern India.[27] Their results suggest that reductions in black carbon emissions might have led to a delay in the outbreak of Indian summer monsoon. In addition, some studies have shown that black carbon can either enhance or suppress the length and intensity of urban pollution episodes by altering the atmospheric dynamics near the surface.[28]

3.6 *Present-Day and Historical Effects of SLCPs*

In the latest IPCC AR6, there is no estimation for combined effect for SLCP contribution on human-induced climate warming.[29] However, based on chemistry-climate model simulations (see Section 1.4), the individual ERF and surface temperature estimates are provided for each SCLF species. The total global surface air temperature change due to anthropogenic activities was estimated to be 1.3 °C between 1750 and 2019.

Out of all SLCPs, methane has had the strongest warming effect on the global climate since pre-industrial times. The global mean ERF for methane is

26 IPCC AR6 (n1).

27 Linyi Wei and others, Black carbon-climate interactions regulate dust burdens over India revealed during COVID-19' (2022) 13 Nat Commun, Article 1839.

28 A. J. Ding and others, 'Enhanced haze pollution by black carbon in megacities in China' (2016) 43 Geophysical Research Letters 6, 2873–2879; Jessica Slater and others, 'The effect of BC on aerosol–boundary layer feedback: potential implications for urban pollution episodes' (2022) 22 Atmos. Chem. Phys. 4, 2937–2953.

29 IPCC AR6 (n1).

TABLE 1.2 The ERF and corresponding global surface air temperature change estimates between 1750 and 2019

Substance	Radiative forcing [W/m2]	Estimated contribution to temperature change
CO_2	2.156±0.259[a]	
O_3	0.47 [0.24 to 0.71][a]	~0.2 °C [a]
CH_4	0.54 [0.44 to 0.65][a] or 1.19 [0.81 to 1.58][b]	~0.6 °C [b]
HFCS	0.04[a]	
Black Carbon	0.11 [-0.20 to 0.42][b]	Less than 0.1 °C [b]

The values are retrieved from the IPCC AR6 (Chapters 6 and 7)[c]. The superscript 'a' indicates that the numerical value is from the abundance-based estimate (AR6 Chapter 7), and 'b' indicates that the value is from the emission-based estimate (AR6 Chapter 6).
c Ibid.

estimated to be 0.5 [0.4 to 0.7] W/m^2 (abundance-based estimate) or 1.2 [0.8 to 1.6] W/m^2 (emission-based estimate), depending on the modelling approach. Besides direct effects, indirect effects such as ozone-related chemistry enhance the methane ERF. The emission-based ERF for methane translates into an approximately 0.6 °C increase in global surface air temperature.

The changes in O_3 abundance are estimated to have resulted in an ERF of 0.47 [0.24 to 0.71] W/m^2. This translates into the human-induced changes in O_3 to have had a warming effect of 0.23 [0.11 to 0.39] °C on global surface air temperature since pre-industrial times. This makes O_3 the second most important anthropogenic compound after well-mixed greenhouse gases. The estimate of the O_3 warming effect has increased since AR5, due to improved estimates of its precursor emissions.[30]

In AR6, the best estimate for global ERF due to black carbon is 0.1 [-0.2 to 0.4] W/m^2 compared to pre-industrial times, which is lower than in AR5. The negative value of the lower bound highlights the uncertainty related to black carbon-induced warming. Moreover, as mentioned in section 1.3.4, the simultaneous changes in cooling aerosol species, such as OC, can lead to even more negative values when considering combined aerosol effects. The

30 IPCC AR6 (n1).

estimated average value for the warming due to black carbon is less than 0.1 °C, without including co-emitted species. When considering all aerosol species, IPCC AR6 estimates that the changes in aerosols have primarily contributed to cooling compared to pre-industrial times, which has masked some of the human-induced warming. In other words, though black carbon has had globally a small warming effect compared to other SLCPs, the total effect of all aerosols has been estimated to be net negative. However, because the climatic effects of black carbon vary strongly with geographical location and are enhanced above snow and ice (see Section 1.3.4), the impacts of black carbon in, e.g., the Arctic may differ from the global value.[31] From a policy perspective, the contribution of black carbon emissions to air pollution should also be noted, as explained below.

3.6.1 Present-Day Health Effects Due to SLCFs

Climate change and air pollution are strongly interlinked, as many of the pollutants can affect both. Many SLCFs are either considered as air pollutants or can contribute to air pollution indirectly. Air pollutants, such as fine particulate matter ($PM_{2.5}$) and O_3, can have severe impacts on human health. $PM_{2.5}$ originates from both anthropogenic activities and natural sources, and includes various chemical compounds, such as organic carbon, sulfate, black carbon, mineral dust, and sea salt. When inhaled, fine particulate matter enters human lungs and from there can enter the human blood circulation. Both short-and long-term exposure can cause adverse health effects, for instance diseases related to respiratory and lung functioning, or heart-related diseases.[32] Similarly, elevated O_3 concentrations affect the lungs and cause breathing problems, triggering asthma and other respiratory diseases.

Air pollution is known to provoke millions of excess deaths globally each year.[33] For instance, Fuller et al. estimate that in 2019, there were over 6 million (6.67 [5.90–7.49] million) premature deaths due to household and outdoor fine particulate and ozone pollution.[34] Out of the 6 million, ozone was associated with 0.4 [0.2–0.6] million, ambient fine particulate matter with 4.1

31 Knut von Salzen and others, 'Clean air policies are key for successfully mitigating Arctic warming' (2022) 3 Commun Earth Environ, Article 222.

32 GBD 2015 Risk Factors Collaborators, 'Global, regional, and national comparative risk assessment of 79 behavioural, environmental and occupational, and metabolic risks or clusters of risks, 1990–2015: A systematic analysis for the global burden of disease study 2015' (2016) 388 The Lancet 10053, 1659–1724.

33 Ibid.

34 Richard Fuller and others, 'Pollution and health: a progress update' (2022) 6 The Lancet Planetary Health, 6, e535–e547.

[3.5–4.8] million and household air pollution with 2.3 [1.6–3.1] million premature deaths. Burnett et al. attributed over 8.9 million premature deaths to ambient fine particulate pollution in 2015.[35] Due to the severe health issues, air pollution is regulated with policies and guidelines. The World Health Organization (WHO) has recently announced new, more ambitious, guidelines for air pollution. The update is based on the latest scientific evidence of the health impacts of air pollution.[36]

4 Climate Modelling of SLCFS

The most robust method for estimating the climate effects of SLCFS is climate modelling. For past and present climate, observational estimates can also be made. However, for obtaining future projections of the climate, a model of some level of complexity must be used. Such models can range from a model which describes the whole Earth as one "box" to Earth system models which aim at including all relevant processes in the Earth system in three-dimensional frameworks. A comprehensive assessment of the climate effects of SLCFS can only be made using global three-dimensional models. The climate effects of SLCFS depend on a multitude of characteristics: their physical and chemical properties, distribution in all three dimensions in the atmosphere, and how they enter and exit the atmosphere. For example, sizes of atmospheric aerosol particles range over several orders of magnitude and since climate effects of aerosols depend on aerosol size, the whole size range should be simulated in climate models. Another aspect which adds complexity in simulating SLCFS is that the number of chemical compounds in the atmosphere is vast. Especially, the number of organic compounds which contribute to aerosol cloud interactions, can be counted in hundreds or even thousands.

4.1 *Structure of Climate Models*

The core of Earth System Models consists of atmospheric, land, and ocean models which in turn are coupled with sub-models which simulate, e.g., atmospheric chemistry, carbon cycle, and vegetation. SCLPS are simulated in the atmospheric aerosol and chemistry sub-models coupled to the atmospheric

35 Richard Burnett and others, 'Global estimates of mortality associated with long-term exposure to outdoor fine particulate matter' 115, Proceedings of the National Academy of Sciences 38, 9592–9597.

36 World Health Organisation, 'WHO global air quality guidelines: Particulate matter ($PM_{2.5}$ and PM_{10}), ozone, nitrogen dioxide, sulfur dioxide and carbon monoxide.' (WHO 2021).

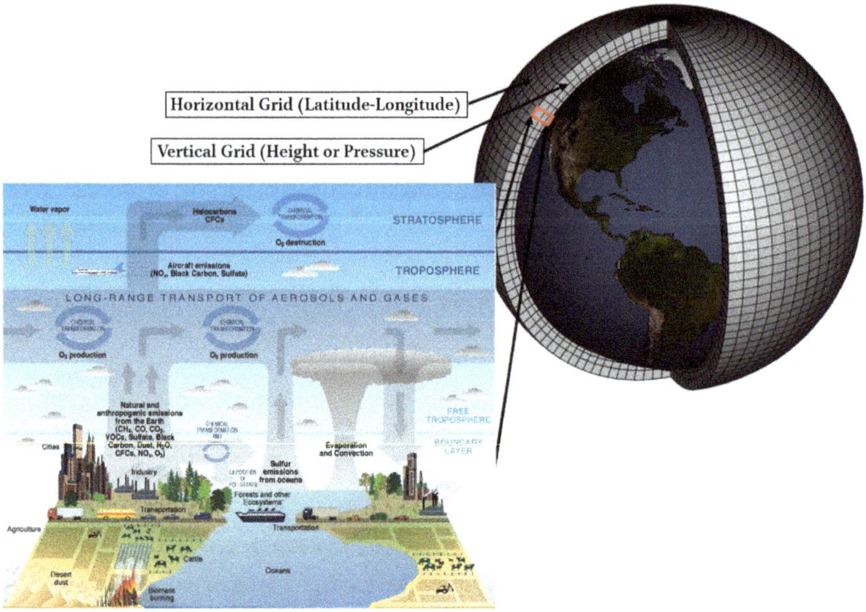

FIGURE 1.1 Schematic of a global atmospheric model grid (top right) and a schematic of processes that are solved in atmospheric global models

component of Earth System Models. The atmosphere is divided to a three-dimensional grid and the sub-models solve all relevant physical and chemical processes in each grid cell. Figure 1.1 illustrates the grid structure of a global atmospheric model as well as the processes that are included in such a model. In current global aerosol and chemistry models, the number of grid cells can amount to hundreds of thousands, making models computationally extremely expensive. Due to the above-mentioned complexity of SLCF properties, the description of gases and aerosols in Earth System Models is simplified. Simplifications include reducing the number of chemical compounds, reducing the accuracy of solving physical and chemical equations, and using coarse spatial resolution in simulating the atmosphere. All these simplifications have significant implications on the uncertainty of the estimates on radiative forcings of SLCFs. On the other hand, increasing details in model routines does not necessarily translate into improved model results.[37] SLCFs can be modelled in more detail when only the atmospheric part of the Earth system is

37 G.W. Mann and others, 'Intercomparison of modal and sectional aerosol microphysics representations within the same 3-D global chemical transport model' (2012) 12 Atmospheric Chemistry and Physics 10, 4449–4476.

modelled. In this case we talk of an atmosphere-only, or atmospheric global circulation model.

Aerosol and chemistry sub-models of Earth System Models and global circulation models describe the full life cycle of SLCFs providing their properties to influence incoming sunlight and outgoing thermal radiation emitted by the Earth's surface. In addition, these sub-models simulate how SLCFs alter the physical properties of clouds which in turn also affect incoming and outgoing radiation, i.e., the Earth's radiation balance. Once these properties are simulated for pre-industrial and present-day conditions, the radiative forcing of different SLCFs can be determined.

4.2 *Simulating the SLCFs in Climate Models*

In the models, gases and aerosols are introduced to the atmosphere through emission routines which are either prescribed based on emission data bases or calculated in the model. Emission databases provide emission strengths for individual compounds. These include, e.g., anthropogenic emissions and forest fire emissions. Sea salt aerosol emissions are an example, where aerosol emissions are calculated in the model based on the simulated wind speeds. There are also very complicated emission modules, for example for considering the emission of substances from vegetation, which depends on ambient conditions like temperature and humidity. Regarding future projections of the climate, uncertainties in emission strengths can cause a much larger uncertainty than the lack of knowledge of Earth system processes or model inaccuracies. This is because it is difficult to estimate how humans will change their emissions in the future and what kind of new innovations will emerge from reducing emissions of climate forcers.

Once compounds are emitted into the atmosphere, model routines calculate the evolution of these compounds in the atmosphere, their transport, and modification by chemical and physical processes (see also Section 1.3). For example, the climate effects of black carbon are heavily dependent on such processes. Studies show that different global models have very large variability and uncertainty in simulating the properties of black carbon which dictate the ability of black carbon to affect the Earth's energy balance through absorbing incoming sunlight. Chemical and physical processing of black carbon aerosol influences both its optical properties and transport from source regions to remote regions (e.g., Arctic regions).[38]

38 Junfeng Liu and others, 'Evaluation of factors controlling long-range transport of black carbon to the Arctic' 116 Journal of Geophysical Research: Atmospheres D4.

In addition to the direct effects of SLCFs on radiation, their interactions with clouds also have significant implications on climate. As explained above, cloud droplets form via condensation of water vapor on soluble aerosol particles and ice particles on or around certain kinds of aerosol particles (e.g., atmospheric dust). The challenge in simulating aerosol-cloud interactions accurately comes from the coarse grid sizes of global scale models, which are currently horizontally of the order between tens and hundreds of kilometres. However, as we can see watching the clouds in the real atmosphere, over a span of hundred kilometres there can be several different types of clouds. In addition, many of the cloud processes happen at even smaller scales. This mismatch between model resolution and process length scales means that simulating clouds and their interactions with aerosol has to be simplified and cloud properties as well as aerosol-cloud interactions are represented as an average or a distribution of what occurs within a model grid box. A part of this challenge is resolved through the quick progress in supercomputing as it allows for making simulations at higher spatial resolution, although it will still take several years to increase the resolution to match those of cloud scale processes.

Parameterizations of aerosol-cloud interactions provides the change in optical properties of clouds due to changes in aerosol concentrations, which allows for estimating the ERF of aerosols (see also Section 1.2). In addition to the effects on the Earth's radiative balance, models simulate how aerosol affects global and regional precipitation which in turn affects the removal of SLCFs from the atmosphere. As mentioned above, removal processes affect the transport of SLCFs and determine the deposition on ice and snow, e.g., in the case of absorbing aerosol. This in turn affects the albedo of Earth's surface. Deposition of absorbing aerosol also has implications on melting of snow and ice.

4.3 *Estimating Radiative Forcing from Climate Model Simulations*

IPCC bases their forcing estimates on model simulated radiative forcing from climate model simulations. Since one model simulation cannot provide robust values, the estimate is based on several Earth System Model and global circulation model simulations. Because climate variability is large, each model runs an ensemble of simulations, i.e., several simulations of the same time span with slightly altered starting conditions. The average over such an ensemble is more robust than a single simulation. The coupled model intercomparison project (commonly referred to as CMIP) provides a protocol for multi-model experiments, which provides the model estimates for radiative forcing of SLCFs. The best estimates for forcings are calculated from the distribution of values of all model simulations and the uncertainty is derived from the variability of this distribution. The IPCC model estimated present-day radiative forcing values are determined as the value due to changes between pre-industrial times and present-day. This means that obtaining an accurate estimate for radiative forcing, conditions for both time periods should be known. Even though present-day properties can be constrained fairly well based on observations, model simulated SCLF properties can significantly differ from observed values. For pre-industrial conditions, the uncertainty in how well models simulate SLCFs is even larger, and this translates into a large uncertainty in radiative forcing estimates. Out of all climate forcers, the variability between the models is the largest for aerosols. Especially, uncertainties in aerosol-cloud interactions cause a major uncertainty in the model estimated radiative forcing of aerosol.

The uncertainty in the aerosol radiative forcing in turn impedes our projections of future climate change since it translates into uncertainty of the climate sensitivity. Despite extensive efforts on narrowing down the uncertainty in the temperature change due to a doubling of pre-industrial CO_2 concentrations, it has remained persistent.[39] Between the IPCC AR5 and AR6, the estimated range has increased from 2.0–4.7 K to 1.8–5.5 K.[40] However, there are strong indications that the latter range has an unrealistically high upper bound. Strong aerosol radiative forcing has its part to play in this range of climate sensitivities.[41] For example, the coupled model intercomparison project models need to reproduce past temperature records, and models with too high climate sensitivity can still reproduce them well if the model has strong aerosol forcing as it counteracts the greenhouse gas induced warming. One could consider that improving the parameterizations of aerosol processes in climate models would improve the skill of models to simulate atmospheric aerosol and these advances would reduce the uncertainty in aerosol forcing. However, in multi-model experiments even a more detailed description of aerosol size distribution does not translate into improved predictions of the properties of atmospheric aerosol.

39 Mark D. Zelinka and others, 'Causes of Higher Climate Sensitivity in CMIP6 Models' (2020) 47 Geophysical Research Letters 1, p. e2019GL085782.

40 Clare Marie Flynn and Thorsten Mauritsen, 'On the climate sensitivity and historical warming evolution in recent coupled model ensembles' (2020) 20 Atmospheric Chemistry and Physics, 13, 7829–7842.

41 Meinrat O. Andreae, Chris D. Jones, and Peter M. Cox, 'Strong present-day aerosol cooling implies a hot future' (2005) 435 Nature 7046, 1187–1190.

5 Future Effects of SLCFs

Because the future development of human behaviour is unknown, analysing effects of anthropogenic activities in climate modelling requires certain assumptions and restrictions. For this purpose, projections of the future have been developed that can be used when estimating plausible emission scenarios for SLCPs. In the IPCC framework, the future emission scenarios are based on five Shared Socio-economic Pathways (SSPs)[42] which frame different future assumptions for various socio-economic factors, such as economic growth, population, technological development, and urbanization. The scenarios vary from stringent climate change mitigation (SSP1) to projections with very high level of fossil fuel usage (SSP5), and also consider regional (in)equality in regional development.

For the next two decades (2020–2040), the outcome from IPCC AR6 indicates that the SLCF emission changes will result in an additional warming relative to 2019. A net warming effect is present in the case of all scenarios (from SSP1 to SSP5), though with varying magnitude. The warming is caused by increased contributions of methane and ozone and decreased contributions of cooling aerosol species like sulfate. The reductions in sulfur emissions are expected due to more stringent legislation and policies for energy production and the industrial sector, and due reductions of the sulfur content of fuel used in shipping.[43] Furthermore, the projections for SLCF climatic effects at the end of the century had varying results for global surface air temperature changes. For the "middle way", moderate scenario SSP2, the temperature changes due to SLCF relative to 2019 was estimated to be 0.2 to 0.5 °C, which consists mostly of warming due to aerosol reductions.

Furthermore, in the near future, the IPCC AR6 reports that decarbonization strategies are not projected to be sufficient to achieve the new WHO air quality guidelines for fine particulate matter. At the end of the century, implementation of air quality controls could lead to significant improvements in air quality compared to climate change-orientated mitigation strategies. Nevertheless, even in the case of air quality-focused mitigation, the air pollution levels are projected to remain at levels that exceed the WHO guidelines for major parts of the global population.

---

42 Keywan Riahi and others, 'The Shared Socioeconomic Pathways and their energy, land use, and greenhouse gas emissions implications: An overview' (2017) 42 Global Environmental Change, 153–168.

43 IPCC AR6 (n1).

6 Uncertainties

Policy-making benefits from accurate estimates on how much each forcing agent contributes to the total radiative forcing because decision making for, e.g., emission reductions can be targeted more precisely. However, due to the complexity of the Earth system, large uncertainties remain in the estimates of the radiative forcing of individual SCLFS. In this section we summarize and expand upon the aspects of uncertainties related to the radiative forcing and the climate effects of SLCFS.

In natural sciences, any measured value can never be entirely precise: repeated measurements yield a range of values. This range is expressed using a best estimate (e.g., the mean value) and an uncertainty, which is a measure of the spread of all measured values. Because the computation of the outcomes of physical processes is based on measured values, the uncertainties related to these measured values must be incorporated in the calculations, which means that also the results of computed values are expressed as a best estimate and an uncertainty. For instance, in IPCC AR6[44] the ERF for black carbon is estimated to be 0.1 [-0.2 to 0.4] W/m^2, where the mean value is 0.1 and [-0.2 to 0.4] is the associated uncertainty interval.

In climate science there are additional sources of uncertainty. For instance, the climate system is highly chaotic, meaning that small changes in an initial condition can lead to very different final results. Furthermore, many atmospheric processes are not fully understood or suffer from problems like model resolution or lack of computational power. Therefore, different models may treat different atmospheric processes differently, which leads to differences between results from different models and this is ultimately expressed as an uncertainty.

The uncertainty ranges reported in the IPCC assessment reports are a combination of several sources of uncertainty: scientific uncertainties, uncertainties caused by simplifications of Earth's processes, model structural limitations (e.g., coarse spatial resolution of models), and randomness in the variability of Earth system processes as well as internal variability in climate models. As explained in Section 3, when IPCC reports the model confidence in radiative forcings of individual SLCPS, the provided uncertainty value is based on the variability between an ensemble of models which also have run an ensemble of simulations.

44 Ibid.

The reason why radiative forcing estimates require many model simulations with many different climate models is that processes governing the global Earth system are so complex and sensitive to how a model is initialized, that an insignificantly small change in initial model parameters can lead to a significantly different model result. An ensemble refers to a set of climate model simulations using the same or several climate models, which span the same time period but use slightly altered starting conditions. The individual ensemble members do not accurately repeat or predict the actual evolution of the real Earth system, but instead each represent one possible evolution. Therefore, an ensemble will provide a distribution of values which gives us a good idea of the most likely value or range of values. This means that despite the differences between the individual model ensemble members, we can get estimates for forcings of SCLFs that can be very robust. The probable values of radiative forcing and their uncertainty can be further narrowed down based on expert judgement and using observations of past climate. This is done in order to rule out unrealistic modelled radiative forcing values by comparing if past real-world behaviour matches the simulations.[45]

7 Conclusion

Short-lived climate pollutants, which are a subgroup of SLCFs, are known to impact both global climate and human health. Because SLCPs and SLCFs are often emitted from the same sources, their climate and air quality effects are usually considered jointly in natural sciences. Some of the SLCPs have a stronger contribution to global warming (e.g., methane), whereas other compounds critically affect air quality and are therefore more harmful to human health (e.g., ozone). Therefore, reductions in SLCP emissions can bring either improved air quality or reduced warming of the climate, or in some cases, both.

Estimating the global and regional effects of SLCF emissions requires a sophisticated modeling framework and sets of numerous climate model simulations, which are then combined to produce more robust climate projections. The outcomes of these simulations, however, include a certain level of uncertainty which is due to various aspects, such as lack of knowledge of emission sources, uncertainty related to the model parametrization, and natural

45 Reto Knutti and others, 'Constraints on radiative forcing and future climate change from observations and climate model ensembles' (2002) 416 Nature, 719–723, https://doi.org/10.1038/416719a ; K.S. Carslaw and others, 'Climate models are uncertain, but we can do something about it' (2018) Eos, 99.

variability of Earth system processes. For some compounds, such as aerosols and especially black carbon, the uncertainty is relatively large and therefore the range of estimates is wide. For other compounds, such as methane, the uncertainty related to the estimates is smaller.

In the near future, the combined effects of the changes in all anthropogenic SLCFs (which includes both reductions and increases in cooling as well as warming agents) are projected to have a warming effect on the global climate. Therefore, reductions in anthropogenic SLCPs, and especially methane, provide an opportunity to slow down global warming in the near future. However, in the long term, well mixed greenhouse gases like CO_2 will play the dominant role in global warming and their mitigation cannot be neglected.

Bibliography

Agathokleous E and others, 'Ozone affects plant, insect, and soil microbial communities: A threat to terrestrial ecosystems and biodiversity' 6 Science Advances 33, eabc1176.

Andersen SO, Halberstadt ML and Borgford-Parnell N, 'Stratospheric ozone, global warming, and the principle of unintended consequences—An ongoing science and policy success story' (2013) 63 Journal of the Air & Waste Management Association 6, 607–647.

Andreae MO, Jones CD, and Cox PM, 'Strong present-day aerosol cooling implies a hot future' (2005) 435 Nature 7046, 1187–1190.

Arctic Monitoring and Assessment Programme (AMAP), *AMAP Assessment 2015: Black carbon and ozone as Arctic climate forcers* (AMAP 2015).

Burnett R and others, 'Global estimates of mortality associated with long-term exposure to outdoor fine particulate matter' 115 Proceedings of the National Academy of Sciences 38, 9592–9597.

Cailleret M and others, 'Ozone effects on European forest growth—Towards an integrative approach' (2018) 106 J Ecol. 4, 1377–1389.

Carslaw KS and others, 'Climate models are uncertain, but we can do something about it' (2018) Eos, 99.

Ding AJ and others, 'Enhanced haze pollution by black carbon in megacities in China' (2016) 43 Geophysical Research Letters 6, 2873–2879.

Flynn CM and Mauritsen T, 'On the climate sensitivity and historical warming evolution in recent coupled model ensembles' (2020) 20 Atmospheric Chemistry and Physics, 13, 7829–7842.

Fullerand R others, 'Pollution and health: a progress update' (2022) 6 The Lancet Planetary Health, 6, e535–e547.

GBD 2015 Risk Factors Collaborators, 'Global, regional, and national comparative risk assessment of 79 behavioural, environmental and occupational, and metabolic risks or clusters of risks, 1990–2015: a systematic analysis for the global burden of disease study 2015' (2016) 388 The Lancet 10053, 1659–1724.

Hurwitz MM and others, 'Ozone depletion by hydrofluorocarbons' (2015) 42 Geophys. Res. Lett. 20, 8686–8692.

Intergovernmental Panel on Climate Change (IPCC), *Climate Change 2021: the Physical Science Basis. Contribution of Working Group I to the Sixth Assessment Report of the Intergovernmental Panel on Climate Change* (CUP 2021).

IPCC, *Climate Change 2013: the Physical Science Basis. Contribution of Working Group I to the Fifth Assessment Report of the Intergovernmental Panel on Climate Change* (CUP 2013).

Knutti R and others, 'Constraints on radiative forcing and future climate change from observations and climate model ensembles' (2002) 416 Nature, 719–723 <https://doi .org/10.1038/416719a>.

Kühn T and others, 'Effects of black carbon mitigation on Arctic climate' (2020) 20 Atmos. Chem. Phys., 5527–5546.

Liu J and others, 'Evaluation of factors controlling long-range transport of black carbon to the Arctic' (2011) 116 Journal of Geophysical Research: Atmospheres D4.

Mann GW and others, 'Intercomparison of modal and sectional aerosol microphysics representations within the same 3-D global chemical transport model' (2012) 12 Atmospheric Chemistry and Physics 10, 4449–4476.

Miinalainen T, Kokkola H, Lehtinen KEJ and Kühn T, 'Comparing the radiative forcings of the anthropogenic aerosol emissions from Chile and Mexico' (2021) 126 Journal of Geophysical Research: Atmospheres 10, e2020JD033364.

Mills G and others, 'Evidence of widespread effects of ozone on crops and (semi-) natural vegetation in Europe (1990–2006) in relation to AOT40-and flux-based risk maps' (2011) 17 Global Change Biology, 592–613.

Riahi K and others, 'The Shared Socioeconomic Pathways and their energy, land use, and greenhouse gas emissions implications: an overview' (2017) 42 Global Environmental Change, 153–168.

Seinfeld JH and Pandis SN, *Atmospheric chemistry and physics: from air pollution to climate change* (John Wiley & Sons, 2016).

Slater J and others, 'The effect of BC on aerosol–boundary layer feedback: potential implications for urban pollution episodes' (2022) 22 Atmos. Chem. Phys. 4, 2937–2953.

Velders GJM, Fahey DW, Daniel JS, Andersen SO and McFarland M, 'Future atmospheric abundances and climate forcings from scenarios of global and regional hydrofluorocarbon (HFC) emissions' (2015) Atmospheric Environment, Volume 123, Part A, 2015, Pages 200–209, ISSN 1352–2310, https://doi.org/10.1016/j.atmosenv.2015.10.071.

von Salzen K and others, 'Clean air policies are key for successfully mitigating Arctic warming' (2022) 3 Commun Earth Environ, Article 222.

Wei L and others, 'Black carbon-climate interactions regulate dust burdens over India revealed during COVID-19' (2022) 13 Nat Commun, Article 1839.

World Health Organisation, 'WHO global air quality guidelines: Particulate matter ($PM_{2.5}$ and PM_{10}), ozone, nitrogen dioxide, sulfur dioxide and carbon monoxide.' (WHO 2021).

Zelinka MD and others, 'Causes of Higher Climate Sensitivity in CMIP6 Models' (2020) 47 Geophysical Research Letters 1, p. e2019GL085782.

PART 1

Global Perspectives on Law and Policy of SLCPS

CHAPTER 2

A Conceptual History of SLCPs

Niklas Löther

1 Introduction

Short-lived climate pollutants (SLCPs) encompass a vast range of substances with highly diverse properties – so how did they all come to be included under this one label? As the previous chapter shows, there is more that divides than unites them scientifically speaking, so their grouping under one category has political reasons as well, rendering SLCPs a *policy concept* rather than a purely scientific term. This chapter traces the history of this concept by analysing how these pollutants have been framed over time, first individually and later as one category, and tracing the scientific and political drivers behind this process.

Such a *conceptual history* of SLCPs had not been written before, but offers crucial insights to those aiming to promote their governance – in particular as it is a tale of ups and downs that reveal the concept's strengths and weaknesses in terms of political effect. After all, like the following chapters show, the politico-legal response to SLCPs has much room for improvement – so it is worthwhile investigating the concept's merits. This chapter thus delves into the connection between the alarming scientific inputs, reviewed before, and political outputs that fail to live up to them, discussed thereafter, all with the aim of drawing lessons for the future.

In particular, such a history sheds light on the political dimension of conceptual innovations like SLCPs. Concepts exist to simplify the world, which is necessary to render it governable, but also imposes a framing on it and thereby introduces an element of politics. They always have a normative content and are never purely descriptive.[1] SLCPs are a perfect example of this: The short acronym contains a plethora of pollutants with highly diverse properties, but only highlights those aspects that matter most to policy-makers – that they are all short-lived, pollute the air, and also impact the climate. Such simplifications help decision-makers, in this case by suggesting that substances which contribute to several environmental problems deserve special attention. However,

1 James Meadowcroft and Daniel Fiorino, 'Conceptual Innovation in Environmental Policy' in J Meadowcroft and D Fiorino (eds.), *Conceptual Innovation in Environmental Policy* (MIT Press 2017) 31f.

they also render the concept itself political by prioritising some problems over others, which may furthermore be seen as casting responsibility on certain actors – a fact that has repeatedly obstructed the international response to SLCPs. The politics of this concept will consequently be a key theme in this history and something that those promoting it should be acutely aware of.

In short, this chapter thus analyses the history of how and why various strands of science were combined under the label of SLCPs, what political implications this has, and uses this to draw lessons on where we should go next.

1.1 *Theoretical Background*

The history of SLCPs is approached here through a *global environmental governance* lens, which posits that how we govern the environment is not just shaped by lawmakers, but rests on a wider societal debate among numerous stakeholders, including many private actors.[2] In this particular case, scientists play an especially important role, since the concept in focus derives from scientific research and assessments.

A key concept for this chapter is therefore the *science-policy interface*, meaning the processes of interaction between scientists and policy-makers, through which information may be exchanged and jointly constructed in order to enrich decision-making with scientific expertise.[3] Such arrangements are common in environmental policy due to the complexity of this field requiring expert-involvement – and as the previous chapter shows, SLCPs are particularly complex. Hence, theory on science-policy interfaces informed the focus of this research: At the international level, scientists and policy-makers frequently interact through the medium of scientific assessment reports requested by governments, but written by experts.[4] The concept of SLCPs has its origins in such documents, so they play a key role in this history.

Furthermore, it has frequently been shown that scientific information is particularly effective at crossing the science-policy interface if so-called *epistemic communities* are promoting it.[5] These are transnational networks of experts who share both causal beliefs about a particular problem and a policy

2 Frank Biermann and Philipp Pattberg, 'Global Environmental Governance: Taking Stock, Moving Forward' (2008) 33 *Annual Review of Environment and Resources* 277.

3 Sybille van den Hove, 'A Rationale for Science-policy Interfaces' (2007) 39 *Futures* 7, 815.

4 Henrik Selin and Noelle Eckley, 'Science, Politics, and Persistent Organic Pollutants: The Role of Scientific Assessments in International Environmental Co-operation' (2003) 3 International Environmental Agreements 17; Ronald Mitchell and others, '*Global Environmental Assessments: Information and Influence* (MIT Press 2006).

5 Emanuel Adler and Peter Haas, 'Conclusion: Epistemic Communities, World Order, and the Creation of a Reflective Research Program' (1992) 46 International Organization 367;

agenda that they promote in response to it.[6] They are characterised by intense exchanges of information within the community and active outreach to policy-makers, all of which goes beyond purely professional requirements.[7] In scientifically complex fields like the climate and pollution, they may wield particularly strong influence, as governments require advice on these matters.[8] Indeed, my previous research shows that such a community has formed around SLCPS as well.[9] This particular epistemic community arose from scientific assessment reports that first framed SLCPS and is now promoting these framings to policy-makers. Hence, the following historiography of the concept's emergence and diffusion is also the story of this community.

Given that SLCPS were formulated as a concept by scientists in reports requested by policy-makers, it responds to both scientific and political demands. This renders it a *boundary object*, meaning it has to fulfil the expectations of scientists and decision-makers alike – requiring an often precarious balance between scientific credibility and political relevance.[10] These concepts and the theories behind them informed this chapter.

1.2 *Methodology*

In line with the theoretical framework, the main sources for this historiography were both the scientific reports that have shaped the SLCP agenda and political proclamations on the subject by states. This covers each side of the science-policy interface and allows to trace how the epistemic community's arguments and framings developed, how they were received by governments, and how the concept as we know it today ultimately resulted from interactions and co-production between these realms. These documents were furthermore supplemented with seven key informant interviews and existing literature on the subject.

Mai'a Davis Cross, 'Rethinking Epistemic Communities Twenty Years Later' (2012) 39 *Review of International Studies* 137.

6 Peter Haas, 'Introduction: Epistemic Communities and International Policy Coordination' (1992) 46 International Organization 1.

7 Mai'a Davis Cross, 'The Limits of Epistemic Communities: EU Security Agencies' (2015) 3 *Politics and Governance* 90, 92.

8 Davis Cross (n5) 139.

9 Niklas Löther, 'The Long Debate around Short-lived Climate Pollutants: History of a Policy Concept and its Impact on Global Environmental Governance' (MSocSci thesis, University of Eastern Finland 2022).

10 David Guston, 'Boundary Organisations in Environmental Policy and Science: An Introduction' (2001) 26 Science, Technology, and Human Values 399; Simo Sarkki and others, 'Balancing Credibility, Relevance and Legitimacy: A Critical Assessment of Trade-offs in Science–policy Interfaces' (2014) 41 Science and Public Policy 194.

Relevant international assessments of SLCPs have been identified in previous research and include in particular those by the Arctic Monitoring and Assessment Programme (AMAP), the UN Environment Programme (UNEP), and the Intergovernmental Panel on Climate Change (IPCC).[11] To keep the dataset manageable, only their official summaries were analysed, which condense the framings they promote most clearly. To capture governments' responses, official statements by the Climate and Clean Air Coalition (CCAC) were analysed, a public-private partnership of over 70 states, civil society groups, research institutes, and private sector organisations.[12] The Coalition was founded in direct response to the assessment reports promoting SLCP governance, so it is essentially a forum where the epistemic community interacts with a broad range of stakeholders.[13] Since its communiqués are drafted by government officials, they clearly reflect how information and framings of SLCPs have spread from the scientific into the political realm. Primary documents were supplemented with existing literature where available and, as the written record still leaves gaps, seven interviews conducted with some of those involved, including scientific and policy experts as well as policy-makers. Interviews were unstructured as their primary purpose was gathering information not discernible from other sources and each interviewee's professional background – summarised in anonymised form in the annex – differed significantly. All analysed documents can be found under "Primary Sources" in the bibliography, while the annexed list of interviewees also labels each interview with a number by which they are cited in the following.

Primary documents were first subjected to a framing analysis, meaning a qualitative content analysis of how SLCPs were portrayed over time in scientific assessments and CCAC statements. Following Entman's[14] definition of "framing" as highlighting certain problems under the status quo at the expense of others and suggesting solutions to them, as well as causal and normative reasons to support this view, guiding questions for this analysis were: What problems are SLCPs perceived to cause (if any)? What solutions are suggested to this? And why do (or don't) these substances deserve special attention in the first place? Passages that answer these were coded over an iterative reading process and, where several codes tend to occur together, that was considered a

---

11 Löther (n9) 28, 88.

12 CCAC, 'About' (2022) <https://www.ccacoalition.org/en/content/about> accessed 10/06/2022.

13 Löther (n9) 51f.

14 Robert Entman, 'Framing: Toward Clarification of a Fractured Paradigm' (1993) 43 *Journal of Communication* 51.

framing.[15] Finally, the prevalence of different framings over time and across various sources was analysed to gain an understanding of how the concept's present articulation came to be and who may have contributed to this. Interviews did not feed into the framing analysis per se, but were used to gather important contextual information.

To identify the root causes behind identified changes in framing, the description yielded by this analysis was finally subjected to process tracing.[16] For this, it was considered in the context of secondary literature and interviews and, using all sources in conjunction with one another, a timeline of events was created. Process tracing then involved going backwards through this chain of events to identify the original impulses that led to observed changes in the framing, whether they be political, scientific, or both. Causality was only considered as established where multiple sources suggested the same root cause and this both sufficiently and necessarily explains observed outcomes. Where sources are insufficient or inconsistent, this is explicitly noted in the text.

2 Linking Climate Change and Air Pollution: 1990s–2000s

To start this history, it is helpful to compare where we are now in terms of the framing of SLCPs to where we have come from. The concept is still fairly young, with its first formulation only dating back around 15 years, but it represents a fundamental challenge to how the problems of climate change and air pollution are traditionally framed.

While we now know that SLCPs contribute significantly to global warming and are among the main health risks of our age, they were all perceived to be fairly unimportant to both these challenges up until the 1990s: Black carbon was then considered a problem of the industrial past, already dealt with at least in Western countries, and its climate impacts were underestimated.[17] Methane was known to be a climate forcer and ozone precursor, but also considered fairly benign due to its low atmospheric concentration and reactivity – and as those concentrations were hardly rising at the time, it was also seen

15 Sandra Halperin and Oliver Heath, *Political Research: Methods and Practical Skills* (OUP 2012) 318–327.

16 David Collier, 'Understanding Process Tracing' (2011) 44 *Political Science and Politics* 4, 823–830.

17 Tica Novakov and Hal Rosen, 'The Black Carbon Story: Early History and New Perspectives' (2013) 42 Ambio 840; Spencer Weart, 'Aerosols: Volcanoes, Dust, Clouds and Climate' (2021) <https://history.aip.org/climate/pdf/Aerosol.pdf> accessed 16/01/2022.

as resolved.[18] HFCs, by contrast, were a problem for the future, documented to have a high warming potential, but still hardly in use.[19] All this stands in stark contrast to how SLCPs are framed as a category of pollutants today. Synthesised from the primary textual sources for this chapter according to Entman's definition of framing – highlighting certain problems and solutions and providing causal and normative reasons to back this up[20] – this framing is summarised below.

Firstly, scientific assessments and political statements on SLCPs today naturally highlight two problems: Climate change and the health risks of air pollution. They vary in the extent to which they focus on one or the other, but nearly always thematise them together. Causally, they support this holistic focus by showing that SLCPs are important to both issues (hence their label as *climate pollutants*) and, increasingly, quantifying their effects on them. Suggested solutions involve the targeted mitigation of these pollutants, generally by using different technologies or techniques. For instance, these include filters or newer motors for black carbon, certain best practices in fossil fuel production and agriculture against methane, and replacing HFCs with alternative substances.

Normatively, such policies are promoted as they often deliver co-benefits for both human health and the climate – but also for economic reasons, as they rely on proven techniques and technologies that can generally be implemented at low or even negative cost. Furthermore, due to the short-lived nature of SLCPs, they yield results much faster than the mitigation of CO_2 emissions. Later assessments and statements even go as far as to say that they are necessary to reach our collective climate goal of limiting global warming to 1.5°C above pre-industrial levels, as this requires precisely such immediate changes.

Scientific assessments acknowledge there is some uncertainty about all this but still argue that we know enough to act now, precisely due to the low costs of SLCP-mitigating actions and high potential for co-benefits. A further caveat, present repeatedly in all main assessments, is that these policies must be additional to continuing CO_2-reductions and not replace them. Despite the caveats, all this clearly represents a significant reframing of the pollutants we now call SLCPs compared to their earlier perception. This was only possible through a string of discoveries around the turn of the millennium, which are the subject of this section.

---

18 Spencer Weart, 'Other Greenhouse Gases' (2022) <https://history.aip.org/climate/pdf/Othergas.pdf> accessed 18/01/2022.

19 IPCC, *Second Assessment – Climate Change 1995: Synthesis Report* (CUP 1995) 21.

20 Entman (n14).

2.1 *Early Discoveries: Black Carbon and the Asian Brown Cloud*

The most significant early discoveries connecting climate change and air pollution were made in the UNEP-sponsored "Indian Ocean Experiment" (INDOEX), the first comprehensive study of air pollution over South and East Asia.[21] Rapidly growing populations in the region – and an associated rise in the use of fossil fuels, traditional cookstoves, and agricultural burning – had led to visibly increased air pollution there, sparking concerns about local health and climate effects.[22] Soot particles, i.e. black carbon, which accounted for much of this phenomenon, have long been known to be a health risk and it was also posited that they may distort temperatures and rainfall by dimming the sunlight as it passes through the atmosphere.[23] However, their effects had been vastly underestimated as it was also believed that they rapidly rain back to the ground soon after emission, leaving no longer-term, wider impacts.[24] Through large-scale, concerted measurements from ships, planes, and satellites, INDOEX showed this to be a flawed and incomplete picture.

The experiment revealed that particles can stay airborne longer than previously thought and thus spread much further, seasonally leading to aggregations of soot and other pollutants that can cover much of South and East Asia, dubbed "brown clouds" by researchers.[25] The previously unforeseen scale and density of these clouds, it was now argued, could not only dim the surface, but even distort regional weather patterns to such an extent as to divert the entire monsoon, which sustains agriculture in the region, increasing the risk of droughts and harvest failures.[26] The new data also showed that – even while cooling the surface below – soot particles measurably heat the atmosphere above by absorbing solar radiation otherwise reflected back into space, thus contributing to global warming, too.[27] The implications were clear: Air pollution is not merely a local health concern, but can also change the climate on a regional and even global scale.

21 Novakov and Rosen (n17) 10; Weart, 'Aerosols' (n17); Interview 5.

22 John Fialka, 'Discovery of "Asian Brown Cloud" Sets off Fight' *The Wall Street Journal* (New York, 6 May 2003) <https://www.wsj.com/articles/SB105216877389201500> accessed 12/12/2021.

23 Novakov and Rosen (n17) 10.

24 ibid; Fialka (n22).

25 Fialka (n22); The Economist, 'Pollution and Global Warming: Climate Change in Black & White' (London, 17 February 2011) <https://www.economist.com/science-and-technology/2011/02/17/climate-change-in-black-and-white> accessed 11/12/2021.

26 Weart, 'Aerosols' (n17).

27 Fialka (n22); Novakov and Rosen (n17) 10.

How novel this insight was is corroborated by the framing of particulate climate forcers in the IPCC's earlier reports: Neither of its two assessments published before INDOEX even specifically mention black carbon, instead vaguely talking about aerosols as a general category – which then are only ascribed a dimming and thus cooling effect, with no mention of the potential for some particles to also absorb heat.[28] Where specific aerosols are mentioned, the focus is only on sulfates, which genuinely do have a significant cooling effect by virtue of their much brighter, more reflective colour than black carbon.[29] This lack of concern reflects a then still common assumption among atmospheric scientists that particles would not play a significant role in global warming going forwards – and not without reason: While CO_2 emissions were continuously rising, those of particles actually held relatively stable at the time.[30] Given the much longer atmospheric lifetime of CO_2, it is easy to see why such trends would lead one to believe the effect of short-lived particles would be negligible in the future.[31] However, the conclusions of INDOEX that the climate effect and concentrations of black carbon had been underestimated and could actually be significant forced a re-evaluation of this thinking.[32]

2.2 *Taking a Closer Look at Trace Gases: Methane and HFCs Re-examined*

Around the same time, scientists were also gaining a greater understanding of the outsize impacts certain trace gases can have.[33] In particular, methane was rising considerably on both the climate and air pollution agendas since analyses of ancient air trapped in the ice of Greenland showed that its concentration over time correlated with historic changes in the climate much stronger than had previously been realised.[34] Even though it still only makes up a miniscule fraction of the atmosphere, a better understanding of methane thus became crucial to the modelling of future warming and it attracted increasing scientific attention.[35]

28 IPCC, *First Assessment Report Overview and Policymaker Summaries and 1992 IPCC Supplement* (CUP 1992) 78; IPCC, *Second Assessment* (n19) 21f.
29 ibid; Weart, 'Aerosols' (n17).
30 Spencer Weart and James Hansen, 'James Hansen: Session II' (2000) <https://www.aip.org/history-programs/niels-bohr-library/oral-histories/24309-2> accessed 16/01/2022.
31 ibid; Weart, 'Aerosols' (n17).
32 ibid.
33 Weart, 'Other Greenhouse Gases' (n18).
34 ibid; Gavin Schmidt, 'La Fulgurante Ascension du Méthane' (2004) 378 La Recherche 48, 50–53.
35 Schmidt (n34) 53.

Later research furthermore implicated elevated methane concentrations as the cause of a notable rise in global background levels of tropospheric ozone, contributing to dangerous high-pollution episodes commonly known as smog.[36] Methane alone creates only little ozone as it reacts slowly, so it was previously thought to be relatively benign to health, but its increased atmospheric concentration – more than doubled since pre-industrial times – has evidently raised the baseline of pollution upon which more reactive ozone precursors then build, thereby lowering the threshold for smog creation.[37]

Beyond this, atmospheric concentrations of HFCs also started rising faster than had been expected around the mid-2000s, as developing countries were transitioning to the new chemicals.[38] Prospects for their future contribution to climate change thus shot up and added to the generally dawning conclusion that even trace gases can play a major role in changing the climate. Together, all the above observations supported INDOEX's claims that global warming and air pollution are linked, opening possibilities for co-benefits between the policies addressing them.

2.3 *Reframing Climate Change for the 21st Century*

The first to pull together these and other strings of research into a policy-relevant argument was the influential climate scientist James Hansen. He had built his public profile as one of the first experts to draw political attention to the warming impacts of CO_2, but was now shifting his focus to other climate forcers.[39] In an article boldly entitled "Global Warming in the 21st Century", he even went as far as to argue that policy-makers should *prioritise* these other forcers – in particular black carbon, methane, and chlorofluorocarbons, a list that is very close to what we now call SLCPs – as CO_2 emissions would inevitably rise over the next half century anyways.[40] Without actually coining the concept, this article anticipated key arguments later attached to SLCPs, in particular that their mitigation can deliver immediate results and buy time for

36 Jason West and Arlene Fiore, 'Management of Tropospheric Ozone by Reducing Methane Emissions' (2005) 39 Environmental Science & Technology 4685, 4685.

37 ibid.

38 UNEP, *HFCs: A Critical Link in Protecting Climate and the Ozone Layer* (UNEP 2011) 9f; Weart, 'Aerosols' (n17).

39 Jonathan Mingle, *Fire and Ice: Soot, Solidarity, and Survival on the Roof of the World* (St. Martin's Press 2015) 356.

40 James Hansen and others, 'Global Warming in the Twenty-First Century: An Alternative Scenario' (2000) 97 PNAS 9875.

decarbonisation, while also delivering benefits for human health – and all this already in the year 2000.[41]

However, this proved highly controversial because Hansen's argument lacked important nuances and was released into an already charged political atmosphere: In his native US, the article became embroiled in concurrent presidential elections, alluded to by George W. Bush to counter his opponent Al Gore's demands for more ambitious cuts in CO_2, and was consequentially shunned by environmentalists as well as many fellow scientists.[42] Meanwhile internationally, some developing countries led by India denounced the research it was based on, particularly INDOEX, as essentially a ploy by Western governments to divert from their responsibility for climate change through historic CO_2-emissions and shifting blame onto subsistence farmers in the global South.[43]

In the context of already tense domestic and North-South debates over the US's refusal to ratify the Kyoto Protocol as it entailed no substantial obligations for developing nations, this argument gained enough traction to temporarily block further studies into the brown cloud phenomenon UNEP had envisioned – setting back international SLCP science for the next several years.[44] Nonetheless, the nucleus of a future epistemic community had already been formed: UNEP would go on to become a key node for international investigations into SLCPs – a decision that can be directly traced back to its early involvement in INDOEX and other science cited above.[45] However, this was ten years after the initial controversy and, until then, most research into the issue was funded by the US and European governments on a regional, not global scale.[46]

3 The Concept's Arctic Origins: 2007–9

The first articles to unite the above science under one cohesive concept were two technical reports published in 2008 by AMAP,[47] an advisory scientific working group of the Arctic Council, followed by a summary report for

41 ibid.
42 Mingle (n39) 356f.
43 ibid 360–362; Fialka (n22).
44 ibid; Interview 5.
45 The Economist (n25).
46 ibid; Interviews 1 and 5.
47 AMAP, 'The Impact of Short-Lived Pollutants on Arctic Climate' (2008) <https://www.amap.no/documents/download/974/inline> accessed 14/01/2022; AMAP, 'Sources and Mitigation Opportunities to Reduce Emissions of Short-Term Arctic Climate Forcers'

policy-makers in 2009.[48] These cover black carbon, methane, and other ozone precursors under the label "short-lived climate *forcers*" (SLCFs), which later became SLCPs.[49] Some today make a distinction between SLCFs as all short-lived pollutants with a climate effect – even if they cool temperatures – and SLCPs as only those with a warming effect.[50] However, AMAP essentially focused on what we now call SLCPs under the label of SLCFs – so its work may be seen as both concepts' origin.

Given previous controversies, it only made sense for the concept to emerge in the global North, where virtually all funding was coming from: AMAP's 2008 reports have been gestated at a workshop organised by National Aeronautics and Space Administration (Nasa) and were thus sponsored directly by the US government.[51] Indeed, even some within AMAP still questioned the virtue of such research, perceiving it as a potential distraction from CO_2 as previous critics had, and it was only upon the continued urging of the US – which also provided initial funding – that these reports came to be.[52]

However, it was also science, not just politics, that determined the concept would specifically be born in an Arctic context: The high North warms faster than more southerly latitudes, and there were indications that SLCPs contributed to this – particularly black carbon, which not only heats the atmosphere there (as was the case over the Indian Ocean), but also the surface, as it significantly darkens the ice-sheets it eventually lands on.[53] Hence, the concept of SLCPs clearly emerged at the science-policy interface, from scientific reports responding to political priorities – particularly those of the US at this early stage.

3.1 *AMAP's Contributions to the SLCP Debate*

Like Hansen, AMAP focused on the potential for SLCP cuts to immediately slow down climate change, particularly in the Arctic, while also protecting human health.[54] However, having learned from earlier controversies, its reports also

(2008b) <https://www.amap.no/documents/doc/sources-and-mitigation-opportunities-to-reduce-emissions-of-short-term-arctic-climate-forcers/13> accessed 14/01/2022.

48 AMAP, 'Update on Selected Climate Issues of Concern: Observations, Short-lived Climate Forcers, Arctic Carbon Cycle, and Predictive Capability' (2009) <www.amap.no/documents/doc/amap-2009-update-on-selected-climate-issues-of-concern/752> accessed 14/01/2022.

49 AMAP, 'Update' (n48).

50 IPCC, *Global Warming of 1.5°C* (CUP 2018) 118.

51 AMAP, 'The Impact of SLCPs' (n47).

52 Interviews 3 and 1.

53 David Stone, *The Changing Arctic Environment: The Arctic Messenger* (CUP 2015) 240f.

54 Hansen and others (n40); AMAP, 'Update' (n48).

consciously put front and centre that such policies must be additional to ongoing decarbonisation efforts and should not replace them – and this new framing has been very effective.[55]

Indeed, a former AMAP official argues these were some of the most influential reports in the organisation's history because they inspired the Council's ongoing involvement in SLCP governance:[56] At the 2009 Arctic ministerial meeting in Tromsø, its member states for the first time noted that cutting the emissions of "shorter-lived climate forcers such as black carbon, methane and tropospheric ozone precursors" may "slow the rate of Arctic snow, sea ice and sheet ice melting", even while CO_2 remains the most important issue – in large parts copying AMAP's argumentation.[57] As further credit to the impact of AMAP's early work, this framing analysis shows that all aspects it focused on – co-benefits, immediate rewards, and the continuing importance of CO_2 – remain central pillars of the concept even now.

Nevertheless, several important features of SLCPs as they are currently portrayed are still missing in these first reports. Most notably, they did not yet include HFCs and lacked some crucial details in their assessment of the other pollutants – in particular their health impacts, which are mentioned, but not elaborated on, as most of AMAP's experts were climate scientists.[58] Furthermore, even the more detailed assessment of the pollutants' climate impacts at this stage lacked solid numbers: While writing that SLCFs "may have a combined effect comparable to that of CO_2",[59] scientists did not hazard to quantify this, instead noting repeatedly that there is "considerable uncertainty" around it.[60] Everything that was included, meanwhile, was limited to a regional scope only, given AMAP's Arctic focus.

As a result of these many knowledge gaps, there was also hardly any practical policy advice in these reports apart from a call for further research, so their findings were not yet politically actionable.[61] At least this limited advice was followed when the Arctic Council set up a Task Force on SLCFs to further study the issue and provide concrete policy advice by 2011.[62] AMAP's early

55 Interview 3.
56 Stone (n53) 240f.
57 Arctic Council, 'Tromsø Declaration' (2009) <https://oaarchive.arctic-council.org/handle/11374/91> accessed 17/01/2022.
58 Interview 3.
59 AMAP, 'Update' (n48) 14.
60 AMAP, 'Update' (n48) v, 7, 14.
61 ibid; Interview 3.
62 Arctic Council, 'Tromsø Declaration' (n57) 3.

assessments must thus be seen as scoping exercises that laid the groundwork for future research rather than presenting solid findings themselves.[63]

3.2 *Wider Political Impact of Arctic Research*

Despite its limitations, AMAP's work did start a larger conversation as it happened at a politically opportune moment: Global climate negotiations hit a low-point at the Copenhagen climate summit mere months later, prompting a search for new approaches to complement these stalling efforts.[64] Promises of a new global climate agreement by 2009 had not been met, leaving many in the policy-sphere frustrated with the UNFCCC process and making the idea of slowing warming to buy more time for decarbonisation, a central pillar of AMAP's reports and current arguments around SLCPS, seem very appealing.[65] Earlier controversies were thus put aside in this moment, allowing UNEP – which had never lost interest in the climate-pollution nexus since INDOEX but had been politically blocked from pursuing it – to re-engage.[66]

The result are two ambitious new assessments on the impacts of black carbon, methane, and tropospheric ozone published by UNEP in 2011.[67] Their results and framings dominated the SLCP agenda for years to come and still echo strongly today – even though they also still called them SLCFS. These reports frequently reference AMAP's assessments and cite the Arctic Council's calls for action as part of their underlying rationale,[68] but also went beyond what AMAP had been able to achieve with its organisational limitations and the limited data available at the time. While AMAP started an intergovernmental debate on the substances we now call SLCPS, it was only UNEP's reports that ultimately made this an actionable concept and launched it into the global policy sphere.[69]

63 Interviews 1 and 3.

64 Charlotte Unger, Kathleen Mar, and Konrad Gürtler, 'A Club's Contribution to Global Climate Governance: The Case of the Climate and Clean Air Coalition' (2020) 6 Palgrave Communications 99, 2; Interview 5.

65 ibid.

66 The Economist (n25).

67 UNEP, *Near-term Climate Protection and Clean Air Benefits: Actions for Controlling Short-Lived Climate Forcers* (UNEP 2011); UNEP and WMO, *Integrated Assessment of Black Carbon and Tropospheric Ozone: Summary for Decision Makers* (UNEP and WMO 2011).

68 UNEP and WMO (n67) 5.

69 Interviews 5 and 6.

4 Concept Launch through UNEP and the CCAC: 2011–12

Much like AMAP, UNEP still emphasised the potential to slow warming and achieve health co-benefits by mitigating SLCF emissions – which it still understands to not include HFCs. Also like previously, its assessments stress that this should be additional to ongoing CO_2 reductions. However, as this section shows, they offer much more detail and context on each of these aspects and managed to quantify the impacts of mitigating SLCF pollution, providing a stronger impetus for action.[70]

4.1 *Conceptual Development in UNEP's Assessments*

UNEP's reports build on AMAP's work in four crucial ways. Firstly, while still emphasising the pollutants' impacts on the Arctic and often referencing AMAP in doing so, they complement this with data on their effect in other regions, particularly the Himalayas – another glaciated region and consequently impacted in similar ways – building on the organisation's previous work with INDOEX.[71] UNEP thus constructed a new, global framing of SLCFs, without losing sight of their well-established regional dimensions. Secondly, its reports also place much greater emphasis on non-climate co-benefits than AMAP did, which was presumably possible as UNEP drew on a broader range of experts not limited to climate scientists. Hence, the reports include significantly more detail on which SLCPs have what health effects, as well as where people are most affected by this.[72]

Further setting itself apart from earlier studies, UNEP thirdly suggests a concrete list of policies – 16 in total – targeting most important sources of SLCPs, focused especially on fossil fuel production, agriculture, waste management, as well as residential heating and transport.[73] Fourthly and finally, the reports' authors managed to quantify what impacts these measures would have, with the two headline facts being that full implementation of proposed policies could prevent 2.4 million premature deaths each year as well as around 0.5°C of global warming by 2050 – the first time concrete numbers entered the SLCP debate, making a powerful case for action.[74]

Beyond just building on AMAP's work, UNEP also constructed two new arguments that have frequently been repeated since and become further pillars of

70 UNEP and WMO (n67); UNEP, *Near-term Climate Protection* (n67).
71 See for example UNEP, *Near-term Climate Protection* (n67) xvi; UNEP and WMO (n67) 2.
72 UNEP, *Near-term Climate Protection* (n67) XII–XV.
73 ibid, 9f.
74 ibid, XII–XIII.

the concept: That policies to tackle SLCFs are both practical and cost-effective. Their practicality is repeatedly emphasised in the reports' claims that many recommended policies are already in use in diverse countries and rely on existing, proven techniques – for example emissions standards for cars to reduce black carbon and the capture of methane emissions from landfills.[75] Cost-effectiveness, meanwhile, refers to UNEP's assertions that such policies can often be implemented at low or – as in the case of methane capture, which can be used to generate energy – even negative cost.[76] This, too, has been quantified by UNEP in their second report, which argues that half of the suggested policies would save money in the medium- to longer-term.[77] These arguments have proven to be quite popular with many governments, who to this day often repeat them through the CCAC, as analysed later in this chapter.

With this, following ten years of increasing interest in non-CO_2 climate forcers, UNEP was the first organisation to articulate all the main elements of the SLCP concept as it is framed today: That mitigating these pollutants slows climate change and protects lives, that it can be done relatively easily and cost-effectively, and that it must be additional to ongoing decarbonisation efforts. By combining this with a concrete list of actions to be considered by governments, the reports launched this concept into the global policy sphere, where it remains in a very similar form to this day.

4.2 *Emergence of an Epistemic Community for SLCPs and the CCAC*

As a side-effect of UNEP's reports, from 2011 onwards it also makes sense to speak of an epistemic community promoting the governance of what we now call SLCPs: Previously largely disconnected research and independently operating researchers, e.g. from the Arctic and South Asia, were brought together in the UNEP assessments and given a shared policy agenda through the 16 concrete actions they recommend. These scientists may not directly cooperate like this very often, given the complexity and diversity of SLCPs, but they are aware of one another's work and share a desire to bring more prominence to these pollutants – so all conditions for an epistemic community are fulfilled.[78]

Less than a year after UNEP's assessments, this group of experts was also given a political outlet for their work through the launch of the CCAC – a public-private partnership specifically dedicated to promoting SLCP governance. The Coalition is discussed further in Chapter 6, but for this conceptual history of

75 See for example UNEP and WMO (n67) 2.
76 ibid, 3; UNEP, *Near-term Climate Protection* (n67) x.
77 UNEP, *Near-term Climate Protection* (n67) xvi.
78 Interviews 3 and 4.

SLCPs, it is mostly relevant for two additions it made to the concept: While otherwise taking over framings of these substances from UNEP, the CCAC was the first organisation to include HFCs under this framing *and* the first to actually use the label of SLC*P*s for them, rather than SLC*F*s.

Up to this point, HFCs had been addressed by separate assessments and framed in a distinct way from other SLCPs.[79] For example, early IPCC publications explicitly referred to them as "*long-lived* gases" alongside CO_2,[80] and major pre-2011 reports about HFCs lack some of the main arguments made for the mitigation of other SLCPs, such as the potential for immediate benefits. This was partly for historical reasons, as HFCs were generally studied by scientists specialised in ozone depletion – a separate group from the climate and pollution scholarships – but also based in the science itself: Unlike other SLCPs, HFCs cause no widespread, direct health effects (though they indirectly cause ill-health through global warming) and some of them can indeed be quite long-lived, longer even than methane.[81]

The reason for HFCs' inclusion in the concept – and for its relabelling as SLCPs, not SLCFs – was political: This was around the time that negotiations about these substances started under the Montreal Protocol and the CCAC was used as a vehicle to push these forwards.[82] As is often the case in the history of SLCPs, the political impetus for this came mostly from Washington, DC: While the CCAC has six co-founders – including also Bangladesh, Canada, Ghana, Mexico, and Sweden – the US was the instigator and driving force behind its launch.[83] Initially, the US turned to Canada and Mexico for support, with whom they already closely cooperate on environmental matters through the North American Commission on Environmental Cooperation, whereas the other founding members were invited later to ensure geographical balance.[84]

US domestic politics may also be why the new label of SLCPs became attached to the concept: According to multiple sources, the Obama administration was actively trying to link global warming and air pollution because

79 IPCC and TEAP, *Safeguarding the Ozone Layer and the Global Climate System* (CUP 2005); TEAP, '2010 Report of the Technology and Economic Assessment Panel' (2010) <https://ozone.unep.org/sites/default/files/2019-05/TEAP-Assessment-report-2010.pdf> accessed 20/01/2022; UNEP, *HFCs: A Critical Link in Protecting Climate and the Ozone Layer* (UNEP 2011).

80 IPCC, *Second Assessment* (n19) 21.

81 Interview 4; IPCC and TEAP (n79) 7.

82 CCAC, 'Vienna Communiqué' (2016) <https://www.ccacoalition.org/en/resources/vienna-communique> accessed 20/01/2022; Interviews 2 and 5.

83 Interviews 5, 6, and 7.

84 Interview 7.

the latter is much less controversial than the former in American political discourse – so this link was seen as a way of creating bipartisan support for climate change mitigation.[85] Hence, *climate pollutants* may have replaced *climate forcers* in the new label of SLCPs in order to make this link explicit in the vocabulary used to discuss the substances included under it.

Interestingly, the concept appealed to the CCAC's middle-and low-income members for exactly the opposite reason: Very broadly speaking, they were more concerned with air pollution and perceived richer countries to be overly focused on the climate – so for them, the *climate pollutants* label became a way of refocusing global environmental debates more towards human health.[86] Therein lies a key strength of the SLCP concept: By combining two issues in one term, it also unites these different political coalitions behind a shared agenda. This delicate balance was only possible since AMAP and UNEP made clear that *both* SLCPs *and* long-lived greenhouse gases must be mitigated and, as the following section shows, it enabled the concept's widespread diffusion in global environmental policy circles.

5 Reception and Diffusion in the Policy Sphere since 2012

UNEP's framing of SLCPs was taken up by governments nearly unchanged and persists in large parts to this day: Not only was the CCAC founded in direct response to its assessments, but state partners of the Coalition also generally repeat its arguments and conclusions in their communiqués.[87] For example, the first such statement explicitly cites UNEP's reports to call for "urgent action" against SLCPs to "address near-term climate change, improve air quality and public health", as well as attain some economic benefits – though also

85 Mingle (n39) 356f; Interviews 6 and 7.

86 Interviews 6 and 7.

87 CCAC 'Oslo Communiqué' (2013) <https://www.ccacoalition.org/en/resources/oslo-communique> accessed 20/01/2022; CCAC, 'Paris Communiqué' (2015) <https://www.ccacoalition.org/en/resources/paris-communique> accessed 20/01/2022; CCAC, 'Climate and Clean Air Coalition Five-Year Strategic Plan' (2015) <https://www.ccacoalition.org/en/resources/climate-and-clean-air-coalition-five-year-strategic-plan> accessed 20/01/2022; CCAC, 'Marrakech Communiqué' (2016) <https://www.ccacoalition.org/en/resources/marrakech-communique> accessed 20/01/2022; CCAC, 'Vienna Communiqué' (2016) <https://www.ccacoalition.org/en/resources/vienna-communique> accessed 20/01/2022; CCAC, 'Bonn Communiqué' (2017) <https://www.ccacoalition.org/en/resources/bonn-communique> accessed 20/01/2022; CCAC, 'Talanoa Statement' (2018) <https://www.ccacoalition.org/en/resources/talanoa-statement-and-joint-submission-climate-clean-air-coalition-partners> accessed 20/01/2022.

cautioning that this must be a "complement to ambitious global reductions of long-lived greenhouse gases".[88] It furthermore describes initiatives through which the CCAC will promote SLCP mitigation in various sectors, including all those UNEP assessed to be most important – the fossil fuel industry, agriculture, waste management, transport, and residential heating – as well as the HFC industry, its own addition.[89] The problem definition, suggested solutions, and interpretation of the facts advanced by state partners of the Coalition thus all parallel those of UNEP's reports.

Indeed, these arguments appear to have been very popular among governments: Just within its first year of existence, the CCAC grew to include over 50 state partners (a number that has since risen to 80, as of 2023).[90] Around the same time, the first international legal regimes also took note of SLCPs, with negotiations on HFCs beginning under the Montreal Protocol and black carbon being included in the Gothenburg Protocol.[91] The Arctic Council meanwhile intensified its SLCP action through the "Framework for Action on Enhanced Black Carbon and Methane Reductions", which establishes an iterative process of expert review of member states' policies on these pollutants and thereby formalised and strengthened its previous Task Force.[92] All these initiatives are discussed in further detail elsewhere in this volume.

Nonetheless, there are important differences in emphasis between scientific assessments and official government positions on SLCPs. Firstly, it should be noted that not all states stick to the same framing and there is a general pattern that developed countries focus overwhelmingly on SLCPs' climate impacts, while developing ones pay more attention to their consequences for human health.[93] This is not reflected in their joint communiqués, which combine both viewpoints, but even those emphasise different aspects of the concept than initial scientific reports had: Most notably, there is less focus on concrete action in these official communiqués than there had been in the UNEP reports: While the 2011 assessments recommended a list of 16 policies to tackle SLCPs, early CCAC statements stop short of promoting any particular

88 CCAC, 'Oslo Communiqué' (n87) 1.
89 ibid, 1f.
90 CCAC, 'About' (n12).
91 UNECE Executive Body Decision 2012/2 (4 May 2012) UN Doc ECE/EB.AIR/111/Add.1.
92 Arctic Council, 'Enhanced Black Carbon and Methane Reductions: An Arctic Council Framework for Action' (2015) <https://oaarchive.arctic-council.org/handle/11374/610> accessed 18/01/2021.
93 Interviews 5, 6, and 7.

actions.[94] Apart from the sectoral initiatives launched in the first communiqué, which were formulated rather vaguely to omit specific commitments, the Coalition still provided very little information on what should actually be done about the problem they identified.[95]

5.1 *The "Paris Effect" on the SLCP Debate and Scientific Progress*

From 2016 onwards, governments' communications on SLCPs through the CCAC suddenly become significantly more urgent and action oriented – a change largely owed to the 2015 Paris Agreement, but also significant scientific progress.[96] The Paris Agreement's key contribution towards this was the introduction of a global collective goal of limiting warming to well below 2°C and ideally 1.5°C above pre-industrial temperatures: These numbers require rapid and ambitious action and have since been taken up in many national laws and even private company policies, creating significant momentum behind climate mitigation that has been dubbed the "Paris Effect".[97] As we are on track to overshoot 1.5°C, every decimal degree that can be spared matters – particularly so in the near-term – which is why the argument that SLCP governance can slow warming by half a degree by 2050 became highly appealing once again.[98]

This new urgency manifests both in CCAC statements' language and their substantive contents: From 2016, they become much more concrete about mitigating SLCPs, no longer just identifying the problem and vaguely calling for action, but actively promoting specific policies to tackle it: For example, the Marrakech Communiqué focuses on policies to reduce black carbon emissions from transport through fuel and technological standards, while the Bonn Communiqué highlights options to reduce methane from agriculture and waste management.[99] Furthermore, their tone is increasingly pressing: Where, in 2015, the Coalition still referred to SLCP governance as merely an "effective and pragmatic complement to aggressive mitigation of CO_2" that "*could* help reduce near-term warming",[100] they start acknowledging it as a

94 CCAC, 'Oslo Communiqué' (n87); CCAC, 'Paris Communiqué' (n87); CCAC, 'Five-Year Strategic Plan' (n87).

95 ibid.

96 Interviews 3, 5, and 6.

97 Julia Turner, Mark Meldrum, and Jeremy Oppenheim, 'The Paris Effect: How the Climate Agreement is Reshaping the Global Economy' (2020) <https://www.systemiq.earth/wp-content/uploads/2020/12/The-Paris-Effect_SYSTEMIQ_Full-Report_December-2020.pdf> accessed 15/03/2022.

98 Interviews 3, 5, and 6.

99 CCAC, 'Marrakech Communiqué' (n87) 2; CCAC, 'Bonn Communiqué' (n87) 2.

100 CCAC, 'Paris Communiqué' (n87) 1 (emphasis added).

"*necessary* complement [...] in order to achieve the temperature goals in the Paris Agreement" that can "*substantially* slow down" climate change a year later.[101] This is the origin of a new argument for SLCP mitigation: Ever since the 1.5°C goal became a global point of reference, cutting SLCPs is being framed as a necessity to reach this target. This made for a powerful new rallying cry and, next to HFCs, constitutes the only significant recent addition to the concept as it was framed by UNEP in 2011.

The new urgency was further intensified by scientific progress, as certainty around SLCPs' impacts rose and estimates quantifying them were revised upwards: The number of degrees of warming projected to be prevented by fully implementing recommended policies rose from 0.5°C to 0.6°C,[102] while estimates of avoided deaths through this was revised to at least 3.5 million per year, up from previously 2.4 million.[103] Scientific progress is also evident in AMAP's continuing work on SLCPs, whose conclusions are presented in increasingly more certain language than its highly tentative early reports.[104] By 2015, they even put forth a first quantification for black carbon's climate effect specifically in the Arctic, estimating this at 0.25°C of warming already by 2025.[105] This kind of modelling, focusing on a particular forcer in a particular region, had previously eluded scientists due to the sheer complexities involved, so the field has progressed significantly – though some uncertainty remains around this number.[106]

Even the IPCC, which had previously been sceptical of aerosols' warming potential, acknowledged in its fifth assessment report that it had significantly under-estimated the effect of black carbon in this regard.[107] Indeed, in 2018 it went on to write one of the assessments most cited by those promoting SLCP governance today: Its *Special Report on Global Warming of 1.5°C* found no realistic scenarios that reach the Paris Agreement's goals without "deep reductions

---

101 CCAC, 'Marrakech Communiqué' (n87) 1 (emphasis added).

102 CCAC, ‚Paris Communiqué' (n87) 2.

103 CCAC and WHO, *Reducing Global Health Risks through Mitigation of Short-Lived Climate Pollutants: Scoping Report* (CCAC and WHO 2015) 2.

104 AMAP, 'The Impact of Black Carbon on Arctic Climate' (2011) <https://www.amap.no/documents/doc/the-impact-of-black-carbon-on-arctic-climate/746> accessed 14/01/2022; Task Force on Short-Lived Climate Forcers, 'Recommendations to Reduce Black Carbon and Methane Emissions to Slow Arctic Climate Change' (*Arctic Council* 2013) <https://oaarchive.arctic-council.org/handle/11374/80> accessed 18/01/2022; AMAP, *Arctic Climate Issues 2015: Short-lived Climate Pollutants – Summary for Policy Makers* (AMAP 2015).

105 AMAP, 'Arctic Climate Issues 2015' (n104).

106 Interview 3.

107 IPCC, *Assessment Report 5* (CUP 2014) 44.

in emissions of methane and black carbon (35% or more of both by 2050 relative to 2010)".[108] This provided scientific backing to the argument that SLCP mitigation is necessary to avoid dangerous warming and definitively ended the debate about whether policies targeting them are merely a distraction from CO_2, which had been hindering the concept's promotion from the start.[109] While the IPCC remains somewhat sceptical of the epistemic community's framing, especially around black carbon, their respective overall conclusions are now fully in line with one another.[110] Nevertheless, it should be noted that science on the matter continues to evolve and estimates of black carbon's warming effect were revised downwards in the latest IPCC report, while those for methane rose further still.[111]

Notwithstanding its now more ambitious rhetoric, it is also important to point out that the CCAC is still a fractious coalition – which has become particularly evident in its post-Paris communiqués: Unlike previously, there is an "à la carte" quality to these statements, where rather than all endorsing the same message, different groupings of states undersign different parts of it. For example, the afore-mentioned section on mitigating black carbon from transport comes with its own list of signatures that differs from that of the document as a whole.[112]

5.2 *Recent Developments: Shifting the Focus from Black Carbon to Methane*

While the concept's overall framing has remained relatively stable, the political priority attached to different SLCPs has fluctuated over time. According to people involved in the CCAC, states initially focused largely on black carbon since it lay at the centre of some of the most shocking early discoveries on the climate-pollution nexus.[113] This was followed by a period of intense international interest in HFCs, starting when negotiations under the Montreal Protocol became more serious and lasting until 2016, when an agreement on the Kigali Amendment[114] was reached.[115] Recently, however, both black carbon and HFCs faded into the background, while methane gained ever greater

108 IPCC, *1.5°C* (n50) 19.
109 Interviews 3, 5, and 6.
110 Interview 6.
111 IPCC, *Climate Change 2021: Technical Summary* (CUP 2021) 9.
112 CCAC, 'Marrakech Communiqué' (n87) 2.
113 Interviews 3, 5, 6, and 7.
114 Meeting of the Parties to the Montreal Protocol Decision XXVIII/1 (15 October 2016).
115 Inverviews 2, 3, 5, 6, and 7.

importance.[116] This culminated in the Global Methane Pledge, initiated by the US, wherein over 100 states politically committed to reducing the gas's global emissions by 30% this decade.[117] This last shift in focus reflects the fact that methane's atmospheric concentration and thereby estimates of its future climate impact both shot up recently.[118] As SLCPs' emissions can generally be cut more cheaply than CO_2, and methane was found to have such an outsize effect, it soon became known as the "low-hanging fruit" of climate policy.[119]

Despite the clear advantages of mitigating methane, this new focus may become politically contentious for several reasons. Firstly, it must be noted that reducing methane is easier in some sectors than others: While there are easy fixes for the fossil fuel industry, such as better leak detection in pipelines, techniques to mitigate its emissions in agriculture are still at an earlier stage of development.[120] Consequently, the shift to methane may be perceived as politically motivated: The instigator of the Pledge were the US, who have a large natural gas industry that makes it easy to meet this commitment, while the initiative has garnered relatively little support in Asia, where agricultural emissions play a more important role.[121] Furthermore, methane's connection to human health – generally the main concern of the CCAC's medium- and low-income members – is less direct than that of other SLCPs since its main impact in this regard stems from secondary ozone pollution, not methane itself. Hence, this new focus may also disrupt the delicate balance between developed countries (who care mostly about climate change) and developing countries (more concerned with pollution) that lies at the heart of the concept's acceptability.[122] This once again illustrates that even scientifically-informed concepts always have political contents and raises the prospect for conflict about the future direction of the SLCP agenda.

116 ibid.

117 Global Methane Pledge, 'Fast Action on Methane to Keep a 1.5°C Future within Reach' (2022) <https://www.globalmethanepledge.org> accessed 20/05/2022.

118 IPCC, *Climate Change 2021* (n111) 9; Interviews 3, 4, and 5.

119 Interviews 3 and 5.

120 Interviews 5 and 6.

121 Interview 6.

122 Interview 7.

6 Conclusion

In conclusion, this history shows that the concept of SLCPs emerged at the science-policy interface and was co-produced by both scientific and political actors. To be more precise, tracing the concept's framing over time has revealed that the scientific input to it largely comes from a growing epistemic community that emerged and communicated gradually through the medium of international assessment reports, ultimately finding its home in the CCAC, while the political priorities they responded to were often those of the US.

This Western bias sparked intense controversy in the concept's early and pre-history, when research into the climate-pollution nexus was obstructed at the global level by some developing countries' objections. Ultimately, the concept was therefore developed in an Arctic context and only became popularised globally through later assessments by UNEP, at a moment when traditional climate policy was in doubt following the 2009 Copenhagen climate summit. UNEP's framings proved highly convincing and SLCPs were quickly put at the centre of a new, rapidly growing climate club – the CCAC. Despite this Coalition's reach, however, states continue emphasising different aspects of the concept based on their own national priorities. Lately, for example, the US has been using the Coalition in particular to promote cuts to methane emissions, which are much easier to mitigate there than in many developing countries – so even now that a global coalition has formed around the concept, the potential for controversy persists. This history of ups and downs can teach those promoting the governance of SLCPs three important lessons.

Firstly, it should be noted that uncertainty is an inescapable fact of the SLCP agenda. This is due to its high complexity – encompassing numerous pollutants of diverging properties, each with their own uncertainties attached – and because scientific interest in untangling these complexities only arose relatively recently. Such uncertainty was particularly problematic in the concept's early history, when there was even outright disagreement about whether to conduct further studies into it. While this opposition subsided with scientific progress and we can now be certain that SLCPs need to be mitigated to prevent dangerous warming and health effects, reasonable debates still remain around which specific SLCP contributes how much to these issues and what are the best policies for tackling them. Those promoting the governance of SLCPs should be keenly aware of this.

Secondly, precisely because of these complexities, the concept cannot be seen as a purely scientific category, but is steeped in politics. Like all such conceptual innovations, it highlights some issues over others and therefore has a normative content: Using SLCPs as a policy-concept rests on the implicit value judgements that these pollutants should be prioritised in environmental policy and that the science behind them is strong enough to justify this. It may also be seen as implicating certain actors, or countries, as responsible, opening the potential for conflict. Even beneath the surface of cooperation through the CCAC, different countries thus promote distinct framings of the concept according to their own interests. As the dominant normative dimension of SLCPs has essentially grown out of domestic US politics, these tensions often pit developed against developing countries – another factor that should not be forgotten when discussing the concept.

Thirdly and lastly, all this goes to show that having roots in both science and politics has been a strength and a weakness for the SLCP agenda: As the scientific assessments that framed the concept responded to political demands, they were automatically policy relevant, explaining their successful transition into the policy realm. However, this close link to politics is also what has made SLCPs controversial at times, particularly early on in this history. In order maintain a stable balance between scientific credibility and political relevance, those promoting the concept should thus pay equal attention to its scientific *and* political dimensions.

Overall, this means the central challenge for those promoting the governance of SLCPs is to contextualise the science for decision-makers and turn it into policy-relevant advice without being perceived as overly politicising it. This, in turn, requires a greater focus on global equity and inclusiveness when discussing these pollutants and how they should be tackled. In the past, such nuances were sometimes lacking and the concept's history was plagued by allegations of a Western bias. To prevent this controversy from recurring in the future, acknowledging this history and learning its lessons is an important first step.

Annex: List of Interviews

- **Interview 1:**
  With a former senior AMAP official; conducted 19/11/2019
- **Interview 2:**
  With a European negotiator for the Montreal Protocol; conducted 03/03/2022
- **Interview 3:**
  With a climate scientist and expert on black carbon, involved in Arctic Council, UNEP, and IPCC assessments; conducted 11/03/2022
- **Interview 4:**

With a scientist and national official involved in the Arctic Council's work on SLCPs; conducted 17/03/2022

- **Interview 5:**
  With the former director of an NGO involved in the CCAC with long-time experience in promoting SLCP governance; conducted 18/03/2022
- **Interview 6:**
  With an expert in air pollution regulation serving on the CCAC's advisory committee; conducted 09/06/2022
- **Interview 7:**
  With an expert in air pollution and former delegate to the CCAC of one of its founding governments; conducted 08/07/2022

Bibliography

Primary Sources

AMAP, *Arctic Climate Issues 2015: Short-lived Climate Pollutants – Summary for Policy Makers* (AMAP 2015).

AMAP, 'The Impact of Black Carbon on Arctic Climate' (2011) <https://www.amap.no/documents/doc/the-impact-of-black-carbon-on-arctic-climate/746> accessed 14/01/2022.

AMAP, 'Update on Selected Climate Issues of Concern: Observations, Short-lived Climate Forcers, Arctic Carbon Cycle, and Predictive Capability' (2009) <www.amap.no/documents/doc/amap-2009-update-on-selected-climate-issues-of-concern/752> accessed 14/01/2022.

AMAP, 'The Impact of Short-Lived Pollutants on Arctic Climate' (2008a) <https://www.amap.no/documents/download/974/inline> accessed 14/01/2022.

AMAP, 'Sources and Mitigation Opportunities to Reduce Emissions of Short-Term Arctic Climate Forcers' (2008b) <https://www.amap.no/documents/doc/sources-and-mitigation-opportunities-to-reduce-emissions-of-short-term-arctic-climate-forcers/13> accessed 14/01/2022.

Arctic Council, 'Enhanced Black Carbon and Methane Reductions: an Arctic Council Framework for Action' (2015) <https://oaarchive.arctic-council.org/handle/11374/610> accessed 18/01/2021.

Arctic Council, 'Tromsø Declaration' (2009) <https://oaarchive.arctic-council.org/handle/11374/91> accessed 17/01/2022.

CCAC, 'Talanoa Statement' (2018) <https://www.ccacoalition.org/en/resources/talanoa-statement-and-joint-submission-climate-clean-air-coalition-partners> accessed 20/01/2022.

CCAC, 'Bonn Communiqué' (2017) <https://www.ccacoalition.org/en/resources/bonn-communique> accessed 20/01/2022.

CCAC, 'Marrakech Communiqué' (2016a) <https://www.ccacoalition.org/en/resources/marrakech-communique> accessed 20/01/2022.

CCAC, 'Vienna Communiqué' (2016b) <https://www.ccacoalition.org/en/resources/vienna-communique> accessed 20/01/2022.

CCAC, 'Paris Communiqué' (2015a) <https://www.ccacoalition.org/en/resources/paris-communique> accessed 20/01/2022.

CCAC, 'Climate and Clean Air Coalition Five-Year Strategic Plan' (2015b) <https://www.ccacoalition.org/en/resources/climate-and-clean-air-coalition-five-year-strategic-plan> accessed 20/01/2022.

CCAC 'Oslo Communiqué' (2013) <https://www.ccacoalition.org/en/resources/oslo-communique> accessed 20/01/2022.

CCAC and UNEP, 'Global Methane Assessment: Summary for Decision-Makers' (2021) <https://www.ccacoalition.org/en/resources/global-methane-assessment-summary-decision-makers> accessed 15/02/2022.

CCAC and WHO, *Reducing Global Health Risks through Mitigation of Short-Lived Climate Pollutants: Scoping Report* (CCAC and WHO 2015).

IPCC, *Climate Change 2021: Technical Summary* (CUP 2021).

IPCC, *Global Warming of 1.5°C* (CUP 2018).

IPCC, *Assessment Report 5 – Synthesis Report: Climate Change 2014* (CUP 2014).

IPCC, *Assessment Report 4 – Climate Change 2007: Synthesis Report* (CUP 2007).

IPCC, *Third Assessment Report – Climate Change 2001: Synthesis Report* (CUP 2001).

IPCC, *Second Assessment – Climate Change 1995: Synthesis Report* (CUP 1995).

IPCC, *First Assessment Report Overview and Policymaker Summaries and 1992 IPCC Supplement* (CUP 1992).

IPCC and TEAP, *Safeguarding the Ozone Layer and the Global Climate System* (CUP 2005).

Task Force on Short-Lived Climate Forcers, 'Recommendations to Reduce Black Carbon and Methane Emissions to Slow Arctic Climate Change' (*Arctic Council* 2013) <https://oaarchive.arctic-council.org/handle/11374/80> accessed 18/01/2022.

TEAP '2010 Report of the Technology and Economic Assessment Panel' (2010) <https://ozone.unep.org/sites/default/files/2019-05/TEAP-Assessment-report-2010.pdf> accessed 20/01/2022.

UNEP, *Near-term Climate Protection and Clean Air Benefits: Actions for Controlling Short-Lived Climate Forcers* (UNEP 2011a).

UNEP, *HFCs: A Critical Link in Protecting Climate and the Ozone Layer* (UNEP 2011b).

UNEP and WMO, *Integrated Assessment of Black Carbon and Tropospheric Ozone: Summary for Decision Makers* (UNEP and WMO 2011).

Secondary Sources

Adler E and Haas P, 'Conclusion: Epistemic Communities, World Order, and the Creation of a Reflective Research Program' (1992) 46 *International Organization* 1, 367–390.

Biermann F and Pattberg P, 'Global Environmental Governance: Taking Stock, Moving Forward' (2008) 33 *Annual Review of Environment and Resources*, 277–294.

CCAC, 'About' (2022) <https://www.ccacoalition.org/en/content/about> accessed 10/06/2022.

Collier D, 'Understanding Process Tracing' (2011) 44 *Political Science and Politics* 4, 823–830.

Davis Cross M, 'The Limits of Epistemic Communities: EU Security Agencies' (2015) 3 *Politics and Governance* 1, 90–100.

Davis Cross M, 'Rethinking Epistemic Communities Twenty Years Later' (2012) 39 *Review of International Studies* 1, 137–160.

Entman R, 'Framing: Toward clarification of a fractured paradigm' (1993) 43 *Journal of Communication* 4, 51–58.

Fialka J, 'Discovery of "Asian Brown Cloud" over Indian Ocean Sets off Fight' (*The Wall Street Journal* 2003) <https://www.wsj.com/articles/SB105216877389201500> accessed 12/12/2021.

Global Methane Pledge, 'Fast Action on Methane to Keep a 1.5°C Future within Reach' (2022) <https://www.globalmethanepledge.org> accessed 20/05/2022.

Guston D, 'Boundary Organisations in Environmental Policy & Science: an Introduction' (2001) 26 *Science, Technology, and Human Values* 4, 399–408.

Haas P, 'Introduction: Epistemic Communities and International Policy Coordination' (1992) 46 *International Organization* 1, 1–35.

Halperin S and Heath O, *Political Research: Methods and Practical Skills* (OUP 2012).

Hansen J, Sato M, Ruedy R, Lacis A and Dinas V, 'Global Warming in the Twenty-First Century: an Alternative Scenario' (2000) 97 *Proceedings of the National Academy of Sciences* 18, 9875–9880.

Hove S, 'A Rationale for Science-policy Interfaces (2007) 39 *Futures* 7, 807–826.

Löther N, 'The Long Debate around Short-lived Climate Pollutants: History of a Policy Concept and its Impact on Global Environmental Governance' (MSocSci thesis, University of Eastern Finland 2022).

Meadowcroft J and Fiorino D, 'Conceptual Innovation in Environmental Policy' in Meadowcroft J and Fiorino D (eds.), *Conceptual Innovation in Environmental Policy* (MIT Press 2017).

Mingle J, *Fire and Ice: Soot, Solidarity, and Survival on the Roof of the World* (St. Martin's Press 2015).

Mitchell R, Clark W, Cash D and Dickson N, *Global Environmental Assessments: Information and Influence* (MIT Press 2006).

Novakov T and Rosen H, 'The Black Carbon Story: Early History and New Perspectives' (2013) 42 *Ambio* 7, 840–851.

Sarkki S, Niemelä J, Tinch R, Hove S, Watt A and Young J, 'Balancing Credibility, Relevance and Legitimacy: a Critical Assessment of Trade-offs in Science–policy Interfaces' (2014) 41 *Science and Public Policy* 2, 194–206.

Schmidt G, 'La Fulgurante Ascension du Méthane' (2004) 378 *La Recherche*, 48–53.

Selin H and Eckley N, 'Science, Politics, and Persistent Organic Pollutants: the Role of Scientific Assessments in International Environmental Co-operation' (2003) 3 *International Environmental Agreements*, 7–42.

Stone D, *The Changing Arctic Environment: the Arctic Messenger* (CUP 2015).

The Economist, 'Pollution and Global Warming: Climate Change in Black & White' (2011) <https://www.economist.com/science-and-technology/2011/02/17/climate-change-in-black-and-white> accessed 11/12/2021.

Turner J, Meldrum M and Oppenheim J, 'The Paris Effect: How the Climate Agreement is Reshaping the Global Economy' (2020) <https://www.systemiq.earth/wp-content/uploads/2020/12/The-Paris-Effect_SYSTEMIQ_Full-Report_December-2020.pdf> accessed 15/03/2022.

Unger C, Mar K and Gürtler K, 'A Club's Contribution to Global Climate Governance: the Case of the Climate and Clean Air Coalition' (2020) 6 Palgrave Communications 99.

Weart S, 'Other Greenhouse Gases' (2022) <https://history.aip.org/climate/pdf/Othergas.pdf> accessed 18/01/2022.

Weart S, 'Aerosols: Volcanoes, Dust, Clouds and Climate' (2021) <https://history.aip.org/climate/pdf/Aerosol.pdf> accessed 16/01/2022.

Weart S and Hansen J, 'James Hansen: Session II' (2000) <https://www.aip.org/history-programs/niels-bohr-library/oral-histories/24309-2> accessed 16/01/2022.

West J and Fiore A, 'Management of Tropospheric Ozone by Reducing Methane Emissions' (2005) 39 Environmental Science & Technology 4685.

CHAPTER 3

The International Climate Change Regime

Right Home for SLCPs?

Yulia Yamineva and Veera Pekkarinen

1 Introduction

The climate impacts of SLCPs' emissions suggest the international climate change regime as a potential avenue for their global regulation and governance. The UNFCCC, adopted in 1992, is the core of this regime defining its scope and main principles and provisions. Two treaties have been adopted under the Convention's auspices – the Kyoto Protocol of 1997 and the Paris Agreement of 2015. Further, it is relevant to consider the decisions taken by the main governance bodies of these treaties – Conference of the Parties (COP), Conference of the Parties serving as the meeting of the Parties to the Kyoto Protocol (CMP), and Conference of the Parties serving as the meeting of the Parties to the Paris Agreement (CMA). The decisions operationalize the provisions of the treaties and detail their implementation. Although formally such decisions are not legally binding, they are often treated by states similarly to binding international law.[1]

The international climate regime follows the framework-protocol model common for governing other global environmental problems, for instance acid rain and the depletion of the stratospheric ozone layer.[2] According to this model, framework conventions outline only broad principles and procedures while substantive obligations are defined in subsequent protocols. In reality, the UNFCCC sits somewhere in-between as it contains more substantive provisions than a typical framework convention would.[3]

The international climate change regime ('UNFCCC regime') has significantly evolved over the past two decades. Its development can be viewed in four phases, where the 1990s is described as agenda-setting (first phase), and

1 Jutta Brunnée, 'COPing with Consent: Law-Making Under Multilateral Environmental Agreements' (2002) 15 Leiden Journal of International Law 1.

2 Daniel Bodansky, Jutta Brunnée and Lavanya Rajamani, *International Climate Change Law* (Oxford University Press 2017) 119.

3 ibid 119–120.

the negotiation of a framework convention (1991–1994)[4] as a constitutional phase (second phase). Next followed the negotiation and operationalization of the Kyoto Protocol from 1995 to 2004 (third phase), when it entered into force. Finally, the last fourth stage focused on the development of the regime after 2012 which marks the end of the Protocol's first commitment period – this phase culminated in the adoption of the Paris Agreement.[5] Thus, the second, third and fourth stages of international change climate regime development are manifested in three different treaties.

Two matters are important to highlight in the discussion of the UNFCCC regime: the issue of legal bindingness, and the principle of common but differentiated responsibilities and respective capabilities. On the first matter – legal bindingness – legal experts distinguish between the legal form of the overall instrument and the legal character of its specific provisions. Accordingly, all three instruments of the international climate regime are inter-state treaties and hence legally binding for their Parties. However, their provisions considerably vary in legal force ranging from declarations to legal obligations.[6] This is an important distinction in the discussion of national commitments taken under international treaties on climate change, whether they exist and what exactly they contain.

Concerning the second matter, the principle of common but differentiated responsibilities and respective capabilities underpins the UNFCCC regime. At its core, the principle aims to define the extent to which responsibilities of developed and developing countries are common and to which they are different. However, the operationalization of the principle is still a hotly debated issue in the climate change negotiations and 'there is very little agreement on its rationale, core content, and application in particular situations'.[7] At the same time, the approach to differentiation among countries has evolved over time. The UNFCCC and the Kyoto Protocol follow annex-based differentiation where developed country Parties are listed in Annex I to the Convention whereas developing countries are referred to as non-Annex I Parties. In contrast, the Paris Agreement has a more flexible approach to differentiation between developed and developing countries, 'which takes into account changes in a

---

4 Entry into force.
5 Bodansky, Brunnée and Rajamani (n 2) 96.
6 ibid 18–19.
7 ibid 27.

country's circumstances and capacities and is operationalized differently for different elements of the regime'.[8]

This chapter outlines whether and how different SLCPs are covered in international climate treaties, namely the Convention, the Kyoto Protocol and the Paris Agreement, and discusses opportunities for strengthening the regulation and governance of SLCPs through these avenues. The chapter is structured according to the legal instruments, starting first with the Convention and the Kyoto Protocol, and continuing with a more detailed discussion on the Paris Agreement. The main findings are summarised in the conclusion.

2 UNFCCC

The Convention's objective is defined as limiting greenhouse gas concentrations in the atmosphere to such a level so as to 'prevent dangerous anthropogenic interference with the climate system'.[9] The legal standing of the objective remains unclear, and Parties to the Convention have not been able to agree on what greenhouse gas concentrations can be considered as safe.[10] Instead, the objective has been operationalized in terms of temperature targets and long-term emissions in the Paris Agreement (see Section 4 of this chapter).

The Convention has a broad scope covering the entire spectrum of climate change related issues such as mitigation, adaptation, finance, technology, and capacity building. Concerning mitigation, an important note is that the Convention follows *a comprehensive approach* where all sources and sinks of greenhouse gases are addressed collectively.[11] This approach was justified in the negotiations of the Convention on the grounds that it allows states to choose which gases and sinks to focus on and determine the most cost-effective mitigation measures nationally, as well as eliminates incentives to switch from one polluting activity to another.[12]

Relating to which gases are covered under the UNFCCC, the text of the treaty does not give a precise list. However, its article 4.2 (on Annex I Parties' mitigation commitments) gives the following guidance: 'anthropogenic emissions

8 Daniel Bodansky, 'The Paris Climate Change Agreement: A New Hope?' (2016) 110 American Journal of International Law 4 <http://papers.ssrn.com/abstract=2773895> accessed 30 August 2016.

9 Art 2, UNFCCC.

10 Bodansky, Brunnée and Rajamani (n 2) 126.

11 ibid 133.

12 ibid 133–134.

of carbon dioxide and other greenhouse gases not controlled by the Montreal Protocol'.[13] This suggests that the Convention prioritizes reducing emissions of CO_2 while at the same time covering those non-CO_2 gases which are outside of the scope of the Montreal Protocol. For SLCPs, this means the UNFCCC includes such short-lived gases as methane and HFCs but – if one reads the text literally[14] – does not include aerosols like black carbon.

The comprehensive approach takes into account multiple greenhouse gases; however, they considerably differ in their atmospheric lifetime and climate impacts. For this reason, different greenhouse gases are expressed through a common emission metric. There is no single metric, and according to the IPCC, 'the choice of metric, including time horizon, should reflect the policy objectives for which the metric is applied'.[15] At the same time, Global Warming Potentials (GWP) over 100-years have been the prevalent metric in the UNFCCC to account for non-CO_2 gases in their CO_2-equivalent (CO_2 eq). The application of this metric has been criticized for not accounting for the short-term climate impacts of SLCPs,.[16] [17] This occurs because the warming caused by SLCPs – due to their short life in the atmosphere – depends on their ongoing rate of emissions rather than their cumulative emissions.[18] The metric also ignores other important impacts of SLCPs on human health and ecosystems.[19] Other metrics have been proposed to better account for different climate impacts of non-CO_2 gases but their wider application in climate policy is still contested.[20]

The issue of appropriate metrics for reporting greenhouse gases has been under continuous discussion in the UNFCCC under Subsidiary Body for Scientific and Technological Advice (SBSTA) Methodologies agenda item on 'Common metrics'. In parallel, relevant work is under way in the IPCC Task Force on National Greenhouse Gas Inventories on preparing a Methodology

13 United Nations Framework Convention on Climate Change (UNFCCC), New York, 9 May 1992, in force 21 March 1994, 31 *International Legal Materials* (1992) 849 <http://unfccc.int> art 4.2(b).

14 See however our discussion on the possibilities of including black carbon under NDCs below.

15 Andy Reisinger and others, 'Cross-Chapter Box 2 GHG emission metrics' in Priyadarshi R. Shukla and others (eds), *Climate Change 2022: Mitigation of Climate Change* (IPCC AR6 WGIII report, CUP 2022), p. 226 after Plattner et al 2009.

16 Kathleen A Mar, 'Putting the Brakes on Climate Change – It's about More than Just CO_2' [2021] Climanosco <https://www.climanosco.org/published_article/putting-the-brakes-on-climate-change-its-about-more-than-just-co2/> accessed 16 September 2021.

17 Reisinger and others (n15), 226–227.

18 ibid.

19 Mar (n 16).

20 Reisinger and others (n15), 226–228.

Report on Short-lived Climate Forcers (see also Section 4.1 for the discussion on emission metrics in the Paris Agreement).

Concerning the actions to be taken by Parties, the UNFCCC sets different types of commitments for different groups of countries – in line with the principle of common but differentiated responsibilities. These include: general commitments applicable to all Parties (Articles 4.1, 5, 6, 12.1); mitigation and reporting commitments applicable to Annex I Parties (Articles 4.2, 12.2); and specific commitments on financial and technology support extending only to Annex II Parties (Article 4.3–4.5). General commitments and those of Annex I Parties are particularly relevant to consider in the discussion on SLCPs.

Concerning general mitigation commitments, these are general 'not only in their application to all Parties but also in the content'.[21] Consequently, the Convention only asks Parties to 'formulate, implement, publish and regularly update national and, where appropriate, regional programmes containing measures to mitigate climate change'.[22] At the same time, general commitments relating to national inventories and reporting are seen as significant.[23] This is because all Parties are required to prepare, periodically update and publish their national inventories of emissions by sources and removals by sinks of all greenhouse gases greenhouse gases, using methodologies agreed by the COP (Article 4.1). Comprehensive reporting of emissions at a country level is essential for developing mitigation actions including on SLCP emissions.

On top of general commitments, Annex I Parties also have specific mitigation commitments: they must adopt national policies and measures to limit GHG emissions and to protect and enhance their sinks and reservoirs, with the goal of returning emissions to 1990 levels by the year 2000, as well as coordinate relevant economic and administrative instruments and identify and periodically review their policies and practices that contribute to increased GHG emissions.[24]

Overall, the Convention outlines the general contours of the international mitigation regime without defining the specifics. Its scope clearly includes non-CO_2 greenhouse gases such as methane and HFCs though the general focus remains on mitigating CO_2. Yet, the issue of emission metrics to be applied is still unresolved and has a direct relevance to mitigating SLCP emissions.

21 Bodansky, Brunnée and Rajamani (n 2) 130.
22 UNFCCC (n13) art 4.1(b).
23 Bodansky, Brunnée and Rajamani (n 2) 130.
24 UNFCCC (n13) art 4.2 (a)(b)(e).

3 Kyoto Protocol

The Kyoto Protocol was the first treaty adopted under the UNFCCC to operationalize its broad provisions and principles. It is regarded as 'one of the most complex and ambitious environmental agreements ever negotiated'.[25] The core of the Protocol are the legally binding quantitative emissions reduction targets for Parties included in Annex I to the UNFCCC, which are mostly developed countries and so-called economies in transition. The targets applied to the first commitment period running from 2008 to 2012. The Protocol is often described as a 'top-down' instrument in comparison to a presumably more effective 'bottom-up' Paris Agreement. This juxtaposition is not accurate as it confuses substance and process: although indeed the emission reduction targets in the Kyoto Protocol had a binding, prescriptive nature, they were developed in a bottom-up fashion not dissimilar to the Paris Agreement and its Nationally Determined Contributions (NDCs).[26]

The history of the Protocol has been contentious with the lack of the US support and long negotiations on a second commitment period. The Doha amendment on emissions reduction targets for 2013–2020 was adopted in 2012, though it only entered into force in 2020. With the adoption of the Paris Agreement, the political significance of the Kyoto Protocol has diminished and its future remains highly uncertain. However, it is widely agreed that the Protocol has played a critical role in the evolution of the international climate regime, containing many innovative provisions and providing lessons for future climate agreements .[27]

The scope of the Kyoto Protocol is narrowly on climate mitigation, where the coverage of gases was one of the main issues in its negotiation.[28] Specifically, countries disagreed on whether the Protocol should: apply only to CO_2; include three greenhouse gases (plus methane and nitrous oxide); or follow a more comprehensive approach. The last option is adopted in the Protocol which initially included six greenhouse gases (CO_2, methane, nitrous oxide, hydrofluorocarbons (HFCs), perfluorocarbons, and sulfur hexafluoride),

25 Bodansky, Brunnée and Rajamani (n 2) 161.

26 Joanna Depledge, 'The "Top-down" Kyoto Protocol? Exploring Caricature and Misrepresentation in Literature on Global Climate Change Governance' [2022] International Environmental Agreements: Politics, Law and Economics <https://doi.org/10.1007/s10784-022-09580-9> accessed 6 June 2022.

27 Bodansky, Brunnée and Rajamani (n 2) 161.

28 ibid 164.

supplemented later by a seventh one – nitrogen trifluoride. These gases are considered as a basket – in line with the above-mentioned Convention's comprehensive approach – so Parties have flexibility as to which gases (and sectors) to focus on in meeting their mitigation commitments.[29]

Additional flexibility was provided by the Protocol through the possibility of achieving mitigation targets via market-based mechanisms. Two of these – Clean Development Mechanism[30] and Joint Implementation[31] – involved investment in and development of emission reduction and removal enhancement projects outside of national borders – in developing countries (Clean Development Mechanism) and developed countries (Joint Implementation). The achieved emissions reductions or removals could then be counted towards national mitigation targets, although such market-based mechanisms should have been only supplemental to domestic mitigation actions. The two above mentioned mechanisms have had an important role in spreading HFC and methane mitigation technologies through their projects both in Annex I and developing countries.[32]

To sum up, from the perspective of reducing SLCP emissions, the Kyoto Protocol in principle covers two of them, namely methane and HFCs. However, it has a limited geographical coverage extending only to (some) developed countries whereas it is developing countries which are projected to be the key sources of future methane and HFC emissions (see Chapter 1). Therefore, the treaty is not an effective instrument in reducing global SLCP emissions.[33] Furthermore, as mentioned earlier, the political fate and future role of the Protocol are uncertain while the Paris Agreement has taken the main stage now as the major international framework for climate action.

---

29 Farhana Yamin and Joanna Depledge, *The International Climate Change Regime : A Guide to Rules, Institutions and Procedures* (Cambridge University Press 2004) 78.

30 Kyoto Protocol to the United Nations Framework Convention on Climate Change (adopted 11 December 1997, entered into force 16 February 2005) 2303 UNTS 148, art 12.

31 ibid, art 6.

32 Veera Pekkarinen, 'Going beyond CO_2: Strengthening Action on Global Methane Emissions under the UN Climate Regime' (2020) 29 (3) Review of European, Comparative & International Environmental Law 464.

33 Yulia Yamineva and Kati Kulovesi, 'Keeping the Arctic White: The Legal and Governance Landscape for Reducing Short-Lived Climate Pollutants in the Arctic Region' (2018) 7 Transnational Environmental Law 201.

4 Paris Agreement

4.1 *Mitigation Action in the Paris Agreement*

The already-mentioned Paris Agreement has been described as 'a considerable achievement in multilateral diplomacy'[34] and has now a near universal support with 193 countries having joined it by 2022. Without going into details on the various elements of the Agreement's architecture, this section discusses only the provisions of the treaty that are relevant to mitigating emissions of SLCPS.

The Agreement 'aims to strengthen the global response to the threat of climate change', as stated in its Article 2. The treaty is wide in its scope containing provisions on mitigation, adaptation, loss and damage, finance, technology development and transfer, capacity building, and transparency of action and support. However, despite the broad coverage, the Agreement treats these issues in different ways with the legal character of individual provisions also varying.[35] Notably, the Paris Agreement departs from the annex-based approach to differentiation among countries that was set in the UNFCCC and the Kyoto Protocol, offering instead a more nuanced and tailored method of country differentiation across different issues of its scope.[36]

The Agreement follows a long-term temperature target in interpreting its mitigation goals:[37] as such, it aims at holding 'the increase in the global average temperature to well below 2°C above pre-industrial levels and to pursue efforts to limit the temperature increase to 1.5°C above pre-industrial levels'.[38] To achieve this, countries agreed to aim 'to reach global peaking of greenhouse gas emissions as soon as possible' to achieve 'a balance between anthropogenic emissions by sources and removals by sinks of greenhouse gases in the second half of the century'.[39]

---

34 Bodansky, Brunnée and Rajamani (n 2) 209.

35 Lavanya Rajamani, 'The 2015 Paris Agreement: Interplay Between Hard, Soft and Non-Obligations' (2016) 28 Journal of Environmental Law 337.

36 Bodansky, Brunnée and Rajamani (n 2) 232.

37 ibid 228.

38 Article 2.1(a) of the 'Paris Agreement' (2015). The combined effect of national plans submitted in 2015 has been estimated as consistent with staying below an increase in temperature of 3–3.2°C by the end of the century. Thus, the UNFCCC regime is still not on track to meet the 2 degree target it has set for itself. See UNEP, 'The Emissions Gap Report 2016' (2016) UNEP Synthesis Report.

39 Paris Agreement (adopted 12 December 2015, entered into force 4 November 2016) 55 ILM 740 art 4(1).

While the 1.5°C target was reportedly a last-minute insertion in the negotiation text by the Alliance of Small Island States (AOSIS), a negotiation coalition of low-lying island and coastal nations, and viewed by some as unrealistic against the current ambition conveyed by NDCs,[40] its importance appears to have grown recently in the global policy discussion. This observation is important for the governance and regulation of SLCPs, as, according to IPCC, greenhouse gas emission pathways that limit warming to 1.5°C with no or limited overshoot (i.e. temporarily exceeding the temperature goal) 'involve deep reductions of methane and black carbon emissions, 35 per cent or more of both by 2050 relative to 2010'.[41] This implies that if Parties to the Paris Agreement are serious about aiming for limiting the temperature increase to 1.5°C above pre-industrial levels, this will demand ambitious and focused measures to mitigate emissions of methane and black carbon by mid-century. It has to be mentioned that even a less ambitious 2°C temperature target is not guaranteed by current mitigation actions. According to UNEP estimates, the full implementation of national mitigation targets announced under the Paris Agreement will still lead to 2.4°C of warming by 2050.[42]

The Paris Agreement follows a country-driven approach to mitigation in which Parties define and regularly update their climate action plans, known as NDCs. While countries can determine the scope and the contents of their NDCs, the Agreement includes strong procedural obligations concerning these national submissions.[43] Each country must communicate an NDC every five years and pursue domestic measures to achieve the commitments.[44] In addition, each NDC must represent a progression beyond existing pledge and reflect the highest possible ambition.[45] Parties can adjust their NDCs at any time, but only with a view to enhancing the level of ambition.[46] This is part

40 Joanna Depledge, 'Keeping expectations realistic for COP26 in Glasgow' (Cambridge University Press Blog, 2021) <https://www.cambridgeblog.org/2021/10/keeping-expectations-realistic-for-cop26-in-glasgow/> accessed 2 March 2023.

41 Intergovernmental Panel on Climate Change, 'Summary for Policymakers' in V. Masson-Delmotte and others (eds.), *Global warming of 1.5°C. An IPCC Special Report on the impacts of global warming of 1.5°C above pre-industrial levels and related global greenhouse gas emission pathways, in the context of strengthening the global response to the threat of climate change, sustainable development, and efforts to eradicate poverty* (IPCC 2018), 14 para. C.1.2.

42 UNEP, *Emissions Gap Report 2022: The Closing Window* (UNEP 2022), p. 35.

43 Sebastian Oberthür and Ralph Bodle, 'Legal Form and Nature of the Paris Outcome' (2016) 6 Climate Law 40.

44 Paris Agreement (n39), art 4(9).

45 ibid, art 4(3).

46 ibid, art 4(11).

of the Paris Agreement's 'ambition cycle' that is designed to promote progressively stronger NDCs over time.[47] In this cycle, the results of the global stocktake,[48] a process that will assess the collective progress toward the Paris Agreement's long-term goals, together with the requirements of individual and collective progression,[49] are designed to guide the determination of the successive NDCs.[50] Such global stocktake should occur every five years, with the first one to be conducted by the decision-making body of the Agreement – Conference of the Parties serving as the meeting of the Parties to the Paris Agreement (CMA) – in 2023.

While countries have significant freedom in determining their domestic mitigation actions to be reported in NDCs under the Paris Agreement, they are still guided by the NDC guidance contained in COP decisions, first of all the COP21 decision accompanying the Paris Agreement[51] and the Paris rulebook,[52] adopted by COP24. These rules define the general characteristics of country submissions and suggest the types of information that could be provided 'to facilitate clarity, transparency and understanding of' NDCs. For instance, they propose NDCs to communicate information on the baselines, timeframes, scope, assumptions and methodological issues, among other matters.[53] These provisions have a recommendatory nature and do not bind countries as to what substances have to be covered in NDCs: in other words, there is nothing preventing Parties from including SLCPs in their NDCs.

Another element relevant to SLCPs concerns emissions metrics (see also Section 2). Under the transparency framework for action and support, Parties to the Paris Agreement agreed to use the GWP values with the 100-year time horizon based on the IPCC Fifth Assessment Report for reporting aggregate emissions and removals of greenhouse gases, expressed in CO_2 eq.[54] This, however, excludes the GWP value for fossil methane.[55] Indeed, some recently developed metrics show 'greater climate benefits from rapid and sustained

47 Bodansky, Brunnée and Rajamani (n 2) 235.
48 Paris Agreement (n39) art 14.
49 ibid, art 3, 4(3) and 9(3).
50 Bodansky, Brunnée and Rajamani (n 2) 234–235.
51 UNFCCC, 'Decision 1/CP.21, Adoption of the Paris Agreement' UN Doc FCCC/CP/2015/10/Add.1 (29 January 2016).
52 UNFCCC, 'Decision 4/CMA.1, Further Guidance to the Mitigation Section of Decision 1/CP.21' UN Doc FCCC/PA/CMA/2018/3/Add.1 (19 March 2019).
53 ibid, Article 9.
54 UNFCCC, Decision 18/CMA.1, annex, paragraph 37.ecision 5/CMA.3, paragraph 25 and Decision 18/CMA.1, annex, paragraph 37.
55 Decision 5/CMA.3, paragraph 25.

methane reductions over the next few decades than if such reductions are weighted by GWP100'.[56] The use of different metrics has serious policy implications: for instance, the proponents of using natural gas (of which methane is a primary component) underline its lesser climate impacts using the GWP100 metric whereas these impacts are in fact significant if the GWP20 metric (that is with a 20-year time horizon) is applied.[57] The discussion on the appropriate metric for methane in the UNFCCC is so far ongoing, as noted above.

4.2 *NDC Experiences to Date*

Thus far, most countries have submitted two consecutive national reports: the intended NDCs in advance of COP21 in 2015, and then updated these or submitted new reports in 2020 in line with the five-year ambition cycle. The following part discusses the treatment of SLCPs in these two rounds of NDCs.

By July 2018,[58] 174 countries had submitted their first NDCs to the UNFCCC. Given the flexible, nationally driven nature of the contributions, they greatly varied in their contents, scope and approaches. While some contained quantified absolute emission reduction targets, others were phrased in qualitative terms only. Further, many NDCs from developing countries were conditional on the provision of international support which brought further caveats to the level of their climate mitigation ambitions.

Concerning the scope of NDCs, most of these focused generally on CO_2 but many also included methane. Of the first NDCs, 69 NDCs covered both methane and HFCs. Mexico's first NDC also covered black carbon.[59]

There are three main approaches as to how SLCPs were included in national reports: as part of a quantitative economy-wide greenhouse gas emissions reduction target; by setting a SLCP-specific quantitative outcome for emission reductions; or by setting policies and actions directed toward specific SLCPs.[60] These approaches are demonstrated in the following paragraphs.

---

56 Reisinger and others (n15), p. 227.

57 Mar (n 16).

58 The timeframe for which the analysis of SLCPs in the first NDCs is available: see Ross and others, 'Strengthening Nationally Determined Contributions to Catalyze Actions That Reduce Short-Lived Climate Pollutants' <https://www.wri.org/research/strengthening-nationally-determined-contributions-catalyze-actions-reduce-short-lived> accessed 3 May 2022.

59 Katherine Ross and others, 'Strengthening Nationally Determined Contributions to Catalyze Actions That Reduce Short-Lived Climate Pollutants' 12 <https://www.wri.org/research/strengthening-nationally-determined-contributions-catalyze-actions-reduce-short-lived> accessed 3 May 2022.

60 Ross and others (n 58).

Most commonly, SLCPs were included in an absolute economy-wide mitigation target, which covers all greenhouse gases.[61] For example, in the EU's first NDC, methane and HFCs were included in the quantitative greenhouse gas emissions reduction target: 'The EU and its Member States are committed to a binding target of an at least 40 percent domestic reduction in greenhouse gas emissions by 2030 compared to 1990.'[62] The scope of this target included all seven greenhouse gases covered by the UNFCCC, including methane and HFCs. However, as in the case of the EU's NDC, as these targets were typically expressed in aggregate CO_2 eq, applying GWP100, identification of the quantity of reductions for SLCPs or other compounds is not possible. This makes the targets ambiguous[63] and the evaluation of the effects of the emission reductions difficult since different greenhouse gases act to warm the climate in different ways (see the discussion on emission metrics in Sections 2 and 4.1).

Only nine of the 174 countries set a separate target for methane.[64] For example, in its first NDC, Canada pledges to reduce methane emissions from the oil and gas sector, including offshore activities, by 40–45 percent by 2025.[65] Out of these 174 NDCs, only China's report contained a specific quantitative target for HFC emissions: the country pledged to 'phase down the production and consumption of HCFC-22 for controlled uses, with its production to be reduced by 35 percent from the 2010 level by 2020, and by 67.5 percent by 2025 and to achieve effective control on emissions of HFC-23 by 2020.'[66]

Mexico was the only country to include black carbon specifically in the first NDC: it committed to reduce 25 percent of its GHG and SLCP emissions below business as usual for the year 2030. This commitment included a reduction of 22 percent in greenhouse gases and a reduction of 51 percent in black carbon emissions.[67]

Without any quantitative indicators, many countries listed policies and actions that will reduce SLCPs from various sectors. In such a way, Cambodia listed promoting 'more efficient cookstoves' as a key sectoral mitigation action

61 ibid.

62 Intended Nationally Determined Contribution of the EU and its Member States (2015), 1.

63 Myles R Allen and others, 'A Solution to the Misrepresentations of CO_2-Equivalent Emissions of Short-Lived Climate Pollutants under Ambitious Mitigation' (2018) 1 npj Climate and Atmospheric Science 16.

64 Ross and others (n 58) 16.

65 Canada, 'Canada's 2017 Nationally Determined Contribution Submission to the United Nations Framework Convention on Climate Change' (Revised submission 2017) 3.

66 Enhanced Actions on Climate Change: China's Intended Nationally Determined Contributions (2016), 8.

67 Mexico, Intended Nationally Determined Contribution (2016), 2.

for its 2030 mitigation contribution.[68] This is indeed one of significant ways to reduce SLCP emissions as replacing traditional biomass-based cooking with improved or clean-burning biomass cookstoves or moving to clean-burning cooking and heating fuels such as liquefied petroleum gas can reduce indoor air pollution and with it emissions of black carbon, providing multiple benefits for human health (see also Chapter 9).[69] Canada committed to 'finalizing regulations to phase down the use of HFCs in line with the Kigali Amendment to the Montreal Protocol.'[70] To reduce methane emissions, Nigeria pledged to 'work towards ending gas flaring by 2030.'[71]

The overview above shows that only few countries focused specifically on SLCPs in their first NDCs and the way SLCPs were treated was mostly general and vague. Methane and HFCs were commonly included in absolute economy-wide GHG emission mitigation targets; however, describing specific compounds within the targets is not possible, and hence how exactly methane and HFCs are targeted is uncertain. Further, while many countries listed policies and actions to reduce SLCPs, these were not accompanied by clear objectives and implementation plans, and as a result, their effectiveness remains unclear.

In line with the five-year cycle, Parties with NDCs running to 2025 were requested to communicate a new NDC by 2020, and Parties with NDCs running to 2030 were requested to continue their existing NDCs or update it.[72] By September 2022, 142 new or updated NDCs had been communicated by 169 Parties.[73] Considering all 166 available NDCs, including the new or updated 142 NDCs, 91 percent cover methane and 53 percent cover HFCs.[74] Out of the total number, 11 percent provided information on SLCPs.[75] This includes several countries such as Bangladesh, Benin, Chile, Colombia, Costa Rica, Cote d'Ivoire, Dominican Republic, Eswatini, Mali, Mexico, Nigeria and Zimbabwe, which covered black carbon in their updated NDCs. It is noteworthy that these countries were assisted by CCAC in revising their NDCs to enhance their ambition to achieve the Paris Agreement temperature goals by including SLCPs

68 Cambodia's Intended Nationally Determined Contribution (2017), 6.
69 Ross and others (n 58) 29.
70 Canada (n 65), 3.
71 Nigeria's Intended Nationally Determined Contribution (2015), 3.
72 UNFCCC, 'Decision 1/CP.21, Adoption of the Paris Agreement' UN Doc FCCC/CP/2015/10/Add.1 (29 January 2016) paras 23–24.
73 UNFCCC, 'Nationally Determined Contributions under the Paris Agreement. Synthesis Report by the Secretariat' (October 2022).
74 ibid, p. 4.
75 ibid, p. 15.

actions (see also Chapter 6).[76] Further, in the revised NDCs, some Parties included additional information on approaches for estimating SLCPs or precursor emissions (see Chapter 1).[77]

To sum up, current NDCs in their majority cover individual SLCPs: first of all methane and to a less extent HFCs. Several NDCs include black carbon. However, in most cases, these measures cannot be described as strong as there are no specific targets or timelines attached.

4.3 *What Are the Opportunities for Strengthening SLCP Mitigation Action under the Paris Agreement?*

Policy literature has entertained several opportunities on how to integrate stronger action on SLCPs under the Paris Agreement: some of these concern NDCs, and others involve other elements of the Agreement's architecture. This section discusses these options, presenting their pros and cons.

Given that mitigation actions are determined at the national level, orchestrating a stronger focus on SLCPs in NDCs appears to be the first natural option. The summary above indicates that while many NDCs cover methane and HFCs, only few countries focus specifically on SLCPs in their first and revised NDCs. Indeed, '(j)ust because SLCPs are included in the first NDC does not necessarily mean that their mitigation potential and associated development benefits are being fully exploited.'[78]

There are several concrete opportunities for integrating actions on SLCPs under the Paris Agreement. First, all countries could include methane and HFCs in their absolute economy-wide targets.[79] Contrary to the first round of NDCs,[80] all of the revised or updated NDCs provide information on the scope and coverage of the NDC, including sectors and gases covered,[81] but not all of them cover methane and HFCs.[82] Black carbon cannot be included in the absolute economy-wide targets, because black carbon is not a GHG covered by the UNFCCC.

Second, in addition to the absolute economy-wide emission reduction targets in NDCs, it would be useful for countries to set individual targets for

76 'Increasing Ambition of NDCs' (*Climate & Clean Air Coalition*) <https://www.ccacoalition.org/en/content/increasing-ambition-ndcs> accessed 3 August 2022.
77 UNFCCC, 'Nationally Determined Contributions under the Paris Agreement. Synthesis Report by the Secretariat' UN Doc FCCC/PA/CMA/2021/8 (17 September 2021) para 91.
78 Ross and others (n 58) 13.
79 ibid 16.
80 Ross and others (n 58).
81 UNFCCC 'Nationally Determined Contributions under the Paris Agreement' (n77) para 68.
82 ibid, para 71.

each GHG, including short-lived ones, and specify how those targets will be achieved.[83] This would make the commitments clear and enable evaluation of the net benefits of mitigation measures.[84] This way, also the formation of tropospheric ozone could be estimated from the predicted quantity of its precursors in the atmosphere.[85] The gas-by-gas reporting requirements of past emissions and future projections of greenhouse gases under the Paris Agreement's transparency framework provide a strong basis for this recommendation.[86] Specific SLCP targets could be included in the form of a separate economy-wide target, sector-specific target or targets based on implementing specific SLCP measures.[87]

From a legal point of view, the inclusion of a separate target for each climate pollutant, including SLCPs in NDCs, could first be developed through Parties' voluntary action. The CMA will consider further guidance on the NDCs at its seventh session in 2024[88] and this will offer for an opportunity to deliberate the inclusion of individual targets in formal guidance for all countries.

Individual targets for each climate pollutant in NDCs would provide important input for the global stocktake under the Paris Agreement. The global stocktake will be carried out every five years to assess 'collective progress' towards achieving the Agreement's long-term goals.[89] In addition to this, the stocktake could address specific climate pollutants, such as SLCPs. This would help giving SLCPs the attention they need and provide insights into SLCP emissions and mitigation needs.

83 Myles R Allen and others, 'New Use of Global Warming Potentials to Compare Cumulative and Short-Lived Climate Pollutants' (2016) 6 Nature Climate Change 773; Stephen M Smith and others, 'Equivalence of Greenhouse-Gas Emissions for Peak Temperature Limits' (2012) 2 Nature Climate Change 535.

84 Climate and Clean Air Coalition (CCAC), 'Annual Science Update: Methane Briefing Report' (2018) <http://www.ccacoalition.org/en/resources/2018-annual-science-update-methane-briefing-report> 6.

85 Malley, C., et al, 'Opportunities for Increasing Ambition of Nationally Determined Contributions through Integrated Air Pollution and Climate Change Planning: A Practical Guidance document' (2019) Climate and Clean Air Coalition, Ghana and Stockholm Environment Institute, https://www.ccacoalition.org/en/resources/opportunities-increasing-ambition-nationally-determined-contributions-through-integrated, 36.

86 UNFCCC, 'Decision 18/CMA.1. Modalities, Procedures and Guidelines for the Transparency Framework for Action and Support Referred to in Article 13 of the Paris Agreement' UN Doc FCCC/PA/CMA/2018/3/Add.2 (19 March 2019) Annex paras 47 and 92.

87 ibid.

88 UNFCCC 'Decision 4/CMA.1, Further Guidance to the Mitigation Section of Decision 1/CP.21' UN Doc FCCC/PA/CMA/2018/3/Add.1 (19 March 2019) para 20.

89 Paris Agreement (n39), art 14(1–2).

The procedural obligations related to NDCs are complemented by requirements of transparency and reporting. The Paris Agreement's enhanced transparency framework[90] will likely advance more effective SLCP mitigation, as it established legally binding measurement, reporting and verification (MRV) provisions that are applicable to all countries, providing more information on the levels and sources of SLCP emissions. The Paris Agreements' MRV system provides for 'built-in flexibility' for those developing countries that 'need it in the light of their capacities'.[91] For example, all Parties 'shall' report seven greenhouse gases, including methane and HFCs, but those developing countries that need flexibility can instead report at least three gases: methane, carbon dioxide and nitrous oxide.[92]

While countries are not required to report their black carbon emissions, under the Paris rulebook, Parties may provide information on other substances that have an impact on climate as well.[93] Effectively, this means that under the Paris Agreement, countries can voluntarily report their black carbon emissions already now. The Subsidiary Body for Scientific and Technological Advice will review and update the modalities, procedures, and guidelines for the transparency framework no later than 2028.[94] This will provide for an opportunity to consider the adoption of the requirement of black carbon reporting for all Parties. Also, as already noted, the IPCC is currently developing methodologies for SLCP measurement and reporting[95] – this work is expected to further improve SLCP reporting in the future.

Under the Paris Agreement, in addition to the NDCs, Parties should communicate long-term Low Emissions and Development Strategies by 2020.[96] Long-term strategies provide an opportunity to view both near-and long-term benefits and strategies of SLCP mitigation. Indeed, 'while SLCPs themselves last only a short while in the atmosphere, the infrastructure that produces them can persist for decades.'[97] Thus, the inclusion of SLCP strategies in long-term policy planning and strategies is well-justified.

90 ibid, art 13.
91 ibid, art 13(1–2).
92 UNFCCC 'Decision 18/CMA.1. Modalities, Procedures and Guidelines for the Transparency Framework for Action and Support Referred to in Article 13 of the Paris Agreement' UN Doc FCCC/PA/CMA/2018/3/Add.2 (19 March 2019) Annex, para 48.
93 ibid, Annex, para 52.
94 ibid, para 2.
95 IPCC, 'Methodology Report on Short-Lived Climate Forcers – IPCC' <https://www.ipcc.ch/report/methodology-report-on-short-lived-climate-forcers/> accessed 2 August 2022.
96 Paris Agreement (n39), art 4(19).
97 Ross and others (n 58) 11.

Finally, it is worth noting the Global Methane Pledge – the initiative to reduce global methane emissions driven by the EU and the US, and announced on the sidelines of COP26. Countries joining the Global Methane Pledge commit to a collective goal of reducing global methane emissions by at least 30 percent from 2020 levels by 2030 and moving towards using best available inventory methodologies to quantify methane emissions. According to the website, delivering on the Pledge would reduce warming by at least 0.2 degrees Celsius by 2050.[98] As of January 2023, more than 150 countries have joined the Pledge, including EU, US, UK, Nigeria, Canada, Indonesia, Philippines, Mexico, Brazil, Saudi Arabia, and Pakistan: this includes some of the top 20 methane emitters, representing about 50 per cent of global methane emissions. At the same time, some of the major emitters, such as China, India and Russia, have not joined the coalition. The Global Methane Pledge has a voluntary nature, and although it contains a collective target to reduce methane emissions, this is not translated into individual targets per country. Further, other details like governance, accountability and – crucially – the relationship with the UNFCCC process remain somewhat unclear at the point of writing the chapter.

5 Conclusion

Overall, the general focus of the international climate regime has been on mitigating CO_2, and no concerted effort to integrate SLCPs as a whole has taken place. However, when looking at individual pollutants, the picture becomes varied. The Convention and Paris Agreement, for instance, clearly integrate non-CO_2 greenhouse gases such as methane and HFCs in their reporting and transparency system.

The focus on long-term greenhouse gases has several implications. For instance, methodologies for estimating emissions, in particular the issue of emission metrics to be applied, are significant in the discussion on SLCPs – yet ones that still remain unresolved at the global level. Selecting an appropriate metric has a direct impact on the 'value' of mitigating SLCPs for securing a climate safe future. The current choice of CO_2eq metric prioritizes mitigation of long-lived greenhouse gases, and indeed their mitigation is critical for slowing down global warming in the longer term. However, this metric does not

98 Global Methane Pledge, 'Fast Action on Methane to Keep a 1.5°C Future within Reach' <https://www.globalmethanepledge.org> accessed 02/03/2023.

account well for substances with a shorter atmospheric lifetime, while ignoring non-climatic effects- which in the case of SLCPs have a strong policy relevance.

Concerning national mitigation pledges under the Paris Agreement's NDCs, only few countries focus specifically on SLCPs in their first NDCs, and this is mostly done in a generic way. Methane and HFCs are commonly included in absolute economy-wide GHG emission mitigation targets: but since their composition is not specified, it remains uncertain how exactly methane and HFCs are targeted. Further, even though these NDCs list policies and actions to reduce SLCPs, information on their objectives and implementation is not available, casting doubt on their effectiveness.

This chapter – and the book's conclusions – posit that a separate pathway for regulating and governing each substance among SLCPs should be pursued globally. This applies especially to black carbon: given the scientific uncertainties regarding the combined climate impact of black carbon emissions reductions and the fact that black carbon is emitted as a component of particulate matter, it seems wise to prioritize the relevant legal frameworks on preventing air pollution rather than the climate regime. The same goes for HFC emissions which are now firmly housed under the Montreal Protocol's Kigali amendment (see Chapter 4).

Against this, what is the role of the UNFCCC in mitigating SLCPs globally? For the immediate future, the biggest potential of the international climate regime seems to be in enhancing action on methane emissions' mitigation. This is supported by a growing political momentum for a stronger action on methane emissions illustrated by multiple policy steps taken recently at global, EU and national levels. The Convention's regime will not be the only global avenue for governing methane emissions but it may fill some of the regulatory and governance gaps in the current patchwork of international and transnational arrangements (see Chapter 13).

Bibliography

Allen MR and others, 'New Use of Global Warming Potentials to Compare Cumulative and Short-Lived Climate Pollutants' (2016) 6 Nature Climate Change 773.

Allen MR and others, 'A Solution to the Misrepresentations of CO_2-Equivalent Emissions of Short-Lived Climate Pollutants under Ambitious Mitigation' (2018) 1 npj Climate and Atmospheric Science 16.

Bodansky D, 'The Paris Climate Change Agreement: a New Hope?' (2016) 110 American Journal of International Law <http://papers.ssrn.com/abstract=2773895> accessed 30 August 2016.

Bodansky D, Brunnée J and Rajamani L, *International Climate Change Law* (Oxford University Press 2017).

Brunnée J, 'COPing with Consent: Law-Making Under Multilateral Environmental Agreements' (2002) 15 Leiden Journal of International Law 1.

CCAC, 'Increasing Ambition of NDCs' (Climate & Clean Air Coalition) <https://www.ccacoalition.org/en/content/increasing-ambition-ndcs> accessed 3 August 2022.

Depledge J, 'The "Top-down" Kyoto Protocol? Exploring Caricature and Misrepresentation in Literature on Global Climate Change Governance' [2022] International Environmental Agreements: Politics, Law and Economics <https://doi.org/10.1007/s10784-022-09580-9> accessed 6 June 2022.

Mar KA, 'Putting the Brakes on Climate Change – It's about More than Just CO_2' [2021] Climanosco <https://www.climanosco.org/published_article/putting-the-brakes-on-climate-change-its-about-more-than-just-co2/> accessed 16 September 2021.

'Methodology Report on Short-Lived Climate Forcers – IPCC' <https://www.ipcc.ch/report/methodology-report-on-short-lived-climate-forcers/> accessed 2 August 2022.

Oberthür S and Bodle R, 'Legal Form and Nature of the Paris Outcome' (2016) 6 Climate Law 40.

Rajamani L, 'The 2015 Paris Agreement: Interplay Between Hard, Soft and Non-Obligations' (2016) 28 Journal of Environmental Law 337.

Reisinger A and others, 'Cross-Chapter Box 2 GHG emission metrics' in Priyadarshi R. Shukla and others (eds), Climate Change 2022: Mitigation of Climate Change p. 2–16. (IPCC AR6 WGIII report, CUP 2022).

Ross K and others, 'Strengthening Nationally Determined Contributions to Catalyze Actions That Reduce Short-Lived Climate Pollutants' <https://www.wri.org/research/strengthening-nationally-determined-contributions-catalyze-actions-reduce-short-lived> accessed 3 May 2022.

Smith SM and others, 'Equivalence of Greenhouse-Gas Emissions for Peak Temperature Limits' (2012) 2 Nature Climate Change 535.

UNEP, 'The Emissions Gap Report 2022' (UNEP Synthesis Report, 2022).

Yamin F and Depledge J, *The International Climate Change Regime: a Guide to Rules, Institutions and Procedures* (Cambridge University Press 2004).

Yamineva Y and Kulovesi K, 'Keeping the Arctic White: the Legal and Governance Landscape for Reducing Short-Lived Climate Pollutants in the Arctic Region' (2018) 7 Transnational Environmental Law 201.

CHAPTER 4

Strengthening the Global Regulation of Hydrofluorocarbons under the Montreal Protocol

Louise du Toit

1 Introduction

The production and consumption of hydrofluorocarbons (HFCs) have increased significantly as a result of actions taken by member parties under the Montreal Protocol on Substances that Deplete the Ozone Layer (1987).[1] While HFCs have a low potential to deplete stratospheric ozone and remain in the atmosphere for significantly less time than carbon dioxide (CO_2),[2] many are potent greenhouse gases and, together with methane, black carbon, and tropospheric ozone, are classified as short-lived climate pollutants (SLCPs).[3] Reducing emissions of HFCs is thus important in regard to climate change mitigation. In a significant move, the Parties to the Montreal Protocol, in 2016, agreed to the addition of HFCs to the list of substances controlled by the Montreal Protocol.

This chapter first provides an overview of HFCs and emphasises their contribution to climate change. The section following discusses the international law regime for stratospheric ozone depletion and its application to HFCs. In doing so, it considers the events leading up to the development of the international ozone regime and provides an overview of this regime, focusing particularly on the Montreal Protocol. It also discusses the effectiveness of the ozone regime generally, as well as gaps that have been identified in relation to HFCs, and highlights potential ways in which these gaps could be addressed. The

1 Montreal Protocol on Substances that Deplete the Ozone Layer (signed 16 September 1987, entered into force 1 January 1989) 1522 UNTS 3.

2 While the average lifetime of HFCs is generally relatively short, the lifetime of HFC-23 (a by-product of the manufacture of HCFC-22) is 228 years: World Meteorological Organisation (WMO), 'Scientific Assessment of Ozone Depletion: 2018' (Global Ozone Research and Monitoring Project – Report No. 58, 2018) <https://www.esrl.noaa.gov/csl/assessments/ozone/2018/> accessed 10 December 2021, Appendix A.

3 CCAC, 'Short-lived Climate Pollutants (SLCPs)' <https://www.ccacoalition.org/en/content/short-lived-climate-pollutants-slcps> accessed 10 February 2022.

DOI:10.1163/9789004684089_006

chapter goes on to explore how the global regulation of HFCs under the ozone regime could be further strengthened. Concluding thoughts are provided in the final section.

2 HFCs

HFCs are a group of chemicals that contain hydrogen, fluorine and carbon. They are used in various applications including in air conditioning, refrigeration and fire protection systems and in metered dose inhalers. Their use in air conditioning and refrigeration accounts for over 80 per cent of total HFC consumption.[4] In contrast to other substances controlled by the Montreal Protocol, such as chlorofluorocarbons (CFCs) and hydrochlorofluorocarbons (HCFCs), HFCs do not contain chlorine, which is implicated in the destruction of stratospheric ozone.[5] Thus, HFCs do not deplete stratospheric ozone. However, many HFCs are potent greenhouse gases, with a global warming potential (GWP)[6] hundreds to thousands of times greater than that of CO_2.[7] The most abundant HFC, HFC-134a, is used in mobile air conditioning, foam blowing, and domestic refrigerators,[8] and has a GWP of 1 360.[9] The next most abundant HFCs are HFC-23, HFC-32, HFC-125, and HFC-143a.[10] Their respective GWPs are 12 690, 705, 3 450, and 5 080.[11] Reducing emissions of HFCs is thus important to climate mitigation efforts, especially efforts to limit the global temperature increase to just 1.5° Celsius.[12] In 2021, the top consumer of

4 CCAC, 'Hydrofluorocarbons (HFCs)' <https://www.ccacoalition.org/en/slcps/hydrofluorocarbons-hfcs> accessed 3 December 2021.

5 Mario Molina and Frank Rowland, 'Stratospheric Sink for Chlorofluoromethanes: Chlorine Atom-catalysed Destruction of Ozone' (1974) 249 Nature, 810–812.

6 The GWP is 'a metric for determining the relative contribution of a substance to climate warming'; see WMO (n2), ES.13.

7 ibid, Appendix A.

8 Sergey Gulev and others, 'Changing State of the Climate System' in V Masson-Delmotte and others (eds) *Climate Change 2021: The Physical Science Basis. Contribution of Working Group I to the Sixth Assessment Report of the Intergovernmental Panel on Climate Change* (2021), 2–22.

9 ibid.

10 ibid; Gulev and others (n8), Table 2.2, pp. 2–19.

11 WMO (n2), Appendix A.

12 Valerie Masson-Delmotte and others (eds), *Global Warming of 1.5°C: An IPCC Special Report on the Impacts of Global Warming of 1.5°C above Pre-industrial Levels and Related Global Greenhouse Gas Emission Pathways, in the Context of Strengthening the Global Response to the Threat of Climate Change, Sustainable Development, and Efforts to Eradicate Poverty* (Intergovernmental Panel on Climate Change 2018), 118.

HFCs was China, followed by the European Union, Brazil, Mexico and India respectively.[13]

In turn, global warming due to the increasing emission of greenhouse gases may lead to stratospheric cooling and the formation of polar stratospheric clouds, which play a critical role in the formation of the ozone hole.[14] Furthermore, research shows that increasing greenhouse gas concentrations have caused the stratosphere to contract, with stratospheric contraction of 1.3 kilometres projected by 2080.[15] This highlights the interconnections between different planetary processes.[16] In light of these interconnections, it is important to ensure that introducing solutions to one problem does not shift the problem elsewhere.[17]

It is notable that since HFCs were only commercialised in the early-1990s, their presence in the atmosphere is currently low.[18] However, their abundance is increasing. From 2011 to 2019, levels of the most prevalent HFCs increased by more than 140 per cent.[19] Reasons for the increase in HFC emissions include the fact that HFCs are replacing HCFCs, which have been almost completely phased out in developed country Parties,[20] except in regard to essential uses and for the servicing of existing refrigeration, air conditioning, fire suppression and fire protection equipment and in further specific applications.[21] Rising

---

13 United Nations Environment Programme (UNEP) Ozone Secretariat, 'Country Data' (2023) <https://ozone.unep.org/countries/data-table> accessed 1 August 2023.

14 Susan Solomon, 'Stratospheric Ozone Depletion: A Review of Concepts and History' (1999) 37 Reviews of Geophysics, 286.

15 Petr Pisoft and others, 'Stratospheric Contraction Caused by Increasing Greenhouse Gases' (2021) 16 Environmental Research Letters 064038.

16 Johan Rockström and others, 'A Safe Operating Space for Humanity' (2009) 461 Nature 24, 472–475; Johan Rockström and others, 'Planetary Boundaries: Exploring the Safe Operating Space for Humanity' (2009) 14 Ecology and Society 32; Will Steffen and others, 'Planetary Boundaries: Guiding Human Development on a Changing Planet' (2015) 347 Science 6223, 736.

17 On problem shifting, see Rakhyun Kim and Harro van Asselt, 'Global Governance: Problem Shifting in the Anthropocene and the Limits of International Law' in E Morgera and K Kulovesi (eds), *Research Handbook on International Law and Natural Resources* (Edward Elgar 2016) 473–495.

18 CCAC (n4).

19 This percentage has been calculated based on the figures provided in Gulev and others (n8), Table 2.2, p. 2–19).

20 Hannah Flerlage, Guus Velders, and Jacob de Boer, 'A Review of Bottom-up and Top-down Emission Estimates of Hydrofluorocarbons (HFCs) in Different Parts of the World' (2021) 283 Chemosphere 131208, 1–2.

21 Montreal Protocol on Substances that Deplete the Ozone Layer (adoped 16 September 1987, entered into force 1 January 1989) 1522 UNTS 3, Art. 2(f).

HFC emissions can also be explained by growing demand for motor vehicles, air conditioners and refrigerators – primarily due to economic growth in developing countries.[22] It is projected that the combination of increased warming and growing populations will further increase demand for refrigeration and air conditioning,[23] which will contribute to further increases in HFC emissions.[24] It has been projected that 'the global stock of air conditioners in buildings will grow to 5.6 billion by 2050',[25] and it is estimated that annual HFC emissions could increase to 4.3 gigatonnes (Gt) of CO_2 equivalent by 2050.[26]

The following section outlines the regulation of HFCs at the global level.

3 The Global Regulation of HFCs under the Ozone Regime

HFCs are included as a controlled substance under the Montreal Protocol; and they are also listed as a greenhouse gas under the 1997 Kyoto Protocol[27] and included under the 2015 Paris Agreement.[28] The role of HFCs under the international climate change regime is dealt with in chapter 3 and, therefore, this section focuses on HFC regulation under the ozone regime, with a particular emphasis on the Montreal Protocol. First, the background to the development of the ozone regime is traced.

3.1 *Events Leading to the Development of the Ozone Regime*[29]

Chlorofluorocarbons (CFCs) were invented in 1928 as a safer and more stable alternative to other substances, such as sulfur dioxide and ammonia, for use

22 Flerlage, Velders, and de Boer (n20) 2.

23 Paul Newman, 'The Way Forward for Montreal Protocol Science' (2018) 350 Comptes Rendus Geoscience, 442–447.

24 CCAC (n4).

25 ibid.

26 Pallav Purohit and others, 'Electricity Savings and Greenhouse Gas Emission Reductions from Global Phase-down of Hydrofluorocarbons' (2020) 20 Atmospheric Chemistry and Physics 11305–11327, 11320.

27 Kyoto Protocol to the United Nations Framework Convention on Climate Change (adopted 11 December 1997, entered into force 16 February 2005) 2303 UNTS 162.

28 Paris Agreement (adopted 12 December 2015, entered into force 4 November 2016) 3156 UNTS 54113.

29 This section draws on my earlier research; see Louise Du Toit, 'Stratospheric Ozone Depletion' in French, D and Kotzé, LJ (eds) *Research Handbook on Law, Governance and Planetary Boundaries* (Edward Elgar 2021) 261–277.

as home refrigerants.[30] Their use on a large scale began in the 1930s[31] and, by 1985, total CFC production exceeded 1 million tons.[32] During this time, there was growing concern regarding increasing CFC emissions and their potential role in depleting stratospheric ozone. Destruction of stratospheric ozone allows ultraviolet (UV) radiation, primarily UV-B, to reach the Earth's surface. Excessive UV-B radiation can cause skin cancer and cataracts in humans, stunting in plants, and harm to animals integral to the marine food chain.[33] In 1974, Mario J Molina and FS Rowland noted that CFCs had been added to the atmosphere in increasing amounts over the past few decades and proposed that when CFCs are released into the atmosphere, they are broken down by UV radiation, resulting in the release of chlorine.[34] Chlorine then reacts with ozone, leading to the destruction of ozone in the atmosphere.[35] It should be noted that this process had not actually been observed outside of the laboratory, nor had actual environmental harm due to this process.[36]

Over the following years, further research on the impacts of CFCs was carried out by other scientists and bodies, including the US National Academy of Scientists and the United Nations Environment Programme (UNEP), which supported the 'Molina–Rowland hypothesis'.[37] Velders et al argue that the early warning provided by Molina and Rowland led to citizen action and national regulations to restrict ozone-depleting substances (ODSs).[38] For example, in the US, the Clean Air Act was amended in 1977 to empower the Environmental Protection Agency (EPA) to regulate substances that were

30 Lani Sinclair, 'The Science of Ozone Depletion: From Theory to Certainty' in Andersen, SO and Madhava Sarma, K (eds) Protecting the Ozone Layer: The United Nations History (Earthscan 2002) 4.

31 Rishav Goyal and others, 'Reduction in Surface Climate Change Achieved by the 1987 Montreal Protocol' (2019) 14 Environmental Research Letters 124041, 1.

32 Alexander Gillespie, *Climate Change, Ozone Depletion and Air Pollution: Legal Commentaries with Policy and Science Considerations* (Martinus Nijhoff Publishers 2006) 21.

33 Ved Nanda, 'Stratospheric Ozone Depletion: A Challenge for International Environmental Law and Policy' (1989) 10 Michigan Journal of International Law, 489–490.

34 Molina and Rowland (n5).

35 The chemical reactions involved in this process are set out in Molina and Rowland (n5). See also Frank Rowland, 'Chlorofluorocarbons and the Depletion of Stratospheric Ozone' (1989) 77 American Scientist 36–45.

36 Elizabeth DeSombre, 'The Experience of the Montreal Protocol: Particularly Remarkable, and Remarkably Particular' (2000) 19 Journal of Environmental Law, 50.

37 Sinclair (n30) 11–13.

38 Guus Velders and others, 'The Importance of the Montreal Protocol in Protecting Climate' (2007) 104 PNAS 12, 4814.

reasonably anticipated to impact the stratosphere and adversely affect public health or welfare.[39]

In 1985, Farman and colleagues publicly confirmed that spring-time levels of ozone in Antarctica had fallen considerably.[40] Although a link between the concentration of chlorine-containing substances in the atmosphere and ozone depletion had not yet been conclusively proven, Farman et al suggested that CFCs were the likely cause.[41] Following the discovery of the Antarctic ozone hole, it took several more years for the link between CFCs and ozone depletion to be conclusively established. In August 1987, data obtained during an Antarctic expedition revealed the lowest levels of ozone that had ever been recorded and directly implicated CFCs in the enormous loss of ozone over Antarctica.[42]

Against this background of uncertainty, as well as disagreement over whether a precautionary approach should be followed, or whether conclusive evidence of ozone depletion should first be required,[43] there was no coordinated international response for several years. Since the science was not certain, there was significant resistance[44] and scepticism.[45] Nevertheless, there were several initiatives in the 1970s, including a 1976 tripartite agreement regarding the monitoring of the stratosphere between the governments of the United States, France and the United Kingdom, as well as the 1977 World Plan of Action on the Ozone. Discussions on a draft international convention to address stratospheric ozone depletion began in 1981.[46]

39 Gillespie (n32) 155.

40 Joseph Farman, Brian Gardiner, and Jonathan Shanklin, 'Large Losses of Total Ozone in Antarctica Reveal Seasonal ClO_x/NO_x Interaction' (1985) 315 Nature, 207–210.

41 Susan Solomon, 'Stratospheric Ozone Depletion: A Review of Concepts and History' (1999) 37 Reviews of Geophysics, 283.

42 Sinclair (n30) 22.

43 Gillespie (n32) 152–157.

44 Stephen Andersen, Marcel Halberstadt, and Nathan Borgford-Parnell, 'Stratospheric Ozone, Global Warming, and the Principle of Unintended Consequences – An Ongoing Science and Policy Success Story' (2013) 63 Journal of the Air & Waste Management Association, 613.

45 Ben Lieberman, 'Stratosperic ozone depletion and the Montreal Protocol: A critical analysis' (1994) 2 Buffalo Environmental Law Journal, 1–32; Robert Falkner, 'The Business of Ozone Layer Protection: Corporate Power in Regime Evolution' in DL Levy and PJ Newell (eds), *The Business of Global Environmental Governance* (MIT Press 2005) 105–134.

46 The international process leading to the finalisation of the Vienna Convention is discussed in detail in Stephen Andersen and K Madhava Sarma (eds), *Protecting the Ozone Layer: The United Nations History* (Earthscan 2002).

3.2 *The Vienna Convention*

In view of this uncertainty, it was significant that the Vienna Convention for the Protection of Ozone[47] was agreed to in March 1985. Parties to the Vienna Convention, in the Preamble, noted the potentially harmful impact of the modification of the ozone layer on human health and the environment, and the importance of international co-operation and action as well as scientific and technical considerations in developing measures to protect the ozone layer from human-caused modifications. Parties resolved to protect human health and the environment from adverse effects arising from the ozone layer's modification. 'Adverse effects' are defined to include 'changes in the physical environment or biota, *including changes in climate*, which have significant deleterious effects on human health or on the composition, resilience and productivity of natural and managed ecosystems, or on materials useful to mankind'.[48]

The prevailing uncertainty is reflected in the language of the Vienna Convention, which obliges Parties to take appropriate measures to protect human health and the environment against adverse effects 'resulting or likely to result from human activities which modify or are likely to modify the ozone layer'.[49] The Vienna Convention sets out several general obligations for Parties,[50] including undertaking research and scientific assessments (article 3 read with Annex I) and specifically acknowledges the potential impacts of the modification of ozone on the climate.[51] It furthermore requires Parties to continually review the implementation of the Convention and to consider and undertake additional actions that may be necessary to achieve the Vienna Convention's purposes.[52]

Despite not providing for any controls on ODSs, it was considered 'a promising first step, for it signified recognition by the world community that it must act promptly on this environmental challenge before the occurrence of any actual damage'.[53]

47 Vienna Convention for the Protection of the Ozone Layer (agreed 22 March 1985, entered into force 22 September 1988) 1513 UNTS 293.
48 ibid, Article 1(2), own emphasis.
49 ibid, Article 2 (1).
50 ibid, Articles 2–5.
51 ibid, Articles 2–3 read with Annex I.
52 ibid, Article 6(4).
53 Nanda (n33) 500.

3.3 *The Montreal Protocol*

3.3.1 Introduction

The Montreal Protocol was signed two years later in September 1987. The negotiation process – with regard to both the Vienna Convention and the Montreal Protocol – has been described as 'particularly impressive' since negotiations were carried out (and agreement reached) 'under conditions of uncertainty, both over the existence and extent of environmental harm and the costliness of taking action to mitigate it'.[54] It should be noted that while there were initially only 23 state Parties to the Montreal Protocol, following its continual strengthening and refinement (elaborated on below), the Montreal Protocol became the first international treaty to be universally ratified in 2010.[55]

3.3.2 Overview of the Main Provisions of the Montreal Protocol

Parties to the Montreal Protocol, in the Preamble, recognised that global emissions of certain substances can significantly deplete and modify the ozone layer so as to result in adverse effects to human health and the environment, and noted the potential climatic effect of such emissions. Parties were furthermore '[d]etermined to protect the ozone layer by taking precautionary measures to control equitably total global emissions of substances that deplete it, with the ultimate objective of their elimination'.[56]

The Montreal Protocol sets out control measures for Parties in relation to their consumption and production of the various controlled substances included under the Montreal Protocol. Controlled substances are defined as 'substance[s] in Annex A, Annex B, Annex C, Annex E or Annex F to this Protocol, whether existing alone or in a mixture. It includes the isomers of any such substance, except as specified in the relevant Annex, *but excludes any controlled substance or mixture which is in a manufactured product* other than a container used for the transportation or storage of that substance'.[57] 'Consumption' is defined as 'production plus imports *minus exports of controlled substances*'.[58] 'Production' is defined as 'the amount of controlled substances produced, minus the amount destroyed by technologies to be approved by the Parties and *minus the amount entirely used as feedstock in the*

54 DeSombre (n36) 49.

55 Sophie Godin-Beekmann, Paul Newman and Irina Petropavlovskikh, '30th anniversary of the Montreal Protocol: From the safeguard of the ozone layer to the protection of the Earth's climate' (2018) 350 *Comptes Rendus Geoscience*, 331.

56 Montreal Protocol (n1) Preamble.

57 ibid, Article 1(4), own emphasis.

58 ibid, Article 1(6), own emphasis.

manufacture of other chemicals. The amount recycled and reused is not to be considered as "production"'.[59]

The Montreal Protocol originally set out control measures in relation to the consumption and production of only CFCs and halons,[60] as these were the only substances that had been identified as being ozone-depleting. However, over time, more chemicals were identified as being responsible for ozone depletion.[61] As a consequence, the Montreal Protocol has been continually strengthened since it came into effect in 1989 through numerous adjustments and amendments.[62] Adjustments are a noteworthy feature of the Montreal Protocol, and they allow for binding adjustments to be made – for example, of the reductions of controlled substances – with the consent of only two-thirds of the Parties.[63] These adjustments and amendments have had the effect of, firstly, accelerating phase-out schedules – for instance, the Montreal Protocol originally called for the consumption of CFCs to be decreased to 50 percent of 1986 levels by 1999, but this was adjusted to require a complete phase-out by 1996; and, secondly, bringing more chemicals under the control of the Montreal Protocol.[64]

CFCs and halons were gradually replaced by hydrochlorofluorocarbons (HCFCs).[65] Since HCFCs are still ozone-depleting, they were included under the Montreal Protocol in 1992, as noted in Table 4.1 below. As a consequence, HCFCs are being replaced by HFCs.[66] While HFCs are not ozone-depleting, they have a high potential to warm the climate, and their GWPs range from 53 to 14 800. This is taken up further below. The additional chemicals that have been brought under the Montreal Protocol, together with their ozone-depleting potentials (ODPs)[67] and global warming potentials (GWPs) are depicted in Table 4.1 immediately below.

---

59 ibid, Article 1(5), own emphasis.

60 ibid, Article 2.

61 Gillespie (n32) 164; Mark Roberts, 'Finishing the Job: The Montreal Protocol Moves to Phase Down hydrofluorocarbons' (2017) 26 RECIEL, 221.

62 Adjustments may be made in terms of article 2(9)(a) read with article 6; while substances may be added to (or removed from) any annex in terms of article 2(10) read with article 6. See also DeSombre (n36) 54.

63 Montreal Protocol (n1) Article 2(9)(c) and (d).

64 Tina Birmpili, 'Montreal Protocol at 30: The Governance Structure, the Evolution, and the Kigali Amendment' (2018) 350 Comptes Rendus Geoscience, 427.

65 Godin-Beekmann, Newman and Petropavlovskikh (n55) 332.

66 ibid.

67 The ODP is 'a metric for determining the relative strength of a chemical to destroy ozone': WMO (n2) ES.13.

TABLE 4.1 Substances brought under the control of the Montreal Protocol[a]

Year	Amendment	New substances brought under the control of the montreal protocol	ODP	GWP
1990	London Amendment[b]	Other fully halogenated CFCs	1.0	4 370 – 13 900
		Carbon tetrachloride	1.1	2 110
		Trichloroethane	0.1	153
1992	Copenhagen Amendment[c]	Hydrochlorofluorocarbons (HCFCs)	0.001–0.52	77 – 2 310
		Hydrobromofluorocarbons	0.02–7.5	
		Methyl bromide	0.57	2
1999	Beijing Amendment[d]	Bromochloromethane	0.12	4.7
2016	Kigali Amendment[e]	Hydrofluorocarbons (HFCs)	0	53 – 14 800

a The values contained in this table have been obtained from the Montreal Protocol and WMO (n2).

b United Nations Environment Programme (UNEP), *Report of the Second Meeting of the Parties to the Montreal Protocol on Substances that Deplete the Ozone Layer* (UNEP/OzL.Pro.2/3, 1990) <https://ozone.unep.org/Meeting_Documents/mop/02mop/MOP_2.shtml> accessed 5 May 2022.

c UNEP, *Report of the Fourth Meeting of the Parties to the Montreal Protocol on Substances that Deplete the Ozone Layer* (UNEP/OzL.Pro.4/15, 1992) <https://ozone.unep.org/sites/default/files/2019-04/MOP-4-15E.pdf> accessed 5 May 2022.

d UNEP, *Report of the Eleventh Meeting of the Parties to the Montreal Protocol on Substances that Deplete the Ozone Layer* (UNEP/OzL.Pro.11/10, 1999) <https://ozone.unep.org/sites/default/files/2019-04/MOP-11-10E.pdf> accessed 5 May 2022.

e UNEP, *Report of the Twenty-Eighth Meeting of the Parties to the Montreal Protocol on Substances that Deplete the Ozone Layer* (UNEP/OzL.Pro.28/12, 2016) <https://ozone.unep.org/sites/default/files/2019-08/MOP-28-12E.pdf> accessed 5 May 2022.

Article 4 of the Protocol deals with trade in ODSs. While it deals separately with each of the groups of controlled ODSs, it essentially prohibits the export and import of controlled substances to and from countries that are not Parties to the Montreal Protocol. Article 4 also prohibits the import of products either containing or produced with controlled substances. It furthermore discourages the export of technologies to either produce or utilise certain controlled substances.

Article 5 of the Montreal Protocol deals with the special situation of developing countries and entitles developing countries (also referred to here as article 5 countries), whose annual consumption of controlled substances was less than 0.3 kilograms per capita after the entry into force of the Montreal Protocol (and until 1 January 1999) – in order to meet their basic domestic needs – to delay their compliance with the control measures of the Montreal Protocol.[68] The special situation of developing countries is discussed in further detail in Section 3.3.3 below.

Article 6 of the Montreal Protocol makes provision for the assessment of the control measures contained in article 2 and articles 2A–2J and it provides for Parties to convene panels of experts which will report their conclusions to the Parties. The Montreal Protocol requires Parties to report to the Secretariat on their annual emissions of all controlled substances (including HFCs) 'and, separately, for each substance, … [a]mounts used for feedstocks'.[69] In relation to HFC-23 specifically (also dealt with below), the Montreal Protocol provides that Parties shall report to the Secretariat on their annual emissions of HFC-23 per facility.[70] Article 8 makes provision for the development of procedures and institutional mechanisms to deal with instances of non-compliance. Cooperation in regard to research, development, public awareness and exchange of information is addressed in article 9. Article 10, which was inserted in 1990, provides for the establishment of a financial mechanism. This financial mechanism is elaborated on in Section 3.3.3 below. Furthermore, article 10A provides for the transfer of environmentally safe substitutes and related technologies to developing country Parties.

These provisions are reflected on in more detail in Section 4 below.

3.3.3 Facilitating the Participation of Developing Countries

At the outset, only three developing countries – Egypt, Mexico, and Uganda – signed the Montreal Protocol. At the time, the consumption and production of ODSs in developing countries was insignificant, but was expected to increase substantially. The Montreal Protocol did not initially provide for a financial mechanism and, as DeSombre argues, without 'sufficient incentives to join the agreement, developing countries showed every sign of remaining outside the regulatory system'.[71] Consequently, provision for a financial mechanism was made in 1990 in terms of the London Amendment, and the Multilateral

68 Montreal Protocol (n1) Articles 5(1) and 5(8 *bis*) – 5(8 *qua*).
69 ibid, Article 7.
70 ibid, Article 7(3ter).
71 DeSombre (n36) 69.

Fund (which receives contributions from developed country Parties)[72] was established in 1991. Consequently, China, India and Brazil joined the Montreal Protocol, followed by almost all other developing countries.[73]

Further provisions have arguably facilitated the participation of developing countries. The Multilateral Fund is managed by an Executive Committee, which has equal numbers of developing and developed country Parties.[74] Where it is not possible to take decisions by consensus, the Protocol requires that decisions are taken by a two-thirds majority vote, representing a majority of developing and developed country Parties.[75] The Montreal Protocol also provides that developing country compliance with the control measures of the Protocol depends on the effective implementation of the Multilateral Fund and the transfer of technology.[76] The Montreal Protocol allows a certain amount of production of controlled substances to 'satisfy the basic domestic needs' of developing country Parties.[77]

It has been argued, on the basis of these provisions, that the Montreal Protocol has given effect to the principle of common but differentiated responsibilities.[78] Since developed countries were responsible for the bulk of the production and consumption of ODSs, it was essential that they took responsibility by starting first while allowing developing countries to address their development priorities.[79]

3.3.4 The Role of Industry

While, initially, there was significant resistance from ODS producers and even attempts to discredit the ozone depletion hypothesis,[80] industry came to play a very important role in the success of the ozone regime. As highlighted above, prior to the agreement on the Vienna Convention, national regulations regarding the limitation of ODSs had already been developed in some countries, including the United States, which 'strongly influenced the role industry

---

72 Multilateral Fund for the Implementation of the Montreal Protocol <http://www.multilateralfund.org/default.aspx> accessed 20 December 2022.

73 ibid, 71.

74 Montreal Protocol (n1) Article 10(5).

75 ibid, Article 10(9).

76 ibid, Article 5(5).

77 ibid, Articles 2(d)–2(j).

78 Marco Gonzalez, Kirsten Taddonio, and Nancy Sherman, 'The Montreal Protocol: How Today's Successes Offer a Pathway to the Future' (2020) 5 Journal of Environmental Studies and Sciences, 124–125.

79 DeSombre (n36).

80 Falkner (n45) 108.

played in the process'.[81] For example, the strict domestic regulation in the US incentivised US CFC industries to call for international regulation so that they would not be at a disadvantage in comparison to CFC industries in other countries subject to less stringent domestic regulation. Furthermore, the hefty excise tax that was imposed on ODSs in the US motivated industry to develop substitutes. Indeed, after the Montreal Protocol was adopted, ODS producers such as AT&T and DuPont swiftly developed substitute substances.[82] Industry was further incentivised by the prospect of capturing an emerging market for ODS substitutes.[83] Following the adoption of the Montreal Protocol, industry has continued to play a positive role, including by undertaking joint research programmes.[84]

3.3.5 Governance under the Montreal Protocol

Several institutions established under the ozone regime have been integral to its success. The Ozone Secretariat, which was established under the Vienna Convention, also administers the Montreal Protocol. Amongst other things, it organises Conferences of the Parties under the Vienna Convention and Meetings of the Parties under the Montreal Protocol and manages the implementation of decisions arising from such conventions and meetings. Three assessment panels – the Environmental Effects Assessment Panel (EEAP), the Scientific Assessment Panel (SAP) and the Technology and Economic Assessment Panel (TEAP) – have been established under the Montreal Protocol. The EEAP assesses the effects of ozone depletion and advises the Parties on new developments. The SAP assesses relevant atmospheric science issues and the status of ozone depletion and prepares regular reports and highlights scientific issues of importance for consideration at the Meetings of Parties under the Montreal Protocol. The TEAP provides technical information regarding alternative technologies. As noted above, the Multilateral Fund provides financial assistance to developing countries. The Executive Committee of the Multilateral Fund has played an important role in facilitating the phase-out of ODSs in developing countries. For example, following China's continued construction of plants to produce halons while also applying for funding to retrofit one halon plant, the Executive Committee decided to restrict funding for the phase-out of ODS production while other ODS production was ongoing.[85]

---

81 DeSombre (n36) 57.
82 ibid, 57–60.
83 ibid, 60; Falkner (n45) 105.
84 Falkner (n45) 109–110; see also The Alliance for Responsible Atmospheric Policy <https://alliancepolicy.org/> accessed 20 December 2022.
85 DeSombre (n36) 74.

3.4 *The Kigali Amendment*

3.4.1 Events Leading to the Adoption of the Kigali Amendment

As HFCs were developed to replace HCFCs (discussed above), the consumption of HFCs increased from almost zero in 1990 to more than 1 200 million tonnes of CO_2 equivalent by 2010; and the replacement of HCFCs by HFCs was therefore contributing to climate change.[86] Already in 2009, the G8 countries at the time (France, Germany, Italy, Japan, Russia, the United Kingdom, and the United States) recognised that the phase-out of HCFCs was leading to rapidly rising HFC use and undertook to 'work with [their] partners to ensure that HFC emissions reductions are achieved under the appropriate framework'.[87] Furthermore, in 2009, a proposal to amend the Montreal Protocol to include HFCs was submitted by the Federated States of Micronesia and Mauritius.[88] However, there was resistance particularly from other developing countries, including China, India, Malaysia and the Dominican Republic, who, *inter alia*, argued that HFCs should be dealt with under the climate change regime and that implementation issues relating to the phase-out of HCFCs should first be resolved.[89] In 2010, further proposals were submitted by the Federated States of Micronesia as well as by Canada, Mexico, and the United States and significant debate ensued.[90] Those supporting the inclusion of HFCs under the Montreal Protocol (including Canada, the Federated States of Micronesia, Kenya, Macedonia, Mexico, the Philippines, Tuvalu (on behalf of Pacific Island countries), and the United States) argued, *inter alia*, that there was a legal and moral responsibility to address HFCs under the Montreal Protocol and that such efforts would not diminish responsibility under the UNFCCC. Arguments

86 Roberts (n61) 224; Rakhyun Kim and Klaus Bosselmann, K 'Operationalising Sustainable Development: Ecological Integrity as a *Grundnorm* of International Law' (2015) 24 RECIEL 194–208, 200.

87 Group of Eight (G8), 'Responsible Leadership for a Sustainable Future' (2009) <http://www.g8.utoronto.ca/summit/2009laquila/2009-declaration.pdf> accessed 22 December 2022.

88 International Institute for Sustainable Development (IISD), 'Summary of the Twenty-eighth Meeting of the Parties to the Montreal Protocol: 10–14 October 2016' (2016) <https://enb.iisd.org/events/montreal-protocol-mop-28/summary-report-10-14-october-2016> accessed 5 May 2022, p. 15.

89 IISD, 'Summary of the Twenty-seventh Meeting of the Parties to the Montreal Protocol: 1–5 November 2015' (2015) <https://enb.iisd.org/events/montreal-protocol-mop-27/summary-report-1-5-november-2015> accessed 5 May 2022, pp. 12–13; Arunabha Ghosh, 'Making Sense on its Own Terms: India in the HFC and Aviation Negotiations' in NK Dubash (ed), *India in a Warming World* (Oxford University Press 2019) 232.

90 IISD, '28th Meeting' (n89) 15.

by those opposing the inclusion of HFCs (including Argentina, Brazil, China, Cuba, India and Malaysia) included that HFCs lay outside the scope of the Montreal Protocol, resources under the Montreal Protocol are limited, and, furthermore, that any decision on HFCs under the Montreal Protocol should await the finalisation of discussions under the UNFCCC regarding whether HFCs would be included in the new commitment period under the Kyoto Protocol.[91] It is notable that under the Clean Development Mechanism, established under the Kyoto Protocol, developing countries were able to claim carbon credits to destroy emissions of HFC-23. This created a 'perverse incentive' to produce more HFC-23 (as a by-product of HCFC-22 production) which could then be destroyed to earn more carbon credits. China and India were major producers of HCFC-22. However, the European Union banned HFC-23 carbon credits in the European Trading Scheme in 2013.[92]

Further discussions were held in 2014, and in 2015 the Parties to the Montreal Protocol agreed to establish a contact group to consider the feasibility of and ways to manage HFCs.[93] Resistance began to diminish. For example, in 2016, India and the United States issued a joint statement regarding their intention 'to work to adopt an HFC amendment in 2016 with increased financial support from donor countries to the Multilateral Fund to help developing countries with implementation'.[94] While it is not possible to point to a single factor in the shift or the eventual agreement on the Kigali Amendment, the proactive and behind-the-scenes role of the Ozone Secretariat in facilitating discussions

91 IISD, 'Summary of the Twenty-second Meeting of the Parties to the Montreal Protocol: 8–12 November 2010' (2010) <https://enb.iisd.org/ozone/mop22/> accessed 12 September 2022; UNEP, *Report of the Twenty-Second Meeting of the Parties to the Montreal Protocol on Substances that Deplete the Ozone Layer* (UNEP/OzL.Pro.22/9) (2010) <https://ozone.unep.org/Meeting_Documents/mop/22mop/MOP-22-9E.doc> accessed 12 September 2022.

92 Ghosh (n90) 235.

93 UNEP, *Report of the Thirty-fifth Meeting of the Open-ended Working Group of the Parties to the Montreal Protocol on Substances that Deplete the Ozone Layer* (UNEP/OzL.Pro.WG.1/35/6) (5 May 2015) <https://ozone.unep.org/system/files/documents/OEWG-35-6E.pdf> accessed 5 May 2022, para. 126.

94 The White House 'Joint Statement: The United States and India: Enduring Partners in the 21st Century' (7 June 2016) <https://obamawhitehouse.archives.gov/the-press-office/2016/06/07/joint-statement-united-states-and-india-enduring-global-partners-21st> accessed 12 September 2022.

on HFCs (from as early as 2009) has been highlighted.[95] Furthermore, during negotiations, delegates emphasised the historical success of the ozone regime and the potential for an amendment dealing with HFCs to be 'the Montreal Protocol's next success'.[96] Such submissions also appealed to the sense of responsibility and pride of 'the ozone family'.[97] Furthermore, although measures to address HFCs had been introduced in many countries,[98] Parties recognised that a global and holistic response to the problem would be most beneficial.[99] Significantly, in 2016, at the twenty-eighth Meeting of the Parties in Kigali, the Parties agreed to the insertion of article 2J (and Annex F) which provides for the phase-down of HFCs beginning in 2019.[100]

3.4.2 Overview of the Kigali Amendment

Article 2J provides that, commencing on 1 January 2019, Parties shall ensure that their annual consumption of HFCs (or production of HFCs – in respect of Parties producing HFCs), expressed in CO_2 equivalents, shall, by 2036, not exceed 15 per cent of the annual average of their consumption of HFCs for the years 2011, 2012 and 2013, plus 15 per cent of their consumption of HCFCs, expressed in CO_2 equivalents.[101] Notwithstanding these provisions, Parties may decide that a party may commence its phase-down of HFCs from 1 January 2020 so that by 2036 its annual consumption of HFCs (or production of HFCs – in respect of Parties producing HFCs), expressed in CO_2 equivalents, does not exceed 15 per cent of the annual average of its consumption of HFCs for the years 2011, 2012 and 2013, plus 25 per cent of its consumption of HCFCs, expressed in CO_2 equivalents (article 2J(2) and (4)).[102] Annex F lists 18 different

95 Jannah Wijermars, *Facilitation for the Future: The Ozone Secretariat's Role During the Kigali Amendment Negotiations* (MSc thesis, Utrecht University 2022) <https://studenttheses.uu.nl/bitstream/handle/20.500.12932/42445/MScThesis_Wijermars_5717280%20%28for%20online%20publication%29.pdf?sequence=1&isAllowed=y> accessed 12 September 2022.

96 IISD, '28th Meeting' (n89) 5.

97 ibid, 17; Birmpili (n64).

98 e.g. Duncan Brack, 'National Legislation on Hydrofluorocarbons' (11 September 2015) <http://www.igsd.org/documents/NationalLegislationonHydrofluorocarbons_9.11.151.pdf> accessed 20 December 2022.

99 UNEP, *35th Meeting* (n94); UNEP, *Report of the Twenty-Eighth Meeting of the Parties to the Montreal Protocol on Substances that Deplete the Ozone Layer* (UNEP/OzL.Pro.28/12, 2016) <https://ozone.unep.org/sites/default/files/2019-08/MOP-28-12E.pdf> accessed 5 May 2022.

100 UNEP, *28th Meeting* (n100).

101 Montreal Protocol (n1) Article 2J (1) and (3).

102 ibid, Article 2J (2) and (4).

HFCs, including HFC-23, HFC-32, HFC-125, HFC-134a, and HFC-143a (all of the five most abundant HFCs). The Montreal Protocol makes provision for Parties to decide to allow the production or consumption of HFCs in regard to uses that are agreed to be exempted.[103]

HFC-23 – a potent greenhouse gas with a GWP of 12 690 – is produced incidentally as a by-product of the production of HCFC-22.[104] While the Montreal Protocol does not generally include controls in regard to HFCs that are produced as by-products, it does oblige Parties that manufacture HCFCs or HFCs to ensure that HFC-23 emissions generated in production facilities that manufacture HCFCs or HFCs 'are destroyed to the extent practicable',[105] and furthermore requires that Parties provide statistical data to the Secretariat on their annual emissions of HFC-23 per facility.[106]

While article 4, which deals with the control of trade with non-Parties, does not yet explicitly ban or restrict the import or export of HFCs (perhaps because the Kigali Amendment provides for the phase-down, rather than phase-out, of HFCs), it does for example require that to the fullest extent practicable, Parties discourage the export of any technology for producing or using, amongst others, HFCs to States that are not party to the Protocol.[107]

These provisions are reflected on in Section 4 below.

3.4.3 Participation under the Kigali Amendment

In contrast to other amendments to the Montreal Protocol, which have been almost universally ratified, the Kigali Amendment has been ratified by only 151 countries. However, the Kigali Amendment was accepted by China in June 2021; it was ratified by India in September 2021; and it was ratified by the United States and accepted by Brazil in October 2022.[108] Thus, all of the top consumers of ODSs have ratified the Kigali Amendment.[109] It should be noted that Parties that have not yet ratified the Amendment are not bound to phase down their consumption and production of HFCs or report on their HFC consumption to the Ozone Secretariat.

103 ibid, Article 2J (5).
104 WMO (n2), ES. 20.
105 Montreal Protocol (n1) Article 2J (6).
106 ibid, Article 7(3*ter*).
107 ibid, Article 4(5).
108 UNEP Ozone Secretariat, 'All Ratifications' (2022a) <https://ozone.unep.org/all-ratifications> accessed 20 December 2022.
109 ibid; UNEP Ozone Secretariat (n13).

The effectiveness of the ozone regime – in regard to its strengths and weaknesses – is now considered.

4 Evaluating the Effectiveness of the Ozone Regime

4.1 *Strengths of the Ozone Regime*

Overall, the Montreal Protocol has been described as 'a landmark in the ongoing development of international environmental law'[110] and it is widely considered to be one of the most successful international environmental law regimes.[111] By 2018, 99 per cent of ODSs (controlled by the Montreal Protocol) had been phased out.[112] Ozone levels have not declined further since the late-1990s, and are actually beginning to recover, and it has been projected that global ozone will return to 1980 levels by around mid-century.[113]

As the above discussion reveals, one of the strengths of the ozone regime is that its provision for adjustments and amendments has enabled the Montreal Protocol to 'adapt to changing environmental conditions, scientific and technical understanding, and political realities'.[114] As a result, the regime has been continually refined and strengthened, and further ODSs have been brought under its control.

The ozone regime has also had important climate benefits. Velders et al argue that, as of 2007, '[t]he climate protection already achieved by the Montreal Protocol alone is far larger than the reduction target of the first commitment period of the Kyoto Protocol'.[115] In addition, Goyal et al project the avoidance of a global temperature increase of at least 1°C (they state that this estimate is conservative) by 2050 as a result of the Montreal Protocol.[116] In regard to the Kigali Amendment specifically, it has been argued that due to its adoption, the Montreal Protocol 'evolved from strictly an ozone protection agreement into an ozone and climate agreement'.[117] It has further been argued that the

110 Nanda (n33) 510.

111 Stephen Andersen and others, 'Narrowing Feedstock Exemptions under the Montreal Protocol has Multiple Environmental Benefits' (2021) 118 PNAS 49, 1.

112 Birmpili (n64) 427.

113 WMO (n2), ES-1 at ES.16, ES.42.

114 DeSombre (n36) 57; Birmpili (n64) 430; John Dryzek, 'Institutions for the Anthropocene: Governance in a Changing Earth System' (2016) 4 British Journal of Political Science, 943.

115 Velders and others (n38) 414.

116 Goyal and others (n31).

117 Newman (n23) 442; see also Velders and others (n38).

Kigali Amendment will help to 'ensure that the restoration of the ozone layer does not come at the expense of the global climate'[118] and it has been projected that global warming of 0.2°C–0.4°C will be avoided by 2100 due to the Amendment.[119]

Further factors contributing to the success of the Montreal Protocol include, as also noted above, its commitment to the principle of common but differentiated responsibilities;[120] the participation of developing countries;[121] and the positive involvement of industry.[122] Rockström et al argue that '[o]n balance, the case of stratospheric ozone is a good example where concerted human effort and wise decision making seem to have enabled us to stay within [the] planetary boundary [for stratospheric ozone depletion]'.[123]

Despite these strengths, the ozone regime also contains several gaps, which are now outlined.

4.2 *Gaps in the Ozone Regime*

4.2.1 The Montreal Protocol Does Not Regulate Banks of HFCs

In the first place, the Montreal Protocol does not control the 'banks'[124] of ODSs that are contained in, amongst others, air conditioning, refrigeration and firefighting equipment, which will eventually leak into the environment.[125] In contrast to CFCs, which were largely used in 'rapid-release applications' such as spray cans and solvents, HFCs are primarily contained in applications that involve containment, particularly refrigerators and air conditioners.[126]

This weakness contributes to the fact that 'once produced, ODSs are in "no treaty territory"'.[127] Velders, Solomon and Daniel[128] demonstrate that HFC

118 Roberts (n61) 220.
119 WMO (n2), ES.3.
120 Gonzalez, Taddonio, and Sherman (n79) 124–125.
121 DeSombre (n36) 69–75.
122 Falkner (n45); Birmpili (n64) 427.
123 Rockström and others, 'Planetary Boundaries' (n16) 12.
124 Banks are 'reservoirs of produced and stockpiled, but not yet emitted, chemicals'; see Benjamin Sovacool and others, 'Climate change and industrial F-gases: A critical and systematic review of developments, sociotechnical systems and policy options for reducing synthetic greenhouse gas emissions' (2021) 141 Renewable and Sustainable Energy Reviews 110759.
125 Gonzalez, Taddonio, and Sherman (n79) 123, 127; Megan Lickley and others, 'Quantifying Contributions of Chlorofluorocarbon Banks to Emissions and Impacts on the Ozone Layer and Climate' (2020) 11 Nature Communications 380.
126 Guus Velders, Susan Solomon and John Daniel, 'Growth of climate change commitments from HFC banks and emissions' (2014) 14 Atmos. Chem. Phys. 9, 4564.
127 Gonzalez, Taddonio, and Sherman (n79) 127.
128 Velders, Solomon, and Daniel (n127) 4569.

emissions continue to be released for 20 years after production is phased out and, furthermore, that HFCs continue to contribute to radiative forcing for a further several decades. Thus, 'the buildup of HFC banks [for example, in refrigerators and air conditioners] represents a new challenge to climate change prevention efforts'.[129] Furthermore, developing countries are required to only begin to phase down HFCs from 2029 onwards. In the meantime, the production and consumption of HFCs are increasing, and accumulating in banks, which will leak at unknown future dates.

In response to this concern, it has been proposed that HFCs contained in, *inter alia*, refrigeration and air-conditioning equipment should be recovered and destroyed.[130] However, Velders, Solomon and Daniel[131] point out that many millions of refrigeration and air conditioning units exist, which makes the subsequent recovery and destruction of HFC banks more complex than reducing production in the first place. They, therefore, argue that maximum benefits can be achieved through the destruction of HFC banks combined with the phase-out of HFCs, which would reduce the number of HFC banks.[132]

4.2.2 The Montreal Protocol Does Not Adequately Regulate HFCs Produced as By-Products

As discussed above, HFC-23 is a potent greenhouse gas as well as a by-product of HCFC-22 production. Although the Protocol requires the destruction of HFC-23 to the extent practicable, observations show that HFC-23 emissions are increasing – contrary to countries' reports that HFC-23 is being phased out.[133] Indeed, from 2011 to 2019, the atmospheric abundance of HFC-23 increased by 35 per cent.[134] It has been argued that Parties are not destroying their emissions of HFC-23 and reporting on such emissions as required under the Montreal Protocol.[135] It has been argued that if the emission of HFC-23 does not decline soon, this will undermine the successes of the Montreal Protocol.[136]

---

129 Gonzalez, Taddonio, and Sherman (n79) 127.

130 ibid, 126.

131 Velders, Solomon, and Daniel (n127) 4565.

132 ibid, 4570; Susan Solomon, Joseph Alcamo, and Akkihebbal Ravishankara, 'Unfinished Business after Five Decades of Ozone-layer Science and Policy' (2020) 11 Nature Communications 4272, 4.

133 Kieran Stanley and others, 'Increase in Global Emissions of HFC-23 Despite Near-total Expected Reductions' (2020) 11 Nature Communications 397, 4570.

134 Gulev and others (n8) 22.

135 Jane Palmer, 'The HFC Challenge: Can the Montreal Protocol Continue Its Winning Streak?' (Mongabay, 5 May 2021) <https://news.mongabay.com/2021/05/the-hfc-challenge-can-the-montreal-protocol-continue-its-winning-streak/> accessed 8 December 2021.

136 Solomon, Alcamo and Ravishankara (n133).

To address this weakness, the Montreal Protocol should arguably restrict the production of HFC-23 in the first place, for example, by 'requiring de minimis HFC emissions from HCFC-22'.[137]

4.2.3 The Montreal Protocol Does Not Control Substances that Are Used as Feedstocks

Related to the above concern, the Montreal Protocol does not control or restrict the production of ODSs, when produced purely to manufacture other substances. As discussed above, 'production' is defined in the Montreal Protocol so as to exclude ODSs that are used entirely as feedstock in the manufacture of other chemicals.[138] HCFC-22, which has a GWP of 1 780[139] and results in the emission of HFC-23 as a by-product, is manufactured and used as a feedstock to produce other substances such as Teflon;[140] and its atmospheric abundance has increased by at least 15 per cent from 2011 to 2019.[141] Other ODSs – including CFC-113, HFC-143a, HCFC-142b, which have GWPs of 6 080, 5 080 and 2 070 respectively[142] – are used as feedstocks to produce various materials, including plastics.[143] While '[t]he feedstock exemptions were premised on the assumption that feedstocks presented an insignificant threat to the environment; experience has shown that this is incorrect'.[144]

In response to this concern, it has been proposed that the scope of feedstock exemptions be narrowed.[145] However, critical uses of feedstocks could still be exempted, such as the production of substances to rapidly replace high-GWP HFCs and the use of HCFC-22 to produce polytetrafluoroethylene (PTFE) for medical applications until appropriate alternatives are found.[146] Andersen et al argue that this is consistent with the approach under the Montreal Protocol 'where requirements are strengthened in response to new scientific findings and technological advances'.[147]

---

137 Gonzalez, Taddonio, and Sherman (n79) 126.
138 Montreal Protocol (n1), Article 1(5).
139 WMO (n2), Table A-1.
140 Palmer (n136).
141 Gulev and others (n8) Table 2.2, pp. 2–19.
142 WMO (n2) Table A-1.
143 Andersen and others (n112) Table 2, p. 3.
144 ibid, 1.
145 Gonzalez, Taddonio, and Sherman (n79) 126; Andersen and others (n112).
146 Andersen and others (n112) 7.
147 ibid, 6.

Amending the Montreal Protocol to narrow such exemptions would have socio-ecological benefits, arising not only from reduced ozone depletion and greenhouse gas emissions, but also from the reduced production of plastics.[148] This would also contribute to reducing the unauthorised and illegal production of, *inter alia*, HFCs.[149]

This process could be guided by assessments produced by the various assessment panels established under the Montreal Protocol, including the TEAP, the SAP and the EEAP.[150]

4.2.4 Substitute Substances May Give Rise to Other Problems

Although the Montreal Protocol has addressed one case of environmental problem shifting,[151] namely rising greenhouse gas emissions due to the increased uptake of HFCs, there is the potential for further problem shifting to arise as a result of the substances that are used to replace HFCs, such as hydrofluoroolefins (HFOs). While HFOs have low ODPs *and* low GWPs, they degrade to produce trifluoroacetic acid (TFA), a 'persistent toxic chemical'.[152] Their presence has been detected in humans; plants, including crops consumed by humans; and aquatic environments; and may accumulate in sensitive ecosystems like wetlands.[153] TFA has been found to be 'toxic to many organisms and can in principle lead to acidification of water bodies. … These persistent and mobile compounds have been identified as reason for concern, as they lead to irreversible contamination'.[154] Pickard et al also suggest that 'CFC replacements introduced as a result of the Montreal Protocol are likely the major source of TFA to the Arctic'.[155] HFOs also degrade to produce ozone, which contributes to ground-level pollution, particularly in urban areas. Their potential long-term impacts are not yet known,[156] and it has been argued that HFOs 'cannot be

148 ibid, 4–5.
149 ibid, 7.
150 ibid, 5.
151 Kim and van Asselt (n17).
152 Stephen Montzka, 'Hydrofluorocarbons (HFCs)' in WMO (n2) 2.4.
153 Heidi Pickard and others, 'Ice Core Record of Persistent Short-chain Fluorinated Alkyl Acids: Evidence of the Impact from Global Environmental Regulations' (2020) 47 Geophysical Research Letters e2020GL087535, 2.
154 Flerlage, Velders, and de Boer (n20) 12–13.
155 Pickard and others (n154) 7.
156 Montzka and others (n153) 2.34.

regarded as overall sustainable alternatives'.[157] Measurements of atmospheric concentrations reveal that the consumption of HFOs is increasing,[158] and it is projected that the deposition of TFA in the environment will increase further as HFC-134a (used in mobile air conditioners) is replaced by HFO-1234yf.[159]

Steffen et al argue that '[t]he risks associated with the introduction of novel entities into the Earth system are exemplified by the release of CFCs (chlorofluorocarbons), which are very useful synthetic chemicals that were thought to be harmless but had unexpected, dramatic impacts on the stratospheric ozone layer.[160] In effect, humanity is repeatedly running such global-scale experiments but not yet applying the insights from previous experience to new applications'.[161] Arguably, such 'global-scale experiments' are being repeated with the introduction of HFO-1234yf.

In addition, natural refrigerants (which occur naturally in the environment), including hydrocarbons, ammonia, water and CO_2, have been (re-)introduced to some extent in certain sectors. However, they are not necessarily unproblematic. For example, most are flammable, and ammonia is toxic.[162] Furthermore, while CO_2 has a significantly lower GWP than HFCs, it does remain a greenhouse gas.

In response to these concerns, De Graaf et al note that the use of natural refrigerants would require the introduction of appropriate safety measures and trained personnel.[163] More broadly, Flerlage, Velders and De Boer note the importance of considering '[a]dditional safety and environmental concerns beyond global warming' in the analysis of HFC alternatives.[164] Pickard et al recommend that the persistence and mobility of chemicals should be considered before replacing one class of chemicals with another.[165] Similarly, the

157 Daniel de Graaf, 'Hydrofluorocarbon Emission Reduction: A Crucial Contribution to Climate Protection: Proposals to Enhance European Climate Ambition' (2021) <https://www.umweltbundesamt.de/sites/default/files/medien/2546/publikationen/2021-05-04_scientific_opinion_paper_hfcs_climate_protection_contribution_final.pdf> accessed 15 December 2021, 9.

158 Flerlage, Velders, and de Boer (n20) 12.

159 Pickard and others (n154) 7.

160 Will Steffen and others, 'Planetary Boundaries: Guiding Human Development on a Changing Planet' (2015) 347(6223) Science 736.

161 Steffen and others (n16).

162 de Graaf (n158) 8.

163 ibid, 9.

164 Flerlage, Velders, and de Boer (n20) 13.

165 Pickard and others (n154) 7.

importance of examining the '"life-cycle" impacts' of substitute substances – in relation to both society and the environment – has been highlighted.[166]

4.2.5 Obtaining Accurate Data Is Complex

In terms of the Montreal Protocol, as discussed above, Parties are required to report on their production as well as imports and exports of ODSs. Under the climate regime, Parties are required to report on their HFC emissions.[167] However, Parties to the Montreal Protocol that have not ratified the Kigali Amendment are not required to report on their production, imports and exports of HFCs. This means that obtaining a complete picture is challenging.

In regard to HFC-23 specifically, research reveals a large discrepancy (of 24.4 gigagrams (Gg) between 2015 and 2017) between the HFC-23 emissions that were reported and those that were actually observed in the atmosphere.[168] While it is not possible to identify the precise cause, Stanley et al suggest that 'it is highly likely that developing countries have been unsuccessful in meeting their reported emissions reductions. Alternatively, or additionally, there may be substantial unreported production of HCFC-22 at unknown locations resulting in unaccounted-for HFC-23 by-product being vented to the atmosphere'.[169]

Similarly, in regard to HFCs generally, there is a discrepancy between the HFC emissions reported by developed countries and the global HFC emissions that have been estimated based on atmospheric measurement data. Thus, the emission estimates of HFCs provided by Annex I (developed) countries to the UNFCCC account for less than half of the emissions that have been estimated based on atmospheric data.[170] While China's HFC emissions are estimated to account for approximately 56 per cent of the HFC emissions of non-Annex I (developing) countries, there is still an unexplained gap, and '[n]umerous studies … share the conclusion that China is not the only big non-Annex I emitter causing the gap in emissions between reported values from Annex I countries to the UNFCCC and global emissions derived from atmospheric measurements'.[171]

166 UNEP, *HFCs: A Critical Link in Protecting Climate and the Ozone Layer* (2011) <https://www.unep.org/resources/report/hfcs-critical-link-protecting-climate-and-ozone-layer> accessed 9 December 2021, 12.

167 United Nations Framework Convention on Climate Change (UNFCCC) (signed 4 June 1992, entered into force 21 March 1994) 1771 UNTS 107, Articles 4(1) and 12(1).

168 Stanley and others (n134) 4.

169 ibid, 2.

170 Flerlage, Velders, and de Boer (n20) 7.

171 ibid, 13.

The research of Flerlage, Velders and De Boer[172] illustrates the difficulty of obtaining accurate data including due to the use of different methods to estimate emissions, the unavailability of data in certain regions, the inconsistency in reporting, the one-off nature of atmospheric studies, and the seasonal variability of some HFCs. In addition, emissions of certain HFCs are not reported to the UNFCCC due to confidentiality issues (to protect businesses' competitiveness).[173] Furthermore, exports of products or waste containing HFCs are not included in the inventories of exporting (likely developed) countries that are reported to the UNFCCC. 'While the export may be better recorded, it may be that imports into waste processing countries are not accounted for in bottom-up estimates'.[174] While not confirmed, this could partly explain the gap between reported and observed HFC emissions.[175] In addition, since the emissions 'would be accounted for in countries where only the disposal happens but the benefits of the product were not used, this method of accounting raises fairness issues'.[176]

In response to these concerns, it has been proposed that measurement methods be harmonised and, furthermore, that strategically locating measurement stations would enable additional data to be obtained, thereby enabling emissions from further regions to be quantified and decreasing the uncertainty of top-down atmospheric emission estimates.[177]

5 Strengthening the Global Regulation of HFCs: Enhancing Cooperation under International Law

In addition to addressing the gaps identified above, a more substantive shift relates to enhancing the coordination of measures related to HFC regulation under international law. Although HFCs are regulated directly under the ozone regime – which has been the focus in this chapter – 'this does not mean that

172 ibid.
173 Environmental Protection Agency (EPA) 'Revisions and Confidentiality Determinations For Data Elements Under the Greenhouse Gas Reporting Rule' (21 June 2022) <https://www.federalregister.gov/documents/2022/06/21/2022-09660/revisions-and-confidentiality-determinations-for-data-elements-under-the-greenhouse-gas-reporting> accessed 15 September 2022.
174 Flerlage, Velders, and de Boer (n20) 5.
175 ibid, 5–6.
176 ibid, 6.
177 ibid, 13; see also Sovacool and others (n125).

HFCs are outside the scope of the UNFCCC or the Paris Agreement'.[178] Indeed, HFCs are a listed greenhouse gas under the Kyoto Protocol and, importantly, they fall under the enhanced transparency framework established by the Paris Agreement,[179] which includes obligations in regard to reporting. Furthermore, many countries have dealt with HFCs in their nationally determined contributions (see Chapter 3 of this book). This points to the need to coordinate their regulation under both the ozone and climate regimes, including to address the 'no treaty territory'[180] that ODSs, including HFCs, fall into once produced.

There has previously been cooperation between bodies under the climate and ozone regimes. For example, the Intergovernmental Panel on Climate Change and the TEAP under the Montreal Protocol together prepared a Special Report regarding the impacts of ODS substitutes on the global climate system.[181] Furthermore, the TEAP's Energy Efficiency Task Force is exploring the potential coordination of measures to phase down HFCs and enhance energy efficiency, which would also have climate co-benefits. In addition, the Task Force has suggested that developing countries switch directly from HCFCs to low-GWP alternatives, thereby bypassing HFCs.[182]

Furthermore, Parties under the Montreal Protocol explicitly acknowledge the potential climatic effects of emissions of ODSs[183] and have, in several decisions, acknowledged the link between the ozone and climate regimes. For example, already in 2007, Parties agreed that projects that focused on substitutes that 'minimize other impacts on the environment, including the climate, taking into account global-warming potential, energy use and other relevant factors' should be prioritised.[184]

---

178 Dario Piselli and Harro van Asselt, 'Planetary Boundaries and Regime Interaction in International Law' in French, D and Kotzé, LJ (eds) *Research Handbook on Law, Governance and Planetary Boundaries* (Edward Elgar 2021) 137.

179 Paris Agreement (n28) Article 13.

180 Gonzalez, Taddonio, and Sherman (n79) 127.

181 Bert Metz and others (eds), *Safeguarding the Ozone Layer and the Global Climate System: Issues Related to Hydrofluorocarbons and Perfluorocarbons* (Cambridge University Press 2005).

182 IISD, 'Summary of the Second Part of the 43rd Meeting of the Open-ended Working Group of the Parties to the Montreal Protocol: 14–17 July 2021' (2021) <https://enb.iisd.org/sites/default/files/2021-07/enb19156e.pdf> accessed 12 September 2022; Sovacool and others (n125); Pallav Purohit and others, 'Achieving Paris Climate Goals Calls for Increasing Ambition of the Kigali Amendment' (2022) 12 Nature Climate Change 339–342.

183 Montreal Protocol (n1) Preamble.

184 UNEP, 'Decision XIX/6: Adjustments to the Montreal Protocol with regard to Annex C, Group I, substances (hydrochlorofluorocarbons)' (UNEP/OzL.Pro.19/7) (21 2007) <https://ozone.unep.org/Meeting_Documents/mop/19mop/MOP-19-7E.pdf> accessed 5 May 2022, para. 11(b).

Further cooperation and the seeking of co-benefits to deal with some of the challenges identified above should be encouraged. For example, it has been proposed that a GWP-limit for substances used in, *inter alia*, air conditioning and refrigeration systems should be specified.[185] Under the climate regime, ensuring that HFCs are specifically included in country Parties' nationally determined contributions could strengthen HFC-related action.[186] This is also elaborated on in Chapter 3 of this book. In addition, further greenhouse gas emissions could be avoided by improving energy efficiency in refrigeration and air conditioning equipment and by improving insulation materials and building designs so that there is a reduced need for air conditioning.[187] Purohit et al project that '[w]hen fully implementing the technical potential for energy efficiency improvements, we estimate that compliance with the [Kigali Amendment] can bring electricity savings that correspond to more than 20% of the world's entire future electricity consumption'.[188] This would have further (co-)benefits in the form of reduced emissions of sulfur dioxide, nitrogen oxides and particulate matter with associated positive implications for human health and ecosystems.[189] Furthermore, since ODSs, including HFCs, are used in the production of plastics,[190] cooperation under the Montreal Protocol and a new globally binding treaty on plastics[191] should ideally be promoted.

6 Conclusion

Hailed as one of the most successful international environmental law agreements to date, the Montreal Protocol has thus far been successful in regard to protecting the ozone layer. Furthermore, even though HFCs do not deplete stratospheric ozone, they have been brought under the control of the Montreal

185 de Graaf (n158) 16.

186 Katherine Ross and others, 'Strengthening Nationally Determined Contributions to Catalyze Actions that Reduce Short-lived Climate Pollutants' (2018) <https://www.wri.org/research/strengthening-nationally-determined-contributions-catalyze-actions-reduce-short-lived> accessed 6 December 2021, 23–24.

187 see CCAC (n4).

188 Purohit and others (n26) 11321.

189 ibid, 11322.

190 Andersen and others (n112).

191 United Nations Environment Assembly of the United Nations Environment Programme (UNEA) *Draft Resolution: End Plastic Pollution: Towards an International Legally Binding Instrument* (UNEP/E.A.5/L.23/Rev.1) (2022) <https://wedocs.unep.org/bitstream/handle/20.500.11822/38525/k2200647_-_unep-ea-5-l-23-rev-1_-_advance.pdf?sequence=1&isAllowed=y> accessed 4 March 2022.

Protocol, with the result that the Montreal Protocol has also been beneficial for the climate. Despite these successes, several gaps have been identified under the Montreal Protocol. While some gapss could be addressed, for example, through the refinement of existing definitions and closing of loopholes, on a broader scale, it will also be important that further opportunities to coordinate efforts under different international law regimes are harnessed to ensure the continued effectiveness of the ozone regime and to guard against future problem shifting.

Bibliography

Andersen, SO 'Lessons from the Stratospheric Ozone Layer Protection for Climate' (2015) 5 *Journal of Environmental Studies and Science* 143–162.

Andersen, SO, Gao, S, Carvalho, S, Ferris, T, Gonzalez, M, Sherman, NJ, Wei, Y and Zaelke, D 'Narrowing Feedstock Exemptions under the Montreal Protocol has Multiple Environmental Benefits' (2021) 118 PNAS 49.

Andersen, SO, Halberstadt, ML and Borgford-Parnell, N 'Stratospheric Ozone, Global Warming, and the Principle of Unintended Consequences – An Ongoing Science and Policy Success Story' (2013) 63 *Journal of the Air & Waste Management Association* 607–647.

Andersen, SO and Madhava Sarma, K (eds) *Protecting the Ozone Layer: the United Nations History* (Earthscan 2002).

Biden, JR 'A Message to the Senate on the Amendment of the Montreal Protocol on Substances that Deplete the Ozone Layer' (16 November 2021) <https://www.whitehouse.gov/briefing-room/statements-releases/2021/11/16/a-message-to-the-senate-on-the-amendment-to-the-montreal-protocol-on-substances-that-deplete-the-ozone-layer/> accessed 11 February 2021.

Birmpili, T 'Montreal Protocol at 30: the Governance Structure, the Evolution, and the Kigali Amendment' (2018) 350 *Comptes Rendus Geoscience* 425–431.

Brack, D 'National Legislation on Hydrofluorocarbons' (11 September 2015) <http://www.igsd.org/documents/NationalLegislationonHydrofluorocarbons_9.11.151.pdf> accessed 20 December 2022.

Centre for Climate and Energy Solutions (C2ES) 'Short-lived Climate Pollutants' (no date) <https://www.c2es.org/content/short-lived-climate-pollutants/> accessed 10 December 2021.

Climate & Clean Air Coalition (a) 'Hydrofluorocarbons (HFCs)' <https://www.ccacoalition.org/en/slcps/hydrofluorocarbons-hfcs> accessed 3 December 2021.

Climate & Clean Air Coalition (b) 'Short-lived Climate Pollutants (SLCPs)' <https://www.ccacoalition.org/en/content/short-lived-climate-pollutants-slcps> accessed 10 February 2022.

De Graaf, D, Elsner, C, Hoffmann, G, Martens, K, Thalheim, D and Plehn, W 'Hydrofluorocarbon Emission Reduction: a Crucial Contribution to Climate Protection: Proposals to Enhance European Climate Ambition' (2021) <https://www.umweltbundesamt.de/sites/default/files/medien/2546/publikationen/2021-05-04_scientific_opinion_paper_hfcs_climate_protection_contribution_final.pdf> accessed 15 December 2021.

DeSombre, ER 'The Experience of the Montreal Protocol: Particularly Remarkable, and Remarkably Particular' (2000) 19 *Journal of Environmental Law* 49–81.

Dryzek, JS 'Institutions for the Anthropocene: Governance in a Changing Earth System' (2016) 4 *British Journal of Political Science* 937–956.

Du Toit, L 'Stratospheric Ozone Depletion' in French, D and Kotzé, LJ (eds) *Research Handbook on Law, Governance and Planetary Boundaries* (Edward Elgar 2021) 261–277.

Environmental Protection Agency (EPA) 'Revisions and Confidentiality Determinations For Data Elements Under the Greenhouse Gas Reporting Rule' (21 June 2022) <https://www.federalregister.gov/documents/2022/06/21/2022-09660/revisions-and-confidentiality-determinations-for-data-elements-under-the-greenhouse-gas-reporting> accessed 15 September 2022.

Falkner, R 'The Business of Ozone Layer Protection: Corporate Power in Regime Evolution' in Levy, DL and Newell, PJ (eds) *The Business of Global Environmental Governance* (MIT Press 2005) 105–134.

Farman, JC, Gardiner, BG and Shanklin, JD 'Large Losses of Total Ozone in Antarctica Reveal Seasonal ClO_x/NO_x Interaction' (1985) 315 *Nature* 207–210.

Flerlage, H, Velders, GJM and De Boer, J 'A Review of Bottom-up and Top-down Emission Estimates of Hydrofluorocarbons (HFCs) in Different Parts of the World' (2021) 283, *Chemosphere* 131208.

Ghosh, A 'Making Sense on its Own Terms: India in the HFC and Aviation Negotiations' in Dubash, NK (ed) *India in a Warming World* (Oxford University Press 2019) 230–249.

Gillespie, A (2006) *Climate Change, Ozone Depletion and Air Pollution: Legal Commentaries with Policy and Science Considerations* (Martinus Nijhoff Publishers 2006).

Godin-Beekmann, S, Newman, P and Petropavlovskikh, I, '30th anniversary of the Montreal Protocol: from the safeguard of the ozone layer to the protection of the Earth's climate' 350 *Comptes Rendus Geoscience* 7.

Gonzalez, M, Taddonio, KN and Sherman, NJ 'The Montreal Protocol: How Today's Successes Offer a Pathway to the Future' (2020) 5 *Journal of Environmental Studies and Sciences* 122–129.

Goyal, R, England, MH, Sen Gupta, A and Jucker, M 'Reduction in Surface Climate Change Achieved by the 1987 Montreal Protocol' (2019) 14 *Environmental Research Letters* 124041.

Group of Eight (G8), 'Responsible Leadership for a Sustainable Future' (2009) <http://www.g8.utoronto.ca/summit/2009laquila/2009-declaration.pdf> accessed 22 December 2022.

Gulev, SK, et al 'Changing State of the Climate System' in Masson-Delmotte, V, et al (eds) *Climate Change 2021: the Physical Science Basis. Contribution of Working Group I to the Sixth Assessment Report of the Intergovernmental Panel on Climate Change* (2021) <https://www.ipcc.ch/report/ar6/wg1/#FullReport> accessed 10 December 2021.

International Institute for Sustainable Development (IISD) 'Summary of the Twenty-second Meeting of the Parties to the Montreal Protocol: 8–12 November 2010' (15 November 2010) <https://enb.iisd.org/ozone/mop22/> accessed 12 September 2022.

International Institute for Sustainable Development (IISD) 'Summary of the Twenty-seventh Meeting of the Parties to the Montreal Protocol: 1–5 November 2015' (8 November 2015) <https://s3.us-west-2.amazonaws.com/enb.iisd.org/archive/download/pdf/enb19115e.pdf?X-Amz-Content-Sha256=UNSIGNED-PAYLOAD&X-Amz-Algorithm=AWS4-HMAC-SHA256&X-Amz-Credential=AKIA6QW3YWTJ6YORWEEL%2F20220513%2Fus-west-2%2Fs3%2Faws4_request&X-Amz-Date=20220513T132434Z&X-Amz-SignedHeaders=host&X-Amz-Expires=60&X-Amz-Signature=45d53e909320d6a1f17ac2c58a634b33b9e89110949857 25af704e6c08027333> accessed 5 May 2022.

International Institute for Sustainable Development (IISD) (2016) 'Summary of the Twenty-eighth Meeting of the Parties to the Montreal Protocol: 10–14 October 2016' (18 October 2016) <https://s3.us-west-2.amazonaws.com/enb.iisd.org/archive/download/pdf/enb19131e.pdf?X-Amz-Content-Sha256=UNSIGNED-PAYLOAD&X-Amz-Algorithm=AWS4-HMAC-SHA256&X-Amz-Credential=AKIA6QW3YWTJ6YORWEEL%2F20220513%2Fus-west-2%2Fs3%2Faws4_request&X-Amz-Date=20220513T132029Z&X-Amz-SignedHeaders=host&X-Amz-Expires=60&X-Amz-Signature=80bca9fd92c0c777d32670d9e9f061d2f0d7ffc6273ca96efd8f8ec8695abf95> accessed 5 May 2022.

International Institute for Sustainable Development (IISD) 'Summary of the Second Part of the 43rd Meeting of the Open-ended Working Group of the Parties to the Montreal Protocol: 14–17 July 2021' (2021) 19(156) <https://enb.iisd.org/sites/default/files/2021-07/enb19156e.pdf> accessed 12 September 2022.

Kim, RE and Bosselmann, K 'Operationalising Sustainable Development: Ecological Integrity as a *Grundnorm* of International Law' (2015) 24 RECIEL 194–208.

Kim, RE and Van Asselt, H 'Global Governance: Problem Shifting in the Anthropocene and the Limits of International Law' in Morgera, E and Kulovesi, K (eds) *Research Handbook on International Law and Natural Resources* (Edward Elgar 2016) 473–495.

Kyoto Protocol to the United Nations Framework Convention on Climate Change (1997) 2303 UNTS 148, opened for signature 16 March 1998, entered into force 16 February 2005 <https://treaties.un.org/doc/Treaties/1998/09/19980921%2004-41%20PM/Ch_XXVII_07_ap.pdf> accessed 24 March 2022.

Lieberman, BC 'Stratosperic ozone depletion and the Montreal Protocol: a critical analysis' (1994) 2 *Buffalo Environmental Law Journal* 1–32.

Lickley, M, Solomon, S, Fletcher, S, Velders, GJM, et al 'Quantifying Contributions of Chlorofluorocarbon Banks to Emissions and Impacts on the Ozone Layer and Climate' (2020) 11 *Nature Communications* 380.

Masson-Delmotte, V, et al (eds) *Global Warming of 1.5°C: an IPCC Special Report on the Impacts of Global Warming of 1.5°C above Pre-industrial Levels and Related Global Greenhouse Gas Emission Pathways, in the Context of Strengthening the Global Response to the Threat of Climate Change, Sustainable Development, and Efforts to Eradicate Poverty* (Intergovernmental Panel on Climate Change 2018).

Metz, B, Kuijpers, L, Solomon, S, Andersen, SO, Davidson, O, Pons, J, De Jager, D, Kestin, T, Manning, M and Meyer, E (eds) *Safeguarding the Ozone Layer and the Global Climate System: Issues Related to Hydrofluorocarbons and Perfluorocarbons*. (Cambridge University Press 2005).

Molina, MJ and Rowland, FS 'Stratospheric Sink for Chlorofluoromethanes: Chlorine Atom-catalysed Destruction of Ozone' (1974) 249 *Nature* 810–812.

Montreal Protocol on Substances that Deplete the Ozone Layer (1987) 1522 UNTS 3, opened for signature 16 September 1987, entered into force 1 January 1989 <https://ozone.unep.org/sites/default/files/2019-12/The%20Ozone%20Treaties%20EN%20-%20WEB_final.pdf> accessed 10 December 2021.

Montzka, SA, et al 'Hydrofluorocarbons (HFCs)' in *Scientific Assessment of Ozone Depletion: 2018* (Global Ozone Research and Monitoring Project – Report No. 58) (2018) <https://csl.noaa.gov/assessments/ozone/2018/downloads/2018OzoneAssessment.pdf> accessed 9 December 2021 (World Meteorological Organisation 2018) 2.1–2.56.

Nanda, VP 'Stratospheric Ozone Depletion: a Challenge for International Environmental Law and Policy' (1989) 10 *Michigan Journal of International Law* 482–525.

Newman, PA 'The Way Forward for Montreal Protocol Science' (2018) 350 *Comptes Rendus Geoscience* 442–447.

Ozone Secretariat 'Institutions' <https://ozone.unep.org/institutions> accessed 12 September 2022.

Palmer, J 'The HFC Challenge: Can the Montreal Protocol Continue Its Winning Streak?' (*Mongabay*, 5 May 2021) <https://news.mongabay.com/2021/05/the-hfc-challenge-can-the-montreal-protocol-continue-its-winning-streak/> accessed 8 December 2021.

Pickard, HM, et al 'Ice Core Record of Persistent Short-chain Fluorinated Alkyl Acids: Evidence of the Impact from Global Environmental Regulations' (2020) 47 *Geophysical Research Letters* e2020GL087535.

Piselli, D and Van Asselt, H 'Planetary Boundaries and Regime Interaction in International Law' in French, D and Kotzé, LJ (eds) *Research Handbook on Law, Governance and Planetary Boundaries* (Edward Elgar 2021) 125–146.

Pisoft, P, Sacha, P, Polvani, LM, Añel, JA, De la Torre, L, Eichinger, R, Foelsche, U, Huszar, P, Jacobi, C, Karlicky, J, Kuchar, A, Miksovsky, J, Zak, M and Rieder, HE 'Stratospheric Contraction Caused by Increasing Greenhouse Gases' (2021) 16) *Environmental Research Letters* 064038.

Polvani, LM, Previdi, M, England, MR, Chiodo, G and Smith, KL 'Substantial Twentieth-century Arctic Warming Caused by Ozone-depleting Substances' (2020) 10 *Nature Climate Change* 130–133.

Purohit, P, and others, 'Achieving Paris Climate Goals Calls for Increasing Ambition of the Kigali Amendment' (2022) 12 Nature Climate Change 339–342.

Purohit, P, and others, 'Electricity Savings and Greenhouse Gas Emission Reductions from Global Phase-down of Hydrofluorocarbons' (2020) 20 Atmospheric Chemistry and Physics 11305–11327.

Roberts, MW 'Finishing the Job: the Montreal Protocol Moves to Phase Down hydrofluorocarbons' (2017) 26 RECIEL 220–230.

Rockström, J, Steffen, W, Noone, K, Persson, Å, et al 'A Safe Operating Space for Humanity' (2009a) 461(24) *Nature* 472–475.

Rockström, J, Steffen, W, Noone, K, Persson, Å, et al 'Planetary Boundaries: Exploring the Safe Operating Space for Humanity' (2009b) 14 *Ecology and Society*, article 32.

Ross, K, and others, 'Strengthening Nationally Determined Contributions to Catalyze Actions that Reduce Short-lived Climate Pollutants' (2018) <https://www.wri.org/research/strengthening-nationally-determined-contributions-catalyze-actions-reduce-short-lived> accessed 6 December 2021.

Sherwood Rowland, F 'Chlorofluorocarbons and the Depletion of Stratospheric Ozone' (1989) 77 *American Scientist* 36–45.

Sinclair, L 'The Science of Ozone Depletion: from Theory to Certainty' in Andersen, SO and Madhava Sarma, K (eds) *Protecting the Ozone Layer: the United Nations History* (Earthscan 2002) 1–41.

Solomon, S 'Stratospheric Ozone Depletion: a Review of Concepts and History' (1999) 37 *Reviews of Geophysics* 275–316.

Solomon, S, Alcamo, J and Ravishankara, AR 'Unfinished Business after Five Decades of Ozone-layer Science and Policy' (2020) 11 *Nature Communications* 4272.

Sovacool, BK, Griffiths, S, Kim, J and Bazilian, M, 'Climate change and industrial F-gases: a critical and systematic review of developments, sociotechnical systems and policy options for reducing synthetic greenhouse gas emissions' (2021) 141 *Renewable and Sustainable Energy Reviews* 110759.

Stanley, KM, Say, D, Mühle, J, Harth, CM, et al 'Increase in Global Emissions of HFC-23 Despite Near-total Expected Reductions' (2020) 11 *Nature Communications* 397.

Steffen, W, Richardson, K, Rockström, J, Cornell, SE, et al 'Planetary Boundaries: Guiding Human Development on a Changing Planet' (2015) 347(6223) *Science* 736.

The White House 'Joint Statement: the United States and India: Enduring Partners in the 21st Century' (7 June 2016) <https://obamawhitehouse.archives.gov/the-press-office/2016/06/07/joint-statement-united-states-and-india-enduring-global-partners-21st> accessed 12 September 2022.

United Nations Climate Change 'Nationally Determined Contributions Registry' <https://unfccc.int/NDCREG> accessed 20 December 2022.

United Nations Environment Assembly of the United Nations Environment Programme (UNEA) *Draft Resolution: End Plastic Pollution: towards an International Legally Binding Instrument* (UNEP/E.A.5/L.23/Rev.1) (2 March 2022) <https://wedocs.unep.org/bitstream/handle/20.500.11822/38525/k2200647_-_unep-ea-5-l-23-rev-1_-_advance.pdf?sequence=1&isAllowed=y> accessed 4 March 2022.

United Nations Environment Programme (UNEP) *Report of the Second Meeting of the Parties to the Montreal Protocol on Substances that Deplete the Ozone Layer* (UNEP/OzL.Pro.2/3) (29 June 1990) <https://ozone.unep.org/Meeting_Documents/mop/02mop/MOP_2.shtml> accessed 5 May 2022.

United Nations Environment Programme (UNEP) *Report of the Fourth Meeting of the Parties to the Montreal Protocol on Substances that Deplete the Ozone Layer* (UNEP/OzL.Pro.4/15) (25 November 1992) <https://ozone.unep.org/sites/default/files/2019-04/MOP-4-15E.pdf> accessed 5 May 2022.

United Nations Environment Programme (UNEP) *Report of the Eleventh Meeting of the Parties to the Montreal Protocol on Substances that Deplete the Ozone Layer* (UNEP/OzL.Pro.11/10) (17 December 1999) <https://ozone.unep.org/sites/default/files/2019-04/MOP-11-10E.pdf> accessed 5 May 2022.

United Nations Environment Programme (UNEP) 'Decision XIX/6: Adjustments to the Montreal Protocol with regard to Annex C, Group I, substances (hydrochlorofluorocarbons)' *Report of the Nineteenth Meeting of the Parties to the Montreal Protocol on Substances that Deplete the Ozone Layer* (UNEP/OzL.Pro.19/7) (21 September 2007) <https://ozone.unep.org/Meeting_Documents/mop/19mop/MOP-19-7E.pdf> accessed 5 May 2022.

United Nations Environment Programme (UNEP) *Report of the Twenty-Second Meeting of the Parties to the Montreal Protocol on Substances that Deplete the Ozone Layer* (UNEP/OzL.Pro.22/9) (26 November 2010) <https://ozone.unep.org/Meeting_Documents/mop/22mop/MOP-22-9E.doc> accessed 12 September 2022.

United Nations Environment Programme (UNEP) *HFCs: a Critical Link in Protecting Climate and the Ozone Layer* (2011)<https://www.unep.org/resources/report/hfcs-critical-link-protecting-climate-and-ozone-layer> accessed 9 December 2021.

United Nations Environment Programme (UNEP) *Report of the Thirty-fifth Meeting of the Open-ended Working Group of the Parties to the Montreal Protocol on Substances that Deplete the Ozone Layer* (UNEP/OzL.Pro.WG.1/35/6) (5 May 2015) <https://ozone.unep.org/system/files/documents/OEWG-35-6E.pdf> accessed 5 May 2022.

United Nations Environment Programme (UNEP) *Report of the Twenty-Eighth Meeting of the Parties to the Montreal Protocol on Substances that Deplete the Ozone Layer* (UNEP/OzL.Pro.28/12) (15 November 2016) <https://enb.iisd.org/events/montreal-protocol-mop-28/summary-report-10-14-october-2016> accessed 5 May 2022.

United Nations Environment Programme (UNEP) Ozone Secretariat 'All Ratifications' (2022a) <https://ozone.unep.org/all-ratifications> accessed 20 December 2022.

United Nations Environment Programme (UNEP) Ozone Secretariat 'Country Data' (2022b) <https://ozone.unep.org/countries/data-table> accessed 15 September 2022.

United Nations Framework Convention on Climate Change (UNFCCC) (1992) 1771 UNTS 107, opened for signature 4 June 1992, entered into force 21 March 1994 <https://treaties.un.org/pages/ViewDetailsIII.aspx?src=TREATY&mtdsg_no=XXVII-7&chapter=27&Temp=mtdsg3&clang=_en> accessed 28 March 2022.

United Nations Framework Convention on Climate Change (UNFCCC) *Adoption of the Paris Agreement* (FCCC/CP/2015/L.9/Rev.1) (12 December 2015) <https://unfccc.int/resource/docs/2015/cop21/eng/l09r01.pdf> accessed 5 May 2022.

United Nations Framework Convention on Climate Change (UNFCCC) *Report of the Conference of the Parties Serving as the Meeting of the Parties to the Kyoto Protocol on its Eighth Session, Held in Doha from 26 November to 8 December 2012* (FCCC/KP/CMP/2012/13/Add. 1) (28 February 2013) <https://unfccc.int/resource/docs/2012/cmp8/eng/13a01.pdf#page=2> accessed 5 May 2022.

Velders, GJM, Andersen, SO, Daniel, JS, Fahey, DW and McFarland, M 'The Importance of the Montreal Protocol in Protecting Climate' (2007) 104(12) PNAS 4814–4819.

Velders, GJM, Solomon, S, and Daniel, JS, 'Growth of climate change commitments from HFC banks and emissions' (2014) 14 Atmos. Chem. Phys. 9.

Vienna Convention for the Protection of the Ozone Layer (1985) 1513 UNTS 323, opened for signature 22 March 1985, entered into force 22 September 1988 <https://ozone.unep.org/sites/default/files/2019-12/The%20Ozone%20Treaties%20EN%20-%20WEB_final.pdf> accessed 10 December 2021.

Wijermars, J *Facilitation for the Future: the Ozone Secretariat's Role During the Kigali Amendment Negotiations* (MSc thesis, Utrecht University 2022) <https://studenttheses.uu.nl/bitstream/handle/20.500.12932/42445/MScThesis_Wijermars_5717280%20%28for%20online%20publication%29.pdf?sequence=1&isAllowed=y> accessed 12 September 2022.

World Meteorological Organisation (WMO) *Scientific Assessment of Ozone Depletion: 2018* (Global Ozone Research and Monitoring Project – Report No. 58) (2018) <https://www.esrl.noaa.gov/csl/assessments/ozone/2018/> accessed 10 December 2021.

CHAPTER 5

The Regulation of Short-Lived Climate Pollutants under the Convention on Long-Range Transboundary Air Pollution and Its Gothenburg Protocol

Adam Byrne

1 Introduction

The 1979 Convention on Long-Range Transboundary Air Pollution (1979 CLRTAP),[1] negotiated under the auspices of the United Nations Economic Commission for Europe (UNECE), is a major regional multilateral environmental agreement in force for forty years, under which eight protocols have been negotiated. The 1984 EMEP Protocol,[2] the first protocol adopted under this framework, provides funding to the European Monitoring and Evaluation Programme (EMEP),[3] a programme that has successfully aided the Convention process through air pollution monitoring, measuring and modelling.[4] Over time, seven pollution protocols emerged, with the major pollutants covered now being: sulphur oxides (SO_X), nitrogen oxides (NO_X), non-methane volatile organic compounds (VOCs), ammonia (NH_3), industrial dust and particulate matter (PM), including fine particulate matter ($PM_{2.5}$), heavy metals (lead, cadmium, mercury), and persistent organic pollutants (POPs). The CLRTAP regime has a rich history of focusing on the health and environmental effects of acidification, photochemical smog, ground-level ozone, eutrophication and contamination by toxic chemicals.

1 Convention on Long-Range Transboundary Air Pollution (adopted 13 November 1979, entered into force 16 March 1983) 1302 UNTS 217.

2 Protocol to the 1979 CLRTAP on Long-Term Financing of the Co-operative Programme for Monitoring and Evaluation of the Long-Range Transmission of Air Pollutants in Europe (EMEP) (adopted 28 September 1984, entered into force 28 January 1988) 1491 UNTS 167.

3 The EMEP area now covers predominantly Europe, Turkey, the South Caucasus and Central Asia.

4 Adam Byrne, 'Trouble in the Air: Recent Developments under the 1979 Convention on Long-Range Transboundary Air Pollution', (2017) 26 (3) *Review of European, Comparative & International Environmental Law* 210 <https://doi.org/10.1111/reel.12219>.

 | DOI:10.1163/9789004684089_007

The UNECE framework ties together a heterogeneous range of contemporary regional groupings: North America, Europe, and parts of West and Central Asia.[5] Presently, there are 51 Parties to the Convention, whilst participation in the Protocols varies. Since the 1990s after the end of the USSR it has not been possible to achieve high state participation rates in the protocols outside of Western and Northern Europe, and North America.[6] This is a result of the end of Cold War diplomacy which had secured Soviet participation, the legacy of the USSR's focus on controlling emissions near the European border, the limited interest in LRTAP from the newly independent states, and an indifference from the leading Western European states to air pollution in the Eastern UNECE regions.[7] As I have previously noted, "the less developed states in the Eastern region did not receive adequate financial assistance, technology transfer or joint implementation".[8]

On climate change, an important step forward for the CLRTAP regime was the entry into force of the 2012 Amendments to the 1999 Protocol to Abate Acidification, Eutrophication and Ground-level Ozone (1999 Gothenburg Protocol).[9] In this chapter, I will be focusing primarily on Executive Body (EB) Decision 2012/2 which contained the major revisions and required formal acceptance by the Parties (henceforth the 2012 Amendments). The EB is the Convention's governing body composed of representatives of the Parties to the Convention.[10] By 2019 the Gothenburg Protocol had 29 Parties and entered into force in 2005, whilst by 2022 there were 26 Parties to the 2012 Amendments which entered into force in 2019.[11] The Amendments added black carbon to

5 ibid, 210.

6 ibid, 210.

7 Adam Byrne, 'The 1979 Convention on Long-Range Transboundary Air Pollution: Assessing Its Effectiveness as a Multilateral Environmental Regime after 35 Years', (2015) 4 (1) *Transnational Environmental Law* 37, 59 <https://doi.org/10.1017/S2047102514000296>.

8 ibid, 59–60.

9 Protocol to the 1979 CLRTAP to Abate Acidification, Eutrophication and Ground-Level Ozone (adopted 30 November 1999, entered into force 17 May 2005) 2319 UNTS 81.

10 See UNECE, 'Executive Body' (*Unece.Org*, 2022) <https://unece.org/executive-body> accessed 4 October 2022.

11 2012 Gothenburg Protocol Amendments, UNECE/EB, *Report of the Executive Body on Its Thirtieth Session**. Geneva, 30 April–4 May 2012. Addendum. Decisions Adopted at the Thirtieth Session. Decisions 2012/1 Amendment of Annex I; 2012/2 Amendment of the Text of and Annexes II to IX and the Addition of New Annexes X and XI; 2012/3 Adjustments under the Gothenburg Protocol to Emission Reduction Commitments or to Inventories for the Purposes of Comparing National Total Emissions with Them; 2012/4 Provisional Application of Amendment to the Protocol. ECE/EB.AIR/111/Add.1** (Geneva: UNECE, 1 November 2012). Decision 2012/2 contained the major revisions and required acceptance by the Parties, entering into force 7 October 2019, UNTC Registration No. 21623. A consolidated text is

the Protocol's remit (as an element of $\text{PM}_{2.5}$). There has been a long standing interest in the 1979 CLRTAP regarding climate change which predates the 2012 Amendments, mainly emanating from, although not limited to, environmental scientists.[12] Although there have been international attempts to bring climate change and air pollution together, most notably through the Climate and Clean Air Coalition (CCAC), launched in 2012, legally and institutionally there have not been many major developments to bring the two together in law,[13] apart from the CLRTAP regime. The 2015 Paris Agreement does not reference air pollution, for example.[14] Interest in the CLRTAP and its protocols has therefore increased due to the lack of an overarching international framework on air pollution.[15]

---

available at: <https://unece.org/environment-policy/air/protocol-abate-acidification-eutrophication-and-ground-level-ozone> accessed 3 February 2023. UNECE/EB, *1999 Protocol to Abate Acidification, Eutrophication and Ground-level Ozone to the Convention on Long-range Transboundary Air Pollution, as amended on 4 May 2012. Executive Body for the Convention on Long-range Transboundary Air Pollution.* ECE/EB.AIR/114 *(Geneva: UNECE, 6 May 2013).*

12 Rob Swart and others, 'A Good Climate for Clean Air: Linkages between Climate Change and Air Pollution. An Editorial Essay' (2004) 66 (3) *Climatic Change* 263; Willemijn Tuinstra, Leen Hordijk, and Carolien Kroeze, 'Moving Boundaries in Transboundary Air Pollution Co-Production of Science and Policy under the Convention on Long Range Transboundary Air Pollution' (2006) 16 (4) *Global Environmental Change* 349 <https://doi.org/10.1016/j.gloenvcha.2006.03.002>; Helen ApSimon and others, 'Synergies in Addressing Air Quality and Climate Change', (2009) 9 (6) *Climate Policy* 669 <https://doi.org/10.3763/cpol.2009.0678>; Stefan Reis and others, 'From Acid Rain to Climate Change' (2012) 338 (6111) *Science* 1153; Sabrina Shankman, 'The Most Important Climate Treaty You've Never Heard Of' (*Inside Climate News*, 11 April 2018) <https://insideclimatenews.org/news/11042018/climate-treaty-gothenburg-protocol-air-pollution-regulations-global-warming-science-black-carbon-lrtap/> accessed 7 May 2022; Peringe Grennfelt and others, 'Acid Rain and Air Pollution: 50 Years of Progress in Environmental Science and Policy' (2020) 49 (4) *Ambio* 849 <https://doi.org/10.1007/s13280-019-01244-4>; Elizabeth Moses, Beatriz Cardenas, and Jessica Seddon, 'The Most Successful Air Pollution Treaty You've Never Heard Of' (*wri.org*, 25 February 2020) <https://www.wri.org/insights/most-successful-air-pollution-treaty-youve-never-heard> accessed 7 May 2022.

13 Yulia Yamineva and Seita Romppanen, 'Is Law Failing to Address Air Pollution? Reflections on International and EU Developments' (2017) 26 (3) *Review of European, Comparative & International Environmental Law* 189 <https://doi.org/10.1111/reel.12223>; see the Climate & Clean Air Coalition website <https://www.ccacoalition.org/en> accessed 12 December 2022.

14 Paris Agreement (adopted 12 December 2015, entered into force 4 November 2016) 3156 UNTS.

15 See James Longhurst and others, 'Analysing Air Pollution and Its Management through the Lens of the UN Sustainable Development Goals: A Review and Assessment' (2018) 230 *WIT Transactions on Ecology and the Environment* 3 <https://doi.org/10.2495/AIR180011>.

In this chapter I explore three main issues, looking at: how and why black carbon was introduced into the Gothenburg Protocol, the nature of the provisions, and developments on SLCPs since the 2012 Amendments with particular attention on the recent review and possible updating of the Protocol and the possibility of the further regulation of methane. Table 5.1 contains information on organisational aspects of the regime which will be referred to in the chapter. As the chapter explores, the Gothenburg Protocol offers a possible route to a long-term framework on SLCPs in the UNECE region, but this potential has not yet been realised.

TABLE 5.1 The main organisational elements of the CLRTAP featuring in this chapter[a]

Organisation/Body	Description
UNECE	The United Nations Economic Commission for Europe is the institutional home of the CLRTAP.
EB	The Executive Body is the governing body of the Convention composed of representatives of Parties to the Convention.
EMEP	The Cooperative Programme for Monitoring and Evaluation of the Long-range Transmission of Air Pollutants in Europe provides scientific support to the Convention on atmospheric monitoring and modelling, emission inventories and emission projections, and integrated assessment.
Working Group on Effects	Provides information on the degree and geographic extent of the impacts of major air pollutants on human health and the environment.
Working Group on Strategies and Review (WGSR)	The principal negotiating body for the Convention assisting the Executive Body.
The Task Force on Integrated Assessment Modelling	Working under EMEP, the task force models cost-effective emission control strategies.
The Task Force on Techno-economic Issues	Working under WGSR, the task force updates and assesses information on emission abatement technologies and costs.

a Information taken from UNECE, 'Air' (*unece.org*, 2022) <https://unece.org/environment-policy/air> accessed 12 December 2022.

2 Understanding Why Black Carbon Was Introduced into the Gothenburg Protocol

The CLRTAP regime has been viewed as separate to international climate law, given the CLRTAP's unique history and scope. Prior to the 2012 Gothenburg Protocol Amendments, over the decades, the regime has indirectly touched on the regulation of SLCPs. The objective in Article 2 of the 1979 CLRTAP, part of the "fundamental principles", was that the "Contracting Parties, taking due account of the facts and problems involved, are determined to protect man and his environment against air pollution and shall endeavour to limit and, as far as possible, gradually reduce and prevent air pollution including long-range transboundary air pollution." Under this general framework, the Convention and its Protocols have a fairly developed history of targeting pollutants which contribute to tropospheric ozone, and PM/particulates. For the first decade or so of the regime, particulates as a general description was the preferred word used in the Protocols, and PM has tended to be used from the late 1990s onwards, with an associated move towards denoting particle size (e.g. PM_{10}) for accuracy. Table 5.2 contains details of the CLRTAP Protocols direct and indirect engagement with climate change and pollutants which are components of SLCPs. These pollutants were addressed because of their negative impacts on ecosystems and public health, rather than climate change. The 2012 Gothenburg Protocol Amendments changed this, and directly addressed the issue of radiative forcing and climate.

As Table 5.2 details, the CLRTAP regime developed an extensive regulatory approach to tropospheric ozone and PM. In the 1990s, the Protocols began to acknowledge climate change and the UNFCCC. The climate elements of the 2012 Gothenburg Protocol Amendments can therefore be considered a development in keeping with the regime's history of expanding the range of the pollutants and environmental problems regulated by the Protocols. Although not discussed in great deal in this chapter, the control of tropospheric ozone continues to have a central place in the amended Gothenburg Protocol. The negotiations for the 2012 Gothenburg Protocol Amendments lasted five years,[16] and were described by the UNECE as "wide-ranging and intense".[17] Prior to the

16 Christer Ågren, 'New Gothenburg Protocol Adopted' (*Acid News*, June 2012) <http://www.airclim.org/acidnews/new-gothenburg-protocol-adopted> accessed 2 February 2023.

17 UNECE, 'Parties to UNECE Air Pollution Convention Approve New Emission Reduction Commitments for Main Air Pollutants by 2020' (*unece.org*, 3 May 2012) <https://unece.org/press/parties-unece-air-pollution-convention-approve-new-emission-reduction-commitments-main-air> accessed 10 May 2022.

TABLE 5.2 Early encounters with climate change and SLCPs by the CLRTAP Protocols

1988 Protocol concerning the Control of Emissions of Nitrogen Oxides or their Transboundary Fluxes[a]
– Aimed to stabilize emissions or transboundary fluxes of NOx so they did not exceed 1987 levels by 1994.
– The non-mandatory Technical Annex mentioned particulate pollution, fly ash, and dust.
– Introduced the 'critical loads' concept (Article 1, paragraph 7), a "quantitative estimate of the exposure to one or more pollutants below which significant harmful effects on specified sensitive elements of the environment do not occur according to present knowledge".
1991 Protocol concerning the Control of Emissions of Volatile Organic Compounds or their Transboundary Fluxes[b]
– 20 Parties agreed to reduce non-methane VOC emissions by 30% on the base-year (a choice from 1984 to 1990) by 1999.
– By way of a compromise, Canada and Norway agreed to reduce non-methane VOC emissions by 30% in their Tropospheric Ozone Management Areas (i.e. areas that contributed to transboundary pollution only, instead of the entire territory).
– In addition, Canada, Norway, Bulgaria and Hungary agreed to limit national emissions to 1988 levels.
– Article 3 was the first time climate change appeared in a Protocol text: "Measures required by the present Protocol shall not relieve Parties from their other obligations to take measures to reduce total gaseous emissions that may contribute significantly to climate change".
– Climate change was mentioned in the non-binding Annex II Control measures for emissions from stationary sources, where Parties were asked, when designing compound-specific measures, to take into account "other effects on the environment (e.g. global climate change) and on human health".
– Particulate pollution was mentioned in the non-binding Annex III Control measures for emissions from on-road motor vehicles, specifically on diesel.
1994 Protocol on Further Reduction of Sulphur Emissions[c]
– Preamble noted that under the UNFCCC 1992 "there is agreement to establish national policies and take corresponding measures to combat climate change, which can be expected to lead to reductions of sulphur emissions".
– Particulates and fly ash were mentioned in the guidance Annex IV Control technologies from stationary sources.

TABLE 5.2 Early encounters with climate change and SLCPs by the CLRTAP Protocols (*cont.*)

1998 Protocol on Heavy Metals[d]
– Set in law limit values and product control measures of emissions of 'particulate matter' as a proxy for heavy metal pollution (note that this is the first time that a protocol had used the phrase) for major stationary sources (e.g., industry). These were specified in the mandatory Annex V.
2012 Heavy Metals Protocol Amendments[e]
– PM/dust emissions from new and existing industrial installations were given more stringent limits.
1999 Protocol to Abate Acidification, Eutrophication and Ground-level Ozone[f]
– Parties were required to control and reduce emissions of NOx and VOCs, alongside sulphur and ammonia, and were given emission ceilings/targets for 2010 which were based on critical loads/levels, using 1990 as the base year.
– Climate change was mentioned once in the preamble, where the commitments that Parties had taken under the UNFCCC were noted.
– PM was included in the limit values for fuels and new mobile sources in the mandatory Annex VIII (Article 3), with a specific focus on diesel vehicles and heavy duty vehicles.
– In a first for the regime, Methane (CH_4) was included in the European limit values included in the mandatory Annexes VI and VIII for petrol storage and distribution, and heavy duty vehicles using the European transient cycle test.

a Adopted 31 October 1988, entered into force 14 February 1991, 1593 UNTS 287.
b Adopted 18 November 1991, entered into force 29 September 1997, 2001 UNTS 187.
c Adopted 14 June 1994, entered into force 5 August 1998, 2030 UNTS 122.
d Adopted 24 June 1998, entered into force 29 December 2003, 2237 UNTS 4.
e UNECE/EB 'Decision 2012/5 on Amendment of the Text of and Annexes other than III and VII to the 1998 Protocol on Heavy Metals'; 'Decision 2012/6 on Amendment of Annex III to the 1998 Protocol on Heavy Metals' UN Doc ECE/EB.AIR/113/Add.1 (13 December 2012). Decision 2012/5 required acceptance by the Parties and entered into force 8 February 2022, UNTC Registration No. 21623.
f Adopted 30 November 1999, entered into force 17 May 2005, 2319 UNTS 81.

negotiations, the EB initiated a review in 2005 to report in 2007.[18] This was formally done under Article 10 of the 1999 Gothenburg Protocol, where Parties

18 UNECE/EB, *Report of the Twenty-Third Session of the Executive Body*, ECE/EB.AIR/87 (Geneva: UNECE, 27 January 2006).

are required to "keep under review the [protocol] obligations", including their adequacy and progress in achieving them.

During the review there was increasing attention on the relationship between climate change and air pollution which may have contributed to a consensus on the issue. For example, a major workshop was held on 'Air pollution and its relations to climate change and sustainable development' in Gothenburg in March 2007 (Gothenburg Workshop).[19] Work was also being done by the subsidiary bodies to the Convention. A report by the Working Group on Effects,[20] for example, highlighted the need to reduce uncertainty on the interaction between air pollutants and climate change.[21] Also in 2007, the CLRTAP EB established a 'Task Force on Reactive Nitrogen',[22] reporting to the Working Group on Strategy and Review (WGSR, the principal negotiating body for the Convention).[23] This was in order to, *inter alia*, "develop a better understanding of the integrated, multi-pollutant nature of reactive nitrogen".[24] Amongst its many effects, reactive nitrogen can produce secondary particulate matter ($PM_{2.5}$) and can affect the balance of greenhouse gases in the atmosphere.[25]

2.1 *The Revision of the 1999 Gothenburg Protocol (2008–2012)*

The Gothenburg Protocol review was concluded in 2007, the major outcome being that the EB mandated the WGSR to begin negotiations on the revision

19 This was organized by the Swedish programme on International and national abatement strategies for transboundary air pollution (ASTA), in collaboration with the EB Bureau of the CLRTAP 1979, the European Commission and the EU Atmospheric Composition Change European Network of Excellence (ACCENT) programme. UNECE, *Gothenburg Workshop on Air Pollution and Its Relations to Climate Change and Sustainable Development, ECE/EB.AIR/GE.1/2007/5* (Geneva: UNECE, 13 June 2007).

20 See *Byrne* (n 7) 51; and UNECE, 'Working Group on Effects' (*unece.org*, 2022) <https://unece.org/environment-policy/air/working-group-effects> accessed 4 October 2022.

21 UNECE/EB, *Revised Review Report of the Working Group on Effects, ECE/EB.AIR/WG.1/2007/14/Rev.1* (Geneva: UNECE, 27 September 2007).

22 UNECE/EB, *Decision 2007/1 Establishment of a Task Force on Reactive Nitrogen, ECE/EB.AIR/91/Add.1* (Geneva: UNECE, 2007).

23 See UNECE, 'Working Group on Strategies and Review' (*unece.org*, 2022) <https://unece.org/environment-policy/air/working-group-strategies-and-review> accessed 24 May 2022.

24 *UNECE/EB* (n 22) 2.

25 UNEP, 'Why Nitrogen Management Is Key for Climate Change Mitigation' (*unep.org*, 22 October 2019) <http://www.unep.org/news-and-stories/story/why-nitrogen-management-key-climate-change-mitigation> accessed 7 December 2022.

of the Protocol.[26] From the very beginning the EB had decided that "any revision or new protocol should take into account new scientific knowledge about primary PM and PM precursors, the hemispheric transport of air pollution, and the potential synergies and trade-offs to climate change and the nitrogen cycle".[27] To some extent, the notion of trade-offs was a presumption, with the expectation being that new data and scientific models would clarify the relationship. What might the trade-offs between climate change and air pollution be? At the 2007 Gothenburg Workshop, for example, concerns were raised over the air pollution implications of carbon capture and storage and integrated gasification combined cycle technologies.[28] The idea of trade-offs, however, more likely is referencing that scientifically the concept of SLCPS can "include compounds that are cooling the atmosphere, i.e. small secondary aerosols, e.g. sulphate particles" that reflect sunlight and increase the reflectiveness of clouds.[29] Grennfelt et al. note that air pollutants can have different climatic effects, contributing to both warming and cooling. Consequently a "reduction in sulphur dioxide emissions, although highly desirable from health and ecosystems perspectives, will therefore contribute to warming.... [A] reduction of black carbon will be a win–win solution".[30] With the implementation of the CLRTAP, in particular its sulphur reduction protocols and commitments, the masking, or dampening effect on warming through the action of sulphate particles was ended, particularly for the Arctic.[31] The idea of a climate benefit from air pollution raises ethical questions which most participants in international climate policy are keen to avoid, although the issue has relevance to discussions of geoengineering (i.e. putting sulphate particles into the stratosphere to reduce warming through greater reflection).[32] The issue of sulphur emissions underlines the difficulties in reframing the CLRTAP regime in terms of climate change. There is some evidence that the implementation of the CLRTAP

---

26 UNECE/EB, *Report of the Executive Body on Its Twenty-Fifth Session Held in Geneva from 10 to 13 December 2007, ECE/EB.AIR/91* (Geneva: UNECE, 27 February 2008), 21.

27 ibid, 20.

28 *UNECE* (n 19) 5; See also European Environment Agency, *Air Pollution Impacts from Carbon Capture and Storage* (*CCS*). *EEA Technical Report No 14/2011* (Copenhagen: Publications Office of the European Union, 2011).

29 *Grennfelt and others* (n 12) 855.

30 ibid 861.

31 EMEP, *EMEP Status Report 1/2016: Transboundary Particulate Matter, Photo-Oxidants, Acidifying and Eutrophying Components.* (Oslo, Norway: Norwegian Meteorological Institute, 13 September 2016), vi.

32 Paul Voosen, 'In a Paradox, Cleaner Air Is Now Adding to Global Warming' (*science.org*, 20 July 2022) <https://www.science.org/content/article/paradox-cleaner-air-now-adding-global-warming> accessed 26 September 2022.

Protocols may have contributed to modest reductions in carbon dioxide,[33] so the issue is not clear-cut. It would be surprising nonetheless to see this complex conceptual issue resolved through the revision process.

It was initially unclear whether the Protocol revisions were going to be binding or non-binding aspirational goals.[34] For PM, an Expert Group led by Germany and the UK explored the policy options.[35] The incorporation of $PM_{2.5}$ was raised "in particular due to its effects on human health", as opposed to climate change.[36] Other points raised included the need to use the latest scientific knowledge, air pollution from shipping, and the idea of the development of some kind of "metric to indicate co-benefits of air pollution controls to climate change abatement".[37] The main considerations for the revision were: the addition of PM, "the implications of developments in other forums including co-benefits and potential trade-offs of climate change policies, and the introduction of flexibility to promote ratifications by EECCA [Eastern Europe, the Caucasus and Central Asia] and SEE [South-Eastern Europe] countries".[38] Whilst the main focus was on targets for 2020, "aspirational non-binding targets for 2050 for Parties within the geographic scope of EMEP" were suggested.[39] By 2009, a draft text of the amended Gothenburg Protocol was produced by the WGSR.[40] Integrated assessment modelling was undertaken to aid the revision of Annex II on emission ceilings, but the Task Force on Integrated Assessment Modelling was hindered in the development of the baseline scenario for the Gothenburg Protocol because of the failure of the 2009 Copenhagen Summit on Climate Change, the effects of the global economic crisis, and inconsistent data from the Parties.[41]

Further momentum was provided by the publication of a major scientific report on the Hemispheric Transport of Air Pollution in 2010, produced

---

33 Aurélie Slechten and Vincenzo Verardi, 'Measuring the Impact of Multiple Air Pollution Agreements on Global CO_2 Emissions' (2016) 92 (3) *Land Economics* 534.

34 *UNECE/EB* (n 26) 20.

35 ibid 22.

36 UNECE/EB, *Report of the Executive Body on Its Twenty-Sixth Session Held in Geneva from 15 to 18 December 2008, ECE/EB.AIR/96* (Geneva: UNECE, 22 June 2009), 18.

37 ibid 19.

38 ibid 20.

39 ibid 19.

40 UNECE/EB, *Report of the Executive Body on Its Twenty-Seventh Session Held in Geneva from 14 to 18 December 2009, ECE/EB.AIR/99* (Geneva: UNECE, 10 May 2010).

41 ibid 16.

separate to the revision process (HTAP 2010).[42] This assessment focused on the science of intercontinental transport of air pollutants in the Northern Hemisphere. Part A considered ozone and PM, and the findings were presented via an Executive Summary to the EB.[43] The report appears to have had a significant impact, with the EB describing it as "a milestone in the understanding of intercontinental transport of air pollution and the first comprehensive assessment of intercontinental transport of ozone, PM, mercury and POPs".[44] The Co-Chairs of the Task Force on Hemispheric Transport of Air Pollution drew specific attention to "the need for further reductions of ozone precursors ... the importance of methane and carbon monoxide (CO)... and the contribution of tropospheric ozone, methane, other ozone precursors and black carbon... to climate change, and the potential benefits of further emission controls".[45]

2.1.1 Black Carbon, Methane and Carbon Monoxide in the Revision Process

Crucial to the developments on black carbon was the EB Decision 2009/5 to establish an ad hoc expert group to explore the issue, reporting the following year in order to inform the revision.[46] The US and Norway offered to lead the group, with the Norwegian delegation offering to contribute $50,000 to the work (mainly EMEP related work). Considering that a draft text of the amended Gothenburg Protocol had already been prepared, this development was slightly late in the revision process, but the revisions to the Annexes had not been completed, however. The ad hoc expert group on black carbon reported the following year.[47] The report was produced quickly, and under different

---

42 Produced by a Task Force established in 2005, and reporting to the EMEP Steering Body. See HTAP, 'The Task Force on Hemispheric Transport of Air Pollution (TF HTAP)' (*Htap.Org*, 2022) <http://htap.org/> accessed 25 May 2022.

43 HTAP, *Hemispheric Transport of Air Pollution 2010 Executive Summary, ECE/EB.AIR/2010/10 Corrected*, Informal Document No.10, Convention on Long-range Transboundary Air Pollution Executive Body 28th Session <https://unece.org/fileadmin/DAM/env/documents/2010/eb/wg5/wg47/Informal%20documents/Info%2016_Hemispheric%20Transport%20of%20Air%20Pollution%202010_Executive%20Summary.pdf> accessed 3 February 2023.

44 UNECE/EB, *Report of the Executive Body on Its Twenty-Eighth Session, Geneva, 13–17 December 2010, ECE/EB.AIR/106* (Geneva: UNECE, 24 February 2011), 6.

45 ibid 6.

46 *UNECE/EB* (n 40) 17.

47 UNECE/EB, *Black Carbon: Report by the Co-Chairs of the Ad Hoc Expert Group on Black Carbon, ECE/EB.AIR/2010/7* (Geneva: UNECE, 30 September 2010); see also Erika Rosenthal and Robert Watson, 'Multilateral Efforts to Reduce Black Carbon Emissions: A Lifeline for the Warming Arctic?' (2011) 20 (1) Review of European Community & International Environmental Law 3, 10 <https://doi.org/10.1111/j.1467-9388.2011.00705.x>.

circumstances and perhaps more time, may well have driven the black carbon agenda further. The overall vision for the regime was that the EB "should continue to seek health driven reductions in 'climate cooling' pollutants (e.g., sulphates) while also pursuing reductions in 'climate warming' pollutants (e.g., black carbon)".[48] Moreover, the report included concern over the impact of Arctic warming on indigenous people's way of life, particularly on the issue of food security. Whilst noting scientific uncertainties, the report recommended the inclusion of black carbon in the Gothenburg Protocol revisions and also provided a series of recommendations to ensure that the inclusion would be successful. These included the need to improve emission inventories, determine the parameters of EMEP black carbon monitoring, and to establish a group to develop legal options and technological options for black carbon control. The report was ambiguous on whether the legal provisions would be binding or voluntary, but did recommend to the EB mandatory monitoring and reporting requirements for black carbon and organic carbon emissions. It also made recommendations on improving state participation in the protocol, outreach activities including to non-UNECE countries, and suggested tentative contacts with the International Maritime Organization (IMO) on the issue of black carbon and the Arctic environment.[49]

At EB28, December 2010, "[a] number of delegations expressed appreciation for the high quality of the report that had been produced within such a short time".[50] The EU interpreted the report as reflecting longer-term ambitions; it was Norway however that continued to take the lead with the Norwegian delegation supporting the inclusion of black carbon, methane and CO in the revised Protocol. There were, however, technical aspects that needed to be completed. The Centre for Integrated Assessment Modelling (part of EMEP), was working on hybrid scenarios requested by the WGSR and would need a couple of months to work on black carbon and radiative forcing. Whilst it appears to have been generally accepted that new substances could be included in the Gothenburg Protocol revision under the Annex specification system, the Chair of the WGSR noted a difficulty in setting emission ceilings for black carbon and suggested a "flat reduction rate, e.g.,-30% compared to a reference year, as a possible solution".[51] The Chair further suggested that "[w]hen national inventories for BC

48 ibid 9.
49 ibid 3–4.
50 *UNECE/EB* (n 44) 6.
51 ibid 8.

[black carbon] were established in future, the Gothenburg Protocol could be updated, possibly with setting emission ceilings".[52]

Support for inclusion of black carbon, CO and methane was not overwhelming. The EU was concerned about the level of progress on the revisions, noting many outstanding issues, and expressed a desire that the revisions were completed by the end of 2011. EU opposition was a major problem as the EU "could not commit to including binding ceilings and strict obligations on BC [black carbon] … in view of the rather limited information on the impacts and policy options available". The EU was, however, "willing to discuss text on prioritizing measures that also reduce BC [black carbon]. The Convention should pursue technical and science work with the aim of including specific measures for BC [black carbon] at a later stage".[53] This view was supported by the US which similarly saw it as a longer-term issue, with Switzerland and Canada more supportive on the inclusion of black carbon. The best that could be agreed at this stage was "to include consideration of BC [black carbon], as a component of particulate matter (PM), in the process of the revision" (Decision 2010/2). Methane and CO were in effect kicked into the long grass to be considered by the subsidiary bodies to the Convention over the long-term, and no major revisions would be made.

What direction did the negotiations take in 2011? The Norwegian leadership continued with for example, the Nordic Council of Ministers for the Environment agreeing to cooperate on actions on SLCPs, including black carbon, through "identifying national measures, developing emission inventories and exchange of national plans of action".[54] In the 2011 Gothenburg Protocol options documents prepared by the Secretariat for the WGSR, outstanding issues remained over the inclusion of references to 'climate change' and the nature of the commitments on black carbon.[55] At EB29 in December 2011, the latest version of the revised Protocol text was considered and a number of modifications were made, but there remained 'pending issues', and a breakout

52 ibid 8.

53 ibid 8–9.

54 UNECE/EB, *Report of the Executive Body on Its Twenty-Ninth Session, Geneva, 12–16 December 2011. ECE/EB.AIR/109* (Geneva: UNECE, 31 January 2012), 4.

55 UNECE/EB, *Options for Revising the 1999 Gothenburg Protocol to Abate Acidification, Eutrophication and Ground-Level Ozone. Working Group on Strategies and Review, Forty-Ninth Session Geneva, 12–16 September 2011. ECE/EB.AIR/WG.5/2011/7* (Geneva: UNECE, 17 June 2011); UNECE/EB, *Options for Revising the 1999 Gothenburg Protocol to Abate Acidification, Eutrophication and Ground-Level Ozone. Executive Body for the Convention on Long-Range Transboundary Air Pollution, Twenty-Ninth Session Geneva, 12–16 December 2011. ECE/EB.AIR/2011/8* (Geneva: UNECE, 29 September 2011).

group worked on black carbon.[56] This effort produced results with most of the provisions on black carbon being agreed to, although references to climate change in the revised text remained on the whole undecided.[57] Norway formally proposed to amend the Gothenburg Protocol, feeling that enough progress had been made. This proposal would therefore be discussed at the next EB session, whilst the Chair of the WGSR (Richard Ballaman, Switzerland) "proposed to continue to work on the text … to try to reach consensus".[58] Whilst progress was made on the main text, further work was needed on the technical annexes and Annex II (national emission ceilings).[59] During discussion over the timetable for the conclusion of the negotiations, EU pressure to bring the negotiations to a faster conclusion was notable.[60] EB30 was set by consensus for the 30 April to 4 May 2012 "with the sole purpose of finalizing negotiations and adopting the amendments to the Gothenburg Protocol" in Decision 2011/1.[61] Table 5.3 summarises the key developments between 2007 and 2012 discussed in this section.

3 Discussion of the 2012 Gothenburg Protocol Amendments

EB30 in 2012 was a success in the sense that the Gothenburg Protocol was amended by four EB Decisions.[62] The UNECE was keen in its press release to tout the climate change aspects of the Amendments,[63] but how significant are they? There is no doubt that the inclusion of the word 'climate' in the overall objective of the amended Gothenburg Protocol 2012, contained in Article 2, was ground-breaking (although note, the inclusion of the phrase 'climate

56 *UNECE/EB* (n 54) 5.

57 UNECE/EB, *Options for Revising the 1999 Gothenburg Protocol to Abate Acidification, Eutrophication and Ground-Level Ozone. Note by the Secretariat. Executive Body for the Convention on Long-Range Transboundary Air Pollution Thirtieth Session Geneva, 30 April–4 May 2012 Item 4 of the Provisional Agenda. ECE/EB.AIR/2012/1* (Geneva: UNECE, 2 February 2012).

58 UNECE/EB, *Report of the Executive Body on Its Twenty-Ninth Session, Geneva, 12–16 December 2011. Corrigendum. ECE/EB.AIR/109/Corr.1* (Geneva: UNECE, 30 May 2012), 1.

59 Leonardo Massai, '1. Transboundary Air Pollution' (2011) 22 (1) *Yearbook of International Environmental Law* 193 <https://doi.org/10.1093/yiel/yvs077>.

60 *UNECE/EB* (n 58) 2.

61 UNECE/EB, *Report of the Executive Body on Its Twenty-Ninth Session, Geneva, 12–16 December 2011. Addendum. Decisions Adopted at the Twenty-Ninth Session. ECE/EB.AIR/109/Add.1* (Geneva: UNECE, 31 January 2012).

62 2012 Gothenburg Protocol Amendments (n 11).

63 *UNECE* (n 17).

TABLE 5.3 Timeline of the key developments on the 2012 Gothenburg Protocol Amendments

Year	Event
2005–07	Gothenburg Protocol reviewed by the EB.
2007	EB established the Task Force on Reactive Nitrogen.
2008	Gothenburg Protocol revision process begins.
2009	Draft text of the amended Gothenburg Protocol is produced. Ad hoc expert group on BC is created by the EB.
2010	Publication of the scientific Report on the Hemispheric Transport of Air Pollution. Ad hoc expert group on BC recommends the inclusion of BC in the Gothenburg Protocol.
2011	Gothenburg Protocol Options Document produced. Majority of BC provisions agreed at EB29. Norway formally proposed to amend the Gothenburg Protocol.
2012	The Gothenburg Protocol revision is concluded at EB30, with the adoption of the Amendments.

change' was far more controversial, and a number of references present in the earlier revision options did not make it into the final text).[64] Article 2 states:

> The objective of the present Protocol is to control and reduce emissions of sulphur, nitrogen oxides, ammonia, volatile organic compounds and particulate matter that are caused by anthropogenic activities and are likely to cause adverse effects on human health and the environment, natural ecosystems, materials, crops and the climate in the short and long term, due to acidification, eutrophication, particulate matter or ground-level ozone as a result of long-range transboundary atmospheric transport

The second part of Article 2 requires Parties "to ensure, as far as possible, that in the long term and in a stepwise approach, taking into account advances in scientific knowledge, atmospheric depositions or concentrations do not exceed [the Critical loads/levels in Annex I]". The Amendments created

64 *UNECE/EB*, ECE/EB.AIR/WG.5/2011/7 (n 55), 6.

emissions ceilings for '2020 and beyond', contained in the binding Annex II, for the existing pollutants SO_2, NO_X, ammonia and VOCs, and added commitments for $PM_{2.5}$. For ozone and PM, the Amendments maintain a separation between the EMEP area and North America. For North America, the Canadian Ambient Air Quality Standards and the US National Ambient Air Quality Standards are directly referenced in the protocol text. The Amendments do not expand the coverage of methane emissions. European Union (EU) Member States are jointly required to reduce SO_2 emissions by 59%, NO_X emissions by 42%, ammonia by 6%, VOCs by 28%, and $PM_{2.5}$ by 22%. Annexes V–VI and X contain limit values for NO_X, VOCs, and PM from stationary sources. Annex VIII contains limit values for fuels and new mobile sources, including NO_X and PM.

The Amendments clarified the definition of 'Particulate Matter' used in the protocol as meaning equal to or less than PM_{10}, including $PM_{2.5}$ (Art. 1.11 bis). The Amendments also added definitions for black carbon[65] and ozone precursors.[66] An interesting aspect of the 2012 Amendments was the inclusion in the Preamble of a somewhat cryptic clause on "Taking into account the scientific knowledge about ... the potential synergies with and trade-offs between air pollution and climate change". The main provisions in the protocol, however, do not return to the notion of trade-offs and the issue was therefore successfully side-lined to some extent. The Preamble could justifiably state that the "Protocol is the first agreement under the Convention to deal specifically with reduced nitrogen compounds and particulate matter, including black carbon", although admittedly for PM the word 'specifically' is the main source of credibility for the claim, as the pollutant had first been included in the 1998 Protocol on Heavy Metals (see Table 5.2 above). Article 7.3(c) expanded the role of EMEP and other subsidiary bodies to provide information to the EB on the "[a]dverse effects on human health, natural ecosystems, materials and crops, including interactions with climate change and the environment related to the substances covered by the present Protocol", and on progress in achieving environmental and human health improvements.

3.1 *Black Carbon in the Amended Gothenburg Protocol 2012*

On black carbon, the 2012 Amendments paint a fairly confusing picture which could be viewed as verging on the disappointing. The pollutant is treated as an element of PM; the commitments on $PM_{2.5}$ are binding and are listed in

65 Defined in Art. 1.11 ter as 'carbonaceous particulate matter that absorbs light', 2012 Gothenburg Protocol Amendments (n 11).

66 Defined in Art. 1.11 quarter as 'nitrogen oxides, volatile organic compounds, methane and carbon monoxide', 2012 Gothenburg Protocol Amendments (n 11).

the Annex II emission reduction commitments for the Parties. As I will show, the focus on black carbon is highly dependent on national circumstances and specific black carbon emission reduction commitments are not included in Annex II. Black carbon features in the majority of the Articles of the amended Protocol where it is to be treated as a priority by the Parties, including: the Protocol objective; the basic obligations; the exchange of information and technology; on raising public awareness; the strategies, policies, programmes, measures and information; reporting; research, development and monitoring; and the Protocol reviews by the Parties.[67] The black carbon provisions are weakened, however, by the presence of qualifying clauses and soft law expressions that create vagueness. That being said, the regime has a long history of using this approach in order to build consensus, and so the vague nature of the black carbon provisions are not necessarily a negative outcome as such drafting techniques enabled the pollutants inclusion.[68] Although the regulatory and technological solutions for the reduction of black carbon are effectively the same as for $PM_{2.5}$,[69] the Amendments lack ambition on both black carbon and $PM_{2.5}$. Indeed, a general critique of the 2012 Gothenburg Protocol Amendments across all the pollutants was that they were not stringent enough, with the Parties concerns over economic factors in the aftermath of the Great Recession being dominant.[70] The emission reduction targets for $PM_{2.5}$ are highly varied for the Parties, ranging from a 46% reduction on 2005 levels for Cyprus (a low emitter) to only a 10% reduction for Italy (a high emitter). The leadership of the Nordic countries is also evident, with those Parties agreeing to around a 30% reduction target for 2020 and beyond for $PM_{2.5}$.

Looking at the provisions in more detail, Article 2.2 contained a rather loosely worded and flexible general objective on prioritising black carbon, and it is here where reference to climate change is made. Assessing the implementation of this commitment could present some difficulties:

> Parties should, in implementing measures to achieve their national targets for particulate matter, give priority, to the extent they consider

67 Articles 2–8 and 10, 2012 Gothenburg Protocol Amendments (n 11).

68 *Byrne* (n 7) 44.

69 See Markus Amann and others, 'Reducing Global Air Pollution: The Scope for Further Policy Interventions' (2020) 378 *Philosophical Transactions of the Royal Society A: Mathematical, Physical and Engineering Sciences*, 1; and Climate & Clean Air Coalition, 'Black Carbon' (ccacoalition.org, 2022) <https://www.ccacoalition.org/en/slcps/black-carbon> accessed 9 December 2022.

70 *Byrne* (n 7) 50.

> appropriate, to emission reduction measures which also significantly reduce black carbon in order to provide benefits for human health and the environment and to help mitigation of near-term climate change.[71]

Article 3.1 qualifies the commitment on black carbon, stating "In taking steps to reduce emissions of particulate matter, each Party should seek reductions from those source categories known to emit high amounts of black carbon, to the extent it considers appropriate".[72] The phrase "to the extent it considers appropriate" indicates that the Amendments have given a great deal of leeway to states in the interpretation of the commitment. Similarly, Article 3.6, the requirement to apply best available techniques to mobile and stationary sources, a linchpin of the regime across the Protocols, is again qualified by to the extent "it [the Party] considers appropriate" for black carbon and Parties are only required to take into account guidance adopted by the Executive Body.[73]

Black carbon is specifically mentioned in relation to the creation of "favourable conditions" for the exchange of information and technology (Article 4), and the promotion of the provision of information to the general public on national pollution emissions and progress on compliance (Article 5). These obligations are weakened however with a qualifying statement that such activities will be conducted by each Party "in a manner consistent with its laws, regulations and practices," which is a fair way from unified action. Black carbon gets a specific mention in the overall Article 6 commitments to create strategies, policies, programmes, measures and provide information, which is qualified by the phrase "as necessary and on the basis of sound scientific and economic criteria," to the extent that it could be considered non-binding. In Article 6, black carbon gets a specific mention for each Party to "develop and maintain inventories and projections for emissions of black carbon, using guidelines adopted by the Executive Body", but this is qualified again by the phrase "to the extent it [the Party] considers appropriate".[74] Where black carbon emission inventories and projections are available, the Party should report these, again using guidelines adopted by the Executive Body (Article 7).[75]

Article 8 contains a commitment for Parties to encourage research, development, monitoring and cooperation. PM and black carbon are included in the objective to improve emissions databases and pollution monitoring. Article

71 2012 Gothenburg Protocol Amendments (n 11), 9.
72 ibid, 9.
73 Ibid, 10.
74 ibid, 13.
75 Ibid, 14.

8(d bis) specifies this on the "improvement of the scientific understanding of the potential co-benefits for climate change mitigation associated with potential reduction scenarios for air pollutants (such as methane, carbon monoxide and black carbon)", whilst Article 8(k) specifies "the quantification and, where possible, economic evaluation of benefits for the environment, human health and the impacts on climate" resulting from emission reductions of sulphur, NO_X, ammonia, VOCs and PM.[76] Article 8, combined with the undertaking contained in Article 10 for the EB to evaluate the mitigation measures for black carbon emissions no later than at the second EB session after entry into force of the Amendments,[77] and the overall weak phraseology on black carbon, demonstrates the contested nature of this attempt to overtly regulate black carbon. There is clearly a tension in the text between 'climate' and 'climate change', hence the Article 8 requirements for further research.

Given the above discussion, it is not surprising to find some controversy in the academic literature on the legal nature of the black carbon commitments. Khan and Kulovesi,[78] for example, argue that because the amended Gothenburg Protocol 2012 contains binding commitments on $PM_{2.5}$, and black carbon is included in this, the Gothenburg Protocol is "the first environmental agreement to set legal limits on this pollutant [black carbon]." Shapovalova, after reviewing the Amendments concluded, however, "that whilst the Gothenburg Protocol is a legally binding instrument, its BC [black carbon] provisions are voluntary" and further argued that "the regulation of BC [black carbon] … is more characteristic of soft law".[79] When considering compliance and commitments in this specific instance, it is acceptable to take a broad reading of the spirit of the law.[80] It is clear from the Amended Gothenburg Protocol 2012 that Parties are to give special attention to black carbon; it is reasonable to expect, in the assessment of implementation, significant reductions in black carbon as part of the overall target to reduce $PM_{2.5}$. Whether the provisions are binding or

76 Ibid, 15.

77 Ibid, 16.

78 Sabaa Ahmad Khan and Kati Kulovesi 'Black Carbon and the Arctic: Global Problem-solving through the Nexus of Science, Law and Space' (2018) 27 (1) *Review of European Comparative & International Environmental Law* 5, 9 <https://doi.org/10.1111/reel.12245>.

79 Daria Shapovalova, 'The Effectiveness of the Regulatory Regime for Black Carbon Mitigation in the Arctic' (2016) 7 (2) *Arctic Review on Law and Politics* 136, 139 <https://doi.org/10.17585/arctic.v7.427>.

80 See Edith Brown Weiss, 'Understanding Compliance with International Environmental Agreements: The Baker's Dozen Myths' (1998) 32 *U. Rich. L. Rev.* 1555; W. Bradnee Chambers, 'Towards an Improved Understanding of Legal Effectiveness of International Environmental Treaties', (2003) 16 *Geo. Int'l Envtl. L. Rev.* 501.

non-binding is therefore less relevant to the intention of the Protocol, even after taking into account the numerous qualifying statements. This is also confirmed by the emphasis placed on the black carbon provisions by the UNECE and the CLRTAP EB. Therefore, assessment of the Protocol should include whether reductions in black carbon are occurring. In this context, it is perhaps better to consider the 2012 Amendments as the start of a process rather than a definitive regulatory regime, although this is predicated on the hope of further negotiations and amendments.[81]

4 Developments since the Gothenburg Protocol Amendments (Post-2012)

In this final section I consider developments on air pollution and climate change under the Gothenburg Protocol and the CLRTAP regime since the adoption of the Amendments, considering entry into force, outreach activities with external organisations, black carbon emissions reporting, the production of guidance documents on black carbon, and recent developments on methane. The section also considers in detail the twists and turns of the Gothenburg Protocol Review which was triggered by the Amendments entry into force in 2019. The review has the potential to lead to another round of revisions of the Gothenburg Protocol, possibly integrating air pollution and climate change further, and making the framework more ambitious. In this account, the years after the negotiations are striking for their reliance on bureaucracy (e.g. Task Forces, numerous review groups etc.) and a noticeable lack of political leadership. That is not to say that such processes will not eventually deliver, but they are marked by small incremental change which may build into momentum with time. What the exact outcomes of these processes will be remains unclear. Table 5.4 contains a summary timeline of the major events on the Gothenburg Protocol review from 2016 onwards, discussed in this Section.

4.1 *The Long Wait for Entry into Force of the Amendments, External Outreach, and Black Carbon Guidance*

The most important issue for the EB and for the consideration of compliance was that the Amendments entered into force, and to some extent the years directly after the revision were unusual in their quietness. This is surprising

81 For a general discussion on the possible future of global cooperation on air pollution, see *Yamineva and Romppanen* (n 13) 197–99.

TABLE 5.4 Timeline of the key developments on the Gothenburg Protocol (2016 onwards)

Year	Event
2016	Joint report from the EMEP Steering Body and Working Group on Effects 'Towards Cleaner Air: Scientific Assessment Report 2016' published. EB establishes an ad hoc policy review group of experts.
2017	The ad hoc policy review group of experts recommended that the Gothenburg Protocol should be reviewed and updated following the entry into force of the Amendments with additional commitments.
2018	The ad hoc policy review group of experts submits a draft revised long-term strategy for the Convention and makes suggestions on the possible updating of the Amended Gothenburg Protocol 2012. The EB adopts a weaker version of the long-term strategy for the Convention.
2019	The 2012 Amendments to the Gothenburg Protocol entered into force. The EB decides to initiate the review of the Gothenburg Protocol (as amended). The EB adopts the 'Declaration on Clean Air for 2020–2030 and beyond in the United Nations Economic Commission for Europe region'.
2020	Gothenburg Protocol review group created.
2021	Gothenburg Protocol review group produces its draft review report. The Working Group on Strategies and Review begins to consider methane.

because failure to achieve entry into force would likely have prompted a crisis and called into question the Protocol's contemporary usefulness. Failure to at least achieve entry into force by the Annex II emissions target date of 2020 would have been disconcerting. The majority of the Amendments required two thirds of the Parties to the original Protocol to accept, with entry into force occurring ninety days after this threshold had been reached. The Amendments would only apply to those that accepted them, however. By 2016 only one country had accepted the Amendments: Sweden. A "special segment" at EB36 in December 2016 considered progress in the entry into force of the Protocol Amendments, with the obvious intent of improving ratification, acceptance and approval of, or accession to the Amendments.[82] Much depended on the EU, but the EU deferred its acceptance of the 2012 Gothenburg Protocol Amendments until after it had agreed its 2016 National Emission Ceilings Directive.[83] The Directive incorporated the Gothenburg Protocol 2020 targets but also set more stringent targets for 2030.[84] The EU accepted the 2012 Gothenburg Protocol Amendments in August 2017 and that kick-started acceptance by other Parties which would ultimately lead to entry into force in 2019.

Participation and acceptance by the countries of Southern and Eastern Europe is inconsistent (notably Italy and Poland are not Parties), although this may be symbolic defiance given that they are given targets under EU law. Participation by the post-Soviet states is non-existent for those that did not join the EU, with only Belarus featuring in Annex II of the amended Protocol (although not a Party), with no target or acceptance by Russia thus far. Attempts to promote the participation of the EECCA countries, through for example the EECCA Coordinating group (established in 2010) have tended to focus on increasing cooperation, information exchange and capacity-building through the development of emissions reporting, monitoring and modelling, with the translation of documents into Russian.[85] The ultimate aim has been to raise the political profile of the Convention in the region and encourage ratification of the Convention's latest amended Protocols. Over the past decade the various sessions and workshops have not achieved a great deal beyond getting more ratifications to the EMEP Protocol 1984, which corresponds with an interest in building monitoring and scientific capabilities. In light of Russia's invasion of Ukraine, a new approach to the EECCA may be required, and greater thought as to whether the classification of countries by their shared Soviet past is appropriate in the 2020s.

Whilst waiting for entry into force, the EB and the UNECE attempted to make progress in other areas. In December 2012, a guidance document on the control techniques for emissions of sulphur, NO_X, VOCs and PM (including PM_{10}, $PM_{2.5}$ and black carbon) from stationary sources was adopted (Decision 2012/

---

82 UNECE/EB, *Report of the Executive Body on Its Thirty-Sixth Session, Geneva, 15 and 16 December 2016. ECE/EB.AIR/137* (Geneva: UNECE, 16 March 2017), p. 6.

83 Directive (EU) 2016/2284 of the European Parliament and of the Council of 14 December 2016 on the reduction of national emissions of certain atmospheric pollutants, amending Directive 2003/35/EC and repealing Directive 2001/81/EC [2016] OJ L344/1.

84 See also Seita Romppanen, 'Arctic Climate Governance via EU Law on Black Carbon?' (2018) 27 (1) *Review of European, Comparative & International Environmental Law* 45.

85 See for example Report of the 1st session of the Coordinating Group on Promotion of Actions towards Implementation of the CLRTAP in EECCA, Working Group of Strategies and Review, 48th Session, 11–15 Apr. 2011, Geneva (Switzerland), Informal Doc. No. 21.

8).[86] Outreach activities to external organisations working on climate change and air pollution were undertaken. Kulovesi has argued that "the potential to advance the black carbon mitigation agenda through informal collaboration between the LRTAP and other relevant bodies should not be overlooked".[87] To some extent the EB has been well aware of this potential. For example, in 2014 a representative from the CCAC attended the EB session. The CCAC were particularly interested in cooperating on the "emissions and inventories of black carbon and precursors of tropospheric ozone",[88] and the regional assessment of SLCPs.[89] In 2015 the UNECE became an official non-State partner of the Coalition, and this led to closer ties, with for example, the Convention being mentioned in the Coalition's five-year Strategic Plan.

Likewise, the regime scientific bodies continued to work on climate change and air pollution. In September 2016, a joint session between the EMEP Steering Body and the Working Group on Effects was held with one of the three themes for the session being air pollution and climate change interactions. The joint session points towards the willingness of the Convention scientific bodies to position the Convention as part of a larger coalition, or grouping, with a "considerable part" of the joint session devoted to outreach and cooperation opportunities with what were described as "partner organizations" such as the Arctic Monitoring and Assessment Programme, the CCAC, the Copernicus Atmosphere Monitoring Service (the European Union's Earth Observation Programme) and the North-East Asian Subregional Programme for Environmental Cooperation.[90]

In 2018 the EB decided further guidance on prioritising simultaneous reductions in $PM_{2.5}$ and black carbon was needed and requested the Task Force on Techno-economic Issues and the Task Force on Integrated Assessment

---

86 UNECE/EB, *Report of the Executive Body on Its Thirty-First Session. Geneva, 11–13 December 2012. Addendum. Decisions Adopted at the Thirty-First Session. ECE/EB.AIR/113/Add.1* (Geneva: UNECE, 19 March 2013), p. 19.

87 Kati Kulovesi, 'Exploring Transnational Legal Orders: Using Transnational Environmental Law to Strengthen the Global Regulation of Black Carbon for the Benefit of the Arctic Region', in Veerle Heyvaert and Leslie-Anne Duvic-Paoli (eds) *Research Handbook on Transnational Environmental Law*, (Edward Elgar Publishing, 2020), 18–31, <https://doi.org/10.4337/9781788119634.00010>.

88 UNECE/EB, *Report of the Executive Body on Its Thirty-Third Session. Geneva, 8–11 December 2014. ECE/EB.AIR/127* (Geneva: UNECE, 22 January 2015), p. 14.

89 UNECE/EB, *Report of the Executive Body on Its Thirty-Fifth Session, Geneva, 2–4 May 2016. ECE/EB.AIR/135* (Geneva: UNECE, 31 August 2016), p. 8.

90 Established in 1993 by China, North Korea, Japan, Mongolia, South Korea and Russia. *UNECE/EB* (n 82) 4.

Modelling to develop this.[91] Adopted in 2021 at EB41, the resulting guidance document was developed using Greenhouse Gas and Air Pollution Interactions and Synergies (GAINS) modelling and clarified which sectors to prioritise, such as agricultural waste burning and heating stoves.[92] Whilst this is a useful guidance document, its existence is highly correlated with entry into force of the 2012 Amendments in 2019, its timing is once again suggestive of the slow progress made on black carbon in the years after 2012, related to the seven-year wait for entry into force of the Amendments.

4.2 *The 2017 Policy Review and the Long-Term Strategy for the Convention: towards the Review and Updating of the Gothenburg Protocol*

In 2016, a major joint report from the EMEP Steering Body and Working Group on Effects was published entitled '*Towards Cleaner Air: Scientific Assessment Report 2016*'.[93] In light of this report, Decision 2016/1 established an ad hoc policy review group of experts. The group proposed updates to the long-term strategy for the Convention that would broaden the Convention outlook. The group strongly pushed the development of an "integrated environmental policy" under the Convention, which included "[a]n integrated approach to air pollution and climate change policies and measures".[94] The group also recommended "improving the technical and scientific basis for the Convention and its Protocols by better assessing progress in improving air quality, human health and ecosystem effects … [and] further align monitoring and modelling

91 UNECE/EB, *Report of the Executive Body on Its Thirty-Eighth Session*. Geneva, 10–14 December 2018. ECE/EB.AIR/142* (Geneva: UNECE, 22 February 2019), 8.

92 UNECE/EB, *Prioritizing Reductions of Particulate Matter from Sources That Are Also Significant Sources of Black Carbon – Analysis and Guidance*. Executive Body for the Convention on Long-Range Transboundary Air Pollution, Forty-First Session, Geneva, 6–8 December 2021. Item 4 (b) of the Provisional Agenda, Review of the Implementation of the 2020–2021 Workplan: Policy. ECE/EB.AIR/2021/6*, 23 September 2021, 1; Decision 2021/2, UNECE/EB, *Report of the Executive Body on Its Forty-First Session, Geneva, 6–8 December 2021. ECE/EB.AIR/148* (Geneva: UNECE, 15 June 2022).

93 Rob Maas and Peringe Grennfelt (eds), *Towards Cleaner Air: Scientific Assessment Report 2016* (Oslo: EMEP Steering Body and Working Group on Effects of the Convention on Long-Range Transboundary Air Pollution, 2016).

94 UNECE/EB, *Highlights of Proposed Updates to the Long-Term Strategy for the Convention on Long-Range Transboundary Air Pollution. Submitted by the Ad Hoc Policy Review Group of Experts on the 2016 Scientific Assessment of the Convention. Executive Body for the Convention on Long-Range Transboundary Air Pollution, Thirty-Seventh Session, Geneva, 11–14 December 2017. Item 8 of the Provisional Agenda, Policy Response to the 2016 Scientific Assessment of the Convention. ECE/EB.AIR/2017/4* (Geneva: UNECE, 29 September 2017), 5.

activities for air quality with those undertaken for assessing impacts".[95] The primary recommendation of the group was to increase ratification and implementation of the amended Protocols. A key recommendation was that the 1999 Gothenburg Protocol, as amended in 2012, should be reviewed and updated following the entry into force. The group stated that "[b]ased on the 2016 scientific assessment, these updates should include the consideration of additional commitments for certain pollutants, specifically: particulate matter, including black carbon; ammonia; and ozone precursors, including methane".[96]

The response to the ad hoc policy review group of experts report was mixed at EB37 (December 2017). There was support for improving ratification and implementation of the Amendments, but the idea of new revisions was poorly received by some states. The US representative argued that "it was premature to discuss the updates to the protocols, in particular to the Gothenburg Protocol, before the amendments had entered into force".[97] The EU was cautiously supportive, taking the view that "any move towards revision of the Gothenburg Protocol should be accompanied by a focused drive towards ratification".[98] Canada took a middle position between the US and the EU, arguing that "any updates to or revisions of the Gothenburg Protocol should begin only after the protocol as amended had entered into force," but also noted that "preparatory work could and should begin prior to that time".[99]

In 2018 the ad hoc policy review group of experts submitted its draft revised long-term strategy for the Convention. In this document, countries were reminded that "[p]ursuant to article 10 of the Gothenburg Protocol, the Parties are expected to review the amended Protocol and update it if necessary after its entry into force".[100] The group attempted to shape the direction of travel of the review and any possible updating to the Protocol (as amended). Suggestions for possible updating included:

- "the introduction of mandatory emissions reporting;"
- "[updating] the emission reduction commitments;"

95 ibid 5.
96 ibid 5.
97 UNECE/EB, *Report of the Executive Body on Its Thirty-Seventh Session, Geneva, 11–14 December 2017. ECE/EB.AIR/140* (Geneva: UNECE, 23 April 2018), p. 12.
98 ibid 13.
99 ibid 13.
100 UNECE/EB, *Draft Revised Long-Term Strategy for the Convention, Submitted by the Expert Group. Executive Body for the Convention on Long-Range Transboundary Air Pollution, Thirty-Eighth Session, Geneva, 10–14 December 2018. Item 6 of the Provisional Agenda. Revised Long-Term Strategy for the Convention. ECE/EB.AIR/2018/1/Rev.1* (Geneva: UNECE, 27 November 2018), 10.

- "further measures to reduce black carbon emissions;"
- "further emissions requirements for fine particulate matter, acid rain and ozone precursors already included in the Protocol, in particular strengthened ammonia abatement measures; and the treatment of ozone precursors not yet addressed, such as methane".[101]

The ad hoc policy review group of experts also suggested that the updating could consider, *inter alia*, "shipping emissions (with due consideration for IMO policies and measures); further requirements for hemispheric air pollution; and barriers to implementation, including for existing sources. This review should also include a reflection on the flexibility provisions and their effectiveness".[102] The suggestions amounted to a fairly bold review programme for the Protocol. The group noted that the "completeness and accuracy of emissions inventories and projections needs to be improved", particularly for EECCA.[103] Perhaps somewhat disconcertingly, the group also stressed that the scientific definition of black carbon for both emissions reporting and monitoring of ambient air and effects monitoring needed to improve as "a high priority".[104] On this issue there were specific concerns on the role of hemispheric pollution (i.e. greater than the UNECE region) which EMEP would need to address.

The draft long-term strategy was considered by the EB at EB38 (December 2018). Although most of the suggestions by the ad hoc policy review group of experts were accepted, the EB made subtle changes to the text. The adopted 'Long-term strategy for the Convention on Long-range Transboundary Air Pollution for 2020–2030 and beyond' (through decision 2018/5) appears to suggest that a full review of the Protocol may not be required, instead and somewhat curiously phrased, the review could be limited to "portions".[105] The clarity of the draft strategy on black carbon and the other issues was weakened to "appropriate steps towards reducing emissions of black carbon, methane (as an ozone precursor) and emissions from shipping (with due consideration for IMO policies and measures)".[106] This highlights that limited progress had been made in moving Parties on from the phraseology of the 2012 Amendments (when the idea of appropriateness was dominant, see Section 3.1 above). The

101 ibid 10.
102 ibid 10.
103 ibid 11.
104 ibid 11.
105 UNECE/EB, *Report of the Executive Body on Its Thirty-Eighth Session*, Geneva, 10–14 December 2018. Addendum. Decisions Adopted by the Executive Body.* ECE/EB.AIR/142/*Add.2* (Geneva: UNECE, 22 February 2019), 10.
106 ibid 11.

long-term strategy for 2020–2030 and beyond did not, therefore, contain an explicit aim to revise the Gothenburg Protocol (as amended), only to review it according to Article 10.

In 2019, an opportunity for diplomacy arose at EB39, which included an anniversary event to mark forty years of the Convention. Participants in the event stressed the Convention's strengths, namely its flexible and consensual negotiating process and its science-based approach.[107] There appears to have been a fair amount of goodwill to continue cooperation under the Convention. The EB adopted the 'Declaration on Clean Air for 2020–2030 and beyond in the United Nations Economic Commission for Europe region'.[108] Whilst noting the Convention's successes, in paragraph 5(f) the Declaration urged action on the promotion of "an integrated approach to environmental policymaking, recognizing that air pollution is the central link in the interaction between ground-level ozone, nitrogen, human health, climate change and ecosystem". To some extent the post-2012 years can therefore be seen as when climate change began to be increasingly embedded in the scientific and institutional language of the regime, although this was yet to achieve significant changes in law.

4.3 *The 2nd Gothenburg Protocol Review (2019 Onwards)*

The 2012 Amendments to the Gothenburg Protocol entered into force on 7 October 2019.[109] The amended Article 10 contains a requirement for a general review of the Protocol, but also a specific requirement to evaluate the mitigation measures for black carbon emissions and ammonia control measures, no later than at the second session of the EB after entry into force. In anticipation of this, in May 2019 the WGSR had produced a list of 'potential elements' to inform the Gothenburg Protocol Review based on submissions by the Parties, drawing heavily on the work already undertaken for the long-term strategy (discussed in Section 4.2 above). The WGSR recommended that the EB launch the review.[110] The suggested potential elements of the review were broader than those legally required, including addressing gaps in the Protocol, and scientific and technical issues, including clarifying the definition of black carbon.[111]

107 See UNECE/EB, *Report of the Executive Body on Its Thirty-Ninth Session, Geneva, 9–13 December 2019. ECE/EB.AIR/144* (Geneva: UNECE, 31 January 2020), Annex II, 18–19.

108 See Annex III, ibid 22.

109 ibid 4.

110 UNECE/EB, *Report of the Working Group on Strategies and Review on Its Fifty-Seventh Session, Geneva, 21–24 May 2019. ECE/EB.AIR/WG.5/122* (Geneva: UNECE, 4 October 2019), 5.

111 See Annex I, ibid.

The Annex suggested a great deal of potential complexity on climate change and air pollution which the review would need to resolve. At EB39 (December 2019), the EU proposed to expand the list of potential elements of the review to include, inter alia, the "[a]ir pollution effects on marine ecosystems".[112]

The NGO 'The European Environmental Bureau', who had a right to be present at EB39, made a statement on its expectations for the revision. The ideas presented could provide a useful comparator for any future revisions of the Gothenburg Protocol. This included: the introduction of a long-term vision of zero pollution, with indicative targets for 2035 and 2040; a 2030 commitment that pollution would not exceed the World Health Organisation air quality guidelines for critical levels and loads; binding national emission reduction commitments for 2030; the expansion of pollutants covered by binding reduction commitments (including methane and black carbon); the inclusion of mandatory technical annexes with binding minimum requirements (e.g. emission limit values and abatement measures); a special focus on achieving reductions in agricultural ammonia and methane emissions; and the creation of a new review and revision mechanism, so that the indicative national emission reduction commitments for 2035 and 2040 are reviewed and made binding five years beforehand.[113] Despite the obvious need and desire for an ambitious revision which would produce a new long-term framework agreement, whether the Parties would agree to such a change is an open question.

The EB decided to initiate the review of the Gothenburg Protocol (as amended) at EB39.[114] Work was disrupted by the COVID-19 pandemic in 2020. Nonetheless, the WGSR created the Gothenburg Protocol review group (GP Review Group), which produced a dense preparatory document, of which SLCPs were a small part, including a number of scientific and technical questions to the subsidiary bodies of the Convention on black carbon and methane.[115] At the truncated EB40 (December 2020), conducted in a hybrid format

---

112 *UNECE/EB* (n 107) 7.

113 ibid 27.

114 Decision 2019/4, UNECE/EB, *Report of the Executive Body on Its Thirty-Ninth Session, Geneva, 9–13 December 2019. Addendum. Decisions Adopted by the Executive Body. ECE/EB.AIR/144/Add.1* (Geneva: UNECE, 3 February 2020), 16.

115 See Annex I, UNECE/EB, *Preparations for the Review of the Protocol to Abate Acidification, Eutrophication and Ground-Level Ozone as Amended in 2012* Submitted by the Gothenburg Protocol Review Group. Advance Version. Executive Body for the Convention on Long-Range Transboundary Air Pollution, Working Group on Strategies and Review, Fifty-Eighth Session, Geneva, 14–15 and 17 December 2020. Item 5 of the Provisional Agenda: Review of Sufficiency and Effectiveness of the Protocol to Abate Acidification, Eutrophication and Ground-Level Ozone. ECE/EB.AIR/2020/3–ECE/EB.AIR/WG.5/2020/3* (Geneva: UNECE, 30 September 2020).

due to the pandemic (in person and online), it was decided that "the scope of the review should remain broad at this time, … [and] should focus on information-gathering, scientific and technical inputs and assessing the information collected".[116]

In 2021, the GP Review Group produced a draft review report.[117] The draft report noted that whilst black carbon emissions reporting was voluntary, 40 Parties had provided emission estimates. However, there were "[s]ignificant inconsistencies … between national BC [black carbon] emission estimates, suggesting that the accuracy and completeness of the submissions need to be improved".[118] Reporting and monitoring had been assisted through cooperation with external bodies, such as the Arctic Monitoring and Assessment Programme, and the Copernicus Atmosphere Monitoring Service. EMEP with partners was going to develop a strategy to harmonize black carbon reporting and control strategies at the global level through cooperation with CCAC and the Intergovernmental Panel on Climate Change.[119] The GP Review Group highlighted that the EMEP/European Environment Agency Air Pollutant Emission Inventory Guidebook should be improved, with decisions needed on the metrics for black carbon and inclusion of condensable PM. The emissions methodologies also "need to better account for the influences of climate change".[120] Over 2000–2019, total $PM_{2.5}$ concentrations had reduced by 46% at EMEP long-term observational sites, a reduction described as 'significant'.[121] Total carbonaceous aerosols (which includes black carbon) from observation and modelling of 15 EMEP stations showed an average reduction of 4% per year.[122]

On the general approach to climate change, the GP Review Group noted that "more focus is needed on reducing emissions of air pollutants that have

---

116 Decision 2020/2, UNECE/EB, *Report of the Executive Body on Its Fortieth Session. Geneva, 18 December 2020. ECE/EB.AIR/146* (Geneva: UNECE, 12 February 2021), 8.

117 UNECE/EB, *Draft Report on the Review of the Protocol to Abate Acidification, Eutrophication and Ground-Level Ozone, as Amended in 2012 Submitted by the Gothenburg Protocol Review Group. Executive Body for the Convention on Long-Range Transboundary Air Pollution, Forty-First Session, Geneva, 6–8 December 2021. Item 5 of the Provisional Agenda: Review of Sufficiency and Effectiveness of the Protocol to Abate Acidification, Eutrophication and Ground-Level Ozone. ECE/EB.AIR/2021/4* (Geneva: UNECE, 24 September 2021).

118 ibid 3.

119 UNECE/EB, *Report of the Executive Body on Its Thirty-Seventh Session, Geneva, 11–14 December 2017. Addendum. 2018–2019 Workplan for the Implementation of the Convention. ECE/EB.AIR/140/Add.1* (Geneva: UNECE, 23 April 2018).

120 *UNECE/EB* (n 117) 4.

121 ibid 5.

122 ibid 5.

a warming effect".[123] The group recommended coordinating with the Arctic Council and the CCAC to produce the best SLCP reduction strategy. The group also noted challenges on ozone and methane. The fact that soil NOx emissions for EU member states were specifically excluded from the revised Gothenburg Protocol emission reduction commitments was seen as a barrier to progress.[124] The GP Review Group recommended using and further developing integrated least-cost reduction strategy modelling, such as the GAINS model[125] and the report stipulated the modelling work that would need to be completed by spring 2022.[126] The draft report, which Parties would be commenting on, was fairly descriptive and somewhat repetitive regarding climate change and air pollution challenges and co-benefits, to the extent that not much progress appeared to have been made in broader thinking on the issue over the past ten years. Nonetheless, the EB noted at its 41st session that "excellent progress" had been made on the Gothenburg Protocol review by the subsidiary bodies, and set out the aim of finalizing the review and submitting its conclusions the following year (EB42, scheduled for December 2022).[127]

4.4 *New Developments on the Control of Methane*

An apparent breakthrough on methane occurred in 2021 during the review process. The WGSR was planning on discussing "the need, best approach and potential options to address CH_4 in a future instrument: e.g., if and how to include CH_4 in the Protocol, which emission sources to focus on, and how to link with the forum for international collaboration on air pollution".[128] The WGSR made the request at EB40 (December 2021)[129] to prepare an informal document in collaboration with the Centre for Integrated Assessment Modelling with a focus on air-climate synergies, which was approved by the EB. This document would "inform consideration of methane in a future instrument", with the EB requesting that the scope of the informal document include "methane, black carbon and nitrogen and its compounds".[130]

---

123 ibid 17.

124 ibid 18.

125 See IIASA, 'Greenhouse Gas and Air Pollution Interactions and Synergies (GAINS)' (*International Institute for Applied Systems Analysis*, 2022) <http://iiasa.ac.at/models-and-data/greenhouse-gas-and-air-pollution-interactions-and-synergies> accessed 23 September 2022.

126 *UNECE/EB* (n 117) 18.

127 *UNECE/EB*, ECE/EB.AIR/148 (n 92), 6.

128 *UNECE/EB* (n 117) 17.

129 Once again in hybrid format due to the COVID-19 pandemic.

130 *UNECE/EB*, ECE/EB.AIR/148 (n 92), 6.

At its April 2022 session, the WGSR considered the informal document developed by the GP Review Group on the 'Potential options for addressing methane as an ozone precursor under the Air Convention',[131] the informal document on 'Synergies and interactions with other policy areas'[132] and the latest Draft report on the Gothenburg Protocol Review.[133] The synergies report is a useful document informed by modelling which to some extent bolsters the case for an integrated approach to air pollution and climate change. Fascinatingly, the document once again raises the issue of radiative forcing, noting the cooling effect of sulphur. It resolves this by stating that "[t]o limit the effects of air pollution policy on climate change, a balanced approach is needed, which will mean a focus on reducing emissions of air pollutants that have a warming effect, such as black carbon and ozone precursors … [I]t is of high importance to promote measures addressing … mitigation of carbon dioxide".[134]

The document on methane contained six options/strategies ranging from improving monitoring, to voluntary measures, to the adoption of emission reduction targets. This was a scoping exercise, and although produced by the GP Review Group, it was not the case that the options would be legally binding, as any action could be limited to a guidance document, for example. At the WGSR session where the document was considered, the EU appeared supportive of the process but some opposition could be inferred from the US. The US representative "suggested that not addressing methane under the Gothenburg Protocol be included as an option" and also suggested "marking each option as advantageous or disadvantageous", which does not quite follow as the document was clear that a combination of options could be employed.[135] The

131 UNECE, 'Potential Options for Addressing Methane as an Ozone Precursor under the Air Convention (Gothenburg Protocol Review). Informal Document, Agenda Item 4. 60th Session of the Working Group on Strategies and Review. Gothenburg Protocol Review Group'. (Geneva: UNECE, 2022).

132 UNECE, 'Synergies and Interactions with Other Policy Areas. Working Group on Strategies and Review, Sixtieth Session, 11–14 April 2022. Informal Document No. 1 (Revised 20 March 2022)'. (Geneva: UNECE, 2022).

133 UNECE/EB, *Draft Report on the Review of the Protocol to Abate Acidification, Eutrophication and Ground-Level Ozone, as Amended in 2012*. Submitted by the Gothenburg Protocol Review Group. Executive Body for the Convention on Long-Range Transboundary Air Pollution, Working Group on Strategies and Review Sixtieth Session Geneva, 11–14 April 2022. Item 4 of the Provisional Agenda: Review of Sufficiency and Effectiveness of the Protocol to Abate Acidification, Eutrophication and Ground-Level Ozone.* ECE/EB.AIR/WG.5/2022/3 (Geneva: UNECE, 31 January 2022).

134 *UNECE* (n 132) 2.

135 UNECE/EB, *Report of the Working Group on Strategies and Review on Its Sixtieth Session. Executive Body for the Convention on Long-Range Transboundary Air Pollution, Working*

US appeared keen to explore the idea of voluntary measures and capacity-building programmes. The UK felt that the options "require further development", whilst the Swiss somewhat idealistically saw the document as "an instrument of communication with institutions working on climate change and with countries outside the ECE region".[136] The GP Review Group stressed in the informal document that, whilst "methane is addressed to some extent under the UNFCCC … the UNFCCC was not designed to take into account the health benefits of methane mitigation, nor does it have quantitative commitments to focus particularly on methane as an ozone precursor".[137] It is too early to say whether the process on methane will achieve anything substantial but the general principle that there is scope under the CLRTAP to contribute to methane emissions control which complements the UNFCCC should be an important building block for the regime.

5 Conclusion

The CLRTAP regime continues to have a strong integration of science and policy through the work of the subsidiary bodies. As this chapter has highlighted, the Parties rely on up-to-date scientific data and knowledge on SLCPs. This sophisticated regime has not yet translated knowledge on SLCPs into ambitious action and the effectiveness of the Gothenburg Protocol on black carbon could be improved. The CLRTAP regime has repositioned itself and is now more open to collaboration on SLCPs with external organisations than it perhaps was ten years ago, reflecting broader changes in international environmental law towards transnationalism. The options for further developments in this area appear limited, however, methane may offer an opportunity for increased collaboration. The regulatory approach of an integrated environmental policy has proved to be more difficult to deliver than perhaps first realised. The CLRTAP regime is consistent in its ability to find compromise and consensus, and it should therefore be able to continue to advance SLCP regulation. There is a pressing need to enhance the mechanisms to improve the participation rates of states from the less developed countries in the Eastern UNECE region, and as suggested in this chapter, this could be assisted by ending the post-Soviet EECCA model to a more nuanced collaboration with these countries.

Group on Strategies and Review, Sixtieth Session, Geneva, 11–14 April 2022. ECE/EB.AIR/WG.5/128 (Geneva: UNECE, 16 August 2022), 5.

136 ibid 5.

137 *UNECE* (n 131) 1.

As for the overall Review of the Gothenburg Protocol and the position of black carbon, whether the review does produce the kind of radical revisions that are required is highly uncertain. Assuming the review is concluded in a timely and satisfactory manner, a fairly rapid revision could be concluded by 2025, but given the overall somewhat relaxed approach Parties have had to the regime, it may take longer. It could be argued that the process will be considered a success if the Protocol is revised at all, but there is a clear opportunity to take bold action in this window of opportunity to reduce SLCPs which may not arise for another decade. The Parties made significant revisions in 2012 and there is no reason why major revisions could not occur now. Any revisions should take account the concerns of the less developed countries and offer financial and technological assistance to enable them to reduce their domestic air pollution and transboundary air pollution. The CLRTAP regime remains uniquely placed to improve air pollution for millions of people whilst contributing to the reduction of climate warming pollutants, but its potential is yet to be realised. This can only be achieved through the creation of a new inclusive long-term framework under the Gothenburg Protocol which creates a system of increasing ambition through to 2050 and beyond.

Bibliography

Ågren, C., 'New Gothenburg Protocol Adopted' (*Acid News*, June 2012) <http://www.airclim.org/acidnews/new-gothenburg-protocol-adopted> accessed 2 February 2023.

Amann, M., G. Kiesewetter, W. Schöpp, Z. Klimont, W. Winiwarter, J. Cofala, P. Rafaj, L. Höglund-Isaksson, A. Gomez-Sabriana, C. Heyes, P. Purohit, J. Borken-Kleefeld, F. Wagner, R. Sander, H. Fagerli, A. Nyiri, L. Cozzi and C. Pavarini, 'Reducing Global Air Pollution: the Scope for Further Policy Interventions' (2020) 378 *Philosophical Transactions of the Royal Society A: Mathematical, Physical and Engineering Sciences*, 1.

ApSimon, H., M. Amann, S. Åström, and T. Oxley, 'Synergies in Addressing Air Quality and Climate Change', (2009) 9 (6) *Climate Policy* 669 <https://doi.org/10.3763/cpol.2009.0678>.

Brown Weiss, E., 'Understanding Compliance with International Environmental Agreements: the Baker's Dozen Myths' (1998) 32 *U. Rich. L. Rev.* 1555.

Byrne, A., 'The 1979 Convention on Long-Range Transboundary Air Pollution: Assessing Its Effectiveness as a Multilateral Environmental Regime after 35 Years', (2015) 4 (1) *Transnational Environmental Law* 37, 59 <https://doi.org/10.1017/S2047102514000296>.

Byrne, A., 'Trouble in the Air: Recent Developments under the 1979 Convention on Long-Range Transboundary Air Pollution', (2017) 26 (3) *Review of European, Comparative & International Environmental Law* 210 <https://doi.org/10.1111/reel.12219>.

Chambers, W. B., 'Towards an Improved Understanding of Legal Effectiveness of International Environmental Treaties', (2003) 16 *Geo. Int'l Envtl. L. Rev.* 501.

Climate & Clean Air Coalition (*ccacoalition.org*, 2022) <https://www.ccacoalition.org/en> accessed 12 December 2022.

Climate & Clean Air Coalition, 'Black Carbon' (*ccacoalition.org*, 2022) <https://www.ccacoalition.org/en/slcps/black-carbon> accessed 9 December 2022.

Convention on Long-Range Transboundary Air Pollution (adopted 13 November 1979, entered into force 16 March 1983) 1302 UNTS 217.

EMEP, *EMEP Status Report 1/2016: Transboundary Particulate Matter, Photo-Oxidants, Acidifying and Eutrophying Components*. (Oslo, Norway: Norwegian Meteorological Institute, 13 September 2016).

European Environment Agency, *Air Pollution Impacts from Carbon Capture and Storage* (CCS). *EEA Technical Report No 14/2011* (Copenhagen: Publications Office of the European Union, 2011).

Grennfelt, P., A. Engleryd, M. Forsius, Ø. Hov, H. Rodhe, and E. Cowling, 'Acid Rain and Air Pollution: 50 Years of Progress in Environmental Science and Policy', (2020) 49 (4) *Ambio* 849 <https://doi.org/10.1007/s13280-019-01244-4>.

HTAP, *Hemispheric Transport of Air Pollution 2010 Executive Summary, ECE/EB.AIR/2010/10 Corrected*, Informal Document No. 10, Convention on Long-range Transboundary Air Pollution Executive Body 28th Session <https://unece.org/fileadmin/DAM/env/documents/2010/eb/wg5/wg47/Informal%20documents/Info%2016_Hemispheric%20Transport%20of%20Air%20Pollution%202010_Executive%20Summary.pdf> accessed 3 February 2023.

HTAP, 'The Task Force on Hemispheric Transport of Air Pollution (TF HTAP)' (*Htap.Org*, 2022) <http://htap.org/> accessed 25 May 2022.

IIASA, 'Greenhouse Gas and Air Pollution Interactions and Synergies (GAINS)' (*International Institute for Applied Systems Analysis*, 2022) <http://iiasa.ac.at/models-and-data/greenhouse-gas-and-air-pollution-interactions-and-synergies> accessed 23 September 2022.

Khan, S. A., and K. Kulovesi, 'Black Carbon and the Arctic: Global Problem-solving through the Nexus of Science, Law and Space' (2018) 27 (1) *Review of European Comparative & International Environmental Law* 5, 9 <https://doi.org/10.1111/reel.12245>.

Kulovesi, K., 'Exploring Transnational Legal Orders: Using Transnational Environmental Law to Strengthen the Global Regulation of Black Carbon for the Benefit of the Arctic Region', in V. Heyvaert and L-A. Duvic-Paoli (eds) *Research Handbook on*

Transnational Environmental Law, (Edward Elgar Publishing, 2020), 18, <https://doi.org/10.4337/9781788119634.00010>.

Longhurst, J., J. Barnes, T. Chatterton, L. De Vito, M. Everard, E. Hayes, E. Prestwood and B. Williams, 'Analysing Air Pollution and Its Management through the Lens of the UN Sustainable Development Goals: a Review and Assessment' (2018) 230 *WIT Transactions on Ecology and the Environment* 3 <https://doi.org/10.2495/AIR180011>.

Maas, R., and P. Grennfelt, eds, *Towards Cleaner Air: Scientific Assessment Report 2016* (Oslo: EMEP Steering Body and Working Group on Effects of the Convention on Long-Range Transboundary Air Pollution, 2016).

Massai, L., '1. Transboundary Air Pollution' (2011) 22 (1) *Yearbook of International Environmental Law* 193 <https://doi.org/10.1093/yiel/yvs077>.

Moses, E., B. Cardenas, and J. Seddon, 'The Most Successful Air Pollution Treaty You've Never Heard Of' (*wri.org*, 25 February 2020) <https://www.wri.org/insights/most-successful-air-pollution-treaty-youve-never-heard> accessed 7 May 2022.

Protocol to the 1979 CLRTAP on Long-Term Financing of the Co-operative Programme for Monitoring and Evaluation of the Long-Range Transmission of Air Pollutants in Europe (EMEP) (adopted 28 September 1984, entered into force 28 January 1988) 1491 UNTS 167.

Protocol to the 1979 CLRTAP concerning the Control of Emissions of Nitrogen Oxides or their Transboundary Fluxes (adopted 31 October 1988, entered into force 14 February 1991) 1593 UNTS 287.

Protocol to the 1979 CLRTAP concerning the Control of Emissions of Volatile Organic Compounds or their Transboundary Fluxes (adopted 18 November 1991, entered into force 29 September 1997), 2001 UNTS 187.

Protocol to the 1979 CLRTAP on Further Reduction of Sulphur Emissions (adopted 14 June 1994, entered into force 5 August 1998), 2030 UNTS 122.

Protocol to the 1979 CLRTAP on Heavy Metals (adopted 24 June 1998, entered into force 29 December 2003), 2237 UNTS 4.

Protocol to the 1979 CLRTAP to Abate Acidification, Eutrophication and Ground-Level Ozone (adopted 30 November 1999, entered into force 17 May 2005) 2319 UNTS 81.

Reis, S., P. Grennfelt, Z. Klimont, M. Amann, H. ApSimon, J.-P. Hettelingh, M. Holland, A.-C. LeGall, R. Maas, M. Posch, T. Spranger, M. A. Sutton, and M. Williams, 'From Acid Rain to Climate Change' (2012) 338 (6111) *Science* 1153.

Romppanen, S., 'Arctic Climate Governance via EU Law on Black Carbon?' (2018) 27 (1) *Review of European, Comparative & International Environmental Law* 45.

Rosenthal, E. and R. Watson, 'Multilateral Efforts to Reduce Black Carbon Emissions: a Lifeline for the Warming Arctic?' (2011) 20 (1) Review of European Community & International Environmental Law 3 <https://doi.org/10.1111/j.1467-9388.2011.00705.x>.

Shankman, S., 'The Most Important Climate Treaty You've Never Heard Of' (*Inside Climate News*, 11 April 2018) <https://insideclimatenews.org/news/11042018/climate-treaty-gothenburg-protocol-air-pollution-regulations-global-warming-science-black-carbon-lrtap/> accessed 7 May 2022.

Shapovalova, D., 'The Effectiveness of the Regulatory Regime for Black Carbon Mitigation in the Arctic' (2016) 7 (2) *Arctic Review on Law and Politics* 136 <https://doi.org/10.17585/arctic.v7.427>.

Slechten, A. and V. Verardi, 'Measuring the Impact of Multiple Air Pollution Agreements on Global CO_2 Emissions' (2016) 92 (3) *Land Economics* 534.

Swart, R., M. Amann, F. Raes, and W. Tuinstra, 'A Good Climate for Clean Air: Linkages between Climate Change and Air Pollution. An Editorial Essay' (2004) 66 (3) *Climatic Change* 263.

Tuinstra, W., L. Hordijk, and C. Kroeze, 'Moving Boundaries in Transboundary Air Pollution Co-Production of Science and Policy under the Convention on Long Range Transboundary Air Pollution' (2006) 16 (4) *Global Environmental Change* 349 <https://doi.org/10.1016/j.gloenvcha.2006.03.002>.

UNECE, 'Parties to UNECE Air Pollution Convention Approve New Emission Reduction Commitments for Main Air Pollutants by 2020' (*unece.org*, 3 May 2012) <https://unece.org/press/parties-unece-air-pollution-convention-approve-new-emission-reduction-commitments-main-air> accessed 10 May 2022.

UNECE, 'Air' (*unece.org*, 2022) <https://unece.org/environment-policy/air> accessed 12 December 2022.

UNECE, 'Executive Body' (u*nece.org*, 2022) <https://unece.org/executive-body> accessed 4 October 2022.

UNECE, 'Working Group on Effects' (*unece.org*, 2022) <https://unece.org/environment-policy/air/working-group-effects> accessed 4 October 2022.

UNECE, 'Working Group on Strategies and Review' (*unece.org*, 2022) <https://unece.org/environment-policy/air/working-group-strategies-and-review> accessed 24 May 2022.

UNECE, *Gothenburg Workshop on Air Pollution and Its Relations to Climate Change and Sustainable Development, ECE/EB.AIR/GE.1/2007/5* (Geneva: UNECE, 13 June 2007).

UNECE, 'Potential Options for Addressing Methane as an Ozone Precursor under the Air Convention (Gothenburg Protocol Review). Informal Document, Agenda Item 4. 60th Session of the Working Group on Strategies and Review. Gothenburg Protocol Review Group'. (Geneva: UNECE, 2022).

UNECE, 'Synergies and Interactions with Other Policy Areas. Working Group on Strategies and Review, Sixtieth Session, 11–14 April 2022. Informal Document No. 1 (Revised 20 March 2022)'. (Geneva: UNECE, 2022).

UNECE/EB, *Report of the Twenty-Third Session of the Executive Body, ECE/EB.AIR/87* (Geneva: UNECE, 27 January 2006).

UNECE/EB, *Revised Review Report of the Working Group on Effects*, *ECE/EB.AIR/WG.1/2007/14/Rev.1* (Geneva: UNECE, 27 September 2007).
UNECE/EB, *Report of the Executive Body on Its Twenty-Fifth Session Held in Geneva from 10 to 13 December 2007*, *ECE/EB.AIR/91* (Geneva: UNECE, 27 February 2008).
UNECE/EB, *Decision 2007/1 Establishment of a Task Force on Reactive Nitrogen*, *ECE/EB.AIR/91/Add.1* (Geneva: UNECE, 2007).
UNECE/EB, *Report of the Executive Body on Its Twenty-Sixth Session Held in Geneva from 15 to 18 December 2008*, *ECE/EB.AIR/96* (Geneva: UNECE, 22 June 2009).
UNECE/EB, *Report of the Executive Body on Its Twenty-Seventh Session Held in Geneva from 14 to 18 December 2009*, *ECE/EB.AIR/99* (Geneva: UNECE, 10 May 2010).
UNECE/EB, *Black Carbon: Report by the Co-Chairs of the Ad Hoc Expert Group on Black Carbon*, *ECE/EB.AIR/2010/7* (Geneva: UNECE, 30 September 2010).
UNECE/EB, *Report of the Executive Body on Its Twenty-Eighth Session, Geneva, 13–17 December 2010*, *ECE/EB.AIR/106* (Geneva: UNECE, 24 February 2011).
UNECE/EB, *Options for Revising the 1999 Gothenburg Protocol to Abate Acidification, Eutrophication and Ground-Level Ozone. Working Group on Strategies and Review, Forty-Ninth Session Geneva, 12–16 September 2011. ECE/EB.AIR/WG.5/2011/7* (Geneva: UNECE, 17 June 2011).
UNECE/EB, *Options for Revising the 1999 Gothenburg Protocol to Abate Acidification, Eutrophication and Ground-Level Ozone. Executive Body for the Convention on Long-Range Transboundary Air Pollution, Twenty-Ninth Session Geneva, 12–16 December 2011. ECE/EB.AIR/2011/8* (Geneva: UNECE, 29 September 2011).
UNECE/EB, *Report of the Executive Body on Its Twenty-Ninth Session, Geneva, 12–16 December 2011. ECE/EB.AIR/109* (Geneva: UNECE, 31 January 2012).
UNECE/EB, *Report of the Executive Body on Its Twenty-Ninth Session, Geneva, 12–16 December 2011. Addendum. Decisions Adopted at the Twenty-Ninth Session. ECE/EB.AIR/109/Add.1* (Geneva: UNECE, 31 January 2012).
UNECE/EB, *Options for Revising the 1999 Gothenburg Protocol to Abate Acidification, Eutrophication and Ground-Level Ozone. Note by the Secretariat. Executive Body for the Convention on Long-Range Transboundary Air Pollution Thirtieth Session Geneva, 30 April–4 May 2012 Item 4 of the Provisional Agenda. ECE/EB.AIR/2012/1* (Geneva: UNECE, 2 February 2012).
UNECE/EB, *Report of the Executive Body on Its Twenty-Ninth Session, Geneva, 12–16 December 2011. Corrigendum. ECE/EB.AIR/109/Corr.1* (Geneva: UNECE, 30 May 2012).
UNECE/EB, *Report of the Executive Body on Its Thirtieth Session**. Geneva, 30 April–4 May 2012. Addendum. Decisions Adopted at the Thirtieth Session. Decisions 2012/1 Amendment of Annex I; 2012/2 Amendment of the Text of and Annexes II to IX and the Addition of New Annexes X and XI; 2012/3 Adjustments under the Gothenburg Protocol to Emission Reduction Commitments or to Inventories for the Purposes of Comparing*

National Total Emissions with Them; 2012/4 Provisional Application of Amendment to the Protocol. ECE/EB.AIR/*111/Add.1** (Geneva: UNECE, 1 November 2012).

UNECE/EB, *Report of the Executive Body on Its Thirty-First Session. Geneva, 11–13 December 2012. Addendum. Decisions Adopted at the Thirty-First Session.* ECE/EB.AIR/*113/Add.1* (Geneva: UNECE, 19 March 2013).

UNECE/EB, *1999 Protocol to Abate Acidification, Eutrophication and Ground-level Ozone to the Convention on Long-range Transboundary Air Pollution, as amended on 4 May 2012. Executive Body for the Convention on Long-range Transboundary Air Pollution.* ECE/EB.AIR/*114* (Geneva: UNECE, 6 May 2013).

UNECE/EB, *Report of the Executive Body on Its Thirty-Third Session. Geneva, 8–11 December 2014.* ECE/EB.AIR/*127* (Geneva: UNECE, 22 January 2015).

UNECE/EB, *Report of the Executive Body on Its Thirty-Fifth Session, Geneva, 2–4 May 2016.* ECE/EB.AIR/*135* (Geneva: UNECE, 31 August 2016).

UNECE/EB, *Report of the Executive Body on Its Thirty-Sixth Session, Geneva, 15 and 16 December 2016.* ECE/EB.AIR/*137* (Geneva: UNECE, 16 March 2017).

UNECE/EB, *Highlights of Proposed Updates to the Long-Term Strategy for the Convention on Long-Range Transboundary Air Pollution. Submitted by the Ad Hoc Policy Review Group of Experts on the 2016 Scientific Assessment of the Convention. Executive Body for the Convention on Long-Range Transboundary Air Pollution, Thirty-Seventh Session, Geneva, 11–14 December 2017. Item 8 of the Provisional Agenda, Policy Response to the 2016 Scientific Assessment of the Convention.* ECE/EB.AIR/*2017/4* (Geneva: UNECE, 29 September 2017).

UNECE/EB, *Report of the Executive Body on Its Thirty-Seventh Session, Geneva, 11–14 December 2017.* ECE/EB.AIR/*140* (Geneva: UNECE, 23 April 2018).

UNECE/EB, *Report of the Executive Body on Its Thirty-Seventh Session, Geneva, 11–14 December 2017. Addendum. 2018–2019 Workplan for the Implementation of the Convention.* ECE/EB.AIR/*140/Add.1* (Geneva: UNECE, 23 April 2018).

UNECE/EB, *Draft Revised Long-Term Strategy for the Convention, Submitted by the Expert Group. Executive Body for the Convention on Long-Range Transboundary Air Pollution, Thirty-Eighth Session, Geneva, 10–14 December 2018. Item 6 of the Provisional Agenda. Revised Long-Term Strategy for the Convention.* ECE/EB.AIR/*2018/1/Rev.1* (Geneva: UNECE, 27 November 2018).

UNECE/EB, *Report of the Executive Body on Its Thirty-Eighth Session*. Geneva, 10–14 December 2018.* ECE/EB.AIR/*142* (Geneva: UNECE, 22 February 2019).

UNECE/EB, *Report of the Executive Body on Its Thirty-Eighth Session*, Geneva, 10–14 December 2018. Addendum. Decisions Adopted by the Executive Body.* ECE/EB.AIR/*142/Add.2* (Geneva: UNECE, 22 February 2019).

UNECE/EB, *Report of the Working Group on Strategies and Review on Its Fifty-Seventh Session, Geneva, 21–24 May 2019.* ECE/EB.AIR/WG.*5/122* (Geneva: UNECE, 4 October 2019).

UNECE/EB, *Report of the Executive Body on Its Thirty-Ninth Session, Geneva, 9–13 December 2019. ECE/EB.AIR/144* (Geneva: UNECE, 31 January 2020).

UNECE/EB, *Report of the Executive Body on Its Thirty-Ninth Session, Geneva, 9–13 December 2019. Addendum. Decisions Adopted by the Executive Body. ECE/EB.AIR/144/Add.1* (Geneva: UNECE, 3 February 2020).

UNECE/EB, *Preparations for the Review of the Protocol to Abate Acidification, Eutrophication and Ground-Level Ozone as Amended in 2012* Submitted by the Gothenburg Protocol Review Group. Advance Version. Executive Body for the Convention on Long-Range Transboundary Air Pollution, Working Group on Strategies and Review, Fifty-Eighth Session, Geneva, 14–15 and 17 December 2020. Item 5 of the Provisional Agenda: Review of Sufficiency and Effectiveness of the Protocol to Abate Acidification, Eutrophication and Ground-Level Ozone. ECE/EB.AIR/2020/3–ECE/EB.AIR/WG.5/2020/3* (Geneva: UNECE, 30 September 2020).

UNECE/EB, *Report of the Executive Body on Its Fortieth Session. Geneva, 18 December 2020. ECE/EB.AIR/146* (Geneva: UNECE, 12 February 2021).

UNECE/EB, *Prioritizing Reductions of Particulate Matter from Sources That Are Also Significant Sources of Black Carbon – Analysis and Guidance*. Executive Body for the Convention on Long-Range Transboundary Air Pollution, Forty-First Session, Geneva, 6–8 December 2021. Item 4 (b) of the Provisional Agenda, Review of the Implementation of the 2020–2021 Workplan: Policy. ECE/EB.AIR/2021/6*, 23 September 2021.

UNECE/EB, *Draft Report on the Review of the Protocol to Abate Acidification, Eutrophication and Ground-Level Ozone, as Amended in 2012 Submitted by the Gothenburg Protocol Review Group. Executive Body for the Convention on Long-Range Transboundary Air Pollution, Forty-First Session, Geneva, 6–8 December 2021. Item 5 of the Provisional Agenda: Review of Sufficiency and Effectiveness of the Protocol to Abate Acidification, Eutrophication and Ground-Level Ozone. ECE/EB.AIR/2021/4* (Geneva: UNECE, 24 September 2021).

UNECE/EB, *Draft Report on the Review of the Protocol to Abate Acidification, Eutrophication and Ground-Level Ozone, as Amended in 2012*. Submitted by the Gothenburg Protocol Review Group. Executive Body for the Convention on Long-Range Transboundary Air Pollution, Working Group on Strategies and Review Sixtieth Session Geneva, 11–14 April 2022. Item 4 of the Provisional Agenda: Review of Sufficiency and Effectiveness of the Protocol to Abate Acidification, Eutrophication and Ground-Level Ozone. ECE/EB.AIR/WG.5/2022/3* (Geneva: UNECE, 31 January 2022).

UNECE/EB, *Report of the Executive Body on Its Forty-First Session, Geneva, 6–8 December 2021. ECE/EB.AIR/148* (Geneva: UNECE, 15 June 2022).

UNECE/EB, *Report of the Working Group on Strategies and Review on Its Sixtieth Session. Executive Body for the Convention on Long-Range Transboundary Air Pollution, Working Group on Strategies and Review, Sixtieth Session, Geneva, 11–14 April 2022. ECE/EB.AIR/WG.5/128* (Geneva: UNECE, 16 August 2022).

UNEP, 'Why Nitrogen Management Is Key for Climate Change Mitigation' (*unep.org*, 2019) <http://www.unep.org/news-and-stories/story/why-nitrogen-management-key-climate-change-mitigation> accessed 7 December 2022.

Voosen, P., 'In a Paradox, Cleaner Air Is Now Adding to Global Warming' (*science.org*, 2022) <https://www.science.org/content/article/paradox-cleaner-air-now-adding-global-warming> accessed 26 September 2022.

Yamineva, Y. and S. Romppanen, 'Is Law Failing to Address Air Pollution? Reflections on International and EU Developments' (2017) 26 (3) *Review of European, Comparative & International Environmental Law* 189 <https://doi.org/10.1111/reel.12223>.

CHAPTER 6

The Climate and Clean Air Coalition

A Voluntary Initiative for Climate and Air Quality

Charlotte Unger

1 Introduction

Since the beginning of the millennium, the global environmental and climate governance landscape has broadened significantly and become more complex. Beyond governmental actors, non-traditional, often transnational initiatives have taken over significant roles in environmental policy-making.[1] These initiatives can increase the capacities for mitigation and adaptation within the countries and, on a political level, have the potential to contribute towards the implementation of international commitments;[2] for example, those made under the Paris Agreement or under the recent Global Methane Pledge (see Chapter 3).

This chapter focuses on one of these innovative transnational alliances, namely the Climate and Clean Air Coalition (CCAC). The CCAC is the only global alliance dedicated exclusively to the reduction of SLCPs. Established in early 2012, the CCAC is set up as a multilateral voluntary partnership working on "integrated climate and clean air solutions to stabilize the climate, limit warming to 1.5°C, and drastically reduce air pollution. It focuses on fast action to reduce emissions of short-lived climate pollutants (SLCPs) (...)".[3]

1 Liliana B Andonova, Michele M Betsill and Harriet Bulkeley, 'Transnational climate governance' (2009) 9 Global environmental politics 52; Harriet Bulkeley and Andy Jordan, 'Transnational environmental governance: new findings and emerging research agendas' (2012) 30 Environment and Planning C 556; Frank Biermann and Philipp Pattberg, *Global environmental governance reconsidered* (MIT Press 2012).

2 Kenneth W Abbott and others, *International organizations as orchestrators* (CUP 2015); Richard B Stewart, Michael Oppenheimer and Bryce Rudyk, 'Building blocks: A strategy for near-term action within the new global climate framework' (2017) 144 Climatic Change 1; Lukas Hermwille, 'Making initiatives resonate: how can non-state initiatives advance national contributions under the UNFCCC?' (2018) 18 International Environmental Agreements: Politics, Law and Economics 447.

3 CCAC, 'Factsheet: CCAC 10-Year Anniversary' (2022) <https://www.ccacoalition.org/en/resources/10-years-climate-clean-air-coalition-ccac-factsheet> accessed 05 September 2022.

DOI:10.1163/9789004684089_008

The CCAC's origin is closely connected to activities carried out by the United Nations Environment Programme (UNEP). UNEP and the World Meteorological Organization (WMO) had issued the milestone report *Integrated Assessment of Black Carbon and Tropospheric Ozone* in 2011. It presented strong scientific evidence that mitigating black carbon, ozone, and precursors such as methane, is crucial to limit global warming. It also highlighted the significance of co-benefits obtained additionally from the reduction of SLCPs.[4] The report helped to increase the awareness among the scientific community as well as policy makers about the fact that the United Nation Framework Convention on Climate Change's (UNFCCC) then exclusive focus on CO_2 and equivalents was insufficient to limit global warming. The report thus provided fundamental arguments for launching an organization with a special focus on SLCPs. The increased attention on SLCPs and the formation of the CCAC can be considered as part of the areas in which UNEP has been very successful, in agenda setting on novel environmental issues.[5]

Also, the launch of the CCAC can be seen as part of the general developments in the international climate policy regime. By the end of the first decade of the new millennium, after the UNFCCC Conference of the Parties in Copenhagen in 2009, international negotiations on climate change were stuck in a gridlock. Many policy makers and experts were unsatisfied with the lack of progress for a follow-up treaty to the Kyoto Protocol. In response, alternative initiatives for greenhouse gas mitigation emerged during that time with the perspective of making quicker progress with a selected group of members. Yet, in the beginnings of the CCAC, also critical voices could be heard. For example, some countries were worried about the CCAC's link to the UNFCCC. They perceived the CCAC to be in a competitive relationship with the UNFCCC, and even act as a distraction from CO_2-mitigation.[6] However, this view has changed over the last several years. The CCAC is now seen as a complementary actor to the UNFCCC and their agendas have converged increasingly.[7]

This chapter focuses on the CCAC's role in the international policy landscape and what it can contribute to SLCP governance. After this introduction

4 UNEP, *Integrated assessment of black carbon and tropospheric ozone* (2011) <https://wedocs.unep.org/20.500.11822/8028> accessed 05 September 2022.

5 Maria Ivanova, 'UNEP in global environmental governance: design, leadership, location' (2010) 10 Global Environmental Politics 30; Maria Ivanova, *The Untold Story of the World's Leading Environmental Institution: UNEP at Fifty* (MIT Press 2021).

6 Information obtained from interviews with CCAC members.

7 Charlotte Unger, Kathleen A Mar and Konrad Gürtler, 'A club's contribution to global climate governance: the case of the Climate and Clean Air Coalition' (2020) 6 Palgrave Communications 1.

to the origins of the CCAC, the second section displays the CCAC's objectives, structure and membership, and explains its methodological approach, that is based on the co-benefits concept paired with a sound scientific fundament. The third section focuses on the activities of the CCAC, ranging from practical SLCP project activities to engagement in local, national, and global political discourses, and examines its governance contribution. The last part of this chapter is divided into a discussion of the challenges to the CCAC's governance and a conclusion that also sets the CCAC into the broader international climate political setting.

This chapter is based on existing research in the area of transnational environmental governance. Since analyses of the CCAC are very scarce, the text relies to a large extent on the analysis of material published by the Coalition itself. While such studies, reports, press releases, and website data can provide a good overview about the CCAC's activities, its structure, and goals, they do not present an objective assessment of its actual impacts on climate governance. To complement this, data collected for a previous study were used here.[8] The author had carried out a series of 14 semi-structured interviews with representatives of: CCAC country partners from Latin America, Europe, Central Asia, and Africa; research institutions and NGOs from Europe and Asia; several partners from intergovernmental institutions; and the CCAC secretariat, in the period between April and October 2018.

2 The CCAC's Objectives and Its Structure Are Oriented at Political Feasibility

2.1 *CCAC's Objectives*

The CCAC declared its main objective to be the slowing of the rate of near-term global warming through the reduction of SLCPs. Specifically, it focuses on black carbon, methane, hydrofluorocarbons (HFCs), and tropospheric ozone, which with 45% of global warming are the most important contributors to climate change after carbon dioxide (CO_2).[9] This goal was translated into numbers: cut the current rate of warming in half and avoid approximately 0.6°C of additional warming by 2050.[10] However, the CCAC does not set collective

8 Unger, Mar and Gürtler (n 7).

9 CCAC, 'Short-Lived Climate Pollutants (SLCPs): What are Short-Lived Climate Pollutants?' <https://www.ccacoalition.org/en/content/short-lived-climate-pollutants-slcps> accessed 05 September 2022.

10 CCAC, 'Factsheet' (n 3).

SLCP reduction targets or require its members to establish concrete goals and reduction pathways. Every member can independently decide what it wants to achieve under the CCAC.

In general, the CCAC seeks to emphasize 'quick' action. Behind this approach lies the rationale that because of the short-lived, yet very potent nature of SLCPs, their reduction leads to relatively rapid changes in atmospheric concentration in comparison to CO_2. Another large advantage of SLCPs mitigation is that it would buy time for the world to adapt to a changing climate and avoid climate tipping points with devasting impacts. The main sectors the CCAC focuses its activities on are agriculture, energy (household energy, oil and gas, and also brick production), transportation (first of all, heavy-duty diesel vehicles), cooling (HFCs), and waste.

2.2 *CCAC's Membership and Governance Structure*

The CCAC is an alliance based on voluntary contributions. There is no international treaty that obliges its member to commit to certain activities or targets. Instead, members are required to make a declaration of objectives to join the Coalition and contribute voluntarily either through donations or non-monetary activities, such as knowledge etc. Donations go into the CCAC Trust Fund which provides the financial basis of the CCAC. It is spent mostly for administration and project implementation, mainly in countries of the Global South.[11]

Founded by Bangladesh, Canada, Ghana, Mexico, Sweden, the United States, and UNEP, the CCAC consists of 76 state and 78 non-state partners, as of August 2022.[12] It includes governments, intergovernmental organizations, businesses, scientific institutions, and civil society organizations. From an early beginning, the CCAC has been closely linked to UNEP. UNEP is not only a founding member and cooperation partner in many projects and scientific assessments, it also hosts the CCAC secretariat, which is based in Paris.

The CCAC unites a group of members, relevant to solving the problem of SCLP mitigation. In other words, the CCAC unites countries who are significantly responsible for the problem for climate change (large-emitter members such as Canada, the EU, India, and the USA; CCAC partners cover around 44% of the world's GHG emissions in total) as well as regions with high SLCP and air pollutant emissions (18 out of the 20 most polluted cities, and 6 of the 10

---

11 CCAC, 'Climate and Clean Air Coalition Trust Fund' <https://www.ccacoalition.org/en/content/climate-and-clean-air-coalition-trust-fund> accessed 05 September 2022.

12 CCAC, 'Our Partners' (2022) <https://www.ccacoalition.org/en/partners> accessed 05 September 2022.

world's largest cities are in CCAC countries).[13] The CCAC scores high also in terms of representativeness, as its members come from all continents, including countries from Africa, Asia, and the Americas, which often struggle with air pollution problems. The vast majority of state partners are classified as low-income countries under the UNFCCC.

Also, non-state partners can be counted as part of the CCAC's success. Many members see the transnational character of the CCAC as a great advantage in terms of capacities and knowledge.[14] Research institutes, intergovernmental organisations, and subnational entities add to the CCAC's problem-solving capacity and furthermore increase its legitimacy.

Even though the CCAC has many non-governmental members, it is still a state-led organization. For example, countries have a stronger representation in the decision-making body, *the CCAC Board*. Also, usually countries receive the bulk of attention, when for example, announcements for SLCP reduction strategies, goals, sectors, and funding are made and the political communiqués launched. Non-state actors have first and foremost the role of supporting state-based action through information, analyses, and scientific assessments.

Overall, the degree of activity and engagement varies significantly, and some partners are more engaged than others. Engagement also varies over time, e. g. even though the US was a founding member of the CCAC, participation decreased under the presidency of Trump. More recently, with the presidency of Biden, the US has re-established its commitment, and is now leading the work in many thematic areas. The CCAC's constant growth – it has attracted new partners every year since its establishment – can be seen as proof for its attractiveness. Notwithstanding, some large SLCP emitters, such as China, Brazil and Indonesia are still not CCAC members.

All CCAC members meet annually in *the Working Group* and, usually, *a High-Level Assembly*, where the countries' environmental (or other) ministers and the organizations' directors are invited. *High-Level Assemblies* are held on the sidelines of the UN negotiations on climate change (meetings of the UNFCCC Conferences of the Parties). Here, important outputs such as the work program or the communiqués that set objectives for the CCAC are officially adopted and launched.[15]

The CCAC *Board* has the role of oversight body and the final say in many decisions, for example the funding of project proposals. Member representatives

13 Unger, Mar and Gürtler (n7).

14 Information obtained from interviews with CCAC members.

15 CCAC, 'Governance' <https://www.ccacoalition.org/en/content/governance> accessed 05 September 2022.

can become part of the Board through election. Countries and organisations apply for a seat in the Board and then an election is held. Seats are occupied on a rotating basis for a two-years term. The distribution of seats is the following: ten country, two NGO, two intergovernmental organisation, and one Scientific Advisory Panel seats.[16] All CCAC members vote in their respective category (e.g., countries vote for the country-Board seats).

The CCAC's practical work is organized in several subgroups. Originally named thematic initiatives, the now seven *Thematic Hubs* are smaller forums, in which CCAC members work on a specific area, such as, among others, agriculture, cooling, heavy duty vehicles, oil and gas, household energy, and waste.[17] Here, partners come together for exchange, work together on SLCP projects, present progress and success stories, and develop tools. Partners are free to choose, in which *Hubs* and in what form they want to participate. This structure was developed in 2020/21, leading the CCAC into a new working phase after its ten years of existence. While guaranteeing a regular exchange and close collaboration, it helps to make the CCAC a dynamic partnership.

The governance structure chosen by the CCAC has the advantage that it provides easy access and bears low entrance barriers for countries and organizations. Its established structure, including the regularity of in-person meetings, has helped to build a trustworthy working atmosphere and a strong cooperative network. This network is not only inclusive in that it benefits from the diversity and heterogeneity of its members, it also brings together actors who work both on the technical and political levels.

2.3 *CCAC's Scientific Basis and Science-Policy Interface*

Work realized under the CCAC is supported by the *Scientific Advisory Panel*, an elected international group of scientists with expertise on SLCPs. Scientific Advisory Panel experts are proposed by CCAC members and then selected based on criteria, such as the level and area of expertise, geographical origins, and gender. In comparison with other similar international alliances, the scientific foundation is of outstanding importance within the CCAC. As the mentioning of the 2011 *Integrated Assessment of Black Carbon and Tropospheric Ozone* above has demonstrated, from an early beginning, scientific knowledge has been intrinsically linked to all areas of work. Its purpose is on the one hand to advise and inform the CCAC members and on the other hand ensure the quality of work and generate in-house expertise. Practical examples are

16 Ibid.

17 CCAC, 'Hubs' <https://www.ccacoalition.org/en/initiatives> accessed 05 September 2022.

for instance: expert advisory committees that select project proposals to be funded, scientific experts who accompany policy-making processes,[18] as well as methodologies and tools provided for members, such as the Long-range Energy Alternatives Planning – Integrated Benefits Calculator (LEAP-IBC).[19] In addition, CCAC (in cooperation with other organizations, e. g. UNEP, WMO or World Health Organization) realizes large scientific assessments such as the Regional Assessments for South America, Asia and Africa or the recent Methane Assessment, which attract a far larger audience than CCAC members.[20] Scientific Advisory Panel is an important body, which, through occupying a seat in the Board, forms part of the decision-making procedures and provides information and expertise to the creation of strategies, programmes, and projects.

Overall, it can be argued that maintaining roots and a close relationship with science has increased the credibility of the CCAC as an alliance. It has contributed to creating the 'label of CCAC' that is perceived to stand for a certain quality of work and projects. The reputation tied to the CCAC's name has been described by its members as having a legitimizing effect for certain actions and measures.[21]

Beyond its political aim, the CCAC might be considered an interesting forum for scientific purposes. SLCPs sit at the nexus of climate and air quality, where the science-policy interface has been perceived as weak.[22] For example, important scientific outputs, like the CCAC assessments, e. g. the report *Air Pollution in Asia and the Pacific: Science-based solutions*[23] and *the Global*

18 CCAC, 'Annual report: 2020–2021' (2021) <https://www.ccacoalition.org/content/annual-report-2020-2021-0> accessed 05 September 2022; Clara Mewes and Charlotte Unger, 'Learning by Doing: Co-Benefits Drive National Plans for Climate and Air Quality Governance' (2021) 12 Atmosphere 1184.

19 Mewes and Unger (n 18).

20 CCAC, 'Air Pollution in Asia and the Pacific: Science-based solutions' (2019) <https://www.ccacoalition.org/en/resources/air-pollution-asia-and-pacific-science-based-solutions-summary-full-report> accessed 05 September 2022; CCAC, 'Global Methane Assessment' (2021) <https://www.ccacoalition.org/en/resources/global-methane-assessment-full-report> accessed 05 September 2022.

21 Unger, Mar and Gürtler (n7)

22 Andonova, Betsill and Bulkeley (n 1); Gregory F Nemet, Tracey Holloway and Paul Meier, 'Implications of incorporating air-quality co-benefits into climate change policymaking' (2010) 5 Environmental Research Letters 14007; Annabelle Workman and others, 'The political economy of health co-benefits: embedding health in the climate change agenda' (2018) 15 International journal of environmental research public health 674.

23 CCAC 'Air Pollution in Asia and the Pacific: Science-based solutions' (2019) <https://www.ccacoalition.org/en/resources/air-pollution-asia-and-pacific-science-based-solutions-summary-full-report> accessed 05 September 2022 (n 20).

Methane Assessment received significant attention from press and academia.[24] Cooperation among scientific disciplines, the engagement of policy-related disciplines and humanities in the work on integrated solutions to air pollution and climate change, as well as the links to policymaking processes and governance arrangements are often seen as inadequate.[25] The CCAC's (net-) work might help to bridge existing divides between different scientific areas, as well as science and policy. As described above, its diverse actors create a very large network, in which perspectives and knowledge from all over the world, but also from policy, civil society private sector and science come together. Frequently, this provides the fertile ground for new research, but also for close collaboration.

2.4 *CCAC's Multiple Benefits, or Co-benefits Approach*

The CCAC's name reveals that the alliance is not exclusively focusing on climate change. From its beginning it has targeted multiple goals: air quality, health, food security, human wellbeing, and overall progress in sustainable development, specifically: "(…) preventing millions of premature deaths annually, improving food security by avoiding tens-of-millions of tons of annual staple crop losses, protecting vital ecosystems and ecosystem services, reducing the risk of dangerous and irreversible climate tipping points, and making significant contributions to achieving the 2030 Agenda for Sustainable Development".[26]

This pursuing of multiple goals, the taking into account of multiple sources of impacts, as well as working from diverse regional perspectives, has been built into a more concise and structured approach, named the *Multiple Benefits Pathway Framework*.[27] Behind this approach stands the idea that governments can integrate several goals, like climate, air quality and sustainable development, and design harmonized policies.

---

24 This can be seen, for example in statistics from academic networks such as ResearchGate <https://www.researchgate.net/publication/328630911_Air_pollution_in_Asia_and_the_Pacific_Science-based_solutions> accessed 05 September 2022; see also CCAC, 'Media mentions' <https://www.ccacoalition.org/en/media-mentions> accessed 05 September 2022.

25 Andonova, Betsill and Bulkeley (n 1); Eric Zusman and others, 'One Atmosphere: Integrating Air Pollution and Climate Policy and Governance' (2021) 12 Atmosphere 1570.

26 CCAC, 'Why we need to act now' <https://www.ccacoalition.org/en/content/why-we-need-act-now> accessed 05 September 2022.

27 CCAC, 'Multiple Benefits Pathway Framework' <https://www.ccacoalition.org/en/content/multiple-benefits-pathway-framework> accessed 14 July 2021.

The largest advantage of this approach is that it can satisfy very diverse political interests. Often, the priorities pursued by countries and organizations within the CCAC vary significantly.[28] For example, many European countries set a priority on climate change mitigation, whereas elsewhere, e. g. in the US, exists a strong focus on the combination of climate change mitigation, health and air quality, and countries in Asia or South America often prioritize air quality and local conditions. With an approach that treats the whole of these 'multiple' concerns equally, governments can work more comfortably together and cooperate easily even though national and local interests vary.

This approach is also consistent with research and science. The term 'co-benefits' dates back to the 1990s. It refers to a win-win strategy, where two or more policy goals can be achieved through one single policy.[29] For the Intergovernmental Panel on Climate Change (IPCC), co-benefits are the "positive effects that a policy or measure aimed at one objective might have on other objectives, thereby increasing the total benefits for society or the environment".[30] The concept of co-benefits has received much attention in the scientific community.[31] Within this broad range of research, three varying strands of understanding of the term 'co-benefit' can be identified, according to the country's (or other actor's) political agenda: climate co-benefits, development or climate policy co-benefits, and benefit synergies or co-impacts.[32] In the first category, climate co-benefits are those that arise from policies that do not prioritize climate mitigation or adaptation. The second category consists of additional benefits resulting from climate policies, e.g. as improvements in air, soil and water quality, biodiversity etc. The third category refers to benefit synergies or co-impacts result from policies that are specifically designed to reach two goals simultaneously. Very broadly, the CCAC's approach falls under the third category.

---

28 Unger, Mar and Gürtler (n 7).

29 Jan P Mayrhofer and Joyeeta Gupta, 'The science and politics of co-benefits in climate policy' (2016) 57 Environmental Science Policy 22; Mikael Karlsson, Eva Alfredsson and Nils Westling, 'Climate policy co-benefits: a review' (2020) 20 Climate Policy 292.

30 IPCC, *Global Warming of 1.5°C: An IPCC Special Report on the impacts of global warming of 1.5 C above pre-industrial levels and related global greenhouse gas emission pathways, in the context of strengthening the global response to the threat of climate change, sustainable development, and efforts to eradicate poverty* (CUP 2018); Mewes and Unger (n 18).

31 Diana Ürge-Vorsatz and others, 'Measuring the co-benefits of climate change mitigation' (2014) 39 Annual Review of Environment and Resources 549; Mayrhofer and Gupta (n 29); Karlsson, Alfredsson and Westling (n 29).

32 Karlsson, Alfredsson and Westling (n 29).

Another often-emphasized advantage of the co-benefits approach is its positive framing and functioning as counterweight to the cost-based argument that often blocks climate change policies.[33] In many countries, climate and environmental protection are named simultaneously with economic concerns over mitigation costs or perceived as counterproductive for economic development.[34] The co-benefits concept may alleviate such concerns. Its positive framing of win–win situations bears a strong advocacy potential. Policy makers from the various areas, but also stakeholders, maybe be convinced easier and give their consent, when more than one goal can be achieved. Also, often co-benefits are based on practical evidence, corroborated with substantial scientific data and translated into concrete cost savings.[35] Overall, this approach can improve political feasibility, tying climate policies to local priorities. In its practical work with countries and regions, the CCAC has undertaken many analyses and calculations of co-benefits and brought these into national policy planning; for example, in Nigeria, Ghana and Mexico.[36]

3 The CCAC's Activities and Its Governance Role(s)

Over the years of existence, the CCAC has become a central player in climate, but first and foremost in SLCP governance. It builds knowledge and capacity on SCLPs, supports SLCP policy-making, and coordinates and orchestrates SLCP activities. It furthermore raises awareness on SLPCs at all political levels (from local to global) and complements the UNFCCC in that it raises capacities to increase and implement mitigation targets under the Paris Agreement. Very broadly, the CCAC's activities can be subsumed under two categories: on the one hand, the more practice-oriented work and on the other hand, the policy-making and political activities. Both overlap on many occasions.

First, there are those activities that directly or indirectly achieve SLCP reductions and mostly imply practical, on-the-ground work. At the heart of this

33 Anil Markandya and others, 'Health co-benefits from air pollution and mitigation costs of the Paris Agreement: A modelling study' (2018) 2 The Lancet Planetary Health e126-e133; Karlsson, Alfredsson and Westling (n 29).

34 Barry G Rabe, *Statehouse and greenhouse: The emerging politics of American climate change policy* (Brookings Institution Press 2004).

35 Mayrhofer and Gupta (n 29).

36 Rabe (n 34); Markandya and others (n 33); Government of Nigeria, 'Nigeria's National Action Plan to reduce Short-Lived Climate Pollutants (SLCPs)' (2018) <https://www.ccacoalition.org/en/resources/nigeria%E2%80%99s-national-action-plan-reduce-short-lived-climate-pollutants> accessed 14 July 2021.

work are: projects, including on capacity building,[37] policies and standards,[38] assessment and inventories, especially on black carbon, implementation of technologies, measurements, and guidelines and tools for national planning.[39] Many of these activities are of a lighthouse or model character and meant to be transferred to other regions. For example, after the CCAC supported the development of an SLCPs reduction plan in Ghana, similar plans and programs were launched and are under development in other African countries, such as Nigeria and Cote d'Ivoire.[40]

There are many examples in which this support in methodologies and capacity building has led to domestic regulations and programs, laws, and standards. For example, in the case of assisting Nigeria with the development of its SLCP Action Plan, CCAC experts supported with the assessment and creation of emissions databases, consultation with stakeholders and other governmental agencies, and the formulation of the Plan.[41]

Another overarching area relates to the large scientific assessments the CCAC has realized in certain regions such as Latin America, Asia and Africa or recently on a specific gas – the Global Methane Assessment. These assessments usually do not only calculate the SLCPs' impact, they also suggest and provide details about concrete measures to mitigate SLCPs, and quantify the multiple benefits resulting from these measures.

The above named second broad area of work is tied to political discourse and strategy on the various governance levels, from national and regional to international. Here, the CCAC for example takes part in conferences, ministerial roundtables, negotiations, workshops, and joint press releases etc. For example, it has had a motivating and supporting role for regional ministerial pledges in the Latin American and Caribbean region.[42] Many of these

37 E.g. CCAC, 'Capacity building program for industry stakeholders and policy-makers on HFC-alternative technologies' <https://www.ccacoalition.org/en/activity/conferences-and-workshops> accessed 05 September 2022.

38 E.g. CCAC, 'City waste action program' <https://www.ccacoalition.org/en/activity/city-waste-action-programme> or CCAC, 'Enhancing NDC ambitions with mitigation in the agriculture sector initiative' <https://www.ccacoalition.org/en/activity/enhancing-ndc-ambitions-mitigation-agriculture-sector> both accessed 05 September 2022.

39 E.g. the above-mentioned LEAP-IBC.

40 Rabe (n 34); Government of Nigeria (n 36); Republic of Cote d'Ivoire, 'National Action Planning Document for the Reduction of Short-Lived Climate Pollutants (SLCP)' (2020) <https://www.ccacoalition.org/en/file/6701/download?token=Nd5E3BB0> accessed 05 September 2022.

41 CCAC 'Hubs' (n 17); Mewes and Unger (n 18).

42 CCAC, 'Decision 9: Twentieth Meeting of the Forum of Ministers of Environment for Latin America and the Caribbean' (2016) <https://www.ccacoalition.org/en/resources/decision-9-twentieth-meeting-forum-ministers-environment-latin-america-and-caribbean> accessed 05 September 2022.

activities are linked to international processes and legal frameworks for the environment and climate.

Further, the CCAC has actively contributed to UNEP's work, and has been engaged in its governing body – UN Environment Assembly, e. g. through collaboration in the generation and evaluation of environmental data, expert workshops, and participation. The CCAC's work was recognized on several occasions by the Assembly, e.g. as part of the resolution adopted at the 2017 meeting.[43] This recognition provides not only international attention and awareness to the CCAC, it also improves its credibility as a trustworthy alliance. Another international agreement for which the CCAC has played an advocating role is the Montreal Protocol on Substances that Deplete the Ozone Layer. For example, it was very engaged in pushing for an ambitious amendment to the Montreal Protocol to phase-down HFCs.[44] The outcome of this workstream, Kigali Amendment, was advocated for at CCAC conferences and its adoption lobbied by the CCAC members.[45] The CCAC had also operated a thematic initiative to help countries to phase out HFCs. The CCAC further promotes SLCP reductions as part of international agreements, such as the Montreal Protocol or the UNFCCC; generally via its publications, events and research.[46]

The other large international framework the CCAC has contributed to is the UNFCCC. As initially mentioned, the CCAC has taken a clearly complementary role here, but with diverse functions. On the one hand it provides technical expertise: CCAC's expert knowledge has been fed into the UNFCCC process on several occasions. For instance, the CCAC as institution was involved in the process of the Marrakesh climate action agenda and was recognized as a technical expert under the Ad Hoc Working Group on the Durban Platform

43 UNEP, 'Preventing and reducing air pollution to improve air quality globally' (2017) <https://www.ccacoalition.org/fr/node/2382> accessed 05 September 2022.

44 UNEP, 'Reducing Hydrofluorocarbons via the Montreal Protocol is the most significant climate action the world can take this year' (2016) <https://www.unep.org/news-and-stories/press-release/reducing-hydrofluorocarbons-montreal-protocol-most-significant> accessed 05 September 2022.

45 UNEP, 'Historical Agreement on Hydrofluorocarbons reached in Kigali' (2016) <https://www.unep.org/news-and-stories/news/historical-agreement-hydrofluorocarbons-reached-kigali> accessed 05 September 2022.

46 CCAC, 'Key messages from the Ministerial Roundtable Session in New York, 26 Sep 2018' (2018) <https://www.ccacoalition.org/en/resources/key-messages-ministerial-roundtable-session-new-york-26-sep-2018> accessed 05 September 2022.

for Enhanced Action.[47] Another example is the 2017 Koronivia Joint Work on Agriculture which aims at focusing agricultural development on food security and climate change mitigation, a decision that represented an endorsement of the strategy the CCAC has championed since 2012.[48] As initially mentioned, the CCAC's *High Level Assemblies* are held on the sidelines of the UNFCCC meetings. At such events, ministers and heads of organizations generally endorse a joint political communiqué on SLCPs in line with CCAC priorities, e.g., the Bonn Communiqué of 2017 addressed SLCPs from agriculture and municipal solid waste.[49] These communiques though they do not have a binding character, raise international attention and signal a common objective of the CCAC partners.

The Paris Agreement is occupying a central place in CCAC's work. Not only has the achievement of its goals of keeping global warming under 2 °C been used as a backbone of many communication strategies and political outputs, it has also become a main element of the CCAC's work program for 2020. Furthermore, under the Paris Agreement, some 'bottom-up' integration of SLCPs into the UNFCCC process can be observed. The CCAC supports countries that wish to include SLCPs in their Nationally Determined Contributions (NDCs) under the Agreement. For example, governmental officials from Mexico argued that with the help of the CCAC, Mexico had included a separate goal for the reduction of black carbon into its first NDC.[50] Also, other CCAC country representatives mentioned that they had approached the CCAC seeking support for the development of their NDCs.[51] By 2021, 60 countries had included SLCP reduction in their NDCs. Of these, 60 include methane, 12 black carbon, and 44 HFCs. The CCAC has supported 17 countries to incorporate SLCP measures into their NDCs.[52] Helping countries to integrate SLCPs

47 CCAC 'FACTSHEET: CCAC 10-YEAR ANNIVERSARY' (2022) https://www.ccacoalition.org/en/resources/10-years-climate-clean-air-coalition-ccac-factsheet (n 3).

48 Food and Agriculture Organization of the United Nations, 'Submission by the Food and Agriculture Organization of the United Nations (FAO) to the United Nations Framework Convention on Climate Change (UNFCCC) in relation to the Koronivia joint work on agriculture (4/CP.23) On Topics 2(e) and 2(f)' (2020) <https://www4.unfccc.int/sites/SubmissionsStaging/Documents/202004201455---FAO%20submission%20KJWA%202(e)_2(f)_final.doc.pdf> accessed 05 September 2022.

49 CCAC, 'Hubs' (n 17).

50 Information obtained from interviews with CCAC partners.

51 Information obtained from interviews with CCAC partners.

52 CCAC, 'Annual report: 2020–2021' (n 18).

has become a very important area of work for the CCAC and is named as a working focus in the Coalition's 2030 Vision.[53]

In 2021, at COP26 in Glasgow, the CCAC also contributed to an international initiative, the Global Methane Pledge. This initiative, signed by more than 100 countries, seeks to make an additional contribution to the Paris Agreement through reducing global methane emissions at least 30 percent from 2020 levels by 2030. The CCAC had realized extensive preparatory work, such as the scientific Global Methane Assessment, many political and scientific events, and supporting the launch of several initiatives such as Global Methane Alliance[54] that enabled a good level of awareness and helped to push the EU and the US, who then launched the initiative at COP26.

Through these activities, SLCPs have seen increased attention on the regional and international stage. Beyond examples like the above-mentioned Global Methane Pledge, evidence of this can be seen for example in that SLCPs were taken up by the G7,[55] at a ministerial roundtable on the sidelines of the UN General Assembly,[56] and by the General Assembly of the Parliamentary Confederation of the Americas.[57]

Building knowledge and awareness on the topic of the formerly neglected topic of SLCPs can be claimed a main success of the CCAC. This is an opinion also highlighted by a majority of CCAC partners. They regard the CCAC's work as establishing SLCPs as a topic per se, bringing SLCPs on the political agenda and giving a neglected climate topic a voice internationally and in many national contexts as a main strength.[58]

53 CCAC, 'Climate and Clean Air Coalition adopts new strategy to deliver ambitious climate, clean air, and development goals by 2030' (2020) <https://www.ccacoalition.org/en/news/climate-and-clean-air-coalition-adopts-new-strategy-deliver-ambitious-climate-clean-air-and> accessed 05 September 2022.

54 Government of Nigeria (n 36).

55 CCAC, 'Multiple Benefits Pathway Framework' <https://www.ccacoalition.org/en/content/multiple-benefits-pathway-framework> (n 27).

56 United Nations General Assembly, 'Resolution adopted by the General Assembly on 19 December 2019 [on the report of the Second Committee (A/74/381)] 74/212. International Day of Clean Air for blue skies' (2020) <https://www.ccacoalition.org/en/resources/united-nations-general-assembly-resolution-74212-international-day-clean-air-blue-skies> accessed 05 September 2022.

57 Confederación Parlamentaria de las Américas, 'Committee on the Environment and Sustainable Development Declaration on Short-Lived Climate Pollutants' (2018) <https://www.ccacoalition.org/en/resources/committee-environment-and-sustainable-development-declaration-short-lived-climate> accessed 05 September 2022.

58 Unger, Mar and Gürtler (n7).

A significant advantage of the CCAC for its members is also the increased cooperation and network enhancement for this topic, where many aspects (ranging from science and measurements to policy measures and implementation processes) are still not very well researched. Regular exchange on scientific and technical topics and inputs from non-state partners create a well-informed network and thereby sound basis for action. Here, members can discuss and try out activities and measures, and debate topics in a more informal manner. It can also provide a first step towards further, potentially more formal cooperation and bi-(or multi-) lateral partnerships.

4 Challenges to the CCAC's Work

The previous sections have shown the CCAC as a dynamic, flexible, and non-traditional initiative that has taken over an important role in contributing to SLCP governance. While the advantages of this alliance are numerous, also some challenges should be discussed within this chapter.

Literature on non-traditional and transnational initiatives, like the CCAC, has occasionally argued that their lose, voluntary character leads to weak commitments.[59] Also, under the CCAC only few and non-binding numerical targets have been released. There are no rules that bind countries to implementing the plans stated in their membership applications. Furthermore, many of the CCAC's achievements are difficult to measure, and often, members' emission reductions resulting from projects and policy implementation can only be proven in the future. Overall, there is no control mechanism that guarantees that promises made under the CCAC are kept. This leads to the conclusions that the CCAC is no alternative to an international climate treaty, nor can it be seen as a framing body for global regulations on air quality.

Even though the CCAC might orchestrate and incentivize action on SLPCs, it mostly depends on the individual states whether SLCP emissions are reduced. In spite of the CCAC's successes in awareness raising, it appears that in many countries the topic of SLCPs has not reached the top of political agendas. An example is Germany, where the term 'SLCP' is very rarely used in the political discourse. An explanation for this could be that even though one might think that the reduction of SLCPs is politically very attractive, because, here, the focus lies on the immediate future and positive near-term effects can be

59 Aseem Prakash and Matthew Potoski, 'Collective action through voluntary environmental programs: A club theory perspective' (2007) 35 Policy Studies Journal 773; Ürge-Vorsatz and others (n 31).

expected, SLCP science is rather complex and its scientific understanding, e. g. data and impacts, is incomplete. SLCPs have different impacts than CO_2 (see Chapter 1). For example, methane is 84 times more powerful than CO_2 as a greenhouse gas in the first two decades after it is emitted, yet it is removed after approximately a decade and it is also a precursor to tropospheric ozone, which contributes to air pollution worldwide. These characteristics make policy-making more challenging. Some policy makers may also still fear a competition between the reduction of CO_2 and non-CO_2 emissions (for example, when it comes to the funding of activities or the priorities on the political agenda), even though the CCAC communicates clearly that its aim is to complement the UNFCCC's agenda.

Another challenge lies in the many heterogenous interests that exist within the CCAC, also a feature that is common to such large non-traditional alliances.[60] On the one hand, this may cause the CCAC to pursue a very broad range of topics. On the other hand, varying interests and motivations can be counterproductive and dampen the group's agreement on common objectives. This might be especially relevant, when it comes to the spending of funding; for example, on which type of projects the CCAC's money is to be used. As financial resources are typically constrained in such alliances as the CCAC, priorities need to be set. Overall, the availability of funding and the dependence on donations has limited the activities of the CCAC in the past, e. g. when the major donor, the US government, under former president Trump, had cut donations completely.

Counteracting interests and motivations can also influence the direction of the political dialogue pursued by the CCAC. For example, in 2021 and 2022, a focus was clearly set on methane, a theme pursued by the EU and the US. For some countries, methane might not be an immediate priority. Agreeing with all members and bringing all interests together also often leads to objectives and outputs that are rather broad and soft. This can be seen for example in the communiqués released by CCAC members at the High-Level Assemblies.[61]

The combination of the CCAC's voluntary character with the diverging interests creates the situation where some members are very active, some – only on special occasions, and others – hardly ever. The last group is in principle

---

60 Charlotte Unger and Sonja Thielges, 'Preparing the playing field: climate club governance of the G20, Climate and Clean Air Coalition, and Under2 Coalition' (2021) 167 Climatic Change 41.

61 CCAC, 'Hubs' (n 17); Biermann and Pattberg (n 1); CCAC, 'Paris Communique' (2015) <https://www.ccacoalition.org/en/resources/paris-communique> accessed 05 September 2022.

free-riding: in other words, these members benefit from the activities of the CCAC community, for example, the knowledge sharing, without doing anything themselves. This might become a practical problem, if, for example, not enough members are willing to share the burden of administrative and practical work that needs to be carried out, such as evaluating submitted SLCP project proposals.

There are other practical challenges a large organization such as the CCAC faces, ranging from the balancing of funding for project implementation against administrative costs, to finding adequate leadership (the recent selection of a new head of the CCAC secretariat lasted for almost a year), or the administrative relationship with UNEP. Here, it remains somewhat untransparent how much influence UNEP has on the CCAC secretariat's day-to-day work. Also, in the project implementation work some challenging aspects can be found, for example the control and tracking of the projects' successes or the question of how model projects and methodologies can be upscaled and transferred to other countries, regions, and municipalities.

Last but not least, in the global climate and environmental policy landscape, a trend towards the launching of non-traditional alliances, initiatives and partnerships can be observed.[62] This increases the complexity of the whole climate and environment governance architecture, and additionally bears the risk of creating overlaps among these initiatives. In the best case, alliances benefit from each other through mutual fertilization of topics, the growth of trust, and collaboration. For example, the CCAC invites members of other partnerships, e. g. the NDC Partnership,[63] to join as member or to participate in CCAC working meetings. In a more negative sense, this growth trend can also lead to competition for attention and resources among emerging initiatives. For instance, policy makers who represent their country in multiple initiatives must choose which meetings to attend, and where resources should be spent. In practice, more international alliances also intensify the difficulty to keep track of all their new developments and engagements. As of today, there are only small institutional overlaps.

SLCPs are also one among the items of the Arctic Council's agenda (see Chapter 7). This alliance of nations with territory in the Arctic had its first technical report on the impact of SLCPs in the Arctic released in 2008 and is focused

62 Hermwille (n 2); Thomas Hale, 'Transnational Actors and Transnational Governance in Global Environmental Politics' (2020) 23 Annual Review of Political Science 203.

63 The NDC Partnership is a transnational alliance that aims at supporting countries with the implementation and improvement of their NDCs. See NDC Partnership, 'About Us' <https://ndcpartnership.org/about-us> accessed 05 September 2022.

specifically on methane and black carbon, because their mitigation can slow the rate of Arctic climate change in the near term. The Arctic Council has not a competitive relationship with the CCAC. However, many other initiatives, such as the above-mentioned NDC Partnership are invested in supporting countries with the implementation of the Paris Agreement. Further analyses would have to examine, how much these alliances – including the CCAC – overlap among each other, and close coordination and careful assessment are needed here in order to avoid an overabundance in climate initiatives.

5 Conclusion: the CCAC's Governance Contribution and Possible Future Developments

Throughout its ten years of existence, the CCAC has managed to occupy a niche in climate and environmental governance. Many of its activities have helped to give a politically neglected and scientifically complex issue a voice and brought it to the political agendas at the local – global level. Its role is here that of a pacemaker and awareness raiser that prepares the field of SLCPs for policy-making and the implementation of SLCP reduction.

In comparison to more formal regulatory arrangements, the CCAC's voluntary character and open structure makes it a much more flexible and dynamic governance actor. Even though this easy-access, voluntary contributions-based model might not lead to the generation of more ambitious climate (or environmental) targets, as it includes the mix of very heterogenous – and sometimes counteracting – interests, there is a strong value in this approach. The CCAC is invested in preparing and catalyzing SLCP emissions reductions. Many success stories can be seen in the implementation of a large array of projects on SLCP reductions, such as capacity building, and methodology improvement and some that have resulted in emissions reductions on the ground. These activities have led to more formal policy-making processes: CCAC has supported the development of national laws, regulations, and standards, which promise to reduce emissions in the future.

Also, the combination of voluntary engagement with a strong scientific basis and an approach that communicates the multiple benefits of SLCPs reduction increases the attractiveness of this alliance. In other words, there is 'nothing to lose' when countries join. This can be seen in the transnational, constantly growing membership. Getting more countries on board, especially large emitters like China, and a stronger engagement with the private sector would be beneficial for the CCAC's agenda. Such cooperation can gain more political support for projects, and last but not least might provide an alternative source of funding. Both types of extension can also be regarded from a critical perspective.

The CCAC has also a bridging and integrative function in several ways. First, an integrative, bridging function within the UN system can be assumed. The CCAC has brought together several UN bodies on the topic of clean air (and climate). For example, for several projects, data collection and events, a close cooperation between CCAC, WMO, WHO, and UNEP has taken place. In addition, integrative activity is carried out for specific topics such as: agriculture (where also the UN Food and Agriculture Organization, and UNEP are involved), or household energy (where the United Nations Development Programme and UNEP are involved). Also, the CCAC is contributing to the development and implementation of several international legal frameworks at the same time, ranging from the Montreal Protocol and its Kigali Amendment, resolutions under the United Nations Environment Assembly (UNEA) and the CLRTAP to the UNFCCC and the Paris Agreement.

The CCAC might be seen as an orchestrator of activities here. Stronger exchange among UN agencies and governmental experts who work on the different UN agreements can help to strengthen synergies and avoid trade-offs as well as integrate climate and environmental concerns into other areas of UN policy-making.

Second, the CCAC works at the intersection of air quality and climate policy. The integration of air quality and climate policy still faces many challenges in both policy and science. In the CCAC, governmental officials, scientists and NGO experts from both areas work closely together on this thematic intersection and may overcome existing barriers and fill knowledge gaps etc.

Third, to some degree the CCAC might also function as a broker or an intermediary to help countries access funding from third parties, such as the Green Climate Fund or the German International Climate Initiative. Thematically, some of the CCAC's activities, such as supporting national planning processes may fit under the roof of these climate finance initiatives. The CCAC's name might function as label for a certain project quality, facilitating project acceptance.

The structural change of the CCAC in 2020–2021 is an indication that the CCAC is becoming an even more flexible and dynamic body. For example, the thematic hubs are open to the collaboration with non-CCAC partners. The Focus of the CCAC clearly centers on the Paris Agreement, and most notably on the realization of the Global Methane Pledge – where it plays an advisory role. The CCAC will help to integrate methane reductions and possibly methane targets into countries' NDCs and help countries develop or update a methane reduction action plan by COP27.[64] Also, there is a clear focus on implementation and supporting countries – first of all, countries of the Global South – in the realization of national planning processes, and, mainly, their NDCs.

These objectives may significantly contribute to the goals of the Paris Agreement. On this promising pathway there is still much to do for the CCAC, for both the political and technical sides. One aspect that might help is the increased investment in transferability and adaptation of good practice projects to other regions. The CCAC has created an enormous network with significant knowledge and action capacity. This multiplying and pushing force comes at a moment where it is most urgently needed to cope with the climate crisis, and where, on many occasions, we see a disruption of multilateralism and cooperation through conflict and war. NDC commitments alone are not enough to achieve the Paris Agreement's goals. Nevertheless, also the CCAC is not a surefire success. It depends on members investing their knowledge, time and last but not least financial resources to move the CCAC's program forward; it relies on each individual country to set up domestic policies to implement SLCP objectives and those members who are willing to implement lighthouse projects, set ambitious SLCP goals and policies, and thus provide a model for other members to follow.

Bibliography

Abbott KW and others, *International Organizations as Orchestrators* (CUP 2015).

Andonova LB, Betsill MM and Bulkeley H, 'Transnational climate governance' (2009) 9 Global Environmental Politics 52.

Biermann F and Pattberg P, *Global Environmental Governance Reconsidered* (MIT Press 2012).

Bulkeley H and Jordan A, 'Transnational Environmental Governance: New Findings and Emerging Research Agendas' (2012) 30 *Environment and Planning* C 556.

CCAC, 'Air Pollution in Asia and the Pacific: Science-based solutions' (2019) <https://www.ccacoalition.org/en/resources/air-pollution-asia-and-pacific-science-based-solutions-summary-full-report> accessed 05 September 2022.

CCAC, 'Annual report: 2020–2021' (2021) <https://www.ccacoalition.org/content/annual-report-2020-2021-0> accessed 05 September 2022.

64 CCAC, 'Methane technical assistance' <https://www.ccacoalition.org/en/content/methane-technical-assistance> accessed 05 September 2022.

CCAC, 'Capacity building program for industry stakeholders and policy-makers on HFC-alternative technologies' <https://www.ccacoalition.org/en/activity/conferences-and-workshops> accessed 05 September 2022.

CCAC, 'City waste action program' <https://www.ccacoalition.org/en/activity/city-waste-action-programme> accessed 05 September 2022.

CCAC, 'Climate and Clean Air Coalition adopts new strategy to deliver ambitious climate, clean air, and development goals by 2030' (2020) <https://www.ccacoalition.org/en/news/climate-and-clean-air-coalition-adopts-new-strategy-deliver-ambitious-climate-clean-air-and> accessed 05 September 2022.

CCAC, 'Climate and Clean Air Coalition Trust Fund' <https://www.ccacoalition.org/en/content/climate-and-clean-air-coalition-trust-fund> accessed 05 September 2022.

CCAC, 'Decision 9: Twentieth Meeting of the Forum of Ministers of Environment for Latin America and the Caribbean' (2016) <https://www.ccacoalition.org/en/resources/decision-9-twentieth-meeting-forum-ministers-environment-latin-america-and-caribbean> accessed 05 September 2022.

CCAC, 'Enhancing NDC ambitions with mitigation in the agriculture sector initiative' <https://www.ccacoalition.org/en/activity/enhancing-ndc-ambitions-mitigation-agriculture-sector> accessed 05 September 2022.

CCAC, 'Factsheet: CCAC 10-Year Anniversary' (2022) <https://www.ccacoalition.org/en/resources/10-years-climate-clean-air-coalition-ccac-factsheet accessed> 05 September 2022.

CCAC, 'Global Methane Assessment' (2021) <https://www.ccacoalition.org/en/resources/global-methane-assessment-full-report> accessed 05 September 2022.

CCAC, 'Governance' <https://www.ccacoalition.org/en/content/governance> accessed 05 September 2022.

CCAC, 'Hubs' <https://www.ccacoalition.org/en/initiatives> accessed 05 September 2022.

CCAC, 'Key messages from the Ministerial Roundtable Session in New York, 26 Sep 2018' (2018) <https://www.ccacoalition.org/en/resources/key-messages-ministerial-roundtable-session-new-york-26-sep-2018> accessed 05 September 2022.

CCAC, 'Media mentions' <https://www.ccacoalition.org/en/media-mentions> accessed 05 September 2022.

CCAC, 'Methane technical assistance' <https://www.ccacoalition.org/en/content/methane-technical-assistance> accessed 05 September 2022.

CCAC, 'Multiple Benefits Pathway Framework' <https://www.ccacoalition.org/en/content/multiple-benefits-pathway-framework> accessed 14 July 2021.

CCAC, 'Our Partners' (2022) <https://www.ccacoalition.org/en/partners> accessed 05 September 2022.

CCAC, 'Paris Communique' (2015) <https://www.ccacoalition.org/en/resources/paris-communique> accessed 05 September 2022.

CCAC, 'Short-Lived Climate Pollutants (SLCPs). What are Short-Lived Climate Pollutants?' <https://www.ccacoalition.org/en/content/short-lived-climate-pollutants-slcps> accessed 05 September 2022.

CCAC, 'Why we need to act now' <https://www.ccacoalition.org/en/content/why-we-need-act-now> accessed 05 September 2022.

Confederación Parlamentaria de las Américas, 'Committee on the Environment and Sustainable Development Declaration on Short-Lived Climate Pollutants' (2018) <https://www.ccacoalition.org/en/resources/committee-environment-and-sustainable-development-declaration-short-lived-climate> accessed 05 September 2022.

Food and Agriculture Organization of the United Nations, 'Submission by the Food and Agriculture Organization of the United Nations (FAO) To the United Nations Framework Convention on Climate Change (UNFCCC) In relation to the Koronivia joint work on agriculture (4/CP.23) On Topics 2(e) and 2(f)' (2020) <https://www4.unfccc.int/sites/SubmissionsStaging/Documents/202004201455---FAO%20submission%20KJWA%202(e)_2(f)_final.doc.pdf> accessed 05 September 2022.

Government of Nigeria, 'Nigeria's National Action Plan to reduce Short-Lived Climate Pollutants (SLCPs)' (2018) <https://www.ccacoalition.org/en/resources/nigeria%E2%80%99s-national-action-plan-reduce-short-lived-climate-pollutants> accessed 14 July 2021.

Hale T, 'Transnational Actors and Transnational Governance in Global Environmental Politics' (2020) 23 Annual Review of Political Science 203.

Hermwille L, 'Making initiatives resonate: how can non-state initiatives advance national contributions under the UNFCCC?' (2018) 18 International Environmental Agreements: Politics, Law and Economics 447.

IPCC, *Global Warming of 1.5 C. An IPCC Special Report on the impacts of global warming of 1.5 C above pre-industrial levels and related global greenhouse gas emission pathways, in the context of strengthening the global response to the threat of climate change, sustainable development, and efforts to eradicate poverty* (CUP 2018).

Ivanova M, 'UNEP in global environmental governance: design, leadership, location' (2010) 10 Global Environmental Politics 30.

Ivanova M, *The Untold Story of the World's Leading Environmental Institution: UNEP at Fifty* (MIT Press, 2021).

Karlsson M, Alfredsson E and Westling N, 'Climate policy co-benefits: a review' (2020) 20 Climate Policy 292.

Markandya A and others, 'Health co-benefits from air pollution and mitigation costs of the Paris Agreement: a modelling study' (2018) 2 The Lancet Planetary Health e126–e133.

Mayrhofer JP and Gupta J, 'The science and politics of co-benefits in climate policy' (2016) 57 Environmental Science Policy 22.

Mewes C and Unger C, 'Learning by Doing: Co-Benefits Drive National Plans for Climate and Air Quality Governance' (2021) 12 Atmosphere 1184.

NDC Partnership, 'About Us' <https://ndcpartnership.org/about-us> accessed 05 September 2022.

Nemet GF, Holloway T and Meier P, 'Implications of Incorporating Air-Quality Co-benefits into Climate Change Policymaking' (2010) 5 Environmental Research Letters 14007.

Prakash A and Potoski M, 'Collective Action through Voluntary Environmental Programs: a Club Theory Perspective' (2007) 35 Policy Studies Journal 773.

Rabe BG, *Statehouse and Greenhouse: the Emerging Politics of American Climate Change Policy* (Brookings Institution Press 2004).

Republic of Cote d'Ivoire, 'Natonal Action Plannnig Document for the Reduction of Short-Lived Climate Pollutants (SLCP)' (2020) <https://www.ccacoalition.org/en/file/6701/download?token=Nd5E3BB0> accessed 05 September 2022.

Stewart RB, Oppenheimer M and Rudyk B, 'Building Blocks: a Strategy for Near-term Action within the New Global Climate Framework' (2017) 144 Climatic Change 1.

UNEP, 'Historical Agreement on Hydrofluorocarbons Reached in Kigali' (2016) <https://www.unep.org/news-and-stories/news/historical-agreement-hydrofluorocarbons-reached-kigali> accessed 05 September 2022.

UNEP, 'Preventing and reducing air pollution to improve air quality globally' (2017) <https://www.ccacoalition.org/fr/node/2382> accessed 05 September 2022.

UNEP, 'Reducing Hydrofluorocarbons via the Montreal Protocol Is the Most Significant Climate action the World Can Take This Year' (2016) <https://www.unep.org/news-and-stories/press-release/reducing-hydrofluorocarbons-montreal-protocol-most-significant> accessed 05 September 2022.

Unger C and Thielges S, 'Preparing the Playing Field: Climate Club Governance of the G20, Climate and Clean Air Coalition, and Under2 Coalition' (2021) 167 Climatic Change 41.

Unger C, Mar KA and Gürtler K, 'A Club's Contribution to Global Climate Governance: the Case of the Climate and Clean Air Coalition' (2020) 6 Palgrave Communications 1.

UNEP, *Integrated assessment of black carbon and tropospheric ozone* (2011) <https://wedocs.unep.org/20.500.11822/8028> accessed 05 September 2022.

United Nations General Assembly, 'Resolution adopted by the General Assembly on 19 December 2019 [on the report of the Second Committee (A/74/381)] 74/212. International Day of Clean Air for blue skies' (2020) <https://www.ccacoalition.org/en/resources/united-nations-general-assembly-resolution-74212-international-day-clean-air-blue-skies> accessed 05 September 2022.

Ürge-Vorsatz D and others, 'Measuring the co-benefits of climate change mitigation' (2014) 39 Annual Review of Environment and Resources 549.

Workman A and others, 'The political economy of health co-benefits: embedding health in the climate change agenda' (2018) 15 International Journal of Environmental reseArch Public Health 674.

Zusman E and others, 'One Atmosphere: Integrating Air Pollution and Climate Policy and Governance' (2021) 12 Atmosphere 1570.

CHAPTER 7

How to Tackle Short-Lived Climate Pollutants Regionally

The Experience of the Arctic Council

Timo Koivurova, Medy Dervovic, Mikael Hildén, Stefan Kirchner, Kaarle Kupiainen and Malgorzata (Gosia) Smieszek

1 Introduction

The awareness that climate change progresses much quicker and more intensely in the Arctic became widespread with the release of the Arctic Climate Impact Assessment in 2004, a study that the Arctic Council conducted together with the International Arctic Science Committee. It was also this study that paved the way for various work streams within the Arctic Council, the predominant intergovernmental forum of the region.

The main work under the auspices of the Arctic Council has been scientific assessments on climate change, but there have also been projects addressing the challenge of adapting to climate change consequences in the region. The main activity by the Arctic Council to mitigate Arctic warming is the Framework for Action on Enhanced Black Carbon and Methane Emissions Reduction, which was adopted in 2015 and driven forward by the Expert Group established for this purpose.[1]

There are specific reasons why it was important to focus on black carbon in the Arctic. The Arctic Monitoring and Assessment Programme (AMAP) has reported that the increase in Arctic annual mean surface temperature between 1971 and 2019 was three times higher than the increase in the global average.[2] The main focus in climate change mitigation has been on cutting emission of CO_2 but reducing the emissions of short-lived climate pollutants (SLCP), such as black carbon and methane, can also play a role. Methane has a relatively short lifetime in the atmosphere and is a potent climate forcer.[3] Black

1 Arctic Council, Senior Arctic Officials' Report to Ministers (Iqaluit, Canada, 24 April 2015), 118–130 (hereinafter: Iqaluit 2015 SAO Report).

2 AMAP, 'Arctic Climate Change Update 2021: Key Trends and Impacts. Summary for Policy-Makers' (2021), 2, 4–5.

3 AMAP, 'Impacts of Short-Lived Climate Forcers on Arctic Climate, Air Quality, and Human Health. Summary for Policy-Makers' (2021).

carbon affects particularly ice and snow-surfaces by changing their reflectance whereby it accelerates melting processes. By addressing the SLCPs it is possible to slow Arctic warming in the near term, and actions to reduce black carbon and methane also provide health benefits for local communities.[4]

The possibilities to act on the SLCPs are influenced by the specific nature of the Arctic Council and the Arctic environmental co-operation generally. As the Arctic Council cannot impose legally binding rules on its members,[5] the member states of the Council need to make their own decisions individually or as part of collectives, such as the EU, to address SLCPs. For several issues related to air pollution and climate change, the three Council members that are also EU member states have common policies, making the EU a 'policy hub' for part of the Council members. The US and Canada are sovereign states that are members of the Arctic Council, but in many areas of policy also states or provinces can develop their own policies. Similarly, Russia has sovereign powers in regulating relevant activities. This creates a setting in which individual Council members can experiment with regulation addressing SLCPs, but it also creates a need to harmonize actions and agree on monitoring. The Arctic Council does not have its own processes for specifying rules, regulations, or standards, but relies on open ended voluntary coordination. Such a governance setting can be described as polycentric as there is no designated dominant body that would have been given mandate to develop specific rules for regulating SLCPs.[6]

The chapter proceeds in the following manner. First, it discusses the Arctic Council and the type of climate change work that has been undertaken in this forum. Second, it examines how the SLCPs came to be recognized in the Arctic Council and how the 2015 Framework for reducing black carbon and methane emissions emerged. Finally, it discusses what all this work related to SLCPs has achieved, and what the challenges are. These issues are examined from both theoretical and practical angles.

---

4 Ibid.

5 Arctic Council, Declaration on the Establishment of the Arctic Council (19 September 1996), para. 1: "The Arctic Council is established as a high level forum [...]" (hereinafter: Ottawa Declaration). See also: Rüdiger Wolfrum, 'The Arctic in the Context of International Law' (2009) 69 Zeitschrift für Ausländisches Öffentliches Recht und Völkerrecht 533, 542.

6 Elinor Ostrom, 'Polycentric Systems for Coping with Collective Action and Global Environmental Change' (2010) 20 Global Environmental Change 550; Andrew Jordan and others (eds), *Governing Climate Change: Polycentricity in Action?* (Cambridge University Press 2018).

2 The Arctic Council and Its Work on Climate Change

The Arctic Council consists of eight member states, also referred to as the Arctic Eight (A8): the United States of America, Canada, Denmark, Iceland, Norway, Sweden, Finland, and Russia.[7] It has its origins in the last days of the Cold War. On 1 October 1987, the Soviet leader Mikhail Gorbachev gave a speech in Murmansk in which he outlined his vision of the Arctic as "a zone of peace".[8] This speech, that has to be understood in the context of *Glasnost* and *Perestroika*, which were internal processes within the Soviet Union contributing to its opening towards the West in the late 1980s, opened a door for communication between the Arctic nations. When the Iron Curtain was removed, the vision of a zone of peace presented itself as an opportunity to start a process that would later become known as the Rovaniemi Process,[9] allowing the Arctic states to cross political boundaries and address shared concerns. This idea of cooperation on issues of shared concern was set to guide Arctic cooperation for the next three decades.

As noted above, the Arctic Council can be understood as an example of polycentric governance,[10] a term that also has been used to describe entities such as the EU.[11] One characteristic of polycentric governance approaches, the overlapping of different governance areas,[12] is also found in analyses of shared resources.[13] This feature is not so prominent in the Arctic Council because different regions are governed nationally, either as state territory or as areas under national jurisdiction within the context of the international law of the

7 Arctic Council, 'Arctic States' <https://www.arctic-council.org/about/states/> accessed 16 October 2022.

8 Mikhail Gorbachev, Speech in Murmansk at the Ceremonial Meeting on the Occasion of the Presentation of the Order of Lenin and the Gold Star to the City of Murmansk (1 October 1987) <https://www.barentsinfo.fi/docs/gorbachev_speech.pdf> accessed 16 October 2022.

9 See Markku Heikkilä, 'It All Started in Rovaniemi' Shared Voices Magazine 2016 Special Issue (Rovaniemi, 2016) <https://www.uarctic.org/shared-voices/shared-voices-magazine-2016-special-issue/it-all-started-in-rovaniemi/> accessed 16 October 2022.

10 See instructively Paul Cairney, Tanya Heikkila and Matthew Wood, Making Policy in a Complex World (Elements in Public Policy, Cambridge University Press 2019).

11 See Josephine van Zeben and Ana Bobić (eds), Polycentricity in the European Union (Cambridge University Press 2019).

12 Tanya Heikkila, 'Conflict and Conflict Resolution in Polycentric Governance Systems' in Andreas Thiel, William A. Blomquist and Dustin E. Garrick (eds), Governing Complexity: Analyzing and Applying Polycentricity (Cambridge University Press 2019), 133 – 151.

13 Keith Carlisle and Rebecca L. Gruby, 'Polycentric Systems of Governance: A Theoretical Model for the Commons' (2019) 47(4) Policy Studies Journal 927.

sea. However, there is an overlap of governance areas in terms of substance: air pollution is governed by all states and, as SLCPs cross borders, the regulations in one sovereign state have effects that cross the borders to other states. Strict regulation by one country may help to reduce pollution levels in another country and, *vice versa*, weak regulation in one country will increase pollution levels also beyond its borders. There is also inter- and transnational regulation, for example through international treaties or through the European Union. In addition, the member states of the Arctic Council share concern for the people of the Arctic and the environment on which they depend, creating a base for regulatory cooperation. The fact that the Arctic Council does not provide top-down solutions but instead brings together expertise from across the circumpolar north to search for solutions to problems that affect the entire region is a key characteristic of polycentric governance.

It was the concern for the natural environment of the circumpolar north that brought the A8 together in the Rovaniemi Process. A strong emphasis on scientific perspective facilitated the cooperation and the building of trust in the immediate aftermath of the Cold War as the Soviet Union was falling apart and Russia opened up towards its Arctic neighbours. The Finnish initiative to cooperate on environmental protection between the Arctic states led to adoption of the Arctic Environmental Protection Strategy in 1991.[14]

Within the context of the Arctic Environmental Protection Strategy, several working groups were created that remain operational today. Over time, it became clear that a slightly more formal approach was desirable in order to facilitate cooperation in the Arctic, albeit not at the level of a traditional intergovernmental organisation. In 1996, representatives of all Arctic states met in Ottawa, Canada, and established the Arctic Council. The Ottawa Declaration[15] is the constitutional document of the Arctic Council, and the body would quickly be recognized as the most important international forum for Arctic governance.

The Arctic Council differs from many international organisations not only due to the lack of an international treaty as the foundational document but most notably due to its inclusiveness. In addition to the eight Arctic states that are the members of the Council, six representative organisations of the indigenous peoples of the Arctic (the original residents) are Permanent Participants in the Arctic Council,[16] pursuant to paragraph 2 of the Ottawa

14 Arctic Environmental Protection Strategy, (Rovaniemi, 14 June 1991) <http://library.arcticportal.org/1542/1/artic_environment.pdf> accessed 16 October 2022 (hereinafter: AEPS).

15 Ottawa Declaration (n5).

16 Arctic Council, 'Permanent Participants' <https://www.arctic-council.org/about/permanent- participants/> accessed 16 October 2022.

Declaration, a position that gives them full rights to participate in the deliberations between member states. In addition, numerous intergovernmental and non-governmental organisations, and non-Arctic states have been granted observer status in the Arctic Council.[17] While not full members, the observers contribute to the work of the Council and add not only their views but also their expertise, for example in environmental matters, to the work of the Arctic Council.

The Arctic Council's practical work largely happens within Working Groups.[18] Some of the Working Groups that were created within the framework of the Arctic Environmental Protection Strategy have continued their work while others were established more recently. While there is no single Working Group specifically dedicated to climate change, climate change permeates the work of the Arctic Council – a development that commenced most clearly with the release of the *Arctic Climate Impact Assessment* in 2004, a large scientific assessment conducted under the auspices of the Arctic Council. From the protection of the natural environment to efforts to facilitate sustainable development across the Arctic, climate change permeates the work of the Arctic Council and forms the lens through which large parts of the Council's efforts have to be seen.

But the Arctic Council, which acts based on consensus,[19] has not always been able to be as active in the field of climate change as it has been in other areas. Unlike the conscious exclusion of hard security issues from the Council's remit,[20] this is the consequence of different views on the meaning of climate change for the Arctic. Among the A7 (the A8 minus Russia), climate change is currently seen as a challenge, while Russia, largely neglecting potential threats to Arctic people, has seen the warming as an advantage.[21]

During the Trump Administration, the US government rejected the notion of climate change as a human-made threat. As a result, the 2019 Arctic Council ministerial meeting in Rovaniemi, Finland, failed to agree on a declaration that traditionally marks the end of a country's chairmanship of the Arctic Council.

17 Arctic Council, 'Observers' <https://www.arctic-council.org/about/observers/> accessed 22 April 2022.

18 Arctic Council, 'Working Groups' <https://arctic-council.org/about/working-groups/> accessed 22 April 2022.

19 Ottawa Declaration (n 5), para. 7.

20 Ibid., there footnote 1: *"The Arctic Council should not deal with matters related to military security"*.

21 It should be still noted that recently (prior to the war in Ukraine) Russia's general position in relation to climate change seems to have changed somewhat in 2021 – a new long-term strategy, updated pledge – now recognizing climate change and its risks.

This was due to differences of opinion on climate change – despite its practical importance for the people who live in the Arctic and for the work of the Arctic Council.

On 3 March 2022, the A7 announced that they would temporarily stop their participation in all meetings of the Arctic Council and its subsidiary bodies[22] due to Russia's illegal war of aggression against Ukraine: Russia held the chairmanship of the Council from 2021 until spring 2023. In June 2022, the A7 stated that they are still committed to Arctic Council cooperation and re-commenced those projects of the Council where there is no Russian involvement. In June 2023, Norway took over the Arctic Council chairmanship from Russia. It is still difficult to project in what form and composition the Arctic Council – and the Expert Group will continue in the future. Yet, whatever form and composition, it can be expected that climate change and its socio-ecological consequences will remain a key concern for the members of the Arctic Council.

3 Arctic Council's Work on SLCPs

3.1 *The Emergence of Activities Focusing on SLCPs*

The Arctic Council's AMAP Working Group has already for long worked on SLCPs.[23] The initial focus was on methane, ozone, and other greenhouse gases,[24] which slowly evolved to include soot in 2004,[25] referred to as black carbon from 2008.[26] The more focused work on SLCPs commenced with

22 Arctic Council, 'Home Page' <https://www.arctic-council.org/> accessed 16 October 2022: *"The Arctic Council is pausing all official meetings of the Council and its subsidiary bodies until further notice".*

23 AEPS (n 14); AMAP, 'About' <https://www.amap.no/about> accessed 16 October 2022.

24 AMAP, 'Arctic Pollution Issues: A State of the Arctic Environment Report' (1997) <https://www.amap.no/documents/doc/arctic-pollution-issues-a-state-of-the-arctic-environment-report/67> accessed 16 October 2022.

25 Arctic Climate Impact Assessment (ACIA), *Impacts of a Warming Arctic: Arctic Climate Impact Assessment* (Cambridge University Press 2004), 35.

26 P K Quinn and others, 'The Impact of Short-lived Pollutants on Arctic Climate' (2008) AMAP Technical Report No. 1 <https://www.amap.no/documents/download/974/inline> accessed 16 October 2022; J Bluestein, J Rackley, E Baum, 'Sources and Mitigation Opportunities to Reduce Emissions of Short-Term Arctic Climate Forcers' (2008) AMAP Technical Report No. 2 <https://www.amap.no/documents/download/975/inline> accessed 16 October 2022.

AMAP-led scientific conference in September 2008, from which results were conveyed to the Senior Arctic Official's meeting in the same year.[27]

AMAP provided two technical reports[28] to the 2009 Arctic Council Ministerial meeting in Tromsø, Norway, and the meeting adopted a mandate for policy work to identify how to reduce these substances (see Figure 7.1 for the various stages of this work stream) and established a special Task Force on Short-Lived Climate Forcers.[29] In the same year, the AMAP also established the Expert Group on Short-Lived Climate Forcers. Therefore, from early on this work has been divided into a science track (the AMAP and its Short-Lived Climate Forcers Expert Group) and a policy track (the specifically appointed task forces). The AMAP science work has provided the scientific basis on impacts and emission reduction opportunities; and the Task Forces and later the Expert Group on Black Carbon and Methane (EGBCM) have focused on policy solutions.

In 2011, the results of the work of the Expert Group on Short-Lived Climate Forcers were published in the report titled 'The Impact of Black Carbon on Arctic Climate,'[30] giving further impetus to the policy work in the Task Force, which received a new mandate and name at the 2013 Kiruna ministerial meeting in Sweden: Task Force on Black Carbon and Methane. Its work became more policy oriented and aimed "to develop arrangements on actions to achieve enhanced black carbon and methane emission reductions in the Arctic".[31]

This time the focus was on creating a more comprehensive and lasting way to continue the work on black carbon and methane. The Expert Group on Short-Lived Climate Forcers prepared two reports for the 2015 Ministerial Meeting:

---

27 AMAP, 'Progress report from AMAP for the period 2007–2009 to the Arctic Council Ministerial Meeting in Tromsø, Norway, April 28–29, 2009' (2009), 5 <https://oaarchive.arctic-council.org/bitstream/handle/11374/1597/amap_progress_report_2006-2009.pdf?sequence=1&isAllowed=y> accessed 16 October 2022.

28 Technical Report No. 1 (n 26); Technical Report No. 2 (n 26).

29 Arctic Council, Tromsø Declaration on the Occasion of the Sixth Ministerial Meeting of the Arctic Council the 29th of April, 2009, Tromsø, Norway (2009), 3 <https://oaarchive.arctic-council.org/bitstream/handle/11374/91/06_tromso_declaration_2009_signed%20%281%29.pdf?sequence=1&is Allowed=y> accessed 16 October 2022.

30 P K Quinn and others, 'The Impact of Black Carbon on Arctic Climate' (2011) AMAP Technical Report No. 4 <https://www.amap.no/documents/download/977/inline> accessed 16 October 2022.

31 Iqaluit 2015 SAO Report (n 1), 8 citing Arctic Council, Kiruna Declaration (Kiruna, Sweden, 15 May 2013) (2013), 3.

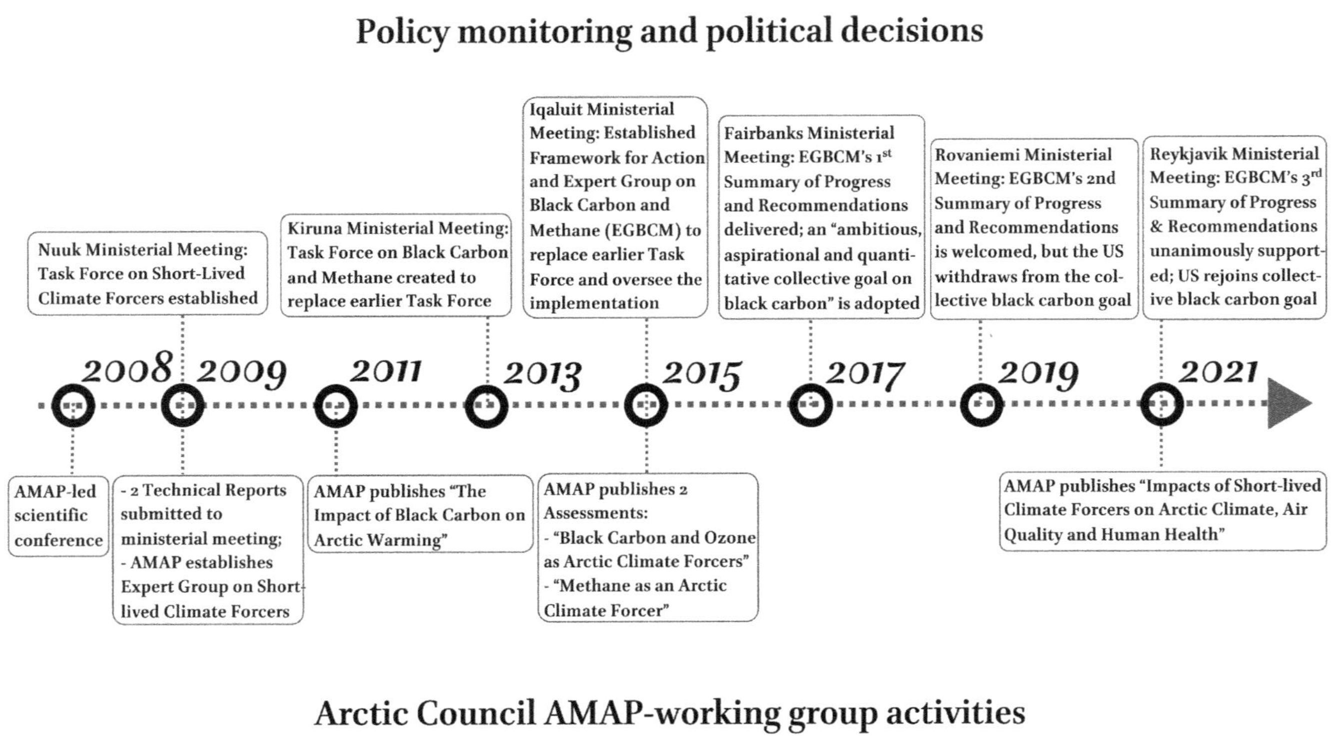

FIGURE 7.1 General timeline illustrating the interaction between the scientific work of the AMAP and the policy decisions and processes led by the senior arctic officials and the ministerial meetings

1) AMAP Assessment 2015: Black carbon and ozone as Arctic climate forcers;[32] and
2) AMAP Assessment 2015: Methane as an Arctic climate forcer.[33]

AMAP science hence provided the scientific fundaments on impacts and emission reduction opportunities to the policy track, but the Arctic Council Framework for Action on Enhanced Black Carbon and Methane emissions reductions was designed independently from the AMAP work, via the Task Force, and was adopted in 2015 at the Iqaluit ministerial meeting.[34]

3.2 *The Establishment of a Framework for Addressing SLCPs*

Through the Framework for Action on Enhanced Black Carbon and Methane emissions reductions, the Arctic states and some observers made a voluntary commitment to "take enhanced, ambitious, national and collective action"[35] to reduce overall black carbon and methane emissions. They also undertook to provide black carbon inventories starting with black carbon and methane emissions, and to adopt "an ambitious, aspirational and quantitative collective goal on black carbon".[36] The latter was agreed at the next ministerial meeting in 2017 in Fairbanks[37] (see Figure 7.1).

The Arctic states also began to share at regular intervals national reports and policies for the purpose of reducing black carbon and methane emissions, measure progress in achieving the collective goal, and jointly identify conclusions and recommendations. Importantly, they also called on the observers to join the action, given the global nature of the challenge. Furthermore, AMAP had demonstrated that the warming effect of black carbon on the Arctic was not limited only to black carbon that originates from the region, but is also due to heated air masses reaching the Arctic from more southern latitudes.[38] Even though the warming effect is proportionally smaller for each ton of emissions

---

32 AMAP, 'AMAP Assessment 2015: Black Carbon and Ozone as Arctic Climate Forcers' (2015) <https://www.amap.no/documents/download/2506/inline> accessed 16 October 2022.

33 AMAP, 'AMAP Assessment 2015: Methane as an Arctic Climate Forcer' (2015) <https://www.amap.no/documents/download/2499/inline> accessed 16 October 2022.

34 Many of the elements for the Framework were visible already in the 2013 progress draft report: Arctic Council, Recommendations to Reduce Black Carbon and Methane Emissions to Slow Arctic Climate Change (2013).

35 Iqaluit 2015 SAO Report (n 1), 119.

36 Ibid.

37 Arctic Council, Fairbanks Declaration (Fairbanks, Alaska, USA, 11 May 2017), para. 24: *"Adopt the first Pan-Arctic report on collective progress to reduce black carbon and methane emissions by the Arctic States and numerous Observer States and its recommendations,* [...]*".* (hereinafter: 2017 Fairbanks Declaration).

38 AMAP, 'Assessment 2015' (n33); AMAP, 'Impacts of SLCFs' (n3).

the further south one goes, there still exists a significant warming effect from emissions from China, India, and the rest of the world as the air masses heated outside the Arctic can be transported and mixed to the area.[39]

The EGBCM supports the implementation of the Framework and monitors progress, but also the Arctic Council's permanent Working Groups have responsibilities in this regard. The AMAP syntheses new science, while the Arctic Contaminants Action Program initiates demonstration projects (for example, on emission reductions). Sector-specific actions are elaborated by the Protection of the Arctic Marine Environment; Emergency Prevention, Preparedness and Response; and Conservation of Arctic Flora and Fauna Working Groups. These actions include initiatives for cleaner shipping, dealing with wildfires or conservation of specific biotopes.

The EGBCM was able to report already in 2017 that all Arctic states and five observer states (France, India, Italy, Spain, and the United Kingdom) had developed and submitted inventories of black carbon and methane emissions, as well as projections for methane emissions.[40] For the Arctic states, these emission inventories and emission projections were to be reported on the basis of the Convention on Long-Range Transboundary Air Pollution (CLRTAP, as regards black carbon) and the United Nations Framework Convention on Climate Change (as regards methane).[41] As the progress report outlined, six out of eight Arctic states provided black carbon projections, along with the United Kingdom.[42] The activities of the Arctic Council have further encouraged countries to develop black carbon emission inventories or projections in fulfilment of the commitments to do so by the Framework and the revised Gothenburg Protocol under CLRTAP (see also Chapter 5).[43] In 2017 the Fairbanks Ministerial Meeting adopted, as recommended by the EGBCM, a quantitative, aspirational collective goal that black carbon emissions be further collectively reduced by

39 AMAP, 'Assessment 2015' (n33).

40 Expert Group on Black Carbon and Methane (EGBCM), 'Summary of Progress and Recommendations 2017' (2017), 4 <https://oaarchive.arctic-council.org/bitstream/handle/11374/1936/EDOCS-4319-v1-ACMMUS10_FAIRBANKS_2017_EGBCM-report-complete-with-covers-and-colophon-letter-size.pdf?sequence=5&isAllowed=y> accessed 16 October 2022.

41 Ibid., 13–14.

42 Ibid., 4, 14, 39.

43 Bradley Matthews and Ville-Veikko Paunu, 'Review of Reporting Systems for National Black Carbon Emissions Inventories: EU Action on Black Carbon in the Arctic' (2019) Technical Report 2 <https://www.amap.no/documents/download/3377/inline> accessed 16 October 2022.

at least 25–33 percent below 2013 levels by 2025.[44] This recommendation was accepted in the ministerial declaration.[45]

The EGBCM developed a limited number of priority recommendations to emphasise steps that can lead to quickest reductions of black carbon and methane. The following sectors were identified: diesel-powered mobile sources (black carbon); oil and gas production (both methane and black carbon); residential biomass combustion appliances (black carbon); and solid waste (methane).[46] During the Finnish chairmanship of the Council in 2017–2019, some additional recommendations were introduced to cover actions in remaining priority sectors such as agriculture (methane and black carbon) and forestry (black carbon due to wildfires).[47]

The second Summary of Progress and Recommendations from the EGBCM to the 2018 Rovaniemi Ministerial Meeting provided an overview of the progress by the Arctic and observer states to reduce emissions of black carbon and methane. It was based on national information submitted in early 2018 and, where relevant, other available data.[48] Most Arctic states continued to associate themselves with the collective mitigation goal on black carbon (except for the US), and this 2019 report placed specific emphasis on tracking policy actions that are likely to affect the trajectory of emissions until 2025.[49] The EGBCM also provided a stocktake of how the priority actions adopted in 2017 had reduced black carbon and methane. Except Russia, states provided an estimate of anticipated reductions in black carbon by 2025 based on current policies.[50]

In 2021, the AMAP prepared a report on Impacts of Short-Lived Climate Forcers on Arctic Climate, Air Quality and Human Health: Summary for Policy-Makers for the Reykjavík Ministerial Meeting held the same year.[51] This AMAP report also informed the third 2021 summary progress report by the EGBCM, which estimated that the Arctic states had reduced black carbon emissions by

---

44 Arctic Council, Senior Arctic Officials' Report to Ministers 2017 (10th Arctic Council Ministerial Meeting, Fairbanks, Alaska, USA, 11 May 2017), 87.

45 2017 Fairbanks Declaration (n 37), paras. 24, 45.

46 EGBCM (n 40), 16.

47 EGBCM, 'Summary of Progress and Recommendations 2019' (2019) <https://oaarchive.arctic-council.org/bitstream/handle/11374/2411/Expert%20Group%20on%20Black%20Carbon%20and%20Methane%20-%20Summary%20Progress%20and%20Recommendations%202019.pdf?sequence=1&isAllowed=y> accessed 16 October 2022.

48 Ibid., 9.

49 Ibid., 10.

50 Ibid.

51 AMAP, 'Impacts of SLCFs' (n3).

20% in 2018, compared to 2013, and were on track to achieve the collective goal set out in 2017.[52,53] Methane emissions on the other hand had increased by 2% between 2013 and 2018, and are projected to continue increasing to 2025.[54] Altogether nine observer states – France, Germany, India, Italy, Japan, Poland, Spain, Switzerland, the United Kingdom – sent in national reports, as well as the European Union.[55]

The summary of progress is based on national information submitted in early 2020 and, where appropriate, other available data.[56] The recommendations build on those outlined in the 2017 and 2019 reports developed by the EGBCM, with minor adjustments, and are offered as a menu of voluntary actions for countries to apply, according to their own national circumstances.[57] In this manner, conjoined expertise forms the basis for decentralised but coordinated decision-making that builds on non-binding expert guidance.

3.3 *Summary of the Work on SLCPs*

To sum up, the Arctic Council provides a unique intergovernmental forum for work on SLCPs by simultaneously catalysing science on the impacts on the Arctic, exploring policy actions, and supporting concrete actions to reduce emissions.[58] But this work is unique also within the Arctic Council. Until now there have been no other policy actions adopted by the Arctic Council in which the member states and observers have agreed and delivered national reports. There have been scientific assessments with related policy recommendations,

---

52 Ibid., 3, 15.

53 EGBCM, '3rd Summary of Progress and Recommendations' (2021) <https://oaarchive.arctic-council.org/handle/11374/2610> accessed 16 October 2022.

54 Ibid., 3, 18.

55 Ibid., 9.

56 Ibid., 3.

57 Ibid.

58 The work on SLCPs can be perceived to have progressed at four different levels: 1) Scientific via the AMAP Short-Lived Climate Forcers Expert Group. This work produces policy relevant scientific assessments, but no direct policy recommendations (it does produce recommendations for further science); 2) Technical civil servant level with the EGBCM. The Expert Group oversees the implementation of the Framework, analyses progress and options for action and makes policy recommendations; 3) The political preparatory level of Senior Arctic Officials, an organ of the Council which prepares the decisions to the taken by the foreign ministers, including the commitments to curtail emissions. 4) The political decision-making level at the level of foreign ministers, to be made at the Ministerial meetings convened after each chairmanship period.

but only two of these have included follow-up procedures,[59] which merely consist of other internal reporting rather than national reporting.

It is also important to point out that the black carbon and methane work has become a cross-cutting activity in almost all working groups of the Council. AMAP has continuously provided scientific knowledge and information of these substances, and their sources and their impacts in the Arctic. Practical demonstration projects have been undertaken in the Arctic Contaminants Action Program Working Group while the Emergency Prevention, Preparedness and Response, and Conservation of Arctic Flora and Fauna Working Groups have considered wildfires, and Protection of the Arctic Marine Environment Working Group – heavy fuel oil.

It is also worth noting that the scope of the activities has generally been the entire territories of the Arctic states, not only those parts defined to be Arctic. This is due to the fact that emissions and impacts of black carbon and methane are not limited to the Arctic, and a significant amount of the substances reach the Arctic through long-range (internal and transboundary) atmospheric transport. Reporting mechanisms for other international treaties also require information on the whole country.[60] The legislative and policy developments generally apply to the whole country. An exception are the regulations on black smoke from ships in ports which have been applied locally or other subnational levels. For example, the State of Alaska limits emissions of 'visible smoke' within three miles of the Alaska coastline.[61]

4 The Arctic Council's Work on SLCPs in a Polycentric Governance Perspective

From the perspective of transnational environmental governance, the Arctic Council is a particular regional body.[62] It is uniquely inclusive in giving

59 Arctic Council, 'Arctic Marine Shipping Assessment 2009 Report' (2009) <https://www.pame.is/images/03_Projects/AMSA/AMSA_2009_report/AMSA_2009_Report_2nd_print.pdf> accessed 16 October 2022; Conservation of Arctic Flora and Fauna (CAFF), 'Arctic Biodiversity Assessment: Status and Trends in Arctic Biodiversity' (2013) <https://oaarchive.arctic-council.org/handle/11374/223> accessed 16 October 2022.

60 Matthews and Paunu (n 43).

61 Alaska Department of Environmental Conservation, Division of Water, 'Cruise Ship Air' <https://dec.alaska.gov/water/cruise-ships/cruise-air/> accessed 16 October 2022.

62 Christoph Humrich, 'Coping with Institutional Challenges for Arctic Environmental Governance' in Kathrin Keil and Sebastian Knecht (eds), Governing Arctic Change (Palgrave Macmillan 2017).

indigenous peoples a formal position in the deliberations and can therefore contribute in particular to what Kay calls constitutive effects: such effects are the formation of collective identity and interests, and mobilisation for collective action.[63] This is of particular interest from the perspective of polycentric environmental governance, which is based on the idea that action on particular issues emerge not in a top-down fashion from a 'supreme' body, but instead bottom-up from different entities that present and develop their approaches partly independently of each other.[64] In the Arctic Council context, these entities are not only the individual member countries, but also indigenous organisations and observers. In addition, for those members that are also members of the EU, the EU is a centre in which a significant part of their air pollution regulation is developed. This demonstrates a general characteristic of polycentric governance: decision-making is dispersed in the sense that actions are not fully harmonised and partly different actions can be taken at different levels of governance.[65]

Jordan and others argue that polycentric processes can be usefully examined in the light of four basic propositions that describe key features of how polycentricity is expected to work and therefore also identify some potential challenges.[66] They specify the propositions as follows:

1. Local Action Governance initiatives are likely to take off at a local level through processes of self-organisation.
2. Mutual Adjustment. Constituent units are likely to spontaneously develop collaborations with one another, producing more trusting interrelationships.
3. Experimentation. The willingness and capacity to experiment is likely to facilitate governance innovation and learning about what works.
4. The Importance of Trust. Trust is likely to build up more quickly when units can self-organise, thus increasing collective ambitions.[67]

The work of the Arctic Council on SLCPs can be examined in the light of the propositions on polycentricity.

63 Tamara Kay, 'Legal Transnationalism: The Relationship between Transnational Social Movement Building and International Law' (2011) 36(2) Law & Social Inquiry 419.

64 Andrew Jordan and others, 'Governing Climate Change Polycentrically: Setting the Scene' in Andrew Jordan and others (eds), *Governing Climate Change: Polycentricity in Action?* (Cambridge University Press 2018).

65 Ostrom (n 6).

66 Andrew Jordan and others (n64).

67 Ibid, 12–20.

4.1 *Local Governance*

In the context of the Arctic Council both national and subnational governance stands for 'local' as opposed to international governance. The main point is that both national and subnational entities can develop their own policy initiatives without being constrained or coerced by the Arctic Council. There is clear evidence of local governance initiatives to address the emissions of SLCPs. There have been various national (regulatory) initiatives in the Arctic Council member countries to reduce emissions of black carbon. For example, regulations to reduce emissions from small-scale domestic heating have been enacted by Arctic states independently from each other. Regulation on emissions from ships in ports have also been national or even local before being debated at the level of the International Maritime Organisation. Additional examples have been documented by the EGBCM.[68] The active interventions to reduce emissions such as those of the Arctic Contaminants Action Program have also been local.[69] They have included activities that have been particularly relevant for indigenous groups. For example, the Nunavut District Heating projects have aimed at reducing local emissions.[70]

Local governance is not unique to the Arctic Council. One can argue that elements of polycentricity have also been introduced under the UNFCCC, in particular with the Paris Agreement that strives to encourage local/national action also outside the formulation of the official emission reduction targets. The Paris Agreement requests each country to outline and communicate their climate actions via Nationally Determined Contributions (NDCs; see Chapter 3).[71] Collectively, the actions included in NDCs determine whether the long-term goals of the Paris Agreement are likely to be achieved or not. The process for specifying NDCs can be seen as a bottom-up process, but there is also an intention "to incentivize and facilitate participation in the mitigation of greenhouse gas emissions by public and private entities" (Article 6, 4b).

Methane is one of the greenhouse gases that is explicitly dealt with under the UNFCCC, and most NDCs cover methane as a priority pollutant for action.[72] Black carbon is still a special case as it is not explicitly recognised in

68 EGBCM, '3rd Summary of Progress and Recommendations' (n53).

69 ACAP, 'Arctic Black Carbon Case Studies Platform' <https://www.arctic-council.org/about/working-groups/acap/home/projects/arctic-black-carbon-case-studies-platform/> accessed 16 October 2022.

70 Nunavut Climate Change Secretariat <https://climatechangenunavut.ca/en/project-type/district-heating-systems-dhs> accessed 16 October 2022.

71 Paris Agreement (adopted 12 December 2015, entered into force 4 November 2016) UNTS 3156, arts. 3–4.

72 See UNFCCC, 'NDC Registry' <https://unfccc.int/NDCREG> accessed 16 October 2022.

the UNFCCC. This is understandable due to the uncertainties that surround the exact climate forcing effects of black carbon. Only a few countries have included black carbon in their NDCs, and the issue on how to account for black carbon under the UNFCCC and the Paris Agreement is still unresolved. This situation opens possibilities for independently developing governance to deal with its emissions. Both methane and black carbon have, on the other hand, been addressed under CLRTAP[73] since the review of its Gothenburg Protocol in 2012 (see Chapter 5).[74] Like the UNFCCC and its reporting framework, the Gothenburg Protocol also provides a process for coordination of national/local actions. It mainly encourages the development of national governance and has so far not imposed strict regulations on emissions of black carbon to be followed by its Parties.

4.2 *Mutual Adjustment*

The Arctic Council can be seen as a forum within which mutual adjustment can occur, for example in setting limit values for emissions of black carbon. It can also be seen from an angle of policy innovation, as a platform encouraging policy diffusion, where different mechanisms of policy diffusion can operate.[75] Policy diffusion refers to the process of 'migrating' policies from one jurisdiction to another. In the context of the Arctic Council, mechanisms of diffusion based on learning or emulation are likely to be significant. The policy-oriented report of the EGBCM provides material for both learning and emulation. The consecutive reports can also provide indications that adjustment (diffusion) takes place.

The Arctic Council's work has interacted with the strategy work in the Arctic countries.[76] For example, Canada[77] has a specific strategy in place for SLCPs,

---

73 Convention on Long-Range Transboundary Air Pollution (adopted 13 November 1979, entered into force 16 March 1983) 1302 UNTS 217.

74 Amendment of the Text and Annexes II to IX to the Protocol to the 1979 Convention on Long-Range Transboundary Air Pollution to Abate Acidification, Eutrophication and Ground-Level Ozone and the Addition of New Annexes X and XI (adopted 4 May 2012, entered into force 7 October 2019).

75 Frances Stokes Berry and William D Berry, 'Innovation and Diffusion Models in Policy Research' in Christopher M Weible and Paul A Sabatier (eds), Theories of the Policy Process (Fourth Edition, Routledge 2018), 253–297.

76 Karin Kindbom and others, Measures to Reduce Emissions of Short-Lived Climate Pollutants (SLCP) in the Nordic Countries (TemaNord 2018:533, Nordic Council of Ministers 2018) <https://norden.diva-portal.org/smash/record.jsf?pid=diva2%3A1236837&dswid=4681> accessed 16 October 2022.

77 Environment and Climate Change Canada, 'Strategy on Short-Lived Climate Pollutants – 2017' (2017) <https://publications.gc.ca/collections/collection_2018/eccc/En4-299-2017-eng.pdf> accessed on 16 October 2022.

while Norway[78] and Finland[79] have developed overarching climate and air pollution strategies with specific recognition of black carbon and methane. The Arctic Council's reporting requirement/encouragement makes countries provide a specific outlook at black carbon and methane specific measures and collect a status update periodically.

In its work on black carbon, the Arctic Council is closely connected with the CLTRAP. One advantage is that the CLRTAP has specific processes for adjustment. Thus, an Ad-hoc Expert Group on Black Carbon was tasked to identify options for potential revisions to the Gothenburg Protocol that would enable the Parties to mitigate black carbon as a component of particulate matter (PM), and the Group delivered their report in 2010.[80] Eventually, the amended Protocol encouraged Parties to prioritise black-carbon-rich sources when planning their $PM_{2.5}$ emission reductions,[81] and develop black carbon emission inventories to complement their inventories of other pollutants.[82] Methane is recognized, but one can argue that the work on methane under the Protocol has not been very extensive yet (see Chapter 5). It has focused on improving the scientific understanding of impacts of methane reductions on concentrations of ground level ozone as well as the co-benefits to climate.

4.3 *Experimentation*

Experimentation can be seen as one part of the local actions, but the attention that the Arctic Council has brought on SLCPs can also be seen to encourage regular research and development activities, supporting and justifying global initiatives such as the zero routine flaring by the World Bank Group or actions of the Climate and Clean Air Coalition (CCAC) that span a wide range of SLCPs. The Arctic Council can, even though it has limited means itself, engage with these initiatives and give them additional visibility. For example, the report and recommendations of the EGBCM have mentioned and endorsed the World Bank activities, and the Arctic Council groups have teamed up with the CCAC

78 Norway's Climate Action Plan for 2021–2030. Meld. St. 13 (2020–2021) Report to the Storting (white paper).

79 Ministry of the Environment 2022. Medium-term Climate Change Policy Plan Towards a carbon-neutral society. Publications of the Ministry of the Environment 2022:20 <http://urn.fi/URN:ISBN:978-952-361-417-8> accessed 16 October 2022.

80 Economic Commission for Europe, 'Black Carbon: Report by the Co-Chairs of the Ad Hoc Expert Group on Black Carbon' 30 September 2010, ECE/EB.AIR/2010/7.

81 Economic Commission for Europe, 1999 Protocol to Abate Acidification, Eutrophication and Ground-Level Ozone to the Convention on Long-Range Transboundary Air Pollution, As Amended on 4 May 2012 (6 May 2013) ECE/EB.AIR/114, art. 2 para. 2.

82 Ibid., art. 6 para. 2*bis*.

and organised, for example, joint side events at meetings of the Conference of the Parties of the UNFCCC. The Arctic Council can also be seen as a test case for policy concepts and arrangements, i.e., the Arctic Council Framework, from which experiences can be taken elsewhere. It is furthermore worth noting that the pool of experts is small globally. Hence, the same experts are involved in the work on reducing emissions of SLCPs and represent their countries in several international bodies and groups.

Also, the practical arrangements with the Arctic Council working groups focusing on specific aspects of SCLPs and the EGBCM exploring the policy implications can be seen as an 'experimental' process in which progress is ensured by actions in relatively small groups. 'Experimentation' can further be viewed to include processes for knowledge production. The Arctic Council's scientific work on black carbon and methane that has been led by AMAP, is also 'experimental' in the sense that scientific assessments of the impacts of short-lived climate forcers, including black carbon and methane have encouraged new scientific work, for example, in developing *in situ* measurements.[83] The mapping of opportunities for policy actions by Arctic Council Task Forces have further supplemented the knowledge base.[84] The Arctic Council has also provided a forum for examining SLCPs, particularly black carbon and methane together, in the Arctic regional context. It has supported the deliberations under the CLRTAP and complemented the work of, for example, the CCAC,[85] whose agenda has been more global.

4.4 *Trust*

The key motivation for the Arctic Council's work has been in building trust. The governance process and its structures, presented in the Arctic Council Framework document, have proven to be relatively robust although governments' commitment to the more political black carbon emission reduction goal has varied. Indeed, past events have shown that trust is probably the most vulnerable element in developing the work to deal with SLCPs. During the Trump administration in the US, the work of the EGBCM suffered significantly

83 AMAP, 'In Situ Observations of BC in the Arctic' <https://bc-policy-landscape.amap.no/areas-of-action/in-situ-observations-of-black-carbon-in-the-arctic> accessed 16 October 2022.

84 See AMAP, 'Areas of Action' <https://bc-policy-landscape.amap.no/areas-of-action> accessed 16 October 2022.

85 For more information on the CCAC: <https://www.ccacoalition.org/en> accessed 16 October 2022.

from the lack of trust in multilateralism that the Trump administration systematically voiced.

The preparation of the EGBCM report in 2019 was hampered by the effort of the US to downplay the recognition of climate change, and by an unwillingness to recognize the value of multilateralism and international cooperation. This led to a hostility towards polycentric approaches such as the synergies between various partly independent processes, including the interacting efforts to limit emissions of black carbon from shipping in the International Maritime Organisation and under the Arctic Council. The US also wished to withdraw from the agreed collective aspirational black carbon mitigation goal. One line of their argument was that Russia had failed to submit data on emissions, and another one that black carbon should not be dealt with as a separate goal but integrated under the general air pollution regulation aiming at the reduction of emissions of particulate matter (rather than referring to climate change, which the Trump administration had problems with). These issues of trust (within the Council), formulated as 'technical' issues, severely reduced the possibilities of US experts to actively participate in the work of the EGBCM. The change of administration in the US made it possible to return to 'normal', and the EGBCM report for 2021 emerged smoothly. The war in Ukraine has demonstrated yet again that the foundation of trust can be lost literally in a few hours.

5 Conclusion: Successes and Weaknesses

Proponents of a polycentric governance argue that it will eventually reach tangible results that are as good as or superior to those that can be reached through more traditional approaches, which first aim at setting international goals that can be enforced. The CLTRAP can be seen to represent a more traditional approach with a focus on legally binding Protocols and decisions by the Parties, whereas the Arctic Council is primarily a purveyor of soft approaches that fit the concept of polycentricity.

In terms of goals, the CLTRAP did not introduce a separate quantitative goal for black carbon, whereas the Arctic Council did. This can be considered as a more ambitious approach; even though it is important to note that the Arctic Council commitment is collective, voluntary and 'aspirational' and not binding under international law. The voluntary nature of the black carbon commitment may have made it easier for countries to get involved and adopt it. Black carbon mitigation goals under the amended Gothenburg Protocol have not yet been ratified by Iceland and Russia, as of January 2023.

The voluntary nature of the Arctic Council goal for black carbon mitigation does not mean that the countries take their commitments light-heartedly. The element of trust implies that the political risk of not joining or contributing to the common effort is relevant. Even when the US withdrew under the Trump administration from the collective goal, it stressed the commitment of the US to reduce emissions of fine particles.[86] Nevertheless, the experience of the Arctic Council demonstrates clearly that a voluntary process is very vulnerable to changes in government which may abruptly shift the countries' level of commitment to the goals and the relevant policy processes.

The jury is still out on which approach leads in the end to the most tangible results, but it is possible to highlight reasons for success in the Arctic Council process that has advanced an agenda reducing emissions of black carbon and methane. One key to success is a well-managed preparatory process, including workshops with reports and scientific papers, and eventually a well-designed but simple enough Framework with clear mandates and roles for the established structures has been the fundament for an operationally successful process. This can be seen to correspond to the concept of *orchestration*,[87] which is about creating a favourable political environment for change. In the case of the Arctic Council, orchestration can be seen in the black carbon related projects that the Council's Working Groups have initiated and which feed into political processes led by the Ministers that participate in the Council deliberations.

In the case of the Arctic Council, the science work to support policymaking included a dedicated AMAP Expert Group with broad membership across the Arctic states and the observer states. The AMAP Expert Group was tasked to conduct periodic scientific assessments and provided crucial support for the science-policy dialogue and eventually the policy discussions by addressing policy relevant issues as well as identifying and filling in knowledge gaps. Also, it is worth noting the significant scientific interest in SLCPs and their climate impacts at the time, which attracted many of the world's leading scientists to take active part in the process. The scientific work has been highly valued by all Parties, including Russia, whose political commitment to emission reductions has been in doubt.

The Arctic Council can be thought of as a 'node' in the global governance of SLCPs. It is generally easier to reach an agreement between a smaller group of relatively like-minded countries on a relatively "narrow" topic (which

86 See footnote 7 in EGBCM (n 47).

87 See Kenneth W Abbott, 'Orchestration: Strategic Ordering in Polycentric Governance' in Andrew Jordan and others (eds), *Governing Climate Change: Polycentricity in Action?* (Cambridge University Press 2018).

nevertheless may be complex). On the other hand, a small group is more vulnerable to abrupt policy changes among Parties.

It is important to note that black carbon and methane mitigation was addressed at the same time also in other policy fora, i.e., the CCAC, the CLRTAP and the Global Methane Initiative, to name a few. Also, the IPCC has included short-lived climate forcers in many of its Assessment Reports. These parallel, partly synergistic processes are compatible with the concept of polycentricity, and synergies among them can be identified.

From a member state government's perspective, the different international policy processes are not operating in isolation from each other. The same delegates often represent their countries in the different work streams and even if this would not be the case, then there is often internal coordination taking place. The level of governments' internal coordination varies, but in many cases, it is made across policy fora if similar topics are addressed. A common concern for governments is often to avoid overlaps and find synergies between the policy processes. This helps to keep an up-to-date overview of the challenge and consider the alternative possibilities for action.

Ultimately, it is difficult to identify which process and approach proves to be the most successful one in reducing emissions of SLCPs. Because there are several parallel and interacting processes with the same goal, close connections among and awareness of work in different fora are beneficial. It can lead to a more rapid adoption of good practices and lessons learnt. One can nevertheless argue that the emission reduction targets for black carbon have been rather modest, and that the regulatory environment is fragmented, even though synergistic features can be identified.[88]

For methane, progress is less evident. It is understandable that the Arctic Council has a specific focus on black carbon given its enhanced importance as a regional pollutant and climate forcer in ice and snow-covered areas like the Arctic. Methane is well mixed in the atmosphere, which is why the location of emissions is not as important for the Arctic climate compared to black carbon. However, for both, there is still a need for more ambitious action. One way to achieve progress could be to encourage more polycentric action. In a world in which trust has been lost between Russia and the other members of the Arctic Council, further local/national experimentation, and mutual adjustment among the willing is likely to be the best way forward for the time being.

88 Yulia Yamineva and Kati Kulovesi, 'Keeping the Arctic White: The Legal and Governance Landscape for Reducing Short-Lived Climate Pollutants in the Arctic Region' (2018) 7(2) Transnational Environmental Law 201.

Acknowledgements

Timo Koivurova would like to express his gratitude to the Japanese funding that enabled him to focus on the topic (Kobe University Strategic International Collaboration Grant Type C (2022)). Mikael Hildén's contribution is based on work for the EU-funded Action on Black Carbon in the Arctic (the EU Partnership Instrument). Furthermore, the help by UEF research assistant Niklas Löther with compiling the timeline is greatly appreciated.

Bibliography

Abbott K W, 'Orchestration: Strategic Ordering in Polycentric Governance' in Andrew Jordan and others (eds), *Governing Climate Change: Polycentricity in Action?* (Cambridge University Press 2018).

ACAP, 'Arctic Black Carbon Case Studies Platform' <https://www.arctic-council.org/about/working-groups/acap/home/projects/arctic-black-carbon-case-studies-platform/> accessed 16 October 2022.

Alaska Department of Environmental Conservation, Division of Water, 'Cruise Ship Air' <https://dec.alaska.gov/water/cruise-ships/cruise-air/> accessed 16 October 2022.

AMAP, 'AMAP Assessment 2015: Black Carbon and Ozone as Arctic Climate Forcers' (2015) <https://www.amap.no/documents/download/2506/inline> accessed 16 October 2022.

AMAP, 'AMAP Assessment 2015: Methane as an Arctic Climate Forcer' (2015) <https://www.amap.no/documents/download/2499/inline> accessed 16 October 2022.

AMAP, 'Arctic Climate Change Update 2021: Key Trends and Impacts. Summary for Policy-Makers' (2021).

AMAP, 'Arctic Pollution Issues: A State of the Arctic Environment Report' (1997) <https://www.amap.no/documents/doc/arctic-pollution-issues-a-state-of-the-arctic-environment-report/67> accessed 16 October 2022.

AMAP, 'Impacts of Short-Lived Climate Forcers on Arctic Climate, Air Quality, and Human Health. Summary for Policy-Makers' (2021).

AMAP, 'Progress report from AMAP for the period 2007–2009 to the Arctic Council Ministerial Meeting in Tromsø, Norway, April 28–29, 2009' (2009) <https://oaarchive.arctic-council.org/bitstream/handle/11374/1597/amap_progress_report_2006-2009.pdf?sequence=1&isAllowed=y> accessed 16 October 2022.

AMAP, 'In Situ Observations of BC in the Arctic' <https://bc-policy-landscape.amap.no/areas-of-action/in-situ-observations-of-black-carbon-in-the-arctic> accessed 16 October 2022.

AMAP, 'Areas of Action' <https://bc-policy-landscape.amap.no/areas-of-action> accessed 16 October 2022.

AMAP, 'About' <https://www.amap.no/about> accessed 16 October 2022.

Arctic Climate Impact Assessment (ACIA), *Impacts of a Warming Arctic: Arctic Climate Impact Assessment* (Cambridge University Press 2004).

Arctic Council, 'Arctic Marine Shipping Assessment 2009 Report' (2009) <https://www.pame.is/images/03_Projects/AMSA/AMSA_2009_report/AMSA_2009_Report_2nd_print.pdf> accessed 16 October 2022.

Arctic Council, 'Declaration on the Establishment of the Arctic Council' (19 September 1996).

Arctic Council, 'Fairbanks Declaration' (Fairbanks, Alaska, USA, 11 May 2017).

Arctic Council, 'Recommendations to Reduce Black Carbon and Methane Emissions to Slow Arctic Climate Change' (2013).

Arctic Council, 'Senior Arctic Officials' Report to Ministers' (Iqaluit, Canada, 24 April 2015).

Arctic Council, 'Senior Arctic Officials' Report to Ministers 2017' (10th Arctic Council Ministerial Meeting, Fairbanks, Alaska, USA, 11 May 2017).

Arctic Council, 'Tromsø Declaration on the Occasion of the Sixth Ministerial Meeting of the Arctic Council the 29th of April, 2009, Tromsø, Norway' (2009) <https://oaarchive.arctic-council.org/bitstream/handle/11374/91/06_tromso_declaration_2009_signed%20%281%29.pdf?sequence=1&is Allowed=y> accessed 16 October 2022.

Arctic Council, 'Home Page' <https://www.arctic-council.org/> accessed 16 October 2022.

Arctic Council, 'Observers' <https://www.arctic-council.org/about/observers/> accessed 22 April 2022.

Arctic Council, 'Working Groups' <https://arctic-council.org/about/working-groups/> accessed 22 April 2022.

Arctic Council, 'Arctic States' <https://www.arctic-council.org/about/states/> accessed 16 October 2022.

Arctic Environmental Protection Strategy (Rovaniemi, 14 June 1991) <http://library.arcticportal.org/1542/1/artic_environment.pdf> accessed 16 October 2022.

Arctic Environmental Protection Strategy, 'Arctic Environmental Protection Strategy' (Rovaniemi, 14 June 1991) <http://library.arcticportal.org/1542/1/artic_environment.pdf> accessed 16 October 2022.

Bluestein J, Rackley J, Baum E, 'Sources and Mitigation Opportunities to Reduce Emissions of Short-Term Arctic Climate Forcers' (2008) AMAP Technical Report No. 2 <https://www.amap.no/documents/download/975/inline> accessed 16 October 2022.

Cairney P, Heikkila T and Wood M, *Making Policy in a Complex World* (Elements in Public Policy, Cambridge University Press 2019).

Carlisle K and Gruby R L, 'Polycentric Systems of Governance: a Theoretical Model for the Commons' (2019) 47(4) Policy Studies Journal 927.

Conservation of Arctic Fauna and Flora (CAFF), 'Arctic Biodiversity Assessment: Status and Trends in Arctic Biodiversity' (2013) <https://oaarchive.arctic-council.org/handle/11374/223> accessed 16 October 2022.

Economic Commission for Europe, 'Black Carbon: Report by the Co-Chairs of the Ad Hoc Expert Group on Black Carbon' (30 September 2010) ECE/EB.AIR/2010/7.

Economic Commission for Europe, 1999 Protocol to Abate Acidification, Eutrophication and Ground-Level Ozone to the Convention on Long-Range Transboundary Air Pollution, As Amended on 4 May 2012 (6 May 2013) ECE/EB.AIR/114.

Environment and Climate Change Canada, 'Strategy on Short-Lived Climate Pollutants – 2017' (2017) <https://publications.gc.ca/collections/collection_2018/eccc/En4-299-2017-eng.pdf> accessed 16 October 2022.

Expert Group on Black Carbon and Methane (EGBCM), 'Summary of Progress and Recommendations 2017' (2017), 4 <https://oaarchive.arctic-council.org/bitstream/handle/11374/1936/EDOCS-4319-v1-ACMMUS10_FAIRBANKS_2017_EGBCM-report-complete-with-covers-and-colophon-letter-size.pdf?sequence=5&isAllowed=y> accessed 16 October 2022.

EGBCM, 'Summary of Progress and Recommendations 2019' (2019) <https://oaarchive.arctic-council.org/bitstream/handle/11374/2411/Expert%20Group%20on%20Black%20Carbon%20and%20Methane%20-%20Summary%20Progress%20and%20Recommendations%202019.pdf?sequence=1&isAllowed=y> accessed 16 October 2022.

EGBCM, '3rd Summary of Progress and Recommendations' (2021) <https://oaarchive.arctic-council.org/handle/11374/2610> accessed 16 October 2022.

Gorbachev M, Speech in Murmansk at the Ceremonial Meeting on the Occasion of the Presentation of the Order of Lenin and the Gold Star to the City of Murmansk (1 October 1987) <https://www.barentsinfo.fi/docs/gorbachev_speech.pdf> accessed 16 October 2022.

Heikkilä M, 'It All Started in Rovaniemi' *Shared Voices Magazine 2016 Special Issue* (Rovaniemi, 2016) <https://www.uarctic.org/shared-voices/shared-voices-magazine-2016-special-issue/it-all-started-in-rovaniemi/> accessed 16 October 2022.

Heikkila T, 'Conflict and Conflict Resolution in Polycentric Governance Systems' in Andreas Thiel, William A. Blomquist and Dustin E. Garrick (eds), *Governing Complexity: Analyzing and Applying Polycentricity* (Cambridge University Press 2019).

Humrich C, 'Coping with Institutional Challenges for Arctic Environmental Governance' in Kathrin Keil and Sebastian Knecht (eds), *Governing Arctic Change* (Palgrave Macmillan 2017).

Jordan A and others, 'Governing Climate Change Polycentrically: Setting the Scene' in Andrew Jordan and others (eds), *Governing Climate Change: Polycentricity in Action?* (Cambridge University Press 2018).

Jordan A and others (eds), *Governing Climate Change: Polycentricity in Action?* (Cambridge University Press 2018).

Kay T, 'Legal Transnationalism: the Relationship between Transnational Social Movement Building and International Law' (2011) 36(2) Law & Social Inquiry 419.

Kindbom K and others, Measures to Reduce Emissions of Short-Lived Climate Pollutants (SLCP) in the Nordic Countries (TemaNord 2018:533, Nordic Council of Ministers 2018) <https://norden.diva-portal.org/smash/record.jsf?pid=diva2%3A1236837&dswid=4681> accessed 16 October 2022.

Matthews B and Paunu V-V, 'Review of Reporting Systems for National Black Carbon Emissions Inventories: EU Action on Black Carbon in the Arctic' (2019) Technical Report 2 <https://www.amap.no/documents/download/3377/inline> accessed 16 October 2022.

Ministry of the Environment 2022. Medium-term Climate Change Policy Plan Towards a carbon-neutral society. Publications of the Ministry of the Environment 2022:20 <http://urn.fi/URN:ISBN:978-952-361-417-8> accessed 16 October 2022.

Norway's Climate Action Plan for 2021–2030. Meld. St. 13 (2020–2021) Report to the Storting (white paper).

Ostrom E, 'Polycentric Systems for Coping with Collective Action and Global Environmental Change' (2010) 20 Global Environmental Change 550.

Quinn P K and others, 'The Impact of Black Carbon on Arctic Climate' (2011) AMAP Technical Report No. 4 <https://www.amap.no/documents/download/977/inline> Accessed 16 October 2022.

Quinn P K and others, 'The Impact of Short-lived Pollutants on Arctic Climate' (2008) AMAP Technical Report No. 1 <https://www.amap.no/documents/download/974/inline> accessed 16 October 2022.

Rantanen M and others, 'The Arctic Has Warmed Nearly Four Times Faster than the Globe since 1979' (2022) 3 Communications Earth & Environment 168.

Stokes Berry F and Berry W D, 'Innovation and Diffusion Models in Policy Research' in Christopher M Weible and Paul A Sabatier (eds), *Theories of the Policy Process* (Fourth Edition, Routledge 2018).

UNFCCC, 'NDC Registry' <https://unfccc.int/NDCREG> accessed 16 October 2022.

van Zeben J and Bobić A (eds), *Polycentricity in the European Union* (Cambridge University Press 2019).

Wolfrum R, 'The Arctic in the Context of International Law' (2009) 69 Zeitschrift für Ausländisches Öffentliches Recht und Völkerrecht 533.

Yamineva Y and Kulovesi K, 'Keeping the Arctic White: the Legal and Governance Landscape for Reducing Short-Lived Climate Pollutants in the Arctic Region' (2018) 7(2) Transnational Environmental Law 201.

CHAPTER 8

From Bilateral Science Diplomacy to Wider Black Carbon Governance?

Norwegian-Chinese and Finnish-Russian Initiatives

Pami Aalto, Gørild Heggelund, Anna Claydon and Minna Hanhijärvi

1 Introduction

In this chapter, we will examine Norwegian-Chinese and Finnish-Russian science diplomacy to mitigate SLCPs, in particular focusing on black carbon emissions. The Norwegian and Finnish science diplomacy initiatives towards China and Russia, respectively, involve various combinations of governmental actors alongside a plethora of public and private sector actors in research, development and innovation (RDI) sectors. These initiatives are of interest for several reasons.

First, the black carbon initiatives of the sender countries Norway and Finland stand out in the international context since initiatives by individual states on black carbon specifically are rare. Second, the target countries, China and Russia, are globally significant emitters of black carbon and other SLCPs, especially so for the Arctic, which forms an important context for Norwegian and Finnish diplomatic practices and foreign policies in general. Third, large and multiple mitigation benefits could be gained domestically in China and Russia. Fourth, the two target countries are differently attuned to bi- or multilateral cooperation with Western countries. Fifth, as the cases also have different outcomes, they can very usefully illuminate the wider multilateral prospects of black carbon and SLCP mitigation.

In the Norwegian-Chinese case, a bilateral project was launched to bolster the science basis of mitigation and support public policies in both countries. In the Finnish-Russian case, bilateral high-level diplomacy led by the Finnish president was combined with similar initiatives in Arctic regional and more global arenas alongside scientific research with Finnish and Russian participants in the multilateral Arctic framework. However, in the Finnish-Russian case, the governmental, science and RDI tracks remained less than optimally integrated. Combined with how Russian domestic structures and foreign policy hampered the Finnish efforts, the outcomes in this case remained unclear.

We seek to shed light on the diverging outcomes and assess lessons learned for wider governance on SLCPs and black carbon. For this end, we first discuss the concept of science diplomacy, situating it into the context of Norwegian-Chinese and Finnish-Russian relations alongside wider structural change in international relations at the turn of the 2020s. In conditions where overall agreement among major actors is increasingly in question, with ramifications for international diplomacy, cooperation and security, we propose an analytical framework wherein the interests and problem definitions of actors assume centrality. In other words, with major tensions and uncertainties prevalent, the conduct of science diplomacy depends on what actors are after in the first place and what problems they identify as calling for attention. This framework is then used to scrutinise the Norwegian-Chinese and Finnish-Russian cases before discussing the implications for wider governance.

2 Science Diplomacy on Black Carbon and SLCPs: Analytical Framework

Science diplomacy is conventionally accepted to involve two aspects. First, the 'science in diplomacy' aspect refers to how scientific knowledge on complex problems such as mitigation of black carbon and SLCPs is needed for diplomacy in these areas to target adept solutions and hence potentially be effective. Second, the 'science for diplomacy' aspect refers to how international scientific cooperation can help to improve interstate relations and by extension, serve the soft power interests of states, that is, being able to exercise subtle influence.[1] Building on this last aspect, some studies suggest that science content can serve trust-building in international relations by means of initiating practices and opening channels for communication through the focus on knowledge production.[2]

We will focus here mostly on the more traditional science in diplomacy aspect while the science for diplomacy aspect will play a secondary role in our scrutiny. In other words, we remain somewhat cautious regarding what the Norwegian and Finnish-initiated science diplomacy can deliver in terms

1 Tim Flink and Nicholas Ruffin, "The Current State of the 'Art' of Science Diplomacy", in Simon, D., Kuhlmann, S. (eds.) *Handbook of Science and Public Policy* (Edward Elgar 2019), 104–121.

2 Ping Su and Maximilian Mayer, 'Science Diplomacy and Trust Building: "Science China" in the Arctic' (2018) 9 Global Policy 23 <https://doi.org/10.1111/1758-5899.12576> accessed 19 September 2022.

of potential soft power gains or mutual trust-building, acknowledging how knowledge production and diffusion do not take place in a neutral territory. Addressing seemingly technical issues such as black carbon can lead parties to fundamental political questions with deep-seated socio-economic path-dependencies involved as the Finnish-Russian case study will also indicate. Such domestic-political constraints can amplify any reservations governments may hold vis-à-vis international cooperation.

Despite this cautious approach, we expect the sender country to seek engagement in 'structured government attempts in initiating or governing the cooperation toward specific ends such as collaborative research, technology transfer, and co-production of technology'.[3] Such outcomes would serve Norwegian and Finnish soft power interests even if the exact results for mitigation would remain uneasily ascertainable or more limited than the science involved would prescribe. In other words, even somewhat limited advances can be highly welcome interim outcomes in international diplomacy.

The Norwegian and Finnish science diplomacies build on both multilateral and bilateral tracks. The chief multilateral track comprises Arctic research institutions. Like Norway and Finland, Russia is a full member in the Arctic Council where China is also an active permanent observer since 2013. However, the Council's full potential all but evaporated when Russia as then its chair country (2021–23) escalated its war in Ukraine in February 2022, after first starting it in 2014. This led to several rounds of sanctions set on Russia by other Arctic Council member states, the EU and other Western states, and to Russia's own countersanctions, resulting in the immediate freezing of Arctic cooperation involving Russia. In these conditions, the other multilateral contexts wherein black carbon mitigation has been prominently pursued, such as the Climate and Clean Air Coalition are of almost equally limited use for engaging Russia even though Russia is a member. China for its part is not a member, despite its participation in the Coalition's scientific work that largely focuses on emission sources in Asia (see Chapter 6).

The bilateral track builds on strong legacies. Finland has a long history of scientific, technological, economic and environmental cooperation with the Soviet Union and Russia. In 2006, Finland initiated the Northern Dimension Environmental Partnership between the EU, Russia, Iceland and Norway.[4]

3 Elif Özkaragöz Doğan, Zafer Uygun and İbrahim Semih Akçomak, 'Can Science Diplomacy Address the Global Climate Change Challenge?' (2021) 31 Environmental Policy & Governance 31, 34 <http://libproxy.tuni.fi/login?url=https://search.ebscohost.com/login.aspx?direct=true&AuthType=cookie,ip,uid&db=bsu&AN=148477343&site=ehost-live&scope=site>.

4 Pami Aalto, Helge Blakkisrud and Hanna Smith, *The New Northern Dimension of the European Neighbourhood* (Centre for European Policy Studies 2008).

Notably, this track survived all major tensions seen in the relations throughout the 2000s between the EU, western states and Russia, until Russia's serious escalation of its war in Ukraine in 2022. Norway's knowledge-based cooperation with China for its part paved the way for China to sign the Minamata Convention in 2013.[5] Overall, the Norwegian activities benefit from China's general tendency of involving scientific cooperation into its foreign relations, as is evident for example in China's ties with developing countries.[6]

Regarding the results the Norwegian and Finnish efforts can yield, the shallow nature of trust in international relations since the late 2010s must be acknowledged. This not only follows from the Russian-initiated war in Ukraine and rounds of mutual sanctions. At issue are also the anxieties held by many powers regarding China's foreign policy ambitions and its quest for leadership in several RDI sectors,[7] and related debates on greater strategic autonomy in connection to Europe's Green Deal agenda, raising questions for multilateralism.[8] On top of these, uncertainties persist on the more generic commitment of major powers to international cooperation, particularly the USA, and their ability to agree on the purposes of global environmental governance. Challenges also emerge questioning their leadership and the hierarchy of states.[9]

While constraints for multilateralism persist, it is important to note how bilateral cooperation can be effective for mitigating black carbon and SLCP emissions.[10] 'Minilateral' or 'club' type arrangements may also work.[11] Bi-or

5 Rosendal, GK, Andresen, S, Heggelund, G, Stensdal, EH, 'The Minamata Convention and Mercury Policy in China: The Role of Science' (2020) 44 Asian Perspective 435.

6 Malgorzata Smieszek, Timo Koivurova, and Egill Thor Nielsson, 'China's Arctic Policy', in Koivurova T and Kopra S, *Chinese Policy and Presence in the Arctic* (BRILL 2020). Pavel Devyatkin 'Russian and Chinese Scientists to Establish Arctic Research Center'. The High North News, April 15 (2019) <https://www.highnorthnews.com/en/russian-and-chinese-scientists-establish-arctic-research-center> accessed 11 December 2022.

7 Andrew B Kennedy and Darren J Lim, 'The Innovation Imperative: Technology and US–China Rivalry in the Twenty-First Century' (2018) International Affairs (London) 94 (3).

8 Eric Van den Abeele, 'Towards a New Paradigm in Open Strategic Autonomy' (2021), ETUI Research Paper 2021.3 <http://dx.doi.org/10.2139/ssrn.3873798> accessed 2 December 2022.

9 E.g. Gabriele Abbondanza and Thomas S Wilkins, *Awkward Powers: Escaping Traditional Great Power and Middle Power Theory* (Springer 2022).

10 Stine Aakre and others, 'Incentives for Small Clubs of Arctic Countries to Limit Black Carbon and Methane Emissions' (2018) 8 Nature Climate Change 85.

11 Seita Romppanen, 'Arctic Climate Governance via EU Law on Black Carbon?' (2018) 27 Review of European Community & International Environmental Law 45; M Sand and others, 'Response of Arctic Temperature to Changes in Emissions of Short-Lived Climate Forcers' (2016) 6 Nature Climate Change 286; Charlotte Unger, Kathleen A Mar and Konrad Gürtler, 'A Club's Contribution to Global Climate Governance: The Case of the Climate and Clean Air Coalition' (2020) 6 Palgrave Communications.

minilateral diplomacies feature potent tools vis-a-vis black carbon, since pairs and clusters of countries continue cross-polluting each other. Because they are affected by each other's emissions, countries in such pairs and regional clusters should have a strong self-interest in mitigation, regardless of how they relate to bi-or minilateral diplomacy in general. When looking at black carbon emissions affecting the Arctic, 90% of abatement can be achieved on grounds of the main polluters acting in self-interest, that is India, China, the EU area, the USA and Russia, in this order. Among them, China would have the largest self-benefits, chiefly for public health and crop yield. The Nordic countries would have the clearest self-benefits in terms of climate, while the collective benefits would relate mostly to climate as well.[12] For black carbon and SLCPs, bilateralism may work much better than in the case of CO_2 or chemical pollution that are more global problems by nature.

The case for bilateralism must also be seen in the context of how summit-based multilateral and global mitigation efforts have proved, as a rule, relatively inefficient.[13] The Paris Agreement of 2015 is a landmark exception, but it is a political agreement outlining overall global targets. Actual mitigation targets are defined nationally and then submitted to the Paris Agreement as part of Nationally Determined Contributions. The Paris agenda furthermore remains inconclusive regarding SLCPs and black carbon that are traditionally treated as 'environmental problems' pertaining to air quality, with ambiguous ramifications on climate politics. SLCPs and black carbon can, however, be reported in Nationally Determined Contributions if the country so wishes (see Chapter 3). With this state of affairs, global governance on SLCPs has consequently remained relatively fragmented and weak, mostly consisting of soft law.[14]

Since multilateralism remains hampered by persisting and possibly deepening constraints for diplomacy, and while the record of global environmental governance remains thin, we propose that it is imperative to look at the problem definitions of actors which are crucial for the take-up and adoption of mitigation actions vis-à-vis black carbon and SLCPs. In short, in the absence of shared understandings of which problems merit most attention, especially as prospects of resolution appear weak, it is unlikely for cooperation to enhance

12 Aakre and others (n 10).

13 Hailey Stevenson, *Global Environmental Politics: Problems, Policy and Practice* (Cambridge University Press 2017).

14 Yulia Yamineva and Seita Romppanen, 'Is Law Failing to Address Air Pollution? Reflections on International and EU Developments' (2017) 26 Review of European Community & International Environmental Law 189.

dramatically. Here we build on Rosendal et al.,[15] postulating that the extent to which the sender country can affect the problem definitions in the target country depends on whether the message is held to be from a *credible* source; whether the underlying knowledge-production is considered *legitimate*, for example co-produced in regional or wider cooperation with the target country's participation; and whether the science communicated is *relevant* in view of the set of target country's national interests.

Our theoretical contribution here pertains to specifying the involved interests. Black carbon mitigation solutions and technologies can serve both public and private sector interests. Following institutional literature, we suggest that such interests are multiple.[16] Here we would mention promotion of *climate neutrality*; *public health interest* of actors responsible for air quality, in cities in particular; *profits* for involved technology and service companies; *fiscal interests* of public sector actors in terms of tax income from both polluting and environmental technology industries; the associated *RDI competence* development and possible *export income*, alongside *wider socio-economic interests* for job creation and taxes paid by industries, not to forget the respective interests of the agricultural sector actors in *crop yield* that can be affected by pollution. Naturally, interests in *foreign policy influence* through science diplomacy are expected to exist.

Although the self-interested calculus of costs and gains should ultimately be in favour of mitigation for most actors, especially in the longer run, the outcomes can also be minuscule. This can be explained by referring to the domestic structural contexts where path-dependencies and lock-ins to existing technologies, infrastructures, institutions and behavioural patterns typically inhibit mitigation initiatives.[17] In summary, our analytical framework postulates that a crucial precondition for science diplomacy to shape black carbon and SLCP mitigation is its capacity to aggregate the various interests involved in sender and receiver countries and support the formation of shared problem definitions. The domestic structural context can furthermore either enable or inhibit shared problem definitions (see Figure 8.1). This framework will be used to examine actors, interests and problem definitions in our two

---

15 Rosendal and others (n 5).

16 Llewelyn Hughes and Phillip Y Lipscy, 'The Politics of Energy' (2013) 16 Annual Review of Political Science 449.

17 Kirsi Kotilainen and others, 'From Path Dependence to Policy Mixes for Nordic Electric Mobility: Lessons for Accelerating Future Transport Transitions' (2019) 52 Policy Sciences 573.

case studies, with references made to the domestic context in the target countries to account for relative successes or failures in science diplomacy.

At the time of writing, shared problem definitions are more limited in the case of black carbon and SLCP mitigation compared to the situation prevailing with CO_2 where a firm epistemic community has formed on mitigation. Therefore, it matters how much or how little the interests of actors meet and to what extent that can facilitate the formation of more congruent problem-definitions internationally. To address this research agenda, we will ask: 1) What are the problem definitions vis-à-vis SLCPs and black carbon characterising the science diplomacy actions of Norwegian and Finnish actors, and which interests shape those problem definitions? 2) What are the respective problem definitions and underpinning interests of their Chinese and Russian counterparts? 3) How do domestic structural contexts shape the prospects of science diplomacy in the target countries; and 4) What are the wider implications for multilateral governance?

The next two sections introduce our case studies. The main bulk of the material comprises previous literature, reports and documents from Norway, Finland, China and Russia. In addition, we benefited from informal communication with Norwegian environmental officials cooperating with Chinese actors. We also used semi-structured interviews conducted with 22 representatives from the Finnish RDI cluster with expertise on black carbon (see Section 4 below). The interview data is anonymised and consists primarily of

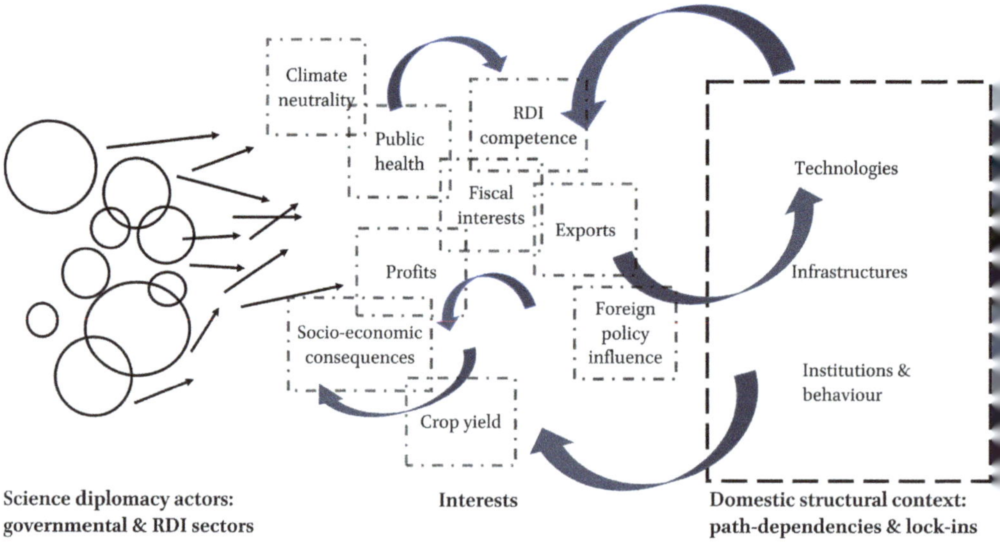

FIGURE 8.1 Problem definition in science diplomacy (developed by authors)

interviews in Finland, as we sought to cover well the Finnish RDI sector that is strong on development, innovation and commercialisation whereas Norway's main strength is the integration of scientific research into diplomacy. The Finnish interviews were fully transcribed, content analysed and coded with atlas.ti software.

3 Norwegian Science Diplomacy towards China

Norwegian interests in global climate and environmental diplomacy spring from several sources since the 1980s. First, Norway suffers from transboundary air pollution from Russia. Second, through diplomacy focusing on global problems, small countries like Norway can increase their power.[18] Third, research in the natural, environmental and social sciences, alongside the expertise and policy continuity of Norwegian environmental authorities lend support for Norway's diplomatic activities in this sphere.[19] Hence, it is natural that Norway was a first runner ratifier of protocols under the Convention on Long-range Transboundary Air Pollution (CRLTAP). As a member of the European Economic Area, Norway participates in the EU's emissions trading scheme that covers about half of the country's emissions and implements several EU directives on climate and air pollution. Overall, Norway's closest partner in these matters is the EU.

Norway implements the national actions of the Paris agenda. The country's Environment Agency produced a report on SLCP reduction in 2014, but neither Norway's updated NDC submission as of 2022 nor any of the country's official policies or targets specifically mention SLCPs or black carbon.[20] Yet, its air pollution and climate change legislation has contributed to large reductions in black carbon and organic carbon emissions since 1990. This is not an entirely atypical situation for advanced countries.[21] Norway has also pushed

---

18 G Kristin Rosendal, 'Norway in UN Environmental Policies: Ambitions and Influence' (2007) 7 International Environmental Agreements: Politics, Law and Economics 439.

19 ibid.

20 Norwegian Environment Agency, Summary of proposed action plan for Norwegian emissions of short-lived climate forcers (2014). M135/2014. <https://www.miljodirektoratet.no/globalassets/publikasjoner/m135/m135.pdf>; Government of Norway, Update of Norway's nationally determined contribution (2022), <https://unfccc.int/sites/default/files/NDC/2022-06/Norway_updatedNDC_2020%20%28Updated%20submission%29.pdf>.

21 See H Christopher Frey, 'Trends in Onroad Transportation Energy and Emissions' (2018) 68 Journal of the Air & Waste Management Association 514 <https://doi.org/10.1080/10962247.2018.1454357>.; M Cheng et al. 'Review of BC/OC emissions and control measures in China and Norway' (2021) ChiNorBC1.

for more guidance and methodology to the related IPCC's work. Moreover, the country is a very active member of the CCAC and the Arctic Council (see also Chapters 6 and 7).

We propose that this global, European and Arctic posture leads to a problem definition whereby particle emissions nearby the Arctic significantly affect the country's environment and have global multiplier effects of grave concern to Norwegian diplomacy given its ambitions regarding climate neutrality, air quality, as well as RDI exports, with consequences for foreign policy interests.[22] Simultaneously Norway's ambitions must come to terms with the country's oil and natural gas exports, not forgetting the corporate interest in continued profits from these sectors. The profits also serve the fiscal interests of the state and municipalities owing to taxes paid to them and dividends obtained from companies, the flagship being the majority state-owned Equinor. As Norway exports emissions, the industry has consistently sought to reduce its domestic emissions. The government for its part has used part of the proceeds incurred for ambitious climate and energy transition policies, including electrification of transport, assisted by the large-scale availability of hydropower.[23]

The Norwegian scientific community has sought to interlink the climate, air quality and health interests, somewhat distinctively from the EU context where climate neutrality most significantly targets CO_2 mitigation, leaving SLCPs to be treated mostly under air quality and health policies.[24] Norwegian scientists have developed bottom-up emission models for measuring black carbon, organic carbon and particulate matter for different sectors, utilised by the Government in the national reporting to the monitoring mechanisms of the Arctic Council and CLRTAP. Several domestic problems have been identified in this respect: 1) combustion of wood mostly in stoves for heating in residential buildings (in 2019, the 'other combustion' category accounted for 37% of Norway's black carbon emissions, of which 75% from domestic combustion); 2) the maritime transport sector (the transport sector overall accounted for 34% of black carbon emissions, of which 57% from coastal navigation); and

22 Government of Norway, 'Better growth, lower emissions – the Norwegian government's strategy for green competitiveness' (Strategy T-1562 E, 2017); Norwegian Ministry of Climate and Environment, *Norway's Climate Action Plan for 2021–2030* (White Paper, Cm 13, 2021); Norwegian Environment Agency, 'Climate mitigation measures up to 2030: Short term climate effects and health effects' (2016).

23 Aalto, Blakkisrud and Smith (n 4); Kotilainen and others (n 17).

24 Nils Hooftman and others, 'A Review of the European Passenger Car Regulations – Real Driving Emissions vs Local Air Quality' (2018) 86 Renewable & Sustainable Energy Reviews 1.

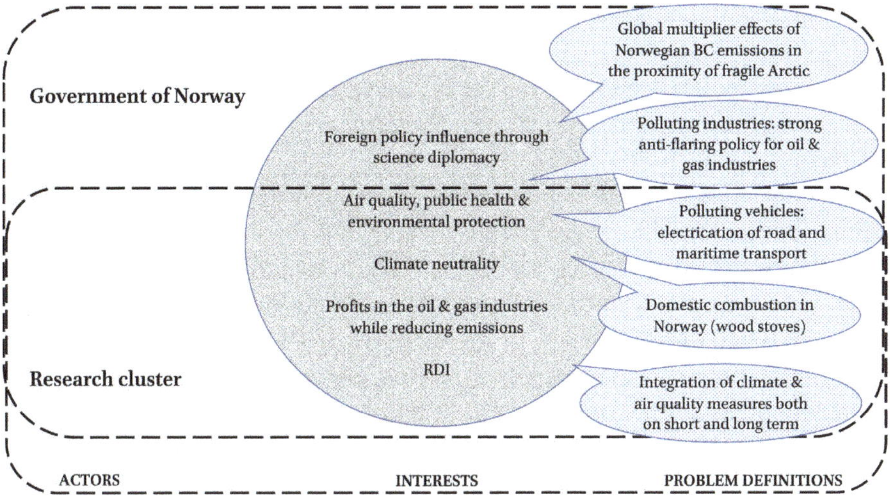

FIGURE 8.2 Norwegian actors, interests and problem definitions

3) the oil and natural gas sectors;[25] here gas flaring is, however, allowed only for safety purposes while methane emissions remain considerably lower than for example those from the production in the UK's continental shelf.[26]

Norway's well-developed research competences in measurement and monitoring practices may be transferable through science diplomacy (see Figure 8.2). Such demand for knowhow can be expected in the Chinese case, given the relatively scarce information on projected black carbon emissions in China.[27]

China's contribution to global and Arctic emissions makes it a natural target for Norway's science diplomacy. East Asia accounts for approximately 30% of the global anthropogenic black carbon emissions annually.[28] China is not

25 M Cheng et al., 'Review of BC/OC emissions and control measures in China and Norway' (2021) ChiNorBC1.

26 Marshall Hall, 'Net Zero Targets and GHG Emission Reduction in the UK and Norwegian Upstream Oil and Gas Industry: A Comparative Assessment' (2020) <https://www.oxfordenergy.org/publications/net-zero-targets-and-ghg-emission-reduction-in-the-uk-and-norwegian-upstream-oil-and-gas-industry-a-comparative-assessment> accessed 2 December 2022.

27 Yulia Yamineva and Zhe Liu, 'Cleaning the Air, Protecting the Climate: Policy, Legal and Institutional Nexus to Reduce Black Carbon Emissions in China' (2019) 95 Environmental Science & Policy 1.

28 Kohei Ikeda and others, 'Evaluation of Anthropogenic Emissions of Black Carbon from East Asia in Six Inventories: Constraints from Model Simulations and Surface Observations on Fukue Island, Japan' (2022) 2 Environmental Science: Atmospheres 416.

only the main polluter here but also an increasingly proactive actor in global environmental diplomacy. However, black carbon remains a recent item on the Chinese policy agenda.[29] The Norwegian science diplomacy addresses this situation, comprising both the science in diplomacy and science for diplomacy aspects.

In 2019, following joint preparation, the Norwegian Ministry of Foreign Affairs granted funding to a Chinese-Norwegian Project on 'Emission, Impact, and Control Policy for Black Carbon and its Co-benefits in Northern China'. The main partners were the Chinese Research Academy of Environmental Sciences, which is affiliated with the Ministry of Ecology and Environment; and the Norwegian Environment Agency, working closely with the Ministry of Climate and Environment. The Chinese Academy of Environmental Planning, the Norwegian Institute of Public Health and CICERO – Centre for International Climate Research also participated.

The project was tasked to 'develop improved emission inventories for black carbon-and OC-emissions in China using the most recent, best available national statistics and measurements obtained in the project'.[30] This information was intended to inform Chinese policy makers of possible policy solutions, in order to maximize co-benefits,[31] and potentially shape Chinese black carbon policies. While Norway's main interest in the project pertains to climate change and China's – to air pollution, finding a common ground is possible, especially given the potency of bilateralism in black carbon mitigation. During 2020, the project was affected by COVID-19. However, since 2021 monthly (digital) meetings were held in good dialogue, with project reports issued.[32] The final report was expected by the end of 2022.[33]

The project was initiated within a favourable structural context on the Chinese side. Chinese policymaking is characterized by a long-term perspective and input from different ministries expressing their interests. That China is governed by the principle of 'Scientific Outlook on Development', equated with Marxist-Leninist thinking in the Communist Party, translates to demand for knowledge-based policy.[34] The research cluster's close association with high-level policymakers supports knowledge dissemination.

29 Yamineva and Liu (n 27).
30 Cheng et al. (n 25).
31 ibid.
32 Jost Wubbeke, 'China's Climate Change Expert Community-Principles, Mechanisms and Influence' (2013) 22 The Journal of Contemporary China 712.
33 Informal communication with Norway's Environment Agency 2022.
34 Li Cheng, *The Power of Ideas: The Rising Influence of Thinkers and Think Tanks in China* (World Scientific Publishing Co Pte Ltd 2017); Wubbeke (n 34).

Mitigation and adaptation vis-à-vis climate warming are of Chinese interest at least since the 2007 National Climate Change Programme.[35] The government and scientific community unequivocally view warming as a threat to socio-economic development. China Meteorological Administration's annual report from 2022 on climate change found China's warming to exceed the global average.[36] Since 2013, Chinese scientists have participated in Arctic cooperation on SLCPs and black carbon, including the widely cited work of the Arctic Contaminants Action Programme.[37] China's Arctic expeditions have expanded from natural scientific research into wider research, development and policy formation exercises. In 2015, a task force was set by a high-level policy advisory body China Council for International Cooperation for Environment and Development to address SLCPs and black carbon.[38] Moreover, scientists involved in the AC's work on black carbon have prominent roles in the Chinese-Norwegian project.

China's governmental problem definition conforms to that of the World Health Organisation, proceeding more generally from $PM_{2.5}$ rather than from specific pollutants, as is evident in the 13th Five-Year Plan (2016–2021). The coal burning power sector, transport and industrial sectors remain priority areas as they were in the 2013–2017 Ambient Air Pollution Prevention and Control Action Plan.[39] In the transport sector, size of the vehicle fleet, technology and standard upgrades featured among the more precise problem definitions in the 2013 Plan, and in the industrial sector, improved emission indicators and tightened entry requirements for new production units.[40] The successor to this

35 National Development and Reform Commission, *China's National Climate Change Programme* (National Development and Reform Commission, June 2007).

36 Gov.cn., 'China Meteorological Administration released the "China Climate Change Blue Book"' (in Chinese, 10 August 2022) <http://www.gov.cn/xinwen/2022-08/10/content_5704792.htm>; Reuters, 'China warns that its temperatures are rising faster than global average' (4 August 2022) <https://www.reuters.com/world/china/china-warns-that-its-temperatures-are-rising-faster-than-global-average-2022-08-04/#:~:text=SHANGHAI%2C%20Aug%204%20(Reuters),mount%2C%20a%20government%20official%20said>.

37 Peoples' Republic of China [PRC], Observer Review Report 2017–2019, Arctic Council (2019), available at: https://oaarchive.arctic-council.org/handle/11374/2251; Peoples' Republic of China [PRC], Observer Review Report 2019–2021, Arctic Council (2021), available at: https://oaarchive.arctic-council.org/handle/11374/2717.

38 Gørild M Heggelund, 'China's Climate and Energy Policy: At a Turning Point?' (2021) 21 International Environmental Agreements: Politics, Law and Economics 9.

39 ibid.

40 State Council, 'Notice of the State Council Distributing the Action Plan for the Prevention and Control of Air Pollution'(10 September 2013) <http://www.gov.cn/zwgk/2013-09/12/content_2486773.htm> retrieved in Chinese 12 May 2022.

Plan, the Action Plan for Winning the Blue Sky War (2018–2020) offered more detail but retained similar problem definition. Largely comparable problem definitions have been transferred into key laws through several amendments while regional level implementation and measures in emission hotspots remain concerning (see Figure 8.3).[41] President Xi has announced that coal use is set to peak in 2025 during the 14th Five-Year plan (2021–2025), to be reduced thereafter.[42] China's '30.60' dual decarbonization goals foresee peaking carbon emissions before 2030 and carbon neutrality by 2060, likely affecting Chinese black carbon emissions. The Chinese-Norwegian project supports this goal by developing emission inventories.

Like in Norway, $PM_{2.5}$ emissions in China are on a decreasing trend even though no major national policy explicitly targets black carbon. At the same time, environmental enforcement remains decentralised to the regions in China, while regional authorities encounter serious path dependencies in transferring the policies and laws into action as they are also responsible for local socio-economic development.[43] Some regions must simultaneously deal with the most polluting form of coal consumption (i.e., coal used in rural heating and small industry), shift away from a coal-based economy, manage job changes for hundreds of thousands of coal-workers, whilst maintaining economic growth. The institutional and behavioural lock-ins of the coal-oriented industry weigh heavily for local authorities, who are supposed to implement the central government's policy targets that are divided among the provinces.[44]

In sum, Norway's bilateral effort led to increased attention and capacity to address the black carbon and SLCP challenges in China. Bilateral scientific collaboration was established on equitable terms with joint implementation of the project. As such, Norway and China's long-term collaboration on environmental and climate issues has enhanced trust between scientific institutions and in that way strengthened diplomatic relationships. Hence the Norwegian-Chinese project illustrates in part also the science for diplomacy aspect in the environmental sector. Importantly, while China is emerging as a central actor

41 Yamineva and Liu (n 27).

42 State Council, 'The People's Republic of China's 14th Five-Year Plan of National Economic and Social Development and Outline of Vision Goals for 2035' <http://www.gov.cn/zhengce/2020-11/03/content_5556991.htm> accessed 16 July 2021, in Chinese; David Stanway & Cate Cadell 'President Xi says China will start cutting coal consumption from 2026' (Reuters, April 22, 2021) <https://www.reuters.com/world/china/chinas-xi-says-china-will-phase-down-coal-consumption-over-2026-2030-2021-04-22/> accessed 9 December 2022.

43 Yamineva and Liu (n 27).

44 Miranda Schreurs, 'Multi-Level Climate Governance in China' (2017) 27 Environmental Policy and Governance 163 <https://doi.org/10.1002/eet.1751> accessed 19 September 2022.

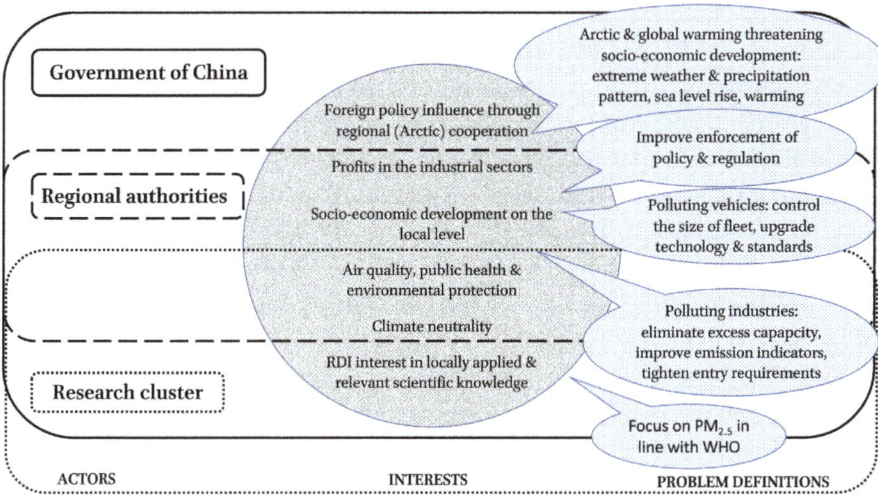

FIGURE 8.3 Chinese actors, interests and problem definitions

in global environmental governance, cooperation with it in these matters can shape the country's efforts and commitments vis-à-vis global agreements.

4 Finnish Science Diplomacy towards Russia

Finnish interests in climate and environmental diplomacy rely, first, on the country's strong climate and environmental policies nationally (see Appendix 1), and as part of the EU. Finland seeks accelerated transition away from black carbon and SLCP emitting fossil fuels, being politically committed to climate neutrality by 2035. Second, Finland has advanced research in meteorology, aerosol physics, and further natural scientific and engineering competences supporting such diplomacy. The Finnish RDI cluster on black carbon comprises publicly funded research institutions, municipal authorities experienced in air quality monitoring and private environmental technology companies ranging from small and mid-size enterprises to stock market listed firms.

Third, an important background factor for Finnish science diplomacy is the country's extensive use of biofuels. Their use raises questions of managing the associated black carbon emissions.[45] Solid and liquid biofuels accounted for

45 Carl Muth, Pami Aalto, Fanni Mylläri, Topi Rönkkö, and Pirkko Harsia, 'Globally and Locally Applicable Technologies to Accelerate Electrification' in Aalto, P. (ed.), *Electrification: Accelerating the Energy Transition* (Academic Press/Elsevier 2021), 25–55.

29.7% of total final energy consumption during 2021.[46] Owing to their availability and capacity for energy storage, biofuels will remain integral for Finland's energy transition. In the power sector, fossil fuels are replaced primarily by weather-dependent wind power that is so far difficult to store, unlike biofuels. In the transport sector, liquid biofuels represent a major transition fuel in national policies.[47] In the residential heating sector, combustion of wood materials is important, being the main source of black carbon emissions as in Norway.[48] Hence, the Finnish RDI cluster will have a domestic market in addition to that emerging globally. Fourth, like Norway, Finland is a net importer of black carbon emissions just like the Nordic countries and most of western Europe.[49]

Despite Finland's global gaze, Russia remains a major source of those imported emissions,[50] and is traditionally a crucial target of Finnish diplomacy. Here the country's president is the main actor. This is so despite the prime minister being responsible for EU affairs and formally the main national actor in the EU's Russia relations. However, the practical legacy of heavily personalised Finnish-Soviet/Russian relations is strong while Finland's semi-presidential system lends the presidency strong rights of foreign policy initiative.[51] Consequently, the initiator of Finnish black carbon diplomacy vis-à-vis Russia is President Sauli Niinistö (2012–), well known of his regular contacts with President Vladimir Putin (2000–2008; 2012–), until Russia's intensified war in Ukraine. Niinistö started the black carbon diplomacy during his first term in office (2012–18); it became particularly intense during Finland's chairmanship of the Arctic Council (2017–19) and continued until Russia's full-scale invasion of Ukraine. In the Arctic Council context, Niinistö reiterates the Arctic-specific climate warming effects of black carbon that were prominent in the IPCC's fifth report:

---

46 Tilastokeskus, 'Energian kokonaiskulutus energialähteittäin (kaikki luokat), 1970–2021' <https://pxweb2.stat.fi/PxWeb/pxweb/fi/StatFin/StatFin__ehk/statfin_ehk_pxt_12vq.px/>.

47 Pasi Toivanen and others, 'Finland's Energy System for 2030 as Envisaged by Expert Stakeholders' (2017) 18 Energy Strategy Reviews 150.

48 Nordic Council of Ministers, 'Policy Brief: Emissions of Short-Lived Climate Pollutants (SLCPs): emission factors, scenarios and reduction potentials' (Nordic Council of Ministers 2019) <http://dx.doi.org/10.6027/Nord2019-013>.

49 Aakre and others (n10).

50 Ibid.

51 Tapio Raunio, 'Semi-Presidentialism and European Integration: Lessons from Finland for Constitutional Design' (2012) 19 Journal of European Public Policy 567; Tapio Raunio and Thomas Sedelius, 'Presidents and Cabinets: Coordinating Executive Leadership in Premier-Presidential Regimes' (2020) 18 Political Studies Review 53.

> Beyond CO_2, however, there are also other factors contributing to climate change. One of them is black carbon, which is particularly relevant for the fate of the Arctic Sea ice. When black carbon falls on the white ice, it immediately accelerates the melting. Yet reducing black carbon emissions has an equally immediate, positive impact.[52]

The Finnish Arctic Council chairmanship also proposed the AC's scientific work on black carbon and methane to be integrated with that of the UNFCCC and IPCC.[53] The more detailed problem definition features Arctic-and Russia-specific emission sources: gas flaring (widespread practice in the Russian oil industry; see Box 1), energy production and Arctic shipping (large part of which relates to Russian energy projects). The related problems are to be tackled with cleaner technologies and processes where Finland has expertise.

BOX 1 The Gas Flaring Problem in Russia's Arctic

The flaring of associated petroleum gas is a side-product of oil extraction, contributing 42% to the annual mean black carbon surface concentrations in the Arctic.[54] Despite commitment to the World Bank's Zero Routine Flaring by 2030 initiative, Russia has for long been the world's largest emitter of these gases.[55]

The respective Russian regulation comprises the pollution fees system. Corporations with activities harmful to the environment must obtain an environmental permit issued by the Russian public

52 President of Finland, 'Speech by the President of the Republic of Finland, Mr. Sauli Niinistö, at the Arctic Forum in St. Petersburg, 9 April 2019' (2019) <presidentti.fi/en/speeches/speech-by-the-president-of-the-republic-of-finland-mr-sauli-niinisto-at-the-arctic-forum- in-st-petersburg-9-april-2019/>.

53 Government of Finland, 'Finland's Chairmanship program for the Arctic Council 2017–2019' (Ministry for Foreign Affairs of Finland 2017) <https://oaarchive.arctic-council.org/server/api/core/bitstreams/cd14f8d1-cba1-4802-ab3e-67ac12b9e544/content>.

54 A Stohl and others, 'Black Carbon in the Arctic: The Underestimated Role of Gas Flaring and Residential Combustion Emissions' (2013) 13 Atmospheric Chemistry and Physics 8833.

55 World Bank, *Global Gas Flaring Tracker Report 2021 – Global Gas Flaring Partnership* (2021) <https://thedocs.worldbank.org/en/doc/1f7221545bf1b7c89b850dd85cb409b0-0400072021/original/WB-GGFR-Report-Design-05a.pdf>; World Bank, *Global Gas Flaring Tracker Report 2022 – Global Gas Flaring Partnership* (2022) <https://thedocs.worldbank.org/en/doc/1692f2ba2bd6408db82db9eb3894a789-0400072022/original/2022-Global-Gas-Flaring-Tracker-Report.pdf>.

authority Rosprirodnadzor, the Russian Federal Service supervising natural resources. Since 2009, Russian oil companies must utilize 95% of their produce of associated petroleum gases. The pollution fee is set for the exceeding 5 percent and for non-metered flaring. For methane emission, 4.5 times the standard environmental fine applies. However, strong institutional lock-ins inhibit enforcement and inspection, combined with technological and infrastructural lock-ins on the part of Russian fossil fuel companies that also have strong lobbying powers. In practice, the industry is obliged to protect the environment only insofar as this does not harm its activities.[56]

Black carbon emissions and volumes of flared gas are correlated.[57] Best Available Technologies and Best Environmental Practices such as reinjection technologies of associated petroleum gases are applicable in at least five oil and gas fields in Russia's Arctic; six further fields have high potential.[58] For example Gazprom Neft uses associated petroleum gas reinjection in its Novoportovskoye field since 2019. By 2025, best available techniques and best environmental practices could reduce SLCP emissions in Russia's Arctic from 25 to 7 million tons of CO_2 equivalents, with significant economic co-benefits. The challenges for scaling up include the geology of the oil and gas fields and lack of incentives in Russia's regulatory system after the 95% utilization target is met for associated petroleum gases.

56 Anna Korppoo, 'Russian Associated Petroleum Gas Flaring Limits: Interplay of Formal and Informal Institutions' (2018) 116 Energy Policy 232 <https://www.sciencedirect.com/science/article/pii/S0301421518300752>.

57 Kristin Böttcher and others, 'Black Carbon Emissions from Flaring in Russia in the Period 2012–2017' (2021) 254 Atmospheric Environment 118390 <https://www.sciencedirect.com/science/article/pii/S1352231021002090>.

58 Arctic Contaminants Action Program (ACAP), 'Mitigation of Short-Lived Climate Pollutants from APG-Flaring. Project: Phase 2 – The Use of New Methodology to Reduce APG Flaring at Remote Fields' (2021) <https://oaarchive.arctic-council.org/handle/11374/2607>; 'Black Carbon and Methane from the Oil and Gas Sector: Webinar Report with Recommendations' (2021) <https://oaarchive.arctic-council.org/bitstream/handle/11374/2605/MMIS12_2021_REYKJAVIK_ACAP_Black-Carbon-Webinar.pdf?sequence=1&isAllowed=y>; 'Mitigation of Short-Lived Climate Pollutants from AGP-Flaring Project: Final report. Phase 1A – Evaluation of potential impact of AÅG flaring on Arctic zone environment by Vygon Consulting' (2018) <https://oaarchive.arctic-council.org/bitstream/handle/11374/2450/FinalReport_APG-flaring-Phase-1A.pdf?sequence=1&isAllowed=y>.

In the UN context, the set of interests expressed by Niinistö expands from climate towards health, wider environmental and socio-economic issues: 'Issues like sustainability, climate change and migration are not only about development and human rights. They are also essential questions of peace and security.'[59] Black carbon becomes a multifaceted security problem, linking climate change with forced migration and famine, raising a need for international cooperation to fill persisting knowledge gaps.

Importantly, these knowledge gaps connect the interests of public and private actors. To shape the market, in the EU context, the Finnish actors participate in industrial lobbies and RDI consortia wherein governmental, university and company funding are combined. This includes for example working groups of the European Committee for Standardisation and the European Commission-initiated information exchange procedures, on areas such as BAT solutions, best available techniques reference documents, and the Industrial Emissions Directive. Direct contacts exist with national and EU level policymakers, and the World Health Organisation. The Finnish cluster specialises on monitoring and measurement devices, and filtering and low-emission solutions for example in engines. The cluster's problem definition highlights less climate neutrality and more air quality and health, covering issues like how scientific knowledge and RDI competence can be transferred to policies, how technological modernization and modification in individual behaviour is required for example in small-scale residential combustion for black carbon-relevant business to emerge.

The knowledge gaps reiterate the calls of the World Health Organisation and concern the measurement and monitoring of relevant parameters (e.g., black carbon, elemental carbon, particle number, ultra-fine particles), in addition to the parameters used in regulation (at the time of the interviews, $PM_{2.5}$; see Chapter 1). The industry foresees a need for medium-priced, durable and reliable measurement technologies to complement standard high-end devices applicable for long-term monitoring needs and more low-end devices. Since the technology market is driven by regulation, only regulation can create a market for such middle-range devices applicable to high-emitting economies such as Russia or China.

59 President of Finland, 'Statement by President of the Republic of Finland Sauli Niinistö at the United Nations General Assembly 73rd General Debate on 25th September 2018' (2018) <presidentti.fi/en/speeches/statement-by-president-of-the-republic-of-finland-sauli-niinisto-at-the-united-nations-general-assembly-73rd-general-debate-on-25th-september-2018/>.

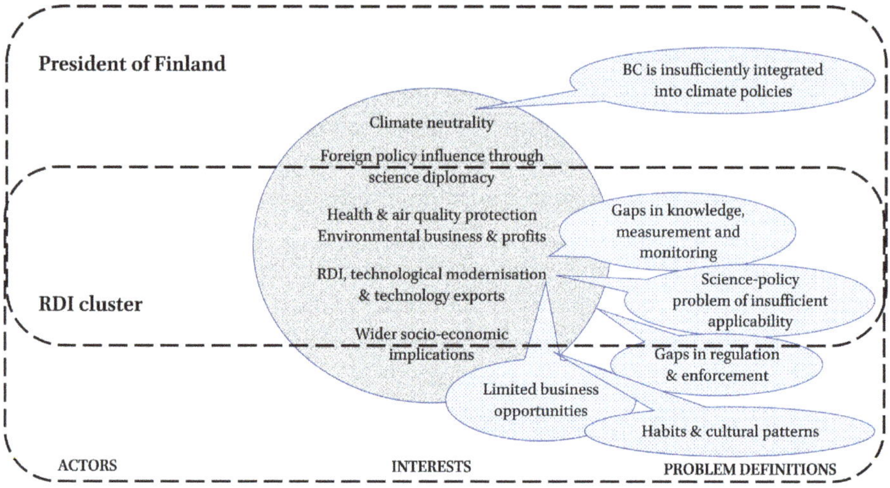

FIGURE 8.4 Finnish actors, interests and problem definitions

The profit interests of the Finnish RDI cluster concern most prominently the EU and Chinese markets. The Indian market is potentially emerging, yet considered a difficult environment. Despite the mentioned, potentially high Russian self-interest in black carbon mitigation, the Finnish RDI cluster expressed at best indifferent, if not outrightly negative, views on the Russian market already well before the 2022 full-scale invasion of Ukraine:

> maybe environmental issues are not as high a priority for policy and decision-makers [in Africa, Russia, Middle East, and India] as they are elsewhere. Sure, the problems there are as big, but they have many other problems there too than those connected to the environment.[60]

The Finnish RDI actors identify a problem of measurement leading to monitoring and mitigation problems. The yet wider problem concerns the interface between science and policy. Taken that the RDI cluster deems health impact the primary area of black carbon mitigation, with the climatic effects remaining uncertain, the lack of respective scientific data becomes problematic. Its availability could be boosted by regulatory means (see Figure 8.4).

In other words, the Finnish RDI actors call for regulation to oblige the take-up and adoption of low black carbon emitting technologies and services. While

60 Interview with a measurement technology manufacturer, 11.9.2019.

BOX 2 Finnish-Russian Bilateral Black Carbon Diplomacy

Monitoring and mitigation of black carbon emissions, and climate change in the Arctic were discussed in May 2019 between the Finnish Ministry of Foreign Affairs and the Russian Ministry for Natural Resources and Ecology. The Russian ministry's Director of the Department of International Cooperation, Nuritdin Inamov reiterated Russia's commitment to the Paris Agreement, referring to the ongoing introduction of BAT practices, for example in the transport, forestry, energy and industry sectors, and indicating interests in public health and environmental protection. The national environmental project 'Ekologiya' (Ecology) was set to reduce the total volume of air pollution in large industrial centres and the most polluted cities by at least 20%. However, the credibility of knowledge formed in the Arctic Council context was questioned by an expert of the Voeikov Main Geophysical Observatory, disputing the global effects of black carbon emissions, instead alleging only rather some (insignificant) regional effects.[61]

During his visit to Finland in August 2019, President Putin acknowledged the agreed intensification of Russian-Finnish environmental cooperation. President Niinistö welcomed the Russian plans to combat black carbon emissions.[62] When meeting the Prime Minister of Russia Dmitry Medvedev in November 2019, Prime Minister of Finland Antti Rinne took up black carbon emissions in the context of the Paris Agreement.[63]

61 Russian Ministry for Natural Resources and Ecology, 'Working meeting between representatives of the Finnish foreign ministry and the embassy of Finland in Russia and the Russian ministry for natural resources and ecology' (Press release, 21 May 2019) <https://www.mnr.gov.ru/press/news/predstaviteli_minprirody_rossii_i_mida_finlyandii_obsudili_voprosy_sokrashcheniya_vybrosov_chernogo_/?sphrase_id=405786> accessed 12 May 2022.

62 President of Finland, 'President of Russia Vladimir Putin visited Finland' (Press release, 21 August 2019), <https://www.presidentti.fi/en/news/president-of-russia-to-make-working-visit-to-finland-3/> accessed 11 July 2022; President of Russia, 'Joint news conference with President of Finland Sauli Niinistö – Vladimir Putin and Sauli Niinistö made press statements and answered media questions following Russian-Finnish talks' (Presidential Executive Office, Press release 21 August 2019) <http://en.kremlin.ru/events/president/news/61349> accessed 11 July 2022.

63 Government of Finland, 'Prime Ministers Rinne and Medvedev met in Moscow' (Press release, 25 November 2019) <https://valtioneuvosto.fi/-/10616/paaministerit-rinne-ja-medvedev-tapasivat-moskovassa?languageId=en_US> accessed 11 July 2022.

science diplomacy is unlikely to achieve such regulatory change, it can affect the knowledge spurring on reform, to the extent that knowledge-based policy-making practices prevail in the target country. In this respect, Russia poses a stern test for Finnish science diplomacy. Despite the legacy of cooperation, and bilateral track (see Box 2) utilised alongside the regional one, no similar project or other institutionalised result has emerged as in the Norwegian-Chinese case.

On the Arctic track, Russian and Finnish experts have jointly contributed to policy-relevant knowledge, as part of the Arctic Contaminants Action Programme and its Expert Group on SLCPs.[64] Russia has moreover signed the 2015 approved Arctic Council Framework for Action on Enhanced Black Carbon and Methane Emissions, which is a soft law document that politically commits Parties to either national action plans or mitigation strategies with a two-year iterative reporting process. However, Russia's only such report is from 2015.[65] Broadly in agreement with Finnish diplomacy, the report identifies the extraction of mineral resources (80%), electricity production, manufacturing industries and transport, as the major sources of black carbon emissions in Russia's Arctic (see Box 1). Yet, the report hints how climate change coupled with the fossil fuels industry's technological development enables it to pursue profits by accessing Arctic resources.

Overall, a dual picture emerges whereby the fossil fuel industry's profit interests co-exist with interest expressed in reducing black carbon emissions from associated petroleum gases, right until the full-scale invasion of Ukraine. For example, the Russian Ministry for Natural Resources and Ecology[66] referred to Arctic Contaminants Action Programme's study that proposed unified national methodologies for identifying, measuring and estimating emissions alongside appropriate reporting. In an Arctic Council plenary meeting in June 2021, the Minister for Natural Resources and Ecology Alexander Kozlov reported on

---

64 Arctic Council Secretariat, Expert group on Black carbon and methane 3rd Summary of Progress and Recommendations Report (2021) <MMIS12_2021_REYKJAVIK_EGBCM_Summary-Report-2021.pdf>; also see Chapter 7.

65 Ministry of Natural Resources and Environment of the Russian Federation, 'National report on the actions on black carbon and methane emissions reduction in accordance with the Framework for Action on Enhanced Black Carbon and Methane reductions' (Report, 24 April 2015) <https://oaarchive.arctic-council.org/handle/11374/1168>.

66 Russian Ministry for Natural Resources and Ecology, 'Video webinar arranged 29 October 2020 in connection of the forthcoming Russian chairmanship of the Arctic Council' (Press release, 29 October 2020) <https://www.mnr.gov.ru/press/news/sokrashchenie_vybrosov_chernogo_ugleroda_i_metana_v_atmosferu_arktiki_rossiya_otkryta_dlya_sotrudnich/?special_version=N> accessed 12 May 2022.

Russian plans for a black carbon emissions monitoring system. This system would include best available techniques practices and would expand and modernise Roshydromet's network of 240 monitoring stations including 172 meteorological stations. Voluntary monitoring of emissions from shipping and installation of meteorological stations was planned for the Arctic Ocean. The minister himself sought to assure that the Russian parties 'will definitely do it'.[67]

Similar duality characterises Russia's wider climate and environmental policies. black carbon and SLCP issues surface here too in the context of air quality and environmental protection rather than climate change. This problem definition is inseparable from the structure of Russian government and society. In Russia's heavily presidential system, science institutions exercise advisory and variable functions in knowledge production. The most influential ones in climate modelling are the Institute of Numerical Mathematics of the Russian Academy of Sciences and Roshydromet, the Russian Federal Service for Hydrometeorology and Environmental Monitoring, which has reported on climate change for the Russian government since 2008 and contributed to IPCC's reports.[68] However, such knowledge is secondary to the profit interests of Russia's fossil fuel industries and other heavy industries, and the socio-economic and foreign policy interests they serve.[69] At the same time, the Russian society features little awareness, if not outright scepticism of the anthropogenic sources of climate change (see Figure 8.5).[70]

---

67 Ibid. (2021).

68 Igor Makarov, 'Does Resource Abundance Require Special Approaches to Climate Policies? The Case of Russia' (2022) 170 Climatic change; Katja Doose, 'Modelling the Future: Climate Change Research in Russia during the Late Cold War and beyond, 1970s–2000' (2022) 171 Climatic Change 6 <https://doi.org/10.1007/s10584-022-03315-0>; Elana Wilson Rowe, 'Climate Science, Russian Politics, and the Framing of Climate Change' (2013) 4 WIREs Climate Change 457 <https://doi.org/10.1002/wcc.235> accessed 19 September 2022.

69 Pami Aalto and Anna Lowry, *Modernization of the Russian Economy: Fossil Fuels, Diversification and the Shackles of International Political Economy* (Routledge 2020); Lada V Kochtcheeva, 'Foreign Policy, National Interests, and Environmental Positioning: Russia's Post Paris Climate Change Actions, Discourse, and Engagement' (2021) ahead-of-print Problems of post-communism 1; Ellen Martus, 'Contested Policymaking in Russia: Industry, Environment, and the "Best Available Technology" Debate' (2017) 33 Post-Soviet Affairs 276.

70 See e.g. Veli-Pekka Tynkkynen and Nina Tynkkynen, 'Climate Denial Revisited: (Re) Contextualising Russian Public Discourse on Climate Change during Putin 2.0' (2018) 70 Europe-Asia Studies 1103; Tatiana Mitrova and Yuriy Melnikov, 'Energy Transition in Russia' (2019) 3 Energy Transitions 73.; Marianna Poberezhskaya, "Russian Climate Change Policy: Increasing Ambitions" (2021), Russian Analytical Digest, 72, 2–5 <https://doi.org/10.3929/ethz-b-000511730>.

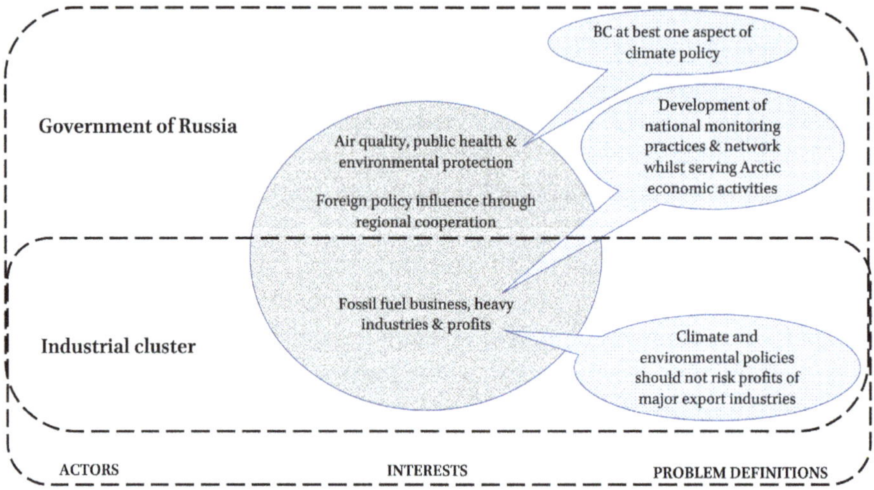

FIGURE 8.5 Russian actors, interests and problem definitions

The same duality applies to Russian companies. They need to demonstrate awareness of the climate and air quality problems of gas flaring to their customers in Western markets. The share of Russian export volumes to such environmentally sensitive markets continued to be decisive until summer 2022. Sanctions, combined with a poor outlook for Russia-West relations and ongoing energy transition in Europe, may well mean such air quality disclosure loses its stature. This can support the simultaneously existing, widespread non-compliance of Russian companies with the respective Russian domestic regulation. This in turn may protect the industry's competitive advantage in those markets that remain accessible for Russian producers.[71] For example, Russia's four largest energy and mineral extraction companies failed to reduce emissions despite declaring environmental safety measures and ambitious climate change targets during 2015–2019 (see Table 8.1). This is so because the fines for violation of environmental legislation are significantly lower than the costs of developing and implementing emission-reducing innovation.[72]

Overall, Russia's domestic structures comprise major technological, infrastructural and institutional-behavioural lock-ins to the fossil fuels economy.

---

71 Korppoo (n 54).

72 VA Tsukerman and SV Ivanov, 'Problems of Reducing Air Pollution from Industrial Enterprises in the Arctic Regions' (2022) 988 IOP Conference Series: Earth and Environmental Science 32006.

TABLE 8.1 Volume of air and greenhouse gas emissions in million tons of CO_2, 2015–2019

Company	2015	2016	2017	2018	2019
PJSC MMC Norilsk Nickel	2064	1963.4	1846.8	1926.6	1952.7
PJSC Severstal (Division Severstal Resources)	214.9	220.8	204.7	219.7	213.3
Arctic PJSC NOVATEK	66.2	121.2	92	70.3	75.6
PJSC ALROSA	9.4	8.9	7.5	9.8	8

SOURCE: MODIFIED FROM VA TSUKERMAN AND SV IVANOV, 'PROBLEMS OF REDUCING AIR POLLUTION FROM INDUSTRIAL ENTERPRISES IN THE ARCTIC REGIONS' (2022) 988 IOP CONFERENCE SERIES: EARTH AND ENVIRONMENTAL SCIENCE 32006

These lock-ins make mitigation a relatively low priority. Adaptation is a timelier goal as the Russian fossil fuel industry is shifting production to the Arctic with the large western Siberian fields depleting, and having to adapt to the rapidly changing Arctic conditions (e.g. permafrost melting, depreciating sea ice cover, heavier storms).[73] In this situation, despite adopting several climate and environmental documents pertaining to the Paris commitments, Russia's emission reduction commitments remain modest (see Table 8.2). At the same time, it is party to several international agreements and a member of transnational partnerships relevant for black carbon and SLCP mitigation (see Appendix 1).

Following the full-scale attack on Ukraine, this late, albeit unimpressive surge in climate policy was followed by depreciating economy with extensive sanctions, withdrawing foreign investment and strengthened anti-Western rhetoric domestically, with significant effects on the communicated decarbonisation plans and technological modernization. During 2022, debates in the Duma called for withdrawing from the Paris Agreement while companies asked for easing of environmental regulation. Russian climate scientists lost access to international research networks and data, thus endangering the future of measuring systems crucial for Arctic climate modelling.

In summary, the Finnish bilateral efforts and Arctic cooperation at best co-contributed, alongside more global pressure, to Russia's adoption of global climate and environmental regulation with relevance for black carbon and SLCP. China's commitment to climate neutrality during Autumn 2021 is significant

73 Michael Bradshaw "Russian energy dilemmas: energy security, globalisation and climate change", in P. Aalto (ed.), *Russia's energy policies: national, interregional and global levels* (Edward Elgar 2012), 206–229.

TABLE 8.2 Russian policies and regulations relevant for BC and SLCP mitigation

Document	Summary
Long-term climate strategy with emissions projections until 2050[a]	Target for net emissions reduction by 80% compared to the 1990 level by 2050, primarily through increasing the absorptive capacity of forests; yet no implementation plan[b]
Federal law on limiting GHG emissions[c]	Mandatory disclosure of information on GHG emissions by companies emitting the equivalent of 150,000 tons of CO_2 a year or more, from 2025 at the latest; legal framework for carbon trading & climate projects; carbon footprint concept; register of GHG emissions incl. methods for quantifying and determining emissions & sequestrations
Climate adaptation action plan until 2022[d]	Framework for adaptation vis-à-vis climate change; yet no sector-specific measures[e]
Energy strategy until 2035[f]	Reducing the environmental impact of the energy system and industry and their adaptation to climate change; Russia presented as one the most ecologically friendly (low carbon) leading economies owing to nuclear power, hydropower and natural gas resources
Regulations regarding BAT[g]	Incentives for companies to modernize; removal of environmental penalties for fully BAT compliant enterprises; investment credits; sanctions for negative environmental impact. Enterprises exceeding BAT regulations required to develop an environmental effectiveness programme and modernized production processes[h]
Decree on limiting atmospheric emissions from flaring and APG with introduction of a 5% limit on flaring of gas as a proportion of total production in 2012[i]	The regulation is based partly on the pollution fees system, set for exceeding the allowed 5 percent, for non-metered flaring and 4.5 times the standard environmental fine for methane emissions[j]

TABLE 8.2 Russian policies and regulations relevant for BC and SLCP mitigation (*cont.*)

a Government of Russia, *Strategiya sotsialno-ekonomicheskogo razvitiya Rossiyskoy Federatsii s nizkim urovnem vybrosov parnikovyh gazov do 2050 goda, ot 29 oktyabrya 2021 g. № 3052-r* (Decree № 3052-r., 2021a) <http://static.government.ru/media/files/ADKkCzp3fWO32e2yAoBhtIpyzWfHaiUa.pdf> accessed 28 March 2022.

b Makarov (n 67).

c Government of Russia, *Federalnyi zakon ot 02.07.2021 № 296-FZ "Ob ogranicsenii vybrosov parnikovyh gazov"* (Federal Law, No 296-FZ., 2021b) <https://legalacts.ru/doc/federalnyi-zakon-ot-02072021-n-296-fz-ob-ogranichenii-vybrosov/> accessed 6 July 2022.

d Government of Russia, *Rasporyazhenie ot 25 dekabrya 2019 goda №3183-r. "Natsionalnyi plan meropriyatiya perbogo etapa adaptatsii k izmeneniyam klimata na period do 2022 goda"* (Decree № 3183-r, 25 December 2019a) <http://government.ru/docs/38739/> accessed 6 July 2022.

e Igor Yakovlev, Kabir, L. S. & Nikulina, S. I. "Climate policy of Russian Federation: international cooperation and national approach" (2020) ("Klimaticheskaya politika Rossiyskoy Federatsii: mezhdunarodnoe sotrudnitsestvo i natsionalniy podhod."), Financial Journal (Financovyi zhurnal) Vol 12 (4), 26–36 (in Russian).

f Government of Russia, *Rasporyazhenie Pravitelstva Rossiyskoy Federatsii ot 9 iyunya 2020 g. № 1523-r "Energeticheskaya strategiya Rossiyskoy Federatsii na period do 2035 года"* (Decree No 1523-r., 2020) <http://static.government.ru/media/files/w4sigFOiDjGVDYT4IgsApssm6mZRb7wx.pdf> accessed 6 July 2022.

g Government of Russia, *Federalnyi zakon ot 21 iyulja 2014 g. № 219-FZ "O vnesenii izmeneniy v Federalnyi zakon "Ob ohrane okruzhajushchey sredy" I otdelnye zakonodatelnye akty Rossiyskoy Federatsii"* (Federal Law № 219-FZ, 21 July 2014a) <http://base.garant.ru/70700466/> accessed 11 July 2022; Government of Russia, *Postanovlenie Pravitelstva RF ot 8 dekabrya 2014 г. № 1458 "O poryadke opredeleniya tehnologii v kachestve nailyshey dostupnpoy tehnologii, a takzhe razrabotki, akualizatsii i opublikovaniya informatsionno-tehnitseskih spravochnikov po nailushym dostunym tehnologiyam"* (Decree № 1458, 8 December 2014b) <http://base.garant.ru/70829288/> accessed 11 July 2022.

h Martus (n 70); PV Roslyakov and others, 'Optimal Choice of the Best Available Technologies for Russian Thermal Power Plants' (2019) 66 Thermal Engineering 268.

i Government of Russia (2009).

j Korppoo (n 54).

here as the country was among the last to do so of the major customers of Russian fossil fuel industry. However, it is possible to propose that for example further joint RDI actions in the Arctic context would be considered relevant nationally, to the extent they could reduce the costs of environmental innovation in Russia. Yet, Russia's war in Ukraine has long-standing repercussions to such a regional cooperation path which earlier would have represented natural continuation to bi-and multilateral projects.

5 Conclusion

In this chapter, we compared the science diplomacies of Norway and Finland towards China and Russia, respectively, on black carbon and SLCP mitigation. In the Norwegian-Chinese case, the diplomacy led to a tangible result in the form of a Norwegian-Chinese project intended to bolster the science basis of mitigation. In the Finnish-Russian case, bilateral high-level diplomacy led by the Finnish president was combined with similar initiatives in Arctic regional and more global arenas as well as scientific work as part of multilateral Arctic cooperation. Despite greater political capital invested, the results in this latter case are not as well ascertainable. It is true that Russia has adopted several black carbon and SLCP relevant regulatory acts. Yet, underpinning these actions are Russia's own modernisation interests while they also represent its long-standing aim to be recognised as one of great powers and contributor to major international processes, even if such processes were taking place in a low-priority-area for Russian foreign policy like environmental governance. At the same time, bilateral and regional cooperation may have played their own role in preparing the ground for these actions. In science diplomacy, and in wider global environmental governance which such diplomacy sustains and seeks to shape, numerous reasons usually underpin outcomes. This applies also to the cases examined here. Our theoretical starting points help to explain some of these reasons.

In the Norwegian-Chinese case, the bilateral scientific project was complemented by the regional track wherein Chinese scientists participated in similar Arctic scientific cooperation until Russia's war in Ukraine froze that track. Together, scientific work along these two tracks can help to improve the credibility of knowledge in this area. This is crucial given the uncertainties of knowledge pertaining to black carbon mitigation in general and more specifically on black carbon emissions in China. The legitimacy of knowledge produced can also improve with the involvement of Chinese science institutions on the two tracks, given their strong links with the Chinese government and its preference for science-based policy in climate and environmental policy. The relevance of the knowledge produced is strong as it responds to the central government's interest in improving air quality as evinced in successive Chinese policy documents. Chinese actors also acknowledge how Arctic air pollution shapes the region's climate system, with effects extending to China. This has repercussions to strengthening Chinese interests in climate change mitigation and adaptation.[74] The links to Norwegian interests in air quality and climate policy

74 Gørild Heggelund and Cheng, H. "China's climate policy: does an Arctic dimension exist?", in Rottem, S.V., Soltvedt, I. (eds) *Arctic Governance III: Norway, Russia and Asian states* (I.B. Tauris 2019), 281–298.

are evident. The main lock-ins standing on the way in China's case concern the way in which the implementation of air quality issues rests with regional authorities that also need to mind the considerable socio-economic interests associated with local polluting industries.

In some contrast to the Norwegian-Chinese case, Finland's high-level black carbon initiative never as decisively shaped knowledge production processes in Russia. The Arctic track for its part was not fully sustained by Russian parties as the country only reported on its black carbon emissions in 2015 and then failed to follow up, as agreed within the Arctic Council Framework for enhanced black carbon and methane emission reductions. It is possible to propose that the bilateral and regional processes did not decisively enough strengthen the credibility of the knowledge the Finnish parties sought to disseminate. Yet, on balance, in this case, the change that needed to be achieved was greater than that in the Norwegian-Chinese case.

For the Finnish official diplomacy, the major interest pertained to climate, and perhaps to some extent the sometimes nationally debated air pollution from Russian fossil fuel production and other industrial sites to Finland. For Russian parties, the credibility of the climate argument vis-à-vis black carbon was never widely enough accepted. Russia's interests in this area mostly pertained to adaptation rather than to mitigation sought by Finnish parties. For improving the legitimacy of knowledge, the work within the two tracks utilised remained inconclusive. No notable bilateral knowledge production process occurred despite the interests of Finnish scientists on cooperation with Russia.[75] No new joint research project or programme was launched by the authorities or science funders despite long-standing scientific and technical cooperation. The official diplomacy track could have integrated science and RDI actors more decisively into the activities, especially considering the RDI cluster's more global approach at the outset that was sceptical of the Russian market. Now that task was largely left to the Arctic multilateral track.

Here one must, however, return to how Russia's system of climate and environmental policy formation is not as open nor transparent for knowledge-based diplomacy and policy as is the Chinese one. It is furthermore crucial to note that very strong lock-ins in terms of fossil fuel technologies, infrastructures, institutions and behaviour persist in Russia, eroding the relevance of Finnish diplomacy's message. This means that in Russia, powerful national interests persist in continued fossil fuel economy and exports – to those markets and

75 Hanna Lappalainen et al., Pan-Eurasian Experiment (PEEX): Towards a holistic understanding of the feedbacks and interactions in the land-Atmosphere-ocean-society continuum in the northern Eurasian region, Atmospheric Chemistry and Physics 16(22): 14421–14461.

product segments remaining outside of the sanctions that were reinforced since Russia's escalation of war in Ukraine and not (yet) subject to efforts to diversify away from Russian suppliers. Such interests easily override potential Finnish interests in exports of environmental technologies and devices. It is furthermore well known that Russian interests in economic diversification are limited, as commodities and products in potential sectors of the economy are bound to be less competitive than those of the fossil fuels industry.[76] In other words, no decisive enough breakthrough took place to sufficiently integrate Finnish and Russian interests.

The lessons for the global governance of black carbon and SLCPs concern the role of knowledge in science diplomacy. Bilateralism can work with congruent enough interests and investment in joint knowledge production that can bolster the credibility and legitimacy of the knowledge. High-level science diplomacy without enough science cooperation created may not have the same effect for knowledge, especially if powerful lock-ins exist in the target country and knowledge-based policy tradition is limited. In terms of interests involved, the sender country should plan its approach carefully. If health and socio-economic health bill are likely to be the primary self-interests for the target country as far air pollution is concerned, focusing the science diplomacy on climate policy may not be helpful, particularly if we assume actors in the target country to know those benefits to be of global nature from their perspective, and think global benefits to weigh less than national ones.

In other words, the diplomatic practice must be tailor-made for each target country to maximise its chances while a mechanism must exist for adapting and learning along the way. Learning by doing has been the actual practice of Arctic cooperation for a long time,[77] but this requires opportunities for such doing. At the time of writing, such opportunities involving Russian parties are becoming fewer than during the Cold War. Overall, the long-term consequences of the Russian offensive in Ukraine will hamper the diffusion of climate and environmental policies and adoption of mitigation technologies that would normally be sought by science diplomacy. Without doubt this development will be instructive to Chinese foreign policy makers as well as Chinese scientists who likely do not want to witness the same while their western

---

76 Clifford Gaddy and Barry Ickes, *Bear Traps on Russia's Road to Modernization* (Routledge 2013); Aalto and Lowry (n 68).

77 Sigve R Leland and Alf Håkon Hoel, "Learning by doing: The Barents cooperation and development of regional collaboration in the north", in Aalto, P., Blakkisrud, H. and Smith, H. (eds) *The New Northern Dimension of the European Neighbourhood* (Centre for European Policy Studies 2009), 36–53.

counterparts cannot afford it. This all should make science diplomacy actors in Norway, Finland and beyond acutely aware of how their sphere of activity depends on international order. As for China, we expect China's science-based energy and environmental policies to make the domestically expected benefits of mitigation more likely to be reaped than in the case of Russia, with more positive outlook for continued international cooperation. Should China instead embark on similar geopolitical adventures like Russia, the outlook for international science diplomacy may be dark.

Appendix 1: Membership in Key International Agreements, Frameworks, and Partnerships Relevant to SLCPs

TABLE 8.3 Membership in key international agreements, frameworks, and partnerships relevant to SLCPs

Binding international agreements	Membership, year of ratification/ joining				
	FI	NO	RUS	CHI	SLCPS concerned
UNFCCC (1992)	1994	1993	1994	1993	CH_4 & HFCS
Kyoto Protocol (1997)	2002	2002	2004	2002	CH_4 & HFCS
Paris Agreement (2015)	2016	2016	2019	2016	Unspecified[a]
UNECE Convention on Long-Range Transboundary Air Pollution (CLRTAP) (1979)	1979	1979	1979	N/A	AP
UNECE CLRTAP (1979) Gothenburg Protocol to Abate Acidification, Eutrophication and Ground-level Ozone (1999), Geneva Amendment (2012)	2017	2019	-	N/A	$PM_{2.5}$, BC
Vienna Convention for the Protection of the Ozone Layer (1985) Montreal Protocol on Substances that Deplete the Ozone Layer (1987) Kigali Amendment (2016)	2017	2017	2020	2021	HFCS

TABLE 8.3 Membership in key international agreements, frameworks (*cont.*)

Binding international agreements	Membership, year of ratification/joining				
International Convention for the Prevention of Pollution from ships (MARPOL 73/78) (1973, 1978)[b]	1983	1983	1984	1983	PM
MARPOL 73/78 (1973, 1978) Protocol of 1997 Annex VI Prevention of Air Pollution from Ships[c]	2005	2005	2011	2006	PM
Voluntary inter-governmental frameworks					
The North-East Asia Clean Air Partnership (NEACAP)[d]	N/A	N/A	2018	2018	$PM_{2.5}$, BC
North-East Asian Subregional Program for Environmental Cooperation (NEASPEC)	N/A	N/A	1993	1993	AP
Arctic Council	1996	1996	1996	2013	BC, CH_4
Arctic Council Framework "Enhanced Black Carbon and Methane Emissions Reductions: An Arctic Council Framework for Action" (2015)[e]	2015, 2017, 2020	2015, 2017, 2020	2015	-	BC, CH_4
Tripartite Environment Ministers Meeting (TEMM) (1990), Tripartite Policy Dialogue on Air Pollution (TPDAP) (2013)	N/A	N/A	N/A	2013	AP, $PM_{2.5}$
Acid Deposition Monitoring Network in East Asia (EANET) (2001)	N/A	N/A	2001	2001	PM
UNEP Action Plan for the Protection, Management and Development of the Marine and Coastal Environment of the Northwest Pacific Region (NOWPAP) (1994)	N/A	N/A	1994	1994	AP, PM_{10}, CH_4
East Asia Summit (EAS) (2005)	N/A	N/A	2011	2005	env. coop.
Asia-Pacific Economic Cooperation (APEC) (1989) Green Supply Chain Cooperation Network (2014)	N/A	N/A	(1998) 2014	(1991) 2014	env. coop.

TABLE 8.3 Membership in key international agreements, frameworks (*cont.*)

Binding international agreements	**Membership, year of ratification/ joining**				
EU-Russia Permanent Partnership Council (2003), PPC on Environment (formal EU-Russia environmental dialogue) (2006)	N/A	N/A	(2003) 2006	N/A	env. coop.
Voluntary public-private/multi-stakeholder partnerships					
Climate and Clean Air Coalition (CCAC) to reduce short-lived climate pollutants (2012)	2012	2012	2014	-	BC, CH_4, TO, HFCS
Global Methane Initiative (GMI) (2004)	2008	2011	2004	2004	CH_4
Asia Pacific Clean Air Partnership (APCAP) (2015)[f] Joint Forum	N/A	N/A	N/A	-	$PM_{2.5}$, O3
Political and economic unions					
European Union (EU) (1992)[g]	1995	-	-	N/A	$PM_{2.5}$, BC
Association of Southeast Asian Nations (ASEAN) (1967) (through Non-ASEAN Ambassadors)[h]	2011	2015	1991	1991	AP, haze
ASEAN + 3 Environment Ministers Meeting (2002)	N/A	N/A	N/A	2002	AP, haze
Inter-governmental organisations					
International Civic Aviation organisation (ICAO) (1947)[i]	1949	1947	1970	1946	AP, PM, nvPM
UN Economic and Social Commission for Asia and the Pacific (ESCAP)	N/A	N/A	1947	1947	AP
Baltic Marine Environment Protection Commission (Helsinki Commission – HELCOM) (1974, 1992)	1974, 1992	N/A	(1974) 1992	N/A	env. coop.
Northern Dimension Environmental Partnership (NDEP) (2001)	2001	2001	2001	N/A	env. coop.
Barents Euro-Arctic Council (BEAC) (1993)	1993	1993	1993	N/A	env. coop.

TABLE 8.3 Membership in key international agreements, frameworks (*cont.*)

Year = member; - = not a member; N/A = not applicable

a The Paris Agreement does not specify mitigated pollutants. However, GHGs, CH4 and HFC are part of the reporting system through the agreement's transparency framework. The voluntary submission of reduction plans on any SLCPs can take place as part of the nationally determined contributions (NDCs).

b The Optional Annexes III, IV, V of the Convention adopted as follows: Finland: Annex III (1992), IV (2003), and V (1988), Norway: Annex III (1992), IV (2003), and V (1988), Russia: Annex III (1992), IV (2003), and V (1988), and China: Annex III (1994), IV (2007), and V (1989)

c IMO 2020 Amendment ("IMO 2020 Sulphur regulation") is applicable to all parties having ratified MARPOL Protocol 1997 Annex VI

d NEACAP comprises science-based, policy-oriented cooperation on transboundary air pollution in North-East Asia. It has received technical support from UNECE CLRTAP

e Finland and Norway have submitted reports in 2015, 2017, and 2019, and Russia in 2015.

f China is not a member; Chinese experts are involved in the scientific panel.

g E.g., the National Emission Ceiling (NEC) Directive of the EU Clean Air Policy Package includes limits for PM2.5 and recommendations for BC. BC is also targeted indirectly through EURO6 vehicle standards.

h Finland's partnership with ASEAN is unspecified (though a partnership exists), Norway is involved as a Sectoral Dialogue Partner, and Russia and China as Dialogue Partners.

i ICAO Committee on Aviation Environmental Protection (CAEP) has introduced a PM standard (PM mass & number) and End Smoke Number Standard; both applicable in 1/2023 (included under Annex 16, Volume II, Chapter 4).

Acknowledgements

We would like to acknowledge the financial support of the 'Black Carbon Footprint (BCFp)' project (Business Finland, 2019–2022, no. 530/31/2019) and the support Pami Aalto obtained during his research visit to the Fridtjof Nansen Institute (FNI) in November 2021, including several invaluable discussions with FNI staff members.

Bibliography

Aakre S and others, 'Incentives for Small Clubs of Arctic Countries to Limit Black Carbon and Methane Emissions' (2018) 8 Nature Climate Change 85.

Aalto P and Lowry A, *Modernization of the Russian Economy: Fossil Fuels, Diversification and the Shackles of International Political Economy* (Routledge 2020).

Aalto P, Blakkisrud H and Smith H, *The New Northern Dimension of the European Neighbourhood* (Centre for European Policy Studies 2008).

Abbondanza, G and Wilkins, T S, *Awkward Powers: Escaping Traditional Great Power and Middle Power Theory* (Springer 2022).

Arctic Contaminants Action Program, *Mitigation of Short-Lived Climate Pollutants from APG-Flaring. Project: Phase 2 – the Use of New Methodology to Reduce APG Flaring at Remote Fields* (Arctic Contaminants Action Programme 2021a) <https://oaarchive.arctic-council.org/handle/11374/2607>.

Arctic Contaminants Action Program, *Black Carbon and Methane from the Oil and Gas Sector: Webinar Report with Recommendations.* (Arctic Contaminants Action Programme 2021b), <https://oaarchive.arctic-council.org/server/api/core/bitstreams/168f1e3f-a237-45d9-8092-720ce8a3fe35/content>.

Arctic Contaminants Action Program, *Mitigation of Short-Lived Climate Pollutants from AGP-Flaring Project: Final report. Phase 1A – Evaluation of potential impact of AÅG flaring on Arctic zone environment* (Final report, VYGON Consulting, 16 November 2018) <https://oaarchive.arctic-council.org/bitstream/handle/11374/2450/FinalReport_APG-flaring-Phase-1A.pdf?sequence=1&isAllowed=y>.

Arctic Council Secretariat, *Expert group on Black carbon and methane 3rd Summary of Progress and Recommendations Report* (Arctic Council Secretariat 2021) <MMIS12_2021_REYKJAVIK_EGBCM_Summary-Report-2021.pdf>.

Arctic Monitoring and Assessment Programme, *Impacts of Short-Lived Climate Forces on Arctic Climate, Air Quality and Human Health Summary for Policymakers* (Arctic Monitoring and Assessment Programme 2021) <https://www.amap.no/documents/download/6760/inline>.

Böttcher K and others, 'Black Carbon Emissions from Flaring in Russia in the Period 2012–2017' (2021) 254 Atmospheric Environment 118390 <https://www.sciencedirect.com/science/article/pii/S1352231021002090>.

Bradshaw, M. "Russian energy dilemmas: energy security, globalisation and climate change", in P. Aalto (ed.), *Russia's Energy Policies: National, Interregional and Global Levels* (Edward Elgar 2012), 206–229.

Cheng L, *The Power of Ideas: The Rising Influence of Thinkers and Think Tanks in China* (World Scientific Publishing Co Pte Ltd 2017).

Cheng, M., Meng, F., Randall, S., Rønning, I., Vestreng, V. "Review of BC/OC emissions and control measures in China and Norway" (2021) ChiNorBC1.

Devyatkin, P, 'Russian and Chinese Scientists to Establish Arctic Research Center' (The High North News, 15 April 2019) <https://www.highnorthnews.com/en/russian-and-chinese-scientists-establish-arctic-research-center> Accessed 6 September 2022.

Doose K, 'Modelling the Future: Climate Change Research in Russia during the Late Cold War and beyond, 1970s–2000' (2022) 171 Climatic Change 6 <https://doi.org/10.1007/s10584-022-03315-0>.

Flink T. and Ruffin N, 'The Current State of the 'Art' of Science Diplomacy', in Simon D and Kuhlmann S (eds.) *Handbook of Science and Public Policy* (Edward Elgar 2019), 104–121.

Frey HC, 'Trends in Onroad Transportation Energy and Emissions' (2018) 68 Journal of the Air & Waste Management Association 514 <https://doi.org/10.1080/10962247.2018.1454357>.

Gaddy C and Ickes B, *Bear Traps on Russia's Road to Modernization* (Routledge 2013).

Gov.cn., 'China Meteorological Administration released the "China Climate Change Blue Book' (in Chinese, 10 August 2022) <http://www.gov.cn/xinwen/2022-08/10/content_5704792.htm>.

Government of Finland, 'Finland's Chairmanship program for the Arctic Council 2017 – 2019' (Ministry for Foreign Affairs of Finland, 2017) <https://oaarchive.arctic-council.org/server/api/core/bitstreams/cd14f8d1-cba1-4802-ab3e-67ac12b9e544/content>.

Government of Finland, 'Prime Ministers Rinne and Medvedev met in Moscow' (Government Communications Department, Press release, 25 November 2019) <https://valtioneuvosto.fi/-/10616/paaministerit-rinne-ja-medvedev-tapasivat-moskovassa?languageId=en_US> accessed 11 July 2022.

Government of Norway, 'Update of Norway's nationally determined contribution' (2022) <https://unfccc.int/sites/default/files/NDC/2022-06/Norway_updatedNDC_2020%20%28Updated%20submission%29.pdf> accessed 2 December 2022.

Government of Norway, *Better Growth, Lower Emissions – the Norwegian Government's Strategy for Green Competitiveness* (Strategy T-1562 E, 2017).

Government of Russia, *Federalnyi zakon ot 02.07.2021 № 296-FZ "Ob ogranicsenii vybrosov parnikovyh gazov"* (Federal Law, No 296-FZ., 2021b) <https://legalacts.ru/doc/federalnyi-zakon-ot-02072021-n-296-fz-ob-ogranichenii-vybrosov/> accessed 6 July 2022.

Government of Russia, *Federalnyi zakon ot 21 iyulja 2014 g. № 219-FZ "O vnesenii izmeneniy v Federalnyi zakon "Ob ohrane okruzhajushchey sredy" I otdelnye zakonodatelnye akty Rossiyskoy Federatsii"* (Federal Law № 219-FZ, 21 July 2014a) <http://base.garant.ru/70700466/> accessed 11 July 2022.

Government of Russia, *Postanovlenie Pravitelstva RF ot 8 dekabrya 2014 г. № 1458 "O poryadke opredeleniya tehnologii v kachestve nailyshey dostupnpoy tehnologii, a takzhe razrabotki, akualizatsii i opublikovaniya informatsionno-tehnitseskih spravochnikov po nailushym dostunym tehnologiyam"* (Decree № 1458, 8 December 2014b) <http://base.garant.ru/70829288/> accessed 11 July 2022.

Government of Russia, *Postanovlenie Pravitelstva RF ot 8 Yanvarya 2009 g. No 7 "O merah po stimulirovaniyu sokrasheniya atmosfernogo vozduha produktami szhiganija popytnogo neftyanogo gaza na fakelnyh ustanovkah"* (Decree № 7, 8 January 2009) <https://www.garant.ru/products/ipo/prime/doc/12064540/> accessed 6 July 2022.

Government of Russia, *Rasporyazhenie ot 25 dekabrya 2019 goda №3183-r. "Natsionalnyi plan meropriyatiya perbogo etapa adaptatsii k izmeneniyam klimata na period do 2022 goda"* (Decree № 3183-r, 25 December 2019a) <http://government.ru/docs/38739/> accessed 6 July 2022.

Government of Russia, *Rasporyazhenie Pravitelstva Rossiyskoy Federatsii ot 9 iyunya 2020 g. № 1523-r "Energeticheskaya strategiya Rossiyskoy Federatsii na period do 2035 года"* (Decree No 1523-r., 2020) <http://static.government.ru/media/files/w4sigFOiDjGVDYT4IgsApssm6mZRb7wx.pdf> accessed 6 July 2022.

Government of Russia, *Strategiya sotsialno-ekonomicheskogo razvitiya Rossiyskoy Federatsii s nizkim urovnem vybrosov parnikovyh gazov do 2050 goda, ot 29 oktyabrya 2021 g. № 3052-r* (Decree № 3052-r., 2021a) <http://static.government.ru/media/files/ADKkCzp3fWO32e2yAoBhtIpyzWfHaiUa.pdf> accessed 28 March 2022.

Hall, M 'Net Zero Targets and GHG Emission Reduction in the UK and Norwegian Upstream Oil and Gas Industry: A Comparative Assessment' (2020) <https://www.oxfordenergy.org/publications/net-zero-targets-and-ghg-emission-reduction-in-the-uk-and-norwegian-upstream-oil-and-gas-industry-a-comparative-assessment/> accessed 2 December 2022.

Heggelund GM, 'China's Climate and Energy Policy: At a Turning Point?' (2021) 21 International Environmental Agreements: Politics, Law and Economics 9.

Heggelund, Gorild and Cheng, H. 'China's climate policy: does an Arctic dimension exist?', in Rottem, S.V., Soltvedt, I. (eds) Arctic Governance III: Norway, Russia and Asian states (I.B. Tauris 2019), 281–298.

Hooftman N and others, 'A Review of the European Passenger Car Regulations – Real Driving Emissions vs Local Air Quality' (2018) 86 Renewable & Sustainable Energy Reviews 1.

Hughes L and Lipscy PY, 'The Politics of Energy' (2013) 16 Annual Review of Political Science 449.

Ikeda K and others, 'Evaluation of Anthropogenic Emissions of Black Carbon from East Asia in Six Inventories: Constraints from Model Simulations and Surface Observations on Fukue Island, Japan' (2022) 2 Environmental Science: Atmospheres 416.

Kennedy AB and Lim DJ, 'The Innovation Imperative: Technology and US–China Rivalry in the Twenty-First Century' (2018) 94 International Affairs (London) 553.

Kochtcheeva LV, 'Foreign Policy, National Interests, and Environmental Positioning: Russia's Post Paris Climate Change Actions, Discourse, and Engagement' (2021) ahead-of-print Problems of Post-communism 1.

Korppoo A, 'Russian Associated Petroleum Gas Flaring Limits: Interplay of Formal and Informal Institutions' (2018) 116 Energy Policy 232 <https://www.sciencedirect.com/science/article/pii/S0301421518300752>.

Kotilainen K and others, 'From Path Dependence to Policy Mixes for Nordic Electric Mobility: Lessons for Accelerating Future Transport Transitions' (2019) 52 Policy Sciences 573.

Lappalainen H et al., 'Pan-Eurasian Experiment (PEEX): towards a holistic understanding of the feedbacks and interactions in the land-Atmosphere-ocean-society continuum in the northern Eurasian region' (2016) Atmospheric Chemistry and Physics 16(22): 14421–14461.

Leland SL and Alf Håkon Hoel, "Learning by doing: The Barents cooperation and development of regional collaboration in the north", in Aalto, P., Blakkisrud, H. and Smith, H. (eds) *The New Northern Dimension of the European Neighbourhood* (Centre for European Policy Studies 2009), 36–53.

Li C, *The Power of Ideas: The Rising Influence of Thinkers and Think Tanks in China* (World Scientific Publishing Co Pte Ltd 2017).

Makarov I, 'Does Resource Abundance Require Special Approaches to Climate Policies? The Case of Russia' (2022) 170 Climatic Change.

Martus E, 'Contested Policymaking in Russia: Industry, Environment, and the "Best Available Technology" Debate' (2017) 33 Post-Soviet Affairs 276.

Ministry of Natural Resources and Environment of the Russian Federation, *National report on the actions on black carbon and methane emissions reduction in accordance with the Framework for Action on Enhanced Black Carbon and Methane reductions* (Government of Russia, Report, 24 April 2015) <https://oaarchive.arctic-council.org/handle/11374/1168>.

Mitrova T and Melnikov Y, 'Energy Transition in Russia' (2019) 3 Energy Transitions 73.

Muth, C, Aalto, P, Mylläri, F, Rönkkö, T, Harsia, P, "Globally and Locally Applicable Technologies to Accelerate Electrification", in Aalto, P. (ed.), *Electrification: Accelerating the Energy Transition* (Academic Press/Elsevier 2021), 25–55.

National Development and Reform Commission, *China's National Climate Change Programme* (National Development and Reform Commission, June 2007) <http://www.ccchina.gov.cn/WebSite/CCChina/UpFile/File188.pdf>.

Nordic Council of Ministers, *Policy Brief: Emissions of Short-Lived Climate Pollutants (SLCPs): emission factors, scenarios and reduction potentials* (Nordic Council of Ministers 2019) <http://dx.doi.org/10.6027/Nord2019-013>.

Norwegian Environment Agency, *Climate Mitigation Measures up to 2030: Short Term Climate Effects and Health Effects* (Norwegian Environment Agency 2016).

Norwegian Environment Agency, *Summary of proposed action plan for Norwegian emissions of shortlived climate forcers* (M135/2014, 2014) <https://www.miljodirektoratet.no/globalassets/publikasjoner/m135/m135.pdf> accessed 2 December 2022.

Norwegian Ministry of Climate and Environment, *Norway's Climate Action Plan for 2021–2030* (White Paper, Cm 13, 2021).

Özkaragöz Doğan E, Uygun Z and Akçomak İS, 'Can Science Diplomacy Address the Global Climate Change Challenge?' (2021) 31 Environmental Policy & Governance 31 <http://libproxy.tuni.fi/login?url=https://search.ebscohost.com/login.aspx?direct=true&AuthType=cookie,ip,uid&db=bsu&AN=148477343&site=ehost-live&scope=site>.

Peoples' Republic of China [PRC], *Observer Review Report 2017–2019, Arctic Council* (2019) <https://oaarchive.arctic-council.org/handle/11374/2251>.

Peoples' Republic of China [PRC], *Observer Review Report 2019–2021, Arctic Council* (2021) <https://oaarchive.arctic-council.org/handle/11374/2717>.

Poberezhskaya, M "Russian Climate Change Policy: Increasing Ambitions" (2021) Russian Analytical Digest Vol 72, 2–5. <https://doi.org/10.3929/ethz-b-000511730>.

President of Finland, 'President of Russia Vladimir Putin visited Finland' (Office of the President of the Republic of Finland, Press release, 21 August 2019) <https://www.presidentti.fi/en/news/president-of-russia-to-make-working-visit-to-finland-3/> accessed 11 July 2022.

President of Finland, *Speech by the President of the Republic of Finland, Mr. Sauli Niinistö, at the Arctic Forum in St. Petersburg, 9 April 2019* (2019) <presidentti.fi/en/speeches/speech-by-the-president-of-the-republic-of-finland-mr-sauli-niinisto-at-the-arctic-forum-in-st-petersburg-9-april-2019/>.

President of Finland, *Statement by President of the Republic of Finland Sauli Niinistö at the United Nations General Assembly 73rd General Debate on 25th September 2018*, available at: <presidentti.fi/en/speeches/statement-by-president-of-the-republic-of-finland-sauli-niinisto-at-the-united-nations-general-assembly-73rd-general-debate-on-25th-september-2018/>.

President of Russia, 'Joint news conference with President of Finland Sauli Niinistö – Vladimir Putin and Sauli Niinistö made press statements and answered media questions following Russian-Finnish talks' (Presidential Executive Office, Press release 21 August 2019) <http://en.kremlin.ru/events/president/news/61349> accessed 11 July 2022.

Raunio T, 'Semi-Presidentialism and European Integration: Lessons from Finland for Constitutional Design' (2012) 19 Journal of European Public Policy 567.

Raunio T and Sedelius T, 'Presidents and Cabinets: Coordinating Executive Leadership in Premier-Presidential Regimes' (2020) 18 Political Studies Review 53.

Reuters, 'China warns that its temperatures are rising faster than global average' (4 August, 2022) <https://www.reuters.com/world/china/china-warns-that-its-temperatures-are-rising-faster-than-global-average-2022-08-04/#:~:text=SHANGHAI%2C%20Aug%204%20(Reuters),mount%2C%20a%20government%20official%20said>.

Romppanen S, 'Arctic Climate Governance via EU Law on Black Carbon?' (2018) 27 Review of European Community & International Environmental Law 45.

Rosendal GK, 'Norway in UN Environmental Policies: Ambitions and Influence' (2007) 7 International Environmental Agreements: Politics, Law and Economics 439.

Rosendal GK and others, 'The Minamata Convention and Mercury Policy in China: The Role of Science' (2020) 44 Asian Perspective 435.

Roslyakov PV and others, 'Optimal Choice of the Best Available Technologies for Russian Thermal Power Plants' (2019) 66 Thermal Engineering 268.

Russian Ministry of Natural Resources and Ecology, 'Arctic Council plenary meeting' (Ministry of Natural Resources and Ecology, Press release, 25 June 2021) <https://www.mnr.gov.ru/press/news/aleksandr_kozlov_vazhno_uchityvat_monitoring_po_chyernomu_uglerodu_i_metanu_seychas_uzhe_obsuzhdaem_/?sphrase_id=405821> accessed 12 May 2022.

Russian Ministry for Natural Resources and Ecology, 'Video webinar arranged 29 October 2020 in connection of the forthcoming Russian chairmanship of the Arctic Council' (Ministry for Natural Resources and Ecology, Press release, 29 October 2020) <https://www.mnr.gov.ru/press/news/sokrashchenie_vybrosov_chernogo_ugleroda_i_metana_v_atmosferu_arktiki_rossiya_otkryta_dlya_sotrudnich/?special_version=N> accessed 12 May 2022.

Russian Ministry for Natural Resources and Ecology, "Working meeting between representatives of the Finnish foreign ministry and the embassy of Finland in Russia and the Russian ministry for natural resources and ecology" (Ministry for Natural Resources and Ecology, Press release, 21 May 2019) <https://www.mnr.gov.ru/press/news/predstaviteli_minprirody_rossii_i_mida_finlyandii_obsudili_voprosy_sokrashcheniya_vybrosov_chernogo_/?sphrase_id=405786> accessed 12 May 2022.

Sand M and others, 'Response of Arctic Temperature to Changes in Emissions of Short-Lived Climate Forcers' (2016) 6 Nature Climate Change 286.

Schreurs M, 'Multi-Level Climate Governance in China' (2017) 27 Environmental Policy and Governance 163 <https://doi.org/10.1002/eet.1751> accessed 19 September 2022.

Smieszek, MG, Koivurova, T, Nielsson, ET, "China's Arctic Policy", in Koivurova T and Kopra S, *Chinese Policy and Presence in the Arctic* (BRILL 2020).

Stanway, D, "President Xi says China will start cutting coal consumption from 2026" (Reuters, 22 April 2021) <https://www.reuters.com/world/china/chinas-xi-says-china-will-phase-down-coal-consumption-over-2026-2030-2021-04-22/>.

State Council, "Notice of the State Council Distributing the Action Plan for the Prevention and Control of Air Pollution" (10 September 2013) <http://www.gov.cn/zwgk/2013-09/12/content_2486773.htm> accessed 12 May 2022, in Chinese.

State Council, "The People's Republic of China's 14th Five-Year Plan of National Economic and Social Development and Outline of Vision Goals for 2035" (2021) <http://www.gov.cn/zhengce/2020-11/03/content_5556991.htm> accessed 16 July 2021, in Chinese.

Stevenson H, *Global Environmental Politics: Problems, Policy and Practice* (Cambridge University Press 2017).

Stohl A and others, 'Black Carbon in the Arctic: The Underestimated Role of Gas Flaring and Residential Combustion Emissions' (2013) 13 Atmospheric Chemistry and Physics 8833.

Su P and Mayer M, 'Science Diplomacy and Trust Building: "Science China" in the Arctic' (2018) 9 Global Policy 23 <https://doi.org/10.1111/1758-5899.12576> accessed 19 September 2022.

Tilastokeskus, 'Energian kokonaiskulutus energialähteittäin (kaikki luokat), 1970-2021' (2022) <https://pxweb2.stat.fi/PxWeb/pxweb/fi/StatFin/StatFin__ehk/statfin_ehk_pxt_12vq.px/>.

Toivanen P and others, 'Finland's Energy System for 2030 as Envisaged by Expert Stakeholders' (2017) 18 Energy Strategy Reviews 150.

Tsukerman VA and Ivanov SV, 'Problems of Reducing Air Pollution from Industrial Enterprises in the Arctic Regions' (2022) 988 IOP Conference Series: Earth and Environmental Science 32006.

Tynkkynen V-P and Tynkkynen N, 'Climate Denial Revisited: (Re)Contextualising Russian Public Discourse on Climate Change during Putin 2.0' (2018) 70 Europe-Asia Studies 1103.

Unger C, Mar KA and Gürtler K, 'A Club's Contribution to Global Climate Governance: The Case of the Climate and Clean Air Coalition' (2020) 6 Palgrave Communications.

Van den Abeele, E, 'Towards a New Paradigm in Open Strategic Autonomy' (ETUI Research Paper 2021.3, 2021) <http://dx.doi.org/10.2139/ssrn.3873798> accessed 2 December 2022.

Wilson Rowe E, 'Climate Science, Russian Politics, and the Framing of Climate Change' (2013) 4 WIREs Climate Change 457 <https://doi.org/10.1002/wcc.235> accessed 19 September 2022.

World Bank, *Global Gas Flaring Tracker Report. Global Gas Flaring Reduction Partnership* (World Bank 2021) <https://thedocs.worldbank.org/en/doc/1f7221545bf1b7c89b850dd85cb409b0-0400072021/original/WB-GGFR-Report-Design-05a.pdf>.

World Bank, *Global Gas Flaring Tracker Report. Global Gas Flaring Reduction Partnership* (World Bank 2022) <2022-Global-Gas-Flaring-Tracker-Report.pdf (worldbank.org)>.

Wubbeke J, 'China's Climate Change Expert Community-Principles, Mechanisms and Influence' (2013) 22 The Journal of Contemporary China 712.

Yakovlev, Igor, Kabir, L. S. & Nikulina, S. I. "Climate policy of Russian Federation: international cooperation and national approach" (2020) ("Klimaticheskaya politika Rossiyskoy Federatsii: mezhdunarodnoe sotrudnitsestvo i natsionalniy podhod."), Financial Journal (Financovyi zhurnal) Vol 12 (4), 26–36 (in Russian). DOI: 10.31107/2075-1990-2020-4-26-36.

Yamineva Y and Liu Z, 'Cleaning the Air, Protecting the Climate: Policy, Legal and Institutional Nexus to Reduce Black Carbon Emissions in China' (2019) 95 Environmental Science & Policy 1.

Yamineva Y and Romppanen S, 'Is Law Failing to Address Air Pollution? Reflections on International and EU Developments' (2017) 26 Review of European Community & International Environmental Law 189.

PART 2

Case Studies of SLCP Mitigation

CHAPTER 9

Regulating Emissions from Cookstoves

Global and National Approaches

Tuula Honkonen and Alice Karanja

1 Introduction

Household cookstoves are used for cooking and heating on a large scale in many parts of the world. It has been estimated that around 2.6 billion people (36 per cent of the total global population) rely on traditional cookstoves.[1] These cookstoves usually burn biomass, such as animal dung, wood and crop waste, or use fossil fuels such as coal or natural gas.[2] As a result, many types of emissions, including SLCPs such as black carbon, are produced.

The air pollution that results from cookstove emissions gives rise to serious and wide-ranging human health risks and costs.[3] In addition, reliance on cookstoves has diverse and large-scale negative social impacts on households and individuals.[4] Burning of solid fuels in combustion-inefficient traditional stoves

1 International Energy Agency (IEA), 'Energy Access Outlook 2017: From Poverty to Prosperity' (IEA 2017) 58 <https://iea.blob.core.windows.net/assets/9a67c2fc-b605-4994-8eb5-29a0ac219499/WEO2017SpecialReport_EnergyAccessOutlook.pdf> accessed 10 August 2022; World Health Organization (WHO), 'Air Pollution Data Portal: Household Air Pollution Data' <www.who.int/data/gho/data/themes/air-pollution/household-air-pollution> accessed 10 August 2022.

2 WHO, 'Household Air Pollution and Health' (WHO Fact sheet 26 July 2022) <www.who.int/news-room/fact-sheets/detail/household-air-pollution-and-health> accessed 11 August 2022.

3 The WHO has estimated that more than three million premature deaths are annually attributable to household air pollution. WHO (n 2). Consequently, it has been estimated that household air pollution is perhaps the most overlooked, widespread health risk of our time. WHO, *Burning Opportunity: Clean Household Energy for Health, Sustainable Development, and Wellbeing of Women and Children* (WHO 2016) <https://apps.who.int/iris/bitstream/handle/10665/204717/9789241565233_eng.pdf?sequence=1&isAllowed=y> accessed 11 August 2022.

4 See, generally, e.g., Venkata Ramana Putti and others, 'The State of the Global Clean and Improved Cooking Sector' (The International Bank for Reconstruction And Development 2015) 34–38 <https://openknowledge.worldbank.org/bitstream/handle/10986/21878/96499.pdf?sequence=1&isAllowed=y> accessed 11 August 2022. Women and children are disproportionately affected by cookstove emissions. See, eg, WHO (n 3); UNEP, *Air Pollution*

DOI:10.1163/9789004684089_011

always contributes to climate change; yet the impacts on climate and ambient (outdoor) air quality are typically more local in character given the short-lived quality of the SLCPs.[5]

Many of the health, climate and weather benefits of reduced black carbon emissions occur locally, near where mitigation takes place.[6] These facts may significantly add up to the motivation of governments to take action for reducing black carbon emissions, and of households to shift to cleaner cooking.

Overall, there are several technical and regulatory strategies through which cookstove emissions can be reduced. Firstly, people can be instructed to use their existing stoves more effectively and in a cleaner manner (e.g. by avoiding burning moist wood which results in incomplete combustion and more emissions). Second, the stoves and their technologies can be upgraded so that cooking on them produces less emissions. Thirdly, people can switch to using cleaner fuels. The regulation of cookstove emissions has to be multi-objective and versatile in nature, recognizing the diversity of the circumstances of the users of cookstoves, being responsive to the associated risks and promoting the benefits from changing to clean cooking.

This chapter looks at the overall setting of and different options for the regulation of cookstove emissions. The problem of pollution from cookstoves is multidimensional, characterized by linkages between different governance and thematic levels. The chapter maps out relevant regulation and its impacts from international and transnational to national levels with India and Kenya as case study countries. In the analysis part, the authors take stock of the current regulatory experiences and challenges, make recommendations on what aspects should be taken into account when countries desire to tackle the cookstove emissions problem effectively, and identify regulatory avenues for more effective cookstove regulation.

---

in Asia and the Pacific: Science-based Solutions (UNEP 2019) 20 <https://www.ccacoalition.org/resources/air-pollution-asia-and-pacific-science-based-solutions-summary-full-report> accessed 11 August 2022.

5 Forrest G Lacey and others, 'Transient Climate and Ambient Health Impacts due to National Solid Fuel Cookstove Emissions' (2017) 114 *PNAS* 1269 doi:10.1073/pnas.161243011. See also Chapter 1 of this book.

6 Noah Scovronick, *Reducing Global Health Risks Through Mitigation of Short-Lived Climate Pollutants. Scoping Report For Policy-makers* (WHO 2015) 19 <http://apps.who.int/iris/bitstream/10665/189524/1/9789241565080_eng.pdf?ua=1> accessed 11 August 2022.

2 Regulatory Responses

2.1 *Starting Point: Multi-level Regulation*

Regulation of cookstove emissions denotes both legal and non-legal means of controlling and influencing behavior and activities that result in emissions from the use of cookstoves. The concept also covers other actors than state as relevant in creating the behavioral changes. The regulation of cookstove emissions is essentially multilevel in nature. The international level sets the relevant legal and policy framework, mainly in terms of global climate change governance, but entrenching to broader human health and sustainable development objectives and policies. Transnational level of regulation has become increasingly significant in the cookstove sector, comprising regulation that is being produced rather than merely applied in a transnational setting, with the involvement of actors that are not state authorities. National level remains, arguably, the most important one in ensuring effective control of cookstove emissions; it is in the best position to account for specific domestic circumstances. In the following, the different regulatory levels with their various approaches and instruments to tackle cookstove emissions will be discussed. Particular attention will be paid to India and Kenya as case study countries in this respect.

2.2 *International Level*

International agreements on air pollution or climate change do not mention cookstove emissions. There are international agreements that address e.g. particle pollution (most notably the Gothenburg Protocol to the Convention on Long-Range Transboundary Air Pollution (see Chapter 5),[7] but they remain rather ineffective in this specific task, especially at the global level.[8]

In the context of global climate change governance, some countries have included SLCPs or black carbon in their nationally determined contributions (NDCs), in which Parties to the Paris Agreement[9] specify their emissions reduction commitments (see Chapter 3).[10] Interestingly, at least 11 Parties

7 Convention on Long-Range Transboundary Air Pollution (adopted 13 November 1979, entered into force 16 March 1983) 18 ILM 1442.

8 Yulia Yamineva and Seita Romppanen: 'Is Law Failing to Address Air Pollution? Reflections on International and EU Developments' (2017) 26 RECIEL 189, doi:10.1111/reel.12223.

9 Paris Agreement to the United Nations Framework Convention on Climate Change (adopted 12 December 2015, entered into force 4 November 2016) 55 ILM 740.

10 At least Chile, Mexico, Columbia and Nigeria have included black carbon in their NDCs.

have specifically included cookstove emissions in their (intended) NDC documents.[11] In many cases, the NDC commitments in relation to cookstoves are mainly justified by lowering the demand for firewood and thereby curbing deforestation, although also the potential for direct greenhouse gas emissions reductions and health benefits is mentioned.

The clean development mechanism (CDM) under the Kyoto Protocol[12] has provided a financing mechanism for cookstove projects in developing countries. The projects generated carbon credits as a result of, for instance, a switch to a cleaner cooking fuel. The long-term sustainability of CDM projects in the cookstove sector has, however, been questioned.[13] Furthermore, the CDM is largely history now with the role of the Kyoto Protocol winding down. In addition to official carbon-offsetting projects under the UNFCCC, clean cooking is being promoted through other types of international financial initiatives, ranging from official development aid to privately funded and commercial projects.

From a broader perspective, the Sustainable Development Goals (SDGs) form a general global framework for action towards limiting air pollution. Reduction of cookstove emissions is inherently linked to the SDG 7 ('Access to clean & affordable energy to everyone by 2030') and Goal 3 ('Ensure health and well-being for all'). Also, Goal 5 ('Achieve gender equality and empower all women and girls') is relevant. If done properly, and sustainably, the introduction of clean cooking technology can drive progress and deliver impact towards implementation of multiple SDGs.[14]

---

11 These countries include Benin (2018), Burkina Faso (2016), Cabo Verde (2021), Lao (2021), Lesotho (2017), Liberia (2021), Mongolia (2016), Morocco (2016), Myanmar (2021), Rwanda (1995) and Uganda (2015).

12 Kyoto Protocol to the United Nations Framework Convention on Climate Change (adopted 11 December 1997, entered into force 16 February 2005) 37 ILM 22.

13 This is the generic risk of project-based clean cooking initiatives, especially if they are not genuinely nationally-driven. See, e.g., Olivia E Freeman and Hisham Zerriffi, 'Carbon Credits for Cookstoves: Trade-offs in Climate and Health Benefits' (2012) 88 The Forestry Chronicle 600 doi:10.5558/tfc2012–112; Luke Sanford and Jennifer Burney, 'Cookstoves Illustrate the Need for a Comprehensive Carbon Market' (2015) 10 Environmental Research Letters 084026, doi:10.1088/1748-9326/10/8/084026.

14 Joshua Rosenthal and others, 'Clean Cooking and the SDGs: Integrated Analytical Approaches to Guide Energy Interventions for Health and Environment Goals' (2018) 42 Energy for Sustainable Development 152, doi:10.1016/j.esd.2017.11.003; Global Alliance for Clean Cookstoves, 'Delivering on the SDGs through Clean Cooking' <https://sustainabledevelopment.un.org/content/documents/11416Global%20Alliance%20for%20Clean%20Cookstoves%20-%20Delivering%20on%20the%20SDGs%20through%20Clean%20Cooking.pdf> accessed 12 August 2022.

The World Health Organization (WHO) represents another kind of global interests and policy authority that touches upon the regulation of cookstove emissions. The WHO has set and regularly updates Global Air Quality Guidelines which concern, inter alia, particulate matter.[15] The Guidelines set an authoritative basis for national air pollution policies and targets all over the world. In addition, the WHO has for years been concerned with household air pollution. The Organization has published reports on clean household energy[16] and on the possible ways to regulate cookstove emissions.[17] The WHO has also issued specific Guidelines for Indoor Air Quality, targeting household fuel combustion, in particular.[18] The Guidelines provide recommendations on the types of cleaner household fuels and technologies that protect health, and effective strategies for their dissemination and adoption.

2.3 *Transnational Level*

Transnational environmental law and governance networks represent an additional layer of policy-making that goes "beyond the state". The rise of transnational environmental law in recent years reflects the broadened sphere of actors and the multiplied levels of governance that nowadays participate or are involved in the efforts to tackle severe environmental problems. The main actors in transnational environmental law are private entities and/or sub-national governments, rather than states or inter-state organizations – which are sometimes also involved. The actors operate across country borders.[19] Transnational environmental law networks may be perceived as self-standing efforts to respond to a state's failure to regulate[20] or more subtly as

---

15 'WHO Global Air Quality Guidelines. Particulate matter ($PM_{2.5}$ and PM_{10}), ozone, nitrogen dioxide, sulfur dioxide and carbon monoxide' (2021) <https://apps.who.int/iris/bitstream/handle/10665/345329/9789240034228-eng.pdf?sequence=1&isAllowed=y> accessed 12 August 2022. The current guideline for the maximum average annual $PM_{2.5}$ concentration is set at 5 µg/m³.

16 See, e.g., WHO, 'Clean Household Energy Solutions Toolkit (CHEST)' <https://www.who.int/tools/clean-household-energy-solutions-toolkit> accessed 12 August 2022.

17 See, e.g., WHO, *Setting National Voluntary Performance Targets for Cookstoves'* (WHO 2021).

18 WHO, *Indoor Air Quality Guidelines: Household Fuel Combustion* (WHO 2014).

19 Kenneth W Abbott, 'Strengthening the Transnational Regime Complex for Climate Change' (2014) 3(1) *Transnational Environmental Law* 57, 60, doi:10.1017/S2047102513000502. See also Gregory Shaffer, 'Transnational Legal Ordering and State Change' in Gregory Shaffer (ed), *Transnational Legal Ordering and State Change* (CUP 2013) 4.

20 Veerle Heyvaert, *Transnational Environmental Regulation and Governance: Purpose, Strategies and Principles* (CUP 2019) 70–71.

complements to the regulation by states and the intergovernmental system.[21] In practice, transnational environmental law networks provide platforms for exchange of best practices and experiences in policymaking and implementation as well as offer guidance and capacity-building for their members.[22]

Several large transnational environmental networks address air pollution and recognize, or even directly deal with, cookstove emissions. The Climate and Clean Air Coalition (CCAC) is a voluntary partnership of governments, intergovernmental organizations, businesses, scientific institutions and civil society organizations which focuses on climate protection and air quality improvement through actions that reduce SLCPs (see Chapter 6). The actions include, inter alia, project funding, policy and planning support, scientific advice and awareness raising. CCAC has a specific Household Energy Initiative which focuses on reducing SLCPs from traditional cookstoves, among other things. In concrete terms, the Initiative works to strengthen awareness, and to mobilize financial aid and support for new technologies, fuels and standards on clean cooking.[23]

Targeting cookstove technologies is a potentially effective way to promote and regulate cleaner cooking solutions. The cookstove industry is active in developing new types of stoves.[24] The Clean Cooking Alliance (CCA) is a partnership organization, involving partners and donors representing government agencies, corporations, researchers, advocacy groups, and investors, that focuses on making clean cooking globally accessible. According to its stated approach, the Alliance seeks to foster clean cooking solutions and create demand and supply for improved stoves and cooking practices. Furthermore, it mobilizes investment and supports policies that boost the clean cooking sector. The CCA has set itself a strategy based on the goal of achieving universal

---

21 Liliana B Andonova, Thomas N Hale and Charles B Roger, 'National Policy and Transnational Governance of Climate Change: Substitutes or Complements?' (2017) 61 *International Studies Quarterly* 253, doi:10.1093/isq/sqx014.

22 See, e.g., Harriet Bulkeley and Michele M Merrill, *Cities and Climate Change: Urban Sustainability and Global Environmental Governance* (Routledge, 2003); Taedong Lee, 'Global Cities and Transnational Climate Change Networks' (2013) 13 *Global Environmental Politics* 1, 108 doi:10.1162/GLEP_a_00156; Kaveh Rashidi and Anthony Patt, 'Subsistence over Symbolism: the Role of Transnational Municipal Networks on Cities' Climate Policy Innovation and Adoption' (2018) 23 *Mitigation and Adaptation Strategies for Global Change* 507, doi:10.1007/s11027-017-9747-y.

23 See CCAC, 'Household Energy' <www.ccacoalition.org/en/initiatives/household-energy> accessed 12 August 2022.

24 See, e.g., CCA, '2022 Clean Cooking Industry Snapshot' (3rd edn, 2022) <https://cleancooking.org/wp-content/uploads/2022/05/CCA-2022-Clean-Cooking-Industry-Snapshot.pdf> accessed 12 August 2022. See also Putti and others (n 4).

access to clean cooking by 2030.[25] The CCA does not engage in standard creation or direct transnational regulatory measures for the cookstove sector.

Another relevant transnational initiative is the Sustainable Energy for All (SEforALL). It is an international organization that works in partnership with the UN and governments, the private sector, financial institutions, civil society and philanthropies with the aim to ensure a sustainable clean energy transition. The initiative has a specific Clean Cooking access programme that focuses on expanding access to clean cooking solutions. According to its website, the programme seeks to advance its agenda mainly by advocating for governments and partners to raise ambition and prioritize access to clean cooking, and by providing reliable data to support investment and decision-making in the sector.[26]

There have also been concerted international efforts to create global standards for cleaner burning cookstoves. The relevant International Organization for Standardization (ISO) standards are the most prominent example in this field. The ISO test protocols,[27] released in 2018, provide a method to compare stove performance. They have established improved quality and comparability for data on cookstove air pollutant emissions, effciency, safety, and durability.[28] Laboratory testing naturally needs to be complemented by field data and information on local circumstances and user preferences. Nevertheless, the ISO standards provide a mechanism for uniform measurement of the effects of different cookstoves – on which basis regulation can be established across countries.

Clean cooking is an issue where national and even local circumstances and practices play a large role. Nevertheless, a transnational setting for exchange of information, experiences and best practices, on one hand, and the possible development of joint regulatory initiatives, on the other hand, certainly entail added value for the network members.

2.4 *National Level*

Cookstove emissions mostly originate in households that are subject to national legislation and policies. The legal and policy setting naturally varies

25 CCA, 'Our Approach' <https://cleancooking.org/our-approach/> accessed 12 August 2022.

26 SEforALL, 'Clean Cooking' <https://www.seforall.org/clean-cooking> accessed 14 February 2023.

27 ISO 19867–1, 'Harmonized laboratory test protocols' (2018).

28 Wyatt M Champion and others, 'Cookstove Emissions and Performance Evaluation Using a New ISO Protocol and Comparison of Results with Previous Test Protocols' (2021) 55 Environ. Sci. Technol. 15333 doi:10.1021/acs.est.1c03390.

from country to country, depending on many factors. There are both top-down and bottom-up approaches, and both public and private governance initiatives. What is common to national regulatory frameworks and specific policy instruments on cookstoves is that they need to be responsive to specific national circumstances. In the following, two case study countries will be examined in more detail.

2.4.1 Case of India[29]

India has traditionally been situated near the bottom of the global rankings on country populations that have access to clean cooking.[30] However, recent years have seen positive developments: in the period 2010–2019, India reduced the percentage of its population that is exposed to household air pollution from 73% to 61%.[31] Nevertheless, the number of Indians relying on polluting stoves for their cooking and heating needs is still remarkable. This results in around 500.000 deaths every year due to indoor air pollution.[32]

Numerous initiatives have been taken at the national level over the years to promote cleaner stoves and cooking habits. These have involved legislation, air quality standards and programs, clean cookstove initiatives, health policy instruments, subsidy policies, and clean cooking campaigns. India has tested a broad selection of regulatory approaches and concrete regulatory instruments to address the problem of cookstove emissions. Experience has been gained from different levels of action and from both public and private governance initiatives.

The relevant national legislation starts from the Constitution of India[33] which expresses the state commitment to protect and improve the environment.[34] Article 21 of the Constitution, which concerns the fundamental right to the protection of life and personal liberty, has been interpreted by the

---

29 For a more detailed account of the Indian legislative and policy framework on reducing cookstove emissions, see Tuula Honkonen, 'Tackling Cookstove Emissions in India: Towards an Enabling Policy Environment and More Effective Legal Solutions' (2020) 16 lead 195, 200 doi:10.25501/SOAS.00033485.

30 Health Effects Institute (HEI), 'State of Global Air 2020. Special Report' (HEI 2021) 12 <https://www.stateofglobalair.org/sites/default/files/documents/2020-10/soga-2020-report-10-26_0.pdf> accessed 12 August 2022.

31 ibid 13.

32 India State-Level Disease Burden Initiative Air Pollution Collaborators, 'Health and Economic Impact of Air Pollution in the States of India: the Global Burden of Disease Study 2019' (2021) 5(1) The Lancet Planetary Health e25, e29 doi:10.1016/S2542-5196(20)30298-9.

33 The Constitution of India, 26 November 1949, as amended.

34 Art. 48A.

Supreme Court of India as to include 'the right of enjoyment of pollution-free water and air for full enjoyment of life'.[35] The main piece of the relevant Indian sectoral legislation, the Air (Prevention and Control of Pollution) Act[36] generally provides for the prevention, control and abatement of air pollution in the country. However, the Act does not address household air pollution and thereby not cookstove emissions either. The same concerns the Indian National Ambient Air Quality Standards and the accompanying National Air Monitoring Programme. The National Clean Air Programme, launched in 2019, includes a time-bound target for particulate matter reduction, but focuses on ambient air pollution, leaving indoor air pollution without much attention. In the same vein, cookstove emissions are not addressed in the Indian climate change policy documents.

National programmes on cookstoves have been the main policy instrument through which India has sought to reduce cookstove emissions. Several government-led programmes have been implemented over the years.[37] Some of them have had a more technical approach by focusing on promoting or even installing improved cookstoves for households while others have taken the energy question as their starting point and sought to facilitate the adoption of alternative and cleaner fuels for stoves.[38] In terms of regulatory instruments, the programmes relied on direct distribution of improved cookstoves to the end-users with the help of NGOs, government subsidies or market mechanisms.[39] Awareness-raising campaigns have also been used in India to educate people on the risks of household air pollution. What has been common to the different cookstove programmes is that they have rarely led to lasting changes in the use of cookstoves at the household level,[40] except for, to some extent,

35 Subhash Kumar v. State of Bihar (1991) AIR 420, 1991 SCR (1) 5.

36 The Air (Prevention and Control of Pollution) Act, No. 14 of 1981.

37 These include the National Program on Improved Cookstoves, implemented from 1980s to early 2000s; the National Biomass Cookstoves Initiative, operational from 2009; the Unnat Chulha Abhiyan Programme active in 2012–2017; the Pradhan Mantri Ujjwala Yojana initiative, launched in 2016; and the National Biogas and Manure Management Programme, operational since 2018.

38 See, e.g., Nimrata Chindarkar, Abhishek Jain and Sunil Mani, 'Examining the Willingness-to-pay for Exclusive Use of LPG for Cooking among Rural Households in India' (2021) 150 Energy Policy 112107, doi:10.1016/j.enpol.2020.112107.

39 See, e.g., Meena Khandelwal and others, 'Why Have Improved Cook-Stove Initiatives in India Failed?' (2017) 92 World Development 13, doi:10.1016/j.worlddev.2016.11.006.

40 RD Hanbar and Priyadarshini Karve, 'National Programme on Improved Chulha NPIC) of the Government of India: an Overview' (2002) 6 Energy for Sustainable Development 49, doi:10.1016/S0973-0826(08)60313-0; Bhaskar Sinha, 'The Indian Stove Programme: an Insider's View – the Role of Society, Politics, Economics and Education' (2002) 48 Boiling Point 23; Khandelwal and others (n 39) 19.

programmes focused on cleaner fuels. The main reasons for the regulatory failure have been both poorly-designed programmes (bureaucratic nature, poor performance of improved cookstoves, non-durability, and lacking repair services) and hard-to-change priorities of cookstove users (in other words, the improved cookstoves not meeting the needs).[41]

Subsidies have been a rather broadly used regulatory instrument to promote cleaner cooking in India.[42] Subsidization has mainly been directed at energy and the fuel that cookstoves use. Residential liquefied petroleum gas (LPG) subsidy programs have significantly lowered the cost of a cleaner fuel used for cooking and heating.[43] The subsidies have been directed at low-income households because they often cannot afford other than firewood or polluting biomass to fuel their stoves.[44] According to estimates, the subsidy policies make sense also economically since the substantial improvements in human health outcomes may significantly exceed the subsidy costs.[45] In terms of their effectiveness in incentivizing people to switch to using LPG to fuel their cookstoves, the subsidy programs have achieved encouraging results in recent years.[46] However, the continuation of the good development is uncertain since the Indian government removed the subsidy for LPG in 2020. This was done because the difference in the price of subsidized and non-subsidized cooking gas had diminished to near zero due to the dramatic decline in global oil prices.[47] However, the price of energy has since reached the previous level and

41 Sinha (n 40).

42 For a summary, see, e.g., WHO, *Opportunities for transition to clean household energy: application of the Household Energy Assessment Rapid Tool (HEART) in India* (WHO 2018) <https://apps.who.int/iris/bitstream/handle/10665/274280/9789241513999-eng.pdf?sequence=1&isAllowed=y>19–20> accessed 12 August 2022.

43 See, e.g., Neeraj Mittal and others, 'Fuel Subsidy Reform in Developing Countries: Direct Benefit Transfer of LPG Cooking Gas Subsidy in India' (Center for Global Development policy paper 114,2017) <www.cgdev.org/sites/default/files/fuel-subsidy-reform-developing-countries-india.pdf> accessed 12 August 2022; Chindarkar and others (n 38).

44 See, e.g., Mittal (n 43) 3.

45 Santosh Harish, 'Renewing India's Air Quality Management Strategy in the shadow of COVID-19' (Centre for Policy Research 2021) 18 <https://cprindia.org/wp-content/uploads/2021/12/AQ-Framing-Paper_270921.pdf> accessed 12 August 2022.

46 See, e.g., S Arun and Ibrahim H Rehman, 'Can Subsidies be a Tool for Strengthening the Improved Cookstoves Market?' (The Energy and Resources Institute (TERI) 2015) <www.teriin.org/policybrief/files/SUBSIDIES_spread/files/downloads/SUBSIDIES_spread.pdf> accessed 12 August 2022.

47 See, e.g., Shruti Sharma and others, 'How to Target LPG Subsidies in India: Step 2. Evaluating Policy Options in Jharkhand' (International Institute for Sustainable Development (IISD) 2021) <www.iisd.org/system/files/2021-04/target-lpg-subsidies-india-jharkhand.pdf> accessed 12 August 2022.

even higher, and thus the need to re-introduce the subsidy program seems necessary again.

India seeks to benefit from transnational networks in its efforts to strengthen the national clean cooking policy. Importantly in this respect, India joined the CCAC in 2019. Upon joining, the Indian government stated that India will work under the CCAC to 'adopt cleaner energy sustainable production and consumption patterns'.[48] India also expressed a commitment to work on best practices and experiences for the effective implementation of the country's National Clean Air Programme with the help of the partnership platform provided by the CCAC.[49] As an example of tangible national action facilitated by the CCAC, India has since 2019 been engaged in a project that aims at developing integrated climate, air pollution and SLCP strategies that would be aligned with political priorities at different scales in the country. In concrete terms, the project seeks to identify the benefits that India can reap from integrated air pollution and climate strategies, which will be used as a vehicle to engage with key decision makers and the private sector. The project addresses one of the main challenges of Indian clean air policies: the fact that the current strategies to mitigate air pollution and climate change are being developed and implemented in silos.[50]

2.4.2 Case of Kenya

In Sub-Saharan Africa, Kenya prides itself as one of the leading countries in the development and commercialization of clean cookstoves, dating from the 1900s.[51] Despite this promising history, 84% of Kenyans (equivalent to 8.1 million households) rely on traditional biomass energy as their primary source of cooking fuel.[52] According to the WHO estimates of 2019, long-term exposure to indoor household air pollution from burning of solid fuels was responsible for

48 UN Environment, 'India Joins the Climate and Clean Air Coalition' (press release, 5 July 2019) <www.unenvironment.org/news-and-stories/press-release/india-joins-climate-and-clean-air-coalition> accessed 12 August 2022.

49 ibid.

50 See CCAC, 'Identifying short-lived climate pollutant mitigation opportunities in India' <www.ccacoalition.org/en/activity/identifying-short-lived-climate-pollutant-mitigation-opportunities-india> accessed 12 August 2022.

51 Karanja, Alice and Alexandros Gasparatos, 'Adoption and impacts of Clean Bioenergy Cookstoves in Kenya' (2019) 102 Renewable and Sustainable Energy Reviews 285, doi:10.1016/j.rser.2018.12.006.

52 Chapter 2 of IEA and others, 'Tracking SDG 7: The Energy Progress Report' (World Bank, 2022) <https://trackingsdg7.esmap.org/data/files/download-documents/sdg7-report2022-ch2-access_to_clean_cooking.pdf> accessed 22 September 2022.

19,000 deaths for children under-5 years each year in Kenya from acute respiratory infections.[53]

The Government of Kenya has an ambitious plan to end this trend by 2028. The country has been taking on a leading role championing for the clean cooking agenda at global high-level political forums, including the Health and Energy Platform for Action and under the UNFCCC.[54]

Kenya has a long history of energy planning and enabling governance ecosystem featuring ambitious targets, dedicated policies and regulations, tailored delivery models, financing for consumers and businesses, technology innovation, capacity building and promotional efforts for increased adoption of efficient and clean cooking technologies. Promulgated in 2010, the Constitution of Kenya[55] and country's Vision 2030[56] contemplate the recognition of rights to a clean and healthy environment through legislative and other measures.

The Ministry of Energy has demonstrated commitment to the cookstoves sector through various strategies and plans including the Sessional Paper No 4 of 2004,[57] Energy Policy, 2018,[58] and the Energy Act, 2019[59] which promote the development and efficiency of renewable energy technologies including biogas, bioethanol and improved biomass stoves. The Kenya Off-Grid Solar Access Project, a flagship project by the Ministry of Energy, was established to deliver higher-tier clean cooking solutions to 150,000 households in the remote, low density, and traditionally underserved areas of the country by 2023.[60] Biogas installations have also been made through various initiatives, including the Kenya Biogas Programme which was started to commercially promote the uptake of biogas at the household level. Since the start of the programme in 2009, over 18,000 bio-digesters have been built across Kenya, of which 88%

---

53 HEI (n 30).

54 See Modern Energy Cooking Services, 'Side event on scaling clean cooking in the SDG7 Pavilion at COP26' <https://mecs.org.uk/join-our-side-event-on-scaling-clean-cooking-in-the-sdg7-pavilion-at-cop26/> accessed 22 September 2022.

55 Constitution of Kenya (2010), section 42.

56 Government of Kenya (GoK), 'Kenya Vision 2030' (2007) <http://www.vision2030.go.ke/about-vision-2030/> accessed 14 February 2023.

57 GoK Ministry of Energy, 'Sessional Paper No. 4 of 2004 on Energy' (2004) <https://repository.kippra.or.ke/handle/123456789/1371> accessed 22 September 2022.

58 GoK Ministry of Energy, 'National Energy Policy 2018' (2018) <https://repository.kippra.or.ke/handle/123456789/1947> accessed 22 September 2022.

59 The Energy Act No.1 of 2019.

60 See GoK Ministry of Energy, 'Kenya Off-Grid Solar Access Project' <https://www.kosap-fm.or.ke/> accessed 14 February 2023.

were still operational in 2020.[61] However, affordability is the main barrier to the uptake of biogas systems in Kenya.

Guided by the Africa SEforAll Hub guidelines for developing national action agendas on energy sector development,[62] the Kenyan Ministry of Energy initiated the development of the Action Agenda and Investment Prospectus[63] in 2014, presenting an energy sector-wide long-term vision spanning the period 2015 to 2030. The Kenya Action Plan outlines Kenya's commitment strategy towards 100% universal access to clean cooking by 2030. The Plan further proposed the establishment of a national cookstoves testing and knowledge center to determine which cookstoves meet international standards set by the ISO for emissions and fuel efficiency, and dissemination of the information through labeling and consumer education.[64] The proposed test center had not yet been established at the time of writing this chapter, and the Kenya Industrial Research and Development Institute, operating under the Ministry of Industrialization and Enterprise Development, has been running the only cookstoves test lab in Kenya with emissions testing capacity. Further, along with partner organizations, the Ministry of Energy has developed standards for biomass and charcoal stoves (focused on efficiency, $PM_{2.5}$ and carbon oxide emissions, durability and safety) that need to be enforced.[65] However, the enforcement of these regulations has been minimal due to a lack of quality air monitoring data, to compare with the standards.

Kenya's National Environmental Management Agency formulated Environmental Management and Coordination (Air Quality) Regulations[66] in 2014 to provide for the prevention, control and abatement of air pollution. These set out the maximum permissible concentrations of different widespread pollutants for residential and industrial areas, but exempts observance

61 See Kenya Biogas Programme <https://kenyabiogas.com/about/> and Gold Standard, 'Kenya Biogas Programme' <https://marketplace.goldstandard.org/products/kenya-biogas-programme> both accessed 22 September 2022.

62 See SEforALL, 'Kenya Action Agenda' (2016) <https://www.seforall.org/sites/default/files/Kenya_AA_EN_Released.pdf> accessed 22 September 2022.

63 GoK Ministry of Energy and Petroleum and SEforAll, 'Kenya's SE4All Action Agenda and the Investment Prospectus Pathways for Concerted Action toward Sustainable Energy for All by 2030' (2015) <https://www.se4all-africa.org/fileadmin/uploads/se4all/Documents/Country_AAs/Kenya_SE4ALL_AA_January_2016.pdf> accessed 22 September 2022.

64 Global Alliance for Clean Cookstoves, 'Kenya Country Action Plan (KCAP)' (2013) <https://cleancooking.org/wp-content/uploads/2021/07/236-1.pdf> accessed 22 September 2022.

65 Standards affecting cooking at the national level include KS 1814–2018 for biomass stoves, KS 2759 – 2018 for ethanol fuel cooking appliances and KS 2520 – 2014 for domestic biogas stoves specification.

66 The Environmental management and coordination (Air Quality) Regulations (2014).

for residential wood burning stoves and wood burning fireplaces. The National Environmental policy of 2013 recognized domestic cooking activities to be among specific deficiencies with respect to the air quality monitoring system in the country.[67] It was further recognized that the majority of the Kenyan households use kerosene and biomass-based fuel (charcoal and firewood) for domestic cooking, which leads to substantial indoor exposure to air pollution. In recognition of health complications associated with indoor air pollution, the legislation made a policy statement that the Government would promote adoption of non-polluting cookstoves and construction of well-ventilated houses.

There have been instances of using economic disincentives or reversing subsidies to reduce the consumption of conventional cooking fuels and promote clean cooking options in Kenya. In 2016, the government reduced import duties for clean cookstoves from 25% to 10%. The budget proposal also enforced a zero value-added tax (VAT) on clean cookstoves, raw materials, and their accessories in an effort to make the cooking technologies more affordable. At the same time, the government increased the kerosene levy to disincentive its use and zero-rated VAT on LPG. In 2021, the government re-introduced the 16% standard rate of VAT on LPG which was scrapped off in 2016. The imposed VAT led to an increase in LPG market prices by 15%, making the commodity unaffordable for many Kenyans and consequently threatening a reversal of the gains made in terms of cookstove emissions and health benefits. In the 2022–2023 financial budget, the Ministry of Finance included a plan to fund the supply of 300,000 LPG cylinders to low-income households over the next three years. This is, however, only a small percentage of the target of three million that was initially outlined.

The wider policies on climate change and energy are a central part of the efforts to reduce cookstove emissions. Kenya enacted a Climate Change Act[68] in 2016 that requires the government to develop five-year National Climate Change Action Plans to guide the mainstreaming of adaptation and mitigation actions into sector functions of the national and county governments. The current National Climate Change Action Plan (2018–2022) presents a framework for Kenya to deliver on its National Adaptation Plan 2015–2030 and its NDC under the Paris Agreement. The National Climate Change Action Plan guides the country to achieve a low-carbon development pathway, including through

67 GoK Ministry of Environment, Water and Natural Resources, 'Kenya National Environment Policy, 2013' (2013) <http://www.environment.go.ke/wp-content/uploads/2014/01/NATIONAL-ENVIRONMENT-POLICY-20131.pdf> accessed 22 September 2022.

68 The Climate Change Act No. 11 of 2016.

the uptake of LPG, ethanol and other clean fuels in urban areas and improved biomass (charcoal and wood) cookstoves in rural areas.[69]

Beyond laws, policies and regulations, Kenya witnesses a growing number of public and private sector initiatives that aim at promoting clean cooking. For instance, the Clean Cooking Association of Kenya[70] has been at the forefront to catalyze the growth of the clean cooking sector and to promote adoption of clean cooking technologies through capacity building, sector coordination, awareness campaigns and behavior change communication. In 2013, a miscellaneous provision related to Improved Biomass Cookstoves was added into Energy Act No 12 of 2006[71] through the intervention of the Association. These regulations apply to (a) licensing of manufacturers, importers, distributors, technicians, and contractors of Improved Biomass Cookstoves, and institutions using biomass fuels for cooking and heating; (b) providing a warranty to customers; and (c) disposing of stoves following other national environmental laws.

In addition, Kenya joined the CCAC in 2014 with a commitment to implement mitigation activities to reduce SLCPs for improved public health and sustainable development. Launched in 2021, the Ministry of Environment and Forestry has been working, in collaboration with the CCAC's Supporting National Planning Initiative, to undertake a national planning process on SLCPs and implement the resulting mitigation measures.[72]

2.4.3 Observations from the Case Studies[73]

2.4.3.1 *Choice of Regulatory Approaches and Instruments*

Cookstove regulation is characterized by reliance on a variety of different types of regulatory approaches and instruments. This has largely been the

---

69 GoK Ministry of Environment and Forestry, 'National Climate Change Action Plan 2018–2022' (2018) <http://www.environment.go.ke/wp-content/uploads/2020/03/NCCAP_2018-2022_ExecutiveSummary-Compressed-1.pdf> accessed 14 February 2023.

70 See Clean Cooking Association of Kenya <https://ccak.or.ke/> accessed 14 February 2023.

71 GoK, 'The Draft Energy (Improved Biomass Cookstoves) Regulations, 2015' made from Energy Act No.1 2 of 2006 <https://www.epra.go.ke/wp-content/uploads/2018/12/The-Draft-Energy-Improved-Biomass-Cook-stoves-Regulations-2015.pdf> accessed 22 September 2022.

72 CCAC, 'Kenya – National planning on short-lived climate pollutants' <http://www.ccacoalition.org/en/activity/kenya-national-planning-short-lived-climate-pollutants> accessed 12 August 2022. The national planning action does not explicitly target clean cooking.

73 On the weaknesses of Indian cookstove regulation, see also Honkonen (n 29). Generally on the implementation challenges of Indian air pollution legislation, see Harish (n 45). On the Kenyan case, see, e.g. Alice Karanja and Alexandros Gasparatos, 'Adoption and impacts of clean bioenergy cookstoves in Kenya' (2018) Renewable and Sustainable

picture in India. Direct legal regulation targeting household air pollution from cookstoves has been scarce; the regulation has been carried out through fixed-period programmes and campaigns, subsidy policies and more general air quality standards and programs. Diversity in approaches and instruments is not necessarily a downside, provided that the different instruments are introduced and implemented, and their effects evaluated, in a coordinated manner. Unfortunately, this aspect has not been fully accounted for in the Indian case.[74]

In Kenya, clean cooking regulation is characterized by multiple instruments and approaches as well. A marked difference in comparison to India is that national standards for biomass and charcoal stoves have been established at the ministerial level. Even if the enforcement of the standards is currently seriously hindered by lacking monitoring data, they have clear potential as a regulatory instrument to shape the national cookstove market. Cookstove quality standards are also an example of a tangible piece of regulation to address emissions from cookstoves.

In both Kenya and India, most of the relevant legislation and stove emission regulation is characterized by general statements of intent. It is remarkable that Kenya, for instance, has established a clear national goal to strive for: the commitment strategy towards 100% universal access to clean cooking by 2030. There is, however, a real need to develop tangible and implementable measures to realize the ambitions. In addition to programmes and projects, attaining the set goals requires high-quality regulation with a long-term vision – and a clear allocation of resources in the national budget lines.

Both India and Kenya have implemented relatively extensive energy subsidy programmes to promote cleaner cooking. In India, while these subsidies have not achieved their full potential in terms of effective and lasting results, they have had positive impacts. Given that the majority of Indian cookstove users have low incomes, LPG subsidies have supported the market and made improved cookstoves available to a larger part of the population than would otherwise have been the case.[75] In Kenya, the subsidy policy has targeted both cooking energy and stoves entering the market. However, both countries have

Energy Reviews 102 285 doi: 10.1016/j.rser.2018.12.006; New Climate Institute, 'The Kenyan Cooking Sector – Opportunities for Climate Action and Sustainable Development' (2021) <https://ambitiontoaction.net/wp-content/uploads/2021/07/A2A_Kenya_CleanCookingStudy_July2021.pdf> accessed 5 January 2023.

74 See Honkonen (n 29) and the studies listed in n 40.

75 Arun and Rehman (n 46) 1.

abolished their subsidy programmes in recent years, which has led to uncertainties in the energy and stove markets as well as at the household level. For both India and Kenya, direct subsidies linked to micro-finance options or reduction of stove VAT and tax-rebates could help enhance user affordability of clean cooking options and increase the reliability of fuel delivery and availability in rural areas.

2.4.3.2 *A Coordinated and Integrated Approach*

Indian experience in the past clean air policy-making shows that acting in silos does not yield lasting impacts. For instance, the most remarkable Indian clean air policies have so far targeted industries, leaving households in a secondary position.[76] In the same vein, the Indian policy-making related to emissions standards for pollution control have been criticized for largely excluding health impact considerations.[77] However, the 2019 National Clean Air Programme could be considered as a change towards a more comprehensive approach. With a view to clean cooking policies in particular, the Indian experience has so far been relatively sectoral with different ministries (on health, energy and environment, respectively) having largely acted independently, focusing on the particular objective of clean cooking policies that is most relevant to their work.[78] There has been some level of centralized federal government leadership,[79] but institutional coordination and policy integration among different ministries, for instance, has been rather scarce or ad hoc.[80] This has clearly hindered the effectiveness of clean cooking policymaking.

In Kenya, the Ministry of Energy has been the dominant player in initiating regulation on cookstove emissions. However, multiple stakeholders are also involved in the Kenyan clean cooking sector, often having different perspectives, interests and agendas in efforts to promote clean cooking.[81] Awareness raising about the availability and benefits of cleaner-burning cookstoves is a key example of where such a multi-stakeholder approach is

---

76 Honkonen (n 29) 209.

77 ibid 208; Ministry of Health and Family Welfare, 'Report of the Steering Committee on Air Pollution and Health Related Issues' (2015) <https://main.mohfw.gov.in/sites/default/files/5412023661450432724_0.pdf> accessed 12 August 2022.

78 See, e.g., Honkonen (n 29) 208.

79 ibid 207.

80 ibid 208.

81 Alice Karanja, Francis Mburu, and Alexandros Gasparatos, 'A Multi-stakeholder Perception Analysis about the Adoption, Impacts and Priority Areas in the Kenyan Clean Cooking Sector' (2020) Sustainability Science 15 333 doi: 10.1007/s11625-019-00742-4.

needed. For example, in the past years, Kenya has successfully implemented market transformation interventions focused on behavior change such as malaria bed nets and hand-washing campaigns. However, current evidence suggests that many consumers are not aware of the health risks associated with the use of traditional biomass and stoves, and their knowledge about the availability of alternatives is not obvious. Thus, it becomes important to capitalize on the synergies between household cooking energy, health and climate mitigation sectors, including their financing strategies. The creation of an overarching institution or coordinating agency in charge of the cooking sector transition could accelerate and enhance coordination of policies and action plans.

2.4.3.3 *Focus on Implementation*

From a legal perspective, only the implementation of legally binding regulation can be required and backed up by legal enforcement measures if needed. In India, the majority of the regulation relevant for tackling cookstove emissions is soft law. This poses challenges to the effectiveness and possibly also to the credibility of the regulation, a fact that has been evidenced in case of the Indian national air quality standards which are routinely violated.[82] The case might be different, however, if technical standards for cookstoves are introduced. If coupled with market access and cooperation with the industry, implementation would have a good chance of success.

As evidenced by the case of the Kenyan cookstove standards, effective monitoring is key to ensure proper implementation of cookstove regulation. Dead letter standards are, in the end, detrimental to the credibility of the whole branch of regulation. Monitoring of cookstove emissions at the household level is nearly impossible in practice, therefore the regulation does better in targeting the stoves, the fuel they use, and the cooking habits of their users.

2.4.3.4 *Information and Participation*

Information plays a crucial role in effective cookstove emission regulation. Firstly, regulation must be based on correct and up-to-date scientific information on the formation and impacts of emissions from cookstoves, and different stove technologies and fuels. Secondly, the manufacturers and users of

---

82 Ministry of Environment, Forest & Climate Change, 'National Clean Air Programme' (2019) <https://moef.gov.in/wp-content/uploads/2019/05/NCAP_Report.pdf> accessed 12 August 2022.

the stoves must be aware of the associated risks of unclean cooking and of the available and potential options of shifting to cleaner cooking. According to studies made in India, even simple health messaging given at the very local level can have significant positive effects on households' adoption of LPG as their cooking fuel.[83]

Many of the government-led clean cooking programmes carried out in India in the past did not pay particular attention to public participation or finding out user preferences in some other ways.[84] Many people and communities (esp. the rural poor, the illiterate, women) were left in a marginalized position with regard to having their voices heard in the context of clean cooking programmes.[85] The more recent clean cooking policies in India have focused on the promotion of clean cooking energy instead of distribution of improved cookstoves. Consequently, the information needs of the regulator regarding local circumstances and user preferences have been smaller.

The Kenyan case study shows that the effectiveness of cookstove regulation does not only depend on the resources used for developing appropriate legislation and everything related directly to its implementation, but it is crucial that the overall air quality management and monitoring system is sufficient and fully operational. Lacking monitoring data keeps the regulator in darkness with regard to the impacts of the regulation. Civil society organizations play a crucial role in stove innovation for emission reduction in terms of awareness raising, learning, and competence-building.[86] For instance, some stove manufacturers and innovators often fail to involve consumers particularly during stove design. This cultural and user mismatch forces consumers to revert to traditional and polluting cooking methods. Increasingly, it is recognized that involvement and understanding of consumer preferences, constraints and behavior can influence the design of clean cooking products and interventions resonating with local cooking needs and cultures.

83 See, e.g., Martina Zahno and others, 'Health Awareness and the Transition towards Clean Cooking Fuels: Evidence from Rajasthan' (2020) 1584) PLoS ONE e0231931, doi:10.1371/journal.pone.0231931.

84 See, e.g., Sinha (n 40).

85 ibid 26.

86 Benard O Muok and Ann Kingiri, 'The Role of Civil Society Organizations in Low-carbon Innovation in Kenya' (2015) 5 Innovation and Development 207, doi: 10.1080/2157930X.2015.1064558.

3 Discussion and Recommendations

3.1 *The Multitude of Objectives, Actors and Governance Levels*

The regulation of cookstove emissions is, like so many other environmental and social problems, subject to regulation that is inherently multi-objective in nature. This means that the regulation aims at fulfilling more than one regulatory objective. In this case, the objectives can be the reduction of negative human health effects of cookstove emissions, promotion of cleaner and more sustainable energy sources, energy security and affordability, amelioration of the social injustices related to cooking with biomass and other highly polluting fuels, advancement of rural and urban development, and tackling climate change. From this, it follows that the regulator may have to make a choice as to which objective to prioritize. The dominant regulatory objective, then, largely determines the regulatory approach and specific instruments to be used. The regulatory objectives may also vary according to the target group of cookstove regulation (e.g., vulnerable groups of a population, all households in a certain area, households using a specific cooking fuel). Nevertheless, the fact that cookstove regulation usually has multiple objectives places high requirements for their communication to the public, and finding the most appropriate implementation design.[87]

Taking due consideration of the multiple objectives of cookstove policies and regulation is challenging, but it can also yield positive effects at the practical and policymaking levels. Air pollution regulation should not be created or implemented in silos, focusing only on one type of sources, effects, or regulatory approaches. An integrated approach to cookstove regulation would mean that emissions from cookstoves are targeted from multiple directions. Accordingly, the regulation would focus on and explicitly emphasize its relevant impacts on and interactions with air quality, climate, energy, health and social policies. At best, the multi-objectivity would result in multiple benefits being accrued from an effectively implemented clean cooking policy, turning the existence of multiple policy objectives from a hindrance to an advantage.

Interestingly, addressing the issue of cookstove emissions through SDGs and national sustainable development planning bears the potential to simultaneously serve multiple objectives and strengthen inter-linkages between policy fields. The multi-objective nature of cookstove emission regulation makes it a fruitful object of sustainable development planning. In practice, cookstove policies would be then coordinated with and possibly integrated into various

87 Honkonen (n 29) 204.

national sustainable development and energy policy plans. This could potentially help secure longer-term clean cooking policies and also attract additional investments to address the cookstove emissions problem.

The multi-objective nature of the regulation contributes to the fact that cookstove emissions are being governed by a host of different actors at different levels of governance. Polycentric governance is a phenomenon that has received increasing scholarly attention in recent years.[88] The main thrust of the concept is that instead of one monocentric unit, there are multiple governing authorities on different scales, each of which quite independently forms part of the governance system in respect of a given issue.[89] The governance units are from the public, private and voluntary sectors, having overlapping areas of responsibility and functional capacities.

The governance levels vary from international and transnational to national and local. Targets and general guidelines may originate at the international level, but the concrete regulatory instruments and strategies need to be tailored to local circumstances. At the national level, cookstove emissions may belong to the mandate and regulatory repertoire of several ministries and administrative branches, from health authorities to environmental and energy ministries and agencies. Households are the usual regulatees, but it is also possible to target cookstove regulation at the relevant industry, or to allow or encourage the industry and the relevant business sectors to self-regulate.

3.2 *A Long-Term View*

The timeframe for the regulatory measures targeting cookstove emissions does matter from an effectiveness perspective. The regulation may be a one-off measure or programme, or it may have been introduced as a long-term policy with interim and final targets, monitoring of progress and the possibility to make adjustments as needed. Another dimension of the long-term nature of cookstove regulation is that it should lead to lasting impacts. This remains a persistent challenge.

Sometimes transitional measures may be needed to carry households over a challenging period. This applies to circumstances where a rapid adoption of

88 Within the environmental governance context, see, e.g., the seminal work of Elinor Ostrom, 'Polycentric Systems for Coping with Collective Action and Global Environmental Change' (2010) 20 Global Environmental Change 550, doi:10.1016/j.gloenvcha.2010.07.004. See also Daniel H Cole, 'Advantages of a Polycentric Approach to Climate Change Policy' (2015) 5 Nature Climate Change 114 doi:10.1038/nclimate2490; Andrew Jordan and others (eds), *Governing Climate Change: Polycentricity in Action?* (CUP 2018).

89 Ostrom (n 88) 552.

clean fuels and technologies is often not possible, particularly in more rural and poorer areas where affordability and the lack of infrastructure are major obstacles. The switch to clean cooking may be more gradual, and intermediate solutions are thus required. In these cases, transitional fuels and technologies – like low-emission biomass cookstoves that are more energy efficient and substantially reduce emissions, yielding benefits for health, climate, and the environment – should be prioritized.[90]

3.3 *Focus on Energy Policies*

Regulation of cookstove emissions is naturally strongly linked to energy policy. The fuel that stoves use largely determines the type and amount of the resulting emissions (of course, also the stove technology and cooking habits matter). Thus, it is straight-forward to focus on energy, especially as energy questions have broader societal and environmental implications and so addressing them is regarded as important beyond the issue of cookstove regulation. For instance, focus on cleaner cooking energy leads to synergies with and co-benefits for climate change mitigation. This may then lead to additional resources to be allocated to the matter, both nationally and at the international/transnational level.

In examining India and Kenya, it is clearly visible that the countries have adopted a strong focus on regulating cookstove emissions through energy policy, promoting LPG and biogas, in particular. These policies have been, by and large, relatively effective. However, a question could be asked as to whether the focus on the energy aspect of the problem of cookstove emissions has been in detriment of other social (gender, for instance) and economic aspects lying behind the use of cookstoves.

3.4 *Targeting Households*

Cookstoves are mainly used at the household level. That is also where the current focus of the regulation lies at the national level. Whereas the general air pollution regulation and policymaking currently target industry-level pollution, like in India,[91] emissions from cookstoves have proved to be a matter to be regulated at the household level. The challenge is that the diverse

90 In identifying such transitional technologies, policy and programmatic decision-makers should use available evidence of performance (e.g., emissions rates), health risks, safety, and user acceptability to secure the widespread and sustained use of such improved technologies.

91 Honkonen (n 29).

circumstances and user preferences should be accounted for in the regulation. That is the only route to broad social acceptability, which is a major precondition to effective cookstove regulation. Reaching it may require unconventional thinking and broad consultation on the part of the governing actors.[92]

The cookstove manufacturing industry would naturally be a more homogenous group of regulatees compared to households even in a single country. The cookstove industry has invested in the development of cleaner stove technologies, albeit largely in the absence of long-term and binding regulation to that effect. Then again, effectively targeting the industry with clean cooking regulation would likely require transnational efforts.

3.5 *Transnational Initiatives*

Reduction of cooking emissions has traditionally been seen as a matter for nation states to take care of. Increasingly, however, the cross-border potential of the regulatory solutions has become visible. Even if the national circumstances and cooking habits vary from country to country, common regulatory elements and strategies can be identified and exchanged among countries and sub-national governments through jointly established platforms and networks. This is already common especially in the field of climate change regulation where a large number of transnational governance networks operate.[93]

The CCA is currently the only larger transnational network that solely focuses on clean cooking. It is a visible actor in the field with the mission to develop a sustainable cooking industry. The CCAC is more engaged with nation states, but clean cooking is only a rather small element of its work. It appears that there is a need for a specific transnational initiative or network specifically focusing on tackling cookstove emissions – with a clear regulatory emphasis in its activities. Unlike CCA, such an initiative could engage interested national and sub-national authorities, complemented with other actors working in the field such as NGOs and industry representatives.

92 ibid 209.

93 See, e.g., Jennifer S Bansard, Philipp H Pattberg and Oscar Widerberg, 'Cities to the Rescue? Assessing the Performance of Transnational Municipal Networks in Global Climate Governance' (2017) 17 International Environmental Agreements: Politics, Law and Economics 229 doi:10.1007/s10784-016-9318-9; Natasha Affolder, 'Transnational Climate Law' in Peer Zumbansen (ed), *Oxford Handbook of Transnational Law* (OUP 2021).

4 Conclusion

Household cookstoves are used for cooking and heating on a large scale in many parts of the world. The air pollution that results from cookstove emissions poses a serious threat to human health and well-being, and contributes to climate change.

The multi-dimensional nature of the problem of cookstove emissions also defines the fittest regulatory responses to it. Furthermore, linkages among different governance and thematic levels, and the consequent multiple regulatory objectives, characterize the overall picture. International law on cookstove emissions is non-existent, and significant progress in that field does not seem likely. The transnational level looks more promising. Although clean cooking is an issue where national and even local circumstances and practices play a large role, exchange of information, experiences and best practices, on one hand, and the possible development of joint regulatory initiatives, on the other hand, in a transnational setting, certainly entail added value for network members. Several large transnational networks address air pollution and recognize or even directly deal with cookstove emissions as a small component of their activities. However, the existing transnational initiatives do not offer much in terms of tangible support to national governments struggling with finding effective ways to address the cookstove emissions problem.

The examined case studies showed that creating and implementing national cookstove regulation that is effective in the long-term is not an easy task. A number of lessons could be pointed out. Firstly, the quality of cookstove regulation comprises not only the level of detail, easiness of implementation, and legal bindingness but also such factors as: the timeframe for the regulatory measures, a versatile toolbox of economic incentives, diverse regulatory approaches and instruments, and tangible implementable measures. Secondly, clean cooking regulation requires a comprehensive approach whereby the relevant policies and implementing agencies coordinate and interact with each other. Thirdly, standards may be an ineffective way to control cookstove emissions if they are not in any way binding or if effective compliance monitoring is lacking. Fourth, the role of information cannot be underestimated, and its importance is evident at both ends of the regulatory relationship.

The chapter also identified a number of regulatory avenues for more effective clean cooking policies. Firstly, regulating the issue through energy policies has proved to be relatively effective in many cases, although challenges are also involved. Secondly, the regulation should successfully target the cookstove users, i.e. households, instead of placing significant regulation primarily on the cookstove-producing industry which acts on the basis of market demand and possible self-regulation in any case. Thirdly, addressing the issue of cookstove emissions through transnational initiatives was identified as a regulatory avenue that could have a larger role in the future. There would be, consequently, room for a new transnational initiative that would have clean cooking exclusively in its focus and target not only the cookstove industry but effectively bring together international organizations, states and sub-state actors. This would also directly correspond to the general trend of polycentric governance of cookstove emissions.

Bibliography

Abbott, KW, 'Strengthening the Transnational Regime Complex for Climate Change' (2014) 3(1) *Transnational Environmental Law* 57, doi:10.1017/S2047102513000502.

Affolder, N, 'Transnational Climate Law' in Zumbansen, Peer (ed), *Oxford Handbook of Transnational Law* (OUP 2021).

Andonova, LB, Hale, TN and Roger, CB, 'National Policy and Transnational Governance of Climate Change: Substitutes or Complements?' (2017) 61 *International Studies Quarterly* 253, doi:10.1093/isq/sqx014.

Arun, S and Rehman, IH, 'Can Subsidies be a Tool for Strengthening the Improved Cookstoves Market?' (The Energy and Resources Institute (TERI) 2015) <www.teriin.org/policybrief/files/SUBSIDIES_spread/files/downloads/SUBSIDIES_spread.pdf> accessed 12 August 2022.

Bansard, JS, Pattberg, PH and Widerberg, O, 'Cities to the Rescue? Assessing the Performance of Transnational Municipal Networks in Global Climate Governance' (2017) 17 International Environmental Agreements: Politics, Law and Economics 229, doi:10.1007/s10784-016-9318-9.

Bulkeley, H and Merrill, MM, *Cities and Climate Change: Urban Sustainability and Global Environmental Governance* (Routledge, 2003).

CCA, 'Kenya Country Action Plan (KCAP)' (2013) <https://cleancooking.org/wp-content/uploads/2021/07/236-1.pdf> accessed 22 September 2022.

CCA, '2022 Clean Cooking Industry Snapshot' (3rd edn, 2022) <https://cleancooking.org/wp-content/uploads/2022/05/CCA-2022-Clean-Cooking-Industry-Snapshot.pdf> accessed 12 August 2022.

CCA, 'Our Approach' <https://cleancooking.org/our-approach/> accessed 12 August 2022.

CCAC, 'Household Energy' <www.ccacoalition.org/en/initiatives/household-energy> accessed 12 August 2022.

CCAC, 'Identifying short-lived climate pollutant mitigation opportunities in India' <www.ccacoalition.org/en/activity/identifying-short-lived-climate-pollutant-mitigation-opportunities-india> accessed 12 August 2022.

CCAC, 'Kenya – National planning on short-lived climate pollutants' <www.ccacoalition.org/en/activity/kenya-national-planning-short-lived-climate-pollutants> accessed 12 August 2022.

Champion, WM and others, 'Cookstove Emissions and Performance Evaluation Using a New ISO Protocol and Comparison of Results with Previous Test Protocols' (2021) 55 Environ. Sci. Technol. 15333, doi:10.1021/acs.est.1c03390.

Chindarkar, N, Jain, A and Mani, S, 'Examining the Willingness-to-pay for Exclusive Use of LPG for Cooking among Rural Households in India' (2021) 150 Energy Policy 112107, doi:10.1016/j.enpol.2020.112107.

Clean Cooking Association of Kenya <https://ccak.or.ke/> accessed 14 February 2023.

Cole, DH, 'Advantages of a Polycentric Approach to Climate Change Policy' (2015) 5 Nature Climate Change 114, doi:10.1038/nclimate2490.

Freeman, OE and Zerriffi, H, 'Carbon Credits for Cookstoves: Trade-offs in Climate and Health Benefits' (2012) 88 The Forestry Chronicle 600, doi:10.5558/tfc2012-112.

Global Alliance for Clean Cookstoves, 'Delivering on the SDGs through Clean Cooking' <https://sustainabledevelopment.un.org/content/documents/11416Global%20Alliance%20for%20Clean%20Cookstoves%20-%20Delivering%20on%20the%20SDGs%20through%20Clean%20Cooking.pdf> accessed 12 August 2022.

Government of Kenya (GoK), 'The Draft Energy (Improved Biomass Cookstoves) Regulations, 2015' (Made from Energy Act No.1 2 of 2006; 2015) <https://www.epra.go.ke/wp-content/uploads/2018/12/The-Draft-Energy-Improved-Biomass-Cookstoves-Regulations-2015.pdf> accessed 22 September 2022.

GoK, Kenya Vision 2030 (2007) <http://www.vision2030.go.ke/about-vision-2030/> accessed 14 February 2023.

GoK Ministry of Energy, 'Kenya Off-Grid Solar Access Project' <https://www.kosap-fm.or.ke/> accessed 14 February 2023.

GoK Ministry of Energy, 'National Energy Policy 2018' (2018) <https://repository.kippra.or.ke/handle/123456789/1947> accessed 22 September 2022.

GoK, 'Sessional Paper No. 4 of 2004 on Energy' (2004) <https://repository.kippra.or.ke/handle/123456789/1371> accessed 22 September 2022.

GoK Ministry of Energy and Petroleum and SE4All, 'Kenya's SE4All Action Agenda and the Investment Prospectus Pathways for Concerted Action toward Sustainable Energy for All by 2030' (2015) <https://www.se4all-africa.org/fileadmin/uploads/se4all/Documents/Country_AAs/Kenya_SE4ALL_AA_January_2016.pdf> accessed 22 September 2022.

GoK Ministry of Environment and Forestry, 'National Climate Change Action Plan 2018–2022' (2018) <http://www.environment.go.ke/wp-content/uploads/2020/03/NCCAP_2018-2022_ExecutiveSummary-Compressed-1.pdf> accessed 14 February 2023.

GoK Ministry of Environment, Water and Natural Resources, 'Kenya National Environment Policy, 2013' (2013) <http://www.environment.go.ke/wp-content/uploads/2014/01/NATIONAL-ENVIRONMENT-POLICY-20131.pdf> accessed 22 September 2022.

Hanbar, RD and Karve, P, 'National Programme on Improved Chulha NPIC) of the Government of India: an Overview' (2002) 6 Energy for Sustainable Development 49, doi:10.1016/S0973-0826(08)60313-0.

Harish, S, 'Renewing India's Air Quality Management Strategy in the shadow of COVID-19' (Centre for Policy Research 2021) <https://cprindia.org/wp-content/uploads/2021/12/AQ-Framing-Paper_270921.pdf> accessed 12 August 2022.

HEI, 'State of Global Air 2020. Special Report' (HEI 2021) <www.stateofglobalair.org/sites/default/files/documents/2020-10/soga-2020-report-10-26_0.pdf> accessed 12 August 2022.

Heyvaert, V, *Transnational Environmental Regulation and Governance: Purpose, Strategies and Principles* (CUP 2019).

Honkonen, T, 'Tackling Cookstove Emissions in India: towards an Enabling Policy Environment and More Effective Legal Solutions' (2020) 16 LEAD 195, 200, doi:10.25501/SOAS.00033485.

IEA, 'Energy Access Outlook 2017: from Poverty to Prosperity' (IEA 2017) <https://iea.blob.core.windows.net/assets/9a67c2fc-b605-4994-8eb5-29a0ac219499/WEO2017SpecialReport_EnergyAccessOutlook.pdf> accessed 10 August 2022.

India State-Level Disease Burden Initiative Air Pollution Collaborators, 'Health and Economic Impact of Air Pollution in the States of India: the Global Burden of Disease Study 2019' (2021) 5(1) The Lancet Planetary Health e25 doi:10.1016/S2542-5196(20)30298-9.

Jordan, A and others (eds), *Governing Climate Change: Polycentricity in Action?* (CUP 2018).

Karanja, A and Gasparatos, A, 'Adoption and impacts of Clean Bioenergy Cookstoves in Kenya' (2019) 102 Renewable and Sustainable Energy Reviews 285, doi:10.1016/j.rser.2018.12.006.

Karanja, A, Mburu, F and Gasparatos, A, 'A Multi-stakeholder Perception Analysis about the Adoption, Impacts and Priority Areas in the Kenyan Clean Cooking Sector' (2020) 15 Sustainability Science 333, doi:10.1007/s11625-019-00742-4.

Khandelwal, M and others, 'Why Have Improved Cook-Stove Initiatives in India Failed?' (2017) 92 World Development 13, doi:10.1016/j.worlddev.2016.11.006.

Lacey, FG and others, 'Transient Climate and Ambient Health Impacts due to National Solid Fuel Cookstove Emissions' (2017) 114 PNAS 1269, doi:10.1073/pnas.161243011.

Lee, T, 'Global Cities and Transnational Climate Change Networks' (2013) *Global Environmental Politics* 13(1) 108, doi:10.1162/GLEP_a_00156.

Ministry of Environment, Forest & Climate Change, 'National Clean Air Programme' (2019) <https://moef.gov.in/wp-content/uploads/2019/05/NCAP_Report.pdf> accessed 12 August 2022.

Ministry of Health and Family Welfare, 'Report of the Steering Committee on Air Pollution and Health Related Issues' (2015) <https://main.mohfw.gov.in/sites/default/files/5412023661450432724_0.pdf> accessed 12 August 2022.

Mittal, N and others, 'Fuel Subsidy Reform in Developing Countries: Direct Benefit Transfer of LPG Cooking Gas Subsidy in India' Center for Global Development policy paper 114 (2017) <www.cgdev.org/sites/default/files/fuel-subsidy-reform-developing-countries-india.pdf> accessed 12 August 2022.

Muok, B O and Kingiri, A, 'The Role of Civil Society Organizations in Low-carbon Innovation in Kenya' (2015) 5 Innovation and Development 207 doi: 10.1080/2157930X.2015.1064558.

Ostrom, E, 'Polycentric Systems for Coping with Collective Action and Global Environmental Change' (2010) 20 Global Environmental Change 550 doi:10.1016/j.gloenvcha.2010.07.004.

Putti, VR and others, 'The State of the Global Clean and Improved Cooking Sector' (The International Bank for Reconstruction And Development, 2015) <https://openknowledge.worldbank.org/bitstream/handle/10986/21878/96499.pdf?sequence=1&isAllowed=y> accessed 11 August 2022.

Rashidi, K and Patt, A, 'Subsistence over Symbolism: the Role of Transnational Municipal Networks on Cities' Climate Policy Innovation and Adoption' (2018) 23 *Mitigation and Adaptation Strategies for Global Change* 507, doi:10.1007/s11027-017-9747-y.

Rosenthal, J and others, 'Clean Cooking and the SDGs: Integrated Analytical Approaches to Guide Energy Interventions for Health and Environment Goals' (2018) 42 Energy for Sustainable Development 152, doi:10.1016/j.esd.2017.11.003.

Sanford, L and Burney, J, 'Cookstoves Illustrate the Need for a Comprehensive Carbon Market' (2015) 10 Environmental Research Letters 084026, doi:10.1088/1748-9326/10/8/084026.

Scovronick, N, *Reducing Global Health Risks Through Mitigation of Short-Lived Climate Pollutants. Scoping Report For Policy-makers* (WHO, 2015) <http://apps.who.int/iris/bitstream/10665/189524/1/9789241565080_eng.pdf?ua=1> accessed 11 August 2022.

SEforALL, 'Kenya Action Agenda' (2016) <https://www.seforall.org/sites/default/files/Kenya_AA_EN_Released.pdf> accessed 22 September 2022.

SEforALL, 'Clean Cooking' <https://www.seforall.org/clean-cooking> accessed 14 February 2023.

Shaffer, G, 'Transnational Legal Ordering and State Change' in Shaffer, G (ed), *Transnational Legal Ordering and State Change* (CUP 2013).

Sharma, S and others, 'How to Target LPG Subsidies in India: Step 2. Evaluating policy options in Jharkhand' (International Institute for Sustainable Development (IISD) 2021) <www.iisd.org/system/files/2021-04/target-lpg-subsidies-india-jharkhand.pdf> accessed 12 August 2022.

Sinha, B, 'The Indian Stove Programme: an Insider's View – the Role of Society, Politics, Economics and Education' (2002) 48 Boiling Point 23.

UN Environment, 'India joins the Climate and Clean Air Coalition' press release (5 July 2019) <www.unenvironment.org/news-and-stories/press-release/india-joins-climate-and-clean-air-coalition> accessed 12 August 2022.

UNEP, *Air Pollution in Asia and the Pacific: Science-based Solutions* (UNEP, 2019) 20 <https://www.ccacoalition.org/resources/air-pollution-asia-and-pacific-science-based-solutions-summary-full-report> accessed 11 August 2022.

WHO, *Indoor Air Quality Guidelines: Household Fuel Combustion* (WHO, 2014).

WHO, *Burning Opportunity: Clean Household Energy for Health, Sustainable Development, and Wellbeing of Women and Children* (WHO, 2016) <https://apps.who.int/iris/bitstream/handle/10665/204717/9789241565233_eng.pdf?sequence=1&isAllowed=y> accessed 11 August 2022.

WHO, 'Exposure to household air pollution for 2016' (version 5 April 2018) <www.who.int/airpollution/data/HAP_exposure_results_final.pdf> accessed 11 August 2022.

WHO, *Opportunities for transition to clean household energy: application of the Household Energy Assessment Rapid Tool (HEART) in India* (WHO 2018) <https://apps.who.int/iris/bitstream/handle/10665/274280/9789241513999-eng.pdf?sequence=1&isAllowed=y>19–20> accessed 12 August 2022.

WHO, *Setting National Voluntary Performance Targets for Cookstoves'* (WHO, 2021).

WHO, 'Air Pollution Data Portal: Household Air Pollution Data', <www.who.int/data/gho/data/themes/air-pollution/household-air-pollution> accessed 10 August 2022.

WHO, 'Clean Household Energy Solutions Toolkit (CHEST)' <https://www.who.int/tools/clean-household-energy-solutions-toolkit> accessed 12 August 2022.

WHO Global Air Quality Guidelines. Particulate matter ($PM_{2.5}$ and PM_{10}), ozone, nitrogen dioxide, sulfur dioxide and carbon monoxide' (2021) <https://apps.who.int/iris/bitstream/handle/10665/345329/9789240034228-eng.pdf?sequence=1&isAllowed=y> accessed 12 August 2022.

Zahno, M and others, 'Health Awareness and the Transition towards Clean Cooking Fuels: Evidence from Rajasthan' (2020) 1584) PLoS ONE e0231931, doi:10.1371/journal.pone.0231931.

CHAPTER 10

An Integrated and Inclusive SLCP Strategy for Asia

Recommended Policy and Institutional Reforms

David D. Sussman, Eric Zusman and Matthew Hengesbaugh

1 Introduction

The health, agriculture, and climate impacts of short-lived climate pollutants (SLCPs)—including black carbon, tropospheric ozone, and methane—are not only sizable but often interrelated.[1] Near-term climate changes, for instance, influence crop yields and food security. In addition, SLCPs often have varying yet underappreciated spatial and social impacts. In fact, women, children, and other vulnerable segments may suffer disproportionately from the impacts of SLCPs. Further, some SLCP control measures that offer the greatest potential to reduce these impacts may impose high costs and restrict the agency of key social groups (i.e. bans on open burning for farmers). Fortunately, the inverse of the above claim may also hold true: an effective SLCP response can yield multiple benefits for multiple stakeholders. While previous research features the potential benefits of sector-specific SLCP solutions, the broader policy and institutional reforms enabling their widespread implementation often fall to the margins of analyses.[2]

This chapter aims to bring policy and institutional considerations to the center of work on SLCPs. Its primary purpose is to suggest policy and institutional reforms needed for an integrated and inclusive SLCP strategy in Asia. The chapter begins by setting the context with a review of the interrelated yet varying impacts of SLCPs. It then underlines how work on 1) the science-policy-society interface; 2) multi-sectoral, multi-level governance; and 3) just

1 UNEP/WMO, 'Integrated Assessment of Black Carbon and Tropospheric Ozone: Summary for Decision Makers' (2011) <http://www.unep.org/dewa/Portals/67/pdf/Black_Carbon.pdf>; CCAC and UNEP, *Short-Lived Climate Pollutants Short-Lived Climate Pollutants in Latin America* (2018); UNEP, Asia Pacific Clean Air Partnership (APCAP) and CCAC, 'Air Pollution in Asia and the Pacific: Science-Based Solutions. United Nations Environment Programme' (2019) <https://www.ccacoalition.org/resources/air-pollution-asia-and-pacific-science-based-solutions-summary-full-report>.

2 Eric Zusman and others, 'One Atmosphere: Integrating Air Pollution and Climate Policy and Governance' (2021) 12 Atmosphere 1.

DOI:10.1163/9789004684089_012

transitions can shed light on policy and institutional reforms underpinning an integrated and inclusive SLCP strategy. These reforms focus more attention on strengthening policy coherence, interagency coordination and vertical integration as well as opening compensatory programmes (for stakeholders adversely affected by SLCPs, in addition to control measures) and deliberative decision-making fora. Embedding key SLCP measures such as inspection/maintenance programmes, clean cookstoves and open burning of biomass residue in these broader institutional and policy reforms is critical for moving work on SLCPs forward in Asia and other regions.

The remainder of the chapter is divided into five sections. Section two focuses on the impacts of SLCPs on health, food production as well as varying impacts across social groups and space. Section three synthesizes research on the science-policy-society interface, multi-sector, multi-level governance, and just transitions to identify policy and institutional reforms supporting the implementation of SLCP measures. Section four applies insights from that research to three measures with significant potential in Asia: 1) inspection and maintenance programmes; 2) clean cookstoves; and 3) open burning of biomass. The final section concludes.

2 The Impacts of SLCPs

2.1 *Impacts Across Sectors*

The starting point for this chapter is the impact of SLCPs on health. It is difficult to overstate the health effects of many of the air pollutants labeled as SLCPs. According to the UN Environment Programme (2022), "air pollution is the greatest environmental threat to public health globally and accounts for an estimated 7 million premature deaths every year".[3] Other assessments using different indicators come to a comparable conclusion; annually, outdoor and indoor air pollution cause the loss of 215.5 million disability-adjusted life years.[4] The State of Global Air (2019) makes a similar point: air pollution was the fourth most important risk factor for death globally, following high blood pressure, tobacco, and diet.[5] The quality of air is of greater consequence for human mortality than many other causes—whether obesity in developed

3 UNEP, 'Air Pollution Note—Data You Need to Know' (2022) <https://www.unep.org/interactive/air-pollution-note/?fbclid=IwAR2KKH_zwwl9nDJFZk0yTny586HoI76dbswRKkuN0yBSJ6uystEHdXkEGLE>.

4 UNEP, APCAP and CCAC (n 1).

5 HFI, 'State of Global Air 2020' (2020).

countries or malnutrition and communicable diseases in less-developed countries.

When it comes to chronic exposure to air pollution, $PM_{2.5}$ (and its constitutive component of black carbon that is one of the key SLCPs) is most closely associated with mortality and other poor health outcomes.[6] The $PM_{2.5}$ exposure-related diseases include acute lower respiratory disease, heart disease, obstructive pulmonary disease, stroke, and lung cancer (WHO 2015, p.1). The first four of these were listed within the WHO's top 10 global causes of death in 2019 (WHO 2020). In addition, air pollution is also tied to other undesirable impacts such as type 2 diabetes and adverse birth outcomes (more on this later).[7] Ischemic heart disease rose from 4th in 1990 to 1st in both 2005 and 2014. Needless to say, air pollution remains an important factor when it comes to loss of healthy years of life.

SLCP's effects, however, do not begin nor end at human health but extend to the health of the planet.[8] In particular, SLCPs affect food systems, and therefore the health of populations, depending on what they eat. SLCPs impact food production in a number of ways: for instance, black carbon emissions impede sunlight required for photosynthesis.[9] In addition to black carbon, ozone pollution can lead to reduced yields of between 3% and 16% in rice, maize, wheat, and soybeans.[10] Air pollution also has serious implications for ecosystems and biodiversity.[11] Not surprisingly, a reduction in SLCPs will not only prevent crop losses, but advance other dimensions of sustainable development.[12]

SLCPs also have effects on the climate (see also Chapter 1).[13] Though recent studies have suggested the global climate impacts of black carbon may be more limited than once thought,[14] regional effects on cloud formation and

6 UNEP, APCAP and CCAC (n 1).
7 HFI (n 5).
8 Mark Elder and Christian Loewe, 'Introduction and Context' in UNEP (ed), *Global Environment Outlook—GEO6: Healthy Planet, Healty People* (United Nations Environment Programme 2019).
9 WHO, 'Reducing Global Health Risks: Through Mitigation of Short-Lived Climate Pollutants: Scoping Report for Policymakers' (2015).
10 ibid.
11 UNEP, 'Air Pollution Note' (n3).
12 Durwood Zaelke, 'Primer on Short-Lived Climate Pollutants' (2013) <http://www.igsd.org>.
13 TC Bond and others, 'Bounding the Role of Black Carbon in the Climate System: A Scientific Assessment.' (2013) 118 Journal of Geophysical Research: Atmospheres 5380.
14 Toshihiko Takemura, 'Return to Different Climate States by Reducing Sulphate Aerosols under Future CO_2 Concentrations' (2020) 10 Scientific Reports.

precipitation patterns are still believed to be significant.[15] Further emissions from black carbon rich sources such as diesel vehicles may be particularly destabilizing.[16] In addition, there is also growing evidence of methane's substantial and even greater than previously estimated impacts.[17]

2.2 *Impacts Across Social Groups*

The main sources of SLCPs are directly connected to the specific groups who suffer from negative health and other impacts. Those most affected are often constrained by where they live and their social station—e.g. women cooking at home, the children they reside with and care for, and the elderly. Though some have drawn attention to these varied effects—suggesting "the burden of disease attributable to air pollution does not fall evenly across age groups"[18]—this can often be the exception that illustrates the rule. To exemplify this point, a 48-page 2016 report by the European Investment Bank considered SLCPs and included "impact of activities" in its title, but did not mention elderly, women, or children.[19] Given this lack of attention, it is critical to disaggregate impact assessments for particular groups.

The starting point for this more disaggregated perspective is people living at lower levels of development. Poor and vulnerable groups are more likely to be exposed to air pollution, and this holds both across and within countries.[20] In general, air pollution from SLCPs is more of a problem in less-developed countries since there are fewer regulations and limited enforcement capacities; the fact that their populations tend to live closer to the sources of pollution

---

15 Lai Nguyen Huy, Ekbordin Winijkul and Nguyen Thi Kim Oanh, 'Assessment of Emissions from Residential Combustion in Southeast Asia and Implications for Climate Forcing Potential' (2021) 785 Science of the Total Environment.

16 Nazar Kholod and Meredydd Evans, 'Reducing Black Carbon Emissions from Diesel Vehicles in Russia: An Assessment and Policy Recommendations' (2016) 56 Environmental Science and Policy 1.

17 IPCC, *Climate Change 2021: The Physical Science Basis. Contribution of Working Group I to the Sixth Assessment Report of the Intergovernmental Panel on Climate Change* (R Yu and B Zhou Masson-Delmotte, V., P. Zhai, A. Pirani, S. L. Connors, C. Péan, S. Berger, N. Caud, Y. Chen, L. Goldfarb, M. I. Gomis, M. Huang, K. Leitzell, E. Lonnoy, J. B. R. Matthews, T. K. Maycock, T. Waterfield, O. Yelekçi ed, 2021).

18 HFI p. 16 (n5).

19 European Investment Bank, 'Short-Lived Climate Pollutants (SLCPs): An Analysis of the EIB's Policies, Procedures, Impact of Activities and Options for Scaling up Mitigation Efforts' (2016).

20 T Failey, 'Poor Communities Exposed to Elevated Air Pollution Levels' (2016) <https://www.niehs.nih.gov/research/programs/geh/geh_newsletter/2016/4/spotlight/poor_communities_exposed_to_elevated_air_pollution_levels.cfm> accessed 6 December 2022.

adds another layer of complexity to the issue.[21] However, this is not simply a developed-developing country debate. More-developed economies also have income-related disparities when it comes to air pollution: those with lower socio-economic status are more likely to live in areas with dirtier air.[22]

Another differentiating dimension is gender. In general, air pollution from SLCPs in households is the greatest cause of non-communicable disease in women.[23] McDuffie et al. (2021) found that the disease burden related to $PM_{2.5}$ from the heating of and cooking in residences was associated with an estimated 770,000 deaths annually.[24] However, such gender-differentiated effects can often be relegated to the footnotes of research. The previously mentioned 2021 report to "provide the first comprehensive estimates of source contributions to exposure to $PM_{2.5}$ and cause-specific disease burden at global, regional, and national scales" actually does not refer to women specifically.[25]

A third at-risk population group to SLCPs is children. Research shows that exposure to air pollution at young ages leads to adverse outcomes at birth (babies born too early and with low weights),[26] and higher incidence of pneumonia-related deaths.[27] A fifth of infant mortality taking place in babies' first month is attributable to air pollution such as ambient $PM_{2.5}$ and ozone, as well as household cooking.[28] To put a firm number on this, globally nearly half a million newborns die annually due to air pollution.[29] Exposure to air pollution does not stop when they age. Exposing children to air pollution continues to burden them with respiratory and immune system difficulties as they move into adulthood.[30]

---

21 UNEP, APCAP and CCAC (n 1).

22 Lara Cushing and others, 'Environmental Equity: Evidence from California's Cap-and-Trade Program' (2018) 15 plos Medicine 1; Anjum Hajat, Charlene Hsia and Marie S O'Neill, 'Socioeconomic Disparities and Air Pollution Exposure: A Global Review' (2015) 2 Current Environmental Health Reports 440 <https://pubmed.ncbi.nlm.nih.gov/26381684/> accessed 6 December 2022.

23 K Akahoshi and E Zusman, 'Bringing Clean Air to 4 Billion People in Asia' *The Diplomat* (23 September 2021) <https://thediplomat.com/2021/09/bringing-clean-air-to-4-billion-people-in-asia/> accessed 6 December 2022.

24 E McDuffie and others, 'Global Burden of Disease from Major Air Pollution Sources (GBD MAPS): A Global Approach' (2021) <http://ovidsp.ovid.com/ovidweb.cgi?T=JS&PAGE=reference&D=emexb&NEWS=N&AN=639091709> accessed 6 December 2022.

25 ibid.

26 HFI (n 5).

27 UNEP, APCAP and CCAC (n 1).

28 McDuffie and others (n 24).

29 HFI (n 5).

30 UNICEF, 'Clean Air for Children' (2016) <https://www.unicef.org/media/49966/file/UNICEF_Clear_the_Air_for_Children_30_Oct_2016.pdf> accessed 6 December 2022;

A final area where these effects vary involves the elderly. An increasing amount of scholarship looks at how air pollution is associated with diseases that affect older populations, particularly among seniors. Not only are these populations more vulnerable due to weakened immune systems, they have also been exposed to air pollutants for longer time periods. Clearly, chronic exposure is tied to pulmonary disease, asthma, as well as emphysema.[31] Even low exposure year after year leads to increased incidence of respiratory disease, heart attacks, and stroke.[32] In addition, there is an association between air pollution, dementia, and chronic kidney disease.[33]

2.3 *Impacts Across Scales and Regions*

SLCPs do not simply affect multiple dimensions of development or social groups; there are also geographic and spatial differences in their effects. Impacts on health, food and other development concerns vary across space for reasons owing to levels of development. In fact, air pollution exposure and its impacts are often connected to a country's level and style of development.[34] Those undergoing rapid development face a larger health burden[35] and differences in development play a part in disparities for both level of exposure and overall health.[36] Even though researchers understand much more about how health is negatively affected by air pollution, geographic disparities persist, with many areas lacking sufficient improvement.[37] There are also gaps in data for some regions, such as Africa.[38]

There are also regional variations within countries. Outdoor air pollution is particularly dangerous in rapidly expanding urban areas.[39] Urbanisation in

---

UNICEF, 'Mongolia's Air Pollution Crisis: A Call to Action to Protect Children's Health' (2018) <https://reliefweb.int/sites/reliefweb.int/files/resources/Mongolia_air_pollution_crisis_ENG.pdf> accessed 6 December 2022; UNICEF, 'Child-Centred Clean Air Solutions: Guide for Asia and the Pacific Region' (2022).

31 Marzia Simoni and others, 'Adverse Effects of Outdoor Pollution in the Elderly' (2015) 7 Journal of Thoracic Disease 34.

32 Mahdieh Danesh Yazdi and others, 'Long-Term Association of Air Pollution and Hospital Admissions among Medicare Participants Using a Doubly Robust Additive Model' (2021) 143 Circulation 1584.

33 McDuffie and others (n 24).

34 HFI (n 5).

35 UNEP, APCAP and CCAC (n 1).

36 HFI (n 5).

37 ibid.

38 UNEP, 'Integrated Assessment of Air Pollution and Climate Change in Africa 2020–2021' (2022).

39 UNEP, APCAP and CCAC (n 1).

these countries can take place quickly and without much planning, which is associated with more ambient air pollution from vehicles.[40] However, "air pollution is not just a problem in cities"; billions in rural areas face exposure to health-damaging $PM_{2.5}$ and more.[41]

The effects can also vary at the even smaller scales—notably the community level. To cite an example covered later in the chapter, a significant number of health problems are attributed to fuels rural populations often use for heating and cooking, ranging from wood, charcoal and coal, to animal dung.[42] Estimates from 2015 show that 2.7 billion people resided in conditions that exposed them to contaminated air.[43] The WHO also observes that "fuel combustion in residential and commercial buildings and transport together account for approximately 80% of anthropogenic black carbon emissions".[44]

Finally, there are regional differences. Generally, air pollution is most dangerous in the Asia-Pacific.[45] The vast majority (more than 90%) of people living in Asia are exposed to dirty air that exceeds WHO guidelines and leads to greater risk of illness and early death.[46] About 91% of premature deaths related to air pollution take place in middle-or lower-income countries, with sizable concentrations in Asia.[47] As a result of having large populations sizes and poor air quality, India and China account for a significant number of deaths caused by air pollution.[48] Due to the sizable impacts and potential benefits in Asia, much of the chapter will refer to examples in the region.

3 Toward an Integrated and Inclusive SLCP Strategy for Asia

The previous section highlighted the serious threat that SLCPs pose to health, food, and climate systems. It also underlined that those impacts are not uniform; they vary across sectors, social groups and locations. This section

40 Simoni and others (n 31).

41 UNEP, APCAP and CCAC (n 1).

42 HFI (n 5).

43 UNEP, APCAP and CCAC (n 1).

44 WHO, 'Reducing Global Health Risks: Through Mitigation of Short-Lived Climate Pollutants: Scoping Report for Policymakers' (n 9).

45 UNEP, APCAP and CCAC (n 1).

46 Elder and Loewe (n 8).

47 WHO, 'Ambient (Outdoor) Air Pollution' (22 September 2021) <https://www.who.int/news-room/fact-sheets/detail/ambient-(outdoor)-air-quality-and-health> accessed 24 May 2022.

48 HFI (n 5).

discusses policy and institutional reforms for a strategy that not only addresses the multiple impacts of SLCPs but captures a range of benefits in the process. To do so, the section draws on three strands of literature that could inform a more integrated and inclusive SLCP strategy: 1) the science-policy-society interface; 2) multi-sectoral, multi-level governance; and 3) just transitions.

3.1 *Strengthening the Science-Policy-Society Interface*

Research on the science-policy-society interface has evolved over three discrete stages. Beginning in the 1960s, the first of these stages implicitly subscribed to an almost "linear" and "unidirectional" view of "science informing policymaking". An arguably more accurate "interactive" second phase followed, emphasizing a science and policy interplay. Most recently, an even more nuanced "embedded" phase has underlined the need to include citizens and other stakeholders in decisions affecting their livelihoods, thereby ensuring greater scrutiny and legitimacy of those decisions. Over the course of this three-stage evolutionary development, there has also been a growing understanding of the factors and actors that support a dynamic interchange between science, policy and wider society.[49]

Table 10.1 summarizes literature on the actors and factors highlighted in relevant studies. In so doing, the table underlines some salient points that subsequently have been reflected in research and initiatives on SLCPs—though this research has a more general focus on society-policy interface. Connections between the findings of this literature and the science-policy-society interface as it relates to SCLPs are further discussed below.

First, Table 10.1 suggests that when it comes to the producers of scientific information, key characteristics of knowledge such as relevance, transparency, accessibility, and timeliness matter for influencing policy. Some of the most persuasive SLCP research has focused on developing clear, cogent, and accessible analyses of how much different mitigation measures deliver tangible benefits. Studies such as *Air Pollution in Asia and the Pacific: Science-based Solutions* has been able to gain traction among policymakers in Asia, in part, because it helps present a robust case for 25 measures that can bring health, food, and climate benefits to the region.[50]

Second, the table shows that work on SLCPs has also paid attention to decision-makers receiving scientific knowledge. This is not only evident in the studies that estimate the benefits of more integrated air pollution and climate

49 Nataliia Sokolovska, Benedikt Fecher and Gert G Wagner, 'Communication on the Science-Policy Interface: An Overview of Conceptual Models' (2019) 7 Publications.

50 UNEP, APCAP and CCAC (n 1).

TABLE 10.1 Science-policy-society interface

Actors	Featured subthemes
1. Producers of Scientific Information	Relevance of Information[a] Openness/Transparency[b] Accessibility[c] Timeliness[d] Inclusiveness[e]
2. Recipients of Scientific Information	Willingness to Accept Information[f] Institutional Capacity[g] Inclusiveness[h]
3. Role of Intermediaries and Co-design[i]	---

a Sharon A Jones, Baruch Fischhoff and Denise Lach, 'Evaluating the Science-Policy Interface for Climate Change Research' (1999) 43 Climatic Change 581; David W Cash and others, 'Knowledge Systems for Sustainable Development' (2003) 100 Proceedings of the National Academy of Sciences of the United States of America 8086; Michael J Spilsbury and Robert Nasi, 'The Interface of Policy Research and the Policy Development Process: Challenges Posed to the Forestry Community' (2006) 8 Forest Policy and Economics 193.

b ibid; Robert T Watson, 'Turning Science into Policy: Challenges and Experiences from the Science-Policy Interface' (2005) 360 Philosophical Transactions of the Royal Society B: Biological Sciences 471.

c Jones, Fischhoff and Lach (n a); Cash and others (n a); Spilsbury and Nasi (n a).

d Spilsbury and Nasi (n a).

e A Gupta and others, *Science Networks* (2012); Yulia Yamineva, 'Lessons from the Intergovernmental Panel on Climate Change on Inclusiveness across Geographies and Stakeholders' (2017) 77 Environmental Science and Policy 244 <http://dx.doi.org/10.1016/j.envsci.2017.04.005>.

f Dhanush Dinesh and others, 'Learning from Failure at the Science–Policy Interface for Climate Action in Agriculture' (2021) 26 Mitigation and Adaptation Strategies for Global Change.

g ibid; Zoë Heritage and Geoff Green, 'European National Healthy City Networks: The Impact of an Elite Epistemic Community' (2013) 90 Journal of Urban Health 154.

h N Castells and J Ravetz, 'Science and Policy in International Environmental Agreements' (2001) International Environmental Agreements: Politics, Law and Economics 405; André Derek Mader and others, 'Country Representatives' Perceptions of the Biodiversity Science-Policy Interface' (2021) 1 Conservation 73; Watson (n b).

i David H Guston, 'Boundary Organizations in Environmental Policy and Science: An Introduction' (2001) 26 Science, Technology, & Human Values 399; Spilsbury and Nasi (n a); GD Gooch and others, 'The Science–Policy–Stakeholder Interface in Sustainable Water Management: Creating Interactive Participatory Scenarios Together with Stakeholders', Science, Policy and Stakeholders in Water Management (Routledge 2010); Lisa Dilling and Maria Carmen Lemos, 'Creating Usable Science: Opportunities and Constraints for Climate Knowledge Use and Their Implications for Science Policy' (2011) 21 Global Environmental

TABLE 10.1 Science-policy-society interface (*cont.*)

Change 680; M Jacob and T Hellström, 'Reviewing the Science-Policy Relationship: The Policy as Theory Alternative (PAST)' (1998) 25 Science and Public Policy 218; Kai Wan and others, 'Science-Policy Interplay on Air Pollution Governance in China' (2020) 107 Environmental Science and Policy 150 <https://doi.org/10.1016/j.envsci.2020.03.003>.

controls; it is also apparent in efforts to build the capacity of decision-makers to use that information. For instance, the Climate Change and Clean Air Coalition (CCAC)—a global network of more than 100 state and non-state partners that was formed more than a decade ago to catalyze action on SLCPs—has offered funding for in-country capacity building work on SLCPs and sought to assure that is consistent with regional and national needs. Many countries have been responsive to this approach; for example, in Asia the Maldives developed SLCP action plans, while Cambodia integrated SLCPs into its clean air initiatives.

Third, there has been an active effort to use intermediaries and co-design to help mainstream SLCPs into national and local planning processes. This is again readily apparent when looking at the work of the CCAC as well as regional initiatives such as the Asia Pacific Clean Air Partnership and Clean Air Asia; all three of these initiatives and organizations have made considerable efforts to mediate between science, policy and wider society in order to demonstrate the multiple benefits achieved by implementing the aforementioned 25 clean air measures.[51]

One of the strengths of research and initiatives on SLCPs is that they have generated estimates of narrow measures that make it easier to communicate and build capacities of policymakers and other stakeholders. An important caveat, however, is that these activities have often paid less attention to the policy and institutional reforms needed to work across sectors and social groups for effectively implementing such measures at scale. The next section will argue that research on multi sectoral, multi level governance and just transitions could complement work on science-policy-society because it pays more attention to these intersectoral and multi-stakeholder dynamics. Bringing in insights from this complementary work stands to not only strengthen relevant research. It can also bridge institutional divides and harness stakeholder energies in ways that drive the widespread implementation of narrower SLCP measures.

51 ibid.

3.2 *Toward an Integrated Strategy: Bringing in Multi-sector, Multi-level Governance*

A line of work that can offer insights into policy and institutional reforms supporting widespread implementation comes from studies on governance. A longstanding observation within this field is that government agencies with different remits may fail to work together even if it is in a country's (broadly conceived) interest to do so.[52] These cross-agency challenges can stem from issues ranging from differences in budgeting allocation formulas to variations in organisational cultures. There have nonetheless been some efforts to bridge these institutional divides. For example, a sizable literature has concentrated on how policies can be made more coherent or integrated by, to illustrate, requiring that environmental considerations are included in economic policies.[53] Other studies have underlined the importance of institutional changes such as interagency coordination mechanisms or multiagency task forces that can lead to more coherent policies.[54] Such institutional changes may also entail data sharing protocols or tagging of public budgets so they reflect impacts on climate, health, and other development needs.

Another coordination challenge concerns aligning actions across different administrative levels. A core insight from work on multi-level governance—sometimes framed as vertical integration—is that local governments often find it easier than national governments to formulate responses to climate and other global challenges.[55] This is, in part, because local governments are better positioned to recognize ways that strategic responses align with other development needs. It may also be because local authorities often find it easier to navigate interagency turf wars and break down the siloes that impede integrated responses in larger and inherently more complex national level organizational

---

52 B Guy Peters, 'The Challenge of Policy Coordination' (2018) 1 Policy Design and Practice 1 <https://doi.org/10.1080/25741292.2018.1437946>; B Guy Peters, 'Managing Horizontal Government: The Politics of Co-Ordination' (1998) 76 Public Administration 295.

53 ibid; Åsa Persson and others, 'Editorial: Environmental Policy Integration: Taking Stock of Policy Practice in Different Contexts' (2018) 85 Environmental Science & Policy 113.

54 B Guy Peters (n52).

55 Michele M Betsill and Harriet Bulkeley, 'Cities and the Multilevel Governance of Global Climate Change' (2006) 12 Global Governance 141; Jan Corfee-Morlot and others, 'Cities, Climate Change and Multilevel Governance' (2009) Cushing L and others, 'Environmental Equity: Evidence from California's Cap-and-Trade Program' (2018) 15 PLOS Medicine 1; Barry G Rabe, 'Beyond Kyoto: Climate Change Policy in Multilevel Governance Systems' (2007) 20 423.

settings.[56] At the same time, local governments are naturally smaller-scale, and face some limitations in their capacity to effectively organize. They also may have specific interests that conflict with broader measures to address pollution. It therefore merits highlighting that national governments can play a critical role in response. For instance, they may offer fiscal and other incentives to help forward-looking local governments advance more integrated responses to climate and other development concerns.[57] They can similarly provide support and resources to local governments that are further behind the learning curve, enabling them to extract and adapt experiences from elsewhere. Provided that there is alignment across levels, international and regional organizations can also offer technical assistance and afford national and local governments a platform for demonstrating integrated actions. This alignment is moreover increasingly important given the need for coordination across different spatial scales to maximize the benefits from solutions.

3.3 *Toward an Inclusive Approach: Bringing in Just Transitions*

Another potentially revealing piece of work on just transitions suggests supporting the implementation of key measures and requires recognizing that impacts and benefits may not only be distributed across different spatial scales but also between different social groups. Research in this area grows from the understanding that some climate policies may leave select groups and regions worse off even if they generate considerable aggregate benefits. This has led to consideration of some remedial policy actions targeting those who suffer employment and other losses due to the closure of industries and sectors. While some of this work highlighted specific kinds of compensatory policies and programmes (i.e. retraining programmes), others have pointed to the need for more expansive social dialogues and interactive discussion among those who are adversely affected, including on efforts to arrive at the compensatory policies.[58]

A related line of work has suggested the need for participatory and deliberative (institutional) fora to advance more sustainable and just transitions. This inclusion could occur at several different entry points—from the local to the

---

56 Edgardo Bilsky, Anna Calvete Moreno and Ainara Fernández Tortosa, 'Local Governments and SDG Localisation: Reshaping Multilevel Governance from the Bottom Up' (2021) 22 Journal of Human Development and Capabilities 713.

57 M Mohieldin and others, 'The Role of Local and Regional Governments in the SDGs: The Localization Agenda', *Business, Government and the SDGs* (Palgrave Macmillan 2023).

58 Béla Galgoczi, 'From Paris to Katowice: The EU Needs to Step Up Its Game on Climate Change and Set Its Own Just Transition Framework' [2018] SSRN Electronic Journal.

national level. There are a few concrete options that might have relevance in this regard. For example, in countries such as Ghana, the government has instituted gender quotas to ensure that women have a seat and voice at the table.[59] Other studies have also pointed to the important role small scale or what some call mini-public deliberative fora can play in increasing the quantity as well as the quality of inputs from affected stakeholder groups.[60] These fora could be built into existing decision-making processes where there are clearly differentiated impacts as well as benefits for key stakeholder groups.

4 Three Measures Where Integration and Inclusion Matter in Asia

The consideration of the above lines of work is particularly relevant to this chapter. As noted previously, SLCPs have not only cross-sectoral but differential impacts across regions and social segments; thus, effective implementation of priority mitigation measures requires additional consideration among the broader set of policies and institutions that drive implementation. This section concentrates on policy and institutional reforms that can support the implementation of three measures that have sizable benefits in Asia. Table 10.2 summarizes some of those main recommendations for a key transport measure, namely the inspection and maintenance programmes for on-the-road vehicles as well as clean cookstoves (see also Chapter 9) and open burning of biomass, all of which are described in the text that follows.

4.1 *Inspection and Maintenance Programmes*

One of the key solutions that cannot only significantly reduce emissions of black carbon but may also have sizable impacts on the well-being of poorer populations is an effective inspection and maintenance (I&M) programme. I&M programmes are critical for controlling SLCPs because they help to curb emissions from a segment of the transportation fleet that contributes disproportionately to pollution. This narrow segment is made of vehicles known as "super-emitters" (such as trucks that are more than 20 years old). Data on

59 Nathan J Cook, Tara Grillos and Krister P Andersson, 'Gender Quotas Increase the Equality and Effectiveness of Climate Policy Interventions' (2019) 9 Nature Climate Change 330 <http://dx.doi.org/10.1038/s41558-019-0438-4> accessed 6 December 2022.

60 Graham Smith and Maija Setälä, 'Mini-Publics and Deliberative Democracy' in Andre Bächtiger and others (eds), *The Oxford Handbook of Deliberative Democracy* (2018) <https://www.oxfordhandbooks.com/view/10.1093/oxfordhb/9780198747369.001.0001/oxfordhb-9780198747369-e-27> accessed 12 June 2022.

TABLE 10.2 Examples of policy and institutional reforms enabling the implementation of key SLCP measures in Asia

	Integration		Inclusion	
	Policy	**Institutional**	**Policy**	**Institutional**
Inspection and Maintenance (I&M) Programmes	Include I&M in climate and air pollution policies	Strengthen interagency coordination between transport and environmental/ climate agencies	Provide subsidies/ compensation for low income drivers of older vehicles for repairs or new vehicles	Create deliberative fora that enable vehicle users to participate in design and implementation of I&M programmes
Residential Energy and Clean Cooking	Include clean cooking programmes in climate and air pollution policies	Strengthen interagency coordination between energy (especially rural energy divisions) and environmental/ climate agencies	Provide subsidies/ compensation for low-income users of traditional stoves to transition to cleaner stoves or fuels	Create deliberative fora that enable vehicle users to participate in design and implementation of cookstove programmes
Open Burning of Agricultural Residue and Biomass	Include open burning prevention in climate and air pollution policies	Strengthen interagency coordination between energy (especially rural energy divisions) and environmental/ climate agencies	Provide subsidies/ compensation for small scale farmers to purchase control technologies or transition to more circular models of crop residue use	Create deliberative fora that enable vehicle users to participate in design and implementation of cookstove programmes

the performance of older and poorly maintained vehicles bears this out: in many developing countries, a small share of 5% to 10% of the total vehicle fleet contributes between 50% to 80% of total vehicle emissions. At the same time, studies have shown that in rapidly motorizing cities such as Bangkok, investments in improving these programmes would deliver benefits that far outweigh the costs.[61]

Though there is growing awareness of this cost-benefit calculus, effective implementation of I&M programs is challenging. Part of the difficulty is technical in nature: testing equipment needs to be compatible with varied driving conditions. However, many of the key challenges involve issues pertaining to wider policy and institutional issues.[62] For instance, there is a need to ensure coherence between climate, air quality and transport policies; often inspection and maintenance is not featured in climate or air quality policies. Furthermore, there may also be a need to support greater governmental coordination between environmental and transport agencies. In addition, mechanisms that support the transfer of funds to local governments can help in strengthening monitoring of implemented programmes. In a similar fashion, I&M programmes would arguably benefit from compensatory measures that, among others, subsidize automotive repairs among low-income groups. A similarly motivated set of reforms could involve fostering opportunities for low-income drivers and advocacy groups to participate in fora where decisions are made over programme implementation.

4.2 *Residential Energy and Clean Cooking*

Another key SLCP measure involves residential energy and cookstoves. In energy-scarce and rural areas, traditional cook stoves are powered by firewood, dung, biomass, and coal. Beyond low levels of combustion, the lack of ventilation from traditional stoves leads to high levels of emissions that contribute to worsening air quality.[63] The knowledge of these adverse impacts has led governments and the international development community to promote a variety

61 Ying Li, 'Evaluating and Improving the Effectiveness of Vehicle Inspection and Maintenance Programs: A Cost-Benefit Analysis Framework' (2017) 08 Journal of Environmental Protection 1541.

62 ibid; Ying Li and Douglas J Crawford-Brown, 'Assessing the Co-Benefits of Greenhouse Gas Reduction: Health Benefits of Particulate Matter Related Inspection and Maintenance Programs in Bangkok, Thailand' (2011) 409 Science of the Total Environment 1774 <http://dx.doi.org/10.1016/j.scitotenv.2011.01.051>.

63 WHO, 'Increasing Access to Clean Cooking through Subsidies' (2022) <https://www.householdenergypolicies.org/assets/subsidies.pdf?sfvrsn=6a5a5a19_5> accessed 6 December 2022.

of solutions. Several solutions involve technical measures like improved cookstoves with fans, electrification, switching to liquified petroleum gas, and biodigesters that generate alternative lower emission fuels.[64]

There have nonetheless been challenges to the widespread uptake of cleaner options. Some of the barriers are again technical in nature, such as a lack of access to cleaner fuels. However, many would benefit from paying greater attention to work across sectors and involving key stakeholders. For instance, residential energy systems do not always fit into climate or even air pollution strategies. Another part of why these issues are often relegated to the margins of policy decisions relates to the absence of key agencies and divisions in relevant discussions. For these reasons, cleaner stove and fuel programmes stand to gain more traction with greater engagement between national, local and even community level governments.[65] Similarly, such programmes would find greater support from targeted subsidy programmes aimed at helping lower-income groups shift to less polluting fuels and technologies;[66] in much the same way, the creation of decision-making fora that enable the meaningful participation of stove users and purchasers would also be useful.[67]

4.3 *Open Burning of Agricultural Residue and Biomass*

A third key SLCP measure involves open burning of agricultural residues. With growing pressures to accelerate planting and harvesting cycles, farmers in many parts of the world often use fire to clear residue (such as rice stalks) from fields. Though expedient, this technique leads to higher emissions of

---

64 K Thoday and others, 'The Mega Conversion Program from Kerosene to LPG in Indonesia: Lessons Learned and Recommendations for Future Clean Cooking Energy Expansion' (2018) 46 Energy for Sustainable Development 71; Kaoru Akahoshi and others, 'Overcoming Barriers to Clean Cooking in Thailand: A Quantitative Assessment' (2022) April-June Asia Pacific Tech Monitor <https://apctt.org/sites/default/files/attachment/2022-09/06_Cookstove_Article_rev10_AB_Edited_DM.pdf>; Huy, Winijkul and Kim Oanh (n 15).

65 Putti Venkata Ramana and others, 'The State of the Global Clean and Improved Cooking Sector' [2015] ESMAP and GACC 1 <https://openknowledge.worldbank.org/bitstream/handle/10986/21878/96499.pdf>.

66 WHO, 'Increasing Access to Clean Cooking through Subsidies' (n 72).

67 So-Young Lee and Eric Zusman, 'Participatory Climate Governance in Southeas Asia: Lessons Learned from Gender-Responsive Mitigation' in Tahseen Jafry (ed), *Routledge Handbook of Climate Justice* (Routledge 2019); Adeladza Kofi Amegah and Jouni JK Jaakkola, 'Household Air Pollution and the Sustainable Development Goals' (2016) 94 Bulletin of the World Health Organization 215; WHO, 'Increasing Access to Clean Cooking through Subsidies' (n 72).

carbonaceous aerosols (both black and organic carbon) that contribute significantly to seasonal air pollution episodes.[68]

Although policymakers and farmers are aware of the combination of factors that contribute to burning, changing the practices runs into a number of difficulties. Some hurdles are technical such as a lack of equipment that can turn residue into mulch or fertilizer. However, similar to the examples cited above, many of the challenges stem from the need for more integrated and inclusive polices and institutions. To illustrate, there is a clear need to ensure that policies promoting increased crop yields and climate mitigation and air pollution control do not operate at cross-purposes. Likewise, institutions focusing on food production and climate protection will require mechanisms facilitating the exchange of knowledge, data and perhaps even funding. Moreover, comparable to previous cases, multi-level cooperation can help to ensure that local governments have the resources they need to monitor burning while rewarding communities for conceiving and making use of alternatives. In line with some of the other solutions, there may also be opportunities to advance more inclusive solutions to burning by bringing farmers into the decision-making process. For instance, climate field schools could help identify workable solutions to climate-related agricultural challenges that could then be adjusted to build consensuses around alternatives to the practices.[69] Similarly, there may be opportunities to build and expand enterprises that convert crop residues into furniture or other products. Building a strong value chain for these products—focused on creating a reliable a sustainable income stream for farmers—would help remedy the impacts.

5 Conclusion

In most policy areas, the more information the better, but at this point it is evident that action to address the harms of SLCPs is also necessary. As UNEP stated in 2019, it is clear "that there is now sufficient evidence for action to

68 Danutawat Tipayarom, Nguyen Thi and Kim Oanh, 'Effects from Open Rice Straw Burning Emission on Air Quality in the Bangkok Metropolitan Region' (2007) 33 339; Kim Oanh N. T, NP Dong and DA Permadi, 'Emissions of Toxic and Climate Forcer Pollutants from Crop Residue Open Burning in Southeast Asia', *A&WMA's 109th Annual Conference & Exhibition* (2016).

69 Matthew Hengesbaugh, Eric Zusman and Peter King, 'Growing Support for Climate-Smart Agriculture by Scaling Up Farmer and Climate Field Schools: Recommended Policy and Institutional Reforms' (2020) <https://www.iges.or.jp/en/publication_documents/pub/policy/en/11007/PB_42_E_1005.pdf>.

reduce the impacts of air pollution on human health in Asia and the Pacific".[70] Appropriate policy response can make a significant difference, and the stakes are high, with hundreds of thousands—even millions—of lives at risk. There is little excuse for inaction. However, there is still scope to ensure that policies and institutions are in place that can drive implementation of those actions.

More specifically, what must be done in terms of enacting these policies? A major step forward would be the comprehensive and well thought out integration of strategies and plans to simultaneously address air pollution and climate change, and their concomitant positive effect on health outcomes. There is overlap between actions in these areas, with the clear potential for mutually beneficial results, whether through steps by national governments and companies that even partially reduce SLCP's contribution to global warming,[71] or at least some reduction in the more than 7 million annual premature deaths tied to air-pollution, not to mention the millions of disability-adjusted life years lost.[72]

Imagining this as a win-win-win solution for air quality, climate and health could motivate action not only by environmental and health experts, but other stakeholders like businesses or politicians focused on cost-effective spending (as well as their re-election to office). Although not explicitly discussed above, the economic motivations and probable net positive economic benefits of reducing pollution for action are worth considering in future research. While any improvements that reduce polluting processes, or even hasten the transition away from reliance on fossil-fuel energy and industrial processes that produce SLCPs may be costly at the outset, there are likely measurable benefits in the reduction of climate-related and improved health outcomes, not to mention long-term financial savings.

This chapter has argued that it is vital that future SLCP strategies focus not only on maximizing benefits, but who benefits (and loses) from those changes. In using a slightly different lens, it may be possible to refine both the policies intended to minimize the health and other impacts of SLCPs as well as mitigate SLCP emissions. Adopting this lens will require more efforts to bring different agencies and stakeholder groups into the modelling, design and implementation of concrete interventions. A final point merits highlighting when thinking about this interface. Moving forward, it will also be useful to more explicitly consider how "inclusiveness" affects the adoption and implementation of different interventions in modelling scenarios. For instance,

70 UNEP APCAP and CCAC (n 1).
71 UNEP/WMO (n 1).
72 McDuffie and others (n 24).

the timing of adoption or diffusion rates of key technologies could be slowed by a failure to understand the needs and concerns of users. A more accurate accounting of the influence of those concerns on benefit estimates may also prompt the research community and policymakers to better understand what inclusiveness means for their work.

Acknowledgements

Eric Zusman would like to extend his appreciation to the "Environment Research and Technology Development Fund of the Environmental Restoration and Conservation Agency Provided by the Ministry of Environment of Japan" for the financial support required to conduct the research featured in this article.

Bibliography

Akahoshi K and others, 'Overcoming Barriers to Clean Cooking in Thailand: A Quantitative Assessment' (2022) April-June Asia Pacific Tech Monitor <https://apctt.org/sites/default/files/attachment/2022-09/06_Cookstove_Article_rev10_AB_Edited_DM.pdf>.

Akahoshi K and Zusman E, 'Bringing Clean Air to 4 Billion People in Asia' *The Diplomat* (23 September 2021) <https://thediplomat.com/2021/09/bringing-clean-air-to-4-billion-people-in-asia/>.

Amegah AK and Jaakkola JJ, 'Household Air Pollution and the Sustainable Development Goals' (2016) 94 Bulletin of the World Health Organization 215.

Betsill MM and Bulkeley H, 'Cities and the Multilevel Governance of Global Climate Change' (2006) 12 Global Governance 141.

Bilsky E, Moreno AC and Tortosa AF, 'Local Governments and SDG Localisation: Reshaping Multilevel Governance from the Bottom Up' (2021) 22 Journal of Human Development and Capabilities 713.

Bond TC and others, 'Bounding the Role of Black Carbon in the Climate System: a Scientific Assessment.' (2013) 118 Journal of Geophysical Research: Atmospheres 5380.

Cash DW and others, 'Knowledge Systems for Sustainable Development' (2003) 100 Proceedings of the National Academy of Sciences of the United States of America 8086.

Castells N and Ravetz J, 'Science and Policy in International Environmental Agreements' [2001] International Environmental Agreements: Politics, Law and Economics 405.

CCAC and UNEP, *Short-Lived Climate Pollutants Short-Lived Climate Pollutants in Latin America* (2018).

Cook NJ, Grillos T and Andersson KP, 'Gender Quotas Increase the Equality and Effectiveness of Climate Policy Interventions' (2019) 9 Nature Climate Change 330 <http://dx.doi.org/10.1038/s41558-019-0438-4>.

Corfee-Morlot J and others, 'Cities, Climate Change and Multilevel Governance' (2009).

Cushing L and others, 'Environmental Equity : Evidence from California ' s Cap-and-Trade Program' (2018) 15 PLOS Medicine 1.

Danesh Yazdi M and others, 'Long-Term Association of Air Pollution and Hospital Admissions among Medicare Participants Using a Doubly Robust Additive Model' (2021) 143 Circulation 1584.

Dilling L and Lemos MC, 'Creating Usable Science: Opportunities and Constraints for Climate Knowledge Use and Their Implications for Science Policy' (2011) 21 Global Environmental Change 680.

Dinesh D and others, 'Learning from Failure at the Science–Policy Interface for Climate Action in Agriculture' (2021) 26 Mitigation and Adaptation Strategies for Global Change.

Elder M and Loewe C, 'Introduction and Context' in UNEP (ed), *Global Environment Outlook—GEO6: Healthy Planet, Healty People* (United Nations Environment Programme 2019).

European Investment Bank, 'Short-Lived Climate Pollutants (SLCPs): an Analysis of the EIB's Policies, Procedures, Impact of Activities and Options for Scaling up Mitigation Efforts' (2016).

Failey T, 'Poor Communities Exposed to Elevated Air Pollution Levels' (2016) <https://www.niehs.nih.gov/research/programs/geh/geh_newsletter/2016/4/spotlight/poor_communities_exposed_to_elevated_air_pollution_levels.cfm>.

Galgoczi B, 'From Paris to Katowice: the EU Needs to Step Up Its Game on Climate Change and Set Its Own Just Transition Framework' [2018] SSRN Electronic Journal.

Gooch GD and others, 'The Science–Policy–Stakeholder Interface in Sustainable Water Management: Creating Interactive Participatory Scenarios Together with Stakeholders', *Science, Policy and Stakeholders in Water Management* (Routledge 2010).

Gupta A and others, *Science Networks* (2012).

Guston DH, 'Boundary Organizations in Environmental Policy and Science: an Introduction' (2001) 26 Science, Technology, & Human Values 399.

Hajat A, Hsia C and O'Neill MS, 'Socioeconomic Disparities and Air Pollution Exposure: a Global Review' (2015) 2 Current Environmental Health Reports 440 <https://pubmed.ncbi.nlm.nih.gov/26381684/> accessed 6 December 2022.

Hausker K, 'Vehicle Inspection and Maintenance Programs: International Experience and Best Practices' (2004).

Hengesbaugh M, Zusman E and King P, 'Growing Support for Climate-Smart Agriculture by Scaling Up Farmer and Climate Field Schools: Recommended Policy

and Institutional Reforms' (2020) <https://www.iges.or.jp/en/publication_documents/pub/policy/en/11007/PB_42_E_1005.pdf>.
Heritage Z and Green G, 'European National Healthy City Networks: the Impact of an Elite Epistemic Community' (2013) 90 Journal of Urban Health 154.
HFI, 'State of Global Air 2020' (2020).
Huy LN, Winijkul E and Kim Oanh NT, 'Assessment of Emissions from Residential Combustion in Southeast Asia and Implications for Climate Forcing Potential' (2021) 785 Science of the Total Environment.
IPCC, *Climate Change 2021: the Physical Science Basis. Contribution of Working Group I to the Sixth Assessment Report of the Intergovernmental Panel on Climate Change* (R Yu and B Zhou Masson-Delmotte, V., P. Zhai, A. Pirani, S. L. Connors, C. Péan, S. Berger, N. Caud, Y. Chen, L. Goldfarb, M. I. Gomis, M. Huang, K. Leitzell, E. Lonnoy, J. B. R. Matthews, T. K. Maycock, T. Waterfield, O. Yelekçi ed, 2021).
Jacob M and Hellström T, 'Reviewing the Science-Policy Relationship: the Policy as Theory Alternative (PAST)' (1998) 25 Science and Public Policy 218.
Jones SA, Fischhoff B and Lach D, 'Evaluating the Science-Policy Interface for Climate Change Research' (1999) 43 Climatic Change 581.
Kholod N and Evans M, 'Reducing Black Carbon Emissions from Diesel Vehicles in Russia: an Assessment and Policy Recommendations' (2016) 56 Environmental Science and Policy 1.
Kim Oanh N. T, Dong NP and Permadi DA, 'Emissions of Toxic and Climate Forcer Pollutants from Crop Residue Open Burning in Southeast Asia', *A&WMA's 109th Annual Conference & Exhibition* (2016).
Lee S-Y and Zusman E, 'Participatory Climate Governance in Southeas Asia: Lessons Learned from Gender-Responsive Mitigation' in Tahseen Jafry (ed), *Routledge Handbook of Climate Justice* (Routledge 2019).
Li Y, 'Evaluating and Improving the Effectiveness of Vehicle Inspection and Maintenance Programs: a Cost-Benefit Analysis Framework' (2017) 08 Journal of Environmental Protection 1541.
Li Y and Crawford-Brown DJ, 'Assessing the Co-Benefits of Greenhouse Gas Reduction: Health Benefits of Particulate Matter Related Inspection and Maintenance Programs in Bangkok, Thailand' (2011) 409 Science of the Total Environment 1774 <http://dx.doi.org/10.1016/j.scitotenv.2011.01.051>.
Mader AD and others, 'Country Representatives' Perceptions of the Biodiversity Science-Policy Interface' (2021) 1 Conservation 73.
McDuffie E and others, 'Global Burden of Disease from Major Air Pollution Sources (GBD MAPS): a Global Approach' (2021) 1 <http://ovidsp.ovid.com/ovidweb.cgi?T=JS&PAGE=reference&D=emexb&NEWS=N&AN=639091709>.

Mohieldin M and others, 'The Role of Local and Regional Governments in the SDGs: the Localization Agenda', *Business, Government and the SDGs* (Palgrave Macmillan 2023).

Persson Å and others, 'Editorial: Environmental Policy Integration: Taking Stock of Policy Practice in Different Contexts' (2018) 85 Environmental Science & Policy 113.

Peters BG, 'The Challenge of Policy Coordination' (2018) 1 Policy Design and Practice 1 <https://doi.org/10.1080/25741292.2018.1437946>.

Peters G, 'Managing Horizontal Government: the Politics of Co-Ordination' (1998) 76 Public Administration 295.

Rabe BG, 'Beyond Kyoto : Climate Change Policy in Multilevel Governance Systems' (2007) 20 423.

Simoni M and others, 'Adverse Effects of Outdoor Pollution in the Elderly' (2015) 7 Journal of Thoracic Disease 34.

Smith G and Setälä M, 'Mini-Publics and Deliberative Democracy' in Andre Bächtiger and others (eds), *The Oxford Handbook of Deliberative Democracy* (2018) <https://www.oxfordhandbooks.com/view/10.1093/oxfordhb/9780198747369.001.0001/oxfordhb-9780198747369-e-27> accessed 12 June 2022.

Sokolovska N, Fecher B and Wagner GG, 'Communication on the Science-Policy Interface: an Overview of Conceptual Models' (2019) 7 Publications.

Spilsbury MJ and Nasi R, 'The Interface of Policy Research and the Policy Development Process: Challenges Posed to the Forestry Community' (2006) 8 Forest Policy and Economics 193.

Takemura T, 'Return to Different Climate States by Reducing Sulphate Aerosols under Future CO_2 Concentrations' (2020) 10 Scientific Reports.

Thoday K and others, 'The Mega Conversion Program from Kerosene to LPG in Indonesia: Lessons Learned and Recommendations for Future Clean Cooking Energy Expansion' (2018) 46 Energy for Sustainable Development 71.

Tipayarom D, Thi N and Oanh K, 'Effects from Open Rice Straw Burning Emission on Air Quality in the Bangkok Metropolitan Region' (2007) 33 339.

UNECE, 'Air Pollution, Ecosystems and Biodiversity' (2022) <https://unece.org/air-pollution-ecosystems-and-biodiversity> accessed 5 October 2022.

UNEP, 'Air Pollution Note—Data You Need to Know' (2022) <https://www.unep.org/interactive/air-pollution-note/?fbclid=IwAR2KKH_zwwl9nDJFZkoyTny586HoI76dbswRKkuNoyBSJ6uystEHdXkEGLE>.

UNEP/WMO, 'Integrated Assessment of Black Carbon and Tropospheric Ozone: Summary for Decision Makers' (2011) <http://www.unep.org/dewa/Portals/67/pdf/Black_Carbon.pdf>.

UNEP/WMO, 'Integrated Assessment of Air Pollution and Climate Change in Africa 2020–2021' (2022).

UNEP, APCAP and CCAC, 'Air Pollution in Asia and the Pacific: Science-Based Solutions. United Nations Environment Programme' (2019) <https://www.ccacoalition.org/resources/air-pollution-asia-and-pacific-science-based-solutions-summary-full-report>.

UNICEF, 'Mongolia's Air Pollution Crisis: a Call to Action to Protect Children's Health' (2018) <https://reliefweb.int/sites/reliefweb.int/files/resources/Mongolia_air_pollution_crisis_ENG.pdf>.

UNICEF, 'Child-Centred Clean Air Solutions: Guide for Asia and the Pacific Region' (2022).

United Nations International Childrens' Emergency Fund (UNICEF), 'Clean Air for Children' (2016) <https://www.unicef.org/media/49966/file/UNICEF_Clear_the_Air_for_Children_30_Oct_2016.pdf>.

Venkata Ramana P and others, 'The State of the Global Clean and Improved Cooking Sector' [2015] ESMAP and GACC 1 <https://openknowledge.worldbank.org/bitstream/handle/10986/21878/96499.pdf>.

Wan K and others, 'Science-Policy Interplay on Air Pollution Governance in China' (2020) 107 Environmental Science and Policy 150 <https://doi.org/10.1016/j.envsci.2020.03.003>.

Watson RT, 'Turning Science into Policy: Challenges and Experiences from the Science-Policy Interface' (2005) 360 Philosophical Transactions of the Royal Society B: Biological Sciences 471.

WHO, 'Reducing Global Health Risks: Through Mitigation of Short-Lived Climate Pollutants: Scoping Report for Policymakers' (2015).

WHO, 'Ambient (Outdoor) Air Pollution' (22 September 2021) <https://www.who.int/news-room/fact-sheets/detail/ambient-(outdoor)-air-quality-and-health> accessed 24 May 2022.

WHO, 'Increasing Access to Clean Cooking through Subsidies' (2022) <https://www.householdenergypolicies.org/assets/subsidies.pdf?sfvrsn=6a5a5a19_5> accessed 6 December 2022.

Yamineva Y, 'Lessons from the Intergovernmental Panel on Climate Change on Inclusiveness across Geographies and Stakeholders' (2017) 77 Environmental Science and Policy 244 <http://dx.doi.org/10.1016/j.envsci.2017.04.005>.

Zaelke D, 'Primer on Short-Lived Climate Pollutants' (2013) <http://www.igsd.org>.

Zusman E and others, 'One Atmosphere: Integrating Air Pollution and Climate Policy and Governance' (2021) 12 Atmosphere 1.

CHAPTER 11

Black Carbon Emissions in International Maritime Shipping

Thomas L. Brewer

1 Introduction

Black carbon contributes about one-fifth of the carbon dioxide equivalent (CO_2e) in shipping's emissions.[1] In the emissions of marine diesel engines, the ratio of black carbon to organic carbon (OC) – which is a 'global coolant' – is about 9:1, which means that the net effect of diesel-powered ships' emissions clearly contributes to global warming.

Black carbon emissions of ships are especially significant in the Arctic region because of their effects on ice melt, not only in the Arctic Ocean, but also in the glaciers of Greenland (see Chapter 1). Between 2015 and 2019, ships' black carbon emissions increased 85%.[2]

In all regions of the world, major portions of ships' black carbon emissions occur near coasts, especially in port areas. Consequently, there are also *significant local and regional health effects*.[3] Ships' black carbon emissions can cause asthma, as well as lung cancer, heart disease, dementia and Alzheimer's disease among older people.[4] There is also accumulating evidence of a causal relationship between local variations in particulate matter, including black

1 Naya Olmer and others, 'Greenhouse gas emissions from global shipping, 2013–2015' (2017) <https://theicct.org/sites/default/files/publications/Global-shipping-GHG-emissions-2013-2015_ICCT-Report_17102017_vF.pdf> accessed 3 May 2022.

2 Brian Comer and others, 'The International Maritime Organisation's Proposed Arctic Heavy Fuel Oils Ban: Likely Implications and Opportunities for Improvement' (2020) <https://theicct.org/publication/the-international-maritime-organizations-proposed-arctic-heavy-fuel-oil-ban-likely-implications-and-opportunities-for-improvement/> accessed 7 March 2023.

3 Thomas Brewer, 'Black Carbon and Other Air Pollutants in Italian Ports and Coastal Areas: Problems, Solutions and Implications for Policy' (2020) 10 Applied Science 23.

4 Susan Anenberg and others, 'Impacts of global, regional, and sectoral black carbon emission reductions on surface air quality and human mortality deaths' (2011) 11 Atmospheric Chemistry and Physics 14, 7253–7267; Susan Anenberg and others, 'A global snapshot of the air pollution-related health impacts of transportation sector emissions in 2010 and 2015' (ICCT, 2019) <https://theicct.org/sites/default/files/publications/Global_health_impacts_transport_emissions_2010-2015_20190226.pdf> accessed 3 July 2019.

 | DOI:10.1163/9789004684089_013

carbon in particular, and the incidence of COVID-19.[5] These direct, local, and virtually immediately-experienced health effects make black carbon emissions distinctive in comparison with the well-known greenhouses gasses (methane, nitrous oxides and carbon dioxide), not only because black carbon emissions occur in the form of particulate matter rather than gases but also because the profiles of the costs and benefits of mitigating them are different from all the other climate change forcing agents.[6]

Globally, all types of emissions from ships in international commerce cause about 60,000 deaths annually and about USD 160 billion in health costs, according to 'conservative estimates'.[7] There are not only health care economic costs, but also economic costs from damage to agricultural crops,[8] in addition to the economic costs of global warming. Black carbon is however co-emitted with other substances with some of them like SO_2 having a cooling impact on the climate.

International shipping's black carbon emissions thus present a wide range of regulatory issues at multiple levels of governance on climate change, public health, and agricultural agendas around the world. Those agendas not only

5 Anushka Bhaskar and others, 'Air pollution, SARS-CoV-2 transmission, and COVID-19 outcomes: A state-of-the-science review of a rapidly evolving research area' (medRxiv 2020) <https://www.medrxiv.org/content/10.1101/2020.08.16.20175901v1> accessed 14 December 2022; Dario Caro, Edoardo Conticini, and Bruno Frediani, "Link between air pollution and coronavirus mortality in Italy could be possible' (Science Daily 2020) <https://www.sciencedaily.com/releases/2020/04/200406100824.htm> accessed 14 December 2022; Silvia Comunian and others, 'Air Pollution and COVID-19: The Role of Particulate Matter in the Spread and Increase of COVID-19's Morbidity and Mortality' (2020) 17 Int. J. Environ. Res. Public Health 4487; Edoardo Conticini, Bruno Frediani, and Dario Caro, 'Can atmospheric pollution be considered a co-factor in extremely high level of SARS-CoV-2 lethality in Northern Italy?' (2020) 261 Environ. Pollut. 114465; Leonardo Setti and others, 'Evaluation of the Potential Relationship between Particulate Matter (PM) Pollution and COVID-19 Infection Spread in Italy' (Società Italiana di Medicina Ambientale 2020) <https://www.aircentre.org/wp-content/uploads/2020/04/Setti_et_al_2020.pdf> accessed 14 December 2022; Xiao Wu and others, "Exposure to Air Pollution and COVID-19 Mortality in the United States: A Nationwide Cross-Sectional Study' (medRxvi 2020) <https://www.medrxiv.org/content/10.1101/2020.04.05.20054502v2> accessed 14 December 2022; Maria Zoran and others, 'Assessing the relationship between surface levels of $PM_{2.5}$ and PM_{10} particulate matter impact on COVID-19 in Milan, Italy' (2020) 738 Sci. Total. Environ. 139825.

6 Thomas Brewer, *Climate Change – An Interdisciplinary Introduction* (Springer, forthcoming).

7 Anenberg and others, 'A global snapshot' (n4).

8 CCAC, 'Fast Track to Improving Food Security and Mitigating Climate Change: The Agriculture Initiative of the Climate and Clean Air Coalition' (2014) <https://www.ccacoalition.org/en/resources/coag-flyer-fast-track-improving-food-security-and-mitigating-climate-change-agriculture> accessed on 20 June 2018; IPCC, *Special Report: Climate Change and Land* (Cambridge University Press 2019).

vary by geography and level of government; they also vary among the many segments of the industry. The industry segments can be defined in terms of three dimensions: type of service; propulsion system, including the fuel used; and size of the vessel. There is no universally accepted, comprehensive list of the types of ships.[9] However, it is common to identify at least six or more types of commercial vessels. A particularly detailed list identified 21 types, not including military ships.[10] Between these low and high examples, a list from the United Nations Conference on Trade and Development (UNCTAD)[11] includes ten (see Table 11.1).

Among the types of vessels in the world fleet, there are highly variable contributions of black carbon emissions. For instance, of the estimated 67 million tonnes of black carbon emitted by the world fleet of 70,000 ships in 2015, 60% of the total was emitted by only three types: container ships (26%), bulk carriers (19%), and oil tankers (15%).[12]

Black carbon regulatory issues are a combination of the *distinctive* issues for each type of vessel and the *common* issues among them. The following section of the chapter addresses the three questions at the *global* level of governance: What is the current state of the international regulatory agenda? What has the regulatory system achieved? How should it be developed in the future? The subsequent sections do the same for each of the other levels of governance: regional, national and local. Although black carbon emissions are regulated at different levels of governance, this chapter also argues that there are overlaps of the governance levels.

2 Global Level: International Maritime Organization (IMO)

2.1 *State of the Regulatory Agenda*

The IMO is a specialized UN agency with 175 member states and many types of regulatory systems in place to limit ships' emissions. However, the IMO as of this writing in mid-2022 has not produced a substantial regulatory system explicitly

9 IMO, 'Prevention of air pollution from ships' (2021) <https://www.imo.org/en/OurWork/Environment/Pages/Air-Pollution.aspx> accessed 25 February.

10 Bryan Comer and others, 'Black carbon emissions and fuel use in global shipping' (ICCT 2017) <https://theicct.org/publications/black-carbon-emissions-global-shipping-2015> accessed 1 March 2021.

11 United Nations Conference on Trade and Development, 'Review of Maritime Transport 2020' (UNCTAD 2021).

12 Comer and others, 'Black Carbon Emissions' (n10).

TABLE 11.1 Types of ships in international maritime shipping and their black carbon emissions (2015)

Ship type ('class')	BC emissions (Mmt)	BC emissions (% of industry)	Number of ships
Container ships	17.4	26.1	5,008
Bulk carriers	12.4	18.6	10,572
Oil tankers	10.0	15.0	5,733
Chemical tankers	4.4	6.6	4,568
General cargo ships	4.3	6.5	9,183
Cruise	4.1	6.1	406
Ferry-ro-pax	2.4	3.6	2,062
Liquified gas tanker	2.0	3.0	1,675
Vehicle	1.7	2.6	820
Service – other	1.6	2.3	6,865
Ro-ro	1.5	2.2	1,055
Fishing	1.3	2.0	7,030
Refrigerator bulk	1.2	1.8	703
Offshore supply	1.2	1.7	4,447
Service tug	0.7	1.0	6,941
Ferry-pax only	0.3	0.5	1,424
Yacht	0.1	0.2	1,530
Total[a]	66.6[a]	100[a]	70,360[a]

a Totals include "others" not itemized separately in this table.

SOURCE: COMPILED BY THE AUTHOR FROM COMER AND OTHERS, 'BLACK CARBON EMISSIONS AND FUEL USE IN GLOBAL SHIPPING' (ICCT 2017) <HTTPS://THEICCT.ORG/PUBLICATIONS/BLACK-CARBON-EMISSIONS-GLOBAL-SHIPPING-2015> ACCESSED 1 MARCH 2021.

focused on black carbon. It received a series of reports from expert workshops organized by the International Council for Clean Transportation (ICCT) over a period of six years. The workshops produced extensive reports on black carbon problems and potential solutions.[13] The reports were acknowledged by relevant IMO committees, but no significant actions were taken.

However, in 2021, the IMO's Marine Environment Protection Committee adopted a resolution on the voluntary use of cleaner fuels in the Arctic, to reduce black carbon emissions.[14] The document 'urges Member States and ship operators to voluntarily use distillate or other cleaner alternative fuels or methods of propulsion that are safe for ships and could contribute to the reduction of Black Carbon emissions from ships when operating in or near the Arctic'.[15] A group of countries spoke in opposition to the resolution – including Russia, China, India, Japan, Saudi Arabia, UAE and Angola – but there were not enough IMO national government members to prevent its passage.[16] The full one-page resolution is attached to this chapter as Annex 8.1. In 2022, the IMO established a correspondence group to "develop draft guidelines on recommendatory goal-based control measures to reduce the impact on the Arctic of Black Carbon emissions from international shipping".[17] Thus, as of mid-2022, there have been two initiatives to reduce black carbon emissions in the Arctic region – but they do not provide any formalized schedule for doing so.

---

13 Bryan Comer, 'Black Carbon and Maritime Shipping: The Long Road to Regulating a Short-Lived Climate Pollutant' (CCAC 2019) <https://www.ccacoalition.org/en/blog/black-carbon-and-maritime-shipping-long-road-regulating-short-lived-climate-pollutant> accessed 2 April 2022; ICCT, '1st workshop on marine black carbon emissions' (2014) <https://www.theicct.org/event/marine-black-crbon-emissions-identifyresearch-gaps/> accessed 15 April 2022; ICCT, '2nd workshop on marine black carbon emissions' (2015) <https://theicct.org/event/2nd-workshop-on-marine-black-carbon-emissions/> accessed 10 April 2022; ICCT, '3rd workshop on marine black carbon emissions' (2016) <https://theicct.org/event/3rd-workshop-on-marine-black-carbon-emissions-measuring-and-controlling-bc-from-marine-engines/> accessed 10 April 2022; ICCT, '4th workshop on marine black carbon emissions' (2017) <https://theicct.org/event/4th-workshop-on-marine-black-carbon-emissions-identifying-appropriate-measurement-methods/> accessed 10 April 2022; ICCT, '5th workshop on marine black carbon emissions' (2018) <https://theicct.org/event/5th-workshop-on-marine-black-carbon-emissions/> accessed 10 April 2022; ICCT, '6th workshop on marine black carbon emissions' (2019) <https://theicct.org/event/6th-workshop-on-marine-black-carbon-emissions/> accessed 10 April 2022.

14 IMO, 'Prevention of Air Pollution' (n9).

15 Resolution MEPC.342(77) of 26 November 2021.

16 Climate Home News, 'How the shipping industry can halve climate-warming black carbon in the Arctic' (2022) <https://www.climatechangenews.com/2021/03/18/shipping-industry-can-halve-climate-warming-black-carbon-arctic/> accessed 14 April 2022.

17 IMO, 'Report to the Marine Environment Protection Committee' (Sub-Committee on Pollution Prevention and Response, Document PPR 9/21, 26 April 2022) <https://www.iadc.org/wp-content/uploads/2022/05/PPR-9-21-Report-To-The-Marine-Environment-Protection-Committee-Secretariat.pdf> accessed 8 June 2022.

BOX 11.1 MARPOL Annex VI

MARPOL Annex VI, first adopted in 1997, limits the main air pollutants contained in ships exhaust gas, including sulfur oxides (SOX) and nitrous oxides (NOx), and it prohibits deliberate emissions of ozone depleting substances (ODS). MARPOL Annex VI also regulates shipboard incineration, and the emissions of volatile organic compounds (VOC) from tankers. These provisions apply to all IMO members.

Following entry into force of MARPOL Annex VI on 19 May 2005, the Marine Environment Protection Committee (MEPC) agreed to revise the Annex VI to strengthen the emission limits in light of technological improvements and implementation experience. As a result, the revised MARPOL Annex VI and the separate but related NOx Technical Code 2008 entered into force on 1 July 2010.

The main changes introduced to MARPOL Annex VI are a progressive reduction globally in emissions of SOX, NOx and particulate matter and the creation of emission control areas (ECAs) to reduce emissions of selected air pollutants in the designated ECAs' sea areas.

The global sulfur limit will be reduced from current 3.50% to 0.50%, effective from 1 January 2020, subject to a feasibility review to be completed no later than 2018. This global limit, which is now in effect, applies to all types of vessels in international commerce, depending on the date of their entry into service. The limits applicable in ECAs for SOX and particulate matter were reduced to 0.10%, from 1 January 2015.

The revised NOx Technical Code 2008 includes a new chapter based on the agreed approach for regulation of existing (pre-2000) engines established in MARPOL Annex VI, provisions for a direct measurement and monitoring method, a certification procedure for existing engines, and test cycles to be applied to Tier II and Tier III engines.

The amendments provide for the Tier III NOx standards to be applied to a marine diesel engine that is installed on a ship constructed on or after 1 January 2016 and which operates in the North American ECA or the U.S. Caribbean Sea ECA that are designated for the control of NOx emissions.

In addition, the Tier III requirements would apply to installed marine diesel engines when operated in other emission control areas which might be designated in the future for Tier III NOx control. Tier III would apply to ships constructed on or after the date of adoption by the Marine Environment Protection Committee of such an emission control area, or a later date as may be specified in the amendment designating the NOx Tier III emission control area.

Revisions to the regulations for ozone-depleting substances, volatile organic compounds, shipboard incineration, reception facilities and fuel oil quality were also made with regulations on fuel oil availability added.

The revised measures are expected to have a significant beneficial impact on the atmospheric environment and human health, particularly for those people living in port cities and coastal communities.

Further, a recent amendment to MARPOL IV concerns the procedures for sampling and verification of the sulfur content of fuel oil and the Energy Efficiency Design Index; the amendment entered into force on 1 April 2022. These relate to in-use and onboard fuel oil sampling and testing, and requiring one or more sampling points to be fitted or designated for the purpose of taking representative samples of the fuel oil being used or carried for use on board of the ship. The representative samples of the fuel oil being used on board are to be taken in order to verify the fuel oil complies with the regulation.

***Source:* IMO**[18]

There are, however, many IMO rules that indirectly reduce black carbon emissions; in particular, the Energy Efficiency Design Index and Ship Energy Efficiency Management Plan are indirect regulations to reduce CO_2. In addition, the International Convention for the Prevention of Pollution from Ships (MARPOL) is the main international convention covering prevention of pollution of the marine environment by ships from operational or accidental causes. It was adopted in 1973, but it had still not entered into force five years later. A series of shipping accidents prompted agreement in 1978, when adoption of the MARPOL Protocol included the convention. MARPOL Annex VI is relevant to the regulation of black carbon as described in Box 11.1.

2.2 *Proposals for Future Developments*

Ships' black carbon emissions can be reduced in many ways. An effective and direct way is to switch from residual fuels, such as heavy fuel oil, to distillate fuels – a switch that can reduce black carbon emissions from shipping in half. The shift can be achieved via fuel quality regulations.[19] However, because black carbon is particulate matter, not a gas, it has been generally relegated to a low

18 ibid.

19 EUA (EU Funded Action on Black Carbon), 'Shipping' (2022) <https://eua-bca.amap.no/maritime-shipping#:~:text=shipping%20emissions%20include%20black%20carbon,of%20shipping%20emission's%20warming%20potential> accessed 3 May 2022; FOEI, WWF, Pacific Environment, and CSC, 'Reduction of the Impact on The Arctic of Black Carbon Emissions from International Shipping Fuels Are Key to Urgent Black

priority on climate change actions; in addition, it has been regarded as principally an air pollution health problem. A study by Chenxi and El-Halwagi[20] of the effects on black carbon emissions of the IMO's new lower 2020 sulfur emission limit concluded: 'The results indicate that the blended fuel aimed at satisfying the IMO 2020 Sulfur Cap does not perform well in [black carbon] emission control'. Further research on this issue is thus needed, as is further development of alternative technologies to reduce multiple types of emissions.

3 International Regional Level: Emission Control Areas (ECAs)

There are four existing regional ECAs, which limit some emissions to lower levels than global agreements and which have been registered by regional groups of national governments, and recognized by the IMO as international agreements that affect IMO-related concerns (see Table 11.2). The Baltic Sea ECA and the North Sea/English Channel ECA connect with one another in the Kattegat between Denmark and Sweden. The North American coasts of both the Atlantic and Pacific Oceans are in one ECA, and US-Caribbean Sea territories are in a separate ECA, which is a uniquely unilaterally developed ECA.

Although the North American and US-Caribbean ECAs officially include limitations to emissions of particulate matter, limiting black carbon emissions is not a policy objective. The purpose of the ECAs is to limit sulfur content. Any unintended limitation of black carbon would depend on the precise chemical content of a specific fuel.

3.1 *Proposal for Future Development: a Mediterranean ECA*

In recent years, the possibility of creating a Mediterranean ECA has been on the international maritime regulatory agenda.[21] A 'Med ECA' of nearly all of the coastal countries, including ports in southern Europe, northern Africa and the eastern Mediterranean, *could reduce the exposure of approximately 200 million*

Carbon Emission Reductions' (Pollution Prevention and Response Sub-Committee 9th Session Agenda, Item 8 ppr 9/8/3, 11 February 2022) <https://cleanarctic.org/2022/02/11/ppr-9-8-3-fuels-are-key-to-urgent-black-carbon-emission-reductions/> accessed 3 May 2022.

20 Ji Chenxi and Mahmoud El-Halwagi, 'A data-driven study of IMO compliant fuel emissions with consideration of black carbon aerosols' (2020) 218 Ocean Engineering 108241.

21 Maritime Executive, 'Environmental Groups Call for Mediterranean ECA' (2018) <https://maritime-executive.com/article/environmental-groups-call-for-mediterranean-eca> accessed 14 December 2022.

TABLE 11.2 Emission control areas (ECAs)

Area covered	**Baltic sea**	**North sea/ English channel**	**North America[a]**	**US-Caribbean territories[b]**
Year agreed	1997	2005	2010	2011
		Emissions Covered		
Particulate Matter	*No*	*No*	*Yes*	*Yes*
NOx	Yes	Yes	Yes	Yes
SOX	Yes	Yes	Yes	Yes
Members	Denmark Estonia Finland Germany Latvia Lithuania Poland Russia Sweden	Belgium Denmark France Germany Netherlands Norway Sweden UK, E. Coast	Canada France US	Puerto Rico and US Virgin Islands

a Includes both the Atlantic and Pacific coasts. The French self-governing territories of Saint Pierre and Miquelon are in the North Atlantic coast near Newfoundland, Canada.
b The US-Caribbean system is a uni-national system, whereas the other MOUs are international regional agreements.

SOURCES: THOMAS BREWER, 'REGULATING INTERNATIONAL MARITIME SHIPPING'S AIR POLLUTING EMISSIONS: MONITORING, REPORTING, VERIFYING AND ENFORCING REGULATORY COMPLIANCE' (2021) 5 JOURNAL OF INTERNATIONAL MARITIME SAFETY, ENVIRONMENTAL AFFAIRS, AND SHIPPING 4,196–207.); KEVIN CULLINANE AND RICKARD BERGQVIST, 'EMISSION CONTROL AREAS AND THEIR IMPACT ON MARITIME TRANSPORT' (2014) 28 TRANSPORTATION RESEARCH PART D: TRANSPORT AND ENVIRONMENT 1.

people in coastal zones to black carbon and other emissions.[22] The national governments of France, Italy and Spain have endorsed the creation of a Med

22 Thomas Brewer, 'A Maritime Emission Control Area for the Mediterranean Sea? Technological Solutions and Policy Options for a "Med ECA"' (2020) 5 Euro-Mediterranean Journal for Environmental Integration 1.

ECA. A French government lab[23] and the European Commission[24] have sponsored research on issues posed by the design and establishment of a Med ECA. Among the many issues needing to be addressed, one is the types of emissions that would be covered. Including black carbon emissions is clearly one option.

4 National Level: Government Participation in the IMO, ECAs, and MOUs

4.1 *State of the Regulatory Agenda*

As they interact with the other levels of governance – global, regional and local – national governments' policies as leaders or laggards are of course often determinative in international and local policymaking processes. Furthermore, national governments' policies are often direct reflections of industry interests and lobbying. At the global level, for instance, within the IMO, several oil exporting countries opposed the IMO resolution calling upon ships in or near the Arctic to take measures such as reducing their speed, but on a voluntary basis, as noted above.[25] At the regional level, the ten ECAs can only function effectively with the cooperation of the scores of national member governments in them. Yet, there are also variations among the ECAs, depending on the particular group of national governments in each of the ECAs – for instance, Nordic governments' support for the creation of the Baltic Sea and North Sea ECAs. Another example is the French government's initiative, along with the support of other EU members, that has been promoting the creation of a Mediterranean ECA. Furthermore, national government relations with local port authorities vary according to the nature of the national political system (e.g. whether 'federal' or not) and the relative significance of the local port in the national economy.

23 Ineris, French National Institute for Industrial Environment and Risks, Cerema, Citepa, and Plan Bleu, 'ECAMED: A Technical Feasibility Study for the Implementation of an Emission Control Area (ECA) in the Mediterranean Sea' (2019) <https://safety4sea.com/wp-content/uploads/2019/03/ECAMED-a-technical-feasibility-study-for-the-implementation-of-an-ECA-in-the-Mediterranean-sea-2019_03.pdf> accessed 14 December 2022.

24 European Commission, 'Reducing Emissions from the Shipping Sector' (2019) <https://climate.ec.europa.eu/eu-action/transport-emissions/reducing-emissions-shipping-sector_en> accessed 25 September 2020.

25 Climate Home News (n16).

4.2 *Achievements*

The government of Denmark and other governments in northern Europe have sponsored studies of existing monitoring systems for measuring ships' emissions. The study for the Danish government by Mellqvist and Conde[26] briefly reviews those studies and reports the results of a study of the surveillance system at the Great Belt Bridge. Although black carbon was not included among the pollutants being sampled, the results for CO_2, SO_2 and NOx are suggestive of the capabilities of monitoring technology that has been operational for several years after their development at Chalmers University of Technology in Sweden and applied at the other large bridge in Denmark over the Oresund that connects Denmark and Sweden where the Baltic Sea connects to a long passage way to the North Sea.[27] These and other studies report large amounts of data about the systems' accuracies, uncertainties and other features, as well as compliance-non-compliance data for the hundreds of ships whose emissions were monitored. Although these studies are not evidence of the effectiveness of black carbon emissions monitoring systems, they offer important experience in the development, deployment and operation of systems in high volume shipping routes. They therefore constitute a technological achievement.

4.3 *Proposals for Future Developments*

Next steps would be for these northern European countries that are members of an ECA – as described in the previous section of the paper to convey to Mediterranean governments perhaps via EU institutions the successes of the Baltic ECA. Members of the Paris regional port inspection Memorandum of Understanding (MOU) – as described in the next section – could be similarly conveyed. Moreover, both of these types of international agreements could be strengthened by explicitly using the technological accomplishments described above as rationales for expanding the ECAs and MOUs through amendments that would incorporate black carbon emission standards and monitoring procedures.

26 Johan Mellqvist and Vladimir Conde, 'Surveillance of Sulfur Fuel Content in Ships at the Great Belt Bridge 2019' (Danish Environmental Protection Agency, Environmental Project No 2142, 2020) <https://research.chalmers.se/en/publication/523048> accessed on 6 May 2022.

27 Johan Mellqvist and others, 'Fixed remote surveillance of fuel sulfur content in ships from fixed sites in the Goteburg ship channel and at Oresund bridge' (CompMon Report, Chalmers University of Technology, 2017) <https://research.chalmers.se/publication/500248/file/500248_Fulltext.pdf> accessed 14 December 2022.

BOX 11.2 Cases of Contaminated Bunker Fuels Delivered to Hundreds of Ships

Houston, 2018

Deliveries of contaminated fuel that began in Houston in early 2018 spread to other ports in the Caribbean and Southeast Asia affected more than 150 ships.[28] The consequences included engine failures and loss of propulsion, thus posing increased risks for ships and their crews. There was also damage to the ships' fuel filters, fuel pumps, engine pistons and other equipment.

Singapore, 2022

In early 2022, there was another similar incident, when about 80 ships had engine, fuel pump and other equipment problems from contaminated bunker fuel (heavy fuel oil) delivered in Houston. A report[29] found more than 140,000 tonnes were contaminated.

Reactions By Port Authorities, National Governments, and the IMO

A report[30] based on an investigation of the 2018 incident by the International Association of Independent Tanker Owners (INTERTANKO) concluded that … the source of the problem is not the ship owners, the ship managers or the ship operators, but rather an apparent complete lack of interest to control the quality of bunkers supplied to ships and a lack of initiative on the part of the authorities to introduce standard investigations when such events occur.

---

28 Intertanko, 'Contaminated Bunkers damage hundreds of ships: Do authorities really care? Prelude to 1 January 2020 safety problems? An INTERTANKO Critical Review' (2018) <https://www.gard.no/Content/26096787/Intertanko%20paper.pdf> accessed 14 April 2022; Vincent Wee, 'Houston bunker contamination spreading worldwide warns Standard Club' (Seatrade Maritime News, Aug 24, 2018) <https://www.seatrade-maritime.com/americas/houston-bunker-contamination-spreading-worldwide-warns-standard-club> accessed 14 April 2022.

29 Marcus Hand, '200 ships bunkered contaminated fuel in Singapore. (Seatrade Maritime News, 3 April 2022) <https://www.seatrade-maritime.com/bunkering/200-ships-bunkered-contaminated-fuel-singapore?> accessed 14 April 2022.

30 Intertanko (n29).

5 Local Level: Port Inspections According to MOUs

5.1 *State of the Regulatory Agenda*

Ten MOUs include hundreds of ports in scores of countries that have agreed to undertake inspections according to standardized procedures and standards. The ten MOUs have been agreed by groups of national governments on a regional basis, and registered with the IMO, which audits the annual reports of the ten. The procedures are implemented by local port authorities. Implementation of the regulatory system thus involves all four levels of governance, with overlapping roles among them.

Although the functioning of the system is typically routine and out of public view, there have been instances of significant systemic failure that gained much attention. In Box 11.2, two cases of contaminated large-scale deliveries of fuel to hundreds of ships are illustrations of the potential importance of local port authorities' inspection procedures. In these instances, the contaminants apparently came from outside the fuel refining and supply chain and were mistakenly poured into bunker fuel storage tanks. The resulting damages to ships and risks to crew were extensive. In the context of this chapter, the incidents illustrate potential failures of a regulatory system that should reduce damage to the environment from ships' emissions, including black carbon.

5.2 *Achievements*

There are two areas of significant achievements: the MOU inspections system, and the speed limits on ships entering and exiting from some ports.

The number of inspections and the numbers of ports and countries covered by the MOU reports are an impressive network of monitoring, review and verification, and evaluation systems. There were more than 80,000 inspections a year during a three-year study of the operations of the systems.[31] More than a hundred countries have training programs for their inspectors, and the details of the inspection procedures are agreed among the MOU signatories, though cases noted in Box 11.2 indicate the potential for failures in the system.

California's ports are among world leaders in their regulations that reduce emissions, including black carbon emissions. The scope of the regulations is notable in the coverage of not only the ships' emissions from main propulsion engines as they enter and leave ports, but also the emissions of their auxiliary

31 Thomas Brewer, 'Regulating International Maritime Shipping's Air Polluting Emissions: Monitoring, Reporting, Verifying and Enforcing Regulatory Compliance' (2021) 5 Journal of International Maritime Safety, Environmental Affairs, and Shipping 4,196–207.

BOX 11.3 Emission Regulations of Ships in or Near California Ports (2001–2022)

2001

Establishment of a voluntary incentive program, 'Vessel Speed Reduction Program', for Los Angeles and Long Beach ports – according to which *ships are* paid to reduce their speed as they approach or depart the ports.

2007

Reduction of emissions from ocean-going ships within 24 nautical miles of the coast in order to reduce auxiliary diesel engine particulate emissions (including black carbon) and other emissions.

2008

Establishment of Clean Truck Program of the San Pedro Bay Ports Clean Air Action Plan, which requires *trucks* entering port areas to meet emission limits.

2010

Shore-power equipped ships must use shore power if available at berth.

2014

All ships are required to change to cleaner-burning fuel within 24 nautical miles of the coast.

Container, cruise and refrigerated cargo ships at six largest ports are required to reduce emissions by cutting auxiliary engines, plugging into shore-side electric sources, or directly reducing emissions from stacks.

2020

Strengthening of 2014 regulations by including auto carriers and fuel tankers, and by adding more ports to be covered by the 2014 regulations. New regulations to be phased in during 2023–2027.

There have inevitably been disagreements about the official and unofficial estimates of the benefits and costs of the regulations. The following are thus illustrative, but not necessarily conclusively precise, estimates. However, the orders of magnitude are indicative of the scale of the economic, health, environmental and other effects at stake in the policies.

2014

Benefits: Reduced auxiliary (diesel) engine emissions at portside from container, cruise and refrigerated cargo ships by 80% in six major ports.

2020

Benefits: Reduces auto-carriers' and tankers' portside emissions by 90% beginning in 2025. Increases coverage of the number of annual ship visits from 4,000 to 6,300. Reductions from ships' diesel engine emissions reduce cancer deaths by half and save US$ 2.32 billion from reduced deaths and hospital expenses.

Costs: US$ 2.23 billion for shore power systems and ships' smokestack scrubbers – or US$ 4.65 per cruise ship ticket, US$ 7.66 per car carried, and less than US$ 0.01 per gallon of fuel in tankers.

Note: Not a comprehensive list. There are also other regulations concerning motor vehicles and trains, and there are interim deadlines in the incremental implementation of some regulations. The biggest ports are Los Angeles (the biggest in the US), Long Beach, and Oakland. Other ports are San Diego, San Francisco and Hueneme (which is in Ventura County between Los Angeles and San Francisco).

SOURCES: BECKER;[32] CLEAN AIR ACTION PLAN;[33] GARD;[34] LITTLEJOHN;[35] MONGELLUZZO;[36] PORT OF LOS ANGELES;[37] SAN PEDRO BAY PORTS[38]

---

32 Rachel Becker, (2020) 'Shape up or ship out: California requires ships, trucks to eliminate thousands of tons of pollution' (CalMatters 2020) <https://calmatters.org/environment/2020/08/california-ships-trucks-pollution-ports/> accessed 15 April 2022.

33 Clean Air Action Plan, 'Ships' (2022) <https://cleanairactionplan.org/strategies/ships/> accessed 15 April 2022.

34 Gard, 'Ports of Los Angeles and Long Beach – Voluntary incentive programme for low sulphur fuel' (Gard News 191, August/October 2008) <https://www.gard.no/web/updates/content/52005/ports-of-los-angeles-and-long-beach-voluntary-incentive-programme-for-low-sulphur-fuel> accessed 15 April 2022.

35 Donna Littlejohn, 'Ports of LA, Long Beach press on as clean air deadlines loom' (Daily Breeze 2022) <https://www.dailybreeze.com/2022/02/01/ports-of-la-long-beach-press-on-as-clean-air-deadlines-loom/> accessed 15 April 2022.

36 Bill Mongelluzzo, 'LA-LB clean-air rules set to become US port industry norm' (2017) <https://www.joc.com/article/la-lb-clean-air-rules-set-become-us-port-industry-norm_20171103.html> accessed 15 April 2022.

37 Port of Los Angeles, 'Vessel Speed Reduction Program' (2022) <https://www.portoflosangeles.org/environment/air-quality/vessel-speed-reduction-program> accessed 15 April 2022; Port of Los Angeles, 'Clean Truck Program' (2022) <https://www.portoflosangeles.org/environment/air-quality/clean-truck-program#:~:text=All%20trucks%20serving%20non%2DRFID,gain%20entry%20into%20the%20terminals> accessed 15 April 2022.

38 San Pedro Bay Ports, 'Clean Air Action Plan' (2022) <https://cleanairactionplan.org/> accessed 15 April 2022.

engines while in port. The regulations also include on-shore equipment, and trucks and trains involved in the transfer of goods. The two-decade long evolution of the off-shore and on-shore regulations is summarized in Box 11.3, along with some estimates of their benefits and costs. They are examples of what can be done to reduce ships' black carbon emissions in large, densely populated harbour areas, where millions of people are exposed to the effects of black carbon emissions.

6 Conclusion

At the global level, the IMO has been slow to address black carbon emissions in a focused, action-oriented policymaking process; it has not yet put in place explicit, mandatory, enforceable limits on ships' black carbon emissions. IMO policymaking has demonstrated a combination of institutional inertia and intermittent, incremental learning with occasional strategic decision-making based on long-term goals, which have been imposed on it by outside arenas such as the UNFCCC. These tendencies have reflected in part an international maritime industry with a strong tradition of family-owned firms that have enjoyed an unusual degree of privacy for such a large and economically important worldwide industry. At the same time, it has also been an industry with progressive firms, especially from Nordic countries, that have pushed the IMO agenda to be more responsive to environmental issues, including black carbon emissions in the Arctic region. The result is a mélange of regulatory policies, many of them with weak enforcement processes.

At the international regional level and at the port level, there have been significant advances in the technologies and policies of measuring, reporting and verification systems, and to a lesser extent enforcement processes. Despite some regional variations, there is much uniformity among the regional ECA systems and the MOU port inspection systems. At both levels, the regulatory systems have developed beyond the politically feasible limits of IMO policymaking processes. Even though the regional and local systems are officially recognized by the IMO, they have actually been established in regulatory domains where it has not been feasible for the IMO to do so. In that respect, it can be said that the pluralistic nature of the overall system has facilitated a functionality that the IMO on its own could not. The multi-level system that has evolved may be a complex hybrid, but it is nevertheless adaptive to the political realities of an international organization with more than a hundred national government members and an industry with a strong tradition of avoiding public scrutiny.

Whether the hybrid organizational arrangements and an industry marked by a mix of tradition-bound and progressive firms are adequate to meet the increasingly urgent challenges of climate change remains to be seen.

At the international level, despite many international workshops and research projects focused on black carbon issues, there were virtually no formal IMO actions taken to reduce ships' black carbon emissions. The only exception was the decision in early 2022 to 'urge' ships to slow down and/or change their fuels while in or near Arctic waters, but this was on a voluntary basis.

At the regional level, there have been regulatory developments that could affect black carbon emissions. The active monitoring systems in Denmark, Finland and Sweden for sulfur emissions in the Baltic Sea include technologies that are land-based, bridge-based, drone-based and ship-based. These technologies could be extended to the monitoring and enforcement of black carbon emission limits if they were put into place. The same can be said of another type of international regional agreements – namely the ten sets of MOUs in which national governments have included their ports, whose annual reports are audited by the IMO. Thus, there are three levels of governance involved. There are agreed check lists of specific inspection actions that need to be made, with records kept of the results. There is a potential for non-compliance penalties, such as port authorities prohibiting an offending ship from exiting a port – entering a port if a ship has an outstanding non-compliance record. There has been some interest in applying the inspections more extensively and explicitly, but there have not yet been tangible expansions in that regard.

Overall, then, significant weaknesses that require future legal and institutional development are the absence of explicit international and regional regulations addressing black carbon emissions, and the generally weak provisions for enforcement measures for ships' emissions.

Acknowledgements

I am indebted to participants in the May 2022 workshop organized by the Centre for Climate Change, Energy and Environmental Law (CCEEL) of the University of Eastern Finland Law School and to Brian Comer of the International Council on Clean Transportation (ICCT) for comments on a draft of the chapter.

Annex 8.1: IMO Resolution MEPC.342(77) of 26 November 2021

ANNEX 3

RESOLUTION MEPC.342(77) (adopted on 26 November 2021)

PROTECTING THE ARCTIC FROM SHIPPING BLACK CARBON EMISSIONS

The Marine Environment Protection Committee,

RECALLING Article 38(a) of the Convention on the International Maritime Organization concerning the functions of the Marine Environment Protection Committee conferred upon it by international conventions for the prevention and control of marine pollution from ships,

RECALLING ALSO that MEPC 62 agreed to a work plan including an investigation of appropriate control measures to reduce the impact on the Arctic of Black Carbon emissions from international shipping,

RECALLING FURTHER that MEPC 77 approved the updated terms of reference for further work on the reduction of the impact on the Arctic of Black Carbon emissions starting with guidelines on goal-based control measures to reduce the impact on the Arctic of Black Carbon emissions from international shipping,

RECOGNIZING that Black Carbon is a potent short-lived contributor to climate warming, and as such was subject to study in the Fourth IMO GHG Study 2020,

HAVING CONSIDERED the threat to the Arctic from ships' Black Carbon emissions and understanding that the development of goal-based guidelines and any mandatory control measures will require further work and time,

RECOGNIZING that the Fourth IMO GHG Study's emission factors show that, when used in the same engine, a switch to distillate reduces Black Carbon emissions per kilogram of fuel consumption,

ENCOURAGING Member States to commence addressing the threat to the Arctic from Black Carbon emissions, and report on measures and best practices to reduce Black Carbon emissions from shipping,

URGES Member States and ship operators to voluntarily use distillate or other cleaner alternative fuels or methods of propulsion that are safe for ships and could contribute to the reduction of Black Carbon emissions from ships when operating in or near the Arctic.

Bibliography

Anenberg S, Miller J, Henze D, and Minjares R, 'A global snapshot of the air pollution-related health impacts of transportation sector emissions in 2010 and 2015' (ICCT,

2019) <https://theicct.org/sites/default/files/publications/Global_health_impacts_transport_emissions_2010-2015_20190226.pdf> accessed 3 July 2019.

Anenberg S, Talgo K, Arunachalam S, Dolwick P, Jang C, and West J, (2011) 'Impacts of global, regional, and sectoral black carbon emission reductions on surface air quality and human mortality deaths' (2011) 11 Atmospheric Chemistry and Physics 14, 7253–7267.

Becker R, (2020) 'Shape up or ship out: California requires ships, trucks to eliminate thousands of tons of pollution' (CalMatters 2020) <https://calmatters.org/environment/2020/08/california-ships-trucks-pollution-ports/> accessed 15 April 2022.

Bhaskar A, Chandra J, Braun D, Cellini J, and Dominici F, 'Air pollution, SARS-CoV-2 transmission, and COVID-19 outcomes: A state-of-the-science review of a rapidly evolving research area' (medR$_x$iv 2020) <https://www.medrxiv.org/content/10.1101/2020.08.16.20175901v1> accessed 14 December 2022.

Brewer T, 'Black Carbon and Other Air Pollutants in Italian Ports and Coastal Areas: Problems, Solutions and Implications for Policy' (2020) 10 Applied Science 23, 8544.

Brewer T, 'A Maritime Emission Control Area for the Mediterranean Sea? Technological Solutions and Policy Options for a "Med ECA"' (2020) 5 Euro-Mediterranean Journal for Environmental Integration 1.

Brewer T, 'Regulating International Maritime Shipping's Air Polluting Emissions: Monitoring, Reporting, Verifying and Enforcing Regulatory Compliance' (2021) 5 Journal of International Maritime Safety, Environmental Affairs, and Shipping 4,196–207.

Brewer T, *Climate Change – An Interdisciplinary Introduction* (Springer, forthcoming).

Caro D, Conticini E, and Frediani B, 'Link between air pollution and coronavirus mortality in Italy could be possible' (Science Daily 2020) <https://www.sciencedaily.com/releases/2020/04/200406100824.htm> accessed 14 December 2022.

CCAC, 'Fast Track to Improving Food Security and Mitigating Climate Change: the Agriculture Initiative of the Climate and Clean Air Coalition' (2014) <https://www.ccacoalition.org/en/resources/ccac flyer fast track improving-food-security-and-mitigating-climate-change-agriculture> accessed on 20 June 2018.

Chenxi J and El-Halwagi M, 'A data-driven study of IMO compliant fuel emissions with consideration of black carbon aerosols' (2020) 218 Ocean Engineering 108241.

Clean Air Action Plan, 'Ships' (2022) <https://cleanairactionplan.org/strategies/ships/> accessed 15 April 2022.

Climate Home News, 'How the shipping industry can halve climate-warming black carbon in the Arctic' (2022) <https://www.climatechangenews.com/2021/03/18/shipping-industry-can-halve-climate-warming-black-carbon-arctic/> accessed 14 April 2022.

Comer B, Olmer N, Mao X, Roy B, and Rutherford D, 'Black carbon emissions and fuel use in global shipping' (ICCT 2017) <https://theicct.org/publications/black-carbon-emissions-global-shipping-2015> accessed 1 March 2021.

Comer B, 'Black Carbon and Maritime Shipping: the Long Road to Regulating a Short-Lived Climate Pollutant' (CCAC 2019) <https://www.ccacoalition.org/en/blog/black-carbon-and-maritime-shipping-long-road-regulating-short-lived-climate-pollutant> accessed 2 April 2022.

Comer B, Osipova L, Georgeff E, and Mao X, 'The International Maritime Organisation's Proposed Arctic Heavy Fuel Oils Ban: Likely Implications and Opportunities for Improvement' (2020) <https://theicct.org/publication/the-international-maritime-organizations-proposed-arctic-heavy-fuel-oil-ban-likely-implications-and-opportunities-for-improvement/> accessed 7 March 2023.

Comunian S, Dongo D, Milani C, and Palestini P, 'Air Pollution and COVID-19: the Role of Particulate Matter in the Spread and Increase of COVID-19's Morbidity and Mortality' (2020) 17 Int. J. Environ. Res. Public Health 4487.

Conticini E, Frediani B, and Caro D, 'Can atmospheric pollution be considered a co-factor in extremely high level of SARS-CoV-2 lethality in Northern Italy?' (2020) 261 Environ. Pollut. 114465.

Cullinane K and Bergqvist R, 'Emission control areas and their impact on maritime transport' (2014) 28 Transportation Research Part D: Transport and Environment 1.

EUA (EU Funded Action on Black Carbon), 'Shipping' (2022) <https://eua-bca.amap.no/maritime-shipping#:~:text=shipping%20emissions%20include%20black%20carbon,of%20shipping%20emission's%20warming%20potential> accessed 3 May 2022.

European Commission, 'Reducing Emissions from the Shipping Sector' (2019) <https://climate.ec.europa.eu/eu-action/transport-emissions/reducing-emissions-shipping-sector_en> accessed 25 September 2020.

FOEI, WWF, Pacific Environment, and CSC, 'Reduction of the Impact on The Arctic of Black Carbon Emissions from International Shipping Fuels Are Key to Urgent Black Carbon Emission Reductions' (Pollution Prevention and Response Sub-Committee 9th Session Agenda, Item 8 PPR 9/8/3, 11 February 2022) <https://cleanarctic.org/2022/02/11/ppr-9-8-3-fuels-are-key-to-urgent-black-carbon-emission-reductions/> accessed 3 May 2022.

Gard, 'Ports of Los Angeles and Long Beach – Voluntary incentive programme for low sulphur fuel' (Gard News 191, August/October 2008) <https://www.gard.no/web/updates/content/52005/ports-of-los-angeles-and-long-beach-voluntary-incentive-programme-for-low-sulphur-fuel> accessed 15 April 2022.

Hand M, '200 ships bunkered contaminated fuel in Singapore. (Seatrade Maritime News, 3 April 2022) <https://www.seatrade-maritime.com/bunkering/200-ships-bunkered-contaminated-fuel-singapore?> accessed 14 April 2022.

ICCT, '1st workshop on marine black carbon emissions' (2014) <https://theicct.org/event/marine-black-carbon-emissions-identifying-research-gaps/> accessed 15 April 2022.

ICCT, '2nd workshop on marine black carbon emissions' (2015) <https://theicct.org/event/2nd-workshop-on-marine-black-carbon-emissions/> accessed 10 April 2022.

ICCT, '3rd workshop on marine black carbon emissions' (2016) <https://theicct.org/event/3rd-workshop-on-marine-black-carbon-emissions-measuring-and-controlling-bc-from-marine-engines/> accessed 10 April 2022.

ICCT, '4th workshop on marine black carbon emissions' (2017) <https://theicct.org/event/4th-workshop-on-marine-black-carbon-emissions-identifying-appropriate-measurement-methods/> accessed 10 April 2022.

ICCT, '5th workshop on marine black carbon emissions' (2018) <https://theicct.org/event/5th-workshop-on-marine-black-carbon-emissions/> accessed 10 April 2022.

ICCT, '6th workshop on marine black carbon emissions' (2019) <https://theicct.org/event/6th-workshop-on-marine-black-carbon-emissions/> accessed 10 April 2022.

IMO, 'Prevention of air pollution from ships' (2021) <https://www.imo.org/en/OurWork/Environment/Pages/Air-Pollution.aspx> accessed 25 February 2022.

IMO, 'International Convention for the Prevention of Pollution from Ships (MARPOL)' (2022) <https://www.imo.org/en/About/Conventions/Pages/International-Convention-for-the-Prevention-of-Pollution-from-Ships-(MARPOL).aspx> accessed 2 May 2022.

IMO, 'Report to the Marine Environment Protection Committee' (Sub-Committee on Pollution Prevention and Response, Document PPR 9/21, 26 April 2022) <https://www.iadc.org/wp-content/uploads/2022/05/PPR-9-21-Report-To-The-Marine-Environment-Protection-Committee-Secretariat.pdf> accessed 8 June 2022.

Ineris, French National Institute for Industrial Environment and Risks, Cerema, Citepa, and Plan Bleu, 'ECAMED: a Technical Feasibility Study for the Implementation of an Emission Control Area (ECA) in the Mediterranean Sea' (2019) < https://safety4sea.com/wp-content/uploads/2019/03/ECAMED-a-technical-feasibility-study-for the implementation of-an-ECA-in-the-Mediterranean-sea-2019_03.pdf> accessed 14 December 2022.

Intertanko, 'Contaminated Bunkers damage hundreds of ships: Do authorities really care? Prelude to 1 January 2020 safety problems? An INTERTANKO Critical Review' (2018) <https://www.gard.no/Content/26096787/Intertanko%20paper.pdf> accessed 14 April 2022.

IPCC, *Special Report: Climate Change and Land.* (Cambridge University Press 2019).

Littlejohn D, 'Ports of LA, Long Beach press on as clean air deadlines loom' (Daily Breeze 2022) <https://www.dailybreeze.com/2022/02/01/ports-of-la-long-beach-press-on-as-clean-air-deadlines-loom/> accessed 15 April 2022.

Maritime Executive, 'Environmental Groups Call for Mediterranean ECA' (2018) <https://maritime-executive.com/article/environmental-groups-call-for-mediterranean-eca> accessed 14 December 2022.

Mellqvist J and Conde V, 'Surveillance of Sulfur Fuel Content in Ships at the Great Belt Bridge 2019' (Danish Environmental Protection Agency, Environmental Project No 2142, 2020) <https://research.chalmers.se/en/publication/523048> accessed on 6 May 2022.

Mellqvist J, Conde V, Beecken J, and Ekholm J, 'Fixed remote surveillance of fuel sulfur content in ships from fixed sites in the Goteburg ship channel and at Oresund bridge' (CompMon Report, Chalmers University of Technology, 2017) <https://research.chalmers.se/publication/500248/file/500248_Fulltext.pdf> accessed 14 December 2022.

Mongelluzzo B, 'LA-LB clean-air rules set to become US port industry norm' (2017) <https://www.joc.com/article/la-lb-clean-air-rules-set-become-us-port-industry-norm_20171103.html> accessed 15 April 2022.

Olmer N, Comer B, Roy B, Mao X, and Rutherford D, 'Greenhouse gas emissions from global shipping, 2013–2015' (ICCT 2017) <https://theicct.org/sites/default/files/publications/Global-shipping-GHG-emissions-2013-2015_ICCT-Report_17102017_vF.pdf> accessed 3 May 2022.

Port of Los Angeles, 'Vessel Speed Reduction Program' (2022) <https://www.portoflosangeles.org/environment/air-quality/vessel-speed-reduction-program> accessed 15 April 2022.

Port of Los Angeles, 'Clean Truck Program' (2022) <https://www.portoflosangeles.org/environment/air-quality/clean-truck-program#:~:text=All%20trucks%20serving%20non%2DRFID,gain%20entry%20into%20the%20terminals> accessed 15 April 2022.

San Pedro Bay Ports, 'Clean Air Action Plan' (2022) <https://cleanairactionplan.org/> accessed 15 April 2022.

Setti L, Passarini F, de Gennaro G, Di Gilio A, Palmisani J, Buono P, Fornari G, Perrone M, Piazzalunga A, Barbieri P, Rizzo E, and Miani A, 'Evaluation of the Potential Relationship between Particulate Matter (PM) Pollution and COVID-19 Infection Spread in Italy' (Società Italiana di Medicina Ambientale 2020) <https://www.aircentre.org/wp-content/uploads/2020/04/Setti_et_al_2020.pdf> accessed 14 December 2022.

United Nations Conference on Trade and Development, 'Review of Maritime Transport 2020' (UNCTAD 2021).

Wee V, 'Houston bunker contamination spreading worldwide warns Standard Club' (Seatrade Maritime News, Aug 24, 2018) <https://www.seatrade-maritime.com/americas/houston-bunker-contamination-spreading-worldwide-warns-standard-club> accessed 14 April 2022.

Wu X, Nethery R, Sabath M, Braun D, and Dominici F, 'Exposure to Air Pollution and COVID-19 Mortality in the United States: a Nationwide Cross-Sectional Study' (medRxvi 2020) <https://www.medrxiv.org/content/10.1101/2020.04.05.20054502v2> accessed 14 December 2022.

Zoran M, Savastru R, Savastru S, and Tautan M, 'Assessing the relationship between surface levels of $PM_{2.5}$ and PM_{10} particulate matter impact on COVID-19 in Milan, Italy' (2020) 738 Sci. Total. Environ. 139825.

CHAPTER 12

Tackling Black Carbon in Road Transport

Towards Global Car Emission Standards

Kateryna Holzer

1 Introduction

Black carbon abatement, which is necessary to improve air quality and support climate change mitigation, is technologically feasible[1] and could nearly halve global annual black carbon emissions from 9 million tons to just over 4 million tons by 2030.[2] At the same time, the regulatory framework in support of this is lacking, especially at the international level, where efforts to reduce black carbon emissions have so far been confined to aspirational goals or, at best, scientific and technical cooperation under multilateral environmental agreements and public-private initiatives. A road map with concrete implementation measures is missing. Rather than discussing international black carbon reduction initiatives,[3] this chapter focuses on national measures affecting black carbon emissions from cars and assesses prospects for their multilateralization through international regulatory cooperation.

The focus on the road transport sector is warranted given that cars are a significant source of black carbon emissions. They are, in fact, the largest source of black carbon emissions in developed countries, responsible for 80% of urban air pollution in some cities.[4] In developing countries, where car ownership has historically been relatively low, road transport contributes a lower but growing share of black carbon emissions, which are projected to rise with the growth in

1 Air pollution and climate change implications of black carbon are discussed in Chapter 1.

2 UNEP, *The Emissions Gap Report* (Nairobi: UNEP, 2017).

3 What concerns black carbon reduction targets, there are very few internationally agreed norms. Those few arrangements that are relevant (e.g. under the Gothenburg Protocol) do not address black carbon directly but set quantified policy targets to reduce $PM_{2.5}$ (see Chapter 5).

4 UNEP, 'Addressing the Used Vehicles Market: Potential Strategies for Importing and Exporting Countries to Improve Safety, Fuel Economy and Emissions Impacts, A Report of the Used Vehicles Working Group of the Partnership for Clean Fuels and Vehicles' (UNEP 2019) <http://airqualityandmobility.org/PDFs/USED_VEHICLES_WORKING_GROUP_REPORT.pdf> accessed 23 November 2022.

DOI:10.1163/9789004684089_014

the transport sector. The number of cars in developing countries may increase 4 or 5-fold by 2050, with a majority of these projected to be second-hand combustion engine vehicles, projected to emit an unsustainable amount of black carbon and other pollutants.[5]

Black carbon emissions in road transport mainly stem from the use of diesel engines, which are responsible for approximately 90% of transportation-related black carbon and 14% of total black carbon emissions (both anthropogenic and natural).[6] Black carbon constitutes a large fraction of diesel soot ($PM_{2.5}$). Although soot also contains organic carbon, which in contrast to black carbon has a cooling effect, diesel engines produce much more black carbon than organic carbon.[7] Against this background, it is clear that black carbon mitigation policies should include restrictions related to the use of diesel engines.

However, not so long ago, diesel engines as more fuel-efficient engines in cars were considered more favorable for the climate than gasoline engines. Many governments stimulated the use of diesel cars, which, for instance, in the EU led to a 51% share of diesel cars in the new registrations in 2010.[8] Over the years, governments, which promoted diesel cars to reduce energy consumption without setting advanced $PM_{2.5}$ emission control requirements, ultimately realized few climate benefits from dieselization. When black carbon emissions are taken into account, an average diesel vehicle is not better for the climate than a gasoline vehicle, whereas the health impacts are devastating.[9] Hence, the attitude toward diesel engines has been changing and various governments are seeking to discourage their use. This is done in two ways, by either combining car exhaust standards requiring the installation of a diesel particulate filter (DPF) with various incentives for the production and consumption of electric and hydrogen fuel cell cars, i.e. zero-emission vehicles (ZEVs), or by raising car emission standards to the levels that amount to bans on fossil fuel cars. Some of these measures are specifically intended to reduce

5 GFEI, 'Securing Global Fleet Transformation – GFEI's Zero Pathway' (GFEI 2021).

6 Ray Minjares and others, 'Alignment of policies to maximize the climate benefits of diesel vehicles through control of particulate matter and black carbon emissions' (2013) 54 Energy Policy, 54–61.

7 Thomas Brewer, 'Black carbon problems in transportation: Technological solutions and governmental policy solutions' (MIT Working paper, 2017).

8 Minjares and others (n6); Different kinds of measures supported this rapid penetration of diesel vehicles, including CO_2 standards for cars, favorable tax rates for diesel fuel and lax car exhaust emissions standards not requiring the installation of particulate filters. The fuel pricing was also favourable for owners of cars with diesel engines.

9 ibid; Exposure to diesel PM is associated with many adverse health impacts, including the risk of cancer, whereas chronic exposure is linked to premature deaths (CCAC 2016).

soot, and hence black carbon, from cars, while others are primarily aimed at reducing CO_2 emissions or exhaust emissions in general, affecting black carbon emissions indirectly.[10]

There is no 'one size fits all' road transport emission reduction measure. Much depends on the specifics of the car market and the country's level of development that may put constraints on setting a maximum permissible emission level. However, to bring about change in black carbon emissions, a minimum standard should at least require the installation of a DPF. DPF and other car emission reduction technologies are already available and cost-effective.[11] But they have not yet penetrated all markets. The lack of minimum international standards and the existing discrepancies in car emission regulations among countries (as most measures are national) are slowing down the diffusion of technologies. Therefore, the adoption of minimum standards and regulations at the international level could facilitate the process of technology diffusion and transition to ZEVs. So long as the costs of alternative technologies are high, strict emissions standards translating into bans on fossil fuel cars pose high risks for car manufacturers, especially for smaller car producers and automakers in developing countries. International regulatory cooperation on the adoption of emission regulations could potentially increase environmental integrity and at the same time lower trade barriers and the incidence of trade disputes associated with these measures.[12]

In light of the foregoing, this chapter aims to examine measures taken by governments to curb road transport emissions, including black carbon, and discuss how trade and regulatory cooperation can improve regulatory outcome and environmental integrity of these measures and support their dissemination and upward convergence among countries. Methodologically, the chapter follows a multilevel governance approach to examining regulatory measures in a transnational context[13] and draws on studies of international regulatory convergence[14] and regulatory

10 Brewer (n7).

11 Joshua Miller and Lingzhi Jin, 'Global Progress Toward Soot-Free Diesel Vehicles in 2018' (ICCT 2018).

12 Kateryna Holzer and Aik Hoe Lim, 'Trade and Carbon Standards: Why Greater Regulatory Cooperation is Needed, in D. Esty and S. Biniaz (eds), *Cool Heads in a Warming World: How Trade Policy Can Help Fight Climate Change* (Yale University 2020) <https://envirocenter.yale.edu/sites/default/files/files/CoolHeads_Holzer(1).pdf> accessed 24 November 2022.

13 Liesbet Hooghes and Gary Marks, *Multi-Level Governance and European Integration* (Rowman & Littlefield Publishers, 2001).

14 David Vogel, *Trading Up: Consumer and Environmental Regulation in a Global Economy* (Harvard University Press, 1995); Debora Spar and David Yoffie, 'A Race to the Bottom or

cooperation.[15] In what follows, Section 2 maps the regulatory landscape for motor vehicle emissions discussing existing and proposed road transport emission reduction measures; Section 3 examines prospects for regulatory alignment of car emission standards among countries focusing on two principal avenues – *de facto* convergence driven by market forces and *de jure* convergence based on an agreement that can be achieved in an international forum; Section 4 offers concluding remarks and recommendations.

2 Regulatory Landscape for Abating Emissions from Cars

The regulatory landscape to control emissions from cars comprises a wide range of measures taken in different national jurisdictions. Enacted by national (and sometimes local) governments, these measures are characterized by different degree of stringency, type and regulatory purpose. In most cases, they are aimed at reducing national air pollution, with governments seeking to mitigate the negative effects of road transport on the local environment and health of the local population. Black carbon is either one of the controlled pollutants or indirectly affected through requirements set for other pollutants, if the source of those pollutants is the same as for black carbon.[16]

Domestic regulations, particularly those related to air pollution controls and permissible emission levels, have significantly contributed to emission reduction in road transport.[17] A study on black carbon emissions from heavy truck freight transportation in some regions of the US showed that without continuous tightening of the national ambient air quality standards by the US Environmental Protection Agency, which included increasingly stringent controls on $PM_{2.5}$, black carbon emissions from this sector would be nearly

Governance from the Top?' in A. Prakash and J. A. Hart (eds) *Coping with Globalization* (London: Routledge, 2000); David Vogel and Robert Kagan, *Dynamics of Regulatory Change: How Globalisation Affects National Regulatory Policies* (UC Berkley, 2002); Anu Bradford, *The Brussels Effect: How the European Union Rules the World* (Oxford University Press, 2020).

15 Bernard Hoekman and Petros Mavroidis, 'Regulatory Spillovers and the Trading System: From Coherence to Cooperation' (E15 Initiative 2015) <https://cadmus.eui.eu/bitstream/handle/1814/35862/E15-Regulatory-OP-Hoekman-and-Mavroidis_2015.pdf?sequence=1&isAllowed=y> accessed 12/01/2023; Holzer and Lim (n12).

16 Brewer (n7).

17 Other contributing factors include changes in people's behavior and habits (reducing travel), as well as availability of technical solutions, such as speed limits on the road.

five times as high as current levels.[18] Between 1977 and 2007 in the Middle-West and North-East regions, freight transportation has increased by a factor of around five, while the emissions factor for black carbon has decreased by nearly 80% over the same historical time period.

In Europe too, emission controls have been instrumental in addressing the problem of emissions from automobiles. Due to the car emissions standards enacted in some European countries in the 1970s, a new European car in the mid-1990s emitted 93% less carbon monoxide (CO) and 85% less nitrogen oxides (NOx) than an equivalent vehicle in 1970.[19] Later, with the adoption of EU-wide car exhaust standards in the early 1990s, capturing black carbon as part of $PM_{2.5}$, the particle mass limit has been reduced by 98%.[20]

While the purpose of road transport emission restrictions in the past was mitigation of air pollution, the growing awareness of negative effects of black carbon on the climate is increasingly influencing present policy decisions. Governments continue to adopt regulatory measures aimed at neutralizing bad environmental and health effects of road transport, but now they also take into account climate change concerns.[21] There is also a growing trend towards the participation of municipalities and private actors, such as automakers, environmental groups and public-private partnerships, in setting a new generation of road transport regulations to achieve a zero-emission future. While national governments remain the main rule-making authorities in the ambit of road transport emissions, the regulatory landscape is gradually expanding outwards and becoming transnational. As regards the types of measures taken to combat road transport emissions, most of them are of the command-and-control type, with car emission standards being the most common.

2.1 *Car Emission Standards*

Emission standards can be defined as binding limits on the emission of specific polluting substances. They are the most widespread instruments of road

---

18 Benjamin Brown-Steiner and others, 'Black carbon emissions from trucks and trains in the Midwestern and Northeastern United States from 1977 to 2007' (2016) 129 Atmospheric Environment 155–166.

19 William Dietrich, 'Harmonisation of Automobile Emission Standards Under International Trade Agreements: Lessons from the European Union Applied to the WTO and the NAFTA' (1996), 20 William and Mary Environmental Law and Policy Review 175.

20 Martin Williams and Ray Minjares, 'A technical summary of Euro 6/VI vehicle emission standards' (ICCT, 2016).

21 In the EU, the ongoing revision of car emission standards is part of the legislative package in support of the EU goal to reduce GHG emissions by 55% by 2030 and achieve a zero-carbon future by 2050.

transport emission reduction. While road transport emission standards also affect black carbon emissions, the reason for introducing them goes beyond the black carbon abatement. Besides mitigating air pollution, some of them are also aimed at supporting climate change mitigation and energy security.

2.1.1 Car Exhaust Emission Standards

In the 1960s, governments of developed countries started introducing standards for emission of air polluting substances from cars with emission thresholds that were regularly lowered. The first country to introduce such standards was the US, followed by Japan, Canada, Australia and some European countries.[22] In the early 1990s, the European Commission introduced the EU-wide car exhaust standards, called Euro. Between the Euro 0 standard of 1990 and the current 'Euro 6/VI' standard,[23] which entered into force in 2013, the maximum permissible emissions for cars have been reduced by 88% for carbon monoxide, 95% for hydrocarbons, 97% for nitrogen oxides and 98% for fine particles.[24] The Commission is currently preparing the next generation of Euro standards – Euro 7/VII – to be implemented from 2025. If adopted, Euro 7/VII, which additionally may cover CO_2 emissions, would eventually ban the sales of fossil fuel cars, thereby complementing the proposed stricter CO_2 emission standards for cars discussed below.

The progressive tightening of national car exhaust standards in different countries[25] has led to the use of ultralow sulfur fuel and the installation of diesel oxidation catalysts (DOC) in engines and DPF in the exhaust tailpipes of cars.[26] These technologies are cost-effective and widely used in newly produced diesel cars. In 2018, 40% of new heavy-duty diesel vehicles sold worldwide were equipped with DOC and DPF. This share was projected to grow to 50% in 2021 (after the adopted Euro 6/VI-equivalent standards had gone into force in India and Mexico) and to 70% (provided China and Brazil also introduce them).[27]

---

22 Asif Faiz and others, 'Air Pollution from Motor Vehicles: Standards and Technologies for Controlling Emissions' (World Bank 1996).

23 Arabic numerals refer to light duty vehicles, whereas Roman numerals refer to heavy-duty vehicles.

24 Williams and Minjares (n20).

25 North American countries have a similar set of car standards, e.g. US Tier 1–3 standards for passenger vehicle emissions and US 2004 and 2010 standards for heavy duty vehicle emissions.

26 DPF is a filter that captures and stores exhaust soot. DOC is a device that reduces carbon monoxide and hydrocarbons in the exhaust gas by oxidizing them but, through the oxidation of hydrocarbons absorbed on particles, DOC also contributes to reducing the particulate mass.

27 Miller and Jin (n11).

Car exhaust standards equivalent to Euro 5 and Euro 6 requiring DOC and DPF have nearly eliminated black carbon emissions from new light-duty vehicles sold in the US, EU, Canada, and Japan.[28]

A major shortcoming of car exhaust standards is that they generally apply only to new vehicles. Older and second-hand vehicles with poorly-maintained engines limit the potential effectiveness of emission reduction strategies, as the absence of adequate car emission regulations for imports of second-hand cars in developing countries limits the global effectiveness of higher standards of developed countries. As car markets of developed countries advance in a green transport transformation through higher road transport emission standards, developing countries' markets increasingly become 'dumping grounds' for polluting technology from developed countries.[29] Even though countries exporting second-hand cars might benefit from some reduction of air pollutants and CO_2, when older vehicles are sold to other countries, the air pollution problem is simply exported to other parts of the world, while bad impacts for the climate will be felt everywhere.[30]

Another problem with car exhaust standards is compliance.[31] Car manufacturers are known to cheat by installing special software that shows a much better emission output when cars were tested in the lab compared to on-the-road situations.[32] To avoid stricter car exhaust standards, carmakers have also colluded on emission reduction technologies in violation of antitrust law.[33]

28 Minjares and others (n6).

29 In Eastern Europe, Central Asia, Africa and Latin America, most motor vehicle sales are second-hand cars from Europe, Japan and the US. For instance, the imports of second-hand cars to Ukraine in 2021 accounted for more than 80% of total car imports. Russia is also a major importer of second-hand cars with a share of 12% of world's second-hand car imports; see Jorge Macias and others, 'Policy Handbook for the Regulation of Imported Second-Hand Vehicles' (GFEI Working Paper 7, 2013).

30 CCAC, 'Cleaning Up the Global On-Road Diesel Fleet: A Global Strategy to Introduce Low-Sulfur Fuels and Cleaner Diesel Vehicles' (CCAC 2016).

31 Jens Müller, 'Dieselgate: The scandal has not been solved' (Heinrich-Böll-Stiftung, 2021).

32 For instance, in 2015 a big 'Dieselgate' scandal broke out, as VW was caught using special software in new cars to meet exhaust emission standards in the US.

33 In 2016, four carmakers – Volvo/Renault, Daimler, Iveco and DAF – were fined with 2,93 billion euros for colluding over 14 years on truck pricing and on passing on the costs of compliance with stricter emission rules. In 2021, BMW and VW Group were fined with 875 million euros for colluding with Daimler on the development of NOx treatment technology. For many years, they held regular technical meetings to discuss the development of AdBlue systems (selective catalytic reduction technology) and agreed to avoid competition on performing better than what was required by law despite the relevant technology being available. See European Commission, 'Antitrust: Commission fines truck producers € 2.93 billion for participating in a cartel' (Press Release, 2016) <https://ec.europa.eu/commission/presscorner/detail/en/IP_16_2582> accessed 23/11/2022.

These cheating practices underscore implementation problems associated with car emissions standards and the need to improve the surveillance systems ensuring truly independent on-the-road testing. For example, the new EU regulation on vehicle type approval[34] with market surveillance should lead to more robust testing and ensuring EU oversight of the activities of national type approval authorities.[35]

2.1.2 Fuel Quality Standards

To the extent that DPFs perform best with a maximum diesel sulfur content of 10 or 15 ppm, the effectiveness of exhaust emission reduction technologies, such as DOC and DPF, depends on the use of low-sulfur diesel fuel.[36] While it is important to reduce sulfur in fuel,[37] the costs of upgrading a refinery to produce low-sulfur fuels are generally substantial and desulfurization may not be economically attractive without stringent fuel quality standards in place. Therefore, car exhaust standards need to be accompanied by fuel quality standards that set a limit on sulfur content.

Combined with the Euro 6/VI car exhaust standard, fuel standards in the EU set a limit of 10 ppm sulfur in diesel. In fact, no country that has adopted the Euro 6/VI standard has a maximum diesel sulfur content above 10 ppm.[38] In the US, where the 2007 and 2010 heavy-duty vehicle emission standards and Tier 3 light-duty vehicle standards have led to the deployment of DPFs, the maximum diesel sulfur level is 15 ppm.[39] Canada's and Chile's fuel standards are harmonized to the US ones. In contrast, developing countries have varying standards in place, with many at 50 ppm or above for diesel fuel.[40] Given that many developing countries are experiencing increased fuel consumption and rapidly growing vehicle fleets, it is important that they move to cleaner fuel standards to minimize health and climate impacts from their fleets. In addition, in support of the reduction of GHG emissions and with a long-term goal

---

34 Vehicle type approval is a process applied by national authorities to certify that a car model meets all safety, environmental and conformity of production requirements before authorizing it to be placed on the market.

35 Regulation (EU) 2018/858.

36 CCAC (n30).

37 Low-sulfur fuel is also required for some systems that control NOx. Moreover, sulfur in fuel is problematic on its own, because it leads to increased air pollution. When diesel sulfur content is high, sulfate particles, formed from combustion of sulfur in diesel, make up a significant share of total fine particulate emissions – from 15% to 50%; see CCAC (n30).

38 CCAC (n30).

39 ibid.

40 ibid.

of transitioning to ZEVs in mind, they might also consider the use of blending fuel requirements for mixing biodiesel and ethanol with traditional fuels. The experience of promoting alternative fuels in the EU and some other countries can offer lots of useful guidance.[41]

2.1.3 Carbon Standards for Cars

Besides the Euro-type standards limiting emissions from engine exhaust and driven primarily by air pollution concerns, governments enact standards to address climate change, either directly by setting limits on CO_2 emission from cars or indirectly by adopting standards for fuel consumption in cars. While the two groups of standards are aimed at different objectives enabling different regulatory outcomes, they both facilitate CO_2 emission reduction and the transition to ZEVs.

The EU introduced mandatory CO_2 emission standards for light-duty vehicles in 2009 as part of its efforts to reduce greenhouse gas emissions by 20% from 1990 levels by 2020.[42] As discussed below, these standards have subsequently been revised and are currently undergoing yet another revision as part of the 'Fit for 55' legislative package designed to achieve an at least 55% emission reduction by 2030. For the time being, up to 2024, they prescribe that the automaker's new fleet must not emit more than an average of 95 g CO_2/km for cars, whereas for vans, the automaker's new fleet is permitted to emit on average 147 g CO_2/km.[43] In the US, carbon standards for cars are designed as fuel economy standards. The US Corporate Average Fuel Economy (CAFE) standards were enacted in 1975 to increase the fuel economy of cars in the wake of the Arab oil embargo. Today, they also pursue the objective of CO_2 reduction. CAFE standards have been tightening over the years and the recently revised standards will require an industry-wide fleet average of approximately 49 mpg (miles per gallon), which correspond to approximately 111 g CO_2/km, for passenger cars and light trucks in model year 2026 by increasing fuel efficiency by

---

41 While blending requirements for biofuels are used globally, their impact on carbon reduction depends on the sustainability of biofuels themselves. After many years of biofuel promotion, the EU has recently put constraints on the use of crop-based biofuels for the purposes of compliance with the EU renewable energy targets. See European Commission, 'Renewable Energy Progress Report' (14.10.2020). <https://data.consilium.europa.eu/doc/document/ST-11866-2020-INIT/en/pdf> (last accessed 23 November 2022).

42 See EU Regulation 443/2009.

43 Starting in the years 2025 and 2030, the EU fleet-wide CO_2 targets will be stricter and defined as a percentage reduction from the 2021 level – for cars, 15% reduction from 2025 and 37.5% reduction from 2030; for vans, 15% reduction from 2025 and 31% reduction from 2030. See EU Regulation 2019/631.

8% annually for model years 2024 and 2025, and 10% annually for model year 2026.[44] Like the EU carbon standards, the US CAFE standards do not apply to every single vehicle but to an automaker's fleet average.

While carbon and fuel economy standards are beneficial for the climate, they create a perverse incentive for extending the use of diesel engines as the most efficient ones.[45] Indeed, in the last two decades, European manufacturers relied heavily on diesel technology to achieve reductions in CO_2 emissions of new cars. This means that if the installation of DPF is not induced by stricter car exhaust standards, carbon standards for cars can lead to higher emissions of black carbon. This relationship between the standards calls for their combination in the emission policy mix.

2.2 *Fossil Fuel Car Bans*

To enable a more rapid phase-out of specific types of technology, governments may impose bans, which are usually implemented by raising standards to a level that makes the use of the technology impossible. This is how the EU and some other countries have recently decided to speed up the transition to ZEVs. Car emission standards will be raised to a level where they amount to a *de facto* prohibition of sales of new fossil fuel vehicles. Unlike bans on sales, bans on the use of fossil fuel vehicles are less common. One of the few examples is the recently announced ban on fossil fuel cars on the roads in Singapore, which is expected to take effect from 2040.[46] In most other cases, however, bans on the use of fossil fuel vehicles are applied in the context of low-or zero-emissions zones in cities.[47] By making owning such vehicles less attractive, they contribute to the phase-out of fossil fuel vehicles indirectly.

---

44 In addition to fines for non-compliance, the so-called gas guzzler tax is levied on individual passenger car models that do not meet CAFE standards. See NHTSA, 'Corporate Average Fuel Economy' <https://www.nhtsa.gov/laws-regulations/corporate-average-fuel-economy> accessed 23 November 2022.

45 Aleksandra Čavoški, 'The unintended consequences of EU law and policy on air pollution' (2017) 26 RECIEL 3, 255–265.

46 Dylan Loh, 'Singapore vows to be first in Southeast Asia to ditch petrol cars' (NIKKEI Asia, 2020) <https://asia.nikkei.com/Spotlight/Environment/Singapore-vows-to-be-first-in-Southeast-Asia-to-ditch-petrol-cars> accessed 23 November 2022.

47 Hongyang Cui, Pramoda Gode, and Sandra Wappelhorst, 'A Global Overview of Zero-Emission Zones in Cities and their Development Progress' (ICCT Briefing, 2021) <https://theicct.org/publication/a-global-overview-of-zero-emission-zones-in-cities-and-their-development-progress/> accessed 23 November 2022.

2.2.1 State Bans on Sales of Fossil Fuel Cars

European countries were among the first to announce plans to phase-out fossil fuel cars and substitute them with ZEVs. Norway has set a national target of eliminating all diesel and gasoline cars by 2025.[48] It will be the first country in the world to end sales of new fossil fuel cars. To facilitate the implementation of this target, Norway has introduced various regulatory incentives for ZEVs, including tax incentives, preferred access to municipal parking facilities, waivers of fees for ferries and toll roads etc. The UK also announced that it would ban sales of new diesel and gasoline cars by 2030.[49] The EU has recently followed suit planning to realize its phase-out of fossil fuel cars through stricter car emission standards.[50] When presenting the 'Fit for 55' legislative package, the European Commission proposed to slash the average CO_2 emissions of new cars by 55% by 2030 (based on 2021 levels) and 100% by 2035.[51] The new 2030 target of cutting CO_2 in new cars by 55% is a large step from the current EU target of cutting emissions from new cars by 37.5% by 2035 against 2021 levels.[52] The revised standards, especially the 100% reduction target in 2035, imply a phase-out of fossil fuel cars and, given the lack of renewable fuels such as hydrogen, a ban on the internal combustion engine as such.[53] Plans to get fossil fuel cars off the road have also been announced in other parts of the world. By 2035, China wants to allow only sales of new cars, which are powered

48 Roadmaps for Energy, 'The Facts on: Norway's Alleged Plans to "Prohibit Sales of All Vehicles Using Fossil Fuels by 2025"' (2016) <https://roadmapsforenergy.eu/norway-fossilfuel-car-ban/> accessed 23 November 2022.

49 Charles Riley, 'Europe aims to kill gasoline and diesel cars by 2035' (*CNN Business*, 14 July 2021).

50 While this plan is to be fulfilled mainly through car carbon standards, the ongoing revision of car exhaust standards will also contribute to this goal.

51 The proposed changes are part of a larger package aimed at steering the EU towards its goal of cutting GHG emissions by at least 55% by 2030 compared to 1990 levels and become the first continent to be climate neutral in 2050. See European Commission, 'European Green Deal: Commission proposes transformation of EU economy and society to meet climate ambitions' (Press Release, 2021) <https://ec.europa.eu/commission/presscorner/detail/en/ip_21_3541> accessed 23 November 2022.

52 See Proposal for a Regulation of the European Parliament and of the Council amending Regulation (EU) 2019/631 as regards strengthening the CO_2 emission performance standards for new passenger cars and new light commercial vehicles in line with the Union's increased climate ambition, COM/2021/556 final.

53 The planned tightening of Euro exhaust emissions standards will also work for this outcome.

by 'new-energy', so that 50% of sales will fall on electric and fuel cell cars and 50% on hybrid cars.[54]

Yet, phasing out fossil fuel cars is a challenging task, especially for developing countries. A major problem is a lack of necessary infrastructure with a sufficient number of renewable energy-based charging and refueling points available to drivers, especially high-power chargers suitable for trucks, which is currently felt even in developed countries.[55] Less developed economies, such as those in Africa and Latin America, would need much more time to establish infrastructure for ZEVs.[56] Another problem is the prices of ZEVs, which are currently much higher than for fossil fuel cars. For less advanced countries with markets filled with cheap second-hand fossil fuel cars, it presents a major obstacle for transition.

To make ZEVs more attractive for consumers, import duty, sale tax and other incentives are used with various degree of success.[57] Rising fuel prices are likely to support the competitiveness of ZEVs.[58] But concerns are also raised about the readiness of the car industry to undergo the transformation. As any other structural changes, a transition to ZEVs entails job losses in the car industry[59] and requires huge investments.[60] The announcement of bans

---

54 Even today half of all electric and 'new energy' cars in the world are being sold in China. See Sean Fleming, 'China joins list of nations banning the sale of old-style fossil-fuelled vehicles' (World Economic Forum, 2020) <https://www.weforum.org/agenda/2020/11/china-bans-fossil-fuel-vehicles-electric/> accessed 23 November 2022.

55 As the currently available infrastructure in the EU is not sufficient for the implementation of the 2035 target, the European Commission also proposed the Alternative Fuels Infrastructure Regulation requiring member states to expand charging capacity in line with ZEV sales and to install charging and fueling points at regular intervals every 60 km for electric charging and every 150 km for hydrogen refueling on major highways. See Proposal for a Regulation of the European Parliament and of the Council on the deployment of alternative fuels infrastructure, and repealing Directive 2014/94/EU of the European Parliament and of the Council, COM/2021/559 final.

56 Jerónimo Callejas and others, 'Welfare and Environmental Benefits of Electric Vehicle Tax Policies in Developing Countries: Evidence from Colombia' (World Bank Group Policy Research Working Paper 10001, 2022).

57 ibid.

58 John Kemp, 'Oil price spike would accelerate U.S. shift to electric vehicles' (Reuters, 2021) <https://www.reuters.com/world/middle-east/oil-price-spike-would-accelerate-us-shift-electric-vehicles-kemp-2021-07-01/> accessed 23 November 2022.

59 It has been estimated that the shift to ZEVs will put 500,000 jobs at risk, while at the same time it will create 226000 new ones by 2035. See Joe Miller, 'European auto suppliers warn shift to electric would put 500,000 jobs at risk' (Financial Times, 2021) <https://www.ft.com/content/1e0040c9-aab2-4881-828b-e992f23a9f3e> accessed 23 November 2022.

60 Riley (n49).

on fossil fuel cars by the EU and other governments has already pushed the world's largest carmakers to earmark dozens of billions of euros for the development and production of ZEVs and use profits from the current sales of diesel and gasoline cars for these purposes.[61] As not all automakers can afford such big investments in new technologies, market stimuli, additional to fossil fuel car bans, including subsidizing sales of ZEVs and the already mentioned consumer tax incentives, are needed.[62]

2.2.2 Local and Private Initiatives

Plans to phase out fossil fuel cars have also been announced by various local governments around the world. The Canadian province of Quebec announced that it would ban the sales of new gasoline-powered passenger cars from 2035, whereas the US state of California plans to ban by that year not only sales of new gasoline passenger cars but also trucks.[63] Some cities also take measures ahead of their national governments. In their action they are driven either by local authority initiatives or by legal challenges brought by citizens or NGOs based on the right to clean air. In a number of disputes, it has been confirmed that citizens have the right to require sub-national authorities to implement measures aimed at achieving compliance with air quality norms. In 2017, the Administrative Court of Stuttgart ordered the state of Baden-Württemberg to consider a year-round ban on diesel-powered vehicles.[64] A year later, the German Federal Administrative Court in Leipzig declared that the cities of Stuttgart and Düsseldorf were allowed to prohibit older diesel vehicles from driving in zones worst affected by pollution.[65] Moreover, the European Court of Justice overturned the 2016 European Commission relaxation of car NOx emission limits to 168 mg/km, which allowed the cities of Brussels, Madrid and Paris to proceed with their plans to reject Euro 6 diesel vehicles from their centers.[66]

---

61 ibid.

62 Callejas and others (n56).

63 Allison Lampert, 'Quebec to ban sale of new gasoline-powered cars from 2035' (Reuters, 2020) <https://www.reuters.com/article/us-autos-canada-emissions-idUSKBN27W289> accessed 23 November 2022.

64 Reuters, 'German court paves way for diesel ban in Stuttgart' (2017) <https://www.reuters.com/article/germany-emissions-idUSF9N1JO01Q> accessed 23 November 2022.

65 France24, 'Court paves way for cities to ban diesel in Germany' (2018) <https://www.france24.com/en/20180227-germany-diesel-air-pollution-court-paves-way-cities-ban-leipzig-stuttgart-dusseldorf> accessed 23 November 2022.

66 Reuters, 'EU court backs cities' complaint, scraps higher NOx limits' (2018) <https://www.reuters.com/article/autos-emissions-eu-idUSL8N1YI1ZP> accessed 23 November 2022.

Business also plays an important role in the transition to ZEVs. It participates in important public-private initiatives, such as the one launched at the climate change conference in Glasgow in November 2021. At COP26, six car manufacturers (German Daimler's Mercedes-Benz, Swedish Volvo, China's BYD, Jaguar Land Rover, a unit of India's Tata Motors and the American automakers Ford and General Motors) and some other companies joined a group of 24 governments (including such developing countries as India, Turkey and Mexico) and some city and province authorities (e.g. New York, California) in signing a declaration calling to speed up the global transition from cars that burn fossil fuels to ZEVs.[67] Their intention is to end the sale of new fossil fuel cars in leading car markets by 2035, and globally by 2040.[68]

Driven by expectations that governments will raise emission standards, some carmakers make their own plans to phase out fossil fuel car production. For instance, Volvo announced that by 2030 it would only sell e-cars and phase out any car in its global portfolio with an internal combustion engine, including hybrids.[69] The Volvo Group with other truck makers pledged to end diesel truck sales by 2040. General Motors plans to go fully electric by 2035.[70] Jaguar Land Rover plans to stop producing diesel and gasoline vehicles under its Jaguar brand by 2025 and switch to electric-only models.[71] There are many

67 See Accelerating to Zero Coalition, 'COP26 declaration on accelerating the transition to 100% zero emission cars and vans' (Policy Paper, 2022) <https://www.gov.uk/government/publications/cop26-declaration-zero-emission-cars-and-vans/cop26-declaration-on-accelerating-the-transition-to-100-zero-emission-cars-and-vans> accessed 23 November 2022.

68 At the same time, the US (the world's biggest car market), China (the second largest car market), and Germany (the largest car producing country and car market in the EU) remained off the list. Germany's transport ministry could not agree with the signatories of the declaration that e-fuels, such as hydrogen, would play no role in the sustainable transport future. See Tom Espiner, 'COP 26: Four major carmakers fail to back zero emissions pledge' (BBC News, 2021) <https://www.bbc.com/news/business-59236613> accessed 23 November 2022.

69 Jack Ewing, 'Volvo Plans to Sell Only Electric Cars by 2030' (The New York Times, 2021) <https://www.nytimes.com/2021/03/02/business/volvo-electric-cars.html> accessed 23 November 2022.

70 Scott Stump, 'GM Pledged to Go All-electric, Including the Gas-guzzling Hummer – Here's How' (Today, 2021) <https://www.today.com/news/gm-pledged-cars-will-electric-2035-rcna5837> accessed 23 November 2022.

71 Edie, 'Jaguar to switch to fully electric vehicle portfolio by 2025' (2021) <https://www.edie.net/jaguar-to-switch-to-fully-electric-vehicle-portfolio-by-2025/> accessed 23 November 2022.

more automakers that have made similar pledges, and there will likely be more in the future.[72]

2.3 *Market-Based and Fiscal Measures*

In addition to command-and-control measures, governments have been experimenting with more innovative measures to reduce negative impacts of road transport on the environment and climate change. Market-based instruments of emission reductions, such as emission trading schemes (ETS), have proven to be an effective tool of climate policy, inducing reduction of CO_2 in the power and some industrial sectors in a cost-effective way.[73] However, things get more complicated when the focus turns to black carbon emissions. Unlike CO_2, impacts from black carbon are short in duration and mainly caused by black carbon concentrations in specific geographical areas rather than by nation-wide quantities (see Chapter 1). This makes designing market-based instruments for black carbon abatement more complicated. The development of market-based measures for black carbon is also hampered by the fact that there are no standard understanding and metrics on black carbon accounting.[74] So long as the methodological problems exist, the use of market-based measures for black carbon abatement is limited.[75] Whether black carbon might be affected through market-based measures designed to reduce CO_2 (as the latter reduce the use of fossil fuels, which are the source of black carbon as well) is not clear.[76] In any case, market-based instruments have not been

72 Some are still hesitant. VW, for instance, did not sign up to the phase-out declaration at COP26 arguing that the environmental benefits of signing up to the pledge are questionable when electricity in the US and China is still produced mainly from fossil fuels. It argues that an accelerated shift to electromobility has to go in line with an energy transition towards 100% renewables. See Espiner (n68).

73 Stefan Weishaar, Kateryna Holzer, and Bingyu Lu, 'Incentivizing carbon transition – a comparison of carbon trading in the EU and China', in J Verschuuren and L Reins (eds), *Research Handbook on Climate Change Mitigation Law* (Edward Elgar 2022).

74 This also hampers the development of a black carbon label based on the emerging concept of black carbon footprint; see Hilkka Timonen and others, 'Adaptation of Black Carbon Footprint Concept Would Accelerate Mitigation of Global Warming' (2019) 53 Environmental Science & Technology 21, 12153–12155.

75 The existing EU ETS, for example, does not cover black carbon emissions. It covers only GHG emissions, such as CO_2 and NOx (but excluding CH_4).

76 As ETSs target mainly CO_2, under the absence of car exhaust standards, the application of emission allowance requirement creates an incentive for diesel engines as less carbon-intensive and more fuel-saving, thereby leading to more black carbon emissions.

widely used in road transport so far, due to their negative effect of raising costs for consumers.[77]

2.3.1 Emissions Trading for Road Transport

One element of the 'Fit for 55' package is the European Commission proposal for an EU-wide ETS for fuel used in road transport and heating, with the aim of incentivizing the use of ZEVs.[78] This ETS is planned as a separate system from the EU ETS currently applied to some industries, as well as the power and air transport sectors.[79] The road transport ETS will apply to upstream fuel suppliers, putting the responsibility on fuel producers to comply with the ETS, rather than requiring individual road transport users to participate directly.[80] The obligation to submit emissions allowances will set a price to reflect the carbon footprint of fuels that apart from reducing carbon emissions can also help to make ZEVs competitive on the market.[81]

The idea of a road transport ETS has raised a great deal of criticism.[82] Given that road transport is characterized by technological barriers to investments in energy efficiency improvements, high upfront costs of emission abatement options and the low-price elasticity of energy demand, the widespread effect of the ETS will be an increase in the price of every kilometer driven resulting in higher business costs and transport prices for citizens. In this respect, questions have been asked whether carbon pricing is the right tool to decarbonize road transport, whether there are alternatives, how the high costs for consumers can be mitigated and what are the prospects for combining (linking) of

77 Magdalena Maj and others, 'Impact on Households of the Inclusion of Transport and Residential Buildings in the EU ETS' (Polish Economic Institute, 2021).

78 Michal Glowacki, 'Emissions trading for road transport and buildings' (Emissions-EUETS .com, 2021) <https://emissions-euets.com/carbon-market-glossary/2168-emissions-trading-for-road-transport-and-buildings> accessed 23 November 2022.

79 The proposal on a road transport ETS does not exclude possible merger of the two trading systems on assessment of the functioning of the new ETS to be conducted after a few years based on information and collected market experience.

80 Fuel suppliers will have to submit emissions allowances acquired at auction within a total cap on emissions reduced over time. The total quantity of allowances should be established for the first time in 2026, to follow a trajectory starting from the value of the 2024 emissions limits calculated on the basis of the reference emissions for this sector in the period from 2016 to 2018. See Glowacki (n78).

81 Some EU Member States (e.g. Germany) and other European countries (e.g. Switzerland) have carbon taxes on fuel and other pricing mechanisms for transport already in place.

82 Maj and others (n77).

the road transport ETS with the general EU ETS.[83] Concerning black carbon emissions specifically, the planned ETS in road transport is unlikely to have an effect as it targets only CO_2 and, had there been no strict exhaust standards in place, it would even create a negative effect on black carbon emissions stimulating consumption of diesel as a less carbon-intensive and more fuel-saving fuel compared to gasoline.

2.3.2 Taxes and Subsidies Supporting Transition to ZEVs

Environmental taxes have long been used in road transport to internalize external costs, especially those associated with the congestion of road networks.[84] They were initially levied on heavy-duty vehicle traffic, particularly in developed countries. Later, carbon taxes, including carbon footprint taxes for fuel and cars, were introduced to address climate change from road transport. Taxes on car purchase or ownership may vary in accordance with the car's emissions rate. For instance, some years ago Mauritius used a CO_2 levy and rebate scheme on motor vehicles[85] stimulating car buyers to import cleaner automobiles.[86] Switzerland, Finland and some other countries link the car's annual registration fee to the car's emissions rate, thereby accelerating the retirement of high-emission vehicles.[87] And irrespective of the carbon footprint, fossil fuel vehicles may be taxed more heavily. Also, as already mentioned, governments stimulate imports of ZEVs, hybrid vehicles and simply more energy-efficient vehicles through reductions of or exemptions from import duties, sales (excise) and registration taxes, road fees etc.[88] At the same time, taxes that directly target black carbon emissions are rare.[89]

---

83 See e.g. ERCST, 'Workshop: The ETS for road transport and buildings: Why yes? Why not?' (2021) <https://ercst.org/event/the-ets-for-road-transport-and-buildings-why-yes-why-not/> accessed 23 November 2022.

84 Kurt van Dender, 'Taxing vehicles, fuels, and road use: Opportunities for improving transport tax practice' (OECD Taxation Working Papers no. 44, 2019).

85 When purchasing a car, a buyer had to pay a levy per gramme of CO_2 per kilometer if the emission value of the car was above a certain threshold. If it was below the threshold, a rebate was paid. The scheme has eventually been abolished under the pressure of some operational and litigation challenges.

86 UNEP, 'Addressing the Used Vehicles Market' (n4).

87 Callejas and others (n56).

88 ibid; The US is currently preparing an extension of tax credits for ZEV purchasers designed in the way that simultaneously stimulates local ZEV production. See CNBC, 'EU, South Korea say U.S. plan for EV tax breaks may breach WTO rules' (2022) <https://www.cnbc.com/2022/08/12/eu-south-korea-say-us-plan-for-ev-tax-breaks-may-breach-wto-rules.html> accessed 23 November 2022.

89 An example is the environmental protection tax in China that covers key components of $PM_{2.5}$, including black carbon and organic carbon; see Xiurong Hu and others, 'The

In sum, the overview of emission control measures in road transport reveals a heterogeneous landscape of national car emission regulations, and at the same time a considerable improvement that has taken place in emission regulation over the last decades. However, the improvement has mainly occurred in the EU, US and some other developed and advanced developing countries, whereas less developed countries are lagging behind. The uneven car emission standards among countries lead to the situation, which is very similar to 'pollution heaven' and carbon leakage.[90] Particularly, it is evident where second-hand cars from developed countries with stringent emissions controls flow to developing countries with lax standards, simply relocating the problem of air pollution to other parts of the world while continuing to spoil the climate for all. Therefore, an alignment of car emission standards among countries with their gradual convergence and, possibly, harmonization at the level of the highest standards is needed.[91] How such an alignment of car emission regulations can happen is discussed below.

3 Prospects for Developing Global Standards for Road Transport Emissions

The argument here is that the worldwide alignment of car emission standards would improve air quality in individual countries and support action on climate change globally. Alignment is also desirable for economic reasons. Varying standards and regulations among countries increase costs of doing business and act as trade barriers, whereas their harmonization would lead to economies of scale and economic efficiencies with positive welfare effects.[92] This section explores two ways, in which global alignment of car emission standards can happen. One is a 'laissez faire' way induced by market forces. The other is an institutional way, which requires an intervention of states entering negotiations on common standards in international and regional fora.

---

impact of environmental protection tax on sectoral and spatial distribution of air pollution emissions in China' (2019) 14 Environmental Research Letters.

90 PMR, 'Carbon Leakage: Theory, Evidence and Policy Design' (Partnership for Market Readiness (PMR) Technical Note 11, 2015).

91 Kateryna Holzer and Thomas Cottier, 'Addressing Climate Change under Preferential Trade Agreements: Towards Alignment of Carbon Standards under the Transatlantic Trade and Investment Partnership' (2015) 35 Global Environmental Change, 514–522.

92 Hoekman and Mavroidis (n15).

3.1 *Market-Induced Alignment*

The market plays an important role in the alignment of product standards among countries. Studies reveal that large consumer markets with greener preferences combined with political and economic power of the greener countries, the readiness of technologies and the leadership of large producers are the main drivers of convergence of environmental standards.[93] The adoption of stricter car emission standards by large markets is basically the first step towards establishing global standards in this field. Standards of a large market create economic incentives for companies from third countries either to follow these standards voluntarily or lobby their government to adopt them as national standards in order to get access to the large market.

An example of a large market is the EU, which has a global regulatory power effect. The 'Brussels Effect' study shows that 'the EU's greatest global influence may not be through multilateral mechanisms and political institutions but instead through unilateral actions, facilitated by markets and private corporations'.[94] A similar regulatory power effect, albeit at a sub-state level, is observed in the US. The market of the US state of California, which has higher environmental standards, is large enough to have the California Effect through exercising market power and induce other US states and the US as a whole to also raise their standards.[95] Regulatory power of large markets has manifested itself in the automobile sector, when California, a significant market within the US, and Germany, a significant market within the EU, coerced vehicle manufacturers through its market power into accepting standards which were stricter than those previously followed. On the other hand, progressive regulations of smaller markets of Denmark and the Netherlands could not influence the direction of the European standards.[96]

The regulatory power effect of the EU as a whole has worked very well in the case of car emission standards. The EU car emission standards have been adopted by many non-EU countries. The North American car exhaust standards (Tiers) are based on similar emission control technologies as in the EU. Mexico has become the first Latin American country to adopt national Euro VI standards for heavy-duty vehicles. India is moving towards nationwide Euro VI standards too, whereas China has already adopted a regulation requiring all new trucks, buses and other heavy-duty vehicles powered by diesel to meet Euro VI equivalent emissions standards. Even Brazil and Argentina, which have

93 Dietrich (n19); Vogel and Kagan (n14).

94 Bradford (n14).

95 Vogel (n14).

96 Dietrich (n19).

little to do with the EU car market, now have car exhaust standards aligned with those of the EU. This happened through the adoption of equivalent US Tiers on which these countries depend, underlining the existence of complex interlinkages that lead to alignment in the end.[97]

As shown in Bradford's study, the adoption of standards of a large market by foreign governments, i.e. harmonization *de jure*, is often preceded by the adoption of standards of a large export market by producers of exporting countries, i.e. harmonization *de facto*.[98] Producers then lobby their governments to incorporate these standards in national legislation, so that *de facto* harmonization becomes *de jure*. Signs of *de facto* harmonization and upward convergence can be seen in today's automobile market. As already mentioned, while expecting the adoption of stricter emission standards by the EU and other countries, automakers from all over the world seek to develop ZEVs to be able to meet the higher standards. This is also true for carmakers having their assembly facilities in developing countries, if their output is exported to the EU and US markets with imminent higher standards. In the past, Korean carmakers also followed standards that were higher than set by their government to be able to export to North America and the EU, just as Russian car manufacturers had started producing cars compliant with Euro 5 standards before the Russian government adopted them.[99]

That said, the regulatory power effect of large markets is not absolute. Countries, like China and India, having big domestic markets and alternative export markets have little need to follow the EU or the US higher standards, except for cars being exported to the EU and the US. The adoption of higher standards by these countries can only be stimulated by their own consumers, if the consumers are willing to pay higher prices for environmental protection.[100] Consequently, such countries will have different standards for cars exported to markets with stricter standards and for cars produced for their own markets. Moreover, companies have also their own motives to follow certain standards, which may not entirely coincide with public interests of emission reduction and other public goals. Given these limitations of market-driven harmonization, government intervention is needed and countries with higher standards should pursue upward convergence through negotiations in international and regional fora.

97 CCAC (n30).
98 Bradford (n14).
99 ibid.
100 Suparna Karmakar, 'Prospects for regulatory convergence under TTIP' (2013) 15 Bruegel Policy Contribution.

3.2 *Alignment through International and Regional Fora*

Car emission standards can become part of a negotiated agreement as a result of treaty-driven harmonization in contrast to market-driven one discussed above.[101] As there is no sector-specific international organization for road transport, car emission standards can potentially be captured by work of a number of international and regional environmental and trade-related fora, such as the United Nations Economic Commission for Europe, the Climate and Clean Air Coalition, the World Trade Organization and regional trade agreements.

3.2.1 United Nations Economic Commission for Europe

The United Nations Economic Commission for Europe (UNECE) is a regional economic organization with the biggest influence on car emission standards worldwide. UNECE, which embraces 56 European and non-European members (including US, Canada, Israel, Turkey and former Soviet republics), hosts three UN agreements on car technical regulations open to any UN member[102] and the World Forum for Harmonization of Vehicle Regulations (WP.29) aimed at pursuing actions towards the worldwide development of technical regulations for vehicles. The harmonization efforts of WP.29 contribute to improving vehicle safety, protecting the environment, promoting energy efficiency and increasing anti-theft performance.

An important milestone in the UNECE formation of the global car emission regulation is the recently adopted uniform car approval regulations.[103] They are based on the Worldwide Harmonized Light Vehicles Test Procedure (WLTP), which is a global standard for determining the levels of air pollutants (including $PM_{2.5}$), CO_2 emissions and fuel consumption of traditional, hybrid and e-cars, aimed to ensure that emissions remain under the set limits whether the vehicle is driven in urban, rural or highway environments.[104] This international

101 A country would pursue a treaty-driven harmonization in cases where its market power or its regulatory capacity is not sufficient, which is usual for a large exporting country that depends on export markets with standards different from its own; see Bradford (n14).

102 The 1958 Agreement concerning the Adoption of Uniform Technical Prescriptions for Wheeled Vehicles, Equipment and Parts which can be Fitted and/or be Used on Wheeled Vehicles and the Conditions for Reciprocal Recognition of Approvals Granted on the Basis of these Prescriptions; the 1998 Agreement concerning the Establishing of Global Technical Regulations for Wheeled Vehicles, Equipment and Parts which can be Fitted and/or be Used on Wheeled Vehicles; the 1997 Agreement concerning the Adoption of Uniform Conditions for Periodical Technical Inspections of Wheeled Vehicles and the Reciprocal Recognition of such Inspections.

103 UN Regulations nos. 83 and 154 and UN Regulation no. 49.

104 WLTP is added as a protocol to the Global Registry (Global Technical Regulations) defined by the 1998 Agreement.

testing standard is beneficial from both an economic and an environmental perspective. For one, car manufacturers get a single approval for all major markets adopting this regulation.[105] For the other, as one of the main goals of WLTP is to better match the laboratory estimates of fuel consumption and emissions with the measures of an on-road driving condition, WLTP addresses the reliability of testing procedures in the wake of the Dieselgate scandal. WP.29 and its Working Party on Pollution and Energy are now actively working to complement the new regulation on WLTP with a globally-agreed Real Driving Emissions Test, which will introduce procedures for testing vehicles in real life conditions on public roads to demonstrate real world compliance in addition to the WLTP test performed in controlled conditions in laboratories.

It is noteworthy that the uniform car approval regulations adopted by the UNECE are based on the Euro 6/VI standard of the EU.[106] This fact demonstrates the unilateral regulatory power of the EU and its global regulatory influence through international organizations and the potential for the worldwide convergence of car emission standards. Due to the diverse membership of UNECE, the Euro standards have already been exported through UNECE to non-EU markets, including India, Mexico and China.[107] Also, as the UN agreements on car technical regulations hosted by the UNECE are open for non-UNECE members as well, these higher car emission regulations can potentially be adopted worldwide. Whether the adoption of stricter car exhaust and CO_2 standards in the EU will prompt the UNECE WP.29 to undertake further steps for harmonization of car emission regulations facilitating the transition to ZEVs at a global scale remains to be seen.

3.2.2 Climate and Clean Air Coalition

The Climate and Clean Air Coalition (CCAC), a public-private partnership that promotes SLCP reduction policies, also supports a universal upward convergence of car emission standards by bringing high-level attention to the policies and technologies available to promote low-sulfur fuels and cleaner diesel vehicles, providing expertise and financial assistance and promoting regional partnerships (see Chapter 6).

105 Besides the majority of UNECE countries, WLTP is also the standard emission and fuel economy test for India, South Korea and Japan.

106 See UN Regulations nos. 83 and 154 containing the technical provisions for the pollutant emissions standards up to Euro 6 for light-duty vehicles and UN Regulation no. 49 containing the technical provisions for the pollutant emissions standards up to EURO VI for trucks and buses.

107 Bradford (n14).

CCAC members adopted a global strategy to introduce low-sulfur fuels and cleaner diesel vehicles, which shows how $PM_{2.5}$ and black carbon from the global on-road diesel fleet could be reduced by over 90% in different regions by 2030 in a cost-effective way through the introduction of low-sulfur fuels and cleaner diesel vehicle standards.[108] It describes four categories of action depending on country's specifics: 'importers', 'refiners', 'vehicle standards' and 'cities first'. In import-dependent countries, implementing higher standards should not take long, as low-sulfur fuels are readily available on the global market. There are also countries that have no longer a problem with low sulfur fuels but still have a problem with appropriate car exhaust standards. These countries can gain from adopting stricter car exhaust standards matching already-available fuel quality, while playing the role of regional leaders sharing their experience with implementing low-sulfur fuel in regional fora. As concerns the 'cities first' approach, some countries, such as China and India, introduce stricter fuel quality only for urban areas, for instance through investments in cleaner public transport, so that lower sulfur fuels are available in cities and some transit corridors prior to ramping up low sulfur fuels in the whole country.

In general, the CCAC strives to implement car exhaust and fuel quality standards equivalent to Euro 4/IV by 2025 and Euro 6/VI by 2030 worldwide.[109] By committing CCAC member countries to adopt higher car exhaust and fuel quality standards, the CCAC makes an important contribution in the alignment of these standards across countries.

3.2.3 World Trade Organization

Although the World Trade Organization (WTO) is not a forum for setting international standards for products, the WTO has a structural unit, the Committee of Technical Barriers to Trade (TBT Committee), which oversights the implementation of rules on the adoption and application of technical regulations and standards (TBT measures), including emission standards for cars. These rules ensure transparency and prevent unnecessary barriers to trade imposed by TBT measures, as well as discrimination of imports. At the same time, these rules promote regulatory harmonization through provisions which stimulate the use of international standards as the basis of national technical regulations and standards and mutual recognition of regulations and conformity

108 CCAC (n30).

109 See CCAC, 'Marrakesh Communique of CCAC 8th High Level Assembly' (14 November 2016) <https://www.ccacoalition.org/en/resources/marrakech-communique> accessed 23 November 2022.

assessment procedures (the basis for the conclusion of mutual recognition agreements). TBT rules will therefore play an important role in promoting compliance with any future car emission standards adopted by UNECE or at any other international forum.

TBT rules also contribute to promoting best regulatory practices, particularly through discussions of specific trade concerns (STCs) at the TBT Committee.[110] Emissions standards for cars and fuels have also been the topic of STCs. These STCs focused on the elimination of trade barriers resulted from the methodology chosen for the calculation of environmental impact, trade restrictiveness of car regulations and some of their implementation features.[111] Also important are requirements of notification for draft technical regulations, which ensure transition periods between the announcement of a technical regulation and its promulgation. The experience with transition to low-sulfur fuel shows that the successful adoption of low-sulfur fuel standards in different countries was preceded by planning and preparation periods of up to 5 years to allow refiners to select strategies for compliance and raise the necessary capital.[112] Allowing transition periods and technical assistance for developing countries to adopt to more stringent regulations for their exports will be important in the transition to ZEVs.

At the same time, WTO is criticized for not paying due attention to environmental issues and its inability to induce upward regulatory harmonization.[113] Stricter standards can be compromised in trade disputes. In *US-Gasoline,* Venezuela and Brazil challenged three U.S. vehicle-related regulations – the luxury car tax, the gas-guzzler tax and the corporate fuel efficiency standards – and the US lost the dispute on the grounds that some requirements for the implementation imposed on imports were found discriminatory.[114] There is therefore a risk that stringent car emission standards will be challenged in the WTO dispute settlement, especially if they are significantly above standards of other countries. Fossil fuel car bans are particularly susceptible to a challenge, as they constitute quantitative restrictions normally prohibited under WTO rules. However, fossil fuel car bans, as long as they apply on sales of all fossil fuel cars (domestically produced and imported), can be justified under the

110 Kateryna Holzer, 'Addressing tensions and avoiding disputes: Specific trade concerns in the TBT Committee' (2019) 14 Global Trade and Customs Journal 3.
111 Holzer and Lim (n12).
112 CCAC (n30).
113 Dietrich (n19).
114 DS2 United States-Standards for reformulated and conventional gasoline, panel and Appellate Body reports issued in 1996.

health and environmental exceptions.[115] Import and export bans on second-hand cars can be justified on the same grounds.[116] They can also be potentially negotiated within the group of willing WTO members under an international (plurilateral) agreement. Prospects for the conclusion of such an agreement require a separate study.

3.2.4 Regional Trade Agreements

Unlike in the WTO setting, harmonization of car emission standards under regional trade agreements[117] (RTAs) gives less reasons to worry about race to the bottom concerns, as long as an RTA party with a larger market power can offer trade concessions in return for accepting higher standards by its RTA partner. Being a package deal, an RTA increases bargaining power needed to adopt a common standard that might be costly for the other party.[118]

According to Dietrich, RTAs can support alignment of car emission standards based on two approaches: domestic treatment and harmonization.[119] Under the first approach, trade in cars under an RTA will only be liberalized if imported cars comply with standards of the importing RTA party. Following the harmonization approach, governments agree on the application of a common standard and, in the case of upward harmonization, raise standards to the highest level of the two. But if RTA Parties accept mutual recognition of standards, there will be no effect on standards' alignment, as governments accept imports of cars under standards of the exporting country.

Some existing RTAs contain provisions on car emissions and air pollution control policies.[120] Some of these provisions are very general, in which RTA Parties just agree to participate in joint work programs on air pollution standards (e.g. COMESA 1993) or reiterate provisions from specific bilateral agreements addressing air pollution (e.g. China–Korea 2015). Some EU RTAs provide for specific car emission standards to be used in trade between Parties (e.g. EU–Montenegro 2007). Many non-EU countries in Southern and Eastern

---

115 Article XX of the General Agreement on Tariffs and Trade (GATT).

116 Jorge Macias and others, 'Policy Handbook for the Regulation of Imported Second-Hand Vehicles' (GFEI Working Paper 7, 2013).

117 RTAs are preferential trade agreements between two or more partners (usually reciprocal). The most widespread form of RTAs is a free trade agreement, under which the parties eliminate barriers in trade between them but pursue independent customs policies against third countries.

118 Holzer and Cottier (n91).

119 Dietrich (n19).

120 Jean-Frédéric Morin and Sikina Jinnah, 'The untapped potential of preferential trade agreements for climate governance' (2018) 27 Environmental Politics 3, 541–565.

Europe (e.g. Ukraine, Serbia, Turkey etc.) have harmonized car emission standards with the corresponding EU standards through RTAs concluded with the EU. However, this does not concern second-hand cars and consequently the average age of fleets in Eastern Europe and Balkans continues to be much older than in Western Europe.

By contrast, the US-Mexico-Canada Agreement (formerly NAFTA) has been irrelevant for both upward harmonization of car emission standards[121] and promoting restrictions on second-hand cars.[122] In fact, US and Canadian standards have been harmonized through bilateral regulatory cooperation outside the RTA.[123] Efforts to bring greater alignment between Canadian and U.S. car emission standards are ongoing through the Canada-US Regulatory Cooperation Council. Regarding standards in Mexico, US standards are adopted through market forces, as automobile plants in Mexico are operated by U.S. firms and many cars are exported to the US.

Finally, it should be mentioned that an opportunity for harmonization of car emission standards was missed once the negotiations of the Transatlantic Trade and Investment Partnership, a mega-regional US-EU trade agreement, had been suspended in 2016. Driven by interests of costs savings from the elimination of differences in product standards, the EU and the US attached considerable importance to achieving regulatory convergence under the bilateral trade negotiations. Obtaining equivalency was extremely difficult, however, particularly for car carbon (fuel economy) standards, where differences existed not only in the design of standards but also in the level of emission reduction they achieve.[124]

4 Conclusion

As the above overview shows, the regulatory landscape addressing road transport emissions comprises diverse and predominantly national measures to combat air pollution or climate change. In most cases, black carbon emissions

121 Dietrich (n19).

122 Macias and others (n116). As expected from an RTA, all restrictions on import of new and second-hand cars among US, Canada and Mexico were eliminated.

123 Due to high integration of the car industry, the countries build vehicles on both sides of the border to the same vehicle safety and emission standards.

124 Currently, the EU car emission standards are stricter than those in the US. The EU 95 g CO_2/km or 4.1 l/100 km norm corresponds to 46.1 mpg or 5.1 l/100 km norm in the US. See Holzer and Cottier (n91).

are only indirectly affected by policies and measures to reduce air polluting substances from cars. Mainly motivated by climate policy considerations, bans on fossil fuel cars are by far the most effective means of reducing road transport emissions and are considered in the EU, China and in an increasing number of other countries. However, they are unlikely to be feasible for many less developed countries in the foreseeable future, as they require investments in necessary infrastructure, such as charging and refueling stations, and consumer ability to pay higher prices for zero emission vehicles. These countries will therefore have to continue relying on alternative measures, particularly on car exhaust standards requiring the installation of diesel particulate filters.

The adoption of the right mix of instruments is crucial. While the protection of climate, environment and health requires reducing both black carbon and CO_2 emissions, CO_2 and black carbon reduction measures are not always compatible. The adoption of higher carbon and fuel economy standards for cars requires a simultaneous adoption of higher car exhaust and fuel quality standards in order to prevent the negative impacts of dieselization. Car exhaust standards and fuel quality standards, in their turn, should constitute one system of emissions controls, given that diesel particulate filters promoted by higher car exhaust standards can only function with low-sulfur fuels. In any case, due to specificities of countries, a mix of policy instruments, tailored to specific needs of countries is required.

While diesel particulate filters and other emission reduction technologies have become cost-effective, existing discrepancies among countries in car emission standards preclude their diffusion on a global scale. This forms an obstacle to addressing domestic air pollution problems and hinders global climate action. The absence of maximum emission levels in road transport together with the lack of restrictions on trade in second-hand cars will slow down the transition to ZEVs. Global alignment of car emission standards with their gradual convergence to the level of the highest standards is therefore an outcome to strive for.

There are two major ways for such alignment to take place. The first is through market forces that induce carmakers to follow higher car emission standards to get access to export markets. The second is through governments negotiating minimum emission levels and common standards in international and regional fora. The two ways can perfectly complement each other: governments can improve where markets fail and steer market-induced regulatory alignment in the direction of mutual economic and environmental interest.

Today, UNECE as a regional organization with a global impact on vehicle regulation provides the best forum for negotiations on car emission standards. It has already managed to adopt uniform car approval procedures and a global standard for car emission testing based on high standards of the EU. Work of public-private partnerships and initiatives, such as CCAC, can facilitate worldwide adoption of higher emission standards for vehicles, contributing through guidance and technical assistance to countries lagging behind. WTO, for its part, can play a useful role by encouraging the use of international standards and promoting good regulatory practices that ensure the quality of regulations and their transparent and non-discriminatory application. Alignment of car emission standards can also be pursued through negotiations on trade liberalization under regional trade agreements, which offer ample scope for bargaining.

If the goal of zero-emission road transport is taken seriously, front-runner countries should seize every opportunity offered by the above-discussed fora to promote higher standards for emissions from vehicles and their worldwide adoption.

Bibliography

Accelerating to Zero Coalition, 'COP26 declaration on accelerating the transition to 100% zero emission cars and vans' (Policy Paper, 2022) <https://www.gov.uk/government/publications/cop26-declaration-zero-emission-cars-and-vans/cop26-declaration-on-accelerating-the-transition-to-100-zero-emission-cars-and-vans> accessed 23 November 2022.

Bradford A, *The Brussels Effect: How the European Union Rules the World* (Oxford University Press, 2020).

Brewer T, 'Black carbon problems in transportation: Technological solutions and governmental policy solutions' (MIT Working paper, 2017).

Brown-Steiner B and others, 'Black carbon emissions from trucks and trains in the Midwestern and Northeastern United States from 1977 to 2007' (2016) 129 Atmospheric Environment, 155–166.

Callejas J and others, 'Welfare and Environmental Benefits of Electric Vehicle Tax Policies in Developing Countries: Evidence from Colombia' (World Bank Group Policy Research Working Paper 10001, 2022).

Čavoški A, 'The unintended consequences of EU law and policy on air pollution' (2017) 26 RECIEL 3, 255–265.

CCAC, 'Cleaning Up the Global On-Road Diesel Fleet: a Global Strategy to Introduce Low-Sulfur Fuels and Cleaner Diesel Vehicles' (CCAC 2016).

CCAC, 'Marrakesh Communique of CCAC 8th High Level Assembly' (14 November 2016) <https://www.ccacoalition.org/en/resources/marrakech-communique> accessed 23 November 2022.

CNBC, 'EU, South Korea say U.S. plan for EV tax breaks may breach WTO rules' (2022) <https://www.cnbc.com/2022/08/12/eu-south-korea-say-us-plan-for-ev-tax-breaks-may-breach-wto-rules.html> accessed 23 November 2022.

Cui H, Gode P, and Wappelhorst S, 'A Global Overview of Zero-Emission Zones in Cities and their Development Progress' (ICCT Briefing, 2021) <https://theicct.org/publication/a-global-overview-of-zero-emission-zones-in-cities-and-their-development-progress/> accessed 23 November 2022.

Dietrich W F, 'Harmonisation of Automobile Emission Standards Under International Trade Agreements: Lessons from the European Union Applied to the WTO and the NAFTA' (1996), 20 William and Mary Environmental Law and Policy Review 175.

Edie, 'Jaguar to switch to fully electric vehicle portfolio by 2025' (2021) <https://www.edie.net/jaguar-to-switch-to-fully-electric-vehicle-portfolio-by-2025/> accessed 23 November 2022.

ERCST, 'Workshop: the ETS for road transport and buildings: Why yes? Why not?' (2021) <https://ercst.org/event/the-ets-for-road-transport-and-buildings-why-yes-why-not/> accessed 23 November 2022.

Espiner T, 'COP 26: Four major carmakers fail to back zero emissions pledge' (BBC News, 2021) <https://www.bbc.com/news/business-59236613> accessed 23 November 2022.

European Commission, 'Antitrust: Commission fines truck producers € 2.93 billion for participating in a cartel' (Press Release, 2016) <https://ec.europa.eu/commission/presscorner/detail/en/IP_16_2582> accessed 23/11/2022.

European Commission, 'European Green Deal: Commission proposes transformation of EU economy and society to meet climate ambitions' (Press Release, 2021) <https://ec.europa.eu/commission/presscorner/detail/en/ip_21_3541> accessed 23 November 2022.

European Commission, 'Renewable Energy Progress Report' (14.10.2020). <https://data.consilium.europa.eu/doc/document/ST-11866-2020-INIT/en/pdf> (last accessed 23 November 2022).

Ewing J, 'Volvo Plans to Sell Only Electric Cars by 2030' (The New York Times, 2021) <https://www.nytimes.com/2021/03/02/business/volvo-electric-cars.html> accessed 23 November 2022.

Faiz A and others, 'Air Pollution from Motor Vehicles: Standards and Technologies for Controlling Emissions' (World Bank 1996).

Fleming S, 'China joins list of nations banning the sale of old-style fossil-fuelled vehicles' (World Economic Forum, 2020) <https://www.weforum.org/agenda/2020/11/china-bans-fossil-fuel-vehicles-electric/> accessed 23 November 2022.

France24, 'Court paves way for cities to ban diesel in Germany' (2018) <https://www.france24.com/en/20180227-germany-diesel-air-pollution-court-paves-way-cities-ban-leipzig-stuttgart-dusseldorf> accessed 23 November 2022.

GFEI, 'Securing Global Fleet Transformation – GFEI's Zero Pathway' (GFEI 2021).

Glowacki M, 'Emissions trading for road transport and buildings' (Emissions-EUETS.com, 2021) <https://emissions-euets.com/carbon-market-glossary/2168-emissions-trading-for-road-transport-and-buildings> accessed 23 November 2022.

Hoekman B and Mavroidis P, 'Regulatory Spillovers and the Trading System: from Coherence to Cooperation' (E15 Initiative 2015) <https://cadmus.eui.eu/bitstream/handle/1814/35862/E15-Regulatory-OP-Hoekman-and-Mavroidis_2015.pdf?sequence=1&isAllowed=y> accessed 12/01/2023.

Holzer K, 'Addressing tensions and avoiding disputes: Specific trade concerns in the TBT Committee' (2019) 14 Global Trade and Customs Journal 3.

Holzer K and A H Lim, 'Trade and Carbon Standards: Why Greater Regulatory Cooperation is Needed, in D. Esty and S. Biniaz (eds), *Cool Heads in a Warming World: How Trade Policy Can Help Fight Climate Change* (Yale University 2020), <https://envirocenter.yale.edu/sites/default/files/files/CoolHeads_Holzer(1).pdf> accessed 24 November 2022.

Holzer K and T Cottier, 'Addressing Climate Change under Preferential Trade Agreements: Towards Alignment of Carbon Standards under the Transatlantic Trade and Investment Partnership' (2015) 35 Global Environmental Change, 514–522.

Hooghes L and G Marks, *Multi-Level Governance and European Integration* (Rowman & Littlefield Publishers, 2001).

Hu X and others, 'The impact of environmental protection tax on sectoral and spatial distribution of air pollution emissions in China' (2019) 14 *Environmental Research Letters.*

Karmakar S, 'Prospects for regulatory convergence under TTIP' (2013) 15 Bruegel Policy Contribution.

Kemp J, 'Oil price spike would accelerate U.S. shift to electric vehicles' (Reuters, 2021) <https://www.reuters.com/world/middle-east/oil-price-spike-would-accelerate-us-shift-electric-vehicles-kemp-2021-07-01/> accessed 23 November 2022.

Lampert A, 'Quebec to ban sale of new gasoline-powered cars from 2035' (Reuters, 2020) <https://www.reuters.com/article/us-autos-canada-emissions-idUSKBN27W289> accessed 23 November 2022.

Loh D, 'Singapore vows to be first in Southeast Asia to ditch petrol cars' (NIKKEI Asia, 2020) <https://asia.nikkei.com/Spotlight/Environment/Singapore-vows-to-be-first-in-Southeast-Asia-to-ditch-petrol-cars> accessed 23 November 2022.

Macias J and others, 'Policy Handbook for the Regulation of Imported Second-Hand Vehicles' (GFEI Working Paper 7, 2013).

Maj M and others, 'Impact on Households of the Inclusion of Transport and Residential Buildings in the EU ETS' (Polish Economic Institute, 2021).

Miller J, 'European auto suppliers warn shift to electric would put 500,000 jobs at risk' (Financial Times, 2021) <https://www.ft.com/content/1e0040c9-aab2-4881-828b-e992f23a9f3e> accessed 23 November 2022.

Miller J and L Jin, 'Global Progress Toward Soot-Free Diesel Vehicles in 2018' (ICCT 2018).

Minjares R and others, 'Alignment of policies to maximize the climate benefits of diesel vehicles through control of particulate matter and black carbon emissions' (2013) 54 Energy Policy, 54–61.

Morin J-F and S Jinnah, 'The untapped potential of preferential trade agreements for climate governance' (2018) 27 Environmental Politics 3, 541–565.

Müller J, 'Dieselgate: the scandal has not been solved' (Heinrich-Böll-Stiftung 2021).

NHTSA, 'Corporate Average Fuel Economy' <https://www.nhtsa.gov/laws-regulations/corporate-average-fuel-economy> accessed 23 November 2022.

PMR, 'Carbon Leakage: Theory, Evidence and Policy Design', (Partnership for Market Readiness (PMR) Technical Note 11, 2015).

Reuters, 'EU court backs cities' complaint, scraps higher NOx limits' (2018) <https://www.reuters.com/article/autos-emissions-eu-idUSL8N1YI1ZP> accessed 23 November 2022.

Reuters, 'German court paves way for diesel ban in Stuttgart' (2017) <https://www.reuters.com/article/germany-emissions-idUSF9N1JO01Q> accessed 23 November 2022.

Riley C, 'Europe aims to kill gasoline and diesel cars by 2035' (*CNN Business*, 14 July 2021).

Roadmaps for Energy, 'The Facts on: Norway's Alleged Plans to "Prohibit Sales of All Vehicles Using Fossil Fuels by 2025"' (2016) <https://roadmapsforenergy.eu/norway-fossilfuel-car-ban/> accessed 23 November 2022.

Spar D and D Yoffie, 'A Race to the Bottom or Governance from the Top?' in A. Prakash and J. A. Hart (eds) *Coping with Globalization* (London: Routledge, 2000).

Stump S, 'GM Pledged to Go All-electric, Including the Gas-guzzling Hummer – Here's How' (Today, 2021) <https://www.today.com/news/gm-pledged-cars-will-electric-2035-rcna5837> accessed 23 November 2022.

Timonen H and others, 'Adaptation of Black Carbon Footprint Concept Would Accelerate Mitigation of Global Warming' (2019) 53 *Environmental Science & Technology* 21, 12153–12155.

Todts W, 'Three reasons why road transport in the ETS is a bad idea' (Transport and Environment, September 2014).

UNEP, 'Addressing the Used Vehicles Market: Potential Strategies for Importing and Exporting Countries to Improve Safety, Fuel Economy and Emissions Impacts, A Report of the Used Vehicles Working Group of the Partnership for Clean Fuels and Vehicles' (UNEP 2019). <http://airqualityandmobility.org/PDFs/USED_VEHICLES_WORKING_GROUP_REPORT.pdf> accessed 23 November 2022.

UNEP, *The Emissions Gap Report* (Nairobi: UNEP, 2017).

van Dender K, 'Taxing vehicles, fuels, and road use: Opportunities for improving transport tax practice' (OECD Taxation Working Papers no. 44, 2019).

Vogel D and R Kagan, *Dynamics of Regulatory Change: How Globalisation Affects National Regulatory Policies* (UC Berkley, 2002).

Vogel D, *Trading Up: Consumer and Environmental Regulation in a Global Economy* (Harvard University Press, 1995).

Weishaar S, K Holzer, and B Liu, 'Incentivizing carbon transition – a comparison of carbon trading in the EU and China', in J Verschuuren and L Reins (eds), *Research Handbook on Climate Change Mitigation Law* (Edward Elgar 2022).

Williams M and R Minjares, 'A technical summary of Euro 6/VI vehicle emission standards' (ICCT, 2016).

CHAPTER 13

Transnational Approaches to Controlling Methane Emissions from Oil and Gas Operations

Tade Oyewunmi

1 Introduction

Methane is a greenhouse gas (GHG) with significant global warming potential. It is also a short-lived climate pollutant (SLCP) and stays in the atmosphere much shorter than carbon dioxide (CO_2).[1] Compared to other SLCPs, methane emissions are much more irregular, emitted intermittently from wetlands, agricultural and animal farming, landfills, and energy-related sources such as fugitive emissions from oil and gas operations, abandoned coal mines, etc.[2] The energy sector – including oil, natural gas, coal, and bioenergy – accounts for around 40% of methane emissions from human activity.[3] According to the International Energy Agency (IEA), China, India, the United States, Russia, and Brazil are the world's five largest methane emitters (from all sources).[4] Likewise, the following countries reported to account for the highest level of energy-related methane emissions globally i.e., China, Russia, the United

1 Climate and Clean Air Coalition (CCAC), 'Methane' <www.ccacoalition.org/en/slcps/methane> accessed 12 May 2021; US Environmental Protection Agency, 'Overview of Greenhouse Gases' (2022) <https://www.epa.gov/ghgemissions/overview-greenhouse-gases> accessed 23 February 2023.

2 See International Energy Agency (IEA), *Global Methane Tracker 2020*, (IEA Publications, 2020) <www.iea.org/reports/methane-tracker-2020> accessed 12 May 2022. Sources of methane emissions can be categorized as natural sources (around 40% of emissions), and those originating from human activity (the remaining 60% – known as anthropogenic emissions). The largest source of anthropogenic methane emissions is agriculture, followed by the energy sector sources.

3 United Nations Environment Programme (UNEP)/CCAC, *Global Assessment: Urgent steps must be taken to reduce methane emissions this decade* (6 May 2021); IEA, *Global Methane Tracker 2022* (IEA Publications, 2022) <https://www.iea.org/reports/global-methane-tracker-2022> accessed 23 February 2023.

4 ibid. The major methane emission sources for these countries vary greatly. For example, a key source of methane emissions in China is coal production, whereas Russia emits most of its methane from natural gas and oil systems. The largest sources of methane emissions from human activities in the United States are oil and gas systems, livestock enteric fermentation, and landfills.

States, Iran, and India.[5] While methane and fugitive emissions may arise in the oil and gas production and supply process, it is worth noting that typically oil and gas resources play a key role in meeting energy demand and as feedstock for industrial and commercial applications in these countries.[6]

There are notable technical and risk management aspects to production and supply operations carried out by industry operators and since different countries have different levels of experience and know-how, it is essential to create platforms for facilitating knowledge sharing and best practices for implementing tested measures for curtailing emissions and other externalities. Primarily, industry operations to produce, process, and supply oil and gas are carried out under relevant national regulatory frameworks, which may comprise prescriptive standards, performance-based, informational, and economic instruments of regulation.[7] Methane control requirements and best practices may also be stipulated under relevant permitting and contractual provisions applicable to private local and international operators.[8] As discussed in this chapter, such industry best practices and operational approaches have become transnational to a significant extent because most firms and governmental institutions in the respective domestic sectors are increasingly engaged in international partnerships and collaborations such as Global Methane Initiative (GMI) and the Oil and Gas Climate Initiative's (OGCI) multi-stakeholder Methane Guiding Principles group.

The GMI is an international public-private partnership framework through which member countries and organizations coordinate their efforts toward

5 ibid.

6 See US Energy Information Administration (EIA), *International Energy Outlook 2021* (October 6, 2021) <https://www.eia.gov/outlooks/ieo/pdf/IEO2021_ReleasePresentation.pdf> accessed 12 May 2022, on the correlation between energy consumption from primary sources such as oil and gas (although utilization of more carbon-intensive sources like coal declines rapidly) and GDP growth rates globally in its outlook to 2050. See also on the challenges and options for addressing oil and gas related methane emissions: IEA, *Driving Down Methane Leaks from the Oil and Gas Industry: A regulatory roadmap and toolkit* (IEA Publications, 2021) <www.iea.org/reports/driving-down-methane-leaks-from-the-oil-and-gas-industry> accessed 12 May 2022.

7 Tade Oyewunmi, 'Natural Gas in a Carbon-Constrained World: Examining the Role of Institutions in Curbing Methane and Other Fugitive Emissions' (2021) 9 LSU Journal of Energy Law & Resources 1; Monika U Ehrman, 'Lights Out in the Bakken: A Review and Analysis of Flaring Regulation and its Potential Effect on North Dakota Shale Oil Production' (2014) 117 West Virginia Law Review 2, 550–90; Arnold W Reitze, Jr., 'The Control of Methane and VOC Emissions from Oil and Gas Operations in the Western United States' (2018) 54 Idaho Law Review 213.

8 IEA (n4).

reducing barriers to recovering and using methane as a valuable energy source.[9] Similarly, the OGCI is a CEO-led organization comprising twelve of the largest international oil and gas companies worldwide, working towards achieving net zero GHG emissions following the Paris Agreement and representing about 30 percent of global oil and gas production. Through networks like the OGCI, frameworks such as the Methane Guiding Principles are created as a set of transnational soft rules guiding multi-stakeholder partnerships between industry, governmental, and non-industry organizations.[10] These platforms, therefore, serve as a useful medium for identifying and sharing knowledge about tried and tested approaches for lowering methane emissions transnationally. As pointed out by the International Energy Association (IEA),[11] there are well-established policy tools that have already been deployed in multiple jurisdictions to drive down emissions such as leak detection and repair requirements, technology standards, and bans on non-emergency 'routine' flaring and venting. Leak detection and repair typically refers to policies that require companies to establish programs for locating and repairing fugitive leaks, including the method and equipment required for leak detection, the frequency of detection campaigns, the identification of which facilities must undertake the inspections, and a requirement to fix leaks within a certain timeframe. Technology standards for emissions mitigation typically refer to policies that set specific guidelines for equipment, technologies, or procedures which also mandate that certain equipment be replaced by a lower-emitting alternative. Zero non-emergency flaring and venting typically refers to policies that either prohibit all non-emergency flaring and venting or that mandate specific processes and procedures which result in less flaring and venting. Within the methane model, this corresponds to the following abatement options: install plunger; install flares; blowdown capture; and vapor recovery units. It is expected that if all countries that have already committed

---

9 Global Methane Initiative (GMI), 'Partner Countries' <https://www.globalmethane.org/partners/index.aspx> accessed 12 May 2022. The GMI Partner Countries account for approximately 70 percent of global manmade methane emissions. These countries offer special expertise and interest in developing solutions for mitigating methane emissions and using methane as a cleaner energy source and producing byproducts that serve as feedstock for various industrial or agricultural applications. These partner countries are encouraged to develop and submit to the Secretariat action plans outlining considerable activities and priorities and provide a mechanism to advance cooperation.

10 Methane Guiding Principles Initiative, 'Methane Guiding Principles' <https://methaneguidingprinciples.org/methane-guiding-principles/> accessed 12 May 2021.

11 IEA, *Curtailing Methane Emissions from Fossil Fuel Operations: Pathways to a 75% cut by 2030* (IEA Publications, 2020) 1 – 56.

to reducing methane emissions were to adopt such policies, methane emissions from global fossil fuel operations could be cut by nearly 15%.[12]

The countries and institutions with limited information and technical know-how and insufficient monitoring and methane abatement technologies or limited access to buyers and consuming markets would typically have higher emissions intensity when compared to countries and companies with access to viable markets, existing supply or storage networks, and detection or abatement technologies. For example, some producing countries such as Norway in Europe and the United Arab Emirates in the Middle East are reported to have low emissions intensity per unit of production. In contrast, other countries such as Turkmenistan and Venezuela have the highest methane emissions intensity.[13] It is reported that if all producing countries matched Norway's emissions intensity, global methane emissions from oil and gas operations would fall by more than 90 percent.[14]

Given the issues highlighted above, this chapter will examine the increasing role of global partnerships amongst private multinational firms and public sector agencies for methane emissions control and mitigation measures. Over the years, the main barriers to effective mitigation and emissions control measures have included informational gaps between private industry operators, public 'regulatory' institutions, and other stakeholders. The chapter identifies various voluntary, national-level, and industry-led efforts, including pledges toward methane reduction targets. In conclusion, decision-makers need to adopt coherent policies and regulatory measures that enable private operators to fulfill their individual emissions control plans and pledges efficiently.

2 The Gas Production and Supply Networks

Natural gas comprises mostly methane; thus, to understand the challenges and potentials for effectively addressing fugitive methane emissions or leaks in the oil and gas context, it is essential to highlight the features of the value chain. The typical gas supply system comprises (i) upstream exploration and production, (ii) the midstream gas (processing, storage, and transportation), and (iii) downstream (sales and distribution) segments. The upstream producers hold a license or a lease granting proprietary rights to explore and produce gas, which is gathered through small-diameter pipelines (gathering lines) from upstream

12 ibid.
13 See IEA, 'Global Methane Tracker 2022' (n4).
14 ibid.

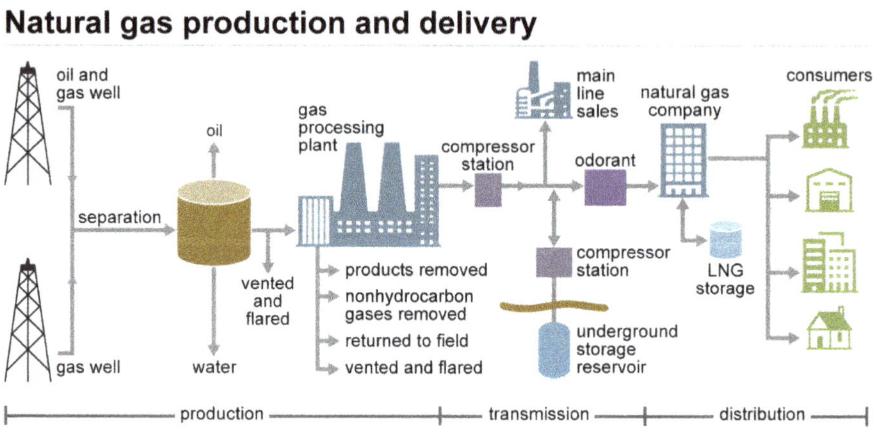

FIGURE 13.1 Natural gas production and supply chain
SOURCE: US EIA, 'NATURAL GAS EXPLAINED' (2022) HTTPS://WWW.EIA.GOV/ENERGYEXPLAINED/NATURAL-GAS/ ACCESSED 23 FEBRUARY 2023

oil and gas fields. The gas molecules then go through the processing facilities to remove water and impurities or by-products, such as natural gas liquids, including ethane, propane, butane, and pentane, some of which are used for heating and petrochemicals. Chemicals called odorants are added to natural gas to detect leaks from pipelines and related facilities. The dry gas is then compressed to flow into large transmission pipelines (midstream) and then transported to offtakers such as gas-fired power generators, storage, or other distribution centers (downstream).[15] Domestic operators engaged in international or cross-border supply arrangements may also take gas from wholesale markets or their upstream production fields and export via pipelines or the Liquified Natural Gas (LNG) value chain.[16]

Produced natural gas comprises mostly methane, thus there are economic, resource conservation, environmental, and energy supply benefits from capturing natural gas which may otherwise be flared, vented, or released into the atmosphere through leaks. An environmental co-benefit of preventing emissions or leaks would be avoiding air pollution and potential climatic impacts. Upstream emissions may arise during 'flaring,' i.e., the controlled combustion of natural gas for operational, safety, or economic reasons, or 'venting,' i.e.,

15 Oyewunmi (n8) pp. 126–196; Donna Peng and Rahmat Poudineh, *A Holistic Framework for the Study of Interdependence Between Electricity and Gas Sectors* (Oxford Institute for Energy Studies, EL 16, November 2015).

16 ibid.

the direct release of natural gas into the atmosphere for similar reasons. The combustion of methane during the process of flaring produces CO_2 emissions and some volatile organic compounds (VOCs). The incomplete combustion of flared gas and venting during upstream oil production operations, or leaks from compressors and processing facilities, could lead to the release of methane into the atmosphere. Such environmental externalities can be curbed if appropriate operational measures and regulatory approaches are implemented to ensure timely detection, regular maintenance and equipment upgrades, and reliable reporting information.

Most flaring and venting in upstream production operations occur in areas with conventional oil and associated gas formations as depicted in Figure 13.2 below.

In such fields, natural gas occurs together with oil, forming a cap over oil in underground reservoirs. Thus, producing oil in such a formation ordinarily presupposes the need to deal with the gas. In places where natural gas pipelines are not available to take away the associated gas produced from the oil wells, the natural gas may be reinjected into the oil-bearing formation, or it may be vented or flared. Reinjecting unmarketable natural gas can help maintain pressure in oil wells to improve oil production. Basins with non-associated gas fields, i.e., reservoirs with gas only, would ordinarily not need to flare or vent. Such fields are not developed unless a specific use or market and connecting

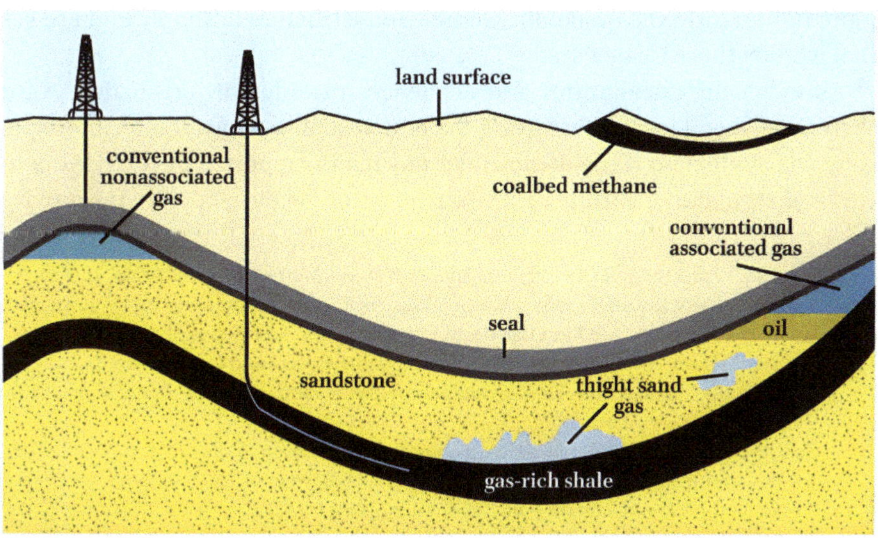

FIGURE 13.2 Geologic formations and natural gas sources
SOURCE: IBID.

pipeline and processing facilities are available. However, the oil producers on associated gas fields will *ab initio* have to factor in utilization and supply projects for gas occurring together with the oil they are trying to produce.

Note that capturing gas that would otherwise escape into the atmosphere is one thing while securing adequate pipeline or storage capacity and eventually selling it in a viable market is another.[17] Unlike crude oil, natural gas is difficult and expensive to store for a long-term duration. Thus, a typical operator producing gas in association with oil would be tempted to flare or use the gas for enhanced oil recovery processes or on-site power generation if there are no adequate gathering lines, processing facilities, and enough transmission pipeline capacity or creditworthy buyers such as an industry or power utility in the downstream energy markets (see Figure 13.1 above). When such supply bottlenecks arise, the challenge can be aggravated when production is in remote areas with limited or non-existing access to necessary supply and storage facilities. Thus, there would be a need to invest in such facilities or at least consider access to such delivery infrastructure when planning production operations. Consequently, the domestic policy and regulatory framework could play an instrumental role in addressing such bottlenecks either by facilitating such access or adopting other tested policy tools mentioned earlier.[18] It is noted that global gas flaring dropped by 5 percent from 150 billion cubic meters (BCM) in 2019 to 142 BCM in 2020 largely due to developments in the US which accounted for about 70 percent of that global decline. The main reported reasons for the decline include a slight fall in oil production and, more importantly, the availability of new infrastructure to supply and use gas that would otherwise be flared.[19]

Although the peculiarities and challenges in different jurisdictions vary, there is a general notion that using the best available mitigation technologies can be cost-efficient if the deployment of such is supported by the right policies and regulatory instruments.[20] Policies could be developed to incentivize

17 See Tade Oyewunmi, *Regulating Gas Supply to Power Markets: Transnational Approaches to Competitiveness and Security of Supply* (Wolters Kluwer International, 2018) 360 at 30 – 78 on the 'Principles and Rationales for Competitive and Secure Gas Markets.'

18 See IEA (n7) on 'Driving Down Methane Leaks from the Oil and Gas Industry.'

19 World Bank/ Global Gas Flaring Reduction Partnership (GGFR), *Global Gas Flaring Tracker Report* (April 2021).

20 See discussions about domestic regulatory approaches and issues in Leon Moller and J.I. Mohammed, 'The Problem of Gas Flaring – A Review of Current Legal and Policy Efforts in the UK and Nigeria' (Oil, Gas & Energy Law Intelligence (OGEL) Journal Special Issue on Law and Policy for Gas Flaring in a Low-carbon Economy, 2022) <www.ogel.org/article.asp?key=4022> accessed 12 April 2022; Magnus Abraham-Dukuma and others, 'Improving Regulatory Approaches for Abating Upstream Gas Emissions in a Low

utilization and abatement technologies or cover repair costs for parts of the transmission facilities that may be prone to leaks and fugitive emissions. Respective governments can adopt informational tools such as training and certificate programs for industry workers; implement measures for monitoring, reporting, and verifying emissions to develop the appropriate economic and technical solutions.[21]

2.1 *Net-Zero Issues in Production and Supply Operations*

The International Energy Agency's (IEA) *World Energy Outlook 2021* (WEO21) includes an outlook on the role of natural gas and other energy resources towards 2040 and beyond.[22] The WEO21 adopts a scenario approach to examine future energy trends. The four scenarios adopted by the report include (i) the Net Zero Emissions by 2050 Scenario (NZE), (ii) the Announced Pledges Scenario (APS), (iii) the Stated Policies Scenario (STEPS), and (iv) the Sustainable Development Scenario (SDS).[23] Under the SDS scenario, a surge in clean energy policies and investment is presumed and expected to put the global energy system on track to achieve sustainability and the Paris Agreement objectives, including universal energy access and air quality goals. Whereas the NZE2050 outlook extends the SDS assumptions, a growing number of countries and companies are assumed to meet their net-zero emissions targets by 2050.

Carbon Era: Case Study of Algeria, Egypt, and Nigeria' (Oil, Gas & Energy Law Intelligence (OGEL) Journal Special Issue on Law and Policy for Gas Flaring in a Low-carbon Economy, 2022) <www.ogel.org/article.asp?key=4021> accessed 12 April 2022.

21 US Department of Energy (DOE), *Natural Gas Flaring and Venting: State and Federal Regulatory Overview, Trends, and Impacts* (Office of Oil and Natural Gas Office of Fossil Energy, 2019) 1–64; World Bank/GGFR, *Global Flaring and Venting Regulations: 28 Case Studies from Around the World*, (GGFR, May 2022) <https://flaringventingregulations.worldbank.org/summary-report> accessed 12 March 2022; Tade Oyewunmi, 'The Regulatory Complexities of Gas Flaring and Venting in the US' (Oil, Gas & Energy Law Intelligence (OGEL) Journal Special Issue on Law and Policy for Gas Flaring in a Low-carbon Economy, 2022) <http://www.ogel.org/article.asp?key=4017> accessed 12 April 2022.

22 IEA, *World Energy Outlook 2021* (IEA Publications, 2021) <www.iea.org/reports/world-energy-outlook-2021> accessed 12 April 2022.

23 The NZE scenario sets out a narrow but achievable pathway for the global energy sector to achieve net zero CO_2 emissions by 2050. Under the APS, it is assumed that all climate commitments made by governments around the world, including Nationally Determined Contributions and longer-term net zero targets, will be met in full and on time. In the STEPS context, the current policy and regulatory framework as well as those that have been announced by governments around the world in the respective countries are deemed be in place during the period the outlook covers.

The WEO21 states that projected reductions in methane emissions are a key tool to limit near-term global warming. These assumptions underscore the importance of concerted efforts from governments, policymakers, and industry to ensure the emissions cuts are necessary to close nearly 15% of the gap required under the NZE scenario. It appears the most cost-effective abatement opportunities are in the energy sector, particularly in oil and gas operations. In both the APS context in which existing and announced policies are known and the ideal NZE context, it can be concluded here that industry operators engaged in gas production and midstream commercialization projects (such as pipelines and LNG) have a significant role in implementing the best practices and meeting relevant NetZero commitments.

According to the US Environmental Protection Agency's (EPA) Global Non-CO_2 Greenhouse Gas Emission Projections & Mitigation Potential: 2015–2050,[24] global methane emissions from natural gas and oil systems increased by 15% as production increased between 1990 and 2015. The report notes that numerous oil and gas initiatives have aimed to reduce emissions over the past decade. As a result, production has grown faster than emissions. The average rates of methane emissions per unit of oil and gas production have decreased because of past deliberate efforts to curtail emissions, especially in countries that have been consistent in seeking the most efficient set of policy instruments and approaches to cutting down emissions.[25] It is noted that as energy utilities and other major consumers sort to reduce their reliance on carbon-intensive coal and heavy oils and the price of gas became considerably cheaper, gas flaring in the US reportedly fell even though oil production increased over the past decade. For instance, in the US state of North Dakota, policies prescribing incremental gas capture targets were set to facilitate a reduction in flaring by producers. Thus, in 2021 about 92.5% of the state's natural gas production was captured, thereby exceeding the state's 91% target capture rate.[26] As noted by the EIA, meeting the capture targets required a buildout of natural gas gathering lines to transport natural gas from wells to processing plants and a buildout of the processing plants that remove impurities and heavier hydrocarbons from the natural gas, including pipelines and storage facilities

24 US EPA, *Non-CO_2 Emission Projections and Mitigation Summary Report: 2015–2050* (EPA-430-R-19-010, 2019) <www.epa.gov/global-mitigation-non-co2-greenhouse-gases/global-non-co2-greenhouse-gas-emission-projections> accessed 5 December 2021.

25 ibid. See also World Bank/GGFR (n22).

26 See US EIA, 'North Dakota's natural gas producers meet the state's natural gas capture target' (December 8, 2021) <https://www.eia.gov/todayinenergy/detail.php?id=50578> accessed 12 June 2022. See also Ehrman (n8).

were key contributing factors to the decline in the emissions intensity of gas production. Nevertheless, routine flaring remains a problem in areas like the Permian basin in Texas and New Mexico where oil production has outpaced the buildout of gathering, storage, and transportation infrastructure required to move the gas to market.[27] Thus, undeliverable associated gas is often vented or flared due to the infrastructural and market access limitations.

Flaring intensity (i.e., the volume of gas flared per barrel of oil produced) indicates the effectiveness of a country's gas utilization policies. The World Bank/GGFR report notes that the volume of gas flared globally decreased by 6 percent from 2012 to 2021, while oil production increased by 4 percent.[28] Flaring intensity and arguably potential emissions that could arise as a result markedly decreased in 10 countries: however, it remained stable or increased in some countries, including large upsurges in Venezuela, Mexico, Argentina, Algeria, Gabon, and Libya (see Graph 13.1 reflecting the flaring intensity in the countries reviewed under the World Bank/GGFR report).[29]

3 National Regulatory Measures and Policies Developments

In the domestic context, two broad categories of regulatory approaches are often used in dealing with the emissions challenge. First, the prescriptive approach focuses on specific and detailed laws and regulations that operators must comply with, including fines and other regulatory requirements. Second is the performance-based approach mixed with an incentive-based framework, which emphasizes collaborative agreement on realistic objectives and targets and having operators demonstrate that they have met stipulated performance standards and goals.[30]

27 US DOE (n24) 1–64; World Bank and GGFR (n24); GaffneyCline/Environmental Defense Fund (EDF), 'Tackling flaring: Learnings from leading Permian operators' (2020) <https://business.edf.org/insights/tackling-flaring-learnings-from-leading-permian-operators/> accessed 6 November 2020; Joe A. Schremmer, 'Regulating Natural Gas Venting and Flaring as Waste: A Review of the New Mexico Approach' (OGEL 2, 2022) <www.ogel.org/article.asp?key=4018> accessed 12 March 2022.

28 World Bank/GGFR (n22).

29 World Bank/GGFR (n22).

30 ibid. See also IEA (n7) on 'Driving Down Methane Leaks from the Oil and Gas Industry'; Tade Oyewunmi, 'The US Gas Supply Boom under Carbon-Constraints: Examining the Role of Regulatory Institutions' in Tade Oyewunmi and others (eds), *Decarbonisation and the Energy Industry: the role of law and regulation in low-carbon and transitional energy markets* (Hart Publishing, 2020).

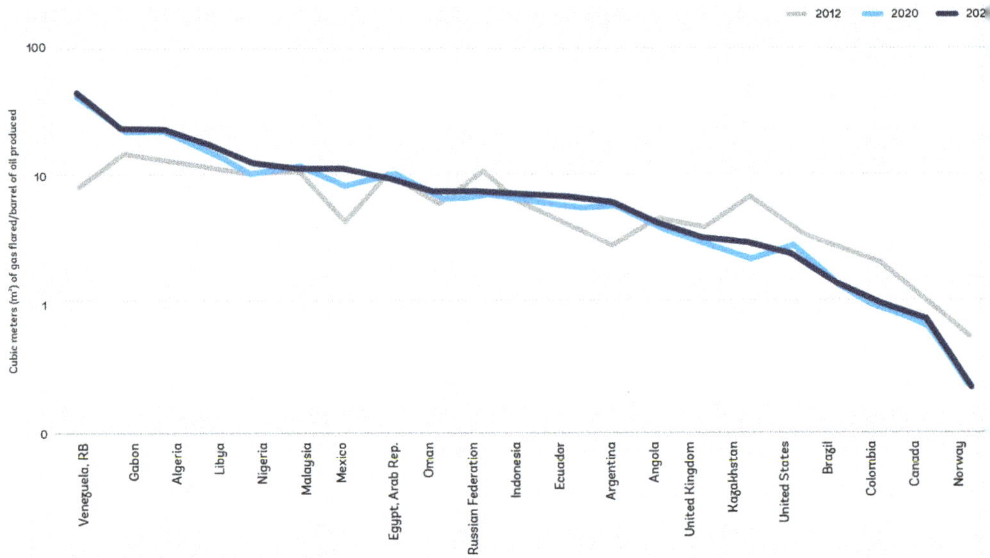

GRAPH 13.1 Flaring intensity in countries reviewed by world bank/GGFR-2012, 2020 and 2021

Most countries have a mixed or hybrid approach to addressing industry-related emissions and environmental regulation frameworks. There is also a growing trend toward economic instruments of regulation such as: (i) emission trading systems and offset credit schemes that allow producers to sell carbon credits by reducing flaring and venting; (ii) green investment funds; and (iii) financial grants for specific emission abatement investments.[31] However, the effectiveness of such economic-based instruments depends greatly on the reliability of monitoring, measuring, and verification processes and pricing of the decreased emissions. In some cases, the framework is designed to lower tax burdens for associated gas utilization and lower or even eliminate royalties for capturing, using, or marketing it.[32] An alternative is to increase the fiscal burden of flaring and venting by levying royalties on gas flared or vented without the regulator's prior approval and imposing carbon taxes on all GHG emissions or, better still, providing certified credits for emissions abatement.[33] The IEA's report on 'Driving Down Methane Leaks from the Oil and Gas Industry' provides a useful categorization of various regulatory approaches and instruments in Table 13.1.

31 World Bank/GGFR (n22).
32 ibid.
33 ibid. See also the US state on North Dakota's scenario in Ehrman (n8).

	Prescriptive					Performance-based				Economic			Information-based		
	Permitting requirements	Leak detection and repair	Restrictions on flaring or venting	Technology standards	Enforcement and related provisions	Strategic targets	Facility or company emissions standards	Process or equipment standards	Flaring or venting standards	Taxes, fees and charges	Emissions trading and credits	Other financial incentives	Emissions estimates	Measurement requirements	Reporting requirements
Brazil	●		●	●	●				●	●	●		●		●
Canada	○	●	○	●	○	●	○	●	○		○	●	●	●	●
China (People's Republic of)	●		●	●	●										
Iraq	●				●										
Iran	●														
Mexico	●		●	●	●	●	●	●	●		●		●	●	●
Nigeria	●		●	●	●	●			●	●		●	●	●	●
Norway	●		●		●					●			●	●	●
Russia	●								●	●					
Saudi Arabia	●			●	●										
United Arab Emirates	●				●										
United States	○	●	○	●	●	○	○	●	○	○		○	●		●

TABLE 13.1 IEA categorization of methane policies in selected producing countries by regulatory approach[a]

SOURCE: IEA, DRIVING DOWN METHANE LEAKS FROM THE OIL AND GAS INDUSTRY: A REGULATORY ROADMAP AND TOOLKIT (IEA PUBLICATIONS, 2021) P. 14. HTTPS://IEA.BLOB.CORE.WINDOWS.NET/ASSETS/465CB813-5BF0-46E5-A267-3BE0CCF332C4/DRIVING_DOWN_METHANE_LEAKS_FROM_THE_OIL_AND_GAS_INDUSTRY.PDF

a The full circle indicates a policy applied at the national level while an empty circle indicates a subnational policy (e.g. at state or provincial level in a federal system). The table reflects entries in the IEA Policies Database as of 18 January 2020

Some notable points that can be deduced from the above table and the review carried out by the IEA and the World Bank's GGFR report is that: (i) policy and regulation can help countries meet emissions goals; (ii) as shown in Figure 13.2 above, there are no one-size-fits-all solutions because the social and economic realities that determine what policies or regulatory instruments will be appropriate in country A would typically differ from country B; (iii) better information can enable more efficient regulatory requirements; and (iv) the countries that have not consistently reduced routine flaring and venting or emissions intensity as shown in Figure 13.1 above would most likely fall under the group of countries without a comprehensive emissions reduction plan, as well as legal, regulatory, and policy framework that is fit-for-purpose.[34] Hence, there is a need for international partnerships and collaborations at the private sector and national institutional levels to facilitate knowledge and information sharing about best practices and guidelines.

3.1 *Highlights from Selected Countries*

To further examine the dynamics of developing and implementing various methane emissions mitigation policy tools and regulatory measures to reduce activities that create emissions such as flaring, it is worth exploring the experiences in selected countries with a considerable level of production and supply operations such as Nigeria, US, Canada, Norway, etc. In Nigeria, laws and regulations aimed at banning gas flaring and venting had been in place since the 1980s, although largely ineffective because the approach of issuing fines made it cheaper for operators to flare and pay the fine rather than developing gas utilization and emission control measures which are more expensive.[35] Nevertheless, the introduction of gas market development reforms in the 2000s to create opportunities for viable domestic utilisation and commercialization schemes, including cross-border pipelines (such as the West African Gas Pipeline) and LNG exports, have considerably impacted flaring and venting reduction in Nigeria.[36] Although the country has remained in the top seven flaring countries, it has nonetheless steadily reduced its flaring by some 70 percent over the past 15 years and saw a reduction from flaring around 25BCM in

34 World Bank/GGFR (n22).

35 Yinka Omorogbe, 'Law and Investor Protection in the Nigerian Natural Gas Industry' (1996) 14 Journal of Energy & Natural Resources Law 179–192; Tade Oyewunmi, 'Examining the Legal and Regulatory Framework for Domestic Gas Utilization and Power Generation in Nigeria' (2014) 7 Journal of World Energy Law & Business 6, 538–557.

36 Oyewunmi (n16) 132–171.

2000 to about 7 BCM in 2020, while oil production has remained essentially flat at around 2 million barrels a day.[37]

In the US, the framework for regulating air pollution is primarily under the Clean Air Act. It includes the New Source Performance Standards for Oil and Gas Systems administered by the US EPA in conjunction with state-level institutions.[38] Most oil and gas operations take place on private land by private operators engaging in a market-based system. To some extent, they are subject to regulation in varying degrees at the federal, state, and local levels.[39] The US Bureau of Land Management manages the Federal government's onshore subsurface mineral estate and some aspects of the oil and gas development for Indian tribes from the Tribal mineral estate. Thus, the Bureau of Land Management imposes royalty payments on flared or vented associated gas that could have been utilized and on gas flared or vented without prior approval. If flaring and venting could have been avoided, the associated gas is considered avoidably lost or wasted and subject to royalties.[40] Notably, North Dakota, the second-biggest oil-producing state in the US and has significant levels of associated gas fields, established incremental targets over several years to increase the amount gas operators must capture. Operators may apply for a flaring exemption if connecting a well to a natural gas gathering line is not economically viable. Without an exemption, violators will pay taxes and royalties on flared gas. Gas is exempt from taxes and royalties for two years and 30 days (25 months) from the first day of production if at least 75 percent of it is used at the well site to generate electricity or collected to produce petrochemicals or fertilizers.[41] By 2020, about 92% of the state's natural gas production was captured, thereby reducing oil production's flaring and emissions intensity.[42]

In discussing regulatory measures relating to oil and gas production in the US alongside other countries, it is important to note that outside of the US, the national government of the respective country typically has absolute ownership and property in all land and oil and gas resources underground in most cases. Further, unlike in the US where operations mostly take place on

37 World Bank/GGFR (n22).

38 See Bradley N. Kershaw, 'Flames, Fixes, and the Road Forward: The Waste Prevention Rule and BLM Authority to Regulate Natural Gas Flaring and Venting' (Winter 2018) 29 Colorado Natural Resources, Energy & Environmental Law Review 1, 115–164; Reitze (n8).

39 See, Joel Eisen et al., 'Oil and Gas Production (Ch 4)' in Joel Eisen and others (eds), *Energy, Economics and the Environment, Cases and Materials* (5th edition, Foundation Press 2019) 147–270.

40 Reitze Jr. (n8); Oyewunmi (n8).

41 World Bank/GGFR (n22).

42 ibid.

private land by private independent companies subject to contractual provisions in a lease agreement and the relevant state laws; other countries invest in oil and gas production and supply through a National Oil Corporation (NOC) and enter into joint ventures or international exploration and production contracts with local or international private corporations.[43] Thus, the government in such jurisdictions often plays commercial, regulatory, and policy-making roles. Such situations could easily become counterproductive and reduce the effectiveness of emissions mitigation measures and regulatory tools such as sanctions imposed by law or under contracts, mandatory payments, progressive penalties, fines, fees, or other means of enforcement for noncompliance with regulations.[44] In Brazil, Colombia, Gabon, the United Kingdom, and certain jurisdictions in Canada and the United States, regulations indicate the situations in which penalties and sanctions should apply and the amounts due. In Mexico, operators must have sufficient financial resources to cover any environmental damages caused by flaring and venting.[45]

Another country with significant oil and gas operations and for instance a major supplier of gas to Europe is Norway. Norway became one of the first countries to introduce a carbon tax that applies to emissions from the combustion of all gas, oil, and diesel in petroleum operations on the continental shelf and CO_2 and natural gas releases.[46] As mentioned earlier, Norway has one of the lowest flaring and emission intensity globally compared to other major producing countries. In 2008, British Columbia implemented Canada's first broad-based carbon tax regulation. With a current value of Can$25.60 per tonne of CO_2e (approximately US$20 as of August 2021), the tax applies to the purchase and use of fossil fuels burned for transportation, home heating, and electricity. The regulation does not include legal requirements for the oil and gas industry. The federal government decided not to apply a carbon tax on flaring or methane emissions in oil and gas operations because doing so could affect the competitiveness of hundreds of small oil and gas producers.

Another example of tried and tested policy measures in a national-level context is in Canada, where Regulated facilities in Alberta, are required to implement specific measures under the Technology Innovation and Emissions Reduction System: reduce their emissions, redeem credits from facilities that

43 IEA, *The Oil and Gas Industry in Energy Transitions* (IEA Publications, 2020) <www.iea.org/reports/the-oil-and-gas-industry-in-energy-transitions> accessed 15 January 2022; Oyewunmi (n17) 14 – 28.

44 World Bank/GGFR (n22); See also IEA (n7).

45 ibid.

46 ibid.

have exceeded their reduction targets, purchase offsets from unregulated entities, or pay into a compliance fund. In British Columbia, the CleanBC Industry Fund supports projects using commercially proven technologies that reduce GHG emissions from large industrial operations that emit more than 10,000 tonnes of CO_2e per year. In Saskatchewan, Canada, the Oil and Gas Processing Investment Incentive offers transferable royalty or freehold production tax credits at 15 percent of eligible program costs to value-added projects in the oil and gas sector, such as gas-gathering transportation infrastructure and methane gathering projects.

According to the World Bank's GGFR report, about twenty-three jurisdictions have set measurement, and reporting standards for the oil and gas sector, including data on flaring and venting that, can be used in proffering solutions and corrective steps. However, despite the increasing recognition of the need to eliminate flaring and venting, only 21 jurisdictions have established outright bans on routine flaring or venting. Just 14 of the 28 jurisdictions reviewed impose monetary fines or use market-based solutions, signaling reluctance to follow through with corrective action.[47] To the extent that these countries have NOCs engaging in international joint ventures, including IOCs and domestic local operators involved in various aspects of the oil and gas production and supply industry in a transnational sense, it can be observed that best practices and approaches for emissions control or abatement are often adopted through the relevant multinational partnerships and intergovernmental initiatives, including provisions in model licensing and contractual frameworks.

As national-level institutions work with local and international companies operating in their jurisdictions to develop tried and tested measures highlighted earlier, such measures become adopted in other developing jurisdictions through the activities of transnational initiatives such as the OGCI mentioned earlier. International operators, NOCs, and their governmental partners in the OGCI recently announced a 2025 methane intensity target reflecting the total methane emissions from oil and gas production as a percentage of the associated volume of gas marketed which could serve as a performance standard to comparatively determine methane emission levels from different actors and segments of the petroleum industry. The initiative outlines a series of methane reduction measures, including a commitment to Zero Routine Flaring by 2030, which may be incorporated into respective national regulatory or policy instruments and frameworks. The overall objective is to be consistent with the Paris goals and approach near-zero methane emissions

47 ibid.

(0.25–0.2%) by 2025 and applies to OGCI members such as BP, Chevron, CNPC, Eni, Equinor, ExxonMobil, Occidental, Petrobras, Repsol, Saudi Aramco, Shell, and Total.

Multinational financial institutions also have a considerable role in facilitating the adoption of best practices into local and regional policy frameworks. For instance, the World Bank's GGFR works with governments in oil-producing countries to develop policies and measures to end routine flaring of associated gas by 2030, such as the Zero Routine Flaring by 2030 initiative mentioned earlier. The main findings from the GGFR review show that:

(a) Global reduction of gas flaring and venting has been much slower than what is possible;
(b) Successful reduction requires strong financial and non-financial incentives, combined with robust monitoring and enforcement capacity; and
(c) If flared and vented gas could be made available in nearby communities, it could replace more-polluting fuels (e.g., biomass and charcoal), thus cutting emissions, improving air quality, and potentially expanding access to energy among those who need it most.
(d) Flaring and venting regulations must consider the capabilities and resources available to the authorities responsible for enforcing them.
(e) About half of the 21 countries analyzed have reduced flaring volumes and flaring intensity since 2012.
(f) Developing an effective regulatory framework requires monitoring, measuring, and enforcement capabilities that may need to be developed by relevant institutions over time.
(g) Penalties should be established at a sufficiently high level to make the alternative of investing in flaring and venting reduction more attractive than paying the fine.[48]

3.2 *National Experiences on Gas Flaring and Methane Reduction Policies*

Gas flaring produces CO_2, carbon monoxide, sulfur dioxide, nitrogen oxides, and other VOCs, depending on the chemical composition of the natural gas in the reservoir and how well the natural gas is burnt in the flare. The incomplete combustion of gas during flaring could lead to the release of some methane

48 ibid.

into the air. Consequently, some oil-producing states in the US, such as North Dakota, New Mexico, etc., and producing countries outside of the US have initiated policies to ban venting while implementing a framework of regulations to curtail routine flaring, including specifying requirements for operators to capture a percentage of gas that would otherwise be flared.[49] Some of the main oil-producing countries now regulate methane emissions from gas flaring and venting as part of their contributions to climate change mitigation efforts. To be reasonably effective, such contributions will need to be carefully determined in light of the respective countries' overarching economic and national policy objectives. Countries such as Algeria, Angola, Gabon, Nigeria, and República Bolivariana de Venezuela have set quantified targets.[50] In addition, Ecuador, Egypt, Mexico, and Oman are reported to only mention gas flaring and venting in their respective NDCs but without setting specific emissions reduction targets. The GGFR report points out that apart from countries such as Nigeria, Norway, some states in the US, and the UK, most of the other relevant countries have not specifically outlined their plans to implement the goal of the Zero Routine Flaring by 2030 initiative. Likewise, only a few have adopted legislation to make new greenfield projects free of routine flaring and venting. Such policies will surely have considerable impact in countries that have traditionally relied on revenues and benefits of oil and gas production for meeting other socio-economic objectives, including employment and social services[51]

Malaysia's Petronas has gradually introduced new emissions control measures requiring all new oil and gas developments to incorporate plans for zero flaring and venting of associated gas.[52] Another major gas producer and supplier to the international market is Algeria, which has adopted an unconditional target of less than 1 percent of total associated gas to be flared by 2030 as part of its NDC. Nigeria has set zero flaring by 2030 as a conditional contribution in its first NDC, updated in 2021. The responsible regulator in the United Kingdom issued guidance in June 2021 requiring all new oil and gas

49 Tade Oyewunmi, 'Editorial OGEL Special Issue on "Law and Policy for Gas Flaring in a Low-carbon Economy' (OGEL 2, 2022) <www.ogel.org/article.asp?key=4016> accessed 12 May 2022.

50 World Bank/GGFR (n22).

51 ibid. The Zero Routine Flaring (ZFR) by 2030 initiative was launched in 2015 via the World Bank and GGFR platform in which the relevant governments and oil companies commit to end routine flaring no later than 2030 see https://www.worldbank.org/en/programs/zero-routine-flaring-by-2030/about#Ben (accessed 12 May 2022).

52 World Bank/GGFR (n22).

developments to incorporate zero routine flaring and venting and gave the industry until 2030 to comply.[53]

Developing the technologies and identifying leaks and fugitive emissions along the gas production and supply networks has received some attention in most jurisdictions. In 2016, Canada, Mexico, and the United States jointly called for a 40–45 percent decrease in methane emissions from their respective oil and gas sectors by 2025. Nigeria's NDC foresees a 60 percent reduction in fugitive methane emissions by 2031 as a conditional contribution. Given the complexities of measures and steps needed to achieve these targets and implement necessary best practices and technological options, there is an obvious need for collaboration and partnerships between private (international and national) industry operators and public sector (regulatory and institutional) stakeholders.

Experiences in the US show that retrofitting parts of the natural gas production and supply network, such as valves and gas-driven pneumatic controllers and pumps, or replacing them with lower-emitting versions can help reduce emissions (EPA, 2019; Oyewunmi, 2021). Another example is Norway, where the Norwegian Oil and Gas Association and the oil and gas companies operating in Norway played a key role in developing and deploying new quantification methodologies and guidelines for reporting methane and other VOCs. The guidelines are made public and used by operating companies to submit environmental data to the authorities (UNECE/GMI, 2019). The Norwegian Environmental Agency initiated a two-year study between 2014 and 2016 to survey methane emission sources at offshore installations. The objective was to quantify emissions, improve quantification, undertake the best assessment techniques, and identify suitable mitigation measures.

Industry operators may be required by law and regulation or act voluntarily to adopt the best emissions reduction or control systems. Technologies for monitoring and leak detection and repair are essential in mitigation efforts. Not all operators and agencies in all the producing countries would have the financial resources and technical expertise to deploy these advanced systems, hence, the need for information sharing and collaborations and a conducive regulatory and policy environment. Recently, 14 European gas infrastructure operators and associations led a project to develop new technologies to curb methane emissions. Such initiatives are against the backdrop of recent EU-level discussions about the best approaches to curb methane emissions from a climate change mitigation perspective. Notwithstanding these initiatives and

53 ibid.

potential mitigation measures, there are still knowledge and informational gaps, cost-related and infrastructural inadequacies that create barriers to effective control of methane emissions globally.

4 Multinational Initiatives and Best Practice Guidelines and Principles

Gas production and supply in producing countries have become more interconnected with international energy markets and consumers over the past two decades. As reflected in IEA's report in Figure 13.2 above and the recent findings from the World Bank/GGFR survey, the regulatory framework and policies for controlling emissions depend largely on the national institutions in the respective national contexts. Consequently, multinational partnerships and knowledge sharing between international and national (public-private sector) stakeholders will be key to understanding and developing best practices and cost-effective solutions. The Global Methane Pledge is a significant example of interested countries coming together and committing to take voluntary actions to support a collective effort to reduce global methane emissions by at least 30 percent from 2020 levels by 2030 (see Chapter 2). National institutions such as the US EPA, Norway's Petroleum Directorate, and the UK's Oil and Gas Authority signed up for the Global Methane Pledge in 2021.[54]

The consolidation of the Global Methane Pledge potentially creates a collaborative platform through which best practices, regulatory approaches, data, and technical expertise can be shared. For instance, the US EPA's non-CO_2 greenhouse gas technical report series provides projected emissions, and technical and economic mitigation estimates of non-CO_2 GHGs (especially methane) from anthropogenic sources for 195 countries and all 50 states in the U.S. Such non-CO_2 GHG datasets provide information that can be used to understand national and sub-national contributions of GHG emissions and mitigation opportunities.[55] Other transnational initiatives typically aim at: (i)

54 European Commission (E.C.), 'Press Release on Launch by United States, the European Union, and Partners of the Global Methane Pledge to Keep 1.5C Within Reach' (2 November 2021) <https://ec.europa.eu/commission/presscorner/detail/en/statement_21_5766> accessed 5 December 2021.

55 Harro van Asselt and Veera Pekkarinen, 'The Global Methane Pledge: a timely new step in global climate governance' (CCEEL Blog, 6 October, 2021) <https://sites.uef.fi/cceel/the-global-methane-pledge-a-timely-new-step-in-global-climate-governance/> accessed 23 February 2023.

facilitating best practices, (ii) gathering reliable data, and (iii) implementing cost-effective strategies to prevent emissions of methane from the oil and gas patch. For instance, GMI is a platform through which relevant international organizations and initiatives collaborate to create synergies to mitigate methane globally. Notably, GMI provides technical support to deploy methane-to-energy projects worldwide, enabling partner countries such as the US, the UK, Saudi Arabia, Nigeria, and Russia to launch methane recovery and use projects. GMI focuses on three key sectors: Oil and Gas, Biogas, and Coal Mines, and works with international organizations such as the United Nations Economic Commission for Europe (UNECE) and the Climate and Clean Air Coalition (CCAC) to research and develop ideas about best practices for reducing global methane emissions.[56]

The oil and gas industry operates based on rules and regulations influencing the conduct of local and international private corporations, government-owned corporations, agencies, and service providers along the production, processing, and supply segments. As a result, operators and governmental institutions are potentially in the best position to facilitate transnational collaborations and partnerships to leverage their diverse expertise and knowledge to establish best practices and guidelines and effectively control methane emissions.

The GMI's *Best Practice Guidance for Effective Methane Management in the Oil and Gas Sector* reviews and recommends best practice measures for methane management within the oil and gas sector. The guidance is intended to be a resource for facility owners, operators, and government policymakers engaged in the international oil and gas industry. It seeks to provide information about cost-effective measures for detecting and mitigating methane emissions along the full oil and gas value chain at the company-and national levels. Guidance for developing and implementing practices for monitoring, reporting, and verifying (MRV) methane emissions is also provided.[57] The major emission sources and the applicable operational or technical mitigation measures are often well-known by most industry operators and institutions with relevant experience and information.

Some of the common methane emission areas and tested mitigation options along with the oil and gas supply networks include: (a) component and

56 UNECE/GMI, 'Regulations and public-private Partnership to improve knowledge about methane emissions and mitigation options – Norway' (Case Study Report, 2019) <www.unece.org/fileadmin/DAM/energy/images/MMNG/Case_Study_V_-_Norway.pdf> accessed 12 April 2022.

57 ibid.

equipment leaks: regular leak detection and repairs are typically a central part of methane mitigation; (b) compressors: various mitigation approaches can be considered including (i) retrofitting to dry seal compressor, (ii) re-routing vent emissions to a low-pressure gas inlet, and (iii) regular replacement of rod packing; (c) unstabilized liquid storage tanks: vapor recovery units can be installed to collect methane and VOC emissions, compress them and transport them for productive use (local power production, export to existing processing facilities, etc.); (d) incomplete combustion from gas flaring, which is best addressed by using the gas and minimizing flaring.[58] The technical know-how, resources, and costs of implementing these mitigation options will vary by country and context. However, it is generally reported that most technological solutions and measures can be implemented cost-efficiently and by adapting or changing operational practices and knowledge sharing. Best practices for detection and mitigation would need to be implemented from the field and corporate level to the level of national policies and regulatory framework.

A major challenge for mitigation efforts in the oil and gas supply systems is that emissions originate from sources spread out across a vast area, and monitoring each source would be prohibitively expensive. Thus, developing policies and economic regulation instruments that support cost-efficient MRV measures and implementing identified mitigation solutions may be helpful. The key conclusions and principles noted from the UNECE/GMI 2019 report include the following:

a) There is considerable uncertainty about the level of methane emissions from oil and gas operations. Private and public sector institutions need increased efforts to reduce the knowledge gap.
b) Quantifying methane emissions is challenging, but technologies to assist in methane detection and quantification are readily available and should be adopted by companies and authorities in their MRV activities.
c) Some oil and gas companies are making progress in quantifying and mitigating emissions. Increased recognition of proper methane management as being important for resource efficiency and environmental protection has led several large companies to undertake an action, unilaterally and through industry associations and public-private partnerships, to address the issue.
d) Host governments and institutions can support effective and cost-efficient policies to address methane emissions from the oil and gas

58 ibid.

sector through regulatory standards, economic instruments, and agreements between the industry and national authorities.

In summary, it is worth noting that cost-efficiency is essential in adopting mitigation measures and technologies. Thus, measures with low abatement costs should be implemented before those with higher ones. In addition, clarity and transparency in rules and procedures for standards, economic instruments, and negotiations and enforcement mechanisms are essential.

The Oil and Gas Methane Partnership (OGMP) methodology was created by the CCAC in 2014 as a voluntary initiative to help companies in a transnational context to reduce methane emissions in the oil and gas sector.[59] Through participation in the OGMP associated reporting, companies were provided with a credible mechanism to address their methane emissions systematically and responsibly and to demonstrate this systematic approach and its results to stakeholders. As part of their efforts to reduce methane emissions from upstream oil and gas operations, member companies developed Technical Guidance Documents on each of the nine core emission sources covered by the OGMP.[60] The guidance documents present suggested methodologies for quantifying methane emissions from each source and describe established mitigation options that Partners should reference when determining if the source is "mitigated." For instance, Technical Guidance Document Number 2 on Fugitive Component and Equipment Leaks deals with fugitive emissions that arise from unintentional leaks from oil and gas operations.[61]

In 2017, a set of Methane Guiding Principles were developed collaboratively by a coalition of industry, international institutions, non-governmental organizations, and academics.[62] The five Methane Guiding Principles focus on priority areas for action along the natural gas supply chain, from production to the final consumer. It includes steps towards continuous emissions reduction and supporting sound regulation and policy initiatives. The signatories to the guiding principles intend for them to be applied concurrently. In the context of these principles, methane emissions refer to venting, fugitive (unintended)

59 UNEP and Oil and Gas Methane Partnership (OGMP), '2.0 Framework' (CCAC, 2020) <https://www.ccacoalition.org/en/resources/oil-and-gas-methane-partnership-ogmp-20-framework> accessed 12 May 2022.

60 CCAC, *Oil and Gas Methane Partnership Technical Guidance Documents*, (2020) <https://www.ccacoalition.org/en/content/oil-and-gas-methane-partnership-technical-guidance-documents> accessed 5 December 2021.

61 ibid.

62 Methane Guiding Principles Initiative (n11).

emissions, and incomplete combustion, including during flaring. The principles focus on areas of action to reduce methane emissions, including recommended guidelines and best practices for production operations on: (i) engineering design and construction; (ii) flaring; (iii) energy use; (iv) equipment leaks; (v) venting; (vi) pneumatic devices; (vii) operational repairs; (viii) continual improvement; (ix) identification, detection, measurement, and quantification; and (x) transmission, storage, LNG terminals, and distribution issues.

The methods for reducing emissions from venting have a lot in common with best practices for reducing emissions from flaring and engineering design. To avoid or minimize venting, for instance, there are recommended best practices in key production aspects relating to hydrocarbon liquid storage tanks, compressor seals and starter motors, glycol dehydrators, removing liquids from gas wells, well-completion operations, and oil well casinghead operations. If methane needs to be released, it is recommended to use vapor recovery or flares rather than venting.

On the other hand, the best practice guidelines for reducing gas flaring are categorized into three. Ideally, waste gas production is prevented. If this is not feasible, waste gas recovery for sale can generate revenue. Otherwise, storing (reinjecting) gases in oil and gas reservoirs is also an alternative. If the waste gas cannot be recovered to be sold as natural gas or natural gas liquid product or stored, it could be used to generate electricity. If flaring cannot feasibly be prevented, then improving the efficiency of flares would be necessary to reduce methane emissions. The design or production systems are also essential in curbing methane emissions by using vapor-recovery units to recover waste gases and trucking the recovered gas to processing facilities.

5 Conclusion

Several oil and gas-producing countries and operators have increasingly engaged in transnational platforms and initiatives to share best practices and know-how on tried and tested methane emissions reduction measures. Major buyers and consumers in the international oil and gas markets, for instance, the EU, have also begun to pay close attention to the emissions intensity of products and supply arrangements. As these trends continue with the aim of curbing emissions of methane, this chapter highlights the importance of developing effective national-level measures and institutional capabilities, while fostering collaborations and knowledge sharing through various transnational platforms.

From the national-level considerations above, it appears economically and technically feasible to eliminate many oil and gas-related methane emissions in most countries. Likewise, in most cases and with the support of the right policy and regulatory instruments, the know-how and resources for achieving deeper reductions are readily available or can be acquired if they are not available in a particular jurisdiction. Going forward, it is also important to remove barriers to necessary infrastructure for capturing, processing, storing, and supplying captured gas/methane. Over the past decade, several oil and gas-producing countries have reduced flaring volumes and intensity after adopting a wide range of legislative and regulatory approaches, some of which creates the right incentives to capture methane rather than allow it to waste from an energy resource and economic standpoint while also polluting the air. Most countries have designated institutions responsible for regulating environmental issues regarding the oil and gas sector. However, varying degrees of know-how, capacities, and resources are needed to be fully effective. The jurisdictions that have efficiently reduced flaring and emissions intensity in oil and gas operations relative to production have a combination of regulatory approaches, including prescriptive and performance-based regulatory systems, using strong economic incentives and disincentives, and giving their regulators the powers to monitor and enforce them. Multinational public-private sector collaboration platforms such as the GMI, CCAC, the World Bank's GGFR, and the OGCI have a key role to play in developing and facilitating best practice measures to ensure operators meet their NetZero emission goals and targets. Such partnerships and approaches can help fill the technical capacity and informational gaps about sources, best practices, and provide pathways through which tried and tested methane emissions abatement measures can be implemented transnationally.

Bibliography

Abraham-Dukuma M and others, 'Improving Regulatory Approaches for Abating Upstream Gas Emissions in a Low Carbon Era: Case Study of Algeria, Egypt, and Nigeria' (Oil, Gas & Energy Law Intelligence (OGEL) Journal Special Issue on Law and Policy for Gas Flaring in a Low-carbon Economy, 2022) <http://www.ogel.org/article.asp?key=4021> accessed 12 April 2022.

CCAC, *Oil and Gas Methane Partnership Technical Guidance Documents*, (2020) <https://www.ccacoalition.org/en/content/oil-and-gas-methane-partnership-technical-guidance-documents> accessed 5 December 2021.

Climate and Clean Air Coalition (CCAC), 'Methane' <www.ccacoalition.org/en/slcps/methane> accessed 12 May 2021.

Ehrman MU, 'Lights Out in the Bakken: a Review and Analysis of Flaring Regulation and its Potential Effect on North Dakota Shale Oil Production' (2014) 117 West Virginia Law Review 2, 550.

Eisen J and others, 'Oil and Gas Production (Ch 4)' in Joel Eisen and others (eds), *Energy, Economics and the Environment, Cases and Materials* (5th edition, Foundation Press 2019) 147–270.

European Commission (E.C.), 'Press Release on Launch by United States, the European Union, and Partners of the Global Methane Pledge to Keep 1.5C Within Reach' (2 November 2021) <https://ec.europa.eu/commission/presscorner/detail/en/statement_21_5766> accessed 5 December 2021.

GaffneyCline/Environmental Defense Fund (EDF), 'Tackling flaring: Learnings from leading Permian operators' (2020) <https://business.edf.org/insights/tackling-flaring-learnings-from-leading-permian-operators/> accessed 6 November 2020.

Global Methane Initiative (GMI), 'Partner Countries' <https://www.globalmethane.org/partners/index.aspx> accessed 12 May 2022.

IEA, *Curtailing Methane Emissions from Fossil Fuel Operations: Pathways to a 75% cut by 2030* (IEA Publications, 2020) 1–56.

IEA, *Driving Down Methane Leaks from the Oil and Gas Industry: a Regulatory Roadmap and Toolkit* (IEA Publications, 2021) <www.iea.org/reports/driving-down-methane-leaks-from-the-oil-and-gas-industry> accessed 12 May 2022.

IEA, *Global Methane Tracker 2022* (IEA Publications, 2022) <https://www.iea.org/reports/global-methane-tracker-2022> accessed 23 February 2023.

IEA, *The Oil and Gas Industry in Energy Transitions*, (IEA Publications, 2020) <www.iea.org/reports/the-oil-and-gas-industry-in-energy-transitions> accessed 15 January 2022.

IEA, *World Energy Outlook 2021* (IEA Publications, 2021) <http://www.iea.org/reports/world-energy-outlook-2021> accessed 12 April 2022.

International Energy Agency (IEA), *Global Methane Tracker 2020*, (IEA Publications, 2020) <www.iea.org/reports/methane-tracker-2020> accessed 12 May 2022.

Kershaw BN, 'Flames, Fixes, and the Road Forward: the Waste Prevention Rule and BLM Authority to Regulate Natural Gas Flaring and Venting' (Winter 2018) 29 Colorado Natural Resources, Energy & Environmental Law Review 1, 115.

Methane Guiding Principles Initiative, 'Methane Guiding Principles' <https://methaneguidingprinciples.org/methane-guiding-principles/> accessed 12 May 2021.

Moller L and Mohammed JI, 'The Problem of Gas Flaring – A Review of Current Legal and Policy Efforts in the UK and Nigeria' (Oil, Gas & Energy Law Intelligence (OGEL) Journal Special Issue on Law and Policy for Gas Flaring in a Low-carbon Economy, 2022) <www.ogel.org/article.asp?key=4022> accessed 12 April 2022.

Omorogbe Y, 'Law and Investor Protection in the Nigerian Natural Gas Industry' (1996) 14 Journal of Energy & Natural Resources Law 179.

Oyewunmi T, 'Editorial OGEL Special Issue on "Law and Policy for Gas Flaring in a Low-carbon Economy' (OGEL 2, 2022) <http://www.ogel.org/article.asp?key=4016> accessed 12 May 2022.

Oyewunmi T, 'Examining the Legal and Regulatory Framework for Domestic Gas Utilization and Power Generation in Nigeria' (2014) 7 Journal of World Energy Law & Business 6, 538.

Oyewunmi T, 'Natural Gas in a Carbon-Constrained World: Examining the Role of Institutions in Curbing Methane and Other Fugitive Emissions' (2021) 9 LSU Journal of Energy Law & Resources 1.

Oyewunmi T, 'The Regulatory Complexities of Gas Flaring and Venting in the US' (Oil, Gas & Energy Law Intelligence (OGEL) Journal Special Issue on Law and Policy for Gas Flaring in a Low-carbon Economy, 2022) <http://www.ogel.org/article.asp?key =4017> accessed 12 April 2022.

Oyewunmi T, 'The US Gas Supply Boom under Carbon-Constraints: Examining the Role of Regulatory Institutions' in Tade Oyewunmi and others (eds), *Decarbonisation and the Energy Industry: the Role of Law and Regulation in Low-Carbon and Transitional Energy Markets* (Hart Publishing, 2020).

Oyewunmi T, *Regulating Gas Supply to Power Markets: Transnational Approaches to Competitiveness and Security of Supply* (Wolters Kluwer International, 2018).

Peng D and Poudineh R, *A Holistic Framework for the Study of Interdependence Between Electricity and Gas Sectors* (Oxford Institute for Energy Studies, EL 16, November 2015).

Reitze AW, 'The Control of Methane and VOC Emissions from Oil and Gas Operations in the Western United States' (2018) 54 Idaho Law Review 213.

Schremmer JA, 'Regulating Natural Gas Venting and Flaring as Waste: a Review of the New Mexico Approach' (OGEL 2, 2022) <http://www.ogel.org/article.asp?key=4018> accessed 12 March 2022.

UNECE/GMI, 'Regulations and public-private Partnership to improve knowledge about methane emissions and mitigation options – Norway' (Case Study Report, 2019) <www.unece.org/fileadmin/DAM/energy/images/MMNG/Case_Study_V _-_Norway.pdf> (accessed 12 April 2022.

UNEP and Oil and Gas Methane Partnership (OGMP), '2.0 Framework' (CCAC, 2020) <https://www.ccacoalition.org/en/resources/oil-and-gas-methane-partners hip-ogmp-20-framework> accessed 12 May 2022.

United Nations Environment Programme (UNEP)/CCAC, *Global Assessment: Urgent steps must be taken to reduce methane emissions this decade* (6 May 2021).

US Department of Energy (DOE), *Natural Gas Flaring and Venting: State and Federal Regulatory Overview, Trends, and Impacts* (Office of Oil and Natural Gas Office of Fossil Energy, 2019).

US EIA, 'Natural Gas Explained' (2022) <https://www.eia.gov/energyexplained/natural-gas/> accessed 23 February 2023.

US EIA, 'North Dakota's natural gas producers meet the state's natural gas capture target' (December 8, 2021) <https://www.eia.gov/todayinenergy/detail.php?id=50578> accessed 12 June 2022.

US Energy Information Administration (EIA), *International Energy Outlook 2021* (October 6, 2021) <https://www.eia.gov/outlooks/ieo/pdf/IEO2021_ReleasePresentation.pdf> accessed 12 May 2022.

US Environmental Protection Agency (EPA), 'Overview of Greenhouse Gases' (2022) <https://www.epa.gov/ghgemissions/overview-greenhouse-gases> accessed 23 February 2023.

US EPA, *Non-CO_2 Emission Projections and Mitigation Summary Report: 2015–2050* (EPA-430-R-19-010, 2019) <www.epa.gov/global-mitigation-non-co2-greenhouse-gases/global-non-co2-greenhouse-gas-emission-projections> accessed 5 December 2021.

van Asselt H and Pekkarinen V, 'The Global Methane Pledge: a timely new step in global climate governance' (CCEEL Blog, (6 October, 2021) <https://sites.uef.fi/cceel/the-global-methane-pledge-a-timely-new-step-in-global-climate-governance/> accessed 23 February 2023.

World Bank/Global Gas Flaring Reduction Partnership (GGFR), *Global Gas Flaring Tracker Report* (April 2021).

World Bank/GGFR, *Global Flaring and Venting Regulations: 28 Case Studies from Around the World*, (GGFR, May 2022) <https://flaringventingregulations.worldbank.org/summary-report> accessed 12 March 2022.

Conclusion

The Past, Present and Future of SLCP Law and Governance

Yulia Yamineva, Kati Kulovesi and Eugenia Recio

Global climate mitigation policy has primarily focused on reducing CO_2 emissions, given their significant contribution to long-term global warming. However, non-CO_2 greenhouse gases and aerosols also contribute to climate warming, albeit over shorter timeframes. In the past decade, there has been a growing recognition of the significant role played by substances grouped under the collective term of short-lived climate pollutants (SLCPs) in effectively mitigating near-term climate change. This term encompasses methane, black carbon, hydrofluorocarbons (HFCs), and tropospheric ozone.

Scientists and policy-makers have deliberated the potential of reducing emissions of methane, black carbon, and hydrofluorocarbons for slowing down near-term climate change and thereby contributing to achieving the more ambitious goal under the Paris Agreement to limit global warming to 1.5°C above pre-industrial levels. Multiple co-benefits of mitigating emissions of black carbon and methane for air quality, public health and the environment have also been seen as attractive from a public policy perspective. Several influential scientific assessments have been published that outline the sources, impacts, and specific policy measures to mitigate emissions of SLCPs. In response to these findings, numerous regulatory and governance efforts have been developed and implemented within intergovernmental and transnational arenas.

The thirteen chapters of the book have provided in-depth discussions on the global law and governance pertaining to the mitigation of SLCP emissions, employing a wide range of topics and approaches. This volume covers all significant instruments and institutions, offering the most comprehensive assessment to date of the global legal and governance landscape concerning SLCPs. This concluding chapter synthesises the findings of the book in debating the three questions posed in the introduction, namely: What is the existing state of global law and governance concerning SLCP mitigation? What accomplishments have been made and what gaps remain? What lies ahead for the SLCP policy agenda? The chapter also offers reflections on potential directions for future research on the topic.

1 What Is the Existing State of Global Law and Governance Concerning SLCP Mitigation?

Several conclusions can be drawn from the various contributions to the volume. Firstly, the chapters emphasize the paramount importance of *the science-policy interface* in driving the development and successful implementation of effective policy responses. Secondly, the chapters explicitly highlight two distinct characteristics of the global legal and governance landscape concerning the mitigation of SLCP emissions. The first characteristic is its *polycentric and fragmented nature*, wherein multiple actors, instruments and institutions play a role. The second characteristic is the growing influence of *transnational law and institutions* in shaping global efforts. These features are further explored and analyzed in the subsequent sub-sections.

2 Science–Policy Interface

All too often, literature on climate and environmental law and governance tends to focus solely on legal norms, norm-making processes, and governing institutions, without establishing a connection to the underlying science of the issue at hand and how that science translates into policy concepts and actions. This book takes a distinctly different approach by integrating a detailed discussion of the underlying knowledge and the interactions between science and policy before delving into specific regulations and governance responses. In particular, when read together, Chapters 1, 'Scientific Overview on SLCPs: Characteristics, Impacts, and Uncertainties,' and 2, 'A Conceptual History of SLCPs,' shed light on the complexity of the science-policy relationship in the rise, evolution, and current status of SLCPs on the global environmental policy agenda.

The inclusion of these chapters is rooted in the recognition that scientific knowledge does not exist in isolation, but rather emerges within the context of broader social and political structures. Drawing upon the language of science and technology studies, knowledge and social order are produced together, and hence 'knowledge and its material embodiments are at once products of social work and constitutive of forms of social life'.[1] In other words, the dynamics between science and policy is often more complex than a one-directional

1 Sheila Jasanoff (ed), *States of Knowledge: The Co-Production of Science and the Social Order* (Routledge 2004) 2.

effect, and there are processes where scientific knowledge and policy responses are co-produced and co-developed. Chapter 2 of the book, in particular, highlights how science has shaped the contours, objectives, and content of the SLCP policy agenda, while also revealing how policymakers, in turn, influence the processes of scientific knowledge production and the interpretation of concepts.

These processes are particularly important for the agenda setting stage. Agenda setting phase as a complex social process involving 'the construction of knowledge, consensus, concern and a sense of urgency, as well as processes of social mobilization, the diffusion of norms and ideas, and the definition and articulation of storylines about causality, blame and the possibilities of collective action around a set of possible policy options.'[2] Furthermore, agenda setting is also 'embedded in larger, ongoing social and political institutions and dynamics'.[3] All of that comes to light in Chapter 2 by Niklas Löther, where he unrolls the evolution of the concept of SLCPs and demonstrates the complexity of translating scientific knowledge into a viable policy concept. He clearly shows that different problem framings associated with SLCPs have been entertained in policy discussion of the last 15 years, and these have complex political drivers behind them. The chapter also clearly demonstrates how the evolution of the concept did not escape the broader political context of: the North – South disagreements about historical responsibility for global warming; the impact of the US domestic politics on global environmental affairs; and the effect of the failure of the Copenhagen climate summit of 2009.

Research on how environmental problems gain international recognition has demonstrated that agenda setting occurs in several stages where identifying anthropogenic impacts and constructing such impacts as a 'problem' are an important starting point.[4] Here, the chapters show that the identification and quantification of impacts has not been a smooth process in the case of SLCPs. First of all, this refers to the multiplicity of impacts. Several of SLCPs not only contribute to climate warming but also to air pollution detrimentally affecting public health and the environment. How to account for these multiple effects – or co-benefits of reducing their emissions – remains a challenge for policymaking. In terms of problem definition, one question here is whether some of SLCPs are a climate problem (and therefore should be addressed through

2 Stacy D VanDeveer, 'Agenda Setting at Sea and in the Air' in Norichika Kanie, Steinar Andresen and Peter M Haas (eds), *Improving Global Environmental Governance: Best Practices for Architecture and Agency* (Routledge 2013).

3 ibid.

4 Ronald B Mitchell, *International Politics and the Environment* (SAGE Publications 2010).

climate policies) or rather an air pollution problem (and should be dealt with via air pollution prevention frameworks). What complicates the affair is that integration between climate and air quality laws is problematic at many levels, and for instance international climate law does not account for air quality links (see also below). Thus far, most of the framing work has focused on short-term climate effects of SLCPs whereas other benefits of their reduction have been mostly considered as additional. Yet, such climate-focused framing places less emphasis on the relationship of SLCP mitigation measures to important development dimensions such as health, agriculture and food security. As a result, social impacts on the vulnerable groups of the society remain underappreciated, as discussed in Chapter 10 'An Integrated and Inclusive SLCP Strategy for Asia: Recommended Policy and Institutional Reforms'. The different emphasis in problem framing also brings to the fore important equity and justice considerations, which are either lost or manifested differently in the viewing of SLCPs through a primarily climate lens.

Another challenge relating to problem framing arises in relation to the impacts of black carbon emissions on the climate. Much of the construction of SLCPs, including black carbon, as a global problem has revolved around their climate impacts, as already mentioned. As chapter 1 explains, the estimate for effective radiative forcing for black carbon has however been downgraded in the IPCC Sixth Assessment Report compared to the previous assessment; therefore, the estimated average value for the warming caused by black carbon emissions is assessed as less than 0.1 °C. This points to a relatively small warming effect of black carbon emissions in global terms. Furthermore, the estimate does not include co-emitted aerosols which have a cooling effect on the climate, and indeed the IPCC estimates that the combined effect of all aerosols is in fact net negative. The story however does not end here. To add a further degree of complexity, climatic effects of black carbon emissions vary strongly depending on their location and are higher in glaciated regions. Black carbon emissions in fact have a significant impact on regional warming in such cases, for instance in the Arctic. Also, the contribution of black carbon as part of particulate matter to air pollution is clear and significant, prompting development of appropriate responses. However, whether such responses should be nested in global climate frameworks is not apparent based on science, and instead exploring air pollution policies could be a more fitting choice. While the scientific history of black carbon is arguably not finished, it is no wonder that against the complexity of estimating its climate impacts, it has been challenging to construct black carbon emissions as a problem, first, belonging to a climate policy world and, second, requiring a global response.

What else the book chapters have demonstrated is the importance and associated challenges of the ways and methods of how scientific knowledge is produced, as well as 'ways of measuring' emissions. Chapter 1 for instance delves into characteristics of modelling and the uncertainties about climate impacts of SLCFs. It explains the many different sources of uncertainty: scientific uncertainties, uncertainties caused by simplifications of Earth's processes, structural limitations of models (e.g., their spatial resolution), internal variability in climate models, and randomness in the variability of Earth system processes. Understanding model limitations and the various types of uncertainties associated with the estimates of SLCP emissions reductions is critical for effective policy-making. In particular, the uncertainty is relatively large and therefore the range of estimates is wide for black carbon and aerosols in general while for methane the uncertainty is smaller.

An example of the problematic link between 'ways of measuring' and their policy implications is demonstrated in Chapter 3 'The International Climate Change Regime: Right Home for SLCPs?' by Yamineva and Pekkarinen. This time the matter relates to emission metrics: due to the comprehensive approach adopted in the UNFCCC, different greenhouse gases are expressed through a common emission metric. The commonly used common emission metric in the UNFCCC has been Global Warming Potentials over 100-years: it is applied to express non-CO_2 gases in their CO_2-equivalent. However, this metric ignores the short-term nature of SLCPs and can at least partly explain the insufficient attention to non-CO_2 gases in the UNFCCC regime.

The dual, intermediary nature of science-policy concepts and institutions is well illustrated in many chapters of the book. The concept of SLCPs is itself neither purely scientific nor political as it is largely a construct resulting from complex interactions between scientific knowledge and policy goals. In this way, it is more like a *boundary object,* being positioned at the boundary of science and policy worlds (see also Chapter 2) where institutions mediating between science and policy are similarly described as *boundary organisations*.[5] Boundary work has been described as providing 'fundamental insights into the dynamic processes by which expertise becomes authoritative'.[6] Considering

5 Clark Miller, 'Hybrid Management: Boundary Organizations, Science Policy, and Environmental Governance in the Climate Regime' (2001) 26 Science, Technology, & Human Values 478; David H Guston, 'Boundary Organizations in Environmental Policy and Science: An Introduction' (2001) 26 Science, Technology, & Human Values 399; Karin M Gustafsson and Rolf Lidskog, 'Boundary Organizations and Environmental Governance: Performance, Institutional Design, and Conceptual Development' (2018) 19 Climate Risk Management 1.

6 Silke Beck and others, 'The Making of Global Environmental Science and Politics' in Ulrike Felt and others (eds), *The Handbook of Science and Technology Studies* (MIT Press

this work from a social construction perspective demonstrates 'how expert organizations establish design rules that create different responsibilities and procedures for producing and legitimizing knowledge, which in turn influence how (and by whom) problems are framed'.[7] Many international and regional institutions and networks have been acting as boundary organisations on SLCPs, including first of all UNEP, CCAC, and Arctic Council, but also UNECE, Asia Pacific Clean Air Partnership and Clean Air Asia.

These organisations have produced a number of scientific assessment reports which have brought SLCPs onto global and regional policy agendas, and framed the related discussion on regulating and governing the mitigation of SLCP emissions. Why have these institutions been successful as science-policy interfaces? Previous scholarship has established that science influences policy when the knowledge, including the process of its production, is viewed by policy-makers as credible, salient and legitimate.[8] Here, credibility refers to the evidence and argumentation seen as scientifically adequate, salience means that the knowledge is policy relevant, and legitimacy implies that the knowledge production process is perceived as inclusive and fair.[9] It has further been proposed in the literature that there is a strong link between inclusive institutional set-ups promoting iterative interaction and deliberation, on the one hand, and credibility, salience and legitimacy of resulting knowledge, on the other. These literature findings help explain the effectiveness of science-policy work performed by the aforementioned institutions: especially UNEP, CCAC and Arctic Council have involved a wide group of scientists and policy-makers, with the CCAC also involving other stakeholders, and engaged with the topic in a policy-salient way. Their intergovernmental status (in the case of CCAC, the state-led status) has played a legitimising role for the work on SLCPs. It appears that the same requirements for credibility, salience and legitimacy also apply to the development of shared problem definitions through bilateral science diplomacy, as shown by Chapter 8 'From Bilateral Science Diplomacy to Wider Black Carbon Governance? Norwegian-Chinese and Finnish-Russian initiatives'.

2016) <http://ebookcentral.proquest.com/lib/uef-ebooks/detail.action?docID=5052910> accessed 5 May 2023.

7 ibid.

8 Ronald Bruce Mitchell and others, *Global Environmental Assessments: Information and Influence* (MIT Press 2006) 15.

9 ibid; David W Cash and others, 'Knowledge Systems for Sustainable Development' (2003) 100 Proceedings of the National Academy of Sciences 8086.

3 Polycentric Features and Fragmentation

If there is one characteristic of the global legal and governance landscape on SLCPs, it is that there is no dominant instrument or institution solely regulating and/or governing the mitigation of SLCPs on a global scale. Instead, a variety of legal instruments, soft law rules, international and transnational institutions, and organisations need to be considered. They span various jurisdictions not only horizontally but also vertically – across inter-and transnational, regional, national, and sub-national levels, pointing to the multilevel nature of regulation and governance of mitigating SLCPs. Here, however, HFCs are an exception as they are now centrally regulated through Kigali Amendment to the Montreal Protocol.

In the literature, such characteristics of the governance complexity and multiplicity of relevant avenues are not unique and have been conceptualised as, for instance, policentric governance,[10] fragmentation of law,[11] and institutional fragmentation,[12] as well as multilevel governance.[13] In addition, policy coherence – also well-researched in the literature[14] – can be a useful analytical concept in the discussion of how well different policy goals are coordinated across different institutions, and bodies of laws and policies. Indeed, these analytical frames are employed by several chapters of the book: policentric governance is discussed as a prevailing feature in relation to the work of the Arctic Council in Chapter 7 and regulating of emissions from cookstoves in Chapter 9, and it is also clearly visible in the evaluations of the law and governance on road transportation (Chapter 12), international shipping (Chapter 11) and methane emissions from oil and gas sector (Chapter 13), while chapter 10 engages with

10 Andrew Jordan and others (eds), *Governing Climate Change: Polycentricity in Action?* (Cambridge University Press 2018); Josephine van Zeben, 'Polycentricity as a Theory of Governance' in Ana Bobić and Josephine van Zeben (eds), *Polycentricity in the European Union* (Cambridge University Press 2019) <https://www.cambridge.org/core/books/polycentricity-in-the-european-union/polycentricity-as-a-theory-of-governance/8C7646D0823AFBA090654C8145285E2D> accessed 4 May 2023.

11 Martti Koskenniemi and Päivi Leino, 'Fragmentation of International Law? Postmodern Anxieties' (2002) 15 Leiden Journal of International Law 553.

12 Fariborz Zelli, 'Institutional Fragmentation' in Philipp Pattberg and Fariborz Zelli (eds), *Encyclopedia of Global Environmental Governance and Politics* (Edward Elgar Publishing 2015)<https://www.e-elgar.com/shop/encyclopedia-of-global-environmental-governance-and-politics> accessed 3 August 2018.

13 Andreas Føllesdal, Ramses A Wessel and Jan Wouters, *Multilevel Regulation and the EU: The Interplay Between Global, European, and National Normative Processes* (Brill 2008).

14 Jale Tosun and Achim Lang, 'Policy Integration: Mapping the Different Concepts' (2017) 38 Policy Studies 553.

the topic of policy coherence. Multilevel governance is also discussed widely across many chapters.

The global governance landscape on SLCPs mitigation is evidently polycentric in its decentralised characteristics and a wide variety of intergovernmental and transnational regimes, institutions and initiatives of different nature at all levels.[15] Polycentric governance has been described in terms of the existence of multiple centres of decision-making which relate to each other in both competitive and cooperative ways.[16] Polycentric governance systems are decentralised as they are constituted of 'a complex combination of multiple levels and diverse types of organizations drawn from the public, private, and voluntary sectors that have overlapping realms of responsibility and functional capacities'.[17]

When examining institutions involved in addressing SLCPs, a significant degree of variation becomes apparent. Several international organizations, whether established by international treaties or not (such as UNEP and IMO), undoubtedly hold crucial positions. Yet, much of the forward-looking and innovative governance of SLCP mitigation has occurred around institutions beyond such international organisations. One is the Arctic Council, a regional intergovernmental forum with strong transnational features, and the other is the CCAC, a state-led transnational network of states and non-state actors.

International institutions vary not only in their constituencies but also in terms of the thematic scope. This ranges from a generic focus on the global environment (e.g., UNEP) or regional policy (e.g., Arctic Council) to regulating an entire sector (IMO) or even a narrow specialisation in SLCPs (CCAC). Mandates also vary heavily, as demonstrated in the book, and so does geographic coverage: although many of relevant international institutions have a global coverage, some of these, like the CCAC or Arctic Council, do not.

Also, from the perspective of sources of law, there is a high variation across relevant instruments and norms in terms of the legal nature, scope, participation, and approaches. Legally binding instruments include international treaties that are traditionally considered in international law scholarship, such as: the UNFCCC and Paris Agreement, Montreal Protocol, and Gothenburg Protocol to CLRTAP. The three international regimes listed deal with various aspects of the atmosphere: climate, ozone layer, or regional air pollution, respectively. Noteworthy is that the climate change and ozone layer protection

15 Jordan and others (n 10).
16 van Zeben (n 10).
17 Michael D McGinnis and Elinor Ostrom, 'Reflections on Vincent Ostrom, Public Administration, and Polycentricity' (2012) 72 Public Administration Review 15.

regimes have a global coverage, while Gothenburg Protocol is a regional instrument that concerns only the countries in the Northern hemisphere, and therefore has no global application. None of the treaties regulate SLCPs as a whole: instead they cover only specific aspects (UNFCCC and Paris Agreement) and/or a specific pollutant (Montreal and Gothenburg Protocols). Importantly, even if treaties are legally binding, specific provisions concerning SLCPs may be worded in a non-binding language and do not lead to states' mitigation obligations. The already mentioned Gothenburg Protocol for instance gives its parties a broad discretion in reducing black carbon emissions.

In addition to legally binding instruments, there are various non-binding norms, or soft law, in the form of policy frameworks (Arctic Council Framework for Action on Enhanced Black Carbon and Methane Emissions Reductions) and guidelines (for instance, WHO Air Quality Guidelines, or GMI's Best Practice Guidance for Effective Methane Management in the Oil and Gas Sector). Despite their non-binding legal nature, these are sometimes worded in a highly specific language as to what type of actions states or other actors need to undertake, and their effect on national policies or transnational actors can be quite substantial. In other words, when considering the global legal and governance landscape on mitigating emissions of SLCPs, one has to take into account multiple instruments and institutions of a highly varying nature, pointing to the high degree of fragmentation.

Fragmentation here refers to 'the increased specialization and diversification in international institutions, including the overlap of the substantive rules and jurisdictions'.[18] Specifically, institutional fragmentation has been discussed as a "a patchwork of international institutions that are different: in their character (organizations, regimes, and implicit norms), their constituencies (public and private), their spatial scope (from bilateral to global), and their subject matter (from specific policy fields to universal concerns)".[19] The multiplicity and diversity of normative instruments and institutions is indeed evident from the overview above.

Fragmentation of law and institutions logically raises questions of its consequences. Fragmentation can have both positive and negative impacts on the state of law and governance, depending on its degree and qualities. In

18 Harro van Asselt, *The Fragmentation of Global Climate Governance: Consequences and Management of Regime Interactions* (Edward Elgar Publishing 2014) 35 <https://www.e-elgar.com/shop/the-fragmentation-of-global-climate-governance> accessed 3 August 2018.

19 Frank Biermann and others, 'The Fragmentation of Global Governance Architectures: A Framework for Analysis' (2009) 9 Global Environmental Politics 14, 16.

this respect, literature has deliberated three types of fragmentation, such as synergistic fragmentation (high degree of integration), cooperative fragmentation (loose connections), and conflictive fragmentation (clear cases of norm conflicts).[20] Elsewhere, we analysed the fragmented nature of the legal and governance landscape on SLCPs in the Arctic context, concluding that this fragmentation has a cooperative or synergistic character and therefore does not pose significant problems for an effective response to the problem.[21] The reason for this is that nearly all relevant treaties or institutions belong to the field of international environmental law, sharing its main principles and approaches, and hence risks of legal incoherence are low. The analysis covered many of the same legal and institutional avenues as in this book, and therefore its conclusions on the relatively unproblematic nature of legal and institutional fragmentation on SLCPs can be extrapolated to the global level.

Yet, if fragmentation per se is not problematic in this area, questions still remain as to the appropriate levels of coordination among relevant instruments and institutions. In the absence of coordination, various inefficiencies can occur. One of them is the competition for attention and resources among the various initiatives. At this point, the overlaps are not critical though there is still room for improved coordination, especially in relation to the various alliances launched to implement the Paris Agreement (see Chapter 6). Further, in a pluralistic governance context, an orchestrating function is important. This can help align goals and actions of various actors to create synergies and avoid trade-offs. It is clear that for SLCPs such function has been performed by CCAC. As Chapter 6 highlights, the Coalition has been intermediating across several UN agencies working on clean air issues including UNEP, WHO, WMO, and others, as well as on agriculture and household energy. One interesting observation is that the polycentric landscape allows for self-adjustment whereby governance gaps or inefficiencies can be addressed through alternative arrangements. This is the conclusion made in Chapter 11 with respect to the adaptiveness of the multilevel system of international shipping governance in light of the conservativeness of the IMO and shipping industry.

A particular manifestation of the legal and institutional fragmentation is the incoherence between climate and air quality policies across many levels. Speaking of international law, the normative, operational and conceptial

20 Biermann and others (n 19).

21 Yulia Yamineva and Kati Kulovesi, 'Keeping the Arctic White: The Legal and Governance Landscape for Reducing Short-Lived Climate Pollutants in the Arctic Region' (2018) 7 Transnational Environmental Law 201.

linkages[22] between the domains of law on climate change and on air pollution are relatively weak.[23] Here, normative linkages include both formative norms in the treaties or other sources governing the regimes and implementation rules adopted by subsidiary bodies. The international climate treaties generally make no mention of air quality linkages. From the air quality side, it is more difficult to make a conclusion as there is no one global treaty or a custodian international organisation responsible for the air quality agenda; although the regional CLRTAP regime has made several attempts to explicitly integrate climate concerns in its Gothenburg Protocol. Operational interactions refer to joint activities of international regimes for instance partnerships and other types of collaboration.[24] 'Robust and dynamic' operational interactions can lead to effective initiatives and outcomes.[25] Conceptual linkages are those interactions which produce and disseminate social knowledge, or 'authoritative ways of understanding and organizing the world.'[26] These include scientific cooperation and any efforts to improve the knowledge basis about climate and air quality interdependencies. In contrast to normative linkages, operational and conceptual linkages between climate change and air pollution policies have been growing, evidenced by a number of scientific assessment reports, science-policy formats, partnerships, and global campaigns. Here, again the CCAC has been playing an important role as a proponent of integration across multiple policy goals, including through a structured approach of the Multiple Benefits Pathway Framework (see Chapter 6). In this respect, CCAC has been assisting national governments with integrated modelling of climate and air quality impacts and designing harmonized policies.

Yet, there are also instances of problematic interactions between climate and air quality agendas. One example relates to climate impacts of air pollution controls as has been the case with reducing sulfur emissions which have a cooling effect. Chapter 3 for instance shows that the implementation of the CLRTAP sulphur reduction commitments has unmasked warming especially in

22 Based on Jeffrey Dunoff, 'A New Approach to Regime Interaction' in Margaret Young (ed), *Regime interaction: international law facing fragmentation* (Cambridge University Press 2015) <http://www.cambridge.org/fi/academic/subjects/law/public-international-law/regime-interaction-international-law-facing-fragmentation> accessed 2 August 2018.

23 Yulia Yamineva, 'International Law at the Nexus of Climate Change and Air Pollution: Normative, Operational and Conceptual Linkages' (2020).

24 Dunoff (n 22).

25 ibid 166.

26 ibid 167.

the Arctic.[27] This suggests that policy responses to climate change and air pollution should be integrated in accounting for all co-pollutants and their total effects on air quality, human health, the climate, and ecosystems.[28]

A siloed approach to climate and air quality in law and policies is not only observable at the international level but also evident at the national level where cross-agency work can be insufficient and organisational cultures are not conducive to integrative approaches.[29] Here, building on the rich policy coherence and integration scholarship, chapter 10 discusses how environmental concerns can be incorporated in various public policies, for instance through the institutional formats of interagency coordination mechanisms and multiagency task forces as well as dedicated budget lines.

4 Transnational Law and Governance

Another observation from the book chapters is the clear evidence of the importance of transnational institutions and networks in the global law and governance of mitigating SLCP emissions. This observation was already made earlier in the Arctic context[30] and more broadly corresponds to general trends in international environmental and climate law.[31]

27 EMEP, *EMEP Status Report 1/2016: Transboundary Particulate Matter, Photo-Oxidants, Acidifying and Eutrophying Components* (Oslo, Norway: Norwegian Meteorological Institute, 13 September 2016), vi.

28 Francesca Dominici and others, 'Protecting Human Health from Air Pollution: Shifting from a Single-Pollutant to a Multi-Pollutant Approach' (2010) 21 Epidemiology (Cambridge, Mass.) 187; Megan L Melamed, Julia Schmale and Erika von Schneidemesser, 'Sustainable Policy – Key Considerations for Air Quality and Climate Change' (2016) 23 Current Opinion in Environmental Sustainability 85.

29 Yulia Yamineva and Zhe Liu, 'Cleaning the Air, Protecting the Climate: Policy, Legal and Institutional Nexus to Reduce Black Carbon Emissions in China' (2019) 95 Environmental Science & Policy 1.

30 Kati Kulovesi, 'Exploring Transnational Legal Orders: Using Transnational Environmental Law to Strengthen the Global Regulation of Black Carbon for the Benefit of the Arctic Region' in Veerle Heyvaert and Leslie-Anne Duvic-Paoli (eds), *Research Handbook on Transnational Environmental Law* (Edward Elgar Publishing 2020) <https://www.elgaronline.com/display/edcoll/9781788119627/9781788119627.00010.xml> accessed 21 April 2023.

31 Veerle Heyvaert, *Transnational Environmental Regulation and Governance: Purpose, Strategies and Principles* (Cambridge University Press 2018) <https://www.cambridge.org/core/books/transnational-environmental-regulation-and-governance/B393A30058A94FD3BD6DD3A63B721562> accessed 21 July 2020; Harriet Bulkeley and others, *Transnational Climate Change Governance* (Cambridge University Press 2014); Frank Biermann and Philipp Pattberg (eds), *Global Environmental Governance Reconsidered*

Indeed, it is clear that international law has been undergoing profound transformations, including through the expansion of actors and institutions engaged in law-making.[32] If traditionally – in the Westphalian paradigm of international law – it is states that regulated relations on the regional and global level, in a globalised world many non-state actors actively develop and implement international norms. Nation-states remain key norm-makers but they no longer solely determine the boundaries and contents of international law.

Law-making and governance beyond states is the characteristic that has especially been discussed in relation to climate and environmental law and governance through various overlapping approaches like transnational law,[33] transnational governance,[34] informal law-making,[35] and others. Much of the conceptual and terminological apparatus of transnational law and governance is still in development, and here SLCPs present (yet another) empirical case of its functioning in the global realm.

In terms of the type of actors involved, these are very diverse. However, it is clear that governments still play a key role: they often lead the governance effort and have an important legitimising function, as is the case for CCAC and AC, for instance. Another observation from the chapters is that transnational actors often have a network format with relatively loose connections among members. As such, they have a highly heterogenous membership and include – in addition to governments – intergovernmental organizations, businesses, scientific institutions, and civil society organizations.

Transnational institutions are highly inclusive and give a broad discretion to their members in determining their actions: for instance, in CCAC members decide on what they bring to the Coalition. This characteristic results in significant rates of participation. Another feature relates to a unique link to local contexts and bottom up approaches, demonstrated in particular in Chapter 9, 10 and 11. This requires a strong alignment across levels, again pointing to multilevel characteristics of governance.

Transnationality has been firmly associated in the literature with the high potential for developing innovative approaches to problems. These own to

(MIT Press 2012) <https://direct.mit.edu/books/book/2969/Global-Environmental-Governance-Reconsidered> accessed 27 April 2023.

32 Terence C Halliday and Gregory Shaffer (eds), *Transnational Legal Orders* (Cambridge University Press 2015) <https://www.cambridge.org/core/books/transnational-legal-orders/147B53A8598444318464D8720A6A859B> accessed 21 July 2020; Joost Pauwelyn, Ramses Wessel and Jan Wouters, *Informal International Lawmaking* (OUP Oxford 2012).

33 Heyvaert (n 31).

34 Bulkeley and others (n 31).

35 Pauwelyn, Wessel and Wouters (n 32).

the flexibility of transnational institutions and their preference for bottom-up actions which is conducive to experimentation. For instance, the Arctic Council and CCAC have been able to connect policy makers and scientists with a range of non-state stakeholders bridging science, policy and concrete actions. This stands in contrast for instance to IMO – a traditional international organisation which has exhibited a strong degree of institutional inertia and bureaucracy on black carbon emissions' mitigation, having been unable to adopt any type of concrete regulatory plan after many years of deliberation.

When discussing transnational institutions, it is important to deliberate their contribution and impact to the global law and governance on SLCPs. In general, governance at the global level requires several functions to be performed: '(1) providing guidance and signal to actors, (2) setting rules to facilitate collective action, (3) enhancing transparency and accountability, (4) offering support (finance, technology, capacity-building), and (5) promoting knowledge and learning.'[36] While not exhaustive, such a list provides a helpful tool to evaluate the work of various institutions in a polycentric setting. Accordingly, it appears that transnational institutions engaged in the global governance of SLCPs primarily perform the functions of providing guidance and signal; and knowledge production, exchange and learning, as well as, to some degree, support. Indeed, such institutions as CCAC and Arctic Council have been instrumental in awareness-raising and formulating the overall goals and frames of action on SLCPs. Further, both institutions have been the key actors in synthesising scientific knowledge for policy use through science assessments and other activities. North-South support has been an important function for CCAC: this is however focused on capacity building. Similar conclusions on the main governance functions can be reached in relation to sectoral transnational arrangements, for instance on clean cookstoves.

There are further important questions about the effectiveness and legitimacy of transnational institutions and law, as highlighted multiple times in the literature and well-illustrated in the various contributions to the volume. Whether transnational institutions and law are more effective than traditional international law and institutions, in addressing climate and environmental problems is not clear. The book chapters demonstrate that while transnational institutions perform important functions, there are gaps in the governance not filled through their mandates. This especially relate to development of norms and related implementation mechanisms, including transparency,

36 Sebastian Oberthür, Lukas Hermwille and Tim Rayner, 'A Sectoral Perspective on Global Climate Governance: Analytical Foundation' (2021) 8 Earth System Governance 100104.

accountability and support. What these institutions did not engage in is the setting of concrete rules in the form of obligations or standards as to how to mitigate SLCP emissions. Instead, transnational institutions often rely on bottom up approaches where participants are themselves responsible for formulating concrete actions to achieve a common goal. Similarly, there are generally no transparency and accountability mechanisms, though the Council went a step beyond here in encouraging Arctic and observer states to submit their national reports. Even if policy targets are adopted by such transnational institutions, they often lack ambition. Literature has also discussed the legitimacy of transnational institutions from the perspective of their membership: private sector and civil society participation in international institutions can for instance be problematic because of the dominance of the Global North NGOs and private sector lobbyism.[37]

The book chapters have further raised questions as to the stability of transnational arrangements, well demonstrated in Chapter 6: the CCAC depends on its members, in particular member states, in terms of setting priorities and that opens them to fluctuations according to changes in domestic political agendas. Similarly, the Arctic Council appears to be vulnerable to domestic political changes.

5 What Accomplishments Have Been Made and What Gaps Remain?

Arguably, the most notable change in global governance regarding SLCPs lies in the realm of agenda setting. The concept of SLCPs emerged relatively recently, only about 15 years ago, but it has now firmly established itself in global climate policy discussions and even gained recognition within some national contexts. An epistemic community comprising scientists, policymakers, and other stakeholders with shared interests has formed, particularly around the transnational partnership of CCAC, while SLCPs have also been incorporated into the reports of the IPCC. The increased policy attention given to mitigating SLCPs can perhaps be attributed to the bundling of these substances under a single label. By packaging various SLCPs together, it becomes easier to draw

37 Jochen von Bernstorff, 'New Responses to the Legitimacy Crisis of International Institutions: The Role of "Civil Society" and the Rise of the Principle of Participation of "The Most Affected" in International Institutional Law' (2021) 32 European Journal of International Law 125; Carole-Anne Sénit, Frank Biermann and Agni Kalfagianni, 'The Representativeness of Global Deliberation: A Critical Assessment of Civil Society Consultations for Sustainable Development' (2017) 8 Global Policy 62.

policy attention compared to addressing each individual substance separately. It can be assumed that if policymakers had to tackle each individual substance independently, garnering policy attention for each one would have been more challenging.

Part of this agenda setting work has been a realisation and a better understanding of climate and air quality linkages. Climate change and air pollution are two of the most important challenges to public health and sustainability, closely linked both in terms of emission sources and impacts.[38] The same sources are responsible for the largest amounts of greenhouse gas emissions and of air pollutants: this for instance relates to burning of fossil fuels and biomass. In addition, some substances have effects both on the climate and air quality. Yet, the climate impacts can be complex and while some pollutants, e.g., sulphur dioxide (SO_2), have a cooling effect, others such as SLCPs warm the atmosphere. For these reasons, climate change and air pollution should be addressed in a coordinated manner. This theme has also become part of the debates about SLCPs, which for instance addressed the potential of integrated approaches to bring multiple co-benefits for climate and air quality, and identify win-win, cost-effective solutions and avoid win-lose options.

A related achievement concerns air pollution governance. First, the rise of the concept of SLCPs with its impacts on the climate has contributed to elevating the air pollution problem to global levels – by clearly demonstrating that air pollution is not merely a local concern but it can also have impacts on the global and regional climates. Furthermore, institutional arrangements on mitigating SLCPs have been filling the gap in the global governance of air pollution. As it is well-known, air pollution is not regulated by an international treaty with a global participation or a custodian international organisation. Instead, there is a heavily fragmented patchwork of regional agreements and policy frameworks, and various international and transnational institutions and networks. Further, most of existing international norms address air pollution in a transboundary context rather than from a global perspective. This implies there is a gap in the global governance of air pollution. Here, the topic of SLCPs serves as a proxy to address air pollution globally in conjunction with climate change.

Also, observable is the growing integration of climate concerns into non-climate frameworks. As Chapter 4 stipulates, the Kigali Amendment transformed the Montreal Protocol from a strictly ozone protection agreement into an ozone and climate protection treaty. The case of the Montreal Protocol is

38 Melamed, Schmale and von Schneidemesser (n 28).

all the more interesting since the Kigali Amendment concerns HFCs which are not regarded as ozone-depleting substances per se and the reason for regulating them relates to their climate impacts. Another example is the Gothenburg Protocol which, through its 2012 amendment, integrates climate protection among its objectives. It already addresses black carbon for its climate impacts and there is an ongoing discussion on strengthening its regulation of methane emissions. There are also debates on integrating climate concerns into non-climate frameworks across transnational arrangements, for instance with respect to clean cooking. Whether this phenomenon is contemplated through the lens of climate co-benefits of non-climate policies or the politics of linkages and climate bandwagoning[39] is a matter for further discussion but one consequence is clear – that the landscape of climate governance is becoming more and more polycentric as a result.

Taking a substance-based approach, there are advancements with respect to at least some SLCPs. It appears that HFCs are now well-covered under the ozone regime with strong mitigation obligations and a clear timetable. There has also been a growing cooperation on methane emissions through the Global Methane Pledge and various transnational arrangements, though the global governance of methane mitigation is arguably still in its infancy. As for black carbon emissions, there are no global legal or governance arrangements per se – this gap is closely linked to associated scientific uncertainties about its climate impacts, on the one hand, and the lack of a global treaty or institution responsible for addressing air pollution, on the other.

6 What Lies Ahead for the SLCP Policy Agenda?

Each of the pollutants within the category of SLCPs deserves dedicated policy attention and global governance. However, this book proposes that a distinct regulatory and governance approach should be adopted for each individual substance within the SLCP umbrella term. This recommendation is primarily rooted in the distinct scientific characteristics exhibited by these pollutants, variations in their sources, and at times, divergent impacts they have on the environment and human health. Consequently, the development of different mitigation strategies becomes imperative.

39 Sikina Jinnah, 'Climate Change Bandwagoning: The Impacts of Strategic Linkages on Regime Design, Maintenance, and Death' (2011) 11 Global Environmental Politics 1.

This applies especially to black carbon: given the scientific uncertainties regarding the combined climate impact of black carbon emissions reductions, and the fact that black carbon is emitted as a component of particulate matter, it seems wise to prioritize measures aiming at reducing particulate matter emissions via the relevant legal frameworks on preventing air pollution rather than the climate regime. In the Northern hemisphere, this speaks to the continuing relevance of the Arctic Council and Gothenburg Protocol. Chapter 5 suggests that the Gothenburg Protocol provides a clear route for tackling SLCPs in the UNECE region. This can be done through more ambitious targets relating to black carbon and particulate matter emissions as well as integrating methane emissions' reductions in the next round of revisions to the Protocol. However, current lack of political leadership places progress in this direction in doubt, and insufficient engagement from countries in Eastern Europe and Eurasia is also troublesome. For other regions of the world, efforts need to be pursued through regional policy forums relating to air pollution, while orchestrating of activities can be continued by CCAC. A related and broader question concerns the need to develop a global agenda on tackling air pollution in the context of the global development and health agenda: this could possibly take a soft governance approach through existing institutional arrangements.[40]

Further, there is a clear need for global regulatory activity to address emissions in specific sectors. Chapter 12 explores different pathways towards globally harmonised standards for road transportation, Chapter 11 suggests a need for explicit international and regional regulations addressing black carbon emissions in the shipping sector, and Chapter 9 suggests a need for a transnational initiative or network on tackling cookstove emissions that would involve national and sub-national authorities and have a clear regulatory emphasis in its activities. Such legal and governance developments would clearly have wide-ranging benefits beyond simply reducing black carbon emissions in mitigating emissions of co-pollutants and – especially in the case of cleaner cookstoves – having positive development impacts.

Concerning methane emissions, it appears that the orchestrating function is still unfulfilled despite the efforts under the Global Methane Pledge. The UNFCCC and Paris Agreement would be a clear candidate for coordinating global efforts on mitigating methane emissions, as discussed in Chapter 2. At the same time, the desirability of such an approach remains unclear. Given the politicized nature of the UNFCCC regime and the sheer number of agenda

40 Yulia Yamineva and Seita Romppanen, 'Is Law Failing to Address Air Pollution? Reflections on International and EU Developments' (2017) 26 Review of European, Comparative & International Environmental Law 189.

items it has to deal with, the option of bringing in yet another major mitigation item may not be the most effective solution from the perspective of actual problem solving. At the same time, it appears that on the regional level at least there are promising developments to address methane as a contributor to air pollution, for instance in the already-mentioned review of the Gothenburg Protocol as well as revisions to the EU legislation on air pollution. This may be a productive path given the concreteness of emissions reduction obligations in the air pollution frameworks that would provide an important complementary avenue to any actions under the UNFCCC relying on bottom up approaches.

Simultaneously, in order to maintain consistency and achieve co-benefits, it is crucial to establish strategic oversight and foster enhanced cooperation among the various frameworks and arrangements. The chapters in this book have suggested the need to develop several linkages, for instance between: the ozone and climate regimes, the ozone regime and a new globally binding treaty on plastics, the IMO and CLRTAP regarding black carbon emissions, as well as CLRTAP, Arctic Council, and CCAC, among others.

Finally, the impact of the recent geopolitical changes prompted by the ongoing Russia's aggression against Ukraine on the governance of SLCPs are critical to consider. There are many dimensions to it, and a comprehensive exploration exceeds the boundaries of this book's scope. To mention one dimension, Russia is one of the top methane emitters globally and responsible for a significant proportion of regional black carbon emissions, the latter particularly important in the Arctic context. To note, the country is party to the UNFCCC and Paris Agreement, and the amended Montreal Protocol, as well as a member of the CCAC. However, it is not party to the Gothenburg Protocol (although party to CLRTAP) and has not joined the Global Methane Pledge. Overall, Russia's role in multilateral environmental agreements has often been passive or that of a laggard, while in domestic policy agenda climate and environmental issues have been peripheral. Against this background, it remains crucial to involve Russia in any global or regional governance arrangements on climate and environmental topics, including to mitigate SLCP emissions. Despite the currently ongoing war and a very difficult geopolitical context, any future dealings with the country need to carve out a space for cooperating on global and regional climate and environmental agenda. Under what principles and according to what model this cooperation can take place is subject to further debates. At the very least, exchange on scientific activities and environmental data needs to restart in the nearest future to everyone's benefit.

7 Research Directions

If the preceding sub-section explored future possibilities for global law and policy concerning the mitigation of SLCPs, this sub-section delves into potential research avenues that arise from the requirements of both policy and academia. While this book highlights the research conducted by the contributors, it is essential to identify the existing gaps in knowledge and determine areas that warrant further scholarly attention.

Integrated approaches to climate change and air pollution are widely acknowledged, but the extent of integration within legislation, law-making processes, and institutions remains an under-researched topic. It is crucial to determine the level of integration currently present, ascertain whether synergies are fully realized, and identify potential trade-offs and effective resolution strategies. Additionally, there is a pressing need for more specific and concrete knowledge regarding the implementation of integrated approaches in various sectors and policy areas. It is also essential to consider regional and national contexts, particularly in developing countries, where air pollution policies may attract more attention from policy-makers than climate agenda.

The chapters in this book have revealed the intricate interactions between SLCPs and various social and development dimensions. The causes and impacts of SLCPs differ among social groups and regions. This also has significant implications for global law and policy, for instance for modelling the impacts of SLCPs, considering development and climate finance, prioritizing capacity building, and developing holistic socio-economic development strategies.

The linkages between climate/environmental and health governance are rising in their importance but remain under-researched in academic literature. What we have not discussed in the book for instance is the role of the WHO which is responsible for developing various standards applicable to the mitigation of SLCPs. The involvement of WHO in global environmental governance and law is not widely explored or adequately acknowledged. Yet, the organisation's impact – through its standard-setting work – on the development and implementation of environmental norms appears to be significant. One example relates to the Global standards for air quality which set the basic parameters for the majority of national air quality regulatory frameworks. However, there is a dearth of understanding regarding their development process, their mechanisms of impact, and crucial matters of accountability and legitimacy surrounding these standards.

Lastly, this book offers a compelling case study illustrating the interconnectedness of the science and policy realms within the environmental and climate law field. It demonstrates how a constructivist approach can be instrumental in unveiling the intricacies involved in the formulation and utilization of policy concepts. This highlights the need for an exchange between the research fields of climate law and governance with science and technology studies. The latter has developed various analytical frameworks and approaches that precisely elucidate these dynamics. While some initial attempts in this direction have yielded intriguing outcomes,[41] there remains ample room for further exploration and advancement.

Bibliography

Beck S and others, 'The Making of Global Environmental Science and Politics' in Ulrike Felt and others (eds), *The Handbook of Science and Technology Studies* (MIT Press 2016) <http://ebookcentral.proquest.com/lib/uef-ebooks/detail.action?docID=5052910> accessed 5 May 2023.

Biermann F and others, 'The Fragmentation of Global Governance Architectures: A Framework for Analysis' (2009) 9 Global Environmental Politics 14.

Biermann F and Pattberg P (eds), *Global Environmental Governance Reconsidered* (MIT Press 2012) <https://direct.mit.edu/books/book/2969/Global-Environmental-Governance-Reconsidered> accessed 27 April 2023.

Bulkeley H and others, *Transnational Climate Change Governance* (Cambridge University Press 2014).

Cash DW and others, 'Knowledge Systems for Sustainable Development' (2003) 100 Proceedings of the National Academy of Sciences 8086.

Dominici F and others, 'Protecting Human Health from Air Pollution: Shifting from a Single-Pollutant to a Multi-Pollutant Approach' (2010) 21 Epidemiology (Cambridge, Mass.) 187.

Dunoff J, 'A New Approach to Regime Interaction' in Margaret Young (ed), *Regime Interaction: International Law Facing Fragmentation* (Cambridge University Press 2015) <http://www.cambridge.org/fi/academic/subjects/law/public-international-law/regime-interaction-international-law-facing-fragmentation> accessed 2 August 2018.

Føllesdal A, Wessel RA and Wouters J, *Multilevel Regulation and the EU: The Interplay Between Global, European, and National Normative Processes* (Brill 2008).

41 Lisa Vanhala, 'Coproducing the Endangered Polar Bear: Science, Climate Change, and Legal Mobilization' (2020) 42 Law & Policy 105; Phillip Paiement, 'Urgent Agenda: How Climate Litigation Builds Transnational Narratives' (2020) 11 Transnational Legal Theory 121.

Gustafsson KM and Lidskog R, 'Boundary Organizations and Environmental Governance: Performance, Institutional Design, and Conceptual Development' (2018) 19 Climate Risk Management 1.

Guston DH, 'Boundary Organizations in Environmental Policy and Science: an Introduction' (2001) 26 Science, Technology, & Human Values 399.

Halliday TC and Shaffer G (eds), *Transnational Legal Orders* (Cambridge University Press 2015) <https://www.cambridge.org/core/books/transnational-legal-orders/147B53A8598444318464D8720A6A859B> accessed 21 July 2020.

Heyvaert V, *Transnational Environmental Regulation and Governance: Purpose, Strategies and Principles* (Cambridge University Press 2018) <https://www.cambridge.org/core/books/transnational-environmental-regulation-and-governance/B393A30058A94FD3BD6DD3A63B721562> accessed 21 July 2020.

IPCC and others, 'Global Warming of 1.5°C. An IPCC Special Report on the Impacts of Global Warming of 1.5°C above Pre-Industrial Levels and Related Global Greenhouse Gas Emission Pathways, in the Context of Strengthening the Global Response to the Threat of Climate Change, Sustainable Development, and Efforts to Eradicate Poverty' (IPCC 2018).

Jasanoff S (ed), *States of Knowledge: the Co-Production of Science and the Social Order* (Routledge 2004).

Jinnah S, 'Climate Change Bandwagoning: the Impacts of Strategic Linkages on Regime Design, Maintenance, and Death' (2011) 11 Global Environmental Politics 1.

Jordan A and others (eds), *Governing Climate Change: Polycentricity in Action?* (Cambridge University Press 2018).

Koskenniemi M and Leino P, 'Fragmentation of International Law? Postmodern Anxieties' (2002) 15 Leiden Journal of International Law 553.

Kulovesi K, 'Exploring Transnational Legal Orders: Using Transnational Environmental Law to Strengthen the Global Regulation of Black Carbon for the Benefit of the Arctic Region' in Veerle Heyvaert and Leslie-Anne Duvic-Paoli (eds), *Research Handbook on Transnational Environmental Law* (Edward Elgar Publishing 2020) <https://www.elgaronline.com/display/edcoll/9781788119627/9781788119627.00010.xml> accessed 21 April 2023.

Mar K and Unger C, 'A Practical Approach to Integrating Climate and Air Quality Policy' (Institute for Advanced Sustainability Studies 2019) Policy Brief.

McGinnis MD and Ostrom E, 'Reflections on Vincent Ostrom, Public Administration, and Polycentricity' (2012) 72 Public Administration Review 15.

Melamed ML, Schmale J and von Schneidemesser E, 'Sustainable Policy – Key Considerations for Air Quality and Climate Change' (2016) 23 Current Opinion in Environmental Sustainability 85.

Miller C, 'Hybrid Management: Boundary Organizations, Science Policy, and Environmental Governance in the Climate Regime' (2001) 26 Science, Technology, & Human Values 478.

Mitchell RB and others, *Global Environmental Assessments: Information and Influence* (MIT Press 2006).

Mitchell RB, *International Politics and the Environment* (SAGE Publications 2010).

Oberthür S, Hermwille L and Rayner T, 'A Sectoral Perspective on Global Climate Governance: Analytical Foundation' (2021) 8 Earth System Governance 100104.

Paiement P, 'Urgent Agenda: How Climate Litigation Builds Transnational Narratives' (2020) 11 Transnational Legal Theory 121.

Pauwelyn J, Wessel R and Wouters J, *Informal International Lawmaking* (OUP Oxford 2012).

Sénit C-A, Biermann F and Kalfagianni A, 'The Representativeness of Global Deliberation: a Critical Assessment of Civil Society Consultations for Sustainable Development' (2017) 8 Global Policy 62.

Tosun J and Lang A, 'Policy Integration: Mapping the Different Concepts' (2017) 38 Policy Studies 553.

van Asselt H, *The Fragmentation of Global Climate Governance: Consequences and Management of Regime Interactions* (Edward Elgar Publishing 2014) <https://www.e-elgar.com/shop/the-fragmentation-of-global-climate-governance> accessed 3 August 2018.

van Zeben J, 'Polycentricity as a Theory of Governance' in Ana Bobić and Josephine van Zeben (eds), *Polycentricity in the European Union* (Cambridge University Press 2019) <https://www.cambridge.org/core/books/polycentricity-in-the-european-union/polycentricity-as-a-theory-of-governance/8C7646D0823AFBA090654C8145285E2D> accessed 4 May 2023.

VanDeveer SD, 'Agenda Setting at Sea and in the Air' in Norichika Kanie, Steinar Andresen and Peter M Haas (eds), *Improving Global Environmental Governance: Best Practices for Architecture and Agency* (Routledge 2013).

Vanhala L, 'Coproducing the Endangered Polar Bear: Science, Climate Change, and Legal Mobilization' (2020) 42 Law & Policy 105.

von Bernstorff J, 'New Responses to the Legitimacy Crisis of International Institutions: the Role of "Civil Society" and the Rise of the Principle of Participation of "The Most Affected" in International Institutional Law' (2021) 32 European Journal of International Law 125.

Yamineva Y, 'International Law at the Nexus of Climate Change and Air Pollution: Normative, Operational and Conceptual Linkages' (2020).

Yamineva Y and Kulovesi K, 'Keeping the Arctic White: the Legal and Governance Landscape for Reducing Short-Lived Climate Pollutants in the Arctic Region' (2018) 7 Transnational Environmental Law 201.

Yamineva Y and Liu Z, 'Cleaning the Air, Protecting the Climate: Policy, Legal and Institutional Nexus to Reduce Black Carbon Emissions in China' (2019) 95 Environmental Science & Policy 1.

Yamineva Y and Romppanen S, 'Is Law Failing to Address Air Pollution? Reflections on International and EU Developments' (2017) 26 Review of European, Comparative & International Environmental Law 189.

Zelli F, 'Institutional Fragmentation' in Philipp Pattberg and Fariborz Zelli (eds), *Encyclopedia of Global Environmental Governance and Politics* (Edward Elgar Publishing 2015) <https://www.e-elgar.com/shop/encyclopedia-of-global-environmental-governance-and-politics> accessed 3 August 2018.

Index

www.ingramcontent.com/pod-product-compliance
Ingram Content Group UK Ltd.
Pitfield, Milton Keynes, MK11 3LW, UK
UKHW021409091026
15624UKWH00009B/61

9 789004 684072